JAMESTOWN NARRATIVES

MW00565345

OTHER PUBLICATIONS BY EDWARD WRIGHT HAILE

The Oresteia of Aeschylus	*a translation*
Where Are The Planets?	*orbital charts of the naked-eye solar system*
Open, not Glass	*poems & essays*
Here on a Mission	*poems*
Where None Before Hath Stood	*a poem of Jamestown*
Virginia Discovered & Discribed by Captayn John Smith, 1608	*a map*
England in America: the Chesapeake Bay from Jamestown to St. Mary's City, 1607–1634	*a map*

LIBRARY OF VIRGINIA

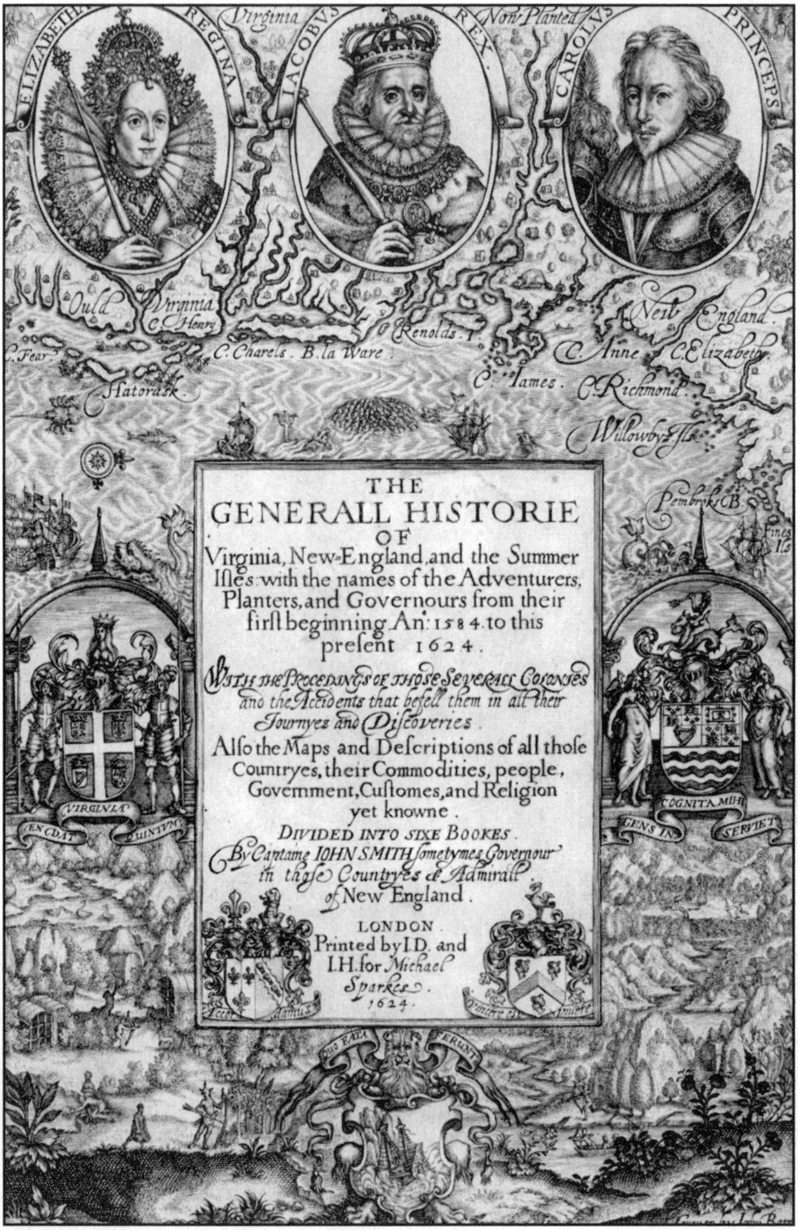

The Generall Historie
John Smith's title page

Jamestown Narratives

Eyewitness Accounts of the Virginia Colony

The First Decade: 1607–1617

Compiled & Edited by
EDWARD WRIGHT HAILE

RoundHouse
Champlain, Virginia

Published by
ROUNDHOUSE
P. O. Box 155, 3079 Daingerfield Landing Road
Champlain, Virginia 22438 Telephone 804-443-4813

© 1998 Edward Wright Haile

First Printing . . . . August 1998
Second Printing. . . . . . September 2001
Third Printing. . . . . .April 2007

Library of Congress Number 98–066423

13 digit ISBN 978-0-9664712-0-5
10 digit ISBN 0-9664712-0-2

Cover design by Sarah Lavicka

All Rights Reserved. No part of this publication may be reproduced, stored in a retrieval system, or transmitted, in any form or by any means, electronic, mechanical, photocopying, recording, or otherwise, without the prior written permission of ROUNDHOUSE.

Printed in the United States of America

Permissions not included in the body of the text:

Passages from the Percy MS of William Strachey's *The Historie of Travell,* including footnotes from the edition of R. H. Major and transcriptions and footnotes from the edition of Louis B. Wright and Virginia Freund; and passages from *The Jamestown Voyages under the First Charter,* Philip L. Barbour, editor, are copied by permission of The Hakluyt Society.

Passages consisting of transcribed margin notes from John Smith's *A True Relation,* from *The Complete Works of Captain John Smith, 1580–1631,* edited by Philip L. Barbour, published for the Institute of Early American History and Culture, copyright © 1986 by the University of North Carolina Press, are used by permission of the publisher.

Passages from *New American World: A Documentary History of North America to 1612,* edited by David B. Quinn, are copied with permission of Ayer Company Publishers, Inc., North Stratford, New Hampshire.

Spanish texts translated by Irene A. Wright are copied by permission of the American Historical Association.

Unattributed passages in the Introduction under "Charters" etc. are taken from Bemiss 1957 and used with permission of the Jamestown-Yorktown Foundation.

for Bess

And then my sweet, who knows I can't forsake her,
is otherwise my only careful acre.

from "Lines Written in Luxurious Late Winter"

Behold Chinquapin, *its riches and its dearth!*

On the sea planet a stretch of sand and earth

Once called New World, cause out this old beehive

Four centuries ago America come alive

Behind the beaches in Algonquian cornfields.

A golden age against tobacco yields

Has come and gone and left old Chinquapin

Leached and haunted, and by a war done in.

Still your African and European folk

Have had a spell to settle in and soak.

Their Old World creeds and loyalties they've shed,

And pretty much live life the same as led

The matchcoat kingdoms of King Powhatan:

Round up a hunt, pray, dip fish, and scratch the land.

—If you find false orthography or broken English, they are small faults in soldiers that not being able to write learnedly only strive to speak truly, and be understood without an interpreter.

THOMAS ABBAY
221

Preface

WHEN the colonists left England in December 1606, and bore away over wintry seas in three ships for America, the Council of Virginia sent with them certain "Instructions by way of advice," one of which read, "You shall do well to send a perfect relation by Captain Newport of all that is done." And well they did. When Newport, after two months in Virginia, weighed anchor off Jamestown to return to England on 22 June 1607, he brought with him in the *Susan Constant* a copious response. Everything in this volume flows from it.

Perfect means "in full," and *relation* means events written down by one who was there. This edition seeks to present every one of them that has survived to the modern age, everything written by those that were at Jamestown, England's first permanent New World colony, from the beginning up to the year 1617—Virginia's first apogee.

Unfortunately the editor has had an easy task. Little survives and much is lost. There are no early bibliographies to give us an idea how much, but the amount is surely vast. Personal correspondence is largely missing. We have no heartfelt letters home or to a spouse. We have only Perkins' letter to "a friend," Whitaker's letter to his friend Crashaw, Percy's begging letter to his brother, the Earl of Northumberland. There must have been hundreds of diaries. We have portions of three, not counting the contributors in Smith's *Map* and *Proceedings*. The rest is official reports to Lord Salisbury and other councilors and high officials—narratives, descriptions, natural resource inventories, policy advisories—all of it earnest attempts to make those in the Old World understand the day-to-day tribulations attending the unbounded promise of the New. Much of it is deeply inspired; a great deal of effort has been put into these official reports.

They make up the American half of the documents historians use to reconstruct the era. The American window. That is to say, as historians assemble sherds to give us a description of the mosaic, here are the sherds for you to assemble. For that reason I give no "history of Jamestown" synopsis for the period they cover. They *are* the history, all anybody knows.

Wonderful and beautiful as this collection is, there is no reason to suppose even the best has come down to us. Samuel Purchas and Captain John Smith made "literary" selections at the time. But Purchas was often a poor judge of what we want to read today, and cuts short many a narrative just when it is getting going. Captain Smith earns more of our gratitude, though he only selected material that would make him look good amid controversy. Neither of them picked as an historian would pick today. The Virginia Company kept good records until it was dissolved in 1624. A lot remained unpublished or uncopied up to that year. Very little of this was looked at for the next two centuries. Meanwhile fire, moth, and neglect took their toll.

In 1819 Smith's *General History* was reprinted by Gilmer in Richmond, Virginia; in the 1830s Peter Force began publishing his *Tracts* in Washington, D. C.—containing, among various Colonial documents, reprints of *Nova Britannia* (1609), *A True Declaration* (1610), and *The New Life of Virginia* (1612), promotionals which contain much "relation," and other pieces. In 1849, 228 years after his death, the Hakluyt Society saw to the first publication of William Strachey's

The History of Travel into Virginia Britannia; a decade later Gabriel Archer's *Relation, Description,* and *Brief Description*—three writings that returned on the *Susan Constant* on the 22nd of June—were published by the American Antiquarian Society. In the next generation, Arber, Neill, Brown, Tyler, and others collected and brought out much of the remainder. Working a hundred years after Peter Force, Susan Myra Kingsbury transcribed and saw through the press the surviving records of the Virginia Company not already in print in Brown's *Genesis of the United States* (1890) or elsewhere. The last great discoverer of America at Jamestown was Philip L. Barbour in his 1969 two-volume *The Jamestown Voyages under the First Charter.*

In the meantime, I am advised one of our manuscripts has gone missing—Spelman's *Relation of Virginia.*

Doubtless during the 400th anniversary in 2007 there will be much focus of attention and energy on our subject; new searches will be made and new material may come forth. Witness two recent discoveries: the "Caert Vande Rivier Powhatan," a 1617 map of the James River, and the addition to the Ferrar Papers, from which three items appear here, one for the first time.

But this is a new edition in which this editor seeks to do two things, namely, to gather the material under one cover for the first time, and to derive a modern text, a text that is verbatim, not literatim, which for nearly all this material will also be the first time. This has long been routine with contemporary editions of Shakespeare and Bacon, the famous literature of the time, let alone the King James Bible.

That said, if the above suggests some difficulty of access hitherto, an exception is surely the works of Captain John Smith. Barbour's masterful *Complete Works* (1986) at the expensive end and Kupperman's *Captain John Smith* (1988), selected writings, at the paperback end, would seem to have done justice to one of our contributors (to name only the most recent publications). One might wonder if his inclusion here is perfunctory.

I include Smith because I include everything from the period. But I thought long and hard about how to do so. His Virginia writings are *A True Relation* (1608), *A Map of Virginia & The Proceedings* (1612), and the third and fourth books of his *General History* (1624). These duplicate and overlap each other extensively. I decided the best way to present Smith was by cutting and combining and spreading his material throughout the book so that the reader gets it all, but gets it all only once. As a result, I present 20% of *A Map* under that title at §16, but the rest under William Strachey's *The History of Travel §41. A True Relation* is wonderful historical writing, full of details he repeats nowhere else, but it has needed an editor worse than anything else in this volume. *The Proceedings* is just as interesting and nearly as bad. Readers have too long neglected these works in favor of the *General History*. Here they are done full justice, each in its own way.

The closest I come to a perfunctory inclusion is Tindall's short letter to Prince Henry. It says little about Virginia. Instead it leaves us in tears for what is lost beyond hazard or recovery. But the rest of our sources remind us time and again that this is a most interesting period of history from any angle.

We often get a number of them. The first voyage to Virginia, the exploration of the James River, trading and negotiating with Powhatan, the capture of Pocahontas, the shipwreck of the *Sea Venture,* the starving time, feud and faction, charge and counter-charge—events come down to us in two, three, four versions, sometimes supplied by the same person. They supplement, they corroborate, they conflict, they attack each other directly, always throwing a different light on the same goings-on. It is the single most interesting characteristic of the material taken as a whole. We are admonished each time how easy it is to write history from one source.

Ralph Hamor in 1614 tells us that things are doing fine, all in all, only to sign the *Answer of the General Assembly* in 1623 (§58), a vast denunciation of the Virginia Company that describes Dale's governorship as a reign of terror. So who's telling the truth and when is he telling it? Can we really believe Smith when he says people preferred starving to working? Or that the Onawmanient Indians were urged from Jamestown to assassinate him? And Smith himself—hero or hoax? He has been called a liar and a braggart so often by so many writers, it begins to sound like the controversy over the authorship of Shakespeare's plays. I suspect it stems more from his personality than his achievements. Archer and Wingfield and Percy were of the anti-Smith faction; Strachey and indirectly Hamor (as well as Crashaw in London) praise him and bolster some of his assertions.

What sort of people were coming over as colonists? We have the clear evidence before us that Virginia has never had such a high proportion of good writers. But every one of them is partisan in describing his fellow colonists. The colonists were employees in various capacities of the Virginia Company. Those in the leadership either owned stock or had connections, or both. At the bottom were hired hands. But among them, Anas Todkill, listed as a carpenter, then as a soldier, in 1607, is one of our best writers and may have contributed to the drafting of Smith's 1612 map of Virginia. William White, listed as a laborer, supplies Smith, Strachey, and Purchas with the text of his eyewitness account of the black boys ceremony among the Quiyoughcohanock. At times it sounds like the bulk of the rank and file are indolent and mutinous; other times it sounds like the personnel problems cluster at the top. More often we just don't know. When Francis West sailed for England with a load of corn from Patawomeck, did he desert the colony in the starving time or was he hijacked by mutineers? He returned a few years later with Lord Delaware, his brother, without a murmur. He later became governor of Virginia. Without a murmur.

In the seventeenth century one would recommend an average guy by saying he was a "gentleman of esteem," whereas today we talk up personality, intelligence, expertise, job experience.

Smith gives us his opinion that, no matter who ran it or who staffed it, the colony as a collective enterprise was bound to fail, whereas each man laboring for his own profit succeeded. But this is not the direction he moved in during his presidency, and, after all, what was the Virginia Company if not a profit-seeking privatization of colony making? And what avail was private enterprise before the introduction of tobacco as a runaway cash crop?

The English had settled in a region of relatively dense native population. We read of Indians everywhere in the land and rivers. For their part, Indians saw a tiny outpost of Europeans as a trade opportunity, possibly as allies with gunpowder against their fierce and powerful Indian enemies. It is only later they come to see a permanent and burgeoning colony as a full-scale invasion competing with them for their homeland. Even then, they assume they have the American safety valve, and can fall back into the interior as a last resort to replace lands lost to settlers.

A few of our sources manifest a real curiosity for native culture. William White went and lived among the Quiyoughcohanock. Whitaker and Strachey, for all their politically correct piety, could not help but be fascinated by the new world of Indian ways and beliefs. At times it looks like the two peoples, after several bitter clashes, were coming to accept a peaceful coexistence. A period of relative tranquility opened up after the marriage of Pocahontas and John Rolfe. Other Englishmen, with or without official leave, lived among the local tribes. Our reporters tell us there was a shortage of males among the native population due to constant warfare; at the same time there were very few Englishwomen at Jamestown. The Spanish ambassador in London, Don Pedro de Zuñiga, sent a diplomatic dispatch to the King of Spain that stands alone from the period:[1]

> SIRE—There is come hither a ship from Virginia. And although some principal men and others suppose that the plantation there doth rather diminish than increase, I have understood by a friend of good credit that they treat and have a determination to marry some of the people that go thither with the Virginians[2]; and he telleth me that there are forty or fifty

[1] Enclosure in a contemporary translation in a dispatch from Sir John Digby, English ambassador to the Court of Spain, to James I. Digby may have made the translation himself. Digby's cover letter to King James reads in part: May 13, 1613. Madrid. – "They have further the last week had a consultation concerning Virginia, but their resolution is not to stir therein until they shall be better informed of the true state thereof. For that here [in Spain] by the advertisements that they have had out of England they are yet in a great hope that the business will fall of itself, though Don Pedro de Çuñiga, at his last being in England, moved that the removing of our plantation might be no longer deferred, as Your Majesty shall see by the copy of a letter sent from him in September last." In Brown 1890:632.

[2] Indians. Brown's 19th-century translator, Maximilian Schele de Vere, renders here and below, "I have been told by a friend, who tells me the truth, that some of the people who have gone there think now some of them should marry the women of the savages of that country." In Brown 1890:572.

persons already married there, and other English intermingled with them[1]; and that the women which were sent over live amongst the Virginians and are received and used kindly by them; and that they wounded[2] a certain zealous minister of their sect for reprehending it.

London, 22 of September [1612].[3] God preserve Your Majesty.

If there were many Pocahontases and many a John Rolfe, the obvious sequel did not occur—two races either becoming one or producing a large mixed population, as happened in French, Spanish, and Portuguese America. The course of events after 1607 is most interesting history, and the reader here has the same contemporary material historians have had to make his own judgments.

On the whole, the English at Jamestown were condescending and contemptuous of native culture. The native people were "simple, savage, thievish, subtle, inconstant, treacherous"—words chosen over and over to describe bad encounters. But there were many good encounters, and on those occasions our reporters regularly reverse themselves and speak of Indians as upright, truthful, possessing uncommon moral and physical courage, full of intelligence, ingenuity, and wisdom. The common opinion was that Indians after a generation or two would get baptized, civilized, and anglicized. In a word, they had more potential than the Irish. Here are two excerpts from Jamestown letters from the years immediately after our period. They contain sympathetic accounts, I think:

TO SIR GEORGE SANDYS—[4]

The great werowance Powhawtan, in his annual progress through his petty provinces, coming to Patowamack, was there as in other places entertained with the greatest honor that nation could. Amongst other shows of solemnity and much mirth, it was ordered that their young men, such as were fit for war,[5] should in a soldier-like manner present themselves before His Majesty, each of these in his turn declaring what worthy exploits by their undaunted valors they had achieved against

---

[1] "... and other Englishmen after being put among them have become savages."

[2] "... was seriously wounded in many places."

[3] The date on Zuñiga's letter is London, August 1, 1612. Rec'd in Madrid, August 18.

[4] Kingsbury 1906c:438.

[5] The inference here is that certain of the other young men were *not* fitted for war.

their enemies, the Massoamacks, and the wild beasts of their forest, everyone striving to strain his actions highest, thereby expecting the greater reward and commendations.

Amongst these, he whose lot was last though not of the least account, having noted his fellows in their extraordinary boastings to devour even more than all that might be said to any purpose in that kind, coming forth, and with a stout and decent behavior making his obeisance, thus related: "And I, my lord, went this morning into a great marsh and there valiantly killed six muskrats, which, though it be no more than the boys do daily, yet this, my liege, is true and most the rest fables."

This moved the whole assembly to laughter; nor was the truth of his mean action either blamed or shamed, for the jest so took the king that this fellow's poor endeavors was most regarded and best rewarded *fabula narratur,*[1] and so I rest.

The true affected servant of your most equisite virtues.
WIL POWELL.

James City, April 12th, 1621.

THE GOVERNOR IN VIRGINIA TO THE COUNCIL IN LONDON—[2]

Being desirous by all good means to continue and enlarge [good feeling with the Indians] as a thing very necessary at the beginning of his government, [I] did, and with the advice and consent of the council, send Captain [George] Thorpe with a message and a present both to the Great King Sasawpen,[3] formerly called Ocatan, and to his brother Apochankano, now Mangopeesomon,[4] whom he found much satisfied with his coming, though they were before, as they confessed, in some jealousy whether our new governor would continue the league or not. Apochankano gave him very good hope of their entertaining of some of our families to live amongst them, and of their sending to cohabit with us, and did confirm a former promise of sending one to be our guide beyond the Falls to certain mines, which we purpose to tie him unto. Captain Thorpe found by discoursing with him that he had more motions of religion in him than could be imagined in so great blindness, for he willingly acknowledged that theirs was not the right way, desiring to be instructed in ours, and confessed that God loved us better than them, and that he thought the cause of His anger against them was their

---

[1] Latin: "The story goes."
[2] Kingsburg 1906c:584.
[3] Or "Sacawpen." (Kingsbury)
[4] Perhaps not a second name but a title or epithet, meaning "Big Peace Pipe."

> custom of making their children "black boys." He found also that he had some knowledge of many of the fixed stars and had observed the North Star and the course of the constellation[s] about that, and called the Great Bear[1] *manguahaian,* which in their language signifies the same; and being then in the middest of his hunting, did in conclusion refer Captain Thorpe touching all matters to a further conference at Pomucke when he had ended his hunting. January 1622.

The Council of Virginia endorsed the sentiments expressed in Robert Johnson's *The New Life of Virginea* by seeing to its publication in May 1612[2]:

> Take their children and train them up with gentleness; teach them our English tongue, and the principles of religion; win the elder sort by wisdom and discretion; make them equal with your English in case of protection, wealth, and habitation, doing justice on such as shall do them wrong. Weapons of war are needful, I grant, but for defense only, and not in this case. If you seek to gain this victory upon them by stratagems of war, you shall utterly lose it, and never come near it, but shall make your names odious to all their posterity. Instead of iron and steel, you must have patience and humanity to manage their crooked nature to your form of civility. For as our proverb is—"Look how you win them; so you must wear them"—if by way of peace and gentleness, then shall you always range them in love to you-wards, and in peace with your English people; and by proceeding in that way, shall open the springs of earthly benefits to them both, and of safety to yourselves.

But Mr. Johnson was never in America. It is difficult to say how serious the Virginia Company was in its evangelical mission, iterated in all three charters. There is much protestation of the primacy of such motives in the propaganda tracts, meaning that sentiment must have been strong in England. But the impetus towards colonizing that led to Jamestown came out of Bristol, Plymouth, and London, not Canterbury, York, and Coventry. The Company sent few preachers, though some good ones, and did not found active

---

[1] The constellation Ursa Major. The same with many other Indian tribes.

[2] Robert Johnson's *The New Life of Virginea* (Force 1836a: 6/18–19). Other selections are at p. 17 & §40–560.

missions, as the Spanish routinely did, and as the Maryland colony did right away under the Jesuit Father Andrew White in the 1630s.

TO THE RIGHT WORSHIPFUL SIR THOMAS SMYTHE, KNIGHT, TREASURER OF VIRG[INIA]—

Whereas the Council and Company have granted to Mr. John Rolfe and the Lady Rebecka—his wife, daughter of King Powhatan, and lately converted to Christian religion—the sum of one hundred pounds, to be paid out of the monies collected for works to be performed for the planting and propagating of Christian religion in those heathen parts, forasmuch as the said sum of one hundred pounds was granted to the said Mr. Rolfe and his lady, partly in doing honor to that good example of her conversion, and to encourage other of her kindred and nation to do the like, and partly upon promise made by the said Mr. Rolfe in behalf of himself and the said lady, his wife, that both by their godly and virtuous example in their particular persons and family as also by all other good means of persuasions and inducements, they would employ their best endeavors to the winning of that people to the knowledge of God and embracing of true religion. Forasmuch also as the said Mr. Rolfe hath promised, as occasion hereafter shall require by his honest and faithful care, to set forward the business of building a college in Virginia for the training up of those heathen children in true religion, accordingly as it shall be hereafter desired—

WE, whose names are hereunder written, by special authority derived unto us by the said Council and Company, well approving of the said grant upon the considerations aforesaid, do desire you that the said sum of one hundred pounds may be paid to Mr. John Rolfe out of the particular cash of the collections aforesaid.

EDWIN SANDYS JHON WROTHE

Copy of the warrant for 100 *librae* to be delivered for the Lady Rebecca out of the money collected for sacred use in Virginia.
10 March 1616.[1]

The Lady Rebecca is, of course, Pocahontas. Indian children in Virginia were receiving Christian schooling. The College of Henrico and the East India School, plans for which fell by the way in the aftermath of the 1622 massacre, were to be classrooms for *Indians,*

[1] Magdalene College: The Ferrar Papers, 72–1611.2

the same as William and Mary three generations later. Our contributors tell us firmly that no real progress can be made in rooting out savagery and heathenism among a native population still in touch with its own priests. All the bad characteristics the English find in the Indians they lay to the instigation and influence of a satanic priesthood. Indian religion was dismissed as devil worship.

Did the English feel a racial as well as cultural superiority to native peoples? It is a difficult distinction. Strachey says Indians are dark only because they dye themselves. Within the first decade at Jamestown it seems to me the rules governing racial apartheid in the South, so associated with African slavery, actually came into being between whites and Indians. It was a cultural separation, not a physical separation, for Indians were everywhere in the streets and homes of the English as if they lived there, and whites were scattered far and wide living in Indian society, with some intermarriage. I am not a student of culture, but having lived in the South all my days, I find in the latter twentieth century the physical separation of the races, all races, to be increasing faster than cultural separation is decreasing, though it is decreasing, thank goodness. Even so, these trends, one bad, one good, are the first seismic shift, I think, since, let us say, 1615. The effect of the 1622 massacre on this was, I think, to dash hopes that cultural apartheid would ever be overcome.

Jamestown was always at pains to fulfill what Bacon called the first priority of colony-making—establishing an economic base. Early profit-taking by investors, too many men drawn off in special projects, or even, if such were the case, scarce resources diverted to support mission work—these might have been the wrong priorities until settlers had the wherewithal to feed and clothe and defend themselves. Self-sufficiency in food? The English were engulfed by the large and often hostile native population. Until they had a secure perimeter, it was surely difficult to get volunteers to expose themselves working in the fields to raise food for hundreds of people, all the while serving as sitting ducks for any passing native war party. Dale frequently mentions projects to "impale" tracts of land. Might such a "Hadrian's Wall" have been set up at Dale's Gift on the Eastern Shore instead of Rochdale on the upper James River? Again, the reader here has all the early sources to make his own judgment.

But judgment should be tempered by a few further considerations. We have only what survives, which is little and is filtered. The Council of Virginia maintained a rigorous censorship over communication coming out of the colony. Colonists could not correspond directly with family and friends at home. A regime of censorship at the same time invites, *demands,* partisan reporting. If rumors were bad it discouraged investors. If rumors were good it aroused Spanish jealousy and encouraged the Dutch and French to get in on the action and plant on the same coast—which they did soon enough!

Hence it appears the wise policy-makers of the Council of Virginia in London had to see to the creation of two images of Virginia, of a propaganda with a twofold thrust, calculated on the positive side to quash rumors and allay fears, and to lure settlers and venture captial as a self-fulfilling prophecy of success. This survives in the form of printed tracts of five to ten thousand words—*A True and Sincere Declaration §19, A True Declaration §25,* Whitaker's *Good News from Virginia §42,* Johnson's *Nova Britannia* and *The New Life of Virginea §40, Saules Prohibition Staid, A Good Speed to Virginia,* Hamor's *Discourse §50,* and more that survive only in name—as well as high-octance sermons by leading preachers—Crakanthorpe, Symonds, Price, Crashaw—also published, who acknowledged commercial advantages but saw overseas colonization as a holy mission to spread what Pedro de Zuñiga called "their sect." They stirred up as much national fury as pious enthusiasm.

The poet laureate Michael Drayton came down with the fever and produced this ode, we guess in 1608, a piece of most complex meter and intense rhyming, an effect which I take as righteous. In recent times the "Ode to the Virginian Voyage" has been set for chorus.

You brave, heroic minds,
Worthy your country's name,
That honor still pursue,
Go and subdue,
Whilst loit'ring hinds
Lurk here at home with shame.

Britons, you stay too long—
Quickly aboard bestow you,
And with a merry gale
Swell your stretch'd sail,
With vows as strong
As the winds that blow you.

Your course securely steer,
West and by south forth keep;
Rocks, lee shores, nor shoals,
When Aeolus scowls,
You need not fear,
So absolute the deep.

And cheerfully at sea
Success you still entice
To get the pearl and gold
And, *ours to hold,*
VIRGINIA—
Earth's only paradise!

Where nature hath in store
Fowl, venison, and fish,
And the fruitfull'st soil
Without your toil:
Three harvests more,
All greater than you wish;

And the ambitious vine
Crowns with his purple mass
The cedar reaching high
To kiss the sky,
The cypress, pine,
And useful sassafras,

To whose the Golden Age
Still nature's law doth give,
No other cares that tend
But them to defend
From winter's age,
That long there doth not live.

LIBRARY OF VIRGINIA

MICHAEL DRAYTON
(1563-1631)

Whenas the luscious smell
Of that delicious land
Above the seas that flows
The clear wind throws
Your hearts to swell,
Approaching the dear strand,

In kenning of the shore
(Thanks to God first given),
O you, the happy'st men,
Be frolic[1] then;
Let cannons roar,
Frighting the wide heaven,

And in regions far
Such heroes bring ye forth
As those from whom we came;
And plant our name
Under that star
Not known unto our north.

And as there plenty grows
Of laurel everywhere,
Apollo's sacred tree,
You it may see,
A poet's brows
To crown that may sing there.

Thy voyages attend,
Industrious HACKLUIT,
Whose reading shall inflame
Men to seek fame,
And much commend
To aftertimes thy wit.

---

[1] Merry.

An easy target for satire, to be sure, but the reader will find all these exuberant claims almost word for word among our contributors: America the land of opportunity and England's destiny. Nevertheless, at the same time, the Council in its wisdom may have been deliberately spreading negative reports in another place, a place always aswarm with spies: at the court of King James—to the effect that things in Virginia were quite bad, in fact falling to pieces. These would be directed at the mortal and ever-present danger of Spain, with her Atlantic squadron. Spain could in one morning wipe out the tiny settlement of English interlopers in Virginia if it showed signs of permanency, as she had the French in Florida. Spain and England had ratified peace agreements in 1604, but they remained adversaries, and Spain insisted on claims to all of North America. On the other hand, if the Spanish were led to believe the new colony was going the way of Roanoke and Sagadahoc and about to collapse on its own, perhaps the peace would tempt them to leave this problem alone to take care of itself. The three Spanish ambassadors in London during our period—Zuñiga, Velasco, Gondomar—while dutifully and continuously urging immediate action to remove the colony, sent a number of dispatches home with this caution also.

And so Jamestown, always threatened, survived and never came under foreign attack. Surely it must be laid down as a great credit to King James that the realm opened a great colonial territory in lands claimed by Spain without firing a shot.

TO THE EARL OF SALISBURY,[1]
MY LORD—

Upon Wednesday morning [13 December 1609], I went to Newmarket, and before the King went to dinner I delivered unto him what I received from Your Lordship concerning etc.

Your Lordship's most assuredly to do you service,
H. SOUTHAMPTON.

The 15 of December.
P.S. Talking with the King, by chance I told him of the Virginia squirrels which they say will fly, whereof there are now divers brought into England; and he presently and very earnestly asked me if none of them

[1] Brown 1890:356–57.

was provided for him, and whether Your Lordship had none for him, saying that he was sure you would get him one of them. I would not have troubled you with this but that you know so well how he is affected to these toys, and with a little inquiry of any of your folks you may furnish yourself to present him at his coming to London, which will not be before Wednesday next; the Monday before to Theobals, and the Saturday before that to Royston.

JAMES I
(1566-1625)
KING OF ENGLAND 1603-1625

This book evolved as it was written. It was shaped and guided by me, the editor, but also substantially it is a product of the people I have been fortunate to work with. My deepest thanks go to Helen Rountree, E. Randolph Turner, III, and J. Frederick Fausz, who each so graciously read the manuscript at a late stage. Thanks go to Dean Simpson of the University of Richmond, who deserves all the credit for the good Latin translations and none of the blame for the bad ones I somehow neglected to show him. Same with my dear, severe copy editor Lisa Chute for so many good corrections. And warmest thanks go to so many libraries and staffs: to my own Essex Public Library; to Alice Moore and Linda Taylor of Rappahannock Community College library, always a pleasure to visit; to Del Moore and the Jamestown Reassessment Project; to Ted Polk and Lee Bagby Viverette and the Library of Virginia; to Aude Fitzsimons, assistant librarian at Magdalene College, Cambridge; to Michael Plunkett and Gayle Cooper and the great Alderman Library (Gayle drew and sent me a confirming sketch of the "Creation of the World"); to E. Lee Shepard and the Virginia Historical Society; to the Library of Congress for the chance to read President Jefferson's papers and to transcribe the Smith/Zuñiga and Velasco maps; to Gil Kelly and the Omohundro Institute of Early American History and Culture for occasion to study the notes and papers of Philip Barbour.

Thanks go to my dear friends, husband and wife, Sarah Lavicka, who did my covers, and Frank Jewell, who lent so much time and valuable advice. To my new friend Dorothy Rouse-Bottom for her timely gift of Preston and Yeandle's *English Handwriting.* It much refined my self-taught knowledge of secretary hand. And to Henry Bond of the Jamestown Settlement for his knowledge of log canoes.

What makes a book like this possible? The Colonial Records Project of the Library of Virginia. Begun by Van Schreeven and Berkeley in the '50s, in two decades it burgeoned into a monster of unmanageable beauty, until Jon Kukla and John Kneebone succeeded, where many others had failed, in devising a means to index and catalog and cross-reference all 14,704 "survey reports." Today you may look up the whole collection of original microfilmed manuscripts by home computer.

The lonely scholar squinting over his desk of papers through days and weeks, nothing is so precious to him as the company he keeps.

"CHESITUXENT," ESSEX COUNTY, VIRGINIA
APRIL 1998

CONTENTS

TEXTS

CONTENTS

CONTENTS

PORTRAITS & ILLUSTRATIONS

MAPS

JAMESTOWN NARRATIVES

EYEWITNESS ACCOUNTS OF THE VIRGINIA COLONY

THE FIRST DECADE: 1607–1617

INTRODUCTION

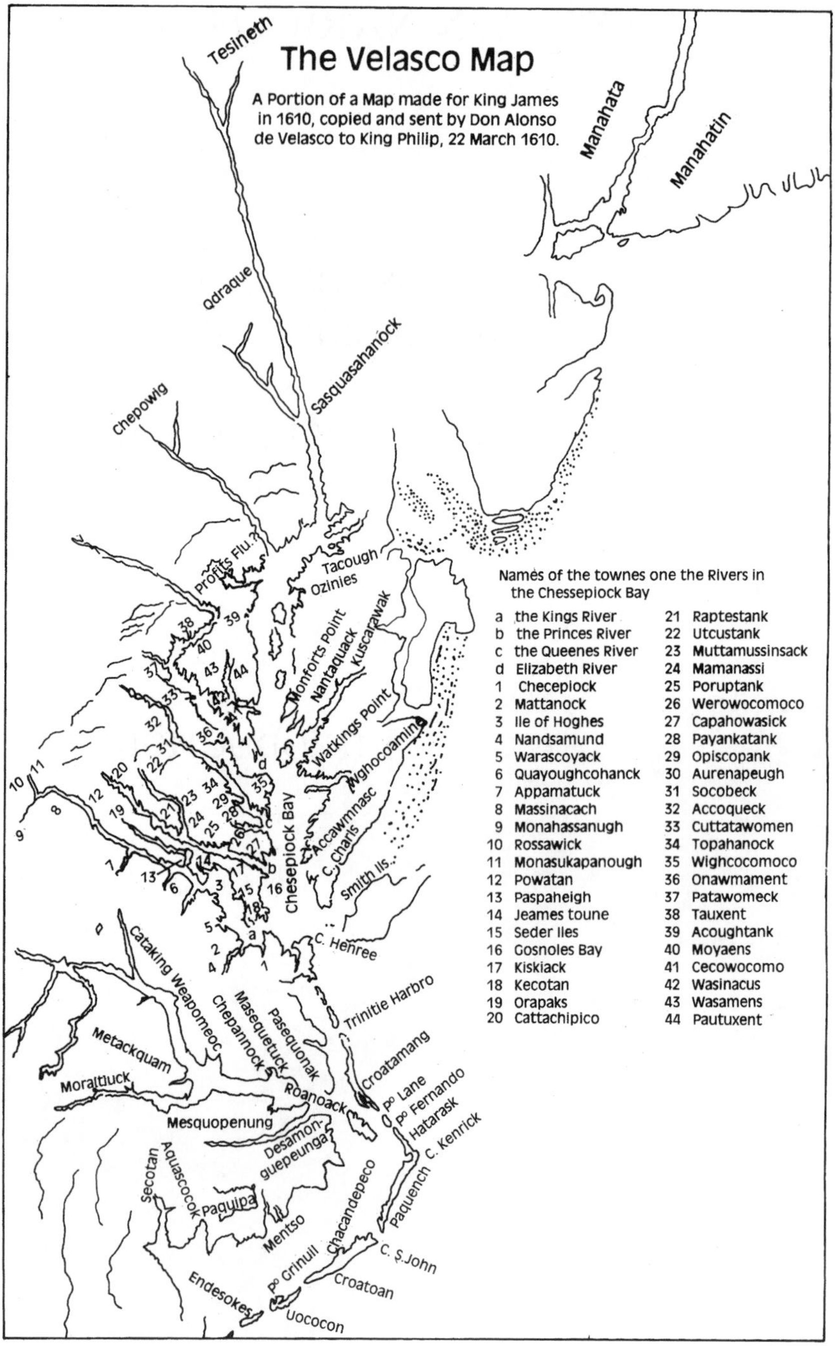
The Velasco Map
A Portion of a Map made for King James in 1610, copied and sent by Don Alonso de Velasco to King Philip, 22 March 1610.
Tesineth
Manahata
Manahatin
Odraque
Sasquasahanock
Chepowig
Profits Flu.?
Tacough
Ozinies
Monforts Point
Nantaquack
Kuscarawak
Watkings Point
Wighcocoamino
Accawmnasc
C. Charls
Smith Ils.
Chesepiock Bay
C. Henree
Trinitie Harbro
Cataking Weapomeoc
Chepannock
Masequetuck
Pasequonak
Metackquam
Moratuck
Roanoack
Croatamang
Pº Lane
Pº Fernando
Hatarask
C. Kenrick
Mesquopenung
Desamon-guepeunga
Secotan
Aquascocok
Paquipa
Mentso
Chacandepeco
Paquench
C. S.John
Pº Grinuil
Croatoan
Endesokes
Uococon
Names of the townes one the Rivers in the Chessepiock Bay
a the Kings River
b the Princes River
c the Queenes River
d Elizabeth River
1 Checepiock
2 Mattanock
3 Ile of Hoghes
4 Nandsamund
5 Warascoyack
6 Quayoughcohanck
7 Appamatuck
8 Massinacach
9 Monahassanugh
10 Rossawick
11 Monasukapanough
12 Powatan
13 Paspaheigh
14 Jeames toune
15 Seder Iles
16 Gosnoles Bay
17 Kiskiack
18 Kecotan
19 Orapaks
20 Cattachipico
21 Raptestank
22 Utcustank
23 Muttamussinsack
24 Mamanassi
25 Poruptank
26 Werowocomoco
27 Capahowasick
28 Payankatank
29 Opiscopank
30 Aurenapeugh
31 Socobeck
32 Accoqueck
33 Cuttatawomen
34 Topahanock
35 Wighcocomoco
36 Onawmament
37 Patawomeck
38 Tauxent
39 Acoughtank
40 Moyaens
41 Cecowocomo
42 Wasinacus
43 Wasamens
44 Pautuxent

Introduction to the Narratives

ENGLAND IN AMERICA

IN MARCH 1496, King Henry VII of England, sorry to have turned down one Genoese, granted letters patent to another, to John Cabot, to claim unknown lands "under our banners and ensigns." Cabot and his sons sailed from Bristol the following year in the *Mathew,* made land, 24 June 1497, at perhaps Nova Scotia, perhaps Newfoundland, explored six or seven degrees of coastline, and returned. Cabot obtained another patent, set out again in the spring of 1498 with four ships, and never returned.

He was the first European to reach North America since Leif Ericson. His voyage lays the basis of England's claim to "Virginia," one which, doubtless due to her good relations with Spain, she made little attempt to realize for most of a century.

His son Sebastian Cabot explored from Labrador southward, possibly as far as Florida, in a voyage of 1508–09. He was convinced he had found the entrance to a northwest passage to the Pacific Ocean (Davis Strait, Hudson Strait, Gulf of St. Lawrence?) when his crewmen forced him to turn back. By now Europe no longer thought America was Asia but a land mass blocking the way to Asia.

In 1524, Giovanni da Verrazano, sailing for France, on his first voyage coasted North America from Cape Fear to Newfoundland. The following year the Spaniard Esteban Gomez explored the Gulf of St. Lawrence and the New England coast. Also in 1525, Luiz Vasquez de Ayllon fitted out a fleet in Hispaniola of 500 colonists, with black slaves, friars, horses, and sailed north to found a settlement, likely on the Cape Fear River. He died, and the settlement was abandoned with 150 survivors in 1526. These three voyages, revealing no valuable commodities, served to turn Spain's attention from North America.

In 1527 the Englishman John Rut's two ships coasted from Labrador to the Spanish West Indies. A decade later Richard Hore led two ships to Newfoundland, lost one, ran out of food, captured and spoiled a French ship there, and returned to England with few survivors.

Jacques Cartier sailing from St. Malo, Normandy, in 1534 explored the Gulf of St. Lawrence. On his second voyage, the year following, he discovered and explored the St. Lawrence River as far as Montreal. The fleet wintered at Stadacona (Quebec) and sailed home in May 1536. Five years later as captain and pilot of an expedition commanded by the Sieur de Roberval, he returned to the "chemin de Canada" and established Charlesbourg-Royal just upstream from Stadacona, which after food shortage and Indian attack was abandoned in the spring of 1542. Roberval, arriving with his party right after Cartier had departed with his, attempted immediate resettlement with nearly 600 new colonists at France-Roy, a site nearby. His party spent a year and departed with survivors in the summer of 1543. These voyages placed Canada in "Nova Francia," the French sphere of the continent.

In testimony to the Spanish explorer Tristan de Luna, a Franco-English prisoner in 1560 described his experience on a French ship some years before:

> He is called John, an Englishman born in Bristol. In the year [15]46, being a boy of ten years, he left Artamua [Dartmouth or Plymouth], which is in England, in a ship of the fleet [a French privateering fleet?]. As it was coming to await the ships which went from the Indies [the Spanish trade fleet from the Indies], a storm struck them which forced them to make the

> land of Florida in 37°. They found a very good bay where they anchored. Soon there came alongside over thirty canoes, in each of which were fifteen to twenty persons with bows and arrows. They would not permit more than two to come on board, and they gave them as many as a thousand marten skins in exchange for knives, fishhooks, and shirts. After two days they went away from there towards the south ...[1]

Thirty-seven degrees is the latitude of the Virginia capes, which makes this the very first account we have of the Chesapeake Bay.

In the second half of the 16th century English privateers, operating on Spanish shipping in the Caribbean and the North American east coast, thoroughly familiarized themselves with American waters.

Richard Eden, in his translation of Peter Martyr's *The Decades of the New World, or West India* (London, 1555), advocated the colonization of North America as a region similar in climate and resources to England and northern Europe.

In 1561 a Spanish ship landed in the Chesapeake Bay and took away the teenage son of a Powhatan werowance. He was baptized Don Luis, sojourned in Mexico and Cuba, and was educated by the Dominicans in Spain. He next accompanied a Jesuit expedition led by Father Juan Segura to found a mission in his homeland, a region the Spanish called "Ajacán" on the bay of "Santa Maria" or "Madre de Dios." They entered the Bay in 1570 and established the mission on the south shore of the York River, probably, between Queen and King creeks. Don Luis, ostensibly in the role of an ambassador, immediately abandoned the group and returned up river to his own people, leaving the missionaries to their fate, which came in February 1571 when all were massacred by the Indians. A lone survivor, a boy, was retrieved a year later by the Spanish, who did not omit to kill eight Indians in revenge.

Still looking for a way around a continent, Martin Frobisher, in three voyages in Arctic waters, 1576–78, discovered Frobisher Bay on Baffin Island and pronounced it the northwest passage.

Richard Hakluyt published *Divers Voyages Touching the Discovery of America,* the book appearing in 1582.

In June 1583, Sir Humphrey Gilbert sailed on his second attempt

---

[1] Quinn 1979a: 218

to reach lands to the west, intending to found a colony. Four ships arrived in St. Johns, Newfoundland—a harbor long popular with European fishermen for drying codfish caught on the Grand Banks. By this time the sails of fisherman and whalers were a familiar sight in North American waters. Gilbert landed settlers among fishermen and claimed the island for England, August 3, 1583. He next reembarked his people, sailed south, lost a ship on the shoals around Sable Island, and decided to go no further. On the return voyage Gilbert went down with the *Squirrel* in a storm near the Azores. The remainder of the fleet arrived home in safety. Newfoundland is deemed England's first colony.

His half brother, Sir Walter Raleigh, now took up England's North American challenge. He obtained a patent from the queen, March 1584, and chose two captains—Philip Amadas and Arthur Barlowe—with Simon Ferdinando (Simão Fernandes) as pilot, to reconnoiter the coast well to the south of Gilbert's voyage. That summer they explored the outer banks and sounds of the North Carolina coast where the people, according to Barlowe, "entertained [us] with all love and kindness, and with as much bounty, after their manner, as they could possibly devise. We found the people most gentle, loving, and faithful, void of all guile and treason, and such as lived after the manner of the Golden Age. The earth bringeth forth all things in abundance, as in the first creation, without toil or labor."

Amadas and Barlowe were back in England in September.

Richard Hakluyt wrote *The Discourse of Western Planting.*

Raleigh changed the local name Windgandcon to "Virginia" with the queen's permission, and organized a colonizing expedition under the command of his kinsman, Sir Richard Grenville. He picked Ralph Lane to be governor of the colony and enlisted and put aboard the scientist Thomas Harriot and the watercolorist John White.

They put out in April 1585 in five ships and two pinnaces with 500 men. After a leisurely voyage through the West Indies taking prizes, 108 colonists landed and established a settlement on Roanoke Island. Grenville and Lane quarreled. Grenville sailed home leaving Lane in charge.

Lane was never satisfied with the site. The water was shallow at the island and "Port" Ferdinando was an exposed anchorage. He scouted for a better situation west and north. Following a tip from the Indians, he sent a party that included Harriot and White (without his brushes) northwards. They reached Hampton Roads and wintered at Skicoak. Meanwhile, doing little to provide for themselves at Roanoke, the English wore out their welcome free-loading on the Indians. Fighting had started when a relief fleet of twenty-three sail arrived in June 1586. It was Sir Francis Drake, fresh from the sack of St. Augustine in Florida, on his way home after a very successful foray on Spanish ports and shipping in the Caribbean.

The nervous Lane asked him to bring off the 103 surviving colonists and two friendly Indians, Wanchese and Manteo; on 18 June 1586 they boarded Drake's ships and sailed for England, abandoning the colony.

Grenville arrived at Roanoke Island behind them in mid July, and finding the fort abandoned he left a small garrison of eighteen led by Coffin and Chapman.

An account of Antonio Espejo's 1583 New Mexico expedition, reporting silver mines, had in the meantime been giving mistaken longitudes so far eastward it seemed they were just in back of the coast of Virginia. The work was brought out by Richard Hakluyt in English. Raleigh immediately began preparations for a second voyage.

A joint stock company was set up and called "The Governor and Assistants of the City of Raleigh in Virginia." John White the artist was named governor. The colonists numbered 89 men, 17 women, and 11 children, including the Dares, White's daughter and son-in-law. They sailed in April 1587 in three ships via the West Indies, Simon Ferdinando commanding the flagship and again acting as pilot as on the previous two voyages. Their intended destination had been the Hampton Roads visited earlier, but Ferdinando regardless brought them back to Port Ferdinando off Roanoke Island. Grenville's garrison had disappeared and the fort had been razed. Lane's cottages were still in good shape. The colonists decided to land and founded the "City of Raleigh" in late July.

After a month in Virginia, during which the governor's

granddaughter Virginia Dare was born—the first English child born in America—Governor White, after consultation, returned alone with Ferdinando and the fleet and after a stormy passage reached Ireland in October.

White was back in England to serve as full-time public relations and supply agent for the colony, and along with Harriot and Raleigh pulled in enough support to form a relief expedition ready to leave in March 1588, but promptly grounded by order of the Privy Council. It was the year of the Armada and England needed all her shipping at home. In April they inveigled permission to depart in two small vessels that were immediately looted and left at sea by a French man-of-war and had to put back.

It was about this time Thomas Smythe, the future treasurer of the Virginia Company, joined the stockholders of the City of Raleigh.

Nothing was done the following year until White succeeded in putting together a relief of three ships and two pinnaces, captained by John Watts. Most of this flotilla set sail in March 1590, as usual via the West Indies on lookout for Spanish prizes.

By August they dropped anchor off Port Ferdinando, off the inlet into Roanoke Island too shallow to admit ships. White took in a landing party only to find the settlement abandoned in ruins, overgrown with grass and vines. On a post by the entrance he found CROATOAN carved in neat capitals, the name of a nearby island inhabited by friendly Indians whose werowance was the anglicized Manteo. But the weather turned bad and the fleet, at Captain Watts' insistence, had to weigh anchor and put to sea before investigating further. White was back in England in October. He died three years later in 1593. No one to this day knows the fate of his Lost Colony.

In June 1588 Vicente Gonzalez coasted northward out of St. Augustine in a packet boat with 30 soldiers and sailors on the lookout for English colonists. He entered the Chesapeake Bay and sailed the length of it, captured two Indians, and returned, touching the coast several times working his way southward. He failed to discover the colonists on Roanoke Island.

Richard Hakluyt published *The Principal Navigations, Voyages, and Discoveries of the English Nation* (1589).

Thomas Harriot published *A Briefe and True Report of the New Found Land of Virginia* (1588), a very copious, readable, unreliably promising description of the new land and its commodities. Two years later, in 1590, it was brought out again in a grander edition with copperplate engravings by Theodor de Bry of the two dozen watercolors White had done of the local Indians, with five more illustrations of "ancient inhabitants of Britain." These last were the "naked savages" that had been the ancestors of the British races, reminding readers what they had been before civilizers arrived on British coasts. Also included were poor renditions of White's two excellent local maps.

The 100-page book was a hit. It circulated throughout Europe for a century and was essential reading for the Jamestown expedition, both for its information and its technique. Harriot's notes are lost, but John White's collection of original watercolors survives complete in the British Library.

It is estimated Raleigh sank £40,000 into the Roanoke venture.

English designs turned to the Gulf of St. Lawrence. In 1597 an expedition under Charles Leigh attacked the Basque settlement in the Magdalen Islands with the intent of supplanting them with a colony of English Brownists (the first Pilgrims) on Ramea, and establishing a base for monopolizing the fishery. The Basques and Bretons fought them off easily; the expedition fell apart; the Brownists fled into exile in the Netherlands. Thereafter French influence came to predominate in the Gulf and in Canada. The English turned south.

Richard Hakluyt published the second edition of his *Principal Navigations* in 1599–1600, expanding the first edition from 700,000 to 1,700,000 words, a reflection of its popularity.

In 1602 the two young Bartholomews, captains and cousins, Gosnold and Gilbert, coasted New England, gave Cape Cod its name, camped at Cuttyhunk, collected some sassafras, skins, cedar.

Gilbert sailed again a year later and was killed by Indians, perhaps on Delaware Bay.

Raleigh sent Samuel Mace to seek "the port of Hatarask" in 1602 and locate survivors of the Lost Colony. He returned with sassafras. He may have killed a werowance on the Rappahannock River (160).

There followed exploratory voyages by Martin Pring and Captain George Waymouth, sojourning on the coast of Massachusetts and

Maine, the latter returning to England with five Indians, 18 July 1605.

So far these had been private ventures and small scale. But general interest in America had reawakened. Englishmen now saw the need to pool commercial resources in a much larger cooperative undertaking, one that would establish and equip colonies of permanent settlement, and sustain long-term commercial development. We do not know the details of the formation of the Virginia companies. We do not know who said what to whom, or who did what and when. Sir John Popham, Lord Chief Justice, and Sir Robert Cecil, recently made the Earl of Salisbury, the king's chief minister and private secretary—two Plymouth men with ties throughout the West Country, and patrons of several previous American voyages—certainly were the principals in getting things under way, rallying and organizing support, including royal support (moral only, but important), and brought together the monied interests of Plymouth, Exeter, and Bristol. Joining them, Sir Thomas Smythe, the most powerful commercial figure of the city, brought with him the backing of the merchants of London. Sir Walter Cope seems to have been the one that kept everybody in touch.

Investors looked at the success of the six-year-old East India Company. It was paying handsome returns. The West Country people saw wealth in developing American fisheries. The gentry hankered to acquire landed estates in the wilderness, as many had already done in Ireland. There were proven commodities which attracted businessmen—timber and naval stores, cedar, wainscot, clapboard, pipe-staves, iron, potash, soap-ashes. Sassafras was a panacea drug with a good market at the time, though this did not last.

Spain was approaching from the south and France from the north. The French did not yet have permanent settlements in Canada, but their activity on the St. Lawrence had recently picked up. It was only a matter of a year or two before Virginia would be staked out by one power or another. If England hesitated, her colonists might face not only Indians but European soldiers.

The westerners favored commercial development with or without settlements. Separatists, Puritans, Catholics—they would be content

LIBRARY OF VIRGINIA

SIR THOMAS SMYTHE

to let these establish agricultural plantations as long as western merchants controlled trade. After the breakup of the Sagadahoc settlement, the Plymouth Company continued to return good profits from New England.

The Londoners, on the other hand, wanted to develop a colonial commonwealth of farms, fisheries, mines, industries, trading with the Indians by opportunity. Their program depended on establishing a permanent settlement—soldiers and laborers, farmers and families.

A charter was drafted with provisions for both approaches. A Council of Virginia would act as overseer and would prevent their activities from degenerating into West Indian privateering, which, of course, was expected to go on covertly.

English imperialism was a national stirring, but promoters stressed three benefits: the exploitation of lands and riches promised in Harriot's *A Brief and True Report*, the Evangelical mission of Protestant Christianity, and the finding of an outlet for a swelling population of poor and unemployed, among whom were now a large number of soldiers and sailors lately discharged and cut off from privateering at the end of the Atlantic war. King James' peace with Spain was an unpopular one.

The charter was sealed 10 April 1606.

The northern group, the Plymouth Virginia Company, got going first and dispatched Henry Challons in the *Richard* with a couple of Waymouth's Indians and twenty-nine colonists in August 1606, bound for "Mawooshen" (the Penobscot Bay area of Maine). He like the others sailed via the West Indies, and with his whole complement was captured by the Spanish and sent to Spain in chains.

Dealt a blow but undaunted, the Company sent out Thomas Hanham and Martin Pring two months later, who explored the Kennebec and selected the site of Sagadahoc, and sailed home.

The southern group, known as the London Virginia Company, now got underway and sent three ships—the *Susan Constant,* the *Godspeed,* and the *Discovery*—in December 1606 via the Caribbean to the Chesapeake Bay, where they arrived in April 1607. Per instructions, they explored the first river inside the capes—the James—and selected a site for settlement on Jamestown Island, principally because of the deep water close inshore, where the expedition disembarked on 13 May 1607, taken as the date of the founding of the Virginia colony.

Newport returned in late July with the news that the place was full of gold and pearl:

12 AUGUST 1607. SIR WALTER COPE TO THE EARL OF SALISBURY[1]—

Right honorable my good lord, if we may believe either in words or letters, we are fall'n upon a land that promises more than the Land of Promise! Instead of milk we find pearl, and gold instead of honey!... here is but a barrelful of the earth, but there seems a *kingdom* full of the ore.... And here by the way give me leave to inform you that there be 50 citizens who have already subscribed to adventure £500 apiece!

... their King of Pamont came with a chain of pearl about his neck, burnt thorough with great holes and spoiled for want of the art to bore them, and showed them shells from whence they were taken.... We showed th' experience made to one Beale, an excellent trier of minerals, who says the trial was ignorantly made, the earth not half tried; for if it had [been] it would have turned black and the gold ran together in the bottom; that this holds 1200[li] in the ton, that there is more in the pot, and he verily thinks it will yield 2000 at the least in the ton!

The Plymouth Company now mounted an expedition of two ships —the *Gift* and the *Mary & John*—with one hundred colonists under the command of George Popham, nephew of the lord chief justice. They arrived at Sagadahoc in August 1607. They had barely fortified themselves when quarrels erupted and factions formed that "bred an unstable resolution and a general confusion"[2] that Popham, an honest man but a weak leader, was unable to contain. It seems Raleigh Gilbert, second son of Sir Humphrey and captain of the *Mary & John,* commanded his own following and began talking of his special rights under his father's patent. It was a very cold winter. Things got to the stage the Indians refused to trade. Sir John Popham, always the prime mover and promoter at home in Plymouth, had died in the summer, and in February President George Popham died at Sagadahoc. Settlers began returning on their own. Gorges sent a relief supply in the summer of 1608, but the heart had

---

[1] from *The Jamestown Voyages under the First Charter,* ed. Barbour, p. 108

[2] Sir Ferdinando Gorges to the Earl of Salisbury in December 1607.

gone out of those remaining. Moreover, Raleigh Gilbert himself determined to go home on learning his brother, Sir John, had died leaving him his father's heir. The colony was abandoned in October 1608, leaving the New England coast for twelve years to the natives and a steady traffic of fishermen, fur traders, mapmakers, and the French.

On 3 July 1608, Samuel de Champlain founded the settlement of Quebec.

SOURCES: Morison 1971, Quinn 1979, Andrews 1984.

THE CHARTERS

THE VIRGINIA COMPANY was a joint-stock enterprise of investors high and low, big and small, called "adventurers," who risked their capital in an attempt to develop commercially profitable colonial ventures in America. It was one of a number of companies set up to deal, trade, and colonize—the East India Company being a famous and successful forerunner set up in 1600 to develop trade in Asia—and it operated in America under a charter granted by King James I in 1606, known as the first charter, superseded in our period by two more in 1609 and 1612, known as the second and third charters.

The first charter, dated 10 April 1606, establishes two companies to be known as the First, or London, Virginia Company (the so-called "Virginia Company") and the Second, or Plymouth, Virginia Company—for the purpose of developing the Crown's North American claims, named by Raleigh, with her permission, "Virginia" in honor of Elizabeth I.

The English are carving out a portion of the continent between Spanish Florida and French Nova Francia, described as lying between 34 and 45 degrees north latitude (Cape Fear to Halifax, Nova Scotia), where colonies may be planted along the coast "within one hundred miles thereof," including islands offshore. The London

Company will have authority to operate from 34 to 41 degrees (up to the eastern tip of Long Island) and the Plymouth Company from 45 to 38 degrees (down to the Maryland/Virginia state line and the mouth of the Potomac River).

The king issues this charter in acknowledgment of the desire of both companies to propagate the Christian religion in America.

They may transport thither "so many of our subjects as shall willingly accompany them," together with adequate supplies and defense, with no restriction on the amount of goods, chattels, munitions, etc. to be taken out of England for the purpose.

They shall have full and exclusive rights to settle the land and enjoy its resources within fifty miles of their settlements, one hundred miles inland from them.

Resolving rights in the area of overlap from 38 to 41 degrees, neither company may make settlements within a hundred miles of the other.

Each colony/company is granted its own seal and is to be governed by two councils of 13, one in England, one in Virginia.

The Crown claims 1/5 of the gold and 1/15 of the value of copper discovered.

The companies may mint coinage.

The colony has the authority to defend itself with arms.

The king grants exclusive trading rights and the right to collect and keep duties for the first 21 years.

Colonists are vouchsafed the same rights in the kingdom as native-born Englishmen.

Ships may not sail from England to Virginia and from there carry cargoes to foreign ports.

The king grants that legal title to land and property in Virginia shall be held the same "of us as of our manor of East Greenwich, in free and common socage only and not in capite." Virginia is not to be a feudal fiefdom.

A second charter was issued 23 May 1609 to the London Virginia Company for the purpose of changing the form of government at Jamestown. The Plymouth Company continued to operate under the first charter.

The second charter recites the first and reaffirms its rights and privileges.

It then incorporates an entity to be known as "The Treasurer and Company of Adventurers and Planters of the City of London for the First Colony of Virginia."

It authorizes the same "to take and hold property, and to settle lands 200 miles north and 200 miles south of Cape, or Point, Comfort" (Cape Fear to Sandy Hook) and through the continent "from sea to sea," including all islands within 100 miles of both coasts.

The offices of the president and council in Virginia are abolished in favor of a single governor appointed by and subject to the authority of a council of fifty-odd sitting in London responsible for laws and appointments, and elected by the members and adventurers of the company.

The new charter authorizes the granting of land to private ownership with due regard for merit and station.

Thomas Smythe is made treasurer, and the treasurer's presence is required for all enactments and appointments.

There are provisions for various duties and taxes, none over 5%, with further waivers and exemptions.

The council is granted authority to pass and enforce laws, to try and to punish offenders, and to declare martial law during unrest.

All colonists must take the oath of supremacy.

No minimum on the amount of money one may invest to become an "adventurer."

The third charter was issued 12 March 1612 to the London Virginia Company. It recites the previous charters, then proceeds vastly to extend the company's boundaries to include unclaimed and uninhabited islands within 300 leagues of the coast between 30 and 41 degrees in order to take in the new settlement on Bermuda, or the Somer Islands. Three years later, 29 June 1615, the Company was to sell out its interest for two thousand pounds and the king granted a separate charter to "The Governor and Company of the City of London for the Plantation of the Somer Islands."

There are provisions for weekly meetings and a court "for handling casual occurrences." Weightier matters will be handled by great, or general, courts convened quarterly.

There is a provision for exportation of necessities duty-free to Virginia for seven years.

The oath of supremacy is required of all colonists.

Answering a specific and strenuous grievance, the charter authorizes the council to track down in England those who have behaved in a disorderly manner in Virginia or have violated the terms of their contract there and have come home without permission, and especially those who have done so and then spread false and vicious rumors about deplorable conditions in Virginia in order to excuse their own behavior. A Company-sponsored publication fulminates against this species:

> And as for those wicked imps that put themselves a-shipboard, not knowing otherwise how to live in England, or those ungracious sons that daily vexed their fathers' hearts at home, and were therefore thrust upon the voyage, which, either writing thence or being returned back, to cover their own lewdness do fill men's ears with false reports of their miserable and perilous life in Virginea, let the imputation of misery be to their idleness, and the blood that was spilt upon their own heads that caused it.[1]

The treasurer and council may "proceed [against them], for all intents and purposes, as is used, in other like cases, within our realm of England," or remand them to Virginia and do with them "as the governor, deputy, or council there shall think meet." Article 12 of the *Laws divine, moral, and martial* (1610–11) had muzzled critics in the colony.

A final provision calls for the Company to set up a lottery in England (voluntary subscriptions had fallen off drastically). It is to operate on their behalf for one year, thereafter to continue at the king's will and pleasure.

The charters were amended and given form by various other instruments. On 20 November 1606, the king issues "articles, instructions, and orders," naming the fourteen members of the King's Council for Virginia, which include (in order) Sir William Wade, Sir

---

[1] Robert Johnson, *The New Life of Virginea* (Force 1836a:6/10–11).

Thomas Smythe, Sir Walter Cope, Sir Francis Popham, Sir Ferdinando Gorges, Thomas la Warr, esquire, and others, with full authority to name and direct the councils of the several colonies.

The colonial councils shall consist of thirteen members maximum, and shall choose a member not of the clergy to be president one year. This body is today the Senate of Virginia.

There is an injunction to spread the faith among the Indians.

Trial procedure is specified. A jury consists of twelve. The council is given authority to punish lawbreakers, and to execute a death sentence for rebellion, mutiny, sedition, murder, manslaughter, incest, rape, and adultery—not for theft despite what Capt. Newport told the Arrohatecks (Archer's *Relation §2–108)*.

For the first five years settlers are to pool supplies in one storehouse, or no more than three, managed by a cape merchant elected yearly by the council.

Two clerks shall be appointed in Virginia for an indefinite term to keep accounts, answered by three more in London.

The adventurers from their own number shall elect members of "companies" living in or near London for a five-year term to manage the colony's supply and its affairs in England.

Colonists must take the oath of obedience.

"Our subjects ... shall from time to time well entreat those savages ... in those parts and use all good means to draw [them] ... to the true service and knowledge of God," or be punished by the president and council as they deem fit.

On 10 December 1606 the Council for Virginia issued "orders and directions" for the Council in Virginia "now bound for that coast to settle His Majesty's First Colony of Virginia."

Captain Christopher Newport is named fleet commander.

Upon arriving in Virginia, "several instruments close sealed" are to be opened which will name the members of the Council in Virginia that will govern ashore. These will then elect a president who will serve one year, have two votes, and govern with a majority of the council.

Newport is required to spend "two months in discovery of such ports and rivers as can be found in that country," and see to the loading of the three ships with whatever merchantable commodities come to hand on the spot. He is then to sail home. Most important for us today, he is required to bring with him "full relation of all that he hath passed in the voyage."

The colonists also took with them the council's "instructions by way of advice." These I give in full:

INSTRUCTIONS GIVEN BY WAY OF ADVICE, BY US WHOM IT HATH PLEASED THE KING'S MAJESTY TO APPOINT OF THE COUNCIL FOR THE INTENDED VOYAGE TO VIRGINIA, TO BE OBSERVED BY THOSE CAPTAINS AND COMPANY WHICH ARE SENT AT THIS PRESENT TO PLANT THERE.

AS WE DOUBT NOT but you will have especial care to observe the ordinances set down by the King's Majesty and delivered unto you under the Privy Seal, so for your better directions upon your first landing we have thought good to recommend unto your care these instructions and articles following.

When it shall please God to send you on the coast of Virginia, you shall do your best endeavor to find out a safe port in the entrance of some navigable river, making choice of such a one as runneth furthest into the land. And if you happen to discover divers portable rivers,[1] and amongst them any one that hath two main branches, if the difference be not great, make choice of that which bendeth most towards the northwest, for that way shall you soonest find the other sea.[2]

When you have made choice of the river on which you mean to settle, be not hasty in landing your victuals and munitions, but first let Captain Newport discover how far that river may be found navigable, that you may make election of the strongest, most fertile and wholesome place. For if you make many removes, besides the loss of time, you shall greatly spoil your victuals and your casks, and with great pain transport it in small boats.

But if you choose your place so far up as a bark of fifty tons will fleet, then you may lay all your provisions ashore with ease, and the better receive the trade of all the countries about you in the land. And such a place you may perchance find a hundred miles from the river's mouth, and the farther up the better. For if you sit down near the entrance, except

---

[1] Good harbors.

[2] The Pacific Ocean.

it be in some island that is strong by nature, an enemy that may approach you on even ground may easily pull you out. And if he be driven to seek you a hundred miles within the land in boats, you shall from both sides of your river where it is narrowest so beat them with your muskets as they shall never be able to prevail against you.

And to the end that you be not surprised as the French were in Florida by Melindus, and the Spaniard in the same place by the French, you shall do well to make this double provision: First, erect a little sconce at the mouth of the river that may lodge some ten men, with whom you shall leave a light boat, that when any fleet shall be in sight they may come with speed to give you warning. Secondly, you must in no case suffer any of the natural people of the country to inhabit between you and the seacoast; for you cannot carry yourselves so towards them but they will grow discontented with your habitation, and be ready to guide and assist any nation that shall come to invade you. And if you neglect this, you neglect your safety.

When you have discovered as far up the river as you mean to plant yourselves, and landed your victuals and munitions, to the end that every man may know his charge, you shall do well to divide your sixscore men into three parts, whereof one forty of them you may appoint to fortify and build, of which your first work must be your storehouse for victual; 30 others you may employ in preparing your ground and sowing your corn and roots; the other ten of these forty you must leave as sentinel at the haven's mouth.

The other forty you may employ for two months in discovery of the river above you, and on the contrary [country?] about you; which charge Captain Newport and Captain Gosnold may undertake of these forty discoverers. When they do espy any high lands or hills, Captain Gosnold may take 20 of the company to cross over the lands, and carrying half a dozen pickaxes to try if they can find any minerals. The other twenty may go on by river, and pitch up boughs upon the bank's side by which the other boats shall follow them by the same turnings. You may also take with them a wherry, such as is used here in the Thames, by which you may send back to the president for supply of munition or any other want, that you may not [be] driven to return for every small defect.

You must observe if you can whether the river on which you plant doth spring out of mountains or out of lakes. If it be out of any lake, the passage to the other sea will be more easy, and it is like enough that out of the same lake you shall find some spring which run the contrary way toward the East India Sea; for the great and famous river[s] of Volga, Tan[a]is, and Dwina have three heads near join'd; and yet the one falleth into the

Caspian Sea, the other into the Euxine Sea, and the third into the Polonian Sea.

In all your passages you must have great care not to offend the naturals, if you can eschew it; and employ some few of your company to trade with them for corn and all other lasting victuals if you [they?] have any; and this you must do before that they perceive you mean to plant among them. For not being sure how your own seed corn will prosper the first year, to avoid the danger of famine, use and endeavor to store yourselves of the country corn.

Your discoverers that passes overland with hired guides must look well to them that they slip not from them. And for more assurance, let them take a compass with them, and write down how far they go upon every point of the compass.[1] For that country having no way nor path, if that your guides run from you in the great woods or deserts, you shall hardly ever find a passage back.

And how weary soever your soldiers be, let them never trust the country people with the carriage of their weapons. For if they run from you with your shot—which they only fear—they will easily kill them all with their arrows.

And whensoever any of yours shoots before them, be sure that they be chosen out of your best marksmen. For if they see your learners miss what they aim at, they will think the weapon not so terrible, and thereby will be bold [...]d to assault you.

Above all things, do not advertise the killing of any of your men, that the country people may know it. If they perceive they are but common men, and that with the loss of many of theirs they may diminish any part of yours, they will make many adventures upon you. If the country be populous, you shall do well also not to let them see or know of your sick men, if you have any, which may also encourage them to many enterprises.

You must take especial care that you choose a seat for habitation that shall not be over burthened with woods near your town. For all the men you have shall not be able to cleanse twenty acres in a year, besides that it may serve for a covert for your enemies round about you.

Neither must you plant in a low and moist place, because it will prove unhealthful. You shall judge of the good air by the people; for some part of that coast where the lands are low have their people blear-eyed and with swollen bellies and legs. But if the naturals be strong and clean made,

---

1 "Professor Taylor comments that 'this is perhaps the first mention of the use of the simple compass traverse in exploration.'" (Barbour)

it is a true sign of a wholesome soil.

You must take order to draw up the pinnace that is left with you under your fort, and take her sails and anchors ashore, all but a small kedge to ride by, lest some ill-disposed persons slip away with her.

You must take care that your mariners that go for wages do not mar your trade. For those that mind not to inhabit for a little gain will debase the estimation of exchange, and hinder the trade forever after. And therefore you shall not admit or suffer any person whatsoever, other than such as shall be appointed by the president and council there, to buy any merchandises or other things whatsoever.

It were necessary that all your carpenters and other suchlike workmen about building do first build your storehouse and those other rooms of public and necessary use before any house be set up for any private person. And though the workman may belong to any private persons, yet let them all work together first for the company and then for private men.

And seeing order is at the same price with confusion, it shall be advisably done to set your houses even and by a line, that your streets may have a good breadth, and be carried square about your marketplace, and every street's end opening into it, that from thence with a few fieldpieces you may command every street throughout; which marketplace you may also fortify if you shall think it needful.

You shall do well to send a perfect relation by Captain Newport of all that is done, of what height you are seated, how far into the land, what commodities you find, what soil, woods, and their several kinds, and so of all other things else to advertise particularly; and to suffer no man to return but by passport from the president and council, nor to write any letter of anything that may discourage others.

Lastly and chiefly, the way to prosper and obtain good success is to make yourselves all of one mind for the good of your country and your own, and to serve and fear God the giver of all goodness. For every plantation which our Heavenly Father hath not planted shall be rooted out.

An ordinance and constitution of 9 March 1607 enlarges the Council of Virginia from fourteen to include sixteen new members —among them Sir Edwin Sandys—for the First Colony and ten more for the Second Colony.

On 15 May 1609, under the second charter (not yet sealed), the Council of Virginia issues these instructions, under thirty-six numbered headings, to Sir Thomas Gates.

Gates is named governor with absolute authority, an office created by the new charter, replacing the president. He is to sail with 600 colonists in eight ships and one pinnace.

He is warned against calling at the West Indies during the voyage, but rather holding his course further north.

The Council in Virginia is named: Sir George Somers, Capt. John Smith ("now president"), Capt. John Ratcliffe, Capt. Peter Winne, Master Matthew Scrivener (who will be secretary), Capt. John Martin, Capt. Richard Waldo, Capt. Wood, and Master Fleetwood. They will be an advisory body with legislative authority.

Since Jamestown is "unwholesome," Gates is urged to use it only as a port and warehouse, and to move settlements to higher ground further inland but to a location accessible by water.

He is to see to converting the Indians to Christianity by procuring their children for instruction, and getting them away from the "*iniocasockes,* or priest."

Instruction 15 is given in full. It reads a bit feverish and is likely inspired by information returned by the Sicklemore and the Powell and Todkill expeditions enjoined in the 1606 instructions. It sounds like the voice of the king in its elaborate concern for the fate his subjects of the Lost Colony, but it could just as well be Raleigh.

> Four days' journey from your fort southwards is a town called Ohonahorn, seated where the river of Choanock divideth itself into 3 branches, and falleth into the sea of Rawnocke in thirty-five degrees. This place—if you seek by Indian guides from James fort to Winocke by water, from thence to Manqueock, some twenty miles from thence to Caththega, as much and from thence to Oconahoen—you shall find a brave and fruitful seat, every way unaccessible by a stranger enemy, much more abundant in *pochon* and in the grass silk, called *soue del lherva,*[1] and in vines than any part of this land known unto us. Here we suppose, if you make your principal and chief seat, you shall do most safely and richly, because you are in the part of the land inclined to the south, and two of the best rivers will supply you.
>
> Besides, you are near to rich copper mines of Ritanoe, and may pass

[1] cf. Strachey's *History §41–598.*

> them by one branch of this river, and by another Peccarecamicke, where you shall find four of the English alive left by Sir Walter Raweley, which escaped from the slaughter of Powhaton of Roanocke, upon the first arrival of our colony,[1] and live under the protection of a *wiroane* called Gepanocon, enemy to Powhaton, by whose consent you shall never recover them.
>
> One of these were worth much labor. And if you find them not, yet search into this country. It is more probable than towards the north.

Each settlement is to have a church and storehouse and "land set out for corn for the public," intersecting streets, and a paved marketplace.

Capt. John Smith is made commander of a fort to be established at Point Comfort. The colonists are again urged not to allow Indians to live between Jamestown and its sea approaches.

Powhatan is not be trusted, and he and all his werowances must be made tributaries. It is hoped the burden of tribute will force the Indians to fell the forest and become cashcrop farmers.

Sons of werowances shall be seized and educated in "manners and religion."

The English must cultivate alliance and trade with tribes furthest from Jamestown—"Monocon, Manahockes, the werowance Cathcatapeius, Masawoymekes, Pocoughtuwonough"—Powhatan's enemies.

Weapons are banned as trade goods, nor may Indians be taught skills, namely blacksmithing, that would allow them to produce their own European weapons.

Colonists shall be organized into gangs with public messes and designated rest periods. They will be called to work by ringing a bell. Militia will be trained by captains of fifty.

Tight censorship over letters and shipments to and from England.

The colony must be made to pay for itself through profits by trade, tribute, and manufacture. A principal means of doing so will be by finding "the south sea or royal mines."

---

[1] It was believed that Powhatan destroyed the Chesapeake tribe around the time the English arrived on the James River in 1607, due to the presence there of survivors of the Roanoke colony. See also Strachey §41–664.

In 1609–10, the Council of Virginia issued fourteen instructions to Sir Thomas West, Lord Lawarr, knight. He is appointed lord governor and captain general of Virginia, and is to sail with three ships and 150 colonists.

Sir Thomas Gates is appointed lieutenant governor, Sir Thomas Dale marshal, Sir George Somers admiral, Captain Christopher Newport vice-admiral.

Once the ships are unloaded at Jamestown, the sailors shall be put to work fishing for sturgeon, etc. The residue of the ships' return freight is to be whatever local commodities are at hand.

Of great advantage will be putting the colonists to work producing food.

The population shall be organized into work and militia details of fifty men.

The same instructions as before in propagating religion among the Indians.

Lord Lawarr is advised to judge "rather upon the right and equity … than upon the niceness and letter of the law," creating a "summary and arbitrary way of justice."

Trade is monopolized by the Company.

Expeditions will be mounted to explore beyond the falls "ten or twelve days' journey."

"Sir Ferdinando Weyneman may have the office of master of the ordnance."

Tight censorship of letters and shipments to and from England.

Here is a list of the commodities with prices the Company felt could guide Virginians in making the infant colony self-supporting, entitled "instructions for such things as are to be sent from Virginia, 1610":[1]

> 1. Small sassafras roots to be drawn in the winter and dried, and none to be meddled with in the summer; and it is worth £50 and better per ton.
>
> 2. Bayberries are to be gathered when they turn black, to be laid abroad and dried, and then put in sacks or cask, or for want of both to be turned into the hold; and is worth per ton £12.

---

[1] C.O. 1/1, folio 86a.

3. *Poecone* to be gotten from the Indians and put up in cask, is worth per ton £100.

4. Galband groweth like fennel in fashion, and there is greatest store of it in Warriscoes country, where they cut walnut tree last. You must cut it down in May or June, and being down it is to be cut into small pieces, and bruised and pressed in your small presses which were sent over for oil, or any other like presses. The juice thereof is to be saved and put into cask, which will be worth here per ton £100 at least.

5. Sarsapilla is a root that runneth within the ground like unto licorice, which beareth a small round leaf close by the ground; which being found, the root is to be pulled up and dried and bound up in bundles like fagots, this to be done towards the end of summer before the leaf fall from the stalk; and it [is] worth here per ton £200.

6. Walnut oil is worth here £30 per ton, and the like is chestnut oil and *chechinkamyne* oil.

7. Wine, a hogshead or two sour as it is, would be sent for a sample, and some of the grapes packed in sand.

8. Silk grass, according to a note formerly given my lord, should be sent in good quantity.

9. Beaver cod [scrotum] is likewise to be cut and dried, and will yield here 5s per lb.

10. Beaver skins being taken in wintertime will yield good profit; the like will otter skins.

11. Oak and walnut tree is best to be cut in the winter, the oak presently to be cleaven into clapboard, but the walnut to be let lie.

12. Pine trees or fir trees are to be wounded within a yard of the ground, or bore a hole with an auger the third part into the tree, and let it run into anything that may receive the same, and that which issues out will be turpentine worth £18 per ton. When the tree beginneth to run softly, it is to be stopped up again for preserving the tree.

13. Pitch and tar hath been made there, and we doubt not but will be again, and some sent for a sample, your own turns being first served.

14. Sturgeon which was last sent came ill conditioned, not being well boiled. If it were cut in small pieces, and powd'red, put up in cask, the heads pickled by themselves, and sent hither, it would do far better.

15. Roes of the said sturgeon make caviary according to instructions formerly given.

16. Sounds [air bladders] of the said sturgeon will make isinglass, according to the same instructions. Isinglass is worth here £6 13s 4d per 100 pounds, and caviary well conditioned is worth £40 per 100 pounds.

For the Colony in Virginia Britannia: Laws Divine, Moral, and Martial, etc.

DRAWN UP BY WILLIAM STRACHEY, in effect in final form as of 22 June 1611, this is the first written manifestation of English common law in America, and, by the way, the only thing with Strachey's name on it to go to press in his lifetime (1612).

He edited the whole, but his hand as writer is seen in the dedicatory prose and the "shakespearean" sonnet, and the 2600-word official prayer to be "said morning and evening upon the court of guard." The poem is worth quoting for matter and measure:

TO THE RIGHT HONORABLE, THE LORDS OF
THE COUNCIL OF VIRGINEA.

NOBLEST OF MEN, though 'tis the fashion now
Noblest to mix with basest for their gain,
Yet doth it fare far otherwise with you,
That scorn to turn to chaos so again,
And follow your supreme distinction still,
Till of most noble you become divine,
And imitate your Maker in His will
To have His truth in blackest nations shine.
What had you been had not your ancestors
Begun to you that make their nobles good?[1]
And where white Christians turn in manners Moors,
You wash Moors white with sacred Christian blood.
This wonder ye that others nothing make!
Forth then, great lords, for your Lord's Saviour's sake!

In his preface, Strachey tells us he brings out the *Laws* as a first installment of his comprehensive account of Virginia. His tone: "Every common eye may … meditate and bethink how safe, quiet, and comely it is to be honest, just, and civil." "No man doth more ill than

[1] A noble is a gold coin.

he that is ignorant [of the civil wisdom of the law]." Some are born with the knowledge of right and wrong, others need instruction. He writes from his "lodging in the Blackfriars." He hoped for some notice as a writer. The Company published the *Laws* to make known that orderly administration now prevailed under strict and absolute authority, and that Virginia was on sound footing.

We guess that the laws are the product of Sir Thomas Smythe, Sir Thomas Gates, and Sir Thomas Dale. Gates probably compiled the first part of the laws moral and divine up to Article 19. Dale wrote the martial law portions. If these are called "Dale's Code," perhaps this is because the marshal was pleased on occasion to enforce them to the letter at Henrico.

And the land they ordered? Half the population died each year, the leadership until the arrival of Gates in 1610 was riven by faction and sedition, food shortages were frequent, hostilities with Indians ongoing, commonplace were mutiny, pilfery, desertion ... The colonists were fresh out of the restraints of an authoritarian society. They were set down footloose on a wild and distant coast under uncertain supervision. This was America; they took the opportunity to decompress. Governor Gates and Marshal Dale were old soldiers; they had risen in life by achievement alone and a smart execution of orders. Their solution was the crackdown, and Virginia became a military colony.

Capt. John Smith had appropriated authoritarian rule, the second charter sanctioned it, the *Laws* were the enabling legislation. They remained in force until rescinded by Governor Yeardley in 1619. Records of their enforcement are lacking. The justice of Thomas Gates is described in Strachey's *True Reportory §22,* that of Thomas Dale in Percy's *True Relation §31,* and in *A Brief Declaration §57.* The governor was advised to decide the law "by right and equity rather than by niceness and the letter."

Articles, laws, and orders, divine, politic, and martial, for the colony in Virginea, first established by Sir Thomas Gates, knight, lieutenant general, the 24th of May, 1610; exemplified and approved by the Right Honorable Sir Thomas West, knight, Lord Lawair, lord governor and captain general, the 12 of June, 1610; again exemplified and enlarged by Sir Thomas Dale, knight, marshal, and deputy governor, the 22 of June, 1611.

THE LAWS DIVINE AND MORAL—

"7 All preachers or ministers ... shall ... preach every Sabbath day in the forenoon, and catechize in the afternoon, and weekly say the divine service twice every day, and preach every Wednesday. Likewise every minister ... shall choose unto him four of the most religious and better disposed as well to inform of the abuses and neglects of the people in their duties and service to God, as also to the due reparation, ... reverent observances thereunto belonging. Likewise every minister shall keep a faithful and true record, or church book, of all christenings, marriages, and deaths ... upon the burthen of a neglectful conscience and upon pain of losing their entertainment [provisions]."

"9 No man shall commit the horrible and detestable sins of sodomy, upon pain of death. And he or she that can be lawfully convict of adultery shall be punished. No man shall ravish or force any woman, maid, or Indian or other, upon pain of death. And know ye that he or she that shall commit fornication, and evident proof made thereof, for their first fault shall be whip'd, for their second they shall be whip'd, and for their third they shall be whip'd three times a week for one month, and ask public forgiveness in the assembly of the congregation."

"12 No ... person shall dare to detract, slander, calumniate, or utter unseemly and unfitting speeches either against [the Company and council for Virginia or its policies and publications], upon pain for the first time ... to be whip'd three several times, and upon his knees to acknowledge his offense, and to ask forgiveness upon the Sabbath day in the assembly of the congregation, and for the second time ...

to be condemned to the galley for three years, and for the third time so offending to be punished with death." Article 13 extends this protection to officials in the colony with the like punishments. Article 14 forbids disgracing and slandering of ordinary individuals, "upon pain of being tied head and feet together upon the guard every night for the space of one month, besides to be publicly disgraced himself, and be made uncapable ever after to possess any place or execute any office."

"18 ... And if any man die and make a will, his goods shall be accordingly disposed. If he die intestate, his goods shall be put into the store, and being valued by two sufficient praisers, his next of kin ... shall from the Company ... receive due satisfaction in monies ...."

"22 There shall no man or woman, launderer or laundress, dare to wash any unclean linen, drive bucks [bleach], or throw out the water or suds of foul clothes, in the open street within the palisadoes or within forty foot of the same, nor rench [rinse] and make clean any kettle, pot, or pan, or suchlike vessel, within twenty foot of the old well or new pump. Nor shall anyone aforesaid within less than a quarter of one mile from the palisadoes dare to do the necessities of nature, since by these unmanly, slothful, and loathsome immodesties the whole fort may be choked and poisoned with ill airs ... upon pain of whipping and further punishment as shall be thought meet ...

"25 Every man shall have an especial and due care to keep his house sweet and clean, as also so much of the street as lieth before his door; and especially he shall so provide and set his bedstead whereon he lieth that it may stand three foot at least from the ground, as he will answer the contrary at a martial court."

"28 No soldier or tradesman but shall be ready, both in the morning and in the afternoon, upon the beating of the drum, to go out unto his work. Nor shall he return home or from his work before the drum beat again, and the officer appointed for that business bring him off, upon peril for the first fault to lie upon the guard head and heels together all night, for the second time so faulting to be whip'd, and for the third time so offending to be condemned to the galleys for a year."

"32 Whosoever, seaman or landman, of what quality or in what place of command soever, shall be employed upon any discovery, trade, or fishing voyage into any of the rivers within the precincts of our colony shall, for the safety of those men who are committed to his command, stand upon good and careful guard for the prevention of any treachery in the Indian; and if they touch upon any shore they shall be no less circumspect and wary.... And when they have finished the discovery, trade, or fishing they shall make haste with all speed ... to James town again, not presuming to go beyond their commission or to carry any such ... ship, etc. for England or any other country ... upon peril to be held an enemy to this plantation and traitor thereunto, and accordingly to lie liable unto such censure of punishment (if they arrive in England) as shall be thought fit.... And if it shall so happen that he or they shall be prevented and brought back hither again into the colony, their treacherous flight to be punished with death." Francis West, brother of Lord Delaware, apparently escaped punishment for doing exactly this, deserting in a ship loaded with corn from Patawomeck in late 1609 or early 1610, just prior to the initial decree, which was in the spring of 1610; also Matthew Somers, who sailed on to England from Bermuda with the body of his uncle George Somers, who had died there in November 1610, after the decree. But Somers had found a block of ambergris the Company was able to sell for £120,000, a colossal sum.

"37 ... Every minister or preacher shall every Sabbath day, before catechizing, read all these laws and ordinances publicly in the assembly of the congregation, upon pain of his entertainment check'd for that week."

Persons forfeit provisions and wages for first offenses of several minor crimes, and for breaking Sabbath, missing the morning and afternoon services, or failing to attend the weekly services held twice daily; also tradesmen who neglect the trade for which they are hired (and for which they are excused from other labor), or perform it grudgingly; also mariners and settlers engaging in unauthorized barter and at rates other than those nailed to the mainmast of the ship, and in certain proscribed articles such as tools, bedding, oatmeal, aqua vitae. There is a legitimate trade under close supervision in limited amounts.

Showing disrespect for clergy is punished by whipping; the same for those careless or lighthanded with tools, or for launderers and laundresses pilfering linen, being made to return it forthwith. Several lesser crimes call for whipping on the second offense.

Each arrival has to check in with his local minister, who is to determine his special religious needs. If the newcomer misses his "Sunday school," he is to be whipped and forced to beg forgiveness.

Tradesmen, especially bakers, cooks, fishermen, and dressers of sturgeon, who bilk customers or colonial authorities do so "upon pain for the first time offending herein of losing his ears, and for the second time to be condemned a year to the galleys, and for the third time offending to be condemned to the galleys for three years."

Another maiming punishment is a bodkin thrust through the tongue for the second offense of blasphemy.

Creditors are to proceed by obtaining a bill of complaint at the marshal's court and "have justice."

Unspecified punishments are pronounced against officers who neglect the twice daily religious instruction of their commands, and against overseers who fail to carry out assignments.

The death penalty falls upon those speaking against the trinity (heretics), uttering traitorous words, despising and deriding the Gospel. Murder, perjury, thievery in general, unauthorized trade with the Indians, unauthorized slaughter of livestock (even one's own, with severe corporal punishment inflicted on accessaries and concealers), sedition and sabotage (and concealers of the guilty), carrying off without leave a ship belonging to the colony, selling or giving goods to mariners to be transported out of the colony, robbing Indians who come to trade—all are capital crimes. The death penalty descends on keepers of stores who embezzle for friends, on those who make off with the belongings of the dead or absent, and on deserters to the Indians. Those sent out to hoe and weed gardens are to die if caught stealing vegetables. Incorrigibles and habitual and three-time offenders advance themselves to the death penalty.

Women are mentioned nearly as often as men, even for punishment in the galleys. In the days when only one in twenty got caught, pity the one who got caught. If things were quiet all in all, much was surely overlooked and commuted. The Company was not in the business of paying people's transportation only to hang them. The law gave the authorities plenty of opportunity to show magnanimous mercy to stumblers or to proceed unhampered against scoundrels and incorrigibles.

THE LAWS MARTIAL—

Everything that comes under the laws moral and politic is "no less subject to the martial law."

"1 No man shall willingly absent himself when he is summoned to take the oath of supremacy [of the Church of England], upon pain of death."

The death penalty is measured out for various forms and degrees of desertion, sleeping on guard duty,[1] allowing prisoners to escape, insubordination, malingering, brawling, quarreling, dueling, with "passing the pikes" as a lighter alternative, that is, running a gauntlet of them.

"12 He that shall waylay any man by advantage taken, thereby cowardly to wound or murther him, shall pass the pikes."

Personal feuding is not only prohibited, even those who accuse the feuding parties of a cowardly turning to authority for redress themselves must pass the pikes. Various light punishments are given to those that look the other way or second dueling.

16 An officer is to be relieved of command for striking a soldier.

"29, 30 No man shall sell, give, embezzle, or play away his arms or any part thereof, upon pain of death; or make away any of his [issued] apparel, under pain of whipping."

"34 That soldier who fighting with an enemy shall lose his arms or

[1] According to Strachey's *History §41–617,* the laws martial of Powhatan's army called for no more than having a sluggish sentry "beaten extremely" by his officer.

run away cowardly, or yield himself but upon apparent and great constraints, or without having performed first the part of a good soldier and an honest man, shall suffer death with the arms which he carrieth."

"37 That soldier, which upon an assault or taking of any town, that shall not follow his colors and the victory, but shall fall to pillage for his private profit, after the place taken, shall suffer death with the arms which he weareth."

"38 No soldier may speak or have any private conference with any of the savages, without leave of his captain, nor his captain without leave of his chief officer, upon pain of death."

"41 No soldier shall unprofitably waste his powder, shot, or match by shooting it idly away, or at birds, beast, or fowl … [first offender] to lie in irons head and heels together eight and forty hours."

"44 Whosoever shall give offense to the Indians in that nature which truly examined shall [be] found to have been cause of breach of their league and friendship, which with so great travail, desire, and circumspection we have … from them … shall be punished with death."

"45 Whosoever shall willfully or negligently set fire on any Indian dwelling house, or *quioquisock* house or temple, or upon any storehouse or garner of grain, or provision of what quality soever, or disvaledge [rob], ransack, or ill-treat the people of the country, where any war, or wherethrough any march, shall be made, except it be proclaimed, or without commandment of the chief officers, shall be punished with death."

"49 Whosoever shall not retreat when the drum or trumpet soundeth the same, whether it be upon any sallies made out of any town or fortress, or in skirmish, or in any encounter, shall be punished with death."

"51 Every captain shall cause to be read all these laws which concern martial discipline every week upon his guard day unto his company, upon pain of censure of a martial court."

Marshal Dale, in the next section, begins at the top, assigning lengthy procedural and disciplinary guidelines, duties (standing orders), and directions (orders) through the ranks in turn to colonel/governor, captain of the watch, captain, lieutenant, ensign, sergeant, corporal, and private soldier—entitled:

Instructions of the marshal for better enhabling of the—— to the executing of his or their charges in this present colony, the 22 of June, 1611.

Under colonel/governor:
" ... All good and wise men, who knowing the grounds of all goodness, cannot but know this, how this hazardous voyage—as yet but in her early days, reflecting only the comfort of fair hopes—is undertaken by you more to honor God, your country, and to profit your knowledges than for any other ends of profit; which speaks for you, in despite of envy and calumny, that you have minds much in love with virtue, and are right noble and worthy instruments to be employed in so sacred and heroic a cause."

The training of soldiers consists as much of religious drill, the source of discipline, as actual parade drill and the manual of arms. There is hardly any description of purely military technical matters.

Under captain of the watch: "When it shall so fall out that the Indians do at any time come in way of trade or visitation unto the camp, town, or fort, he shall leave order with the guards that they suffer not them to enter before such time as they have made him acquainted first of their being there, who shall inform the governor to know his pleasure; which being understood he shall so accomplish at all times, appointing guards upon such Indians, that they do not steal any of our tools, axes, hoes, swords, pieces, or what thing else; and that none of our people talk publicly or privately with them, or that they truck or trade with them, or do any other unorderly act, without leave granted for the same from the governor or chief officer …" This officer is urged to think of himself as the head of a family of those under him.

Under private soldier, here is a section that should interest the general reader throughout: "If in skirmishes, encounters, or surprise of town the enemies be vanquished, let him set all his care and diligence in execution of the victory with his arms, and not in rifling and spoiling for trash, for so he shall be accounted an unruly freebooter, beside innumerable are the disorders and mischiefs which do happen by ravenous pillagers, many times to the dishonor of the action, and to the loss of their lives. Therefore he shall pursue the victory until the enemy be wholly ended, and the place fully carried and possessed, the guards placed, and liberty granted from the chief commander to sack and spoil, wherein by any means let him avoid murther and cruelty and violation of women, for those are odious to God and man. Rather in such cases let him show himself pitiful and merciful unto the vanquished, rather defending the silly women and children than procuring their hurt and damage, for in so doing it will be right acceptable to God and his commanders." But our species had not yet descended to the depths of the twentieth century. The common soldier was also expected to *read* this to himself daily at his leisure.

The matchlock musket and rifle, effective out to a hundred yards, has a faster and more reliable action than the later flintlock, except that carrying the lit match is an awkward inconvenience, albeit handy for a sleepy guard! "When his corporal shall appoint him forth for sentinel, he shall shoulder his piece, both ends of his match being alight, and his piece charged and prined, and bullets in his mouth, there to stand with a careful and waking eye until such time as his corporal shall relieve him; and to let no man pass nor come up to him, but to force him stand, and then to call his corporal." A line of infantry loading buckshot would present a most formidable array.

In sum, the *Laws* are an excellent way to run an army at war, and still are. As for citizens and cities, they represent a lamentable detour.

THE GREAT CHARTER OF 1618

OUR LAST SUMMARY is of the instructions from "the treasurer and company of adventurers and planters of the City of London for the First Colony in Virginia to Captain George Yeardley, elect governor of Virginia," 18 November 1618, at his going out to the colony, "and to the council of state there being or to be."

When the charters were revoked and the Virginia Company was dissolved by King James in 1624, the so-called Great Charter remained in force and continues so today. It lies just beyond our time limit, but its enactments reflect the growth and prosperity described in Rolfe's *True Relation §53,* and its provisions are unmistakably a turn in our direction. Let us set it in balance against the *Laws Divine, Moral,* etc. and Ralph Hamor's theory of justice.

Yeardley is directed to further the colony's welfare "by the settling there of a laudable form of government." The Virginia General Assembly, America's first representative legislature, was elected and convened the following summer (1619).

To reduce taxes, the Company directs laying out public lands whose income will support public administration—the Governor's Land, near Jamestown, and four tracts, each known as the Company's Land, in the four designated boroughs of Jamestown, Charles City, Henrico, and "Kiccowtan"—3000 acres each; similarly glebe tracts of 100 acres to support clergy, and commons, called City or Borough Land, of 1500 acres, in each of the four boroughs.

Particular (private) plantations must be of contiguous land, and may not exist within five miles of a borough or ten miles of one another—Smith's Hundred, Martin's Hundred, Martin's Brandon, Argall's, Delaware's, Lawne's.

And then the foundation of private property in America:

> And that in all these foresaid cities or boroughs, ancient adventurers and planters which [were] transported thither with intent to inhabit at their own costs and charges, before the coming away of Sir Thomas Dale, knight (May 1616), and have so continued during the space of 3 years, shall have upon a first division, to be afterward by us augmented, 100 acres of land for their personal adventure, and as much for every single

> share of £12/10 paid [for their share], allotted and set out, to be held by them, their heirs, and assigns forever. And that for all such planters as were brought thither at the Company's charge to inhabit there, before the coming away of the said Sir Thomas Dale, after the time of their service to the Company on the common land agreed shall be expired, there be set out 100 acres of land for each of their personal adventures to be held by them, their heirs, and assigns forever; paying for every 50 acres the yearly free rent of one shilling ... on the feast day of St. Michael the Archangel, forever. And in regard that by the singular industry and virtue of the said Sir Thomas Dale the former difficulties and dangers were in greatest part overcome, to the great ease and security of such as have been since that time transported thither, we do, therefore, hereby ordain that all such persons as, sithence the coming away of the said Sir Thomas Dale, have at their own charges been transported thither to inhabit and so continued as aforesaid, there be allotted and set out upon a first division 50 acres of land to them and their heirs, forever, for their personal adventure, paying a free rent of one shilling yearly in manner aforesaid.

Ten thousand acres are designated for the establishment of a university at Henrico for Indian children, maintained by the royal treasury.

Yeardley himself receives two grants totaling 2200 acres.

Individuals preferring practicing a trade to farming are to be given a house and four acres.

Those occupying the common lands yield a quarter of the profits and after three years receive fifty acres.

Grant records are to be kept in Virginia, "yet directly forbidding that a charter of land granted to Captain Samuel Argal and his associates, bearing date the 20th of March, 1616, be entered in your records or otherwise at all respected, forasmuch as the same was obtained by slight and cunning; and afterwards, upon suffering him to go governor of Virginia, was by his own voluntary act left in our custody to be canceled upon grant of a new charter which——"

A share in the Company is worth £12/10, or 100 acres of land.

Those who pay for the transportation of others receive 50 acres per head, effective after midsummer's day 1618. From time to time grantees must report the number, names, ages, sex, trades, and conditions of transportees. Sad to say, we have none of these reports.

Boundary surveys and plats are ordered for all land grants.

WATERCRAFT

AFTER SOME RESEARCH on the subject I am afraid I know less than when I started about what is meant by the terms pinnace, shallop, barge, frigate, longboat, catch boat, and so on, in the early seventeenth century, despite the precise dimensions Strachey gives us of the pinnaces constructed on Bermuda (414–15). I venture therefore only the most general remarks.

They were all intended to earn a living carrying cargo. They could strain themselves to make some little progress against a moderate wind and sea, but were designed to sail properly off the wind. Hence we see none of the fine lines of the modern sailing yachts and motor craft that routinely make headway into oncoming waves. Instead sixteenth and seventeenth century vessels were very blunt forward and broad aft in order to have enough flotation in the ends to lift above the nastiest seas when fully burdened with cargo amidships.

The types listed above were between thirty and sixty feet in length overall.

I believe the term "frigate" describes a rig more than a hull type, but I am not sure what rig. Same with catch boat, or ketch; same with "caravel." The longboat was small enough to be carried on a ship's main deck, so that some may have been under thirty feet.

The barge was a narrow-beam, undecked vessel that sacrificed cargo space and sail-carrying ability for the sake of being more handy as a rowed vessel with a shallow draft for putting ashore anywhere along the riverbank. The rough and ready variety would be the vessel of choice for exploring the Chesapeake and its rivers. The shallop was wider, more heavily built, but like the barge it was undecked and only suitable for work in inland waters. It was slower under oars than a barge. Both types likely relied on a very simple sailing rig such as lugsails on one or two short masts. One would not expect to spend much time trying to row a shallop.

A pinnace was a shallop with a deck and with a square-rig. It was the smallest vessel used on sea passages. The *Discovery* is a pinnace. The deck meant that the vessel could take ocean waves aboard in bad weather and shed them just as quickly. A deck also provided shelter for the crew and the cargo on long voyages. The square-rig is very strong and heavy. It makes maximum use of the trade winds and prevailing winds over the oceans so as to run before them.

However, a full length of deck fore and aft and a square-rig add considerable weight topside and that calls for stowing much ballast and cargo to make the vessel sail properly, all which increases draft. A shallop with the same hull shape as a pinnace could go up rivers carrying cargoes where a pinnace would run aground. We hear of pinnaces with their decks removed and shallops being decked over.

Ships were also downwind sailers. The high sterns were like another sail, providing even more windage for pushing the vessel along while protecting her from being "pooped," or getting boarded by big seas astern. Inshore, if the wind and tide were against her, the ship simply dropped anchor and waited. The first fleet to Jamestown anchored in the Downs off the coast of Kent to wait *six weeks* until the wind blew fair to sail down the English Channel. That is longer than many an entire transatlantic voyage under more favorable conditions. We read that ships coming into the Chesapeake out of the Atlantic customarily drifted up the James River on the flood tide without wind assistance.

On the open sea, when conditions were severe, such as during the great hurricane of 1609, a ship would furl all her sails and let the wind blow her high stern downwind so as to "lie to," "lie to-hull," or "lie a-hull"—terms which all mean the same thing, namely, allowing the vessel on her own to round up and point her bows directly into the oncoming waves while drifting backwards. This is why, despite the very high forecastle of early sailing ships, the "stern castle" is always much higher. Unlike modern vessels, power or sail, an old-time ship would not drift broadside to the sea. Her windage would not allow it.

Whether big ship or small shallop, a seventeenth century vessel was designed to strike a balance between cargo capacity (tonnage) and good sea-going ability. No hulls were designed purely to be sleek, fast, or light-weight, since those qualities sacrificed tonnage, not to say strength. At the same time nobody was fool enough to try to hold to a deadline on the high seas. But a vessel had to handle properly in all conditions or regardless of the size of her cargo it might never be delivered. Smith tells us the *Phoenix* made too much leeway, hence she was blown completely off the Virginia capes at the same time that Newport's ship was able to make in. Leeway is a problem in a vessel of shallow draft, that is, one light and fast.

Rigs look complicated compared with modern sloops and ketches, but that is a consequence of short spars and big spreads of sail.

Finally, tonnage refers not to weight but to the number of "tuns" a vessel could stow before she was overloaded. A tun was a liquid container, typically a cask of wine, containing four hogsheads measure. Towards the end of the 17th century a "tun" was taken as roughly a "ton," or as a cask of liquid topping off around 2000 pounds.

Strachey (638–39) ably describes the native log canoe. Cypress trees were favored; further north, white pine. These woods hold up well to repeated wetting and drying, unlike many other nautical species, and grow large enough to produce a single-log vessel with a four or even a six foot beam. The bottom was flat, making for stability. The ends were identical and scow-bowed, not pointed. This will cause poor tracking and difficult steering, but easier stepping off. There were no thwarts. Propulsion was by paddle and pole. The Indians valued them almost with their lives. When Smith began chopping up the canoes of Nansemonds, we hear their cries (276).

WHO'S WHO

Works in this volume are listed in italics beneath each article.

GABRIEL ARCHER (*c.*1575–1609/10)

Of Mountnessing, Essex, attended Cambridge and was admitted to Gray's Inn as a student in 1593, but never called to the bar.

He was Gosnold's recorder, writing a report of his 1602 voyage to New England, and it is by comparing his writing style there that we confidently credit the unsigned *A Relation* to him.

He was a member of the first expedition to Jamestown but was back in England in 1608. He returned to Virginia in June 1609, serving as secretary, or recorder, to the council, and died in the winter of 1609–10, during the "starving time."

Insofar as his brother John was his heir, he must have had no descendants. He was Virginia's first lawyer, and had as good an education as William Strachey.

A relation §2
The description of the now-discovered river & country of Virginia §3
A brief description of the people §4
Letter from Jamestown §18

SIR SAMUEL ARGALL (1580–1626)

Son of Richard Argall (d.1588) of East Sutton, Kent, and Mary (d.1605), daughter of Sir Reginald Scott, he was a double cousin by marriage of Sir Thomas Smythe, treasurer of the Virginia Company, and a brother-in-law of the uncle of Lord Delaware's wife.

His widowed mother married Laurence Washington, esquire, of Maidstone, Kent, the great-great-uncle of John, the emigrant ancestor of "the father of his country."

In 1609 the Virginia Company picked Argall, by then an accomplished mariner, to find the wind for a shorter sailing route to Virginia that would also avoid encounters with the returning Spanish fleets—a task he duly performed from May to October that year, discovering a more direct route well to the north of the West Indies, described in one account as along 28° north longitude.

He succeeded Newport in the office of pilot of Virginia.

He brought Lord Delaware to Virginia, March 1610, surveyed the coast from the Chesapeake to Cape Cod that summer, explored and traded on the Chesapeake in the autumn and winter, and returned to England with the ailing Lord Delaware in late March 1611, arriving in England in June.

A year later, he sailed from England with a commission to rid Virginia of foreign intruders. On a trading voyage, he captured Pocahontas in the winter of 1613 and in July attacked and destroyed the new French Jesuit settlement of Saint Sauveur on Mt. Desert Island in Maine, returning to Jamestown with prisoners.

He made several voyages to Virginia and served there in various capacities, being appointed deputy governor and admiral of Virginia in May 1617, during which time he established the short-lived Argalltown settlement near Jamestown.

Charges are brought against him in 1618 for immoderate self-serving and malfeasance during his deputyship, and later he is "vehemently complained against" by Gondomar, the Spanish ambassador in London, and others, that his ship committed piracy in the West Indies. Nonetheless, he was the Company's most dependable servant year after year, and he must have been the envy of Capt. John Smith.

Lord Delaware died en route coming to relieve him as governor, so his place was taken by Yeardley, who arrived 19 April 1619. Argall, being forewarned that Yeardley would put him under arrest, absconded ahead of time and was back in England in May.

In 1620–21 he was a captain with the fleet in the Mediterranean under Sir Robert Mansell.

He was knighted in 1622.

From October to December 1625, he commanded the flagship in the attack on Cadiz, and died suddenly thereafter.

He left a daughter, Ann, who married twice.

A letter to Hawes, June 1613 §45

WILLIAM BREWSTER (1562–1607)

Our Virginia colonist has been connected in recent times by handwriting analysis with a William Brewster, baptized 31 December 1562 at Castle Hedingham, Essex, son of William Brewster, gentleman (d. 1583). In 1597 he found work as a "keeper of recusants," that is, he was jailer to various prisoners of conscience, including Dr. Allen's seminary priests from Douay, and was to pursue that line of activity with uneven success.

In London in 1599, he married Mary Welles, daughter of John Welles, chief courier in Her Majesty's diplomatic service. She gave him three sons, John (1600), Anthony (1601), and William (1604).

A member of the first Jamestown expedition, at age forty-four he was one of the oldest. In Percy's *Discourse §1* there is the entry: "The tenth day [of August, 1607], died William Brewster, gentleman, of a wound given by the savages, and was buried the eleventh day."

Was he Salisbury's spy?

Letter from Virginia §6

REVEREND RICHARD BUCKE

Crashaw speaks in his behalf in his dedicatory to the *Good News from Virginia.* He sailed for Virginia in June 1609 with Gates and Somers, and was shipwrecked on Bermuda. He reached Virginia in May 1610 and became the minister at Jamestown, and married in Virginia. He married John Rolfe to Pocahontas at Jamestown, 5 April 1614. In 1616 Rolfe writes of his friend that he was "a very good preacher." It was in his church at Jamestown, newly built during Argall's government (1617–19) and wholly paid for by the colonists, that the first general assembly met on 30 July 1619. And "forasmuch as men's affairs do little prosper where God's service is neglected, all the Burgesses stood in the places, until a prayer was said by Mr. Bucke, that it would please God to guide and sanctify all our proceedings to His own glory, and to the good of the plantation." He and his wife were both dead before February 1624. They left four children and much property.

JOHN CLARK (1573 or 1576–1623)

A ship's pilot by profession, he sailed from London for Virginia in March 1611, he tells us in his *Declaration,* arriving "two and a half months later." In June 1611, at Point Comfort, he was ordered to bring a Spanish ship to anchorage under the point. No sooner was he aboard but he found himself detained as a hostage in response to the detention of the Spanish shore party. The ship then sailed for Havana and he became a prisoner for the next five years until exchanged. Digby reported him in Seville by November 1611. He returned to Virginia in 1619, perhaps on the same ship that a year and a half later he piloted to Plymouth, Massachusetts, namely, the *Mayflower.* Brown cites records of the Virginia court in London, 13 February 1622: "'Mr. Deputy acquainted the court that one Mr. John Clarke, being taken from Virginia long since by a Spanish ship that came to discover that plantation" (a good pun, see §35), "that forasmuch as he hath since that time done the Company good service in many voyages to Virginia, and of late went into Ireland for transportation of cattle to Virginia, he was an humble suitor to this court, that he might be admitted a free brother of the Company, and have some shares of land bestowed upon him.' He was admitted and given two shares. He arrived in Virginia, April 10, 1623, with Daniel Gookin's ship, the *Providence,* and soon after this he died in that colony."

Declaration of the Master, etc. §35
Declaration §36
Confession of the English Pilot §42

REVEREND WILLIAM CRASHAW (1572–1626)

"Sometimes classed as a Puritan divine and poet; was baptized at Handsworth, 26 October 1572; educated at Cambridge; prebend in the church of Ripon, 1602; preacher at the Inner Temple, London; at Church of St. Mary Matfellon, or Whitechapel, London, 13 November 1618; died 1626. A good scholar, an eloquent preacher and writer, and a strong Protestant. He was the father of Richard Crashaw the poet and Roman Catholic." (Brown 1890)

Dedicatory to Whitaker's *Good News from Virginia §43*

SIR THOMAS DALE (d. 1620)

He was a mercenary for the Dutch from 1588. In 1595, he was in Scotland in the retinue of the infant Prince Henry, returning to the Netherlands in 1603, where he was commissioned captain of infantry.

In 1606 he was knighted at Richmond by King James.

He married Elizabeth Throckmorton (February 1611); he secured leave of absence from the United Provinces to enter the service of the Virginia Company, remaining in Virginia until May 1616.

He was a man of intense military and civic virtue, and of such severity of person that he never hired friendship. His administration in Virginia as marshal, deputy governor, and governor under the second charter is condemned for harshness on one hand and praised for order and progress on the other. His program of decentralization of settlements, in fact a policy assignment of the Council of Virginia, was only temporarily interrupted after the massacre of 1622.

In November 1617, Dale was chosen fleet commander for the East India Company, and fell sick and died in Java in early 1620.

Lady Fanny Dale was a cousin of the wife of Sir Walter Raleigh and of her own husband's late wife. She accompanied Sir Thomas to Virginia, and patented land in Accowmack Plantation, Charles City, and Shirley Hundred. She died childless in England in 1640.

Letter to the Committees in §40
Letter to the President & Council, 25 May 1611 §32
Letter to Salisbury, 17 August 1611 §38
Letter to Smythe, June 1613 §46
Letter from Henrico, 10 June 1613 §47
Letter to D. M., 18 June 1614 (appended to Hamor's *Discourse §51)*
Letter to Winwood, 3 June 1616 §54

SIR THOMAS GATES (*c.* 1559–1621)

Born at Colyford, in Colyton Parish, Devonshire, he entered the soldier's profession and fought in the Dutch wars. He sailed on Drake's voyage in the Caribbean that brought off the settlers at Roanoke Island, 1585–86, and published the Briggs-Croftes account of this voyage in 1589. He was knighted by Essex in June 1596. He was in the military service of the States in 1604, but was among the first petitioners to King James for a charter to colonize America. He was granted leave from Dutch service, April 1608. Gates was now named the first governor of the colony under the charter of 1609; sailed in June; was cast away on the Bermudas, July 1609–May 1610. He and Somers reached Virginia in safety on May 21st in Bermuda-built vessels, where he remained until returning to England in July.

We then see his hand in the preparation of *A True Declaration §27* in England.

He returned to Virginia as governor in May 1611, with his family. His wife died en route, and he sent his children back with Newport in December following. He remained in Virginia nearly three years, till April 1614. "He had brought his company from the Netherlands and had carried it to Virginia with him in 1609, under the command of Capt. George Yeardley. I cannot say whether he brought it away from Virginia or not; but after aiding in answering the French complaints, he returned to his post in Holland, and was promptly paid all past dues.

"During 1619 he was serving on one of the committees of the Virginia Company in London. In November 1619, Sir Edwin Sandys, in a speech before the quarter court of that company, said that 'Sir Thomas Gates had the honor to all posterity of being the first named in His Majesty's patent and grant of Virginia, and was also the first that, by his wisdom, industry, and valor, accompanied with exceeding pains and patience in the midst of many difficulties, had laid the foundation of the present prosperous state of the colony.'

"November 3, 1620, he was appointed by James I one of 'the first modern and present council established at Plymouth, in the County of Devon, for the planting, ruling, ordering, and governing of New England in America.'" (Brown 1890)

His children were two sons, Thomas and Anthony, and three daughters, Margaret, Mary, and Elizabeth.

His record is nearly all praise, exception being taken only in §57 and §58.

Quotes in *A true declaration §27* and elsewhere.

RALPH HAMOR (1589–1626)

Born February 1589, the son of Ralph Hamor, the elder, a merchant tailor, and his wife Susan. His father was an incorporator and for a time an East India Company director.

He was shipwrecked on Bermuda with Gates and Somers, arriving in Virginia with them in May 1610, staying until June 1614, at which time he sailed with Argall for England.

His father, then in his directorship, died in 1615, and Hamor invested his large inheritance in Virginia. The Company allotted him eight shares of land and he received money for paying transport for five colonists. His brother Thomas, no doubt at his urging, also received money for transporting four.

When he sailed again for Virginia, in March 1617, arriving in May, he transported sixteen colonists, including Thomas Hamor.

He was a member of the council in 1621 when he signed the *Answer of the General Assembly §58,* and in years following.

During the massacre of 1622, he and his brother barely escaped with their lives from the Warraskoyacks, the details to be found in Smith's *General History,* Fourth Book. In the aftermath he was put in charge of Martin's Hundred and Warraskoyack Plantation for the purpose of bringing off survivors to Jamestown.

In May 1622, he was given a commission for trade and plunder in the Bay in the ship *Tiger* in order to obtain corn.

He married Susan Owen, a widow; they had children. He married again before 1623 to another widow, Elizabeth Clements.

A true discourse of the present estate of Virginia §51

CAPTAIN GEORGE KENDALL (*c.* 1570–1607)

Perhaps a Catholic, he served Lord Salisbury as an informer while soldiering in the Netherlands, where he associated with Catholics, Irish partisans, traitors, etc., among whom he lists Salisbury himself. His background and social position easily qualified him to be named to the first council at Jamestown, but it seems likely from the evidence we have that he was discovered there to be an informer for the Spanish (see Maguel §24), perhaps on the testimony of Read the blacksmith. By official accounts he was executed at Jamestown by firing squad for the crime of mutiny. Kendall remains a shadowy figure, but Barbour (1962) seems to have brought to light the essentials about the "mutineer" and the "intelligencer."

FRANCIS MAGUEL

"Probably the same person mentioned in the following abstract from 'English State Papers, Domestic,' Vol. 8, no. 79–

'December 16,1610. Examination of Francis Maguer, sailor of Ratcliffe, near London. His meeting with Father Patrick, who tried to persuade him to join some troops to be sent by the King of Spain to persuade the Irish to rebel. Plots to seize Dublin Castle and to send the Irish regiment from Flanders to Ireland. Met the Earl of Tyrone and Sir William Stanley at the Spanish court.'

"Francis Maguel, Maguer, or Maguire [?] was probably an adventurer or a spy. Tyrone and Stanley were both regarded in England as traitors (one Irish, the other English) to England at the court of Spain, and both were kept informed regarding affairs in England by correspondents." (Brown 1890)

His name does not appear on Smith's passenger lists of colonists, but that is no matter.

Relation §24

DON DIEGO DE MOLINA

"East India Company Records, June 12, 1618: 'Letter read from Henry Bacon, lately returned from Sir Walter Raleigh's voyage, stating that Molina, who was a prisoner in Virginia, incites the King of Spain to send forces to suppress Virginia, by the hopes of a silver mine there, from which he shows a piece to justify the truth thereof.'" (Brown 1890)

Irene Wright reports that by the end of 1616 he was in Spain and the proud recipient of a thousand ducats from his government "in consideration of his long and good service, and the great need in which he finds himself because of his long detention in Virginia."

Percy's *True Relation §31* states that once in England, de Molina quickly returned to Spain "where he was made general of six tall ships, and ... set out [for Virginia] of purpose to supplant us. But having been at sea about a month, a mutiny did grow amongst them insomuch that one of Diego's company stabbed him to death"—ending the expedition.

Letter to Velasco, 28 May 1613 §44
Letter to Velasco, 8 July 1613 §48

Letter to Gondomar, 30 April 1614 §49
Letter to Gondomar, 14 June 1614 §50

CAPTAIN CHRISTOPHER NEWPORT (1560–1617)

We first hear he sailed to Brazil in 1581, jumped ship due to a quarrel, and made his way back to England.

He was a privateer in the West Indies after 1590, and in 1592 with Sir John Burroughs captured the *Madre de Dios* and brought her into Dartmouth.

On December 10, 1606, he was commissioned and given sole command at sea of the Virginia expedition. He made four subsequent voyages to Virginia: 1607–08, 1608–09, 1609–10, and 1611.

Dissatisfied with the way the Virginia Company was supplying the colony, he left to join the service of the East India Company in 1612; in 1613–14 captained the *Expedition* (260 tons) to the Persian Gulf and India on a voyage of trade and exploration, for which he received the highest commendation, and rose to the rank of admiral in the Company's service.

He made another voyage to India, 1615–16.

On his third voyage he died at Bantam on Java, August 1617.

The Virginia Company granted his widow 3,500 acres in 1621.

Three sons lived in Virginia, one of them on his father's lands at Newport's News.

Letter to Salisbury, 29 July 1607 §8

OPECHANCANOUGH (d.1644)

Powhatan's youngest brother, historians have tried hard without success to connect him to Don Luis, the highborn Pamunkey boy kidnapped by the Spanish in 1561. A man of great leadership and martial bearing, his fortunes and prestige rose as that of his brother Powhatan sank in the years following the hostilities of 1610–13. At Powhatan's death, the right of sibling succession by order of age went to the weak Opitchapam, but the effective leader was already Opechancanough, and by 1630, after the death of Opitchapam, the third brother became mamanatowic, or paramount chief, of the Powhatan people, in fact and virtue. Always hostile, always opposed to accommodation with the English invasion of America, he was field commander of the massacre of March 1622 as well as the massacre of April 1644, when he was captured and murdered in his jail cell by a guard—at which time we estimate he was approaching the end of his first century of life.

It is said that at the time a stroke had left him partially paralyzed such that he was borne on a litter and an attendant had to raise his eyelids to let him see.

The 1622 attack came, but for Chanco's warning, as a complete surprise, coordinated to begin at dawn over the length and breadth of the area of white settlement, namely, the whole course of the tidal James River, few places excepted. Considering that the Indians at the time were in the most intimate association with their victims, beside them in their fields and even in their homes and kitchens, the commander had surely instilled a great sense of morale and mission.

The 1644 attack involved again as much coordination but fell for the most part only on the settlements south of the James, and despite the high death toll, the colony was now too large to destroy.

GEORGE PERCY (1580–1632)

"The Percys are almost without a peer even in the peerage of Great Britain; their nobility dates as remotely as the sovereignty of Normandy, and their renown, coeval with their nobility, has flourished in every age and coexisted with every generation since. Not more famous in arms than distinguished for its alliances, the family banner bears a galaxy of heraldic honors altogether unparalleled." (Brown 1890) They would have been kings but for Prince Hal's defeat of Hotspur in single combat at Shrewsbury in 1403, as told in the last act of Shakespeare's *The First Part of Henry the Fourth.*

Born September 4, 1580, homely George Percy was the eighth son of Henry, eighth Earl of Northumberland, by his wife Catherine, oldest daughter of John Neville, Lord Latimer—another great family.

His brother Henry (1564–1632), ninth earl of Northumberland, one of the most highly placed men in England, was serving on the Privy Council in 1603 when he fell under suspicion in the Gunpowder Plot and was committed to the Tower in November 1605, where he remained in genteel confinement until 1621. He was close to his brother George and corresponded with him in Virginia.

George, after soldiery in the Netherlands, joined the first expedition to Virginia in 1606, likely thinking to put some distance between himself and the suspicion that lay on the earl. It is significant that he was not named to serve on the council.

He was governor during the winter of the "starving time," serving from September 1609 until the arrival of Gates in May 1610. When Lord Delaware left Virginia in March 1611, he appointed Percy interim governor pending the arrival of Sir Thomas Dale in May.

Percy left Virginia for the last time in April 1612. In 1620 he sold four of his shares in the Virginia Company to Christopher Martin.

He was back in the Low Countries after war was declared with Spain in 1625, where he did good service, was captain of a company in 1627, and had one of his fingers shot off.

He died unmarried in 1632.

Observations gathered out of a discourse §1
Excerpt §10
A true relation §31
Letter to Northumberland, 17 August 1611 §39

FRANCIS PERKINS

"Came to Virginia with his son in 1608. Smith gives in his list of this supply only two of the name, 'Francis Perkins, gent., and Francis Perkins, laborer.' Smith's gentleman and laborer were probably father and son." (Brown 1890)

Letter to a friend §9

POCAHONTAS (1595?–1617)

Alias Matoaka, Amonute, baptized Rebecca, the daughter of Powhatan, was likely born at Werowocomoco. She was a frequent visitor to the settlement from the earliest days and became an important emissary for her father. Smith credited her with saving his life after his capture by Opechancanough in late 1607.

On a visit to Patawomeck in 1613, she was abducted by Argall and held at Jamestown as a hostage to peace. She was baptized by Rev. Whitaker in 1614, and married by Rev. Bucke to John Rolfe on April 5th of that year in the church at Jamestown, initiating a period of peace with the Indians that lasted until 1622.

She bore a son Thomas in 1615, and the Rolfes sailed for England the following year, staying seven months. The young princess of Virginia, barely twenty years old, drew considerable attention there, and was feted and entertained in the highest circles, short of being given a royal audience. King James, far from condescending to her royalty, was, it is said, vexed that she had married a commoner.

On the point of returning, she fell ill and died at Gravesend, 21 March 1617. Barbour guesses she was a victim of London's notorious air pollution. She was called "nonpareil," matchless in all attributes, a Miranda, a symbol of America's hopeful innocence.

Thomas Rolfe, likely named for Governor Dale, educated in England, returned to Virginia. In 1641 he petitions the assembly for permission to go into Indian country to visit Cleopatra, his mother's sister.

POWHATAN (1550?–1618)

Alias Wahunsonacock, born at the village of Powhatan below the falls of the James, whence his cognomen; mamanatowic of the Powhatan people until his death. During a long career of political and martial preeminence, he expanded his authority from the chieftainship of seven villages inherited from his unknown predecessor to a loose fiefdom obtaining military service and tribute from all of the Indian tribes of the Virginia coastal plain, including the Eastern Shore, but excluding the Chickahominy. When the English arrived in 1607, he was unmistakably the paramount ruler, with his seat at Werowocomoco. As such he attacked and removed the people of Kecoughtan, and mysteriously ordered the extermination of two tributary tribes, the Chesapeakes and Piankatanks. His European-style coronation ceremony in 1609, conducted by Newport, was an English recognition of the royalty of his authority over Virginia. He moved his seat to Orapax soon afterward, and had removed from there to the upper Pamunkey River by the time of Gates's 1613 visit.

Powhatan cuts an immense figure across these pages, a leader not simply of a tribe but a territory of many tribes. His speeches show great dignity, kingly wisdom, and harrowing prescience. He seems to have realized that the last battle would be at Wounded Knee and native peoples would be supplanted. As our story begins, we sense his best days are behind him. After the hostilities of 1610–11 and the abduction of his favorite Pocahontas, the man is tired and resigned to an accommodation by any means with the European invasion. As his powers decline, those of his brother Opechancanough surge upward.

JOHN RATCLIFFE, *alias* SICKLEMORE (157?–1609)

Brown (1890) identifies him with a Captain Ratcliffe taken prisoner with Sir Henry Cary and Captain Pigott at Mülheim in the Low Countries in October 1605.

It remains a mystery why he used an alias. His real name seems to have been Sicklemore and his alias Ratcliffe, reflected in his signature to his letter, but Capt. John Smith, who held a special dislike for him, assures us the reverse.

On September 10, 1607, he was elected president of the council at Jamestown following the removal of Wingfield; he served out his one-year term, and was succeeded by Capt. John Smith on September 10, 1608. He sailed for England in January 1609, but returned to Virginia in June of the same year. The following winter he and his party, on a trading expedition to Powhatan, were lured into ambush and killed but for two survivors.

Letter to Salisbury, 4 October 1609 §19

RICHARD RICH

Illegitimate son of, Robert, 2nd Baron Rich, he married a daughter of John Machell, sheriff of London and was the father of Sir Nathaniel Rich (member of parliament, involved in colonial affairs at the highest level) and five other children who married prominently.

News from Virginia §21

JOHN ROLFE (1585–1622)

His grandparents, Eustacius Rolfe and Joanna Jener, were married in the parish church at Heacham in Norfolk, May 27, 1560. Their son John Rolfe (senior) was baptized there, October 17, 1562.

"He married there, September 24, 1582, Dorothea Mason, and their twin sons Eustacius and John were baptized there, May 6, 1585. Eustacius died an infant.

John (junior), began his adulthood with a wife (1608) and a voyage with her for Virginia in June 1609 with Gates and Somers. They were shipwrecked on Bermuda, and while there a daughter, Bermuda, was born to them, and christened by the Rev. Mr. Bucke, February 11, 1610, Captain Newport, William Strachey, and Mrs. Horton being sponsors. The child, we are told, died an infant. Mrs. Rolfe arriving at Jamestown died soon after.

In 1612, he introduced crop tobacco in Virginia. Rolfe obtained the seeds of a superior strain of Trinidad and Orinoco tobacco that thrived in Virginia soil, developed cultivation as well as curing methods, and successfully marketed the result in England such that at Jamestown was born the world's first commercial tobacco culture. Whitemen learned tobacco with as much swiftness, intelligence, and inspiration as Indians learned horses and firearms. Regardless of who was governor or what the charters said, Virginia after Rolfe had a reason for being. Even the Indian's smoked Orinoco. They continued to use native tobacco, however, for religious purposes.

In a deserved parenthesis in a sketch of this man, I wish to say that his tobacco regardless of fashion remains the world's prettiest leaf and, for all it is abused by addicts and their pandering merchants, one of its purest pleasures, as profound as the grape. It is so sensitive to soil and climate, let alone handling, that a few thousand acres here and there produce all we could call supreme. The best way to take it is still the peaceful pipe.

John Rolfe and Pocahontas were married about the fifth of April 1614 at the church in Jamestown by his friend Rev. Bucke, the minister there. The Rolfes were in England, 1616–17. On the point of returning, Pocahontas fell ill and died at Gravesend. Rolfe continued to Virginia, leaving their son Thomas under the guardianship of his brother, Henry Rolfe, in England.

He served on the council in 1619.

In 1621 Lady Delaware accuses him of mismanaging proceeds due her from tobacco.

His third wife was Jane, daughter of William Pierce.

His will was drawn March 10, 1621, witnessed by his old friend and pastor, the Rev. Richard Bucke. He died a month later, in April 1622, while a passenger aboard the *Neptune* bound for England.

Jane Pierce Rolfe married Capt. Roger Smith, and her daughter Elizabeth Rolfe (born in Virginia in 1621) was living with Capt. Roger Smith at James City, January 24, 1625. Thomas Rolfe, the child of Pocahontas, was still in England.

Letter to Dale, 1614 (appended to Hamor's *Discourse*) *§51*
A true relation of the state of Virginia §53
Letter to Sandys, 8 June 1617 §56

THE EARL OF SALISBURY (1563?–1612)

Robert Cecil, first earl of Salisbury (1605), son of William Cecil, Lord Burghley (Elizabeth's brilliant minister), he was appointed secretary of state in 1596, was sole secretary from 1603 until his death, serving in an embassy to France and in active military service in the Netherlands, from 1608 lord treasurer of the realm—a short, frail man with a crooked back and a splay foot, the queen's "little elf" and the king's "little beagle," of great modesty and hard work, who rose to supreme power.

He filled the place of Walsingham in gathering intelligence through a network of spies in foreign courts.

In 1603 he wrote to his friend, Sir James Harrington:

> Good knight, rest content, and give heed to one that hath sorrowed in the bright luster of a court and gone heavily on even the best-seeming fair ground. 'Tis a great task to prove one's honesty and yet not mar one's fortune. You have tasted a little thereof in our blessed queen's time, who was more than a man and, in truth, sometimes less than a woman. I wish I waited now in your presence-chamber, with ease at my food and rest in my bed. I am pushed from the shore of comfort, and know not where the winds and waves of a court will bear me. I know it bringeth little comfort on earth; and he is, I reckon, no wise man that looketh this way to heaven.

He was all alone in the world.

A prime mover in the establishment of the Virginia Company, at over £300 a major contributor, a member of the Virginia Council, in fact the principal patron of the London group, Salisbury could also be said to stand at the fore of a large contingent of it, namely, those among the nobility and landed gentry who devoted their money and

LIBRARY OF VIRGINIA

ROBERT CECIL, EARL OF SALISBURY

energy to the Virginia enterprise not so much hoping for personal gain but as proud participants in a public undertaking for the good of the nation.

SIR EDWIN SANDYS (1561–1629)

Son of the Archbishop of York, member of Parliament, courtier and royal commissioner at the court of King James, councilor and treasurer of the Virginia Company, knighted in 1603, political thinker and writer, a leader of the so-called liberals, his profound belief and dedication to the cause of popular liberty and republican principals led directly to establishing democracy and legislative government in Virginia in 1619, and the repeal of the harsh "laws divine, moral, and martial." He assisted Sir Thomas Smythe as treasurer of the Virginia Company from 1617 and was elected full treasurer in 1619, but as he was unacceptable to King James, who suspected him of aiming to let loose a popular government in England like the one in Virginia, he was replaced by the Earl of Southampton in 1620. Absent Sandys, it is difficult to say who would have set us so firmly on the road to becoming the land of the free.

A court minute of the quarter court of the Virginia Company of 7 May 1623:

> *Unfitt Gouerment.* They alleadge that ye Gouerment as it now stands is Democraticall and tumultuous and therfore fitt to be altered and reduced to the hands of some few personns.
>
> *Answer.* The Gouerment is no other then by yor Ma^ty^: in yor Letters Patents is prescribed vnto vs: And itt is a bold censure thus to taxe a Gouerment ordayned and constituted by such authority Butt besides, their Allegacon is a slaunder for ye Gouerment is not Democraticall. [I.e., the king always had a veto.]

An early version of the McCarthy hearings. George Yeardley and Francis Wyatt, his governors in Virginia, made sure we emerged from the dissolution of the Company in 1624 still quite a republic, if that is a slander.

CAPTAIN JOHN SMITH (1580–1631)

The central figure in the establishment of the Jamestown colony, Smith over four centuries has been a figure of legend and controversy, a hero and a villain, his estimate now rising, now falling, through several phases, reaching a high in the history of Stith in the 18th century, reaching a low along with everything connected with Virginia and the South after 1865, then rising steadily through the 20th century to peak with the success of Philip Barbour's *The Three Worlds of Captain John Smith* (1964), and today likely headed again downward. Dominating the field of Smith scholarship at the end of the 20th century is Barbour's *The Complete Works* (1986).

He was one of history's extraordinary characters. We have so many facts about him, we can indulge in the luxury of rejecting some of them.

Because John Smith wrote his life down for us to read: He was born to simple yeomanry, was baptized on January 9, 1580, the son of George and Alice (Rickard) Smith, in Willoughby by Alford, Lincolnshire.

He was apprenticed to a merchant in King's Lynn, but left 1596–97 to join English volunteers fighting in the Netherlands and France. By 1599, at the conclusion of peace, he was back in England. He went home and lived alone in the woods to read Marcus Aurelius.

For a few months he was among the attendants of Peregrine Bertie, son of Lord Willoughby, on a trip to France.

In 1600 he left England and found himself touring on a merchant-cum-pirate ship in the Mediterranean. He took a share in the prize of a Venetian trader, and with money on his belt late in the year joined the Austrian forces against the Turks.

In Hungary he was promoted to captain, sent to Transylvania in 1602, fought and beheaded three Turkish officers in three single combats between the armies. He was captured and sold into slavery; acquired by the Lady Charatza Trabigzanda, who fell in love with him and sent him to her brother for training, a man he killed in order to escape. He now made his way on foot through Russia and Poland back to Transylvania, only to find it in enemy hands.

He was rewarded for service by his prince, Zsigmond Báthory, December 1603, and traveled over Europe and as far as Morocco in search of further soldiering.

He was likely in London by the winter of 1604–05, where before long he was caught up in the Virginia adventure. His activities there are thoroughly described in the texts ahead.

His *True Relation* appeared in print without his knowledge in 1608 while he was in Virginia.

Returning to London in late 1609, he wrote and directed the publication of his *Map of Virginia* and *Proceedings* at Oxford in 1612.

In April 1614 he obtained private backing for a voyage to the north Virginia coast, which he named "New England" with the approval of Prince Charles. Apart from an abortive return voyage, he never again went to sea.

He published eight books in his remaining years, living in or near London on the generosity and encouragement of loyal friends. His chief work remains *The General History of Virginia, New-England, & the Summer Isles* (1624) in six books, the second, third, and fourth of which, expanding on his earlier work, appear here in whole or in part as noted.

He was taken ill and died, June 21, 1631, unmarried.

A true relation §12
A map of Virginia §16 (selections)
The general history, third book §17
The general history, fourth book §52 (selections)

SIR THOMAS SMYTHE (1558?–1625)

The first treasurer of the Virginia Company, he functioned as the chief executive of the entire Virginia undertaking until he was replaced in 1619. Born in Oxford, the son of Customer Mr. Thomas Smythe, he early rose by his remarkable talents to great prominence in business and commercial affairs side by side with his equally prominent father.

He was an incorporator of the Turkey Company in 1584; a leading member of the Russia Company in 1587; was at the top of the list of those to whom Raleigh assigned his interest in Virginia in 1589; succeeded his father as master of customs. He lent his aid to send ships to the East Indies in 1591; organized an expedition there in the same decade; in 1600 was an incorporator and first governor of the great East India Company. He was a sheriff of London 1600–1601, then was sent to the Tower under suspicion as a friend of the Earl of Essex and as captain of the trained bands of London. He was soon released and knighted in the Tower in 1603, finding favor with the new monarch precisely for this association. In 1604 he was appointed ambassador to Russia, thereafter a member of parliament, and member of the Virginia Council from 20 November 1606, going on to fill the office of treasurer created under the 1609 charter.

These are the principle achievements of the man up to the year of our undertaking who was probably the most successful businessman of his day, foremost among that special breed of merchant adventurers who laid the basis for the unparalleled expansion of Anglo-Saxon civilization in the years ahead. To the colonists at Jamestown he was simply the CEO of the whole operation, and of uneven popularity.

SIR GEORGE SOMERS (1554–1610)

Born of respectable parentage at Lyme Regis, Dorset, in 1554, he went to sea and from 1595 commanded naval expeditions, and is credited with successful actions in the West Indies.

He was knighted in 1603.

He served in Parliament for Lyme Regis from 1604.

Leaving his seat vacant, he sailed for Virginia as fleet commander in June 1609 with Gates and Newport in the *Sea Venture*, and was wrecked on Bermuda. He landed her people and saw to her salvage for the building of two pinnaces, the *Patience* and the *Deliverance,* in which 150 colonists were brought off safely to Jamestown, May 1610. The voyage places him among the great sailors of history.

In June, he shipped again for Bermuda to obtain a supply of meat for the colony. He died there November 9, 1610, "of a surfeit in eating of a pig." His heart was buried in the island and his body was returned to England.

He had a wife Johanna. He left property in Lyme Regis to a son Matthew.

The London Company had renamed Bermuda "Virginiola," but

changed that to the "Summer Islands" for the mild climate and in his memory.

Letter to Salisbury, 15 June 1610 §23

HENRY SPELMAN (1595–1623)

Once thought to be the "third son of Sir Henry Spelman of Congham, Norfolk (1562–1641), the distinguished antiquary and historian, treasurer of the Guiana Company, and one of the Council for New England," he has now long since been proved to be the son of Erasmus Spelman, brother of the above Henry.

He "was baptized in 1595; landed in Virginia in August 1609; was sold to the Indians soon after, and lived with them until December 1610.

"He returned to England with Lord De La Warr in March 1611, but afterwards went back to Virginia, where he was employed as interpreter to the colony in 1616.

"In 1618 he was again in England, but returned to Virginia on board the *Treasurer* in that year. He 'knew most of the kings of that country, and spake their languages very understandingly.' (Howe's Abridgment)

"In August 1619, he was tried by the House of Burgesses for speaking disparagingly of Governor Yeardley to Opechancanough, and degraded from his office as interpreter, etc.

"He was trading with the Indians along the Potomac at the time of the massacre in March 1622; and about one year after, on March 23, 1623, he was killed by the Anacostan Indians, probably near the present site of Washington, D.C." (Brown 1890)

Relation of Virginia §29
Excerpt §30

WILLIAM STRACHEY (1572–1621)

Born in 1572 in Saffron Walden, Essex, of minor gentry, his father William Strachey (d. 1598) was a man of property who received a grant of arms from the College of Heralds.

He entered Emmanuel College, Cambridge University in 1588.

He married Frances Forster in 1595.

In 1605, he was a member of Gray's Inn (attending law school), and making friends among the London literary set. He was a stockholder in Blackfriars Theater and frequented it often enough to have known the players, which included Shakespeare.

In 1606, he became secretary to Thomas Glover, ambassador to Constantinople and agent of the Levant Company, and went with him to the Turkish capital. Glover proved to be a difficult person to work for; they fell out and Strachey was dismissed, returning to London jobless in 1608.

He bought two shares in the Virginia Company and sailed with Sir Thomas Gates for Virginia in June 1609. The ship was wrecked off Bermuda, stranding the colonists until two new vessels were built and the party sailed for Jamestown, arriving in May 1610.

After Matthew Scrivener drowned, Strachey replaced him as secretary of the colony.

He returned to England early in the fall of 1611, and immediately prepared his draft of the laws promulgated by Gates, Delaware, Cecil, and Dale, *For the Colony in Virginia. Laws Divine, Moral, and Martial*, which appeared early in 1612, and is the only writing of Strachey's published in his lifetime.

Later in the year he hurried to complete his *History*, and sent a manuscript and dedication to the Earl of Northumberland; after that another copy to Sir Allen Apsley; and in 1618, still hopeful, a third copy was presented with a dedication to the philosopher Sir Francis Bacon—each time without success.

He died in London in poverty, June 21, 1621, with nothing to bequeath his second wife Dorothy.

From his last days:

Hark! 'Twas the trump of death that blew—
    My hour is come; false world, adieu!
    Thy pleasures have betrayed me so
    That I to death untimely go.

Laws divine, moral, and martial, etc. (p. 27)
A true reportory §22
The history of travel into Virginia Britannia §41

REV. WILLIAM SYMONDS (1556–1616?)

"D.D., divine, schoolteacher, rector, and author, in 1599 he was presented by Robert Bertie [Lord Willoughby] to the rectory of Halton Holgate, Lincolnshire." (Barbour 1986a) This connects him with Capt. John Smith, who was then in Willoughby's service. While pastor at St. Saviour's, Southwark, he preached two sermons, 1607–09, most eloquent statements of England's colonial mission, which were published by the Virginia Company. In 1612, at the Rev. Crashaw's request, he lent his best offices to find a publisher for Smith's *Map of Virginia & Proceedings §16 & 17.*

ROBERT TINDALL (d.1610)

"Sailor and gunner for Prince Henry, nothing seems to be known about him beyond his sketch map and odd references to him." (Barbour 1986a)

Letter to Prince Henry, 22 June 1607 §7

UTTAMATOMAKKIN (TOMOCOMO)

He married Matachanna, a daughter of Powhatan, so was a brother-in-law to Pocahontas. He was a quiyoughcosough, or priest, who was tolerant of lectures on Christianity. He sojourned in London with the Rolfes at the head of a delegation from Powhatan, and was on familiar terms with him when he met Captain Smith on the street. He returned to Virginia with Argall and Rolfe, and we hear that in his report to Powhatan he had nothing good to say about the English part of the world.

Interview in London §55

THOMAS WEST, BARON DELAWARE (1577–1618)

Born to Thomas West, second Lord Delaware, and his wife Ann, daughter of Sir Francis Knollys, July 9, 1577.

He was a second cousin to Henry, Earl of Dover; his maternal grandmother was a first cousin to the queen.

In 1596 he married Cecily, daughter of Sir Thomas Sherley.

He served with distinction under Essex in the wars in the Netherlands; was implicated in the Essex rebellion in England in 1601, and imprisoned. Essex, however, denied the young man's involvement, and when his father died in 1602, he became third Lord Delaware, and a member of the queen's Privy Council, continuing under James.

From 1608 till his death, he devoted his ten remaining years to the enterprise of founding English Protestant colonies in America, working mostly as a promoter in England, and was a member of the Council of Virginia from 1609. He was named the first governor and captain general of Virginia for life, February 28, 1610, and sailed for Jamestown the March following, remaining until June 1611, at which time he left due to illness, appointing George Percy interim governor.

His health never completely returned. He died of sickness on a voyage back to Virginia, June 7, 1618, perhaps ashore, his ship having, it seems, put in on our coast somewhere north of the Chesapeake.

His son Henry succeeded him, becoming fourth lord.

Letter to Salisbury, rec'd September 1610 §26
Letter to Salisbury, 22 June 1611 §33
A short relation §34

REV. ALEXANDER WHITAKER (1585–1617)

Born at Cambridge, son of the well-known Rev. Dr. William Whitaker, master of St. Johns College, Cambridge University, whom Purchas calls "that worthy and polemical divine."

He received an M.A. from Cambridge in 1604. He secured a good parsonage in the north of England, but rose from a comfortable life to go as a missionary with Sir Thomas Dale to Virginia, March 1611, with the aim of remaining three years.

He became the preacher at Henrico settlement in 1612, living at "Rock Hall" on church land in Coxendale in 1614.

He became the teacher of Pocahontas, 1613–14, and baptized her. There is no evidence he married her to John Rolfe. The service was more likely performed by the Rev. Bucke, minister at Jamestown and a friend of Rolfe.

He was the preacher at Bermuda Nether Hundred in the spring of 1616.

He drowned in the James in March 1617.

Letter to Crashaw, 9 August 1611 §37

Good news from Virginia §43

Letter to Gouge, 18 June 1614 (in Hamor's *Discourse*) §51

WILLIAM WHITE (d. 1624?)

"A laborer who arrived with the original settlers, and who lived with the Indians at some uncertain time. He may be the William White who was buried in Elizabeth City on 12 September 1624, but his not uncommon name and his lack of prominence make it impossible to trace his career." (Barbour 1969)

The Black Boys Ceremony §11

EDWARD MARIA WINGFIELD (*c.*1560–after 1613)

Born into a family famous for their knighthood and ancient nobility, their chief seat being the castle Kimbolton in Huntingdonshire, his father Thomas-Maria, a Catholic, served in parliament for the county during the reigns of Edward VI and Mary.

After, it seems, a period of youthful excesses and premature debt, he followed in the family tradition to become a soldier by profession, serving in Ireland and in the Netherlands against Catholic Spain. He was captured in 1588 at Lisle together with Ferdinando Gorges, later a member of the Council of Virginia. We read that friends petition for the two to be exchanged for Spanish prisoners recently taken in naval actions by Sir Francis Drake and Sir Walter Raleigh.

He returned to service in Ireland.

He is the only member of the London Virginia Company mentioned in the first charter who went in the first expedition to Jamestown. On May 14, 1607, he was elected president of the council, then removed and barred from the council September 10, 1607.

Wingfield left in disgrace, April 10, 1608, and arrived in England May 21st.

He was still living and unmarried in England in 1613.

A discourse of Virginia §13

Excerpt §14

PETER WINNE

He arrived in Virginia with the second supply of September 1608, and was made a member of the council. "He died in Virginia in the spring of 1609 [during the 'starving time']. Not knowing of his death, and reposing especial confidence in him, Sir Thomas Gates, having been wrecked on the Bermudas, selected him from the members of the council in Virginia to be his lieutenant-governor there, and sent to him, by a bark of aviso, a particular commission." (Brown 1890)

Letter to Egerton, 26 November 1608 §15

GEORGE YEARDLEY (*c.*1577–1627)

The second of four sons born to George, merchant tailor, and Rhonda Yeardley of London, *c.*1577–80; was a veteran of the Dutch Wars. He sailed to Virginia with Gates in 1609 and was with him cast away on Bermuda, until arriving at Jamestown in May 1610. He served as interim governor from Dale's departure to the arrival of Argall, April 1616 to May 1617. He returned to England in 1618. He was named governor of Virginia, 18 November 1618, and was knighted six days later. He arrived in Virginia, 19 April 1618, and in accord with Sir Thomas Smythe's instructions he convened the meeting of the Burgesses on 30 July, America's first legislature. He served three years and was replaced in November 1621 by Sir Francis Wyatt. At Wyatt's departure, King Charles named Yeardley again governor, 14 March 1626, which office he held until his death in November 1627.

He married Temperance—— in Virginia in 1618, and in 1625 they were living in Jamestown with three children. She had come to Virginia on the *Faulcon* in 1609. They have numerous descendants.

He died wealthy.

Letter to Peyton, 18 November 1610 §28

SOURCES: Brown 1890: brief biographies, Dictionary National Biography (1950), Barbour 1986a: biographical directory, and others.

THE TEXTS

I HAVE MOSTLY worked with the earliest source, whether original surviving manuscripts or contemporary print publications, exceptions being Spanish language material and Virginia Company tracts.

The text once in hand, my policy has been modern spelling of the *word*, modern indenting and punctuation of the *thought*. Abbreviations are written out. Names and Indian words are left as I found them. My reference throughout has been the *Oxford English Dictionary* (OED), resorting to Webster's for American orthography.

Li-superscript for *libra* refers to a pound of weight or money.

If a writer says "reqwitall" I print "requital"; but if he says "reqwittalle," I take that to be "requittal"—not as current today but really another and parallel form. Strachey writes of "shaling" an oyster, instead of shelling, or shucking. Today we say "interested" but Ralph Hamor used the old form *interessed* and I let him still, and let the others. If another reporter says "spake" or "doth" or puts an *s*-plural on verbs, I get it all down faithfully. If one writer says "shipped" and another says "shipt" I write "shipped" and "ship'd." The *-ed* was often but not always a syllable then. Obviously *-t* never was. Drayton above in meters wanted to make it plain which was which.

We discriminate today in sense and stress between *humane/human, inhumane/inhuman,* but William Strachey wrote only "inhumane" and pronounced it "inhuman." So I write the latter.

There is a tendency to clip inflections. *Start* serves as either a present or past tense. *Highness* and *corpse* can be singular or plural.

Contemporary possessives were done three ways: a simple *s,* an apostrophe *s* (rare), or where the *s* would make a syllable it was customarily written *his* (common). By analogy this became *her* for female possessives. I have treated the *s*-possessives after the modern manner, letting the context determine singular and plural, except I have left the *his*-possessives as they were written.

A select few contemporary names, both Indian and English, have standard spellings nowadays. I attempted to impose one on the rest only to see it slowly collapse. The same writer (or printer) will use two spellings in as many lines. Of the spellings of the three commonest names—Jamestown, Powhatan, Pocahontas—only Powhatan occurs with any frequency. Jamestown is without exception two words. John Rolfe who married her called her Pokahuntas.

As for Jamestown, *town* is I believe invariably written "towne," but I take it for a common, not a proper, noun, and so spell it modern. It is capital or lower case or hyphenated here depending on the style in the text.

Occasionally it seems somebody at the time spells somebody else's name wrong. John Ratcliffe is called Ratliffe or Ratlieffe, etc., and we wonder if he would have corrected the copy. We don't.

These are personal names, and together with less common New World place names I leave them exactly as I find them. On the other hand, if I have allowed Plymouth to remain Plemoth, or France to remain Fraunce, it is an oversight. But Swethland for Sweden, Switzer for Swiss, St. George for São Jorge are different forms of a name and I keep them literatim.

Lord Delaware writes "comforth," even though there is no evidence in the OED that he or anyone else ever pronounced *th* here. So I print "comfort." Conversely, *fifth* then was often written and spoken "fift," and I retain it where I see it. The same writer will say either "fathom" or "fadom." I follow him. All our reporters write "arquebus" for *harquebus;* so do I. The word *lieutenant* is sometimes written "lieftenant," reflecting old as well as modern British pronunciation, so I always spell it modern.

The title *master* is frequently written "maister," *command* is written "commaund" (straunger, daunger, demaund, auncient, chaunce), *account* is nearly always "accompt," *month* is mostly "moneth," but with those and many similar cases old spellings do not indicate an old pronunciation, and I stick to the modern standard .

Persevere was pronounced "persévver."

Devil is usually written "Divel" and mostly capitalized. I'm not sure what is right, but I write "devil." On the other hand *God* is often not capped, and the capitalized divine *His* never is, but I cap them both everywhere.

Than was always written "then."

The old past tense of *eat* is *eat* but pronounced "ate."

Original spelling means something to the scholar, the layman often reads too much into it. False etymology is a common temptation. Some people think savages were called "salvages" because they needed the "salvation" by baptism, and so on. In fact, both spellings were used, even by the same writer. One though I had to keep—John Rolfe's *all-arm!* for *alarm.*

A few previous publications of our texts have been modernized. Most of the rest are semi-literatim—the texts have been partially modernized. Sentence initials are capitalized and periods replace colons, superscripts come down to the line, *j* and *v* replace *i* and *u,* typos are corrected. But *semi* mostly means writing out abbreviations and shorthand, which are profuse in manuscripts of the period. A couple of *p*-derived symbols stood for *per-, pre-, pro-*. *Provide* was written "þuide." The abstract suffix *-tion* was commonly written *-con.* A tilde stood over a vowel to indicate a nasal, that the vowel was to be followed by an *n* or *m* and so on. I have written all of them out, along with personal titles and names. Where it seems there is any doubt of the full form of a name, I bracket the fill.

Middle English *ye* and *yt* are written *the* and *that* since that is what they stand for and that is the way the writer pronounced them.

Several Spanish forms were in later centuries replaced by the French: barricado/barricade, palisado/palisade, ambuscado/ ambuscade or ambush, and so on—a shift of cultural and political winds.

Numbers are either the numeral or the word, according to the original form. A date such as "22th" is not miswritten. It stands for, I suppose, the "two and twentieth." Similarly there is no way to know if "100" is pronounced *a* hundred, *an* hundred, or *one* hundred (sometimes "hundreth"). The 18 of June may be read as either an ordinal or a cardinal. It depends on the writer.

English dates are "old style," ten days behind our calendar. Spanish dates are "new style," matching our calendar.

If there is lost or cut text, I use dots [...]. If there is a blank after a word, typically where the writer failed to supply a name or date, I use a double em-dash [——].

Material in brackets within the text is editorial and supplied by me, either a gloss on the previous word or a phrase connector.

Footnotes were not used in the seventeenth century. Notes and commentary instead were "marginalized." Nowadays it is lavish to allow margins that wide and I have put original margin material in footnotes, but indicate it as such. Of course a footnote can only be inserted at a *point* while a long marginal note of the type common in Purchas can lie against a whole body of text. Then too, some margin notes are starred in the text. But the difference never seems to me to be crucial. The broadness of a commentary, regardless of format, should be obvious.

At any rate Archer and Wingfield, Smith and Strachey—they are the writers, not I. I introduce reader to writer and assume you speak the same language and do not need me as a running interpreter. Which is to say this tries not to be a "footnote edition." Mine are as seldom and as brief as I can make them. Too many and they swerve the attention from the running narrative, as likely as not anticipating confusion or curiosity that is not there. The scattered few notes that come down from the originals are retained if they are commentary and omitted if they merely highlight. I add simple word glosses where they have to go and try to avoid leading the reader with background and opinion. I have not glossed uncommon words found in standard collegiate dictionaries. I am here in the business of making things as brisk as possible. After all, our material was considered light reading in its day.

I aspire to work for a public that wants to read the books they own but are seriously deterred by quaint spelling and meaningless punctuation no matter how good the tale. Quaint originals amuse for a few lines, but a few pages and a barrier comes down that the author never created and that never was there for his contemporary readers.

In fact scholarly editions, all right in their place, are nowadays rendering old copy and old manuscripts with a fidelity not shared by editors of the time, who were regularly depended upon to clean things up. It is pretty easy to tell which of our texts come down from handwriting and which from contemporary print publication without looking at the source. In an old-spelling edition, add up the oddities and the manuscripts will have it five to one.

Or authors—Ralph Hamor appends a table of errata to his *Discourse*. But unlike a modern table, not a single one out of the two dozen changes is a spelling or punctuation correction. They are all *word* corrections. I don't have them all at hand, but I believe the title *The History of Travel* is spelled three ways in three manuscripts, and never that way. Did Strachey care?

If quaintness is a false participation, it also lends a false sense of authenticity. A literatim edition is a concession to scholars who don't want to deal direct with the original. But if it is so important to read "Iames towne" in order to understand an author's intent, we cannot rely on any transcriber no matter what his methods. We have no choice but to go to the original.

I found in reading long manuscript passages that the quaintness so raised up and irksome in crisp modern fonts entirely falls away from the handwriting itself. Not everybody has the time to learn to read old script, and it is always slow going at best, but it lets you see the normal lay of the written language as a sensible convention. *Y* was used for *i* because *y* has two strokes and a tail, much easier to read. But not easier in print! If every *it* is going to be written *yt,* the printed page is soon tedious and really no more "authentic" for it. The final *e,* so common then and common now in main street Olde Towne revitalizations, was simply a balancing curl (it filled in for an *s)* that set the end of one word off from the beginning of another. It all makes sense for quill pen legibility and the reader *does* grow accustomed to that. Handwriting made only one kind of *s* and made a clear distinction between *u* and *v* that printers refused to follow till the nineteenth century. In sum, a literatim edition, or even strict diplomatic copy, to be safe and "of record," should at least be published with facing facsimile.

Which answers the objection some have that if we leave the language alone we should leave the text alone. Unfortunately, funnye spelinges staie funnye. But variety in *language,* variety in the way people say or use *words,* whether old ways or new, is a fact of life and the brain is made to adapt to and familiarize itself with whatever language surrounds us. If the story is good the reader quickly picks up the usage and incorporates it. That is, the longer he goes with it the more normal any usage becomes until, I suppose, it gets as normal as it was to the writer.

THE TEXTS

The texts appear in chronological order. Below the full title is the symbol < followed first by the original and then some published sources. The text that underlies my transcription is in bold type. Below that is a body of commentary in double-indented small type.

Paragraphing and Punctuation

CONTEMPORARY publishers used the same symbols we use but they used them irregularly and to indicate very different quantities of pause. Rated short to long they used comma, period, semicolon, and colon. They indicate pause more than syntax.

There is a heavy use of parenthesis where a modern text hardly displays commas. If it serves any purpose, it indicates a lowered speaking tone, away from the main statement, quite the way most writers use it now. Much of that I retain. Otherwise, parenthesis here indicates the interjected phrase.

Clauses are inverted very spontaneously, no doubt the result of the writer being fluent in Latin. This calls for em-dashes.

Our reporters all seem to assume, rough soldiers and plain speakers though they be, that a thought ends with a stop. If the thought is in its several embellishing facets still coming forth, they deem it is still too soon to put in a full stop. This leaves a modern editor with a page full of dashes and semicolons. The device they are using is nothing more complicated than omitting to repeat the subject noun or pronoun in ensuing independent clauses, and helping themselves along with an overuse of conjunctions, again a trait of Classical composition.

MODERN: He's a friend. I've known him for years. I trust him. And—there he is.

JAMESTOWN: He is my friend, whom I have known for a many a year, wherefore I do trust him, and, indeed, what shall I say but there he is?

On a couple of occasions I have indented a paragraph and inserted a *they* or a *we* in brackets to begin a new sentence with a new breath.

I suggest the reader first time through read swiftly. Most of these writers are more comfortable writing speech than prose, and the reader should listen for speech sense before prose syntax. In fact, it seems most of the prose is in the front matter—dedications, introductions, addresses. These are usually very involved, betraying revision and polishing. Other times the sense and the syntax both go. My bracketed and footnoted helps and glosses try then to piece and repair. In many of these places I found myself stopped a long time. Captain John Smith is always trying to make his case, and his syntax is crammed with *whereas* and *whereat* and *wherefore* and qualifying clauses, a style, I think, suitable for one who has stood on the gallows a couple of times.

Now and then it is hard to say, based on original punctuation, which sentence a clause belongs to—at the end of one or the beginning of the one following. It is impossible for the editor to read more carefully than you, and there are readers who, somewhere in over 700 pages of text, will raise entirely legitimate objections and decry "modern editions." I admit there are some I have flip-flopped on several times. Here's a hard case from Chapter 6 of Smith's Third Book of the *General History §17–276:* "But two or three escaped by rowing, being against their plains: our muskets they found shot further than their bows, for we made not twenty shot ere they all retired behind the next trees." Does a period come after *rowing* or *plains? Plains* means "open land," "cropland" and the sense does not favor the period there. Or again, in the original garments here is Percy's *Discourse §1–92:* "He would fain have had us come to his town, the captain was unwilling; seeing that the day was so far spent he returned back to his ships for that night." It is hard to believe the punctuation, but what choice do we have? We would like to switch them and write "and" after "spent." Strachey's sense is plain, or is it? The original punctuation puzzles us: "In the morning by daybreak (so soon as one might well see from the foretop) one of the sailors descried land about an hour after, I went up and might discover two hummocks to the southward ..." (§22–417) Surely Strachey saw the hummocks an hour after land-ho, which means a period after *land.*

For better or worse, the reader can see these principles applied in action. I give Sir Thomas Dale's letter of 10 June 1613 (§47) photographed in the original, in literatim (not diplomatic) transcription, and in modern text.

Samuel Purchas (1578–1626)

APART FROM the works of Captain John Smith, our largest contemporary printed source consists of the vast publications of the vicar of Eastwood, Essex, later rector of St. Martin's Ludgate in London. He brought out two titles, *Purchas His Pilgrimage, or Relations of the World and the Religions Observed in All Ages and Places,* etc. (1613, 1614, 1617, 1626, under a thousand pages); and an enormous supplement called *Hakluytus Posthumus, or Purchas His Pilgrimes, containing a History of the World in Sea Voyages and Land-Travels by Englishmen and Others,* etc. (1625, over four thousand pages)—each work devoted to the glory of England and her destiny of world maritime and imperial supremacy. Thus the reader must make a fine discrimination between his book called *Pilgrimage* and his book called *Pilgrimes.*

Purchas saw himself as the successor of Richard Hakluyt whose *Principal Navigations* (1589, 1599) and earlier works had done so much to rouse England's interest in colonization. The *Pilgrimage* is mostly Purchas' own writing punctuating short selections written by others. I have included the bulk of Chapter 6 of the 8th Book, "The Religion and Rites of the Virginians" in Percy §10, White §11, Wingfield §14, Spelman §30, Uttamatomakkin §55. Purchas also made use in it of long passages from Smith's *Map of Virginia.*

The later work, *Pilgrimes,* is the more important source of the two, being a compilation of many full-length accounts from all over the world, Purchas serving as the editor/commentator, and frankly a model for my work here. Most are written by Englishmen and recount firsthand exploration, trade, warfare, and pure adventure in far

LIBRARY OF VIRGINIA

REV. SAMUEL PURCHAS

continents and over high seas. Many of these *Pilgrimes* and *Pilgrimages,* including those that deal with Virginia, give all or part of accounts that survive nowhere else—Percy §1, Archer §18, Strachey §22.

Purchas' work holds a great deal of lively reading (his chief editorial criterion), but we would give anything to see what he discarded. Each generation of scholars comes to praise Purchas' zeal as a collector as much as each deplores his editorial scissors. Nor was he as careful as Hakluyt to preserve manuscripts in his possession once he made use of them in print. We tender him an infuriated thanks.

The Language

OUR CHARACTERS all show uncommon writing ability. They are generally easier to read than Shakespeare and the Bible precisely because they have so little writer's training and tend in spite of themselves toward plain speaking. The chief faults seem to be either lack of any revision or too much. Strachey and Hamor try to master the inflated rhetoric of the day and we are sorry. Few out of the bunch can resist typical Elizabethan punning and alliteration and assonance of roots (for lack of a better description) given a page or two ("I move we remove"). Wingfield tries to outdo Shakespeare's sonnet on the word *will.* Smith wants to luxuriate in modern language: "and those suborned to accuse him accused his accusers of subornation." At more leisure, their accents are more balanced and graceful than things today, and only occasionally should quaintness challenge our understanding.

They retain both tenses of *use to.* Today only the past tense survives (but pronounced like a present!): "They use to rake a great number of them" (They usually, customarily rake, etc.).

Their English is modern English, but some familiar words deceive us and some unfamiliar ones need to be introduced. I give a list of them here and will not gloss them in the texts.

Admiral. *Flagship; the fleet commander in the flagship.*
Adventurer. *Investor.*
After. *Afterwards.*
Ancient. *Military rank of ensign.*
Aqua vitae. *Grain alcohol.*
Barrico. *Keg.*
Bastinado. *Cudgel.*
Bought. *River bend.*
Break with. *Divulge to.*
Bruit. *Clamor.*
Burthen. *Burden.*

Calenture. *Sunstroke? "A disease incident to sailors within the tropics, characterized by delirium in which the patient, it is said, fancies the sea to be green fields, and desires to leap into it."* (OED)
Cape merchant. *Storehouse manager.*
Card, Cart. *Chart, map.*
Cautelous. *Cautious.*
Champion. *Flat, open country.*
Charge. *Expense.*
Conceit. *Think, imagine.*
Corn. *Wheat.*
Court of guard, corps de garde, corps du gard. *The guard detail.*
Crevise. *Crawfish.*
Desert. *Uninhabited.*
Discover. *Explore. Uncover.*
Doubt. *Fear.*
Entertain. *Act as host. Put up.*
Entreat. *Ask for. Act as host.*
Fear. *Frighten.*
For that. *Because.*
Green wound. *Flesh wound.*
Happy. *Lucky, happy.*
Height. *Latitude.*
His. *His* or *its.*
Howbeit. *Although.*
Humorist. *Whimsical, impulsive person.*
Hurtleberry. *Huckleberry.*
Impale. *To fence, to stockade.*
Indifferent. *Impartial.*
In fine. *In the end.*
Jealous. *Suspicious; vehement in feeling; jealous.*
Lay by the heels. *Put in irons.*
Marish. *Marsh.*
Middest. *Midst, midmost.*
Midway. *Halfway.*
Misdoubt. *Not believe.*
Miserable. *Miserly; wretched.*
Natural. *Native.*
Painful. *Painstaking, hard-working.*
Piece. *Gun.*
Pine. *Wither.*
Plant. *Establish a settlement.*
Popham side. *The north, or left, bank.*
Pretend. *Intend.*
Prevent. *Anticipate.*
Pumpion. *Pumpkin.*
Raspis. *Raspberry, -ies.*
Salisbury side. *The south, or right, bank.*
Sassafras, saxafrage. *Sassafras, despite various spellings, not saxifrage.*
So that. *As long as.*
Still. *Always.*
Subtle. *Sneaky, cunning.*
Temporize. *Negotiate, wheel & deal.*
Trial. *Investigation.*
Undertaker. *Backer.*
Vent. *Vend, sell.*
Victual. *Food, vittles.*
Want. *Lack.*
Wheat. *Corn.*

Virginia's Indian Contributions to English

POWHATAN, a piece of music spoken by the Indians of Virginia's tidewater region, has supplied more loan words to English than any other Native American language. H. L. Mencken's American Language was Powhatan first.

In the 1907 *American Anthropologist* (new series 9, pp. 87–112), Dr. William R. Gerard exhausts the subject in an article with the title of this section, and gives the following inventory of twenty-four loans. We would like to reproduce his whole paper with its very full discussion of usages, etymologies, histories, spelling varieties, but we do not have the space to do more than this beside his reconstructed original forms:

English	Powhatan
atamasco lily,	*ätamäsku* ("under-grass")
chinquapin	*chichinkwemen* ("rattle nut")
cockarouse (elder)	*kakärusu* ("he speaks at length")
cushaw (yellow squash)	*askushaw* ("unripe" + ?)
hickory	*pakähikâré* ("it is brayed")
hominy	*ûsekutehemen* ("crushed by pounding")
huskanawing (rite of puberty)	*huskinaweu* ("he has a new body")
maycock, maypop	*mäkak* ("hollow receptacle")
matchcoat	*mächikor* (robe, "bad skin")
moccasin	*makäsin* (same meaning)
nondo (angelica)	*wondeu* ("it is boiled")
opossum	*âpäsûm* ("white animal")
persimmon	*pasimenan* ("dried fruit")
poquoson (swamp)	*pâkwesen* ("slightly drained")
pokeberry	*pokan*, see puccoon
pone (cornbread)	*äpân* ("baked")

puccoon	*pa'kon* ("blood")
raccoon	*ärä'kun* ("he scratches with the hands")
roanoke (thin shell-bead money)	*rärenawok* ("smoothed shells")
rockahominy (pemican meal)	*rokehamen* ("softened")
terrapin	*turûpeu* (sea turtle)
tomahawk	*tämehâkan* ("chopper")
tuckahoe	*p'tûkwen* ("it is round")
werowance	*wirowantesu* ("he is wealthy")

And some probables not on Gerard's list:

chum (friend)
pecan
squaw
peak (thick shell-bead money)
wow! (from "*waugh,* their word of wonder" (Strachey word list)).

—for which I do not suggest etymologies, but those who find their interested stirred should look at Siebert (1975) for up-to-date spellings and some second opinions, and much light on the whole subject of Virginia Algonquian.

The English at Jamestown were already familiar with the language. It was very close to the speech of the Indians encountered in the Carolina sounds in the 1580s. Thomas Harriot recorded it there in material now lost but available to Virginia Company colonists who cared to study it prior to landing on a Virginia coast. Harriot himself was still living in 1607.

Nonetheless the Powhatan language is today lost except for two word lists containing between them about a thousand entries recorded before the year 1612 by Captain John Smith and William Strachey, who have also left us examples of a few phrases. Beyond these sources we have a few dozen terms mentioned in our accounts and of course hundreds of place names.

The Smith vocabulary and phrases are published here as part of his *Map of Virginia §16.* The Strachey list, on the other hand, is a much larger collection, too large and too difficult to include here. It is found at the end of both his Bodleian (Apsley) and British Library (Bacon/Sloan) manuscripts of *The History of Travel* in two nearly identical versions. It is lacking in the Princeton manuscript. It is a treasure trove and has been given a great deal of study and analysis in its own right by Geary, Harrington, and above all Siebert (1975). My hunch is that it contains much of the North Carolina material collected by Harriot, now otherwise lost, in addition to specimens Strachey himself heard on the James River.

Neither Smith nor Strachey were fluent speakers. Others who were, such as Henry Spelman, did not trouble to record the language. The one big item we should hope to find—a Bible translation —as far as we can tell was never so much as begun, and represents a signal failing of the stated mission of the Virginia Company. In perspective, though, Smith and Strachey and Harriot, insofar as they were imperfect speakers, might have found it easier to compel the language into Roman letters—hence they left us written lists and phrases—than a fluent speaker who might feel it was a piece of butchery of the sounds he knew so well. Try it yourself: Invent a phonetic system of spelling English!

At any rate, Powhatan was a spoken language into the latter half of the 18th century. During that time, no one else, Indian or non-Indian, took the pains Smith and Strachey did to transmit it to us.

But everybody recorded a little something. Here is a list of Powhatan words that appear over and over in our text:

Apoke. *Tobacco*
Chechinquamins. *Chinquapin.*
Mamanatowic. *Paramount chief.*
Oke, Okee, Oki, Okeus. *Chief deity or its effigy—the wrathful god who governs human affairs.*
Pemminaw. *"we call silk grass."*[1]
Pocones, pochones. *Puccoon.* (141n)
Putchamins. *Persimmon.*
Quiyoughcosough. *Priest. Deity.*

[1] p. 323. Barbour says not so. *Pemminaw* was, however, used to make thread.

Rarowcun, arrahacounes. *Raccoon.*
Werowance. *Chief, viceroy.*
Wighsakan. *Milkweed*
Wingapo. *Hello* (lit.: "Good man!")

These are a few. There are many more terms for prepared foods and edible plants.

JAMESTOWN NARRATIVES

EYEWITNESS ACCOUNTS
OF THE VIRGINIA COLONY

THE FIRST DECADE:
1607–1617

TEXTS

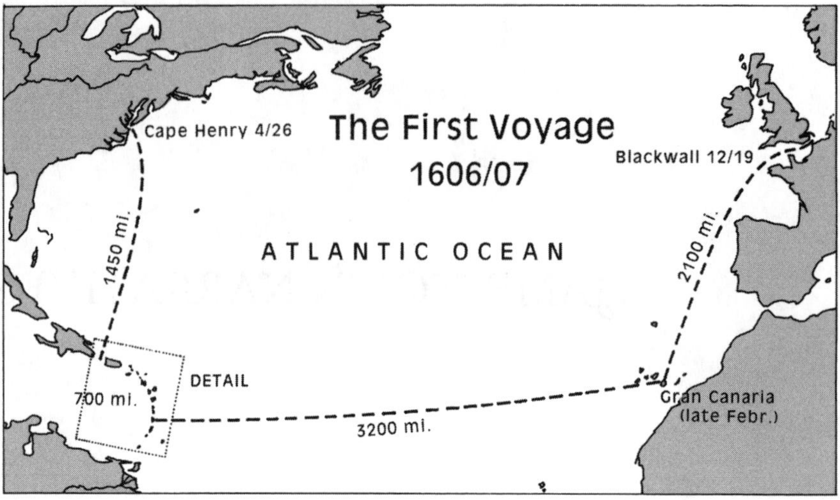
The First Voyage
1606/07
ATLANTIC OCEAN
Cape Henry 4/26
Blackwall 12/19
1450 mi.
2100 mi.
DETAIL
700 mi.
3200 mi.
Gran Canaria
(late Febr.)

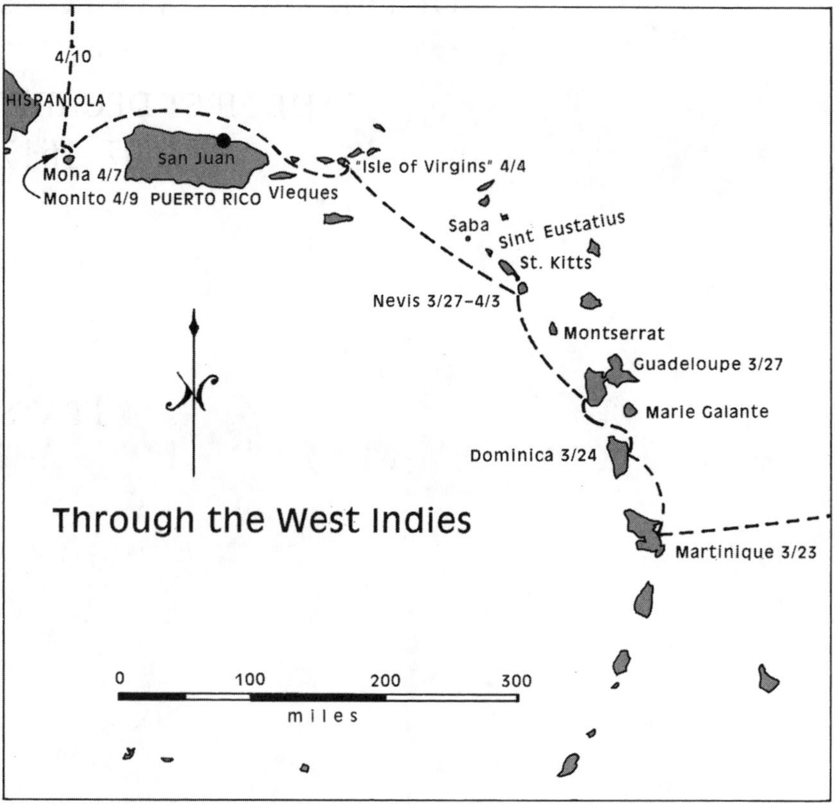
Through the West Indies
4/10
HISPANIOLA
San Juan
Mona 4/7
Monito 4/9
PUERTO RICO
Vieques
"Isle of Virgins" 4/4
Saba
Sint Eustatius
St. Kitts
Nevis 3/27–4/3
Montserrat
Guadeloupe 3/27
Marie Galante
Dominica 3/24
Martinique 3/23
0
100
200
300
miles

1. George Percy

Observations gathered out of a discourse of the plantation of the southern colony in Virginia by the English, 1606. Written by that honorable gentleman, Master George Percy

< **Purchas 1625d:1685,** Arber 1884a:lvii, Brown 1890:152, Quinn 1967, Barbour 1969:129

Here is our fullest account of the first crossing and the arrival in the Chesapeake. Percy's opulence of description in regard to Indian life ranks him with Smith and Strachey.

We read that Tanxpowhatan, werowance of "Powhatan's Tower," was in favor of letting the English live in peace at Jamestown in an American-style Hong Kong.

The account is interrupted by a necrology of the awful summer of 1607, followed by a short narrative of events in September. Let us never forget the ridiculous faith, the groundless courage, the suicidal determination, the awful numbers—it took to establish the beachhead of the United States.

Rev. Purchas has likely cut away much that would have balanced and qualified what we have.

ON SATURDAY, the twentieth of December, in the year 1606, the fleet fell from London, and the fift of January [1607], we anchored in the Downs. But the winds continued contrary so long that we were forced to stay there some time, where we suffered great storms; but by the skillfulness of the captain we suffered no great loss or danger.

The twelfth day of February,[1] at night we saw a blazing star, and presently a storm.

The three and twentieth day, we fell with the island of Mattanenio

---

[1] "The next day Captain Smith was suspected for a supposed mutiny, though never no such matter." (margin note) Purchas has apparently edited out Percy's mention of the matter, but below see the note with Smith's account of their stay on Mevis.

[Martinique] in the West Indies.

The four and twentieth day, we anchored at Dominico within fourteen degrees of the Line—a very fair island, the trees full of sweet and good smells, inhabited by many savage Indians. They were at first very scrupulous to come aboard us. We learned of them afterwards that the Spaniards had given them a great overthrow on this isle. But when they knew what we were, there came many to our ships with their canoas, bringing us many kinds of sundry fruits, as pines,[1] potatoes, plantains, tobacco, and other fruits—and roan cloth abundance[2] which they had gotten out of certain Spanish ships that were cast away upon that island. We gave them knives [and] hatchets for exchange, which they esteem much. We also gave them beads, copper, jewels, which they hang through their nostrils, ears, and lips—very strange to behold. Their bodies are all painted red to keep away the biting of muscetos [mosquitoes]; they go all naked without covering; the hair of their head is a yard long, all of a length pleated in three plaits hanging down to their waists; they suffer no hair to grow on their faces; they cut their skins in divers works; they are continually in wars, and will eat their enemies when they kill them, or any stranger if they take them; they will lap up man's spittle whilst one spits in their mouths, in a barbarous fashion like dogs.[3]

These people and the rest of the islands in the West Indies and Brazil are called by the names of *Canibals,* that will eat man's flesh. These people do poison their arrowheads, which are made of a fish's bone; they worship the devil for their god, and have no other belief.

Whilest we remained at this island we saw a whale chased by a thresher and a swordfish; they fought for the space of two hours. We might see the thresher with his flail lay on the monstrous blows, which was strange to behold. In the end these two fishes brought the whale to her end.[4]

The six and twentieth day, we had sight of Marigalanta, and the

---

[1] Piñas, later called pineapples.

[2] Cloth of Rouen, a fine French linen.

[3] "Brutishness of the Dominicans." (margin note)

[4] "This passage bears a remarkable similarity to William Strachey's *Reportory* [§22-398]. If Percy borrowed from Strachey [and not vice versa], he cannot have written his *Discourse* before 1610." (Barbour)

next day we sailed with a slack sail alongst the Isle of Guadalupa, where we went ashore and found a bath which was so hot that no man was able to stand long by it. Our admiral, Captain Newport, caused a piece of pork to be put in it, which boiled it so in the space of half an hour as no fire could mend it.

Then we went aboard and sailed by many islands, as Mounserot and an island called Saint Christopher, both unhabited about.

About two o'clock in the afternoon, we anchored at the Isle of Mevis [Nevis]. There the captain landed all his men; being well fitted with muskets and other convenient arms, marched a mile into the woods; being commanded to stand upon their guard, fearing the treachery of the Indians, which is an ordinary use amongst them and all other savages on this isle. We came to a bath standing in a valley betwixt two hills, where we bathed ourselves, and found it to be of the nature of the baths in England: some places hot and some colder, and men may refresh themselves as they please. Finding this place to be so convenient for our men to avoid diseases, which will breed in so long a voyage, we encamped ourselves on this isle six days, and spent none of our ship's victual, by reason our men some went a-hunting, some a-fowling, and some a-fishing, where we got great store of conies, sundry kinds of fowls, and great plenty of fish.

We kept sentinels and *courts de gard* at every captain's quarter, fearing we should be assaulted by the Indians that were on the other side of the island. We saw none, nor were molested by any, but some few we saw as we were a-hunting on the island. They would not come to us by any means, but ran swiftly through the woods to the mountain tops; so we lost the sight of them, whereupon we made all the haste we could to our quarter, thinking there had been a great ambush of Indians thereabouts.

We pass'd into the thickest of the woods, where we had almost lost ourselves. We had not gone above half a mile amongst the thick but we came into a most pleasant garden, being a hundred paces square on every side, having many cotton trees growing in it with abundance of cotton wool, and many guaiacum trees. We saw the goodliest tall trees growing so thick about the garden as though they had been set by art, which made us marvel very much to see it.[1]

The third day [of April], we set sail from Mevis.

The fourth day, we sailed along by Castutia [St. Eustatius] and by Saba. This day we anchored at the Isle of Virgins in an excellent bay able to harbor a hundred ships. If this bay stood in England it would be a great profit and commodity to the land. On this island we caught great store of fresh fish and abundance of sea tortoises, which served all our fleet three days, which were in number eightscore persons. We also killed great store of wildfowl. We cut the barks of certain trees which tasted much like cinnamon and very hot in the mouth. This island in some places hath very good ground, straight and tall timber. But the greatest discommodity that we have seen on this island is that it hath no fresh water, which makes the place void of any inhabitants.

Upon the sixt day, we set sail and passed by Becam [Vieques], and by Saint John deportorico.

The seventh day, we arrived at Mona, where we watered, which we stood in great need of, seeing that our water did smell so vildly that none of our men was able to endure it. Whilst some of the sailors were a-filling the casks with water, the captain and the rest of

---

[1] "In this little isle of Mevis more than twenty years ago I have remained a good time together to wood and water and refresh my men. It is all woody, but by the seaside southward there are sands like downs where a thousand men may quarter themselves conveniently. But in most places the wood groweth close to the waterside at a high water mark, and in some places so thick of a soft spongy wood like a wild fig tree you cannot get through it but by making your way with hatchets or falchions [swords]. Whether it was the dew of those trees or of some others I am not certain, but many of our men became so tormented with a burning swelling all over their bodies they seemed like scalded men and near mad with pain. Here we found a great pool wherein bathing themselves they found much ease. And finding it fed with a pleasant small stream that came out of the woods, we found the head half a mile within the land, distilling from a many of rocks, by which they were well cured in two or three days.

"Such factions here we had as commonly attend such voyages, that a pair of gallows was made, but Captain Smith, for whom they were intended, could not be persuaded to use them. But not any one of the inventers but their lives by justice fell into his power to determine of at his pleasure, whom with much mercy he favored that most basely and unjustly would have betrayed him." John Smith, *True Travels* (1630) 56–57. Troubles barely hinted at above.

the gentlemen and other soldiers marched up in the isle six miles, thinking to find some other provision to maintain our victualing. As we marched we killed two wild boars, and saw a huge wild bull. His horns was an ell between the two tops. We also killed *guanas* [iguanas] (in fashion of a serpent and speckled like a toad under the belly).

These ways that we went being so troublesome and vild going upon the sharp rocks, [it happened] that many of our men fainted in the march; but by good fortune we lost none but one Edward Brookes, gentleman, whose fat melted within him by the great heat and drought of the country. We were not able to relieve him nor ourselves, so he died in that great extremity.

The ninth day, in the afternoon we went off with our boat to the isle of Moneta [Monito], some three leagues from Mona, where we had a terrible landing and a troublesome getting up to the top of the mountain, or isle, being a high firm rock step with many terrible sharp stones. After we got to the top of the isle, we found it to be a fertile and a plain ground, full of goodly grass and abundance of fowls of all kinds. They flew over our heads as thick as drops of hail, besides they made such a noise that we were not able to hear one another speak. Furthermore, we were not able to set our feet on the ground but either on fowls or eggs, which lay so thick in the grass. We laded two boats full in the space of three hours, to our great refreshing.

The tenth day, we set sail and disembogued out of the West Indies, and bare our course northerly.

The fourteenth day, we passed the Tropic of Cancer.

The one and twentieth day, about five o'clock at night there began a vehement tempest which lasted all the night with winds, rain, and thunders in a terrible manner. We were forced to lie at hull that night, because we thought we had been nearer land than we were.

The next morning, being the two and twentieth day, we sounded; and the three and twentieth and four and twentieth day—but we could find no ground.

The five and twentieth day, we sounded and had no ground at an hundred fathom.

The six and twentieth day of April, about four o'clock in the morning, we descried the land of Virginia;[1] the same day we ent'red into the Bay of Chesupioc directly without any let or hindrance; there we landed and discovered a little way, but we could find nothing worth the speaking of but fair meadows and goodly tall trees, with such fresh waters running through the woods as I was almost ravished at the first sight thereof.

At night, when we were going aboard, there came the savages creeping upon all four from the hills like bears, with their bows in their mouths, [and] charged us very desperately in the faces, [and] hurt Captain Gabrill Archer in both his hands, and a sailor in two places of the body very dangerous. After they had spent their arrows and felt the sharpness of our shot, they retired into the woods with a great noise, and so left us.

The seven and twentieth day, we began to build up our shallop. The gentlemen and soldiers marched eight miles up into the land; we could not see a savage in all that march; we came to a place where they had made a great fire, and had been newly a-roasting oysters. When they perceived our coming, they fled away to the mountains, and left many of the oysters in the fire. We ate some of the oysters, which were very large and delicate in taste.

The eighteenth day, we launched our shallop; the captain and some gentlemen went in her and discovered up the bay. We found a river on the south side running into the main; we entered it and found it very shoal water, not for any boats to swim.

We went further into the bay and saw a plain plot of ground where we went on land and found the place five mile in compass, without either bush or tree. We saw nothing there but a canoe which was made out of the whole tree, which was five and forty foot long by the rule. Upon this plot of ground we got good store of mussels and oysters, which lay on the ground as thick as stones; we opened some and found in many of them pearls.

We marched some three or four miles further into the woods, where we saw great smokes of fire. We marched to those smokes and

---

[1] "We were driven to try that night, and by the storm were forced near the shore, not knowing where we were." (margin note) *To try* or *to lie atry* means to lie hove to with all sails furled.

found that the savages had been there burning down the grass as, we thought, either to make their plantation there or else to give signs to bring their forces together, and so to give us battle. We pass'd through excellent ground full of flowers of divers kinds and colors, and as goodly trees as I have seen, as cedar, cypress, and other kinds. Going a little further we came into a little plat of ground full of fine and beautiful strawberries four times bigger and better than ours in England. All this march we could neither see savage nor town.

When it grew to be towards night we stood back to our ships. We sounded and found it shallow water for a great way, which put us out of all hopes for getting any higher with our ships, which rode at the mouth of the river. We rowed over to a point of land where we found a channel and sounded six, eight, ten, or twelve fathom, which put us in good comfort; therefore we named that point of land "Cape Comfort."

The nine and twentieth day, we set up a cross at Chesupioc Bay and named that place "Cape Henry."

Thirtieth day, we came with our ships to Cape Comfort, where we saw five savages running on the shore. Presently the captain caused the shallop to be manned; so rowing to the shore, the captain called to them in sign of friendship, but they were at first very timorsome until they saw the captain lay his hand on his heart. Upon that they laid down their bows and arrows and came very boldly to us, making signs to come ashore to their town, which is called by the savages Kecoughtan.

We coasted to their town, rowing over a river running into the main where these savages swam over with their bows and arrows in their mouths. When we came over to the other side, there was a many of other savages which directed us to their town, where we were entertained by them very kindly. When we came first a-land, they made a doleful noise, laying their faces to the ground, scratching the earth with their nails. We did think that they had been at their idolatry. When they had ended their ceremonies, they went into their houses and brought out mats and laid upon the ground. The chiefest of them sat all in a rank; the meanest sort brought us such dainties as they had, and of their bread which they make of their maize, or guinea wheat. They would not suffer us to eat unless we sat down, which we did on a mat right against them.

After we were well satisfied, they gave us of their tobacco, which they took in a pipe made artificially of earth as ours are, but far bigger, with the bowl fashioned together with a piece of fine copper.

After they had feasted us, they showed us in welcome their manner of dancing, which was in this fashion: One of the savages standing in the midst singing, beating one hand against another, all the rest dancing about him, shouting, howling, and stamping against the ground, with many antic tricks and faces, making noise like so many wolves or devils. One thing of them I observed: When they were in their dance they kept stroke with their feet, just one with another, but with their hands, heads, faces, and bodies, every one of them had a several gesture, [and] so they continued for the space of half an hour.

When they had ended their dance, the captain gave them beads and other trifling jewels. They hang through their ears fowls' legs; they shave the right side of their heads with a shell; the left side they wear of an ell long tied up with an artificial knot, with a many of fowls' feathers sticking in it; they go altogether naked, but their privities are covered with beasts' skins beset commonly with little bones or beasts' teeth; some paint their bodies black, some red, with artificial knots of sundry lively colors very beautiful and pleasing to the eye, in a braver fashion than they in the West Indies.

The fourth day of May, we came to the king, of [or] *werowance,* of Paspihe, where they entertained us with much welcome. An old savage made a long oration, making a foul noise, uttering his speech with a vehement action, but we knew little what they meant.

Whilst we were in company with the Paspihes, the werowance of Rapahanna came from the other side of the river in his canoa. He seemed to take displeasure of our being with the Paspihes; he would fain have had us come to his town, [but] the captain was unwilling. Seeing that the day was so far spent, he returned back to his ships for that night.

The next day, being the fift of May, the werowance of Rapahanna sent a messenger to have us come to him. We entertained the said messenger and gave him trifles, which pleased him. We manned our shallop with muskets and targeteers sufficiently; this said messenger guided us where our determination was to go.

When we landed, the werowance of Rapahanna came down to the waterside with all his train, as goodly men as any I have seen of savages or Christians. The werowance, coming before them playing on a flute made of a reed, with a crown of deer's hair colored red in fashion of a rose fastened about his knot of hair, and a great plate of copper on the other side of his head, with two long feathers in fashion of a pair of horns placed in the midst of his crown, his body was painted all with crimson, with a chain of beads about his neck, his face painted blue, besprinkled with silver ore as we thought,[1] his ears all behung with bracelets of pearl, and in either ear a bird's claw through it beset with fine copper or gold; he entertained us in so modest a proud fashion as though he had been a prince of civil government, holding his countenance without laughter or any such ill behavior. He caused his mat to be spread on the ground, where he sat down with a great majesty, taking a pipe of tobacco, the rest of his company standing about him.

After he had rested awhile, he rose and made signs to us to come to his town; he went foremost, and all the rest of his people and ourselves followed him up a steep hill where his palace was settled. We passed through the woods in fine paths, having most pleasant springs, which issued from the mountains. We also went through the goodliest cornfields that ever was seen in any country. When we came to Rapahanno's town,[2] he entertained us in good humanity.

The eight day of May, we discovered up the river; we landed in the country of Apamatica; at our landing there came many stout and able savages to resist us with their bows and arrows in a most warlike manner, with the swords at their backs beset with sharp stones and pieces of iron, able to cleave a man in sunder. Amongst the rest, one of the chiefest, standing before them cross-legged, with his arrow ready in his bow in one hand and taking a pipe of tobacco in the other, with a bold uttering of his speech demanded of us our being there, willing us to be gone. We made signs of peace, which they perceived in the end, and let us land in quietness.

The twelfth day, we went back to our ships and discovered a point

---

[1] Rather antimony paste he likely obtained from Patawomeck.

[2] Called Tappahanock or Quiyoughcohanock in other narratives.

of land called "Archer's Hope," which was sufficient with a little labor to defend ourselves against any enemy; the soil was good and fruitful with excellent good timber; there are also great store of vines in bigness of a man's thigh, running up to the tops of the trees in great abundance; we also did see many squirrels, conies, blackbirds with crimson wings, and divers other fowls and birds of divers and sundry colors of crimson, watchet,[1] yellow, green, murrey,[2] and of divers other hues naturally without any art using; we found store of turkey nests and many eggs. If it had not been disliked because the ship could not ride near the shore, we had settled there to all the colony's contentment.

The thirteenth day, we came to our seating place in Paspiha's country, some eight miles from the point of land which I made mention before, where our ships do lie so near the shore that they are moored to the trees in six fathom water.

The fourteenth day, we landed all our men, which were set to work about the fortification,[3] and others some to watch and ward as it was convenient. The first night of our landing, about midnight, there came some savages sailing close to our quarter; presently there was an alarum given; upon that the savages ran away, and we not troubled any more by them that night. Not long after there came two savages that seemed to be commanders, bravely dress'd with crowns of colored hair upon their heads, which came as messengers from the werowance of Paspihæ, telling us that their werowance was coming and would be merry with us with a fat deer.

The eighteenth day, the werowance of Paspihæ came himself to our quarter with one hundred savages armed, which guarded him in a very warlike manner with bows and arrows, thinking at that time to execute their villainy. Paspihæ made great signs to us to lay our arms away, but we would not trust him so far. He, seeing he could not have convenient time to work his will, at length made signs that he would give us as much land as we would desire to take.

As the savages were in a throng in the fort, one of them stole a

---

[1] Sky blue.

[2] Purple red.

[3] "Their plantation at Jamestown." (margin note)

hatchet from one of our company,[1] which spied him doing the deed, whereupon he took it from him by force, and also struck him over the arm. Presently, another savage seeing that came fiercely at our man with a wooden sword, thinking to beat out his brains. The werowance of Paspiha saw us take to our arms [and so] went suddenly away with all his company in great anger.

The nineteenth day, myself and three or four more walking into the woods, by chance we espied a pathway like to an Irish pace.[2] We were desirous to know whither it would bring us; we traced along some four miles, all the way as we went having the pleasantest suckles, the ground all flowing over with fair flowers of sundry colors and kinds as though it had been in any garden or orchard in England; there be many strawberries and other fruits unknown; we saw the woods full of cedar and cypress trees, with other trees which issues out sweet gums like to balsam; we kept on our way in this paradise.

At length we came to a savage town where we found but few people. They told us the rest were gone a-hunting with the werowance of Paspiha. We stayed there awhile and had of them strawberries and other things. In the meantime, one of the savages came running out of his house with a bow and arrows and ran mainly through the woods. Then I began to mistrust some villainy, that he went to call some company and so betray us; we made all the haste away we could. One of the savages brought us on the way to the wood side, where there was a garden of tobacco and other fruits and herbs. He gathered tobacco and distributed to every one of us; so we departed.

The twentieth day, the werowance of Paspiha sent forty of his men with a deer to our quarter, but they came more in villainy than any love they bare us. They fain would have lain in our fort all night, but we would not suffer them for fear of their treachery. One of our gentlemen having a target which he trusted in, thinking it would bear out a flight-shot,[3] he set it up against a tree, willing one of the savages to shoot; who took from his back an arrow of an ell long, drew it

---

[1] "These savages are naturally great thieves." (margin note)
[2] "A pass through woods between bogs." (Barbour)
[3] Bowshot.

strongly in his bow, shoots the target a foot thorough or better, which was strange, being that a pistol could not pierce it. We, seeing the force of his bow, afterwards set him up a steel target; he shot again and burst his arrow all to pieces; he presently pulled out another arrow and bit it in his teeth, and seemed to be in a great rage, so he went away in great anger.

Their bows are made of tough hazel, their strings of leather, their arrows of canes or hazel, headed with very sharp stones, and are made artificially like a broad arrow. Other some of their arrows are headed with the ends of deers' horns, and are feathered very artificially. Pasphia [Paspiha] was as good as his word, for he sent venison, but the sauce came within few days after.

At Port Cottage,[1] in our voyage up the river, we saw a savage boy about the age of ten years which had a head of hair of a perfect yellow and a reasonable white skin, which is a miracle amongst all savages.

This river which we have discovered is one of the famousest rivers that ever was found by any Christian. It ebbs and flows a hundred and threescore miles where ships of great burthen may harbor in safety.

Wheresoever we landed upon this river we saw the goodliest woods, as beech, oak, cedar, cypress, walnuts, sassafras, and vines in great abundance which hang in great clusters on many trees, and other trees unknown, and all the grounds bespread with many sweet and delicate flowers of divers colors and kinds. There are also many fruits, as strawberries, mulberries, raspberries, and fruits unknown.

There are many branches of this river which run flowing through the woods with great plenty of fish of all kinds; as for sturgeon, all the world cannot be compared to it. In this country I have seen many great and large meadows[2] having excellent good pasture for any cattle. There is also great store of deer, both red and fallow; there are bears, foxes, otters, beavers, musk cats, and wild beasts unknown.

The four and twentieth day, we set up a cross at the head of this

---

[1] Archer had named it "Poor Cottage."

[2] "Low marshes." (margin note)—still used that way in Virginia.

river, naming it "Kings River," where we proclaimed James, King of England, to have the most right unto it. When we had finished, and set up our cross, we ship'd our men and made for James Fort. By the way we came to Pohatan's Tower, where the captain went on shore, suffering none to go with him. He presented the commander of this place with a hatchet, which he took joyfully and was well pleased.

But yet the savages murmured at our planting in the country, whereupon this werowance made answer again, very wisely of a savage: "Why should you be offended with them as long as they hurt you not, nor take anything away by force? They take but a little waste ground which doth you nor any of us any good."

I saw bread made by their women, which do all their drudgery. The men takes their pleasure in hunting and their wars, which they are in continually, one kingdom against another.

The manner of baking of bread is thus: After they pound their wheat into flour, with hot water they make it into paste, and work it into round balls and cakes; then they put it into a pot of seething water; when it is sod throughly, they lay it on a smooth stone; there they harden it as well as in an oven.[1]

There is notice to be taken to know married women from maids: The maids, you shall always see the forepart of their head and sides shaven close, the hinder part very long, which they tie in a plait hanging down to their hips. The married women wears their hair all of a length, and is tied of that fashion that the maids' are.

The womenkind in this country doth pounce and race their bodies, legs, thighs, arms, and faces with a sharp iron which makes a stamp in curious knots, and draws the proportion of fowls, fish, or beasts. Then with paintings of sundry lively colors they rub it into the stamp, which will never be taken away, because it is dried into the flesh, where it is seared.

The savages bear their years well, for when we were at Pamonkie's we saw a savage by their report was above eightscore years of age. His eyes were sunk into his head, having never a tooth in his mouth, his hair all gray, with a reasonable big beard which was as white as

---

[1] This is the Virginia hoecake.

any snow. It is a miracle to see a savage have any hair on their faces. I never saw, read, nor heard any have the like before. This savage was as lusty and went as fast as any of us, which was strange to behold.

The fifteenth day of June, we had built and finished our fort, which was triangle-wise, having three bulwarks at every corner like a half moon, and four or five pieces of artillery mounted in them; we had made ourselves sufficiently strong for these savages. We had also sown most of our corn on two mountains[1]; it sprang a man's height from the ground. This country is a fruitful soil, bearing many goodly and fruitful trees, as mulberries, cherries, walnuts, cedars, cypress, sassafras, and vines in great abundance.

Monday the two and twentieth of June, in the morning Captain Newport in the admiral departed from James Port for England.

Captain Newport being gone for England, leaving us (one hundred and four persons) very bare and scanty of victuals—furthermore in wars and in danger of the savages—we hoped after a supply which Captain Newport promised within twenty weeks.

But if the beginners of this action do carefully further us, the country being so fruitful, it would be as great a profit to the realm of England as the Indies to the King of Spain. If this river which we have found had been discovered in the time of war with Spain, it would have been a commodity to our realm and a great annoyance to our enemies.

The seven and twentieth of July, the King of Rapahanna demanded a canoa, which was restored; lifted up his hand to the sun, which they worship as their god, besides he laid his hand on his heart that he would be our special friend. It is a general rule of these people when they swear by their god, which is the sun, no Christian will keep their oath better upon this promise.

These people have a great reverence to the sun above all other things: At the rising and setting of the same they sit down, lifting up their hands and eyes to the sun, making a round circle on the ground with dried tobacco. Then they began to pray, making many devilish

---

[1] Mounds.

gestures with a hellish noise, foaming at the mouth, staring with their eyes, wagging their heads and hands in such a fashion and deformity as it was monstrous to behold.

The sixt of August, there died John Asbie of the bloody flix.

The ninth day, died George Flowre of the swelling.

The tenth day, died William Bruster [Brewster], gentleman, of a wound given by the savages, and was buried the eleventh day.

The fourteenth day, Jerome Alikock, ancient, died of a wound; the same day, Francis Midwinter; Edward Moris, corporal, died suddenly.

The fifteenth day, there died Edward Browne and Stephen Galthrope.

The sixteenth day, there died Thomas Gower, gentleman.

The seventeenth day, there died Thomas Mounslic.

The eighteenth day, there died Robert Pennington; and John Martine, gentleman.

The nineteenth day, died Drue Piggase, gentleman.

The two and twentieth day of August, there died Captain Bartholomew Gosnold, one of our council; he was honorably buried, having all the ordnance in the fort shot off with many volleys of small shot.

After Captain Gosnol's death, the council could hardly agree by the dissension of Captain Kendall, which afterward was committed about heinous matters which was proved against him.

The four and twentieth day, died Edward Harington and George Walker, and were buried the same day.

The six and twentieth day, died Kenelme Throgmortine.

The seven and twentieth day, died William Roods.

The eight and twentieth day, died Thomas Stoodie [Studley], cape merchant.

The fourth day of September, died Thomas Jacob, sergeant.

The fift day, there died Benjamin Beast.

Our men were destroyed with cruel diseases, as swellings, flixes, burning fevers, and by wars, and some departed suddenly, but for the most part they died of mere famine. There were never

Englishmen left in a foreign country in such misery as we were in this new-discovered Virginia. We watched every three nights, lying on the bare cold ground, what weather soever came, [and] warded all the next day, which brought our men to be most feeble wretches. Our food was but a small can of barley sod in water to five men a day; our drink cold water taken out of the river, which was at a flood very salt, at a low tide full of slime and filth, which was the destruction of many of our men.

Thus we lived for the space of five months in this miserable distress, not having five able men to man our bulwarks upon any occasion.[1] If it had not pleased God to have put a terror in the savages' hearts, we had all perished by those vild and cruel pagans, being in that weak estate as we were, our men night and day groaning in every corner of the fort, most pitiful to hear. If there were any conscience in men, it would make their hearts to bleed to hear the pitiful murmurings and outcries of our sick men without relief every night and day for the space of six weeks, some departing out of the world, many times three or four in a night, in the morning their bodies trailed out of their cabins like dogs to be buried. In this sort did I see the mortality of divers of our people.

It pleased God after a while to send those people which were our mortal enemies to relieve us with victuals, as bread, corn, fish, and flesh in great plenty, which was the setting up of our feeble men; otherwise we had all perished. Also we were frequented by divers kings in the country bringing us store of provision to our great comfort.

The eleventh day, there was certain articles laid against Master Wingfield, which was then president; thereupon he was not only displaced out of his presidentship but also from being of the council. Afterwards Captain John Ratcliffe was chosen president.

The eighteenth day, died one Ellis Kinistone [Kingston], which was starved to death with cold; the same day, at night died one Richard Simmons.

The nineteenth day, there died one Thomas Mouton.

---

[1] "Virginia authorities usually discount malaria as the cause of so many deaths, blaming rather some deficiency disease or typhoid, perhaps associated with beri-beri." (Barbour)

2. Gabriel Archer

A relation of the discovery of our river from James Fort into the main, made by Captain Christofer Newport, and sincerely written and observed by a gentleman of the colony

< **Public Records Office: Colonial Office 1/1–46;** American Antiquarian 1860d:40, Arber 1884a:xl, Barbour 1969:80, Quinn 1979e:274

Historians attach Archer's name to this unsigned narrative as well as §3 and §4, for circumstantial and stylistic reasons, although another possible author is Christopher Newport himself.

This is the best account of Newport's exploration of the James. We have another by Percy §1 and two by Smith §12, §17. By 1607 there had been a lot of European traffic along the coast, but almost no penetration. Here east and west are at a first encounter. The sides are wary but friendly.

Colonists must have written many of these journals of the First Day, full of wonder and optimism.

Right away we hear of native warfare. Worldwide, history-wide, this seems to have been the price of political atomization. Too often what little peace peoples have enjoyed has been an imperial peace.

Newport did not take umbrage at Arrohateck thievery, "Yet he made known unto them the custom of England to be death for such offenses." True for England, but for America the king's "articles, instructions, and orders" under the 1606 charter specify the death penalty only in cases of rebellion, mutiny, sedition, murder, manslaughter, incest, rape, and adultery. Among Virginia's Indians, some groups condoned thievery, others, such as the Pamunkey, condemned it.

Concerning the aqua vitae incident, we have a touchingly humorous account doubtless word of mouth from Newport to Cope back in London:

> One of their kings, sick with drinking our aqua vitae, thought himself poisoned. Newport told him by signs that the next day he should be well, and he was so. And telling his countrymen thereof, they came apace, old men and old women, upon every bellyache, to him to know when *they* should be well.[1]

The "Pawatah" of this relation is Tanxpowhatan, werowance of the village of Powhatan below the Falls (modern Powhite), and son of the great king

[1] from *The Jamestown Voyages under the First Charter,* ed. Barbour, p. 108

(mamanatowic) Powhatan, then living at Werowocomoco on the York River.

The King of Pamaunche we guess is his brother Opechancanough, the great field commander who was mamanatowic after 1618, yet his aspect fails to impress Archer here or Smith later.

THURSDAY, THE XXITH OF MAY [1607], Captain Newport, having fitted our shallop with provision and all necessaries belonging to a discovery, took 5 gentlemen, 4 mariners, and 14 sailors, with whom he proceeded with a perfect resolution not to return but either to find the head of this river, the lake mentioned by others heretofore, the sea again, the mountains Apalatsi, or some issue.

The names of the discoverers are these:

Captain Christofer Newport

[Gentlemen]

George Percye, esquire
Captain Gabriell Archer
Captain John Smyth
Master John Brookes
Master Thomas Wotton

Mariners

Francys Nellson
John Collson
Robert Tyndall
Mathew Fytch

1 Jonas Poole
2 Robert Markham
3 John Crookdeck
4 Olyver Browne
5 Benjamyn White
6 Rychard Genoway
7 Thomas Turnbrydg
8 Thomas Godword
9 Robert Jackson
10 Charles Clarke
11 Stephen
12 Thomas Skynner

13 Jeremy Deale
14 Danyell

Thus from James Fort we took our leave about noon, and by night we were up the river 18 mile at a low meadow point, which I call "Wynauk." Here came the people and entertained us with dances and much rejoicing.

This kingdom Wynauk is full of pearl muskles [mussels].

The King of Paspeiouh and this king is at odds, as the Paspeians told me, and demonstrated by their hurts. Here we anchored all night.

May 22. Friday, omitting no time we passed up some 16 mile further, where we found an islet on which were many turkeys and great store of young birds like blackbirds, whereof we took divers which we brake our fast withal.

Now spying 8 savages in a canoa, we hailed them by our word of kindness *wingapoh,*[1] and they came to us. In conference by signs with them, one seemed to understand our intention, and off'red with his foot to describe the river to us. So I gave him a pen and paper, showing first the use, and he laid out the whole river from the Chesseian Bay to the end of it, so far as passage was for boats. He told us of two islets in the river we should pass by, meaning that one whereon we were, and then come to an overfall of water; beyond that, of two kingdoms which the river runs by; then, a great distance off, the mountains Quirank, as he named them, beyond which by his relation is that which we expected.

This fellow parting from us promised to procure us wheat if we would stay a little before, and for that intent went back again to provide it. But we, coming by the place where he was with many more very desirous of our company, stay'd not as being eager of our good tidings.[2] He, notwithstanding, with two women and another fellow of his own consort followed us some six mile with baskets full of dried oysters, and met us at a point where, calling to us, we went ashore and bart'red with them for most of their victuals.

---

[1] Powhatan: "Good man."
[2] The English were eager to complete the discovery of such a promising river.

Here the shore began to be full of great cobblestones and higher land. The river scants of his breadth 2 mile before we come to the islet mentioned, which I call "Turkey Isle," yet keeps it a quarter of a mile broad most commonly and deep water for shipping.[1]

This fellow with the rest overtook us again upon the doubling of another point. Now they had gotten mulberries, little sweet nuts like acorns (a very good fruit), wheat, beans, and mulberries sod together, and gave us. Some of them desired to be set over the river, which we did, and they parted.

Now we passed a reach of 3 mile ½ in length, high stony ground on Popham side, 5 or 6 fadom 8 oars' length from the shore.

This day we went about 38 mile and came to an anchor at a place I call "Poor Cottage," where we went ashore and were used kindly by the people. We sod our kettle by the waterside within night, and rested aboard.

May 23. Saturday, we passed a few short reaches, and 5 mile off Poor Cottage we went ashore. Here we found our kind comrades again, who had given notice all along, as they came, of us, by which we were entertained with much courtesy in every place.

We found here a *wiroans,* for so they call their kings, who sat upon a mat of reeds with his people about him. He caused one to be laid for Captain Newport; gave us a deer roasted, which according to their custom they seethed again. This people gave us mulberries, sod wheat and beans, and he caused his women to make cakes for us. He gave our captain his crown, which was of deer's hair dyed red. Certifying him of our intention up the river, he was willing to send guides with us. This we found to be a king subject to Pawatah, the chief of all the kingdoms; his name is Arahatec, the country Arahatecoh.

Now as we sat merry banqueting with them, seeing their dances and taking tobacco, news came that the Great King Powatah[2] was come, at whose presence they all rose off their mats—save the King Arahatec—separated themselves apart in fashion of a guard, and with a long shout they saluted him. Him we saluted with silence,

---

[1] "Fishing" is crossed out and "shipping" is written here.

[2] This was not the great king but his son, Parahunt, the werowance of the *village* Powhatan, just below the falls of the James.

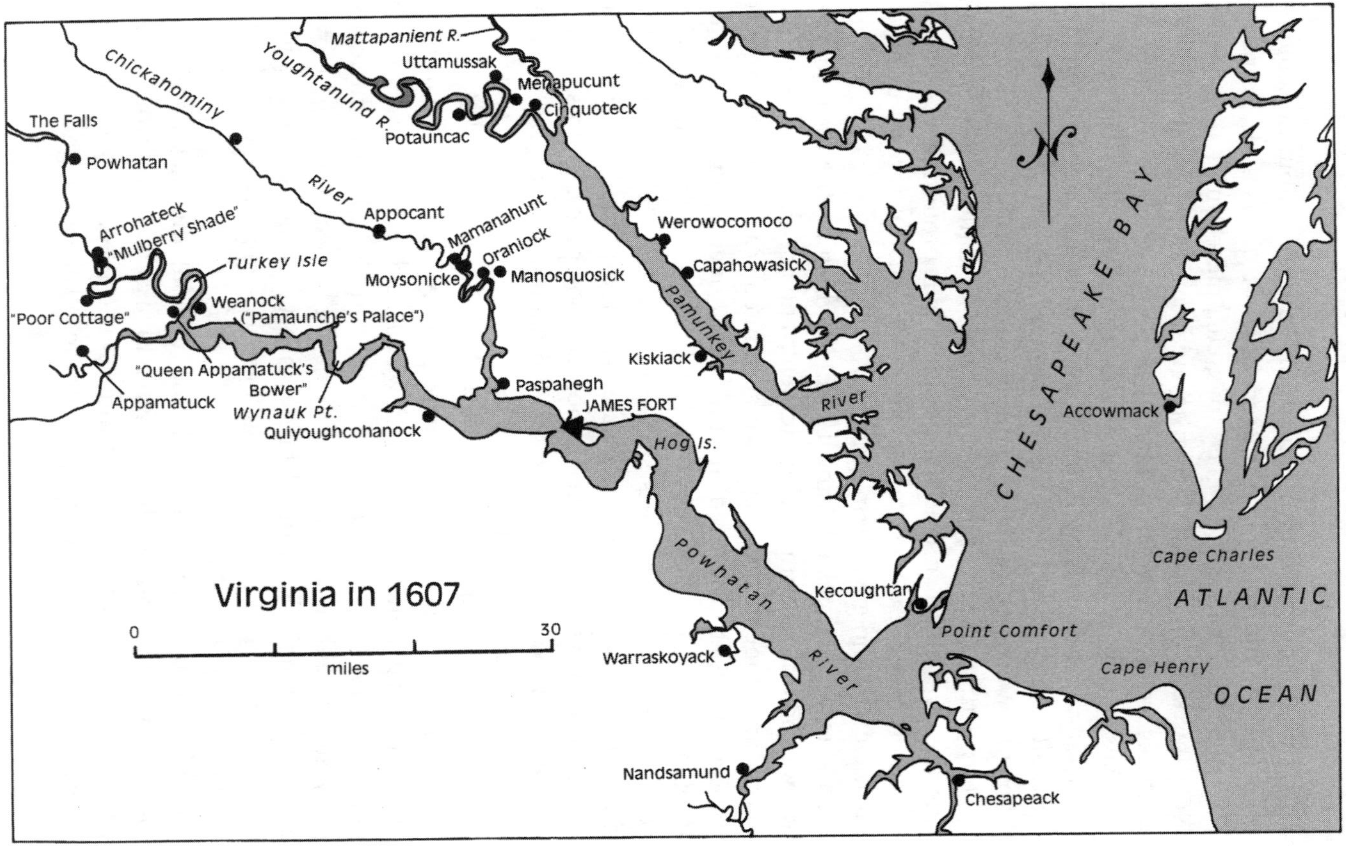
Virginia in 1607
0
30
miles
Mattapanient R.
Uttamussak
Menapucunt
Cinquoteck
Youghtanund R.
Potauncac
Chickahominy
River
The Falls
Powhatan
Appocant
Mamanahunt
Oraniock
Moysonicke
Manosquosick
Arrohateck
"Mulberry Shade"
Turkey Isle
Weanock
("Pamaunche's Palace")
"Poor Cottage"
"Queen Appamatuck's
Bower"
Appamatuck
Wynauk Pt.
Quiyoughcohanock
Paspahegh
JAMES FORT
Hog Is.
Werowocomoco
Capahowasick
Pamunkey
River
Kiskiack
CHESAPEAKE BAY
Accowmack
Cape Charles
ATLANTIC
OCEAN
Cape Henry
Point Comfort
Kecoughtan
Powhatan
River
Warraskoyack
Nandsamund
Chesapeack

sitting still on our mats, our captain in the middest, but presented—as before we did to King Arahatec—gifts of divers sorts, as penny knives, shears, bells, beads, glass toys, etc., more amply than before. Now this king appointed 5 men to guide us up the river, and sent posts before to provide us victual.

I caused now our kind consort that described the river to us to draw it again before King Arahatec, who in everything consented to his draft, and it agreed with his first relation. This we found a faithful fellow; he was one that was appointed guide for us.

Thus parting from "Arahatec's Joy," we found the people on either side the river stand in clusters all along, still proffering us victuals, which of some were accepted as our guides, that were with us in the boat, pleased and gave them requital.

So after we had passed some 10 mile—which by the pleasure and joy we took of our kind entertainment, and for the comfort of our happy and hopeful discovery, we accounted scarce 5—we came to the second islet described in the river, over against which on Popham side is the habitation of The Great King Pawatah, which I call "Pawatah's Tower." It is situate upon a high hill by the water-side, a plain between it and the water 12 [yards] score over, whereon he sows his wheat, bean, peas, tobacco, pompions, gourds, hemp, flax, etc., and were any art used to the natural state of this place, it would be a goodly habitation.

Here we were conducted up the hill to the king, with whom we found our kind King Arahatec. These 2 sat by themselves apart from all the rest, save one who sat by Powatah, and what he was I could not guess, but they told me he was no wiroans. Many of his company sat on either side, and the mats for us were laid right over against the king's. He caused his women to bring us victuals, mulberries, strawberries, etc., but our best entertainment was friendly welcome.

In discoursing with him, we found that all the kingdoms from the——[1] were friends with him and, to use his own word *cheisc*, which is "all one with him" or "under him." Also, we perceived the Chessipian to be an enemy generally to all these kingdoms, upon

---

[1] Word scribbled out. Barbour guesses "Chessipians."

which I took occasion to signify our displeasure with them also, making it known that we refused to plant in their country, and that we had wars with them also, showing hurts scarce whole received by them, for which we vowed revenge, after their manner pointing to the sun. Further we certified him that we were friends with all his people and kingdoms, neither had any of them off'red us ill or used us unkindly. Hereupon he very well understanding by the words and signs we made the signification of our meaning moved of his own accord a league of friendship with us, which our captain kindly embraced, and for concluding thereof gave him his gown, put it on his back himself, and laying his hand on his breast saying, "*Wingapoh chemuze,*" the most kind words of salutation that may be, he sat down.

Now the day drawing on, we made sign to be gone, wherewith he was contented, and sent 6 men with us. We also left a man with him and departed.

But now rowing some 3 mile in shoal water, we came to an overfall impassable for boats any further. Here the water falls down through great main[1] rocks, from ledges of rocks above 2 fadom high, in which fall it maketh divers little islets on which might be placed 100 water milns for any uses.

Our main river ebbs and flows 4 foot even to the skirt' of this downfall. Ships of 200 or 300 ton may come to within 5 mile hereof, and the rest deep enough for barges or small vessels that draw not above 6 foot water. Having viewed this place between content and grief, we left it for this night, determining the next day to fit ourself for a march by land.

So we rode [at anchor][2] all night between Pawatah's Tower and that islet I call—— whereon is 6 or 7 families.

One of our guides which we had from Arahatac's Joy, whose name was Nauirans, and now we found to be brother-in-law to King Arahatec, desired to sleep in the boat with us. We permitted him and used him with all the kindness we could. He proved a very trusty friend, as after is declared.

Now we sent for our man to Pawatah, who coming told us of his

---

[1] Solid.

[2] Written "road," possibly for "rowed," but the sense favors "rode." The islands across the river from the site of Powhatan have long since silted into the west bank.

entertainment, how they had prepared mats for him to lie on, gave him store of victuals, and made as much on him as could be.

May 24. Sunday, Whitsunday, our captain caused two pieces of pork to be sod ashore with peas, to which he invited King Pawatah. For Arahatec, persuading himself we would come down the river that night, went home before dinner for preparation against our coming. But in presence of them both it fell out that we missing two bullet bags, which had shot and divers trucking toys in them, we complained to these kings, who instantly caused them all to be restored, not wanting anything, howbeit they had divided the shot and toys to at least a dozen several persons, and those also in the islet over the water.

One also having stolen a knife brought it again upon this command before we supposed it lost or had made any sign for it. So Captain Newport gave thanks to the kings and rewarded the thieves with the same toys they had stolen, but kept the bullets. Yet he made known unto them the custom of England to be death for such offenses.

Now Arahatec departed. And it being dinner time, King Pawatah with some of his people sat with us, brought of his diet, and we fed familiarly without sitting in his state as before. He ate very freshly of our meat, drank of our beer, aqua vitae, and sack. Dinner done, we ent'red into discourse of the river, how far it might be to the head thereof, where they gat their copper and their iron, and how many days' journey it was to Monanacah, Rahowacah, and the mountains Quirank, requesting him to have guides with us also in our intended march. For our captain determined to have traveled two or 3 days' journey afoot up the river. But without giving any answer to our demands, he showed he would meet us himself at the overfall, and so we [crossed out word, "passed"?] parted.

This Nauirans accompanied us still in the boat. According to his promise he [Pawatah] met us where the fellow, whom I have called our kind consort—he that followed us from Turkey Isle—at the coming of Pawatah made sign to us we must make a shout, which we did.

Now sitting upon the bank by the overfall, beholding the same, he began to tell us of the tedious travel we should have if we proceeded any further, that it was a day and a half journey to Monanacah; and if we went to Quirank we should get no victuals and be tired; and sought by all means to dissuade our captain from going any further. Also he told us that the Monanacah was his enemy, and that he came down at the fall of the leaf and invaded his country.

Now what I conjecture of this I have left to a further experience. But our captain out of his discretion, though we would fain have seen further, yea, and himself as desirous also, check'd his intention and returned to his boat, as holding it much better to please the king, with whom and all of his command he had made so fair way, than to prosecute his own fancy or satisfy our requests.

So upon one of the little islets at the mouth of the falls he set up a cross with this inscription: "Jacobus Rex. 1607," and his own name below. At the erecting hereof we prayed for our king and our own prosperous success in this his action, and proclaimed him king with a great shout.

The King Pawatah was now gone and, as we noted, somewhat distasted with our importunity of proceeding up further, and all the savages likewise, save Nauirans, who seeing us set up a cross with such a shout began to admire.[1] But our captain told him that the two arms of the cross signified King Powatah and himself, the fastening of it in the middest was their united league, and the shout the reverence he did to Pawatah, which cheered Nauirans not a little.

Also, which I have omitted, our captain before Pawatah departed showed him that if he would he would give the wiroans of Monanacah into his hands, and make him king of that country, making signs to bring to his aid 500 men, which pleased the king much; and upon this, I noted, he told us the time of the year when his enemies assail him.

So far as we could discern the river above the overfall, it was full of huge rocks. About a mile off it makes a pretty big island. It runs up between high hills which increase in height one above another so far as we saw. Now our kind consort's relation saith—which I dare well believe, in that I found not any one report false of the river so far as we tried, or that he told us untruth in anything else whatsoever—that

---

[1] Wonder.

after a day's journey or more this river divides itself into two branches, which both come from the mountains Quirank. Here he whispered with me that there *caquassun* was got in the bites[1] of rocks and between cliffs in certain veins.

Having ended thus of the force our discovery, our captain intended to call of King Pawatah; and sending Nauiraus up to him, he came down to the waterside, where he went ashore single unto him, presented him with a hatchet, and staying but till Nauirans had told (as we truly perceived) the meaning of our setting up the cross, which we found did exceedingly rejoice him, he came aboard with the kindest farewell that possible might be. Now at our putting off the boat, Nauirans willed us to make a shout, which we did two several times, at which the king and his company waved their skins about their heads, answering our shout with gladness in a friendly fashion.

This night, though late, we came to Arahatec Joy, where we found the king ready to entertain us, and had provided some victuals for us. But he told us he was very sick and not able to sit up long with us, so we repaired aboard.

May 25. Monday, he came to the waterside and we went ashore to him again. He told us that our hot drinks, he thought, caused his grief, but that he was well again, and we were very welcome. He sent for another deer, which was roasted and after sod for us, as before. Our captain caused his dinner to be dressed ashore also. Thus we sat banqueting all the forenoon.

Some of his people led us to their houses, showed us the growing of their corn and the manner of setting it, gave us tobacco, walnuts, mulberries, strawberries, and raspises. One showed us the herb called in their tongue *wisacan,* which they say heals poisoned wounds. It is like liverwort or bloodwort. One gave me a root wherewith they poison their arrows. They would show us anything we demanded, and labored very much by signs to make us understand their language.

Nauirans our guide and his king's brother made a complaint to Arahatec that one of his people press'd into our boat too violently

---

[1] Bits, bights?

upon a man of ours, which Captain Newport, understanding the proneness of his own men to such injuries, misconstruing the matter, sent for his own man, bound him to a tree before King Arahatec, and with a cudgel soundly beat him. The king, perceiving the error, step'd up and stay'd our captain's hand. And sitting still awhile, he spied his own man that did the injury; upon which he silently rose and made towards the fellow; he seeing him come, run away; after ran the king so swiftly as I assure myself he might give any of our company 6 score in 12. With the king ran also divers others, who all returning brought cudgels and wands in their hands, all to be tewed[1] as if they had beaten him extremely.

At dinner our captain gave the king a glass and some aqua vitae therein, showing him the benefit of the water, for which he thank'd him kindly. And taking our leave of him, he promised to meet us at a point not far off, where he hath another house—which he performed withal, sending men into the woods to kill a deer for us if they could. This place I call "Mulberry Shade."

He caused here to be prepared for us *pegatewk-apoan*,[2] which is bread of their wheat made in rolls and cakes. This the women make, and are very cleanly about it. We had parched meal, excellent good, sod beans, which eat as sweet as filbert kernels in a manner, strawberries and mulberries new shaken off the tree, dropping on our heads as we sat. He made ready a land turtle which we ate, and showed that he was heartly rejoiced in our company.

He was desirous to have a musket shot off, showing first the manner of their own skirmishes, which we perceive is violent, cruel, and full of celerity. They use a tree to defend them in fight, and having shot an enemy that he fall, they maul him with a short wooden sword. Our captain caused a gentleman discharge his piece soldier-like before him, at which noise he started, stop'd his ears, and express'd much fear, so likewise all about him. Some of his people being in our boat leapt overboard at the wonder hereof. But our course of kindness after, and letting him to wit that we never use this thunder but against our enemies, yea, and that we would assist him

---

[1] Tuckered out. *Tew* means to beat.

[2] Or *apyan*.

with these to terrify and kill his adversaries, he rejoiced the more; and we found it bred a better affection in him towards us, so that by his signs we understood he would or [ere] long be with us at our fort. Captain Newport bestowed on him a red waistcoat, which highly pleased him, and so departed, giving him also 2 shouts as the boat went off.

This night we went some—— mile and anchored at a place I call "Kind Woman's Care," which is—— mile from Mulberry Shade. Here we came within night, yet was there ready for us of bread new made, sodden wheat and beans, mulberries, and some fish undressed, more than all we could eat. Moreover, these people seemed not to crave anything in requital, howbeit our captain voluntarily distributed gifts.

May 26. Tuesday, we parted from Kind Woman's Care, and by direction of Nauirans, who still accompanied in the boat with us, went ashore at a place I call "Queen Apumatec's Bower." He carried us along through a plain low ground prepared for seed, part whereof had been lately crop'd; and ascending a pretty hill, we saw the queen of this country[1] coming in selfsame fashion of state as Pawatah or Arahatec, yea, rather with more majesty.

She had an usher before her who brought her to the mat prepared under a fair mulberry tree, where she sat her down by herself with a staid countenance. She would permit none to stand or sit near her. She is a fat, lusty, manly woman; she had much copper about her neck, a crownet of copper upon her head; she had long black hair, which hanged loose down her back to her middle, which only part was covered with a deer's skin, and else all naked; she had her women attending on her adorned much like herself, save they wanted the copper. Here we had our accustomed cates, tobacco, and welcome.

Our captain presented her with gifts liberally, whereupon she cheered somewhat her countenance, and requested him to shoot off a piece, whereat we noted she showed not near the like fear as Arahatec, though he be a goodly man.

She had much corn in the ground. She is subject to Pawatah, as the

---

[1] Opossunoquonuske, the werowansqua of Appamatuck.

rest are, yet within herself of as great authority as any of her neighbor wyoances. Captain Newport stay'd here some 2 hours and departed.

Now leaving her, Nauiraus directed us to one of King Pamaunche's houses, some 5 mile from the Queen's Bower. Here we were entertained with great joy and gladness, the people falling to dance, the women to preparing victuals; some boys were sent to dive for muskles; they gave us tobacco, and very kindly saluted us.

This king, sitting in manner of the rest, so set his countenance striving to be stately as to our seeming he became fool. We gave him many presents, and certified him of our journey to the falls, our league with the Great King Pawatah, a most certain friendship with Arahatec, and kind entertainment of the queen; that we were professed enemies to the Chessepians, and would assist King Pawatah against the Monanacans. With this he seemed to be much rejoiced, and he would have had our captain stay with him all night; which he refused not, but single with the king walked above two flight-shot,[1] showing thereby his true meaning without distrust or fear. Howbeit, we followed aloof off,[2] and coming up to a gallant mulberry tree, we found divers preparing victuals for us. But the king seeing our intention was to accompany our captain, he altered his purpose and waved us in kindness to our boat.

This wyroans Pamaunche I hold to inhabit a rich land of copper and pearl. His country lies into the land to another river, which by relation and description of the savages comes also from the mountains Quirank, but a shorter journey. The copper he had, as also many of his people, was very flexible. I bowed a piece of the thickness of a shilling round about my finger as if it had been lead. I found them nice[3] in parting with any. They wear it in their ears, about their necks in long links, and in broad plates on their heads. So we made no great inquiry of it, neither seemed desirous to have it.

The king had a chain of pearl about his neck thrice double, the third part of them as big as peas, which I could not value less worth than 3 or 400[li], had the pearl been taken from the muskle as it ought

---

[1] Bowshot.

[2] At a distance.

[3] Reluctant.

to be.

His kingdom is full of deer; so also is most of all the kingdoms.

He hath as the rest likewise many rich furs.

This place I call "Pamaunche's Palace," howbeit by Nauviraus his words the King of Winauk is possessor hereof. The plat of ground is bare without wood some 100 acres, where are set beans, wheat, peas, tobacco, gourds, pompions, and other things unknown to us in our tongue.

Now having left this king in kindness and friendship, we crossed over the water to a sharp point which is part of Winauk on Salisbury side. This I call "Careless Point."[1] Here some of our men went ashore with Nauirans, met 10 or 12 savages who offering them neither victuals nor tobacco; they requitted their courtesy with the like and left them.

This night we came to Point Winauk, right against which we rested all night.

There was an old man with King Pamaunche which I omitted in place to specify, who we understood to be 110 year old; for Nauiraus with being with us in our boat had learned me so much of the language, and was so excellently ingenious in signing out his meaning, that I could make him understand me, and perceive him also well-nigh in anything. But this knowledge our captain gat by taking a bough and singling off the leaves let one drop after another, saying *caische,* which is "10"; so first Nauiraus took 11 beans and told them to us, pointing to this old fellow, then 110 beans; by which he answered to our demand for 10 years a bean, and also every year by itself. This was a lusty old man, of a stern countenance, tall and straight, had a thin white beard, his arms overgrown with white hairs, and he went as strongly as any of the rest.

May 27. Wednesday. We went ashore at Point Winauk, where Nauiraus caused them to go a-fishing for us, and they brought us in a short space good store.

These seemed our good friends, but (the cause I know not) here Nauiraus took some conceit and, though he showed no discontent, yet would he by no means go any further with us, saying he would

[1] Jordan Point.

but go up to King Arahatek, and then within some three days after he would see us at our fort. This grieved our captain very deeply, for the loving kindness of this fellow was such as he trusted himself with us out of his own country, intended to come to our fort, and as we came he would make friendship for us before he would let us go ashore at any place, being, as it seemed, very careful of our safety.

So our captain made all haste home, determining not to stay in any place as fearing some disastrous hap at our fort. Which fell out as we expected thus:

After our departure, they seldom frequented our fort but by one or two single now and then, practicing upon opportunity. Now in our absence perceiving there secure carriage in the fort[1]—and the xxvith of May being the day before our return—there came above 200 of them with their king, and gave a very furious assault to our fort, endangering their overthrow, had not the ships' ordnance with their small shot daunted them. They came up almost into the fort, shot through the tents, appeared in this skirmish, which endured hot about an hour, a very valiant people.

They hurt us 11 men, whereof one died after—and killed a boy, yet perceived they not this hurt in us. We killed divers of them, but one we saw them tug off on their backs, and how many hurt we know not. A little after they made a huge noise in the woods, which our men surmised was at the burying of the slain men. Four of the council that stood in front were hurt in maintaining the fort, and our president, Master Wynckfeild, who showed himself a valiant gentleman, had one shot clean through his beard, yet scaped hurt.

Thus having ended our discovery, which we hope may tend to the glory of God, His Majesty's renowm, our country's profit, our own advancing, and fame to all posterity, we settled ourselves to our own safety, and began to fortify, Captain Newport worthily of his own accord causing his seamen to aid us in the best part thereof.

28. Thursday. We labored palisadoing our fort.

---

[1] Ambiguous for either "while we were absent and assumed all there was secure in the fort" [carriage = proceedings] or "while we were absent they (Indians) saw a sure opportunity to *carry* the fort" [carriage = capture].

29. Friday. The savages gave on again, but with more fear, not daring approach scarce within musket shot. They hurt not any of us, but finding one of our dogs they killed him. They shot above 40 arrows into and about the fort.

30. Saturday. We were quiet.

Sunday, they came lurking in the thickets and long grass, and a gentleman, one Eustace Clovell, unarmed, straggling without the fort, shot 6 arrows into him, wherewith he came running into the fort, crying ARM! ARM!—these sticking still. He lived 8 days and died. The savages stayed not, but run away.

June 1. Monday. Some 20 appeared, shot divers arrows at random, which fell short of our fort, and ran away.

2, 3. Tuesday, Wednesday. Quiet and wrought upon fortification, clapboard, and setting of corn.

4. Thursday. By break of day, 3 of them had most adventurously stolen under our bulwark and hidden themselves in the long grass; spied a man of ours going out to do natural necessity, shot him in the head and through the clothes in two places, but missed the skin.

5. Friday. Quiet.

6. Saturday. There being among the gentlemen and all the company a murmur and grudge against certain preposterous proceedings and inconvenient courses, [they] put up a petition to the council for reformation.

7. Sunday. No accident.

8. Monday. Master Clovell died that was shot with 6 arrows sticking in him. This afternoon 2 savages presented themselves unarmed afar off crying *wingapoh!* There were also three more having bow and arrows. These we conjectured came from some of those kings with whom we had perfect league. But one of our gentlemen, guarding in the woods, and having no commandment to the contrary, shot at them; at which, as their custom is, they fell down and after run away. Yet farther off we heard them cry *wingapoh* notwithstanding.

9. Tuesday. In cutting down a great oak for clapboard, there issued out of the heart of the tree the quantity of two barricoes of liquor, in taste as good as any vinegar, save a little smack it took of the oak.

10. Wednesday. The council scanned the gentleman's petition, wherein Captain Newport, showing himself no less careful of our

amity and combined friendship than became him in the deep desire he had of our good, vehemently with ardent affection won our hearts by his fervent persuasion to uniformity of consent, and calmed that (out of our love to him) with ease which I doubt without better satisfaction had not contentedly been carried. We confirmed a faithful love one to another and in our hearts subscribed an obedience to our superiors this day.

Captain Smyth was this day sworn one of the council, who was elected in England.

11. Thursday. Articles and orders for gentlemen and soldiers were upon the court of guard and content was in the quarter.

12. Friday. Cutting down another tree the like accident of vinegar proceeded.

13. Saturday. 8 savages lay close among the weeds and long grass, and spying one or two of our mariners, Master John Cotson and Master Mathew Fitch, by themselves, shot Mathew Fytch in the breast somewhat dangerously, and so ran away this morning.

Our admiral's men gat a sturgeon of 7 foot long, which Captain Newport gave us.

14. Sunday. Two savages presented themselves unarmed, to whom our president and Captain Newport went out. One of these was that fellow I call in my relation of discovery our kind consort, being he we met at Turkey Isle. These certified us who were our friends and who foes, saying that King Pamaunke, King Arahatec, the King of Youghtamong, and the King of Matapoll would either assist us or make us peace with Paspeiouk, Tapahanauk, Wynauk, Apamatecoh, and Chescaik, our contracted enemies. He counseled us to cut down the long weeds round about our fort and to proceed in our sawing. Thus making signs to be with us shortly again, they parted.

15. Monday. We wrought upon clapboard for England.

16. Tuesday. Two savages without, from Salisbury side, being Tapahanauks' country, Captain Newport went to them in the barge, imagining they had been our Sunday friends. But these were Tapahanauks and cried treacherously *wingapoh,* saying their king was on the other side of a point where, had our barge gone, it was so shoal water as they might have effected their villainous plot. But our admiral told them Tapahanauk was *matah* and *chirah,* whereat

laughing they went away.

17, 18, 19, 20. Wednesday, Thursday, Friday, Saturday. No accident.

21. Sunday. We had a communion. Captain Newport dined ashore with our diet, and invited many of us to supper as a farewell.

3. Gabriel Archer

The description of the now-discovered river and country of Virginia, with the likelihood of ensuing riches by England's aid and industry

< **Public Records Office: Colonial Office 1/1–53,** American Antiquarian 1860d:59, Barbour 1969:98, Quinn 1979e:285

There was always the danger that praise of Virginia's *potential* would cause those at home to take it for *actual* and stint on supplies. Archer in §18 for just that reason faults Newport for his glowing reports. Well, no one was guiltier of telling the truth than Archer himself!

THIS RIVER we have named our "King's River" extends itself 160 miles into the mainland between two fertile and fragrant banks two miles, a mile, and, where it is least, a quarter of a mile broad, navigable for shipping of 300 ton 150 miles, the rest deep enough for small vessels of six foot draft. It ebbs and flows 4 foot even to the skirt of an overfall where the water falls down from huge great rocks, making in the fall five or six several islets very fit for the building of water milns thereon. Beyond this not two days' journey it hath two branches which come through a high stony country from certain huge mountains called Quirank, beyond which needs no relation.

This from the overfall was the report and description of a faithful fellow who I dare well trust upon good reasons.

From these mountains Quirank come two less rivers which run into this great one. But whether deep enough for ships or no I yet understand not. Here be many small rivers of brooks which unlade themselves into this main river at several mouths, which veins divide the savage kingdoms in many places, and yield pleasant seats in all the country over by moistening the fruitful mould.

The main river abounds with sturgeon very large and excellent good, having also at the mouth of every brook and in every creek both store and exceeding good fish of divers kinds; and in the large sounds near the sea are multitudes of fish, banks of oysters, and many great crabs rather better in taste than ours, one able to suffice four men. And within sight of land into the sea we expect at time of year to have a good fishing for cod, as both at our first entering we might perceive by palpable conjecture, seeing the cod follow the ship, yea, bite at the—— as also out of my own experience not far off to the northward the fishing I found in my first voyage to Virginia.[1]

This land lieth low at the mouth of the river and is sandy ground, all over beset with fair pine trees. But a little up the river it is reasonable high. And the further we go, till we come to the overfall, it still riseth increasing. It is generally replenish'd with wood of all kinds and that the fairest, yea, and best that ever any of us (traveler or workman) ever saw, being fit for any use whatsoever, as ships, houses, planks, pales, boards, masts, wainscot, clapboard—for pikes or elsewhat.

The soil is more fertile than can be well express'd; it is altogether aromatical, giving a spicy taste to the roots of all trees, plants, and herbs, of itself a black, fat, sandy mould, somewhat slimy in touch and sweet in savor, under which about a yard is in most places a red clay fit for brick, in other marl, in some [places] signification of mineral, in other gravel, stones, and rocks; it hath in divers places fuller's earth, and such [clay] as comes out of Turkey called terra sigillata.

It produceth of one corn of that country wheat sometimes two or

[1] Archer in 1602 sailed with Gosnold to New England.

three stems, or stalks, on which grow ears above a span long, beset with corns at the least 300 upon an ear, for the most part 5, 6, and 700. The beans and peas of this country have a great increase also; it yields two crops a year.

Being temp[t]ed and time taken, I hold it nature's nurse to all vegetables. For I assure myself no known continent brings forth any vendible necessaries which this by planting will not afford. For testimony in part, this we find by proof:

From the West Indies we brought a certain delicious fruit called a *pina*,[1] which the Spaniard by all art possible could never procure to grow in any place but in his natural site. This we rudely and carelessly set in our mould, which fostereth it and keeps it green, and to what issue it may come I know not. Our West Indy plants of oranges and cotton trees thrive well, likewise the potatoes, pumpions, and millions.[2] All our garden seeds that were carefully sown prosper well, yet we only digged the ground half a—— deep, threw in the seeds at random carelessly, and scarce rak'd it.

It naturally yields mulberry trees, cherry trees, vines abundance, gooseberries, strawberries, hurtleberries, raspises, groundnuts, scarrettes [carrots], the root called *sigilla Christi,* certain sweet thin-shelled nuts, certain ground apples (a pleasant fruit), any [and?] many other unknown. So the thing we crave is some skillful man to husband, set, plant, and dress vines, sugar canes, olives, rapes, hemp, flax, licorice, prunes, currants, raisins, and all such things as the North Tropic of the world affords—also saffron, woad, hops, and suchlike.

The commodities of this country, what they are *in esse* is not much to be regarded, the inhabitants having no commerce with any nation, no respect of profit, neither is there scarce that we call *meum et tuum*[3] among them, save only the kings know their own territories and the people their several gardens.

Yet this for the present: By the consent of all our seamen, merely our fishing for sturgeon cannot be less worth than 1000^{li} a year,

---

[1] Pineapple.
[2] Melons.
[3] Private property.

leaving herring and cod as possibilities.

Our clapboard and wainscot (if ships will but fetch it) we may make as much as England can vent; we can send (if we be friends with the savages or be able to force them) 2, 3, 4, or 5000^{li} a year of the earth called terra sigillata; saxafrage, what store we please; tobacco, after a year or two 5000^{li} a year; we have as we suppose rich dyes, if they prove vendible, worth more than yet is nominated; we have excellent furs, in some places of the country great store; we can make pitch, rosin, and turpentine; there is a gum which bleedeth from a kind of maple (the bark being cut) not much unlike a balsam both in scent and virtue; apothecary drugs of divers sorts, some known to be of good estimation, some strange, of whose virtue the savages report wonders; we can by our industry and plantation of commodious merchandise make oils, wines, soap-ashes, wood ashes, extract from mineral earth, iron, copper, etc.; we have a good fishing for muskles, which resemble mother-of-pearl. And if the pearl we have seen in the kings' ears and about their necks come from these shells, we know the banks.

To conclude, I know not what can be expected from a commonwealth that either this land affords not or may soon yield.

4. Gabriel Archer

A Brief Description of the People

< **Public Records Office: Colonial Office 1/1–55,** American Antiquarian 1860d:63, Barbour 1969:102

A brilliant account, full of freshness and insight, tragically brief. At this time no Englishman had met Powhatan.

Different east/west moral attitudes in regard to thievery led to no end of trouble in the years to come. Englishmen condemned thievery in all cases: The thief was punished and goods were restored. Indians, not without exception, felt that while one certainly had a right to claim and defend belongings, once they were stolen possession was, so to speak, nine-tenths of the law. The modern attitude conforms to the English. The Indian attitude has the virtue of consistency in the morality of individuals and nation states.

THERE IS A KING in this land called Great Pawatah, under whose dominions are at least 20ty several kingdoms, yet each king potent as a prince in his own territory. These have their subjects at so quick command as a beck brings obedience, even to the restitution of stolen goods, which by their natural inclination they are loth to leave.

They go all naked save their privities, yet in cool weather they wear deerskins with the hair on loose. Some have leather stockings up to their twists,[1] and sandals on their feet.

Their hair is black generally, which they wear long on the left side, tied up on a knot, about which knot the kings and best among them have a kind of coronet of deer's hair colored red. Some have chains of long link'd copper about their necks, and some chains of pearl. The common sort stick long feathers in this knot. I found not a gray eye among them all. Their skin is tawny, not so born but with dyeing and painting themselves, in which they delight greatly.

---

[1] The crotch.

The women are like the men, only this difference: Their hair groweth long all over their heads, save clip'd somewhat short afore. These do all the labor, and the men hunt and go at their pleasure.

They live commonly by the waterside in little cottages made of canes and reeds, covered with the bark of trees. They dwell as I guess by families of kindred and alliance, some 40ty or 50ty in a *hatto,* or small village, which towns are not past a mile or half a mile asunder in most places.

They live upon sodden wheat, beans, and peas for the most part. Also they kill deer, take fish in their weirs, and kill fowl abundance. They eat often and that liberally.

They are proper lusty, straight men, very strong, run exceeding swiftly; their fight is alway in the wood with bow and arrows, and a short wooden sword. The celerity they use in skirmish is admirable. The king directs the battle and is always in front.

Their manner of entertainment is upon mats on the ground under some tree, where they sit themselves alone in the middest of the mat, and two mats on each side, on which their people sit; then right against him (making a square form) sat we always. When they came to their mat they have an usher goes before them, and the rest as he sits down give a long shout.

The people steal anything comes near them, yea, are so practiced in this art that looking in our face they would with their foot between their toes convey a chisel, knife, piercer, or any indifferent light thing; which having once conveyed, they hold it an injury to take the same from them. They are naturally given to treachery, howbeit we could not find it in our travel up the river, but rather a most kind and loving people.

They sacrifice tobacco to the sun, [a] fair picture, or a harmful thing (as a sword or piece) also; they strinkle some into the water in the morning before they wash.

They have many wives, to whom, as near as I could perceive, they keep constant. The Great King Pawatah had most wives. These they abide not to be touch'd before their face. The great disease[1] reigns in the men generally—full fraught with nodes, botches, and pulpable

[1] Syphilis.

appearances in their foreheads: We found above a hundred.

The women are very cleanly in making their bread and preparing meat.

I found they account after death to go into another world, pointing eastward to the element. And when they saw us at prayer they observed us with great silence and respect, especially those to whom I had imparted the meaning of our reverence.

To conclude, they are a very witty[1] and ingenious people, apt both to understand and speak our language, so that I hope in God, as He hath miraculously preserved us hither from all dangers, both of sea and land and their fury, so He will make us authors of His holy will in converting them to our true Christian faith by His own inspiring grace and knowledge of His deity.

5. The Council in Virginia

Letter to the Council of Virginia, 22 June 1607

< **Northumberland Papers: Alnwick MSS, volume 7,** Brown 1890:106, Barbour 1969:78

Virginia's first report to London lays bare the perennial problem: Of six major tasks in seven weeks, only three ensure comfort and survival. Furthermore, the sailors are already at work "defrauding" the colonists.

---

[1] Cunning.

WE ACKNOWLEDGE ourselves accountable for our time here spent, were it but to give you satisfaction of our industries and affections to this most honorable action, and the better to quicken those good spirits which have already bestowed themselves here, and to put life into such dead understandings or beliefs that must first see and feel the womb of our labor and this land before they will entertain any good hope of us or of the land:

Within less than seven weeks, we are fortified well against the Indians; we have sown good store of wheat; we have sent you a taste of clapboard; we have built some houses; we have spared some hands to a discovery; and still as God shall enhable us with strength we will better and better our proceedings.

Our easiest and richest commodity being sasafrax, roots were gathered up by the sailors with loss and spoil of many of our tools, and with drawing of our men from our labor to their uses against our knowledge to our prejudice. We earnestly entreat you—and do trust—that you take such order as we be not in this thus defrauded, since they be all our waged men. Yet do we wish that they be reasonably dealt withal, so as all the loss neither fall on us nor them. I believe they have thereof two tons at the least which, if they scatter abroad at their pleasure, will pull down our price for a long time. This we leave to your wisdoms.

The land would flow with milk and honey if so seconded by your careful wisdoms and bountiful hands. We do not persuade to shoot one arrow to seek another, but to find them both. And we doubt not but to send them home with golden heads. At least our desires, labors, and lives shall to that engage themselves.

We are set down 80 miles within a river for breadth, sweetness of water, length navigable up into the country, deep and bold channel so stored with sturgeon and other sweet fish as no man's fortune hath ever possessed the like and, as we think, if more may be wished in a river it will be found. The soil [is] most fruitful, laden with good oak, ash, walnut tree, poplar, pine, sweet woods, cedar, and others yet without names that yield gums pleasant as frankincense and experienced amongest us for great virtue in healing green wounds and aches.

We entreat your succors for our seconds with all expedition lest that all-devouring Spaniard lay his ravenous hands upon these gold-showing mountains, which, if it be so enhabled, he shall never dare to think on.

This note doth make known where our necessities do most strike us. We beseech your present relief accordingly. Otherwise, to our greatest and last griefs, we shall against our wills not will that which we most willingly would.

Captain Newporte hath seen all and knoweth all. He can fully satisfy your further expectations, and ease you of our tedious letters.

We most humbly pray the Heavenly King's hand to bless our labors with such counsels and helps, as we may further and stronger proceed in this our king's and country's service.

James town in Virginia, this 22th of June, anno 1607.

Your poor friends,

EDWARD MARIA WINGFEILD	BARTHOLMEWE GOSNOLD
JOHN SMITH[1]	JOHN RATTCLIFFE
JOHN MARTINE	GEORGE KENDALL

[endorsed:] Copy of a Letter from Virginia, dated 22th of June, 1607. The Council there to the Council of Virginia here in England.

1 "It is noteworthy that Smith's name appears immediately below Wingfield's, even though he had just been released from 'restraint' and sworn a member of the council." (Barbour)

6. William Brewster

Letter from Virginia

< **Cecil Papers: Hatfield House, 124/17,** Brown 1898:33, Virginia Magazine 75:4 (1967), Barbour 1969:107

Was there ever a more prophetic piece of rhapsody? He told the truth then, but he tells the truth today. This went back with Newport on June 22nd. In a few weeks Brewster was dead. The page this letter is on has been clipped off below the last line. It is found today in the papers of the Earl of Salisbury, who may have been the addressee.

SIR—It had been my duty to have wrote the whole journey unto you, and so I would have done had not this our ever-renowned captain, Captain Newport, have come himself unto you, who will so justly and truly declare better than I can all this his discovery. This is all I will say to you, that such a bay, a river, and a land did never the eye of man behold; and at the head of the river, which is 160 miles long, are rocks and mountains that promiseth infinite treasure. But our forces be yet too weak to make further discovery. Now is the King's Majesty offered the most stately, rich kingdom in the world, never possess'd by any Christian prince. Be you one means among many to further our seconding to conquer this land as well as you were a means to further the discovery of it, and you yet may live to see England more rich and renowned than any kingdom in all Europa. [the rest is cut off]

[endorsed:] A part of a letter of William Brewster
sent from Virginia.

7. Robert Tindall

Letter to Prince Henry, 22 June 1607

< **British Library: Harleian MS 7007–139r,** Arber 1884a:xxxviii, Brown 1890:108, Barbour 1969:104. The "diurnal of our voyage and draught of our river" are both now lost. Tindall's well-known map of the James and York rivers and the lower Bay, reproduced opposite, is a later product he brought with him when he returned to England in May 1608. Surely its James River portions are based on the missing draft.

MIGHTY PRINCE—I thought it no less than my duty, being employed in this voyage of Verginia, in all humble manner to make Your Princely Self acquainted with those accidents which hath happened to us in this our voyage. May it therefore please Your Grace to accept at the hands of your most humble and dutiful servant a diurnal of our voyage and draft of our river, here enclosed, by us discovered, where never Christian before hath been; and also to let Your Grace understand we are safely arrived and planted in this country by the providence and mercy of God, which we find to be in itself most fruitful, of the which we have taken a real and public possession in the name and to the use of your royal father and our gracious king and sovereign.

Thus ceasing for being too tedious and troublesome unto Your Grace, I in all humble manner commit Your Princely Self to the protection of Almighty God, whom on my knees I daily pray (as I am bound) to bless and prosper your godly and virtuous proceedings.

From James Town in Virginia, this 22 of June, 1607.

By Your Grace's most humble, dutiful, and faithful servant and gunner,

ROBERTE TINDALL.

[endorsed:] To the high and mighty Prince Henry Fredericke, Prince and Heir Apparent of Great Britain, France, Ireland, and Virginia. Tindall, his M[ajesty's] gunner from Virginia.

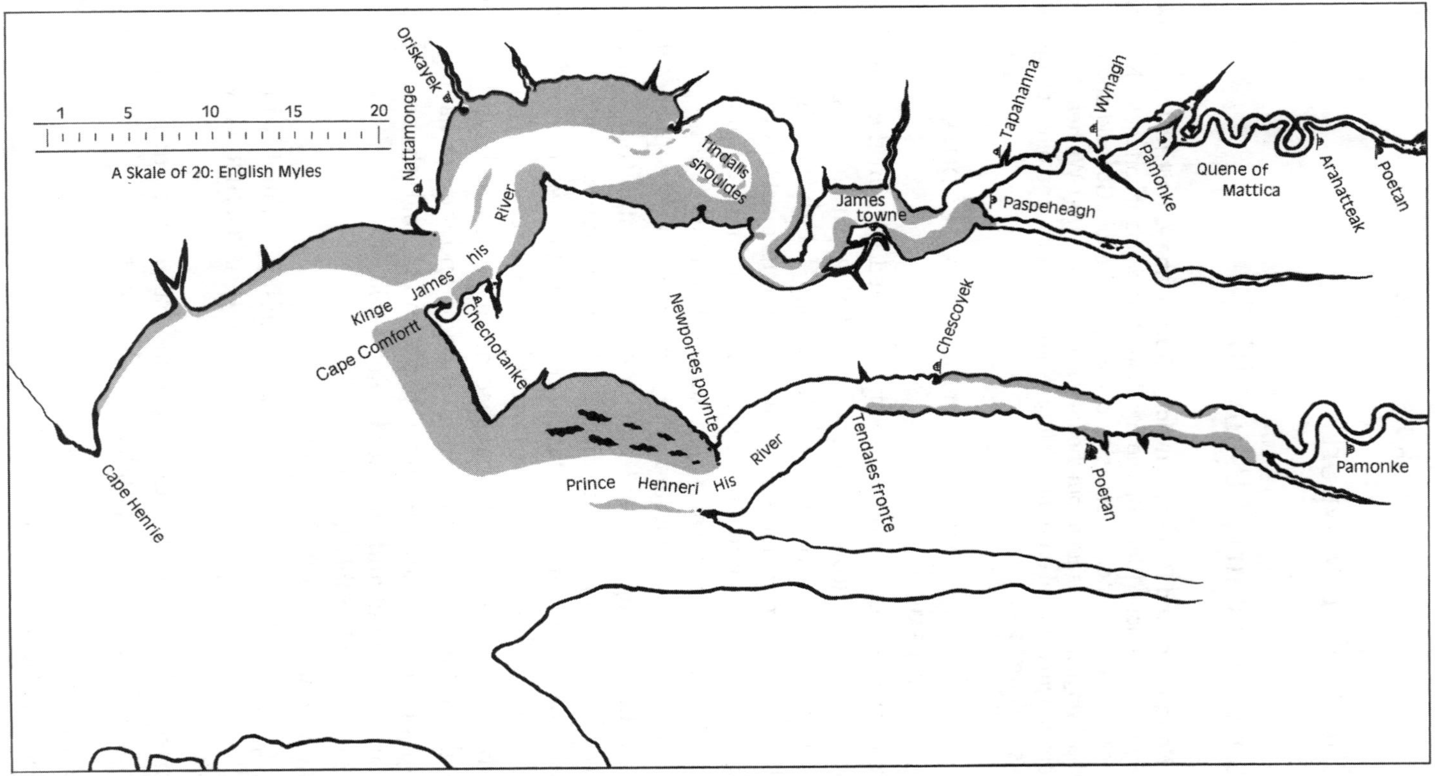

The Draught By Robarte Tindall of Virginia Anno: 1608

8. Christopher Newport

Letter to Salisbury, 29 July 1607

< **Northumberland Papers: Alnwick MSS, volume 7,** Neill 1878:12, Brown 1890:105, Barbour 1969:76. The mention of gold was unfortunate. Newport spoke loosely on another occasion earlier when he told Gosnold and Archer what Wingfield had said about them (*Discourse §13–184)*. We hear the great captain wrote a relation of his visit to Werowocomoco, and other things, but this is all we have.

RIGHT HONORABLE: MY VERY GOOD LORD, MY DUTY IN MOST HUMBLE WISE REMEMB'RED—

It may please Your good Lordship I arrived here in the sound of Plymouth this day from the discovery of that part of Virginia imposed upon me and the rest of the colony for the south part, in which we have performed our duties to the uttermost of our powers; and have discovered into the country near two hundred miles, and a river navigable for great ships one hundred and fifty miles.

The country is excellent and very rich in gold and copper. Of the gold we have brought a say[1] and hope to be with Your Lordship shortly to show it His Majesty and the rest of the lords.

I will not deliver the expectance and assurance we have of great wealth, but will leave it to Your Lordship's censure when you see the probabilities. I wish I might have come in person to have brought these glad tidings, but my inability of body, and the not having any man to put in trust with the ship and that in her, maketh me to defer my coming till wind and weather be favorable.

And so I most humbly take my leave.

From Plymouth this 29th of July, 1607.

Your Lordship's most humbly bounden,
CHRISTOPHER NEWPORTE.

[endorsed:] Copy of a letter to the Lord of Salisbury from Captain Newporte, the 29th of July, 1607, from Plymouth.

---

[1] Ore sample, which proved worthless.

9. Francis Perkins

Letter from Jamestown to a Friend, 28 March 1608
(translated from the Spanish by Maximilian Schele de Vere)

< Simancas Archives E 2586, 111–114; **Brown 1890:173;** Barbour 1969: 158

Originally in English, Perkins' lost original was encrypted in Spanish diplomatic cipher, sent to Spain as a "letter of Virginia to be sent to His Majesty" in a cover with a letter dated 16 June 1608 from Pedro de Zuñiga, the Spanish ambassador in London. In Spain it was deciphered in Spanish so Philip III could read it, and lastly comes to us translated back into English for Brown's *Genesis* a hundred years ago. We can only guess at the original names, such as "Perquin" the writer. I call attention to a few readings in the more recent Barbour translation.

He is arriving with the first supply in the terrible first winter of 1607/08. We cannot tell from this why Perkins has been in difficulties. He mentions debts. There was a category of threadbare gentlemen colonists at this time who expected to stumble over riches if they could only stroll in the New World forest. As for the burden of this chatty letter, he failed in his quest to be appointed to the council. Unlike Maguel's relation, this is not at all the communication of a spy. We have no idea how it came to be spirited away to Spain or what happened to the original, or what became of Perkins.

Nor do we have the addressee, but Barbour writes: "The 'Lady Catherine' was undoubtedly the wife of Sir William Cornwallis the younger, son of Sir Charles (d. 1629). Sir William the elder ... was the older brother of Sir Charles. He lived at Highgate, near the residence of Zuñiga. By his first wife, Lucy Nevill (aunt of George Percy), he had a daughter Elizabeth, who married Sir William Sandys, mentioned later in the letter, undoubtedly a relative of Sir Edwin Sandys of the Virginia Company." (Barbour)

Bracketed material in *italics* is in Schele de Vere, in roman is taken from Barbour.

MOST ILLUSTRIOUS SIR—After my due respects to you, with thanks for the many favors which you have done me, and the trouble you have taken on my account (I being unable to repay them except by praying God and desiring to serve you in every way that I can), I venture to beg of you another favor on the occasion which at this time presents itself (although I have given you just cause to abandon me by not taking leave of so good a friend as you have always been to me on the occasion of my departure!). But the confidence I feel in your unfailing kindness will [I trust] excuse me this time, since that neglect arose only from fear of some impediment in this my long-desired journey.

I shall not fail, however, to make amends in part at least for this mistake, because if I do not succeed in securing your favor and in making my peace with *Madama* [my lady], securing in my absence the success of my wishes (of which I had occasion to speak in petition to you before I left, so much more time being given to solicit this business in person), the whole matter will [otherwise] turn to my great prejudice and injury.

But trusting entirely your usual kindness, I pray you will have the goodness to negotiate with Messrs. William Wade, Thomas Smith, Walter Cope, Thomas Chancellor (Chaloner), George More, and the others, that I be appointed one of the council here in Virginia—as much for my honor as that I may be better able to pay my debts. There are some of the members of the council here who understand state affairs as little as I do and who are no better than I [in business affairs]. It will be a matter of great delight to see coming here so many from our country so richly gifted and enlightened that I would not be worthy to appear among them!

Concerning our voyage and my views of the country, I will state them to you as well as I can: We left Gravesend on Thursday, October 8, 1607. We reached Plymouth the following Thursday, where we remained till Monday; and as the wind was not favorable it became necessary on the next day to make port at Falmouth, where until Friday morning we suffered much from a great storm, after which continuing our voyage. In five weeks and two days (November 29) we reached the island of Santo Domingo [Dominica], which is in the West Indies; and we were there all that day trafficking with the savages, who came on board naked, bringing us potatoes, plantains [bananas], pineapples, which are a very savory fruit, bread which they call *casadra* (made of certain roots), parrots, cocks and hens, and other things, which they gave us in exchange for iron hatchets, saws, knives, rosaries,[1] bells, and other similar trifles which they esteem very highly, and are of great usefulness to those who carry them with them in like voyages.

And thus sailing along the coasts the whole week past the other neighboring islands, we came near the island of San Juan [Puerto Rico] towards the northern part [of the coast], and fourteen days later, on Sunday (December 20), we came in sight of America.

On the following Thursday (December 24), the ship that kept us company, called the *Phœnix,* came to lose us in a very dense fog which rose when we were not more than ten or twelve leagues from the entrance to the port, and we have not been able up to today to hear any news about it. There were in that ship about forty men, who were to remain here with us.

The ship called the *John & Francis,* in which Captain Newport was, came on the 2nd of January to Jamestown. The river is very beautiful and wide, but full of shallows and piles of oyster shells. The land lies low and is full of wood until you reach the coast.

[At first] we always had warm weather, afterwards such bitter colds and such severe frosts that I and several others had our feet frostbitten.

A month after this we came to a land where there was also great frost and snow. The country around there has a great abundance of wild swans, herons, and cranes, wild ducks and other waterfowl, with many other birds, as long as the winter continues, with the prettiest parrots that can be seen. So excessive are the frosts that one night the river froze over almost from bank to bank in front of our harbor, although it was there as wide as that of London. There died from the ice some fish in the river which when taken out after the ice was over were very good and so fat that they could be fried in their own fat without adding any butter or such thing.

After our landing, which took place on a Monday (January 4), there broke out on the following Thursday (January 7) such a fire that growing rapidly it consumed all the buildings of the fort and the storehouse of ammunition and provision, so that there remained only three; and all that my son and I possessed was burnt except

[1] A small coin of the least value.

only a mattress which had not yet been carried on shore.

Thanks to God we are at peace with all the neighboring inhabitants of the country and trade with them in wheat and provisions. They attach very great value to copper which looks at all reddish. Their own great emperor, or the *vuarravance,* which is the name of their kings, has sent us some of his people, that they may teach us how to sow the grain of this country and to make certain tools *[traps?]* with which they are going to fish *[catch fish?]*. And certainly, as far as may be conjectured, there is a great probability that the land is very fertile and good, quite sufficient to support a million of inhabitants in that part which we now occupy; but it is more in clearing out the wood than in the multiplying of the grain that difficulty arises.

I have sent to *Madama* your wife, a pair of tortoises [turtle doves], others to *Madama Catalina* [my Lady Catherine], and others to William Cornwallis, hoping that when our people make another excursion I shall have better things to send. I send you an ear of the grain as it grows here, with two bales of our ordinary flora,[1] and other two to *Madama Catalina,* and others to Master William *[Cornwallis]* the elder. There are found there many small animals with savory *[illegible]* inside (opossum?).[2] When I meet any by chance I shall send them to you that you and your friends may see them.

There is here the greatest abundance of pasturage for any kind of cattle, especially for pigs and goats, even if there were a million of them. There is also to be found all around the fort where we have cut down the trees a great quantity of strawberries and other plants pleasant to the taste.

And, sir, considering that this misfortune of the fire has caused among us a general want of almost all things, especially as far as I am concerned, having suffered much during these past two years—so much in fact that I have not even paper and ink to write to our friends!—I beseech you to see to it that *Madama Catalina* be not angry with me, but that yielding to the natural nobility of her heart and to the affection she has been pleased to show me in the past she

---

[1] Barbour has "... two pots [made] of our ordinary earth."
[2] Barbour has "... many little animals here with skins of fine fur."

will endeavor jointly with you and Master William Cornwallis most earnestly to recommend my claim to be admitted *[to the council in Virginia?]*, especially with Master William *[Thomas?]* Smythe, since he can do more in matters concerning this state than anyone else.

I beg also *Madama Catalina* will have the kindness to get Master William Cornwallis to send me for the value of ten pounds such clothes as he may have that are worn out, whether it be large or small garments, doublets, trousers, stockings, capes, or whatever may appear fit to them, since, the fire having burnt all we possessed, everything is needed and whatever may be sent will be useful.

I beg also you will ask *Madama Catalina* to negotiate, in conformity with the same arrangement, with Master William *Sans* [Sandys], since I promise I will return to them the value of whatever they may send me, whilst I acknowledge that by her kindness and that of these gentlemen I and my people are still alive. And even if this should fall short of supplying the wants of so many, will *Madama* and those gentlemen do me and my son at least this favor out of their liberality, to send us such things as are of little use to them and most valuable to myself.

I beseech you, sir, not to be offended by this my candor and daring boldness, but in your great kindness to remember me who am so far away and cut off from my friends, doing me at the same time the favor in all reasonable things to be kind to my wife if in any emergency she should have recourse to you.

I pray you will communicate the contents of this letter to *Madama Catalina* and let her read it all, if it so please her. And herewith I most humbly commit myself to your protection and that of those gentlemen in whose kindness and favor I put my entire confidence. I pray God may protect you and all.
March 28, 1608.

Your servant for life,
FRANCIS PERQUIN

of Villa James in Virginia.

I am sending to my Lady Catherine and to my lady your wife, to each of them, six pounds of sassafras to use in medicines or between linens. It used to be worth forty *reales* [one pound sterling] the pound not long ago, and is no less efficacious now than then.[1] I shall not fail to send my Lady Catherine, you, and Sir William Cornwallis some trees, fruit, herbs, flowers, and other new things produced by this land, begging you in the meantime to receive what I can now send in the spirit in which I offer it.[2]

10. George Percy

Excerpt published in *Purchas His Pilgrimage*

< **Purchas 1626:844**, Barbour 1969:146

Doubtless here is something Purchas restores among the cuts he made out of the *Discourse §1.*

THEY HAVE[3] a certain herb called *weysake,* like liverwort, which they chew and spit into poisoned wounds that are thereby healed in four and twenty hours. In finding out their medicinal root (it is the relation of Master George Percie), six of them hold together by the arms, and so go singing and withal searching; and when they have found it, sit down singing, crossing the root with their hands for a good space; then gather, chew, and spit.

He thus describeth their dances: One stands in the middest singing and clapping hands; all the rest dance about him, shouting, halloing, stamping, with antic gesture like so many devils, their feet always (and only) agreeing in one stroke.

---

[1] In demand as a remedy for syphilus until about this time.

[2] This postscript is found only in Barbour.

[3] "Virginia Voyage, 1606. MS Master George Percy." (margin note)

Landing at Kecoughtan, the savages entertained them with a doleful noise, laying their faces to the ground, and scratching the earth with their nails.

The werowance of Rapahanna met them, playing on a flute of a reed, with a crown of deer's hair colored red, fashioned like a rose, with a chain of beads about his neck, and bracelets of pearl hanging at his ears, in each ear a bird's claw.

The women are of a modest proud behavior, [and] with an iron pounce and race their bodies, legs, thighs, and arms in curious knots and portraitures of fowls, fishes, beasts, and rub a painting into the same which will never out.

The Queen of Apametica was attired with a coronet beset with many white bones, her ears hanged with copper, a chain thereof six times compassing her neck.

The maids shave their heads all but the hinder part. The wives wear it all of a length. The men wear the left lock long (as is said already), sometimes an ell, which they tie when they please in an artificial knot stuck with feathers, the right side shaven.

The King of Paspahey was painted all black, with horns on his head like a devil.

He [Percy] testifieth of their hard fare: watching every third night, lying on the bare cold ground, what weather soever came, and warding the next day; a small can of barley sodden in water being the sustenance for five men a day; their drink brackish and slimy water —this continued five months.

11. William White

Excerpt published in *Purchas His Pilgrimage:* The Black Boys Ceremony

< **Purchas 1613:640, 1614:766, 1617:952, 1626:841;** Barbour 1969:147

This comes to us in the form reedited by Purchas in four editions of his *Pilgrimage* and includes passages the reader will recognize in Smith and Strachey. Barbour feels that White's unedited account was likely the original that was copied with added details by Smith, who credits no source, and Strachey, who credits Percy.

The name "Black Boys" (written "Blake Boys") is a mystery (= blank? = white?) The ceremony in later times became known as the *huskanaw.* It is the rigorous initiation rite of boys into manhood, but another element of the ceremony seems to have involved ritual child sacrifice. This is denied by other colonists, such as Rolfe, but confirmed by Spelman (487). In the 1626 edition all mention of human sacrifice has been edited out by Purchas.

The unfortunate George Cassen was one of Smith's shipmates in the barge on the Chickahominy River. Accounts also at §16–212 and §41–655.

IN SOME PART OF THE COUNTRY they are said (which since is found false) to have yearly a sacrifice of children. Such a one was performed at Quiyoughcohanock, some ten miles from James Town, in this manner:

Rapahannock werowance[1] made a feast in the woods. The people were so painted that a painter with his pencil could not have done better: Some of them were black like devils, with horns and loose hair, some of divers colors. They continued two days dancing in a circle of a quarter of a mile in two companies, with antic tricks, four in a rank, the werowance leading the dance. They had rattles in their hands. All in the middest had black horns on their heads and green boughs in their hands. Next them were four or five principal men diversly painted which with bastinadoes beat forward such as tired in the dance. Thus they made themselves scarce able to go or stand.

[1] "[The relation of] William White." (margin note)

When they met together they made a hellish noise, and everyone flinging away his bough ran clapping their hands up into a tree, and tare it to the ground, and fell into their order again. Thus they did twice. Fourteen well-favored children or, if you had rather hear Captain Smith, fifteen of the properest young boys between ten and fifteen years of age they painted white. Having brought them forth, the people, saith he, spent the forenoon in dancing and singing about them with rattles. In the afternoon they put these children to the root of a tree, all the men standing to guard them, each with a bastinado of reeds bound together in his hand. Then do they make a lane between them all along, thorough which there were appointed five young men (White calls them priests) to fetch these children. Each of these fetched a child, the guard laying on with their bastinadoes, while they with their naked bodies defend the children to their great smart.

All this time the women weep and cry out very passionately, providing moss, skins, mats, and dry wood, unknown to what purpose.[1] When the children are in this manner fetched away, the guard tears down trees, branches, and boughs, making wreaths for their heads, or bedecking their hair with the leaves. What else was done with the children was not seen. But they were all cast on a heap in a valley as dead, where was made a great feast for all the company.

William White relating this rite[2] saith that they removed them from tree to tree three times, and at last carried them into a valley where the king sat—where they would suffer our men to see, but feasted there two hours. On a sudden all arose with cudgels in their hands, and made a lane as is before said; and the children being laid down under a tree (to their seeming) without life, they all fell into a ring again and danced about the children a good space, and then sat down in a circle about the tree. Raphanna in the mids caused burdens of wood to be brought to the altar made of poles set like a steeple, where they made a great fire which our men thought, but were deceived, was to sacrifice their children to the devil (whom they call Kewase) who, as they report, sucks their blood. They were

[1] After "dry wood" the phrase "... as things fitting the children's funeral." in 1614 was edited out and replaced by the non-committal one in 1617.

[2] "Sacrifice" in 1614.

unwilling to let them stay any longer. They found a woman mourning for young Paspiha sacrificed at the town of Rapahanna. But this Paspiha is now alive, as Mr. Rolph hath since related to me; and the mourning of the women is not for their children's death but because they are for divers months detained from them, as we shall after see. Yea, the Virginians themselves by false reports might delude our men and say they were sacrificed when they were not. For even still they are very inconstant (it is Mr. Rolph's report) in all that they speak of their religion, one denying that which another affirmeth, and either not knowing or not willing that others should know their devilish mysteries.

The werowance (Captain Smith addeth), being demanded the meaning of this sacrifice, answered that the children were not all dead, but that the Oke, or devil, did suck the blood from their left breast who chanced to be his by lot, till they were dead. But the rest were kept in the wilderness by the young men till nine moons were expired, during which time they must not converse with any, and of these were made their priests and conjurers.[1] This sacrifice they held to be so necessary that if they should omit it, their Oke, or devil, and their other *quiyoughcosughes,* or gods, would let them have no deer, turkeys, corn, or fish, and would besides make a great slaughter amongst them.

---

[1] Another version, attributed to "Cap. Smith" and published in 1625, reads: "The werowance being demanded the meaning of this sacrifice answered that the children were not all dead, but the next day they were to drink wighsakon, which would make them mad; and they were to be kept by the last-made black boys in the wilderness where their Oke did suck the blood of those which fell to his lot. The truth is, as I think, that many die with the misery which they endure, for they lie in all weathers in a little hovel naked, and they seldom speak or keep company with any but their keepers, whom they obey, so that if they be bidden sit on the frozen snow they will not rise till they be called; and if they bid them go take fish, flesh, or corn from their mothers or else they are old me[n], this word is so terrible that they will tear their mother's throat but they will have it. Yea, it makes them do whatsoever they are commanded. And much mischief they often do to such as they find straggling, yet hurt they not each other. They continue thus nine months. Then are divers platters of broth set, of which some are poisoned, and he whose divination finds out the poisoned is much esteemed and made a quiyoughcosuck. These are the degrees to become priest or conjurers. This sacrifice they held to be so necessary," etc. (*Purchas His Pilgrimes,* 1702)

They think that their werowances and priests, which they also esteem quiyoughcosughes, when they are dead, do go beyond the mountains towards the setting of the sun, and ever remain there in form of their Oke, having their heads painted with oil and *pocones,*[1] finely trimmed with feathers, and shall have beads, hatchets, copper, and tobacco, never ceasing to dance and sing with their predecessors. The common people, they suppose, shall not live after death.

Some sought to convert them from these superstitions. The werowance of Quiyoughcohanock was so far persuaded as that he professed to believe that our god exceeded theirs as much as our guns did their bows and arrows; and many times did send to the president many presents, entreating him to pray to his god for rain, for his[2] god would not send him any.

William White reporteth these their ceremonies of honoring the sun: By break of day, before they eat or drink, the men, women, and children above ten years old run into the water, and there wash a good space till the sun arise; and then they offer sacrifice to it, strewing tobacco on the land or water; the like they do at sunset.

He also relateth that one George Casson (beforementioned) was sacrificed as they thought to the devil, being stripped naked and bound to two stakes with his back against a great fire. Then did they rip him and burn his bowels, and dried his flesh to the bones, which they kept above ground in a by-room. Many other of our men were cruelly and treacherously executed by them, though perhaps not sacrificed; and none had been left, if their ambushes and treasons had taken effect. Powhatan thus invited[3] Captain Ratliffe and thirty others to trade for corn, and having brought them within his ambush, murthered them.

---

1 "*Pocones* is a small root which dried and beat into powder turneth red. They use it for swellings, aches, and painting." (margin note)

2 "In that extremity of misery which ours since sustained, I have been told that both the savages and fugitives would object our want and their plenty [to be] for theirs and against our religion." (margin note)

3 "Declaration of Virginia." (margin note)

12. John Smith

A True Relation
of such occurrences and accidents of note as hath hap'ned in Virginia since the first planting of that colony which is now resident in the south part thereof, till the last return from thence. Written by Captain Smith, one of the said colony, to a worshipful friend of his in England.

(London: printed for John Tappe, and are to be sold at the Greyhound in Paul's Churchyard by W. W., 1608)

< **Smith 1608,** Arber 1884, Barbour 1969:165, Barbour 1986a:23

This is Smith's account of the period December 1606 to the spring of 1608.

The map and manuscript of *A True Relation,* in the form of a personal letter to a "kind sir," left for England aboard the *Phoenix* on 2 June 1608. Smith was aboard until off Cape Henry when he was lowered over the side in a two ton barge with fourteen men to begin his first exploration of the Chesapeake Bay (§17–254ff). His letter was published later in the year without his knowledge and much cut up by a self-appointed editor.

Among the cuts, the deepest and the only one that has since been restored is the map (pp. 152–53). In the 19th century, the historian and indefatigable searcher Alexander Brown discovered a pen and ink manuscript map in the Simancas Archives in Spain. It had been sent from London to Spain in a diplomatic dispatch in September 1608 by Don Pedro de Zuñiga, the Spanish ambassador there. It is a crude illustration of the milieu of our text. Areas north of the York River have not yet been explored and are drawn by conjecture and information supplied by the Indians.

Smith had opportunity to restore his text in his later works. Instead he waxes fuller in one episode only to lapse into more brevity in another, such that there are details found in the tatters of *A True Relation* not found in *A Map of Virginia, The Proceedings of the English Colony,* or *The General History §16, 17.*

I have studied the facsimile of the British Library text presented in Barbour

1986:32–96, which contains notes in the margin in a very early but unknown hand, most of which are critical and helpful. I include some of them and identify them in footnotes as n., followed by the material in quotation according to Barbour's restorations in places where the rebound margin has been clipped.

Editorial cuts in the text clumsy enough to spot are shown […]. All are according to Barbour, but he suggests more.

TO THE COURTEOUS READER—

COURTEOUS, kind, and indifferent readers, whose willingness to read and hear this following discourse doth explain to the world your hearty affection to the prosecuting and furtherance of so worthy an action, so it is that like to an unskillful actor, who having by misconstruction of his right cue overslip'd himself in beginning of a contrary part, and fearing the hateful hiss of the captious multitude, with a modest blush retires himself in private, as doubting the reprehension of his whole audience in public, and yet, again, upon further deliberation, thinking it better to know their censures at the first and upon submission to reap pardon than by seeking to smother it to incur the danger of a secret scandal, emboldening himself upon the courteous kindness of the best, and not greatly respecting the worst, comes forth again, makes an apology for himself, shows the cause of his error, craves pardon for his rashness, and in fine receives a general applaudity of the whole assembly.

So I, gentle readers, happening upon this relation by chance, as I take it, at the second or third hand, induced thereunto by divers well-willers of the action (and none wishing better towards it than myself), so far forth as my poor ability can or may stretch to, I thought good to publish it.

But the author being absent from the press, it cannot be doubted but that some faults have escaped in the printing, especially in the names of countries, towns, and people, which are somewhat strange unto us. But most of all, and which is the chief error, for want of knowledge of the writer, some of the books were printed under the name of Thomas Watson—by whose occasion I know not unless it were the overrashness or mistaking of the workmen. But since having learned that the said discourse was written by Captain Smith, who is one of the council there in Virginia, I thought good to make the like apology by showing the true author, so far as myself could learn, not doubting but that the wise, noting it as an error of ignorance, will pass it over with patience; and if worthy an applaudity, to reserve it to the author whose pains, in my judgment, deserveth commendations.

Somewhat more was by him written which, being, as I thought, fit to be private, I would not adventure to make it public. What more may be expected concerning the situation of the country, the nature of the clime, number of our people there resident, the manner of their government and living, the commodities to be produced, and the end and effect it may come to—I can say nothing more than is here written, only [that] what I have learned and gathered from the general consent of all that I have conversed withal, as well mariners as others which have had employment that way, is that the country is excellent and pleasant, the clime temperate and healthful, the ground fertile and good, the commodities to be expected, if well followed, many for our people—the worst being already past, these former having endured the heat of the day, whereby those that shall succeed may at ease labor for their profit in the most sweet, cool, and temperate shade—the action most honorable, and the end to the high glory of God, to the erecting of true religion among infidels, to the overthrow of superstition and idolatry, to the winning of many thousands of wand'ring sheep unto Christ's fold, who now and till now have strayed in the unknown paths of paganism, idolatry, and superstition. Yea, I say the action being well followed, as by the grave senators and worthy adventurers it hath been worthily begun, will tend to the everlasting renown of our nation and to the exceeding good and benefit of our weal public in general, whose councils, labors, [and] godly and industrious endeavors I beseech the mighty Jehovah to bless, prosper, and further with His heavenly aid and holy assistance.

Farewell.
I. H.[1]

[1] Perhaps John Healey. Thomas Watson was the likely addressee.

A True Relation

of such Occurrences and Accidents of Note as hath hap'ned in Virginia since the First Planting of that Colony which is now resident in the South Part thereof, till the Last Return.

KIND SIR—Commendations rememb'red, etc.

You shall understand that after many crosses in the Downs by tempests, we arrived safely upon the southwest part of the Great Canaries [...]

Within four or five days after, we set sail for Dominica [...]

The 26 of April, the first land we made, we fell with Cape Henry, the very mouth of the Bay of Chissiapiacke, which at that present we little expected, having by a cruel storm been put to the northward.

Anchoring in this bay, twenty or thirty went ashore with the captain, and in coming aboard they were assaulted with certain Indians, which charged them within pistol shot, in which conflict Captain Archer and Mathew Morton were shot. Whereupon Captain Newport, seconding them, made a shot at them, which the Indians little respected, but having spent their arrows retired without harm.

And in that place was the box opened wherein the council for Virginia was nominated [...]

And arriving at the place where we are now seated, the council was sworn, the president elected—which for that year was Master Edward Maria Wingfield [...] where was made choice for our situation a very fit place for the erecting of a great city, [but] about which some contention passed betwixt Captain Wingfield and Captain Gosnold. Notwithstanding, all our provision was brought ashore, and with as much speed as might be we went about our fortification.

The two and twenty day of April,[1] Captain Newport and myself,

[1] Rather May 21, 1607.

with divers others to the number of twenty-two persons, set forward to discover the river some fifty or sixty miles, finding it in some places broader and in some narrower, the country for the most part on each side plain high ground with many fresh springs, the people in all places kindly entreating us, dancing, and feasting us with strawberries, mulberries, bread, fish, and other their country provisions, whereof we had plenty, for which Captain Newport kindly requited their least favors with bells, pins, needles, beads, or glasses, which so contented them that his liberality made them follow us from place to place, and ever kindly to respect us.

In the midway staying to refresh ourselves in a little isle, four or five savages came unto us which described unto us the course of the river. And after, in our journey, they often met us, trading with us for such provision as we had. And arriving at Arsatecke, he whom we supposed to be the chief king of all the rest most kindly entertained us, giving us in a guide to go with us up the river to Powhatan (of which place their great emperor taketh his name), where he that they honored for king used us kindly.

But to finish this discovery, we passed on further where within an isle[1] we were intercepted with great craggy stones that [stand] in midst of the river, where the water falleth so rudely and with such a violence as not any boat can possibly pass; and so broad disperseth the stream as there is not past five or six foot at a low water, and to the shore scarce passage with a barge. The water floweth four foot; and the freshes[2] by reason of the rocks have left marks of the inundations 8 or 9 foot. The south side is plain low ground and the north side high mountains, the rocks being of a gravelly nature, interlaced with many veins of glist'ring spangles.

That night we returned to Powhatan; the next day, being Whitsunday,[3] after dinner we returned to the falls, leaving a mariner in pawn with the Indians for a guide of theirs. He that they honored for king followed us by the river. That afternoon we trifled in looking upon the rocks and river. Further he would not go, so there we erected a cross. And that night taking our man at Powhatan's, Captain

---

[1] Likely a misprint for "within a mile."

[2] Freshets.

[3] May 24, 1607.

Newport congratulated his kindness with a gown and a hatchet; returning to Arsetecke, and stayed there the next day to observe the height thereof; and so with many signs of love we departed.

The next day, the Queen of Agamatuck kindly entreated us, her people being no less contented than the rest. And from thence we went to another place, the name whereof I do not remember, where the people showed us the manner of their diving for mussels, in which they find pearls.

That night passing by Weanock, some twenty miles from our fort, they according to their former churlish condition seemed little to affect us. But as we departed and lodged at the point of Weanocke, the people the next morning seemed kindly to content us. Yet we might perceive many signs of a more jealousy in them than before.

And also the hind[1] that the King of Arseteck had given us altered his resolution in going to our fort, and with many kind circumstances left us there. This gave us some occasion to doubt some mischief at the fort, yet Captain Newport intended to have visited Paspahegh and Tappahanocke.[2] But the instant change of the wind being fair for our return, we repaired to the fort with all speed, where the first we heard was that 400 Indians the day before had assaulted the fort and surprised it. Had not God beyond all their expectations, by means of the ships at whom they shot with their ordnances and muskets, caused them to retire, they had ent'red the fort with our own men, which were then busied in setting corn, their arms being then in dryfats[3] and few ready but certain gentlemen of their own; in which conflict most of the council was hurt, a boy slain in the pinnace, and thirteen or fourteen more hurt.

With all speed we palisadoed our fort. Each other day for six or seven days we had alarums by ambuscadoes, and four or five cruelly wounded by being abroad. The Indians' loss we know not but as they report three were slain and divers hurt. [...]

Captain Newport, having set things in order, set sail for England the 22 of June, leaving provision for 13 or 14 weeks.

---

[1] Servant. Archer gives his name as Nauirans.

[2] n. "Quiocqahannock."

[3] Large barrels or boxes.

The day before the ships' departure, the King of Pamaunke sent the Indian that had met us before in our discovery to assure us peace, our fort being then palisadoed round and all our men in good health and comfort; albeit that through some discontented humors it did not so long continue, for the president and Captain Gosnold, with the rest of the council, being for the most part discontented with one another, insomuch that things were neither carried with that discretion nor any business effected in such good sort as wisdom would nor our own good and safety required thereby; and through the hard dealing of our president, the rest of the council being diversly affected through his audacious command; [...] and for Captain Martin, albeit very honest and wishing the best good, yet so sick and weak; and myself so disgrac'd through others' malice—through which disorder God being angry with us plagued us with such famine and sickness that the living were scarce able to bury the dead—our want of sufficient and good victuals, with continual watching four or five each night at three bulwarks, being the chief cause. Only of sturgeon we had great store, whereon our men would so greedily surfeit as it cost many their lives—the sack, aqua vitae, and other preservatives for our health being kept only in the president's hands for his own diet and his few associates. [...] Shortly after, Captain Gosnold fell sick and within three weeks died—Captain Ratcliffe being then also very sick and weak, and myself having also tasted of the extremity thereof, but by God's assistance being well recovered.

Kendall about this time for divers reasons [was] deposed from being of the council.

And shortly after, it pleased God in our extremity to move the Indians to bring us corn, ere it was half ripe,[1] to refresh us when we rather expected when they would destroy us.[2]

---

[1] I.e., corn on the cob.

[2] n. "Choapock: weeroance of the Quiocquahanocks did always at our greatest need supply us with victuals of all sorts, which he did notwithstanding the continual wars which we had in the rest of his country, and upon his deathbed charged his people that they should forever keep good quiet with the English. Pippisco now weeroance doth not forget his predecessor's testament."

About the tenth of September, there was about 46 of our men dead; at which time Captain Wingefield having ord'red the affairs in such sort that he was generally hated of all, in which respect, with one consent, he was deposed from his presidency and Captain Ratcliffe according to his course[1] was elected.

Our provision being now within twenty days spent, the Indians brought us great store both of corn and bread ready-made. And also there came such abundance of fowls into the rivers as greatly refreshed our weak estates, whereupon many of our weak men were presently able to go abroad.

As yet we had no houses to cover us, our tents were rotten, and our cabins worse than nought. [...] Our best commodity was iron which we made into little chisels, [...]

The president and Captain Martin's sickness constrained me to be cape merchant, and yet to spare no pains in making houses for the company who, notwithstanding our misery, little ceased their malice, grudging, and muttering. As at this time were most of our chiefest men either sick or discontented, the rest being in such despair as they would rather starve and rot with idleness than be persuaded to do anything for their own relief without constraint [...] our victuals being now within eighteen days spent, and the Indians' trade decreasing, I was sent to the mouth of the river to Kegquouhtan,[2] an Indian town, to trade for corn and try the river for fish. But our fishing we could not effect by reason of the stormy weather.

The Indians, thinking us near famished, with careless kindness off'red us little pieces of bread and small handfuls of beans or wheat for a hatchet or a piece of copper. In the like manner I entertained their kindness and in like scorn offered them like commodities. But the children, or any that showed extraordinary kindness, I liberally contented with free gift such trifles as well contented them.

Finding this cold comfort, I anchored before the town, and the next day returned to trade. But God the absolute disposer of all hearts altered their conceits, for now they were no less desirous of our commodities than we of their corn. Under color to fetch fresh

---

[1] As the last surviving ship's captain.

[2] n. "Keequotancke, Musquasone, Fort Henrie and Fort Charles."

water, I sent a man to discover the town, their corn, and force, to try their intent in that they desired me up to their houses, which well understanding with four shot I visited them. With fish, oysters, bread, and deer they kindly traded with me and my men, being no less in doubt of my intent than I of theirs, for well I might with twenty men have freighted a ship with corn.

The town containeth eighteen houses pleasantly seated upon three acres of ground upon a plain, half environed with a great bay of the great river, the other part with a bay of the other river falling into the great bay, with a little isle fit for a castle in the mouth thereof, the town adjoining to the main by a neck of land of sixty yards. [...]

With sixteen bushels of corn I returned towards our fort. By the way I encount'red with two canoes of Indians who came aboard me, being the inhabitants of Waraskoyack, a kingdom on the south side of the river, which is in breadth 5 miles and 20 mile or near from the mouth. With these I traded, who having but their hunting provision requested me to return to their town where I should load my boat with corn. And with near thirty bushels I returned to the fort, the very name whereof gave great comfort to our despairing company.

Time thus passing away, and having not above 14 days' victuals left, some motions were made about our president's and Captain Archer's going for England to procure a supply; in which meantime we had reasonably fitted us with houses, and our president and Captain Martin being able to walk abroad, with much ado it was concluded that the pinnace and barge should go towards Powhatan[1] to trade for corn. Lots were cast who should go in her: The chance was mine.

And while she was a-rigging, I made a voyage to Topohanack, where arriving there was but certain women and children who fled from their houses; yet at last I drew them to draw near. Truck they durst not, corn they had plenty, and to spoil I had no commission.

In my return to Paspahegh, I traded with that churlish and treacherous nation. Having loaded 10 or 12 bushels of corn, they off'red[2] to take our pieces and swords, yet by stealth. But [with our] seeming

---

[1] The village.
[2] Attempted.

to dislike it, they were ready to assault us. Yet standing upon our guard in coasting the shore, divers out of the woods would meet with us with corn and trade. But lest we should be constrained either to endure overmuch wrong or directly fall to revenge, seeing them dog us from place to place, it being night and our necessity not fit for wars [wares?], we took occasion to return with 10 bushels of corn. Captain Martin after made 2 journeys to that nation of Paspahegh, but each time returned with [only] 8 or 10 bushels.

All things being now ready for my journey to Powhatan, for the performance thereof I had 8 men and myself for the barge, as well for discovery as trading; the pinnace [with] 5 mariners and 2 landmen to take in our ladings at convenient places.

The 9 of November, I set forward for the discovery of the country of Chikhamania, leaving the pinnace the next tide to follow and stay for my coming at Point Weanock, 20 miles from our fort.

The mouth of this river falleth into the great river at Paspahegh, 8 miles above our fort. That afternoon I stayed the ebb in the bay of Paspahegh with the Indians. Towards the evening, certain Indians hailed me. One of them being of Chikahamania off'red to conduct me to his country; the Paspahegheans grudged thereat.

Along we went by moonlight; at midnight he brought us before his town, desiring one of our men to go up with him, whom he kindly entertained and returned back to the barge. The next morning, I went up to the town and showed them what copper and hatchets they should have for corn, each family seeking to give me most content. So long they caused me to stay that 100 at least was expecting my coming by the river with corn. What I liked I bought; and lest they should perceive my too great want, I went higher up the river.

This place is called Manosquosick,[1] a quarter of a mile from the river, containing thirty or forty houses upon an exceeding high land. At the foot of the hill towards the river is a plain wood watered with many springs, which fall twenty yards right down into the river.

---

[1] n. "They moch[mocked?] him, for the name of it is Woo[ze]niuck." Perhaps not if we assume a gap in the text preceding this paragraph. But the objection does agree with both Smith maps.

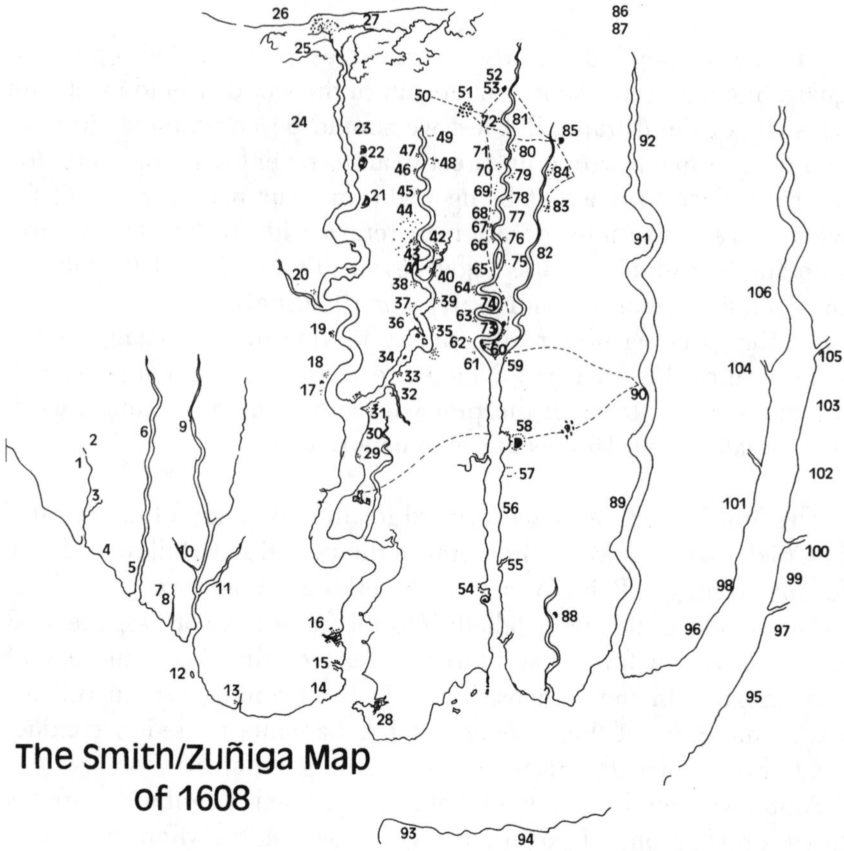

The Smith/Zuñiga Map of 1608

1 pakerakanick
2 here remayne the 4 men clothed that came from roonock to okanahowan
3 rawcoteck
4 aumocawnunt
5 morattico
6 machemenchecock
7 here the king of paspahegh reported our men to be and went to se
8 panawieck
9 ocanahowan
10 uttawmussawone
11 chawwone
12 raonock
13 nihamaock
14 chissapiack
15 nansamund
16 here paspahegh and 2 of our men landed to go to panawieck
17 Tapohanock
18 mantapoyek
19 weanock
20 appamatuck
21 arssateck
22 powhatan
23 monacan 2 days lorney
24 monahassanuck
25 being the south sea
26 amongst theis rocks
27 hear the salt water beateth into the rever

28 kequoughtan
29 namqosick
30 paspahegh
31 cinquaoteck
32 marinough
33 mattapanient
34 Chickahomania
35 ozanieck
36 mansa
37 opahaock
38 mamanahunt
39 werawahone
40 askakip
41 mosonek
42 qosaugh
43 chosicks
44 paspanigh
45 roghtacut *or* yoghtacut
46 nechanicock
47 mattahunt
48 attamuspinck
49 apocant
50 20 miles aboue this C[aptain] S[mith] ~~xxxx~~ was taken
51 rassaweck
52 2 days lorney
53 maskunt
54 kiskieck
55 cantaunkack
56 capohowoseck
57 wighsakan
58 warawocomo[
59 mamanasi
60 cinquaoteck
61 oquonock
62 mattchamins
63 potawunkack
64 weanock
65 pamakeroy
66 righkahauck
67 shamapint
68 parokonosko
69 matunsk
70 manaskunt
71 youghtanan
72 menoughtass
73 manapacunt
74 accossomwinck
75 osamkateck
76 opawnkack
77 askecocack
78 cakkiptaco
79 washasatiack
80 askecack
81 enekent
82 mattapanient
83 amacauncock
84 quacohamaock
85 matoughquaend
86 pocoughtawonauck
87 a saluag people Dwelling vpon this seay beyond this mayne that eateth men & women
88 payankatank
89 moraughtacut
90 Toppohanock
91 nantaughtacun
92 manahocks
93 accawmack
94 accuohack
95 kuskarawaock
96 onamient
97 attamaunk
98 cinquaoteck
99 pokaomonekent
100 pawtuxunt
101 oquotaunk
102 nuntawineck
103 cinquamaxsunt
104 patawomeck
105 moyoonch
106 Tanxesint

The dotted line shows the route Smith was taken as a captive.

Right against the same is a great marsh of 4 or 5 miles circuit, divided in 2 islands by the parting of the river, abounding with fish and fowl of all sorts. A mile from thence is a town called Oraniocke. I further discovered the towns of Mansa, Apanaock, Werawahone, and Mamanahunt, at each place kindly used, especially at the last, being the heart of the country, where were assembled 200 people with such abundance of corn as having laded our barge as also I might have laded a ship.

I returned to Paspahhegh, and considering the want of corn at our fort, it being night, with the ebb by midnight I arrived at our fort where I found our pinnace run aground. [...] The next morning I unladed seven hogsheads into our store.

The next morning I returned again; the second day I arrived at Mamanahunt, where the people, having heard of my coming, were ready with 3 or 400 baskets little and great; of which having laded my barge, with many signs of great kindness I returned.

At my departure they requested me to hear our pieces, being in the midst of the river, which in regard of the echo seemed a peal of ordnance (many birds and fowls they see us daily kill) that much feared them.

So desirous of trade were they that they would follow me with their canoes and for anything give it me rather than return it back. So I unladed again 7 or 8 hogsheads at our fort.

Having thus by God's assistance gotten good store of corn notwithstanding, some bad spirits, not content with God's providence, still grew mutinous insomuch that our president, having occasion to chide the smith for his misdemeanor, he not only gave him bad language but also off'red to strike him with some of his tools, for which rebellious act the smith was by a jury condemned to be hanged. But being upon the ladder, continuing very obstinate, as hoping upon a rescue, when he saw no other way but death with him, he became penitent and declared a dangerous conspiracy, for which Captain Kendall as principal was by a jury condemned and shot to death.

This conspiracy appeased, I set forward for the discovery of the

River of Checka Hamania. This third time I discovered the towns of Matapamient, Morinogh, Ascacap, Moysenock, Righkahauck, Nechanichock, Mattalunt, Attamuspincke, and divers others.[1] Their plenty of corn I found decreased. Yet, lading the barge, I returned to our fort.

Our store being now indifferently well provided with corn, there was much ado for to have the pinnace go for England, against which Captain Martin and myself standing chiefly against it, and in fine after many debatings pro et contra, it was resolved to stay a further resolution.

This matter also quieted, I set forward to finish this discovery, which as yet I had neglected in regard of the necessity we had to take in provision whilst it was to be had. 40 miles I passed up the river, which for the most part is a quarter of a mile broad and 3 fathom and a half deep, exceeding oozy, many great low marshes, and many high lands, especially about the midst at a place called Moysonicke,[2] a peninsule of 4 miles circuit betwixt two rivers, joined to the main by a neck of 40 or 50 yards, and 40 or 50 yards from the high water mark. On both sides in the very neck of the main are high hills and dales, yet much inhabited, the isle declining in a plain fertile cornfield, the lower end a low marsh. More plenty of swans, cranes, geese, ducks and mallards, and divers sorts of fowls none would desire. More plain fertile planted ground in such great proportions as there I had not seen, of a light black sandy mould; the cliffs commonly red, white, and yellow-colored sand, and under, red and white clay; fish great plenty, and people abundance, the most of their inhabitants in view of the neck of land, where a better seat for a town cannot be desired.

At the end of forty miles this river environeth many low islands at each high water drowned for a mile, where it uniteth itself at a place called Apokant, the highest town inhabited. 10 miles higher I discovered with the barge. In the midway a great tree hind'red my passage, which I cut in two. Here the river became narrower—8, 9,

[1] n. "The naturals much abused him, for there is not such a name for any town in all the country saving the first, Matapanient."
[2] n. "No such town."

or 10 foot at a high water, and 6 or 7 at a low—the stream exceeding swift and the bottom hard channel, the ground most part a low plain, sandy soil. This occasioned me to suppose it might issue from some lake or some broad ford, for it could not be far to the head. But rather than I would endanger the barge, yet to have been able to resolve this doubt—and to discharge the imputation of malicious tongues that half suspected I durst not for so long delaying (some of the company as desirous as myself)—we resolved to hire a canoe and return with the barge to Apocant, there to leave the barge secure, and put ourselves upon the adventure, the country only a vast and wild wilderness and but only that town.

Within three or four mile we hired a canoe and 2 Indians to row us the next day a-fowling. Having made such provision for the barge as was needful, I left her there to ride with express charge not any to go ashore till my return.

Though some wise men may condemn this too bold attempt of too much indiscretion, yet if they well consider the friendship of the Indians in conducting me, the desolateness of the country, the probability of some lake, and the malicious judges of my actions at home, as also to have some matters of worth to encourage our adventurers in England, might well have caused any honest mind to have done the like, as well for his own discharge as for the public good.

Having 2 Indians for my guide and 2 of our own company, I set forward, leaving 7 in the barge. Having discovered 20 miles further in this desert, the river still kept his depth and breadth, but much more cumb'red with trees. Here we went ashore, being some 12 miles higher than the barge had been, to refresh ourselves.

During the boiling of our victuals, one of the Indians I took with me to see the nature of the soil, and to cross the boughts of the river; the other Indian I left with Master Robbinson[1] and Thomas Emry, with their matches light and order to discharge a piece for my retreat at the first sight of any Indian. But within a quarter of an hour I heard a loud cry and a holloing of Indians, but no warning piece. Supposing them surprised, and that the Indians had betray'd us, [...]

---

[1] Awarded £100 damages for slander by Wingfield (§13–193).

presently I seized him and bound his arm fast to my hand in a garter, with my pistol ready bent to be revenged on him. He advised me to fly, and seemed ignorant of what was done. But as we went discoursing, I was struck with an arrow on the right thigh, but without harm. Upon this occasion I espied 2 Indians drawing their bows, which I prevented in discharging a French pistol.

By that I had charged again,[1] 3 or 4 more did the like, for the first fell down and fled. At my discharge they did the like. My hind I made my barricado, who offered not to strive. 20 or 30 arrows were shot at me, but short. 3 or 4 times I had discharged my pistol ere the King of Pamaunck, called Opeckankenough,[2] with 200 men environed me, each drawing their bow [...] which done they laid them upon the ground, yet without shot.

My hind treated betwixt them and me of conditions of peace. He discovered me to be the captain. My request was to retire to the boat; they demanded my arms. The rest they said were slain, only me they would reserve. The Indian importuned me not to shoot. In retiring, being in the midst of a low quagmire, and minding them more than my steps, I step'd fast into the quagmire, and also the Indian in drawing me forth. Thus surprised, I resolved to try their mercies: My arms I cast from me, till which none durst approach me. Being seized on me, they drew me out and led me to the king.

I presented him with a compass dial, describing by my best means the use thereof, whereat he so amazedly admired as he suffered me to proceed in a discourse of the roundness of the earth, the course of the sun, moon, stars, and planets. With kind speeches and bread he requited me, conducting me where the canoe lay and John Robbinson slain, with 20 or 30 arrows in him. Emry I saw not, [...] I perceived by the abundance of fires all over the woods, [...]

At each place I expected when they would execute me, yet they used me with what kindness they could, approaching their town, which was within 6 miles where I was taken, only made as arbors and covered with mats, which they remove as occasion requires.

All the women and children, being advertised of this accident,

---

[1] I.e., "By the time I reloaded"

[2] n. "Apachancka[no] was indeed weeraonce but not King of Pa[wm]unckett: for his brother Powh[atan] the emperor was king of that p[lace? people?]."

came forth to meet them, the king well guarded with 20 bowmen, 5 flank and rear, and each flank before him a sword and a piece, and after him the like, then a bowman, then I, on each hand a bowman, the rest in file in the rear; which rear led forth amongst the trees in a *bishion,*[1] each his bow and a handful of arrows, a quiver at his back, grimly painted; on each flank a sergeant, the one running always towards the front, the other towards the rear, each a true pace and in exceeding good order. This being a good time continued, they cast themselves in a ring with a dance, and so each man departed to his lodging, the captain conducting me to his lodging.

A quarter of venison and some ten pound of bread I had for supper. What I left was reserved for me and sent with me to my lodging. Each morning 3 women presented me three great platters of fine bread; more venison than ten men could devour I had. My gown, points and garters, my compass, and a tablet they gave me again. Though 8 ordinarily guarded me, I wanted not what they could devise to content me. And still our longer acquaintance increased our better affection.

Much they threat'ned to assault our fort, as they were solicited by the King of Paspahegh,[2] who showed at our fort great signs of sorrow for this mischance. [...]

The king took great delight in understanding the manner of our ships and sailing the seas, the earth and skies, and of our God. What he knew of the dominions he spared not to acquaint me with, as of certain men clothed at a place called Ocanahonan,[3] clothed like me, the course of our river, and that within 4 or 5 days' journey of the Falls was a great turning of salt water.

I desired he would send a messenger to Paspahegh with a letter I would write, by which they should understand how kindly they used me and that I was well, lest they should revenge my death. This he granted and sent three men in such weather as in reason were unpossible by any naked to be endured.

Their cruel minds towards the fort I had diverted in describing the

---

1 *Bissone* in the *General History,* apparently from Italian *biscione,* "big snake," apparently a military evolution?

2 n. "[W]awinckapunck King of Paspaheygh."

3 n. "as of certain men at a place 6 days' journey beyond Oconahonan."

ordnance and the mines in the fields, as also the revenge Captain Newport would take of them at his return. Their intent I incerted [?incensed = informed] the fort, […] the people of Ocanahonum, and the back sea. This report they after found divers Indians that confirmed.

The next day after my letter, came a savage to my lodging with his sword to have slain me, but being by my guard intercepted. With a bow and arrow he off'red to have effected his purpose. The cause I knew not till the king, understanding thereof, came and told me of a man a-dying, wounded with my pistol. He told me also of another I had slain, yet the most concealed they had any hurt. This was the father of him I had slain, whose fury to prevent, the king presently conducted me to another kingdom upon the top of the next northerly river, called Youghtanan.[1]

Having feasted me, he further led me to another branch of the river, called Mattapament. To two other hunting towns they led me, and to each of these countries a house of the great emperor of Powhatan, whom as yet I supposed to be at the Falls. To him I told him I must go, and so return to Paspahegh. After this four or five days' march, we returned to Rasawrack, the first town they brought me to, where binding the mats in bundles they marched two days' journey and crossed the River of Youghtanan where it was as broad as Thames, so conducting me to a place called Menapacute in Pamaunke, where the king inhabited.

The next day, another king of that nation, called Kekataugh, having received some kindness of me at the fort, kindly invited me to feast at his house. The people from all places flocked to see me, each showing to content me.

By this the great king hath four or five houses, each containing fourscore or an hundred foot in length, pleasantly seated upon an high sandy hill from whence you may see westerly a goodly low country, the river before the which his crooked course causeth many great marshes of exceeding good ground. An hundred houses and many large plains are here together inhabited. More abundance of fish and fowl and a pleasanter seat cannot be imagined.

---

[1] The Pamunkey River.

The king with forty bowmen to guard me entreated me to discharge my pistol, which they there presented me with, a mark at sixscore to strike therewith. But to spoil the practice I broke the cock, whereat they were much discontented, though a chance supposed.

From hence this kind king conducted me to a place called Topahanocke, a kingdom upon another river northward. The cause of this was that the year before a ship had been in the River of Pamaunke,[1] who having been kindly entertained by Powhatan, their emperor, they returned thence and discovered the river of Topahanocke, where being received with like kindness, yet he slew the king and took off his people, and they supposed I were he. But the people reported him a great man that was captain.[2] And using me kindly, the next day we departed.

This River of Topahanock seemeth in breadth not much less than that we dwell upon. At the mouth of the river is a country called Cuttatawomen; upwards is Marraughtacum, Tapohanock, Appamatuck, and Nantaugstacum; at [the] top, Manahocks,[3] the head issuing from many mountains.

The next night I lodged at a hunting town of Powhatam's, and the next day arrived at Waranacomoco upon the River of Pamauncke, where the great king is resident. By the way we passed by the top of another little river which is betwixt the two, called Payankatank. The most of this country though desert [is] yet exceeding fertile, good timber, most hills and dales, in each valley a crystal spring.

Arriving at Werawocomoco, their emperor proudly lying upon a bedstead a foot high, upon ten or twelve mats, richly hung with many chains of great pearls about his neck, and covered with a great covering of *rahaughcums*[4]; at his head sat a woman, at his feet another, on each side sitting upon a mat upon the ground were ranged his chief men on each side the fire, ten in a rank, and behind them as many young women, each a great chain of white beads over their

---

[1] The York River.

[2] A tall man. Smith was short.

[3] The beginning of this phrase is written "at Topmanahocks."

[4] Raccoon pelts. n. "Made of a beast called a *raracoone,* the skin very well dressed and artificially sewed together."

shoulders, their heads painted in red, and [he] with such a grave and majestical countenance as drave me into admiration to see such state in a naked savage.

He kindly welcomed me with good words and great platters of sundry victuals, assuring me his friendship and my liberty within four days. He much delighted in Opechan Comough's relation of what I had described to him and oft examined me upon the same. He asked me the cause of our coming. I told him, being in fight with the Spaniards our enemy, being overpow'red, near put to retreat, and by extreme weather put to this shore, where landing at Chesipiack the people shot us, but at Kequoughtan they kindly used us: We by signs demanded fresh water; they described us up the river was all fresh water. At Paspahegh also they kindly used us: Our pinnace being leak, we were enforced to stay to mend her till Captain Newport, my father, came to conduct us away.[1] He demanded why we went further with our boat. I told him in that I would have occasion to talk of the back sea: that on the other side the main, where was salt water, my father had a child slain, which we supposed Monocan his enemy had done, whose death we intended to revenge.

After good deliberation, he began to describe me the countries beyond the Falls, with many of the rest, confirming what not only Opechancanoyes and an Indian which had been prisoner to Powhatan had before told me, but some called it five days, some six, some eight, where the said water dashed amongest many stones and rocks, each storm which caused ofttimes the head of the river to be brackish. Anchanachuck he described to be the people that had slain my brother, whose death he would revenge. He described also upon the same sea a mighty nation called Pocoughtronack, a fierce nation that did eat men and warred with the people of Moyaoncer and Pataromerke, nations upon the top of the head of the bay under his territories, where the year before they had slain an hundred. He signified their crowns were shaven, long hair in the neck tied on a knot, swords like poleaxes. Beyond them he described people with short coats and sleeves to the elbows, that passed that way in ships

[1] Jamestown was in the territory of Paspahegh.

like ours.

Many kingdoms he described me to the head of the bay, which seemed to be a mighty river issuing from mighty mountains betwixt the two seas. The people clothed at Ocamahowan he also confirmed, and the southerly countries also, as the rest that reported us to be within a day and a half of Mangoge, two days of Chawwonock, 6 from Roonock, to the south part of the back sea. He described a country called Anone where they have abundance of brass and houses walled as ours.

I requited his discourse—seeing what pride he had in his great and spacious dominions, seeing that all he knew were under his territories—in describing to him the territories of Europe, which was subject to our great king, whose subject I was, [and] the innumerable multitude of his ships. I gave him to understand the noise of trumpets and terrible manner of fighting [which] were under Captain Newport, my father, whom I entituled the *meworames*,[1] which they call "king of all the waters." At his greatness he admired and not a little feared. He desired me to forsake Paspaliegh and to live with him upon his river, a country called Capa Howasicke; he promised to give me corn, venison, or what I wanted to feed us; hatchets and copper we should make him, and none should disturb us. This request I promised to perform.

And thus having with all the kindness he could devise sought to content me, he sent me home with 4 men—one that usually carried my gown and knapsack after me, two other loaded with bread, and one to accompany me.

This River of Pamaunke is not past twelve mile from that we dwell on, his course northwest and westerly, as the other. Weraocomoco is upon salt water in breadth two miles, and so keepeth his course without any tarrying some twenty miles, where at the parting of the fresh water and the salt it divideth itself into two parts, the one part to Goughland,[2] as broad as Thames and navigable with a boat threescore or fourscore miles, and with a ship fifty, exceeding crooked

---

[1] Werowance?

[2] Youghtanund?

and many low grounds and marishes, but inhabited with abundance of warlike and tall people.

The country of Youghtomam [is] of no less worth, only it is lower, but all the soil a fat, fertile, sandy ground. Above Manapacumter [are] many high sandy mountains. By the river is many rocks seeming if not of several mines.

The other branch [is] a little less in breadth, yet extendeth not near so far, nor so well inhabited, somewhat lower and a white sandy and a white clay soil. Here is their best terra sigillata.

The mouth of the river,[1] as I see in the discovery thereof with Captain Newport, is half a mile broad, and within four miles not above a musket shot, the channel exceeding good and deep, the river straight to the divisions; Kiskirk the nearest nation to the entrances.

Their religion and ceremony I observed was thus:

Three or four days after my taking, seven of them in the house where I lay, each with a rattle, began at ten o'clock in the morning to sing about the fire, which they environed with a circle of meal, and after, a foot or two from that, at the end of each song, laid down two or three grains of wheat, continuing this order till they have included six or seven hundred in a half circle; and after that two or three more circles in like manner, a hand breadth from other. That done, at each song they put betwixt every three, two, or five grains a little stick, so counting as an old woman her paternoster. One disguised with a great skin, his head hung round with little skins of weasels and other vermin, with a crownet of feathers on his head, painted as ugly as the devil, at the end of each song will make many signs and demonstrations with strange and vehement actions. Great cakes of deer suet, deer, and tobacco he casteth in the fire. Till six o'clock in the evening their howling would continue ere they would depart.

Each morning, in the coldest frost, the principal to the number of twenty or thirty assembled themselves in a round circle a good distance from the town, where they told me they there consulted where to hunt the next day. So fat they fed me that I much doubted

---

[1] The York River.

they intended to have sacrificed me to the *quiyoughquosicke,* which is a superior power they worship. A more uglier thing cannot be described. One they have for chief sacrifices, which also they call *quiyoughquosick.*

To cure the sick, a man with a rattle and extreme howling, shouting, singing, and such violent gestures and antic actions over the patient will suck out blood and phlegm from the patient out of their unable [navel?], stomach, or any diseased place, as no labor will more tire them.

Tobacco they offer [to] the water in passing in foul weather.

The death of any they lament with great sorrow and weeping. Their kings they bury betwixt two mats within their houses, with all his beads, jewels, hatchets, and copper; the other in graves like ours. They acknowledge no resurrection. [1]

Powhatan hath three brethren and two sisters. Each of his brethren succeeded other. For the crown their heirs inherit not, but the first heirs of the sisters, and so successively the women's heirs. For the kings have as many women as they will, his subjects two, and most but one.

From Weramocomoco is but 12 miles, yet the Indians trifled away that day and would not go to our fort by any persuasions. But in certain old hunting houses of Paspahegh we lodged all night.

The next morning ere sunrise, we set forward for our fort, where we arrived within an hour, where each man with the truest signs of joy they could express welcomed me, except Master Archer and some 2 or 3 of his, who was then in my absence sworn councilor, though not with the consent of Captain Martin.

Great blame and imputation was laid upon me by them for the loss of our two men which the Indians slew, insomuch that they purposed to depose me. But in the midst of my miseries it pleased God to send Captain Nuport, who arriving there the same night[2] so

---

[1] n. "This author I find in many errors which they do impute to his not well understanding the language, for they do acknowledge both God and the devil, and that after they are out of this world they shall rise again in another world where they shall live at ease and have great store of bread and venison and other."

[2] January 2, 1608.

tripled our joy as for a while these plots against me were deferred, though with much malice against me, which Captain Newport in short time did plainly see. Now was Master Scrivener, Captain Martin, and myself called councilors.

Within five or six days after the arrival of the ship, by a mischance our fort was burned and the most of our apparel, lodging, and private provision. Many of our old men diseased and of our new for want of lodging perished.

The Emperor Powhatan each week once or twice sent me many presents of deer, bread, *raugroughcuns* [raccoons], half always for my father, whom he much desired to see, and half for me, and so continually importuned by messengers and presents that I would come to fetch the corn and take the country their king had given me,[1] as at last Captain Newport resolved to go see him.

Such acquaintance I had amongst the Indians and such confidence they had in me as near the fort they would not come till I came to them. Every of them, calling me by my name, would not sell anything till I had first received their presents, and what they had that I liked they deferred to my discretion. But after acquaintance they usually came into the fort at their pleasure. The president and the rest of the council they knew not, but Captain Newport's greatness I had so described as they conceived him the chief, the rest his children, officers, and servants.

We had agreed with the King of Paspahegh to conduct two of our men to a place called Panawicke, beyond Roonok, where he reported many men to be appareled [like me]. [...] We landed him at Warraskoyack, where playing the villain and deluding us for rewards, [he] returned within three or four days after without going further.

Captain Newport, Master Scrivener, and myself found the mouth of Pamauncks River some 25 or 30 miles northward from Cape

[1] Capahowasick.

Henrie, the channel good as before expressed.

Arriving at Weramocomoca, being jealous of the intent of this politic savage, to discover his intent the better I with 20 shot armed in jacks[1] went ashore. The bay where he dwelleth hath in it 3 creeks, and a mile and a half from the channel all ooze. Being conducted to the town, I found myself mistaken in the creek, for they all there were within less than a mile.

The emperor's son, called Naukaquawis, the captain that took me, and divers others of his chief men conducted me to their king's habitation. But in the midway I was intercepted by a great creek over which they had made a bridge of grained stakes and rails. The King of Kiskieck and Namontack, who all the journey the king had sent to guide us, had conducted us this passage, which caused me to suspect some mischief: The barge I had sent to meet me at the right landing. When I found myself first deceived, and knowing by experience the most of their courages to proceed from others' fear, though few liked the passage, I intermingled the king's son, our conductors, and his chief men amongst ours, and led forward, leaving half at the one end to make a guard for the passage of the front. The Indians, seeing the weakness of the bridge, came with a canoe and took me in off the middest with four or five more; being landed we made a guard for the rest till all were passed.

Two in a rank we marched to the emperor's house. Before his house stood forty or fifty great platters of fine bread. Being ent'red the house, with loud tunes they all made signs of great joy. This proud savage, having his finest women and the principal of his chief men assembled sat in ranks as before is expressed, [sat] himself as upon a throne at the upper end of the house with such a majesty as I cannot express nor yet have often seen either in pagan or Christian. With a kind countenance he bade me welcome and caused a place to be made by himself to sit. I presented him a suit of red cloth, a white greyhound, and a hat. As jewels he esteemed them, and with a great oration made by three of his nobles (if there be any amongst savages), kindly accepted them with a public confirmation of a perpetual league and friendship.

---

[1] "Leather quilted jackets, often plaited with iron." (Barbour)

After that he commanded the Queen of Apamatuc, a comely young savage, to give me water, a turkey cock, and bread to eat. Being thus feasted, he began his discourse to this purpose: "Your kind visitation doth much content me, but where is your father whom I much desire to see: Is he not with you?"

I told him he remained aboard, but the next day he would come unto him. With a merry countenance he asked me for certain pieces I which promised him[1] when I went to Paspahegh. I told [him] according to my promise that I proffered the man that went with me four demi-culverins, in that he so desired a "great gun"; but they refused to take them, whereat with a loud laughter he desired [me] to give him some of less burthen, as for the other I gave him them, being sure that none could carry them.[2] [...]

"But where are these men you promised to come with you?"

I told him without, who thereupon gave order to have them brought in, two after two, ever maintaining the guard without. And as they presented themselves ever with thanks, he would salute me, and caused each of them to have four or five pound of bread given them. This done, I asked him for the corn and ground he promised me. He told me I should have it, but he expected to have all these men lay their arms at his feet, as did his subjects. I told him that was a ceremony our enemies desired, but never our friends, as we presented ourselves unto him. Yet that he should not doubt of our friendship, the next day my father would give him a child of his in full assurance of our loves. And not only that, but when he should think it convenient, we would deliver under his subjection the country of Manacam and Pocoughtaonack, his enemies.

This so contented him as immediately, with [our] attentive silence, with a loud oration he proclaimed me a werowanes of Powhaton, and that all his subjects should so esteem us, and no man account us strangers nor Paspaheghans, but Powhatans, and that the corn, women, and country should be to us as to his own people. This proffered kindness for many reasons we contemned not, but with the best languages and signs of thanks I could express, I took my leave.

---

[1] I.e., "which I had promised him"

[2] A demi-culverin is a cannon weighing a couple of tons.

The king rising from his seat conducted me forth, and caused each of my men to have as much more bread as he could bear, giving me some in a basket, and as much he sent aboard for a present to my father. Victuals, you must know, is all their wealth and the greatest kindness they could show us.

Arriving at the river, the barge was fallen so low with the ebb [that it was aground] [...] Though I had given order and oft sent to prevent the same, yet the messengers deceived me. The skies being very thick and rainy, [...] the king understanding this mischance sent his son and Mamontack to conduct me to a great house sufficient to lodge me, where ent'ring I saw it hung round with bows and arrows.

The Indians used all diligence to make us fires and give us content. The king's orators presently entertained us with a kind oration, with express charge that not any should steal or take out bows or arrows, or offer any injury.

Presently after, he sent me a quarter of venison to stay my stomach. In the evening, he sent for me to come only with two shot with me. The company I gave order to stand upon their guard and to maintain two sentries at the ports all night. To my supper he set before me meat for twenty men, and seeing I could not eat he caused it to be given to my men. For this is a general custom that what they give, not to take again, but you must either eat it, give it away, or carry it with you.[1] Two or three hours we spent in our ancient discourses, which done, I was with a fire-stick lighted to my lodging.

The next day, the king conducting me to the river, showed me his canoes, and described unto me how he sent them over the bay for tribute beads, and also what countries paid him beads, copper, or skins. But seeing Captain Nuport and Master Scrivener coming ashore, the king returned to his house, and I went to meet him.

With a trumpet before him, we marched to the king, who after his old manner kindly received him, especially a boy of thirteen years old, called Thomas Salvage, whom he gave him as his son. He requited this kindness with each of us a great basket of beans. And entertaining him with the former discourse, we passed away that day and agreed to bargain the next day, and so returned to our pinnace.

---

[1] The Indians were not Indian givers.

The next day, coming ashore in like order, the king having kindly entertained us with a breakfast, questioned with us in this manner: why we came armed in that sort, seeing he was our friend and had neither bows nor arrows: What did we doubt?

I told him it was the custom of our country, not doubting of his kindness any ways. Wherewith, though he seemed satisfied, yet Captain Nuport caused all our men to retire to the waterside, which was some thirty score [paces] from thence. But to prevent the worst, Master Scrivener or I were either the one or other by the barge. Experience had well taught me to believe his friendship till convenient opportunity suff'red him to betray us. But quickly this politician had perceived my absence and cunningly sent for me; I sent for Master Scrivener to supply my place; the king would demand for him; I would again relieve him. And they sought to satisfy our suspicion with kind language, [...]

And not being agreed to trade for corn, he desired to see all our hatchets and copper together, for which he would give us corn. With that ancient trick the Chickahamaniens had oft acquainted me. His offer I refused, offering first to see what he would give for one piece. He, seeming to despise the nature of a merchant, did scorn to sell, but we freely should give him, and he liberally would requite us.

Captain Nuport would not with less than twelve great coppers[1] try his kindness, which he liberally requited with as much corn as at Chickahamania I had for one of less proportion. Our hatchets he would also have at his own rate, for which kindness he much seemed to affect Captain Nuport. Some few bunches of blue beads I had which he much desired; and seeing so few, he off'red me a basket of two pecks; and that which I drew to be three pecks at the least; and yet [he] seemed contented and desired more. I agreed with him the next day for two bushels, for the ebb now constrained us to return to our boat, although he earnestly desired us to stay dinner, which was a-providing. And being ready, he sent [it] aboard after us, which was bread and venison sufficient for fifty or sixty persons.

The next day, he sent his son in the morning [to tell us] not to bring ashore with us any pieces, lest his women and children should

---

1 "Large copper cooking pots used on shipboard." (Barbour)

fear. Captain Nuport's good belief would have satisfied that request, yet twenty or twenty-five shot we got ashore. The king importuning me to leave my arms aboard, much misliking my sword, pistol, and target, I told him the men that slew my brother with the like terms had persuaded me, and being unarmed shot at us and so betrayed us.

He oft entreated Captain Nuport that his men might leave their arms, which still he commanded to the waterside,[1] [...] This day we spent in trading for blue beads, and having near straighted [freighted] our barge. [...]

Captain Nuport returned, with them that came, aboard, leaving me and Master Scrivener ashore to follow in canoes. Into one I got with six of our men, which being launched a stone's cast from the shore stuck fast in the ooze. Master Scrivener, seeing this example, with seven or eight more passed the dreadful bridge, thinking to have found deeper water on the other creek. But they were enforced to stay with such entertainment as a savage, being forced ashore with wind and rain, having in his canoe, as commonly they have, his house and household, instantly set up a house of mats which succored them from the storm.

The Indians seeing me pest'red in the ooze called to me. Six or seven of the king's chief men threw off their skins and to the middle in ooze came to bear me out on their heads. Their importunacy caused me better to like the canoe than their courtesy, excusing my denial for fear to fall into the ooze, desiring them to bring me some wood, fire, and mats to cover me, and I would content them. Each presently gave his help to satisfy my request, which pains a horse would scarce have endured, yet a couple of bells richly contented them.

The emperor sent his seaman Mantiuas[2] in the evening with bread and victual for me and my men. He no more scripulous than the rest, seemed to take a pride in showing how little he regarded that miserable cold and dirty passage, though a dog would scarce have endured it. This kindness I found when I little expected less than a mischief. But the black night parting our companies, ere midnight

[1] I.e., which armed men Newport each time ordered to remain at the waterside.
[2] Error for "his son Naukaquawis"?

the flood [tide] served to carry us aboard.

The next day we came ashore, the king with a solemn discourse causing all to depart but his principal men, [...] and this was the effect whenas he perceived that we had a desire to invade Monacum, against whom he was no professed enemy, [...] yet thus far he would assist us in this enterprise. First, he would send his spies perfectly to understand their strength and ability to fight, with which he would acquaint us himself.

Captain Nuport would not be seen in it himself. Being great werowances, they would stay at home. But I, Master Scrivener, and two of his sons, and Opechankanough, the King of Pamaunke, should have 100 of his men to go before, as though they were hunting. They giving us notice where was the advantage, we should kill them. The women and young children he wished we should spare and bring them to him. Only 100 or 150 of our men he held sufficient for this exploit. Our boats should stay at the Falls, where we might hew timber which we might convey each man a piece till we were past the stones, and there join them [in rafts] to pass our men by water.[1] If any were shot, his men should bring them back to our boats. This fair tale had almost made Captain Nuport undertake by this means to discover the South Sea—which will not be without treachery if we ground our intent upon his [Powhatan's] constancy.

This day we spent in trading, dancing, and much mirth. The King of Pamaunke sent his messenger—as yet not knowing Captain Nuport—to come unto him who had long expected me, desiring also my father to visit him. The messenger stayed to conduct us, but Powhatan, understanding that we had hatchets lately come from Paspahegh, desired the next day to trade with us and [for us] not to go further.

This new trick he cunningly put upon him, but only to have what he listed, and to try whether we would go or stay. Opechankenough's messenger returned [to say] that we would not come. The next day his daughter came to entreat me, showing her father had hurt his leg, and much sorrowed he could not see me.

Captain Nuport, being not to be persuaded to go, in that Powhatan

---

1 The interpretation of this sentence differs from earlier printings.

had desired us to stay, sent her away with the like answer. Yet the next day, upon better consideration, entreaty prevailed and we anchored at Cinquoateck, the first town above the parting of the river, where dwelled two kings of Pamaunke, brothers to Powhatan, the one called Opitchapam, the other Katatough. To these I went ashore, who kindly entreated me and Master Scrivener, sending some presents aboard to Captain Nuport whilst we were trucking with these kings.

Opechankanough, his wife, women, and children came to meet me with a natural kind affection; he seemed to rejoice to see me.

Captain Nuport came ashore. With many kind discourses we passed that forenoon. And after dinner Captain Nuport went about with the pinnace to Menapacant, which is twenty miles by water and not one by land. Opechankanough conducted me and Master Scrivener by land where, having built a feasting house a-purpose to entertain us, with a kind oration after their manner and his best provision kindly welcomed us. That day he would not truck, but did his best to delight us with content. Captain Nuport arrived towards evening, whom the king presented with six great platters of fine bread, and *pansarowmana.*[1] The next day till noon we traded, the king feasted all the company, and the afternoon was spent in playing, dancing, and delight. By no means he would have us depart till the next day he had feasted us with venison, for which he had sent, having spent his first and second provision in expecting our coming. The next day, he performed his promise, giving more to us three than would have sufficed 30; and in that we carried not away what we left, he sent it after us to the pinnace. With what words or signs of love he could express, we departed.

Captain Nuport in the pinnace leaving me in the barge to dig a rock where we supposed a mine at Cinquaoteck, [...] which done, ere midnight I arrived at Weracomoco where our pinnace anchored, being 20 miles from Cinquaotecke.

The next day we took leave of Powhatan, who in regard of his kindness gave him an Indian he well affected to go with him for

---

[1] Virginia succotash. n. "Pansaromanans are accounted a very dainty dish amongst them, being made of the corn when it is green boiled and so mingled amongst beans and so kept all the year, which is when it is boiled, very sweet and wholesome meat."

England, instead of his son. The cause I assure me was to know our strength and country's condition.

The next day, we arrived at Kiskiack. The people so scornfully entertained us, as with what signs of scorn and discontent we could we departed and returned to our fort with 250 bushels of corn.

Our president, being not wholly recovered of his sickness, in discharging his piece brake and split his hand, of which he is not yet well recovered.

At Captain Nuport's arrival we were victualed for twelve weeks. And having furnished him of what he thought good, he set sail for England the tenth of April. Master Scrivener and myself with our shallop accompanied him to Captain Hendrick [Cape Henry]—Powhatan having for a farewell sent him five or six men's loadings with turkeys [in exchange] for swords, which he sent him.

In our return to the fort[1] we discovered the River of Nausamd [Nansemond], a proud, warlike nation, as well we may, testified at our first arrival at Chesiapiack.[2] But that injury Captain Nuport well revenged at his return, where some of them enticing him to their ambuscadoes by a dance, he, perceiving their intent, with a volley of musket shot slew one and shot one or two more, as themselves confess.

The king at our arrival sent for me to come unto him. I sent him word what commodities I had to exchange for wheat, and if he would as had the rest of his neighbors conclude a peace, we were contented. At last he came down before the boat which rid at anchor some forty yards from the shore. He signified to me to come ashore, and sent a canoe with four or five of his men, two whereof I desired to come aboard and to stay, and I would send two to talk with their king ashore; to this he agreed.

The king we presented with a piece of copper, which he kindly accepted and sent for victuals to entertain the messengers. Master Scrivener and myself also after that went ashore. The king kindly

---

[1] This phrase was joined to the former paragraph in earlier printings.

[2] Braided clauses: "We discovered as well as we could the river N., since it is home to a proud, warlike nation, testified at our first arrival …"

feasted us, requesting us to stay to trade till the next day; which having done, we returned to the fort.

This river is a musket-shot broad, each side being shoal bays, a narrow channel but three fadom, his course for eighteen miles almost directly south and by west, where beginneth the first inhabitants. For a mile it turneth directly east, towards the west a great bay and a white chalky island convenient for a fort; his next course south where, within a quarter of a mile, the river divideth in two, the neck a plain high cornfield, the wester bought a high plain likewise, the northeast answerable in all respects. In these plains are planted abundance of houses and people. They may contain 1000 acres of most excellent fertile ground, so sweet, so pleasant, so beautiful, and so strong a prospect for an invincible strong city with so many commodities, that I know as yet I have not seen. This is within one day's journey of Chawwonocke. The river falleth into the Kings River within twelve miles of Cape Hendicke [Henry].

At our fort the tools we had were so ordinarily stolen by the Indians as necessity enforced us to correct their braving thievery. For he that stole today durst come again the next day. One amongst the rest, having stolen two swords, I got the council's consent to set in the bilboes.

The next day, with three more, he came with their wooden swords in the midst of our men to steal. Their custom is to take anything they can seize of—only the people of Pamaunke we have not found stealing. But what others can steal, their king receiveth.

I bade them depart. But flourishing their swords they seemed to defend what they could catch but out of our hands. His pride urged me to turn him from amongst us, whereat he off'red to strike me with his sword, which I prevented, striking him first. The rest, off'ring to revenge the blow, received such an encounter, and fled. The better to affright them I pursued them with five or six shot, and so chased them out of the island—the beginning of this broil little expecting, by his carriage, we durst have resisted, having even till that present not been contradicted, especially them of Paspahegh.[1]

These Indians within one hour, having by other savages then in the fort understood that I threat'ned to be revenged, came presently of themselves and fell to working upon our wares, which were then in hand by other savages, who seeing their pride so encount'red were so submissive and willing to do anything as might be, and with trembling fear desired to be friends within three days after.

From Nawsamond, which is 30 miles from us, the king sent us a hatchet which they had stolen from us at our being there. The messenger, as is the custom, also we well rewarded and contented.

The twenty of April, being at work in hewing down trees and setting corn, an alarum caused us with all speed to take our arms, each expecting a new assault of the savages. But understanding it a boat under sail, our doubts were presently satisfied with the happy sight of Master Nelson, his many perils of extreme storms and tempests [passed]. His ship [was] well, as his company could testify, [and] his care in sparing our provision was well. But the providence thereof, as also of our stones, hatchets, and other tools, only ours excepted which of all the rest was most necessary, which might enforce us to think either a seditious traitor to our action or a most unconscionable deceiver of our treasures [...][2]

This [was a] happy arrival of Master Nelson in the *Phenix,* having been then about three months missing after Captain Nuport's arrival, being to all our expectations lost. Albeit that now at the last having been long crossed with tempestuous weather and contrary winds, his so unexpected coming did so ravish us with exceeding joy that now we thought ourselves as well fitted as our hearts could wish, both with a competent number of men as also for all other needful provisions till a further supply should come unto us.

Whereupon the first thing that was concluded was that myself and Master Scrivener should with 70 men go with the best means we

---

[1] n. "The Paspaheghs were always treacherous villains and ever shall be till they are captives."

[2] Cuts have garbled the passage until one can only guess the meaning: Nelson brought generous supplies, but missing were certain essentials, enough to signal treachery or wholesale embezzlement. He had wintered in the West Indies.

LIBRARY OF VIRGINIA

CAPTAIN JOHN SMITH

could provide to discover beyond the Falls, as in our judgment conveniently we might. Six or seven days we spent only in training our men to march, fight, and skirmish in the woods. These willing minds to this action so quick'ned their understanding in this exercise as in all judgments we were better able to fight with Powhatan's whole force in our order of battle amongst the trees (for thicks there is few) than the fort was to repulse 400 at the first assault with some ten or twenty shot, not knowing what to do, nor how to use a piece.

[But] our warrant being sealed, Master Nelson refused to assist us with the voluntary mariners and himself, as he promised, unless we would stand bound to pay the hire for ship and mariners for the time they stayed; and further there was some controversy through the diversity of the contrary opinions, some alleging that how profitable and to what good purpose soever our journey should portend, yet, our commission commanding no certain design, we should be taxed for the most indiscreet men in the world, besides the wrong we should do to Captain Nuport, to whom only all discoveries did belong, and to no other.

The means for guides beside the uncertain courses of the river, from which we could not err much, each night would fortify us in two hours better than that they first called the fort.[1] Their towns upon the river, each within one day's journey of other, besides our ordinary provision, might well be supposed to add relief for truck and dealing, only but in love and peace, as with the rest. If they assaulted us, their towns they cannot defend nor their luggage so convey that we should not share. But admit the worst, 16 days' provision we had of cheese, oatmeal, and biscuit, besides our rendezvous[2] we could and might have hid in the ground. With six men Captain Martin would have undertaken it himself,[3] leaving the rest to defend the fort and plant our corn. Yet no reason could be reason to proceed forward, though we were going aboard to set sail.

---

[1] The drift of Smith's chopped-up answer seems to be that, despite hazards, guides are available, and the party will keep to the river, and each night set up a more secure perimeter than even that of the first days at Jamestown. And so forth.

[2] Cache.

[3] n. "He that knows n[othing] fears nothing."

These discontents caused so many doubts to some and discouragement to others, as our journey ended. Yet some of us procured petitions to set us forward, [but] only with hope of our own confusions.

Our next course was to turn husbandmen: to fell trees and set corn. Fifty of our men we employed in this service; the rest kept the fort to do the command of the president and Captain Martin, [while] 30 days the ship lay expecting the trial of certain matters which for some cause I keep private.[1]

The next exploit was an Indian, having stolen an ax, was so pursued by Master Scrivener and them next him as he threw it down and flying drew his bow at any that durst encounter him. Within four or five days after, Master Scrivener and I being a little from the fort among the corn, two Indians, each with a cudgel and all newly painted with terra sigillata, came circling about me, as though they would have clubbed me like a hare. I knew their feigning love is towards me not without a deadly hatred, but to prevent the worst, I, calling Master Scrivener, retired to the fort.

The Indians, seeing me suspect them, with good terms asked me for some of their men whom they would beat, and went with me into our fort. Finding one that lay ordinarily with us only for a spy, they offered to beat him.[2] I in persuading them to forbear, they offered to begin with me, being now four—for two other arrayed in like manner came in on the other side the fort—whereupon I caused to shut the ports and apprehend them. The president and council being presently acquainted, rememb'ring at the first assault they came in like manner, and never else but against some villainy, concluded to commit them to prison and expect the event. Eight more we seized at that present. An hour after, came three or four other strangers extraordinarily fitted with arrows, skins, and shooting gloves. Their jealousy and fear bewrayed their bad intent, as also their suspicious departure.

The next day, came first an Indian, then another, as ambassadors for their men. They desired to speak with me. Our discourse was that what spades, shovels, swords, or tools they had stol'n to bring home;

---

1 Barbour suggests "I. H." is here concealing news of gold fever and Ratcliffe's "palace."
2 "The spy was Amocis." (Barbour)

if not the next day, they should hang. The next news was they had taken two of our men ranging in the woods (which mischief no punishment will prevent but hanging) and these they would should redeem their own 16 or 18, thus braving us to our doors. We desired the president and Captain Martin that afternoon to sally upon them, that they might but know what we durst to do; and at night man'd our barge and burnt their towns and spoiled and destroyed what we could; but they brought our men and freely delivered them. The president released one; the rest we brought well guarded to morning and evening prayers. Our men all in arms, their trembling fear then caused them to much sorrow which till then scoffed and scorned at what we durst do. The council concluded that I should terrify them with some torture to know if I could know their intent.

The next day, I bound one in [the ship's] hold to the mainmast and presenting six muskets with match in the cocks forced him to desire life to answer my demands. He could not, but one of his *comovodos*[1] was of the council of Paspahegh that could satisfy me. I releasing him out of sight, I affrighted the other first with the rack, then with muskets, which seeing, he desired me to stay and he would confess to this execution. Master Scrivener come, his discourse was to this effect that Paspahegh, the Chickahamanian, Youghtanum, Pamaunka, Mattapanient, and Kiskiack—these nations were all together a-hunting that took me; Paspahegh and Chicahamanya had intended to surprise us at work to have had our tools; Powhatan and all his would seem friends till Captain Nuport's return; that he had again his man, which he called Namontack, where with a great feast he would so enamor Captain Nuport and his men as they should seize on him, and the like traps would be laid for the rest.

This trap for our tools we suspected the chief occasion was four days before: Powhatan had sent the boy he had to us with many turkeys, to Master Scrivener and me, understanding I would go up into his countries to destroy them. And he doubted it the more in that I so oft practiced my men, whose shooting he heard to his own lodging, that much feared his wives and children. We sent him word we intended no such thing, but only to go to Powhatan to seek stones

---

[1] Co-movers, accomplices?

to make hatchets, except his men shoot at us, as Paspahegh had told us they would; which if they did shoot but one arrow, we would destroy them; and lest this mischief might happen, sent the boy to acquaint him thus much, and request him to send us Weanock, one of his subjects, for a guide.

The boy he returned back with his chest and apparel, which then we had given him, desiring another for him. The cause was he was practicing with the Chikahamanias, as the boy suspected some villainy by their extraordinary resort and secret conference from whence they would send him.

The boy we keep, now [that] we would send him many messengers and presents. The guide we desired he sent us, and withal requested us to return him, either the boy or some other. But none he could have. And that day these Indians were apprehended: His son with others that had loaded [lodged] at our fort returned and, being out of the fort, railed on me to divers of our men to be enemies to him and to the Chikamanias.

Not long after, Weanock, that had been with us for our guide, whom we kept to have conducted us in another journey, with a false excuse returned; and secretly after him Amocis the Paspaheyan, who always they kept amongst us for a spy, whom, the better to avoid suspicion, presently after, they came to beat away. These presumptions induced me to take any occasion not only to try the honesty of Amocis the spy but also the meaning of these cunning tricks of their Emperor of Powhatan, whose true meaning Captain Martin most confidently pleaded.[1]

The confession of Macanoe, which was the councilor of Paspahegh [...] first I, then Master Scrivener, upon their several examinations, found by them all confirmed, that Paspahegh and Chickahammania did hate us and intended some mischief; and who they were that took me; the names of them that stole our tools and swords; and that Powhatan received them they all agreed. Certain volleys of shot we caused to be discharged, which caused each other to think that their fellows had been slain.

---

[1] I.e., Martin wanted to trust Powhatan.

Powhatan, understanding we detained certain savages, sent his daughter, a child of ten years old, which not only for feature, countenance, and proportion much exceedeth any of the rest of his people, but for wit and spirit the only nonpareil of his country. This he sent by his most trusty messenger, called Rawhunt, as much exceeding in deformity of person, but of a subtle wit and crafty understanding. He with a long circumstance told me how well Powhatan loved and respected me and, in that I should not doubt any way of his kindness, he had sent his child, which he most esteemed, to see me, [and] a deer and bread besides for a present, desiring me that the boy might come again, which he loved exceedingly. His little daughter he had taught this lesson also: Not taking notice at all of the Indians that had been prisoners three days till that morning that she saw their fathers and friends come quietly, and [then] in good terms to entreat their liberty.

Opechaukanough sent also unto us that for his sake we would release two that were his friends, and for a token sent me his shooting glove and bracer—which the day our men was taken, upon separating himself from the rest a long time, entreated to speak with me, where in token of peace, he had preferred[1] me the same.

Now all of them, having found their peremptory conditions but to increase our malice, which they seeing us begin to threaten to destroy them, as familiarly as before, without suspicion or fear, came amongst us to beg liberty for their men. In the afternoon, they being gone, we guarded them as before to the church; and after prayer gave them to Pocahuntas, the king's daughter, in regard of her father's kindness in sending her. After having well fed them, as all the time of their imprisonment, we gave them their bows, arrows, or what else they had, and with much content sent them packing. Pocahuntas also we requited with such trifles as contented her to tell that we had used the Paspaheyans very kindly in so releasing them.

The next day, we had suspicion of some other practice for an ambuscado, but perfectly we could not discover it.

Two days after, a Paspaheyan came to show us a glistering mineral

[1] Proffered.

stone and with signs demonstrating it to be in great abundance like unto rocks. With some dozen more [men] I was sent to seek to dig some quantity, and the Indian to conduct me. But suspecting this some trick to delude us for to get some copper of us, or with some ambuscado to betray us, seeing him falter in his tale, being two miles on our way, [I] led him ashore where, abusing us from place to place and so seeking either to have drawn us with him into the woods or to have given us the slip, I showed him copper which I promised to have given him if he had performed his promise, but for his scoffing and abusing us I gave him twenty lashes with a rope and his bows and arrows, bidding him shoot if he durst, and so let him go.

In all this time our men being all or the most part well recovered, and we not willing to trifle away more time than necessity enforced us unto, we thought good for the better content of the adventurers in some reasonable sort to freight home Master Nelson with cedar wood, about which our men going with willing minds was in very good time effected, and the ship sent for England.

We now remaining being in good health, all our men well contented, free from mutinies, in love one with another, and as we hope in a continual peace with the Indians; where we doubt not but by God's gracious assistance, and the adventurers' willing minds and speedy furtherance to so honorable an action, in after times to see our nation to enjoy a country not only exceeding pleasant for habitation but also very profitable for commerce in general, no doubt pleasing to Almighty God, honorable to our gracious sovereign, and commodious generally to the whole kingdom.

FINIS

13. Edward Maria Wingfield

A Discourse of Virginia per Edward Maria Wingfilld

< **Lambeth Palace Library, MSS 250, 382–396;** American Antiquarian 1860a, Arber 1884a:lxxiv, Barbour 1969:213, Quinn 1979e:277

History judges him harshly. Virginia's first chief executive exhibits no qualities of leadership—noblesse without nobility. He returned to England after several months in jail fetters and disgrace, and drops out of history. Here is his apologia. It is a preliminary draft he must have submitted in some form to the Council of Virginia, though we do not know if he did, or if so, how or whether it was answered. We can only say that the sky did not fall upon his enemies.

The *Discourse* launches into a self-serving account of the long, hot summer of 1607, leading up to his removal from office on 10 September. Whatever dignity the man has till then he discards. Granted this is the style of a legal deposition, after long and due consideration, I have come to the conclusion Wingfield should have awarded Ratcliffe his spoonful of beer.

RIGHT WORSHIPFUL AND MORE WORTHY—

My due respect to yourselves, my allegiance (if I may so term it) to the Virginean action, [and] my good heed to my poor reputation thrust a pen into my hands, so jealous am I to be missing to any of them. If it wandereth in extravagance, yet shall they not be idle to those physicians whose loves have undertaken the safety and advancement of Virginia.

It is no small comfort that I speak before such gravity,[1] whose judgment no forerunner can forestall with any opprobrious untruth, whose wisdoms can easily disrobe malice out of her painted garments from the ever-reverenced truth.

I did so faithfully betroth my best endeavors to this noble enterprise as my carriage might endure no suspicion. I never turned my

[1] Persons of high rank.

face from danger or hid my hands from labor, so watchful a sentinel stood myself to myself.

I know well a troop of errors continually besiege men's actions, some of them seized on by malice, some by ignorance. I do not hoodwink my carriage in my self-love, but freely and humbly submit it to your grave censures.

I do freely and truly anatomize[1] the government and governors, that your experience may apply medicines accordingly, and upon the truth of this journal do pledge my faith and life, and so do rest,

Yours to command in all service. [no signature]

Here followeth what happened in James Town in Virginia after Captain Newport's departure for England.

CAPTAIN NEWPORT, having always his eyes and ears open to the proceedings of the colony, 3 or 4 days before his departure, asked the president[2] how he thought himself settled in the government—whose answer was that no disturbance could endanger him of the colony but it must be wrought either by Captain Gosnold or Master Archer. For the one was strong with friends and followers, and could if he would; and the other was troubled with an ambitious spirit, and would if he could. The captain gave them both knowledge of this the president's opinion, and moved them with many entreaties to be mindful of their duties to His Majesty and the colony.

June, 1607. The 22th, Captain Newport returned for England, for whose good passage and safe return we made many prayers to our Almighty God.

June the 25th, an Indian came to us from the Great Poughwaton with the word of peace, that he desired greatly our friendship, that the *wyroaunces* [werowances] Paspaheigh and Tapahanagh should be our friends, that we should sow and reap in peace or else he would make wars upon them with us. This message fell out true, for both those wyroaunces have ever since remained in peace and trade with

---

[1] Analyze, give an account of.

[2] Wingfield himself. He continues to refer to himself thus impersonally until his removal from office.

us. We rewarded the messenger with many trifles, which were great wonders to him.

This Powatan dwelleth 10 miles from us upon the River Pamaonche, which lieth north from us. The Powatan in the former journal mentioned (a dweller by Captain Newport's falls) is a wyroaunce and under this Great Powaton, which before we knew not.[1]

The 3 of July, 7 or 8 Indians presented the president a deer from Pamaonke, a wyroaunce desiring our friendship. They inquired after our shipping, which the president said was gone to Croatoon. They fear much our ships, and therefore he would not have them think it far from us. Their wyroance had a hatchet sent him; they were well contented with trifles.

A little after this came a deer to the president from the Great Powatan. He and his messengers were pleased with the like trifles. The president likewise bought divers times deer of the Indians, beavers, and other flesh, which he always caused to be equally divided amongst the colony.

About this time divers of our men fell sick; we missed above forty before September did see us, amongst whom was the worthy and religious gentleman, Captain Bartholmew Gosnold, upon whose life stood a great part of the good success and fortune of our government and colony. In his sickness time the president did easily foretell his own deposing from his command, so much differed the president and the other councilors on managing the government of the colony.

The seventh of July, Tapahanah, a wyroaunce dweller on Salisbury side, hailed us with the word of peace. The president with a shallop well manned went to him; he found him sitting on the ground crossed-legged, as is their custom, with one attending on him, which did often say, "This is the wyroance Tapahanah," which he did likewise confirm with stroking his breast. He was well enough known, for the president had seen him divers times before. His

[1] Tanxpowhatan, or "Little" Powhatan, Parahunt was the son of Great Powhatan and was the werowance of the village of Powhatan just below the falls of the James River.

countenance was nothing cheerful, for we had not seen him since he was in the field against us. But the president would take no knowledge thereof, and used him kindly, giving him a red waistcoat, which he did desire.

Tapahanah did inquire after our shipping; he received answer as before; he said his old store was spent, that his new was not at full growth by a foot; that as soon as any was ripe he would bring it, which promise he truly performed.

The—— of—— , Master Kendall was put off from being of the council, and committed to prison, for that it did manifestly appear he did practice to sow discord between the president and council.

Sickness had not now left us viable men in our town; God's only mercy did now watch and ward for us. But the president hid this our weakness carefully from the savages, never suff'ring them in all his time to come into our town.

The vith of September, Paspaheigh sent us a boy that was run from us. This was the first assurance of his peace with us, besides we found them no cannibals. The boy observed the men and women to spend the most part of the night in singing or howling, and that every morning the women carried all the little children to the river's sides. But what they did there he did not know.

The rest of the wyroanc[e]s do likewise send our men runagates to us home again, using them well during their being with them, so as now they being well rewarded at home at their return, they take little joy to travel abroad without passports.

The council demanded some larger allowance for themselves and for some sick their favorites, which the president would not yield unto without their warrants.

This matter was before propounded by Captain Martyn, but so nakedly as that he neither knew the quantity of the store to be but for xiii weeks and a half under the cape merchant's hand. He prayed them further to consider the long time before we expected Captain Newport's return, the incertainty of his return, if God did not favor his voyage, the long time before our harvest would be ripe, and the doubtful peace that we had with the Indians, which they would keep no longer than opportunity served to do us mischief.

It was then therefore ordered that every meal of fish or flesh should excuse the allowance for porridge, both against the sick and whole.

The council therefore, sitting again upon this proposition, instructed in the former reasons and order, did not think it fit to break the former order by enlarging their allowance, as will appear by the most voices ready to be showed under their hands.

Now was the common store of oil, vinegar, sack, and aqua vitae all spent, saving two gallons of each: the sack reserved for the communion table, the rest for such extremities as might fall upon us—which the president had only made know[n] to Captain Gosnold, of which course he liked well—the vessels were therefore bunged up. When Master Gosnold was dead, the president did acquaint the rest of the council with the said remnant; but Lord how they then longed for to sup up that little remnant! For they had now emptied all their own bottles and all other that they could smell out.

A little while after this, the council did again fall upon the president for some better allowance for themselves and some few the sick their privates.[1] The president protested he would not be partial, but if one had anything of him, every man should have his portion according to their places, nevertheless that upon their warrants he would deliver what pleased them to demand. If the president had at that time enlarged the proportion according to their request, without doubt in very short time he had starved the whole company. He would not join with them therefore in such an ignorant murder without their own warrant.

The president well seeing to what end their impatience would grow, desired them earnestly and oftentimes to bestow the presidentship among themselves, that he could obey—a private man—as well as they could command. But they refused to discharge him of the place, saying they mought not do it for that he did His Majesty good service in it.

---

[1] Favorites.

In this meantime, the Indians did daily relieve us with corn and flesh, that in three weeks the president had reared up xx men able to work. For as his store increased he mended the common pot. He had laid up besides provision for 3 weeks' wheat beforehand.

By this time the council had fully plotted to depose Wingfeild, the then president, and had drawn certain articles in writing amongst themselves, and took their oaths upon the Evangelists to observe them, th' effect whereof was first:
—To depose the then president;
—To make Master Ratcliff the next president;
—Not to depose the one th' other;
—Not to take the deposed president into council again;
—Not to take Master Archer into the council, or any other, without the consent of every one of them.

To these they had subscribed, as out of their own mouths at several times it was easily gathered.

Thus had they forsaken His Majesty's government set us down in the instructions, and made it a triumvirate.

It seemeth Master Archer was nothing acquainted with these articles, though all the rest crept out of his notes and commentaries that were preferred against the president. Yet it pleased God to cast him into the same disgrace and pit that he prepared for another, as will appear hereafter.

The 10 of September, Master Ratcliff, Master Smyth, and Master Martynn came to the president's tent with a warrant subscribed under their hands to depose the president, saying they thought him very unworthy to be either president or of the council, and therefore discharged him of both. He answered them that they had eased him of a great deal of care and trouble, that long since he had divers times proffered them the place at an easier rate, and further that the president ought to be removed (as appeareth in His Majesty's instructions for our government) by the greater number of xiii voices councilors; that they were but three, and therefore [he] wished them to proceed advisedly. *But they told him if they did him wrong, they must answer it.*[1] Then said the deposed president, "I am at your pleasure; dispose of me as you will without further garboil."[2]

I WILL NOW WRITE what followeth in my own name and give the new president his title. I shall be the briefer, being thus discharged.

I was committed to a sergeant and sent to the pinnace, but I was answered with [words to the effect] if they did me wrong they must answer it.

The 11th of September, I was sent for to come before the president and council upon their court day.

They had now made Master Archer recorder of Virginia. The president made a speech to the colony that he thought it fit to acquaint them why I was deposed. I am now forced to stuff my paper with frivolous trifles, that our grave and worthy council may the better strike those veins where the corrupt blood lieth, and that they may see in what manner of government the hope of the colony now travaileth.

First, Master President said that I had denied him a penny-whittle,[3] a chicken, a spoonful of beer, and served him with foul corn, and with that pulled some grain out of a bag, showing it to the company.

Then start up Master Smyth and said that I had told him plainly how he lied, and that I said though we were equal here, yet if he were in England he would think scorn [t]his man should be my companion.[4]

Master Martyn followed with, He reporteth that I do slack the service in the colony and do nothing but tend my pot, spit, and oven, [saying] "But he hath starved my son, and denied him a spoonful of beer. I have friends in England shall be revenged on him, if ever he come in London!"

I asked Master President if I should answer these complaints, and whether he had aught else to charge me withal. With that, he pulled out a paper-book loaded full with articles against me, and gave them

---

1 By a symbol in the margin it would seem Wingfield wants this underscored.

2 Wrangling? Also below.

3 Knife so worth.

4 Apparently, with a change, "I would think it scornful to make this man my companion." Cf. below.

Master Archar to read. I told Master President and the council that by the instructions for our government our proceedings ought to be verbal, *and I was there ready to answer.*[1] But they said they would proceed in that order. I desired a copy of the articles, and time given me to answer them likewise by writing, but that would not be granted. I bade them then please themselves.

Master Archer then read some of the articles, when on the sudden Master President said, "Stay, stay! We know not whether he will abide our judgment or whether he will appeal to the king," saying to me, "How say you? Will you appeal to the king or no?" I apprehended presently that God's mercy had opened me a way through their ignorance to escape their malice, for I never knew how I might demand an appeal. Besides, I had secret knowledge how they had forejudged me to pay fivefold for anything that came to my hands, whereof I could not discharge myself by writing, and that I should lie in prison until I had paid it.

The cape merchant had delivered me our merchandise without any note of the particularities under my hand, for himself had received them in gross. I likewise as occasion moved me spent them in trade or by gift amongst the Indians. So likewise did Captain Newport take of them, when he went up to discover the Kings River, what he thought good without any note of his hand mentioning the certainty, and disposed of them as was fit for him. Of these likewise I could make no account. Only I was well assured I had never bestowed the value of three penny-whittles to my own use nor to the private use of any other, for I never carried any favorite over with me or entertained any there: I was all one and one to all.

Upon these considerations I answered Master President and the council that His Majesty's hands were full of mercy, and that I did appeal to His Majesty's mercy. They then committed me prisoner again to the master of the pinnace with these words: "Look to him well: He is now the king's prisoner."

Then Master Archer pulled out of his bosom another paper-book full of articles against me, desiring that he might read them in the name of the colony. I said I stood there ready to answer any man's

[1] Margin symbol as above.

complaint whom I had wronged; but no one man spoke one word against me. Then was he willed to read his book, whereof I complained. But I was still answered [that] if they do me wrong they must answer it. I have forgotten the most of the articles, they were so slight (yet he glorieth much in his pen work!). [But] I know well the last; and a speech that he then made savored well of a mutiny. For he desired that by no means I might lie prisoner in the town, lest both he and others of the colony should not give such obedience to their command as they ought to do, which goodly speech of his they easily swallowed.

But it was usual and natural to this honest gent[leman] Master Archer to be always hatching of some mutiny. In my time he might have appeared an author of 3 several mutinies. And he, as Master Pearsie sent me word, had bought some witnesses' hands against me to [substantiate] divers articles,[1] [having bribed them] with Indian cakes, which was no great matter to do after my deposal, and considering their hunger [and his] persuasions and threats. At another time he feared not to say openly and in the presence of one of the council that if they had not deposed me when they did, he had gotten twenty others to himself which should have deposed me. But this speech of his was likewise easily disjested.[2]

Master Crofts feared not to say that if others would join with him, he would pull me out of my seat and out of my skin too.

Others would say (whose names I spare) that unless I would amend their allowance, they would be their own carvers.

For these mutinous speeches I rebuked them openly and proceeded no further against them, considering th' end of men's lives in his king's service there.

One of the council was very earnest with me to take a guard about me. I answered him I would no guard but God's love and my own innocency.

In all these disorders was Master Archer a ringleader.

When Master President and Master Archer had made an end of their articles above mentioned, I was again sent prisoner to the

---

[1] Charges.

[2] Disjected? Digested?

pinnace; and Master Kendall taken from thence had his liberty, but might not carry arms.

All this while the savages brought to the town such corn and flesh as they could spare. Paspaheighe by Tapahanae's mediation was taken into friendship with us. The councilors, Master Smyth especially, traded up and down the river with the Indians for corn, which relieved the colony well.

As I understand by report I am much charged with starving the colony, I did always give every man his allowance faithfully, both of corn, oil, aqua vitae, etc., as was by the council proportioned. Neither was it bettered after my time until towards th' end of March [1608] a biscuit was allowed to every working man for his breakfast, by means of the provision brought us by Captain Newport, as will appear hereafter.

It is further said I did much banquet and riot. I never had but one squirrel roasted, whereof I gave part to Master Ratcliff, then sick, yet was that squirrel given me. I did never heat a fleshpot but when the common pot was so used likewise. Yet how often Master President's and the councilors' spits have night and day been endangered to break their backs so laden with swans, geese, ducks, etc.!—how many times their fleshpots have swelled—many hungry eyes did behold to their great longing. *And what great thieves and thieving there hath been in the common store since my time,*[1] I doubt not but is already made known to His Majesty's council for Virginia.

The 17th day of September, I was sent for to the court to answer a complaint exhibited against me by Jehu Robinson[2] for that when I was president I did say he with others had consented to run away with the shallop to Newfound land; at another time I must answer Master Smyth for that I had said he did conceal an intended mutiny. I told Master Recorder those words would bear no actions, that one of the causes was done without the limits mentioned in the patent granted to us and therefore prayed Master President that I mought

---

[1] Margin symbol as above.

[2] Killed on the Chickahominy when Smith was captured (§12–156, 157).

not be thus lugged[1] with these disgraces and troubles. But he did wear no other eyes or ears than grew on Master Archer's head. The jury gave the one of them £100 and the other two hundred pound damages for slander.[2] Then Master Recorder did very learnedly comfort me that if I had wrong I might bring my writ of error in London; whereat I smiled.

I, seeing their law so speedy and cheap, desired justice for a copper kettle which Master Crofts did detain from me. He said I had given it him; I did bid him bring his proof for that; he confessed he had no proof; then Master President did ask me if I would be sworn I did not give it him; I said I knew no cause why to swear for mine own; he asked Master Crofts if he would make oath I did give it him; which oath he took, and won my kettle from me that was in that place and time worth half his weight in gold. Yet I did understand afterwards that he would have given John Capper the one half of the kettle to have taken the oath for him. But he would no copper on that price.

I told Master President I had not known the like law, and prayed they would be more sparing of law until we had more wit or wealth; that laws were good spies in a populous, peaceable, and plentiful country, where they did make the good men better and stayed the bad from being worse; that we were so poor as they did but rob us of time that might be better employed in service in the colony.

The—— day of——, the president did beat James Read the smith; the smith struck him again.[3] For this he was condempned to be hanged; but before he was turned off the lather he desired to speak with the president in private, to whom he accused Master Kendall of a mutiny, and so escaped himself. What indictment Master Recorder framed against the smith I know not, but I know it is familiar[4] for the president, councilors, and other officers to beat men at their pleasures. One lieth sick till death, another walketh lame, the third crieth

[1] Encumbered.

[2] It is hard believe any colonist, including Wingfield, had that much money with him in Virginia.

[3] I.e., the smith struck him back.

[4] Presuming on their authority.

out of all his bones, which miseries they do take upon their consciences to come to them by this their alms of beating. Were this whipping, lawing, beating, and hanging in Virginia known in England, I fear it would drive many well-affected minds from this honorable action of Virginia.

This smith, coming aboard the pinnace with some others about some business 2 or 3 days before his arraignment, brought me commendations from Master Pearsye, Master Waller, Master Kendall, and some others saying they would be glad to see me on shore. I answered him they were honest gentlemen and had carried themselves very obediently to their governors. I prayed God that they did not think of any ill thing unworthy [of] themselves. I added further that upon Sunday, if the weather were fair, I would be at the sermon. Lastly, I said that I was so sickly, starved, lame, and did lie so cold and wet in the pinnace as I would be dragged thither before I would go thither anymore. Sunday proved not fair; I went not to the sermon.

The day of——, Master Kendall was executed, being shot to death for a mutiny. In th' arrest of his judgment, he alleged to Master President that his name was Sicklemore, not Ratcliff, and so had no authority to pronounce judgment; then Master Martyn pronounced judgment.

Somewhat before this time, the president and council had sent for the keys of my coffers, supposing that I had some writings concerning the colony. I requested that the clerk of the council might see what they took out of my coffers, but they would not suffer him or any other. Under color hereof, they took my books of account and all my notes that concerned the expenses of the colony, and instructions under the cape merchant's hand of the store of provision, divers other books and trifles of my own proper goods, which I could never recover. Thus was I made good prize on all sides.

The—— day of——, the president commanded me to come on shore, *which I refused as not rightfully deposed,*[1] and desired that I mought speak to him and the council in the presence of 10 of the

[1] Margin symbol as above.

best sort of the gentlemen. With much entreaty some of them were sent for. Then I told them I was determined to go into England to acquaint our council there with our weakness; I said further their laws and government was such as I had no joy to live under them any longer; that I did much mislike their triumvirate having forsaken His Majesty's instructions for our government, and therefore prayed there might be more made of the council[1]; I said further I desired not to go into England if either Master President or Master Archer would go, but was willing to take my fortune with the colony; and did also proffer to furnish them with £100 towards the fetching home the colony, if the action was given over. They did like of none of my proffers, but made divers shot at me in the pinnace. I, seeing their resolutions, went ashore to them, where after I had stayed awhile in conference they sent me to the pinnace again.

The 10th of December [1607], Master Smyth went up the river of the Chechohomynaies to trade for corn. He was desirous to see the head of that river, and when it was not passable with the shallop, he hired a canoe and an Indian to carry him up further. The river the higher grew worse and worse. Then he went on shore with his guide, and left Robinson and Emmery, two of our men, in the canoe, which were presently slain by the Indians, Pamaonke's men, and he himself taken prisoner; and by the means of his guide his life was saved; and Pamaonche having him prisoner carried him to his neighbors wyroances to see if any of them knew him for one of those which had been some two or three years before us in a river amongst them northward and taken away some Indians from them by force; at last he brought him to the Great Powaton—of whom before we had no knowledge—who sent him home to our town the viiith of January [1608].[2]

---

[1] I.e., that it be enlarged to have more members than three.

[2] "The date is clearly written, but must be mistaken, since the fire took place afterwards, and that is dated the seventh of January. Newport *arrived* the day of Smith's return, which is clearly deducible from Perkins's letter as the second of January. Brown has guessed that the viiith should stand for the iiiith, but that is the day Newport *landed* his men. Wingfield's memory must have been at fault." (Barbour)

During Master Smythe's absence, *the president did swear Master Archer one of the council,*[1] contrary to his oath taken in the articles agreed upon between themselves (before spoken of) and contrary to the king's instructions, and without Master Martyn's consent, whereas there were no more but the president and Master Martyn then of the council.

Master Archer being settled in his authority sought how to call Master Smyth's life in question, and had indicted him upon a chapter in Leviticus for the death of his two men. He had had his trial the same day of his return and, I believe, his hanging the same or the next day, so speedy is our law there, but it pleased God to send Captain Newport unto us the same evening, to our unspeakable comforts; whose arrival saved Master Smyth's life and mine, because he took me out of the pinnace and gave me leave to lie in the town. *Also by his coming was prevented a parliament*[2] which the new councilor, Master Recorder, intended there to summon. Thus error begot error.

Captain Newport, having landed, lodged, and refreshed his men, employed some of them about a fair storehouse, others about a stove, and his mariners about a church, all which works they finished cheerfully and in short time.

The 7 of January, our town was almost quite burnt with all our apparel and provision. But Captain Newport healed our wants, to our great comforts, out of the great plenty sent us by the provident and loving care of our worthy and most worthy council.

This vigilant captain, slacking no opportunity that might advance the prosperity of the colony, having settled the company upon the former works, took Master Smyth and Master Scrivener—another councilor of Virginia, upon whose discretion liveth a great hope of the action—[and] went to discover the River Pamaonche[3] on the further side, whereof dwelleth the Great Powaton, and to trade with him for corn. This river lieth north from us and runneth east and west. I have nothing but by relation of that matter, and therefore

---

[1] Margin symbol as above.

[2] Margin symbol as above.

[3] The York River.

dare not make any discourse thereof lest I mought wrong the great desert which Captain Newport's love to the action hath deserved, especially himself being present and best able to give satisfaction thereof. I will hasten therefore to his return.

The 9th of March, he returned to James Town with his pinnace well loaden with corn, wheat, beans, and peas, to our great comfort and his worthy commendations.

By this time the council and captain, having intentively looked into the carriage both of the councilors and other officers, removed some officers out of the store and Captain Archer, a councilor, whose insolency did look upon that little in himself with great-sighted spectacles,[1] derogating from others' merits by spewing out his venomous libels and infamous chronicles upon them, as doth appear in his own handwriting; for which and other worse tricks he had not escaped the halter but that Captain Newport interposed his advice to the contrary.

Captain Newport, having now dispatched all his business and set the clock in a true course, if so the council will keep it, prepared himself for England upon the xth of April, and arrived at Blackwall on Sunday, the xxith of May, 1608.[2]

FINIS

I HUMBLY CRAVE some patience to answer many scandalous imputations which malice more than malice hath scattered upon my name, and those frivolous grievances objected against me by the president and council, and though *nil conscire sibi* [3] be the only mask that can well cover my blushes, yet do I not doubt but this my apology shall easily wipe them away.

It is noised that I combined with the Spaniards to the destruction of the colony; that I am an atheist because I carried not a Bible with

[1] A most early reference to the lens as an image magnifier.
[2] Sunday fell on the twenty-second.
[3] "Conscious of no wrong in oneself." (Latin: Horace, *Ep.* 1.1.61)

me and because I did forbid the preacher to preach; that I affected a kingdom; that I did hide of the common provision in the ground.

I confess I have always admired any noble virtue and prowess as well in the Spaniards as in other nations, but naturally I have always distrusted and disliked their neighborhood.

I sorted many books in my house to be sent up to me at my going to Virginia, amongst them a Bible. They were sent me up in a trunk to London, with divers fruit, conserves, and preserves, which I did set in Master Crofte his house in Ratcliff. In my being at Virginia, I did understand my trunk was there broken up, much of my sweetmeats eaten at his table, some of my books which I missed to be seen in his hands; and whether amongst them my Bible was so embezzled or mislaid by my servants, and not sent me, I know not as yet.

Two or three Sundays' mornings the Indians gave us alarums at our town. By that times they were answered, the place about us well discovered, and our divine service ended, the day was far spent. The preacher did ask me if it were my pleasure to have a sermon; he said he was prepared for it. I made answer that our men were weary and hungry, and that he did see the time of the day far past—for at other times he never made such question, but, the service finished, he began his sermon—and that if it pleased him, we would spare him till some other time. I never failed to take such notes by writing out of his doctrine as my capacity could comprehend, unless some rainy day hind'red my endeavor.

My mind never swelled with such impossible mountebank humors as could make me affect any other kingdom than the kingdom of heaven.

As truly as God liveth, I gave an old man, then the keeper of the private store, 2 glasses with salad oil which I brought with me out of England for my private store, and willed him to bury it in the ground, for that I feared the great heat would spoil it. Whatsoever was more I did never consent unto or knew of it. And as truly was it protested unto me that all the remainder before mentioned of the oil, wine, etc., which the president received of me when I was deposed, they themselves poured into their own bellies.

To the president's and council's objections I say that I do know courtesy and civility became a governor. No penny-whittle was asked me, but a knife, whereof I had none to spare: The Indians had long before stolen my knife. Of chickens I never did eat but one, and that in my sickness. Master Ratcliff had before that time tasted of 4 or 5. I had by my own housewifery bred above 37, and the most part of them of my own poultry, of all which at my coming away I did not see three living. I never denied him or any other beer when I had it; the corn was of the same which we all lived upon.

Master Smyth in the time of our hunger had spread a rumor in the colony that I did feast myself and my servants out of the common store, with intent, as I gathered, to have stirred the discontented company against me. I told him privately in Master Gosnold's tent that indeed I had caused half a pint of peas to be sodden with a piece of pork of my own provision for a poor old man, which in a sickness whereof he died he much desired, and said that if out of his malice he [Smith] had given it out otherwise, that he did tell a lie. It was proved to his face that he begged in Ireland like a rogue without license! To such I would not my name should be a companion!

Master Martin's pains during my command never stirred out of our town ten score; and how slack he was in his watching and other duties it is too well known. I never defrauded his son of anything of his own allowance, but gave him above it. I believe their disdainful usage and threats, which they many times gave me, would have pulled some distempered speeches out of far greater patience than mine, yet shall not any revenging humor in me befoul my pen with their base names and lives. Here and there I did visit Master Pearsie, Master Hunt, Master Brewster, Master Pickasse, Master Allicock, old Short the bricklayer, and divers others at several times—I never miscalled at[1] a gentleman at any time.

Concerning my deposing from my place, I can well prove that Master Ratcliff said if I had used him well in his sickness—wherein I find not myself guilty of the contrary—I had never been deposed.

Master Smith said if it had not been for Master Archer's [libels?] I had never been deposed. Since his being here in the town,[2] he hath said that he told the president and council that they were frivolous

[1] Reviled.
[2] In London.

objections they had collected against me and that they had not done well to depose me. Yet in my conscience[1] I do believe him the first and only practicer in these practices.

Master Archer's quarrel to me was because he had not the choice of the place for our plantation, because I misliked his laying out of our town in the pinnace, [and also] because I would not swear him of the council for Virginia, which neither I could do or he deserve.

—Master Smyth's quarrel because his name was mentioned in the intended and confessed mutiny by Galthropp.

—Thomas Wootton, the surgeon, because I would not subscribe to a warrant which he had gotten drawn to the treasurer of Virginia to deliver him money to furnish him with drugs and other necessaries, and because I disallowed his living in the pinnace, having many of our men lying sick and wounded in our town to whose dressings by that means he slacked his attendance.

Of the same men also Captain Gosnold gave me warning, misliking much their dispositions, and assured me they would lay hold of me if they could, and peradventure many because I held them to watching, warding, and working, and the colony generally because I would not give my consent to starve them.[2] I cannot rack one word or thought from myself touching my carriage in Virginia other than is herein set down.

If I may now at the last presume upon your favors, I am an ho[norable] suitor that your own love of truth will vouchsafe to clear me from all false aspersions happening since I embarked me into this affair of Virginia. For my first work, which was to make a right choice of a spiritual pastor, I appeal to the remembrance of my Lord of Canterbury his grace, who gave me very gracious audience in my request. And the world knoweth whom I took with me[3]: Truly, in my opinion, a man not any way to be touched with the rebellious humors of a popish spirit, nor blemished with the least suspicion of a factious schismatic, whereof I had a special care.

For other objections, if your worthy selves be pleased to set me

---

[1] Deepest suspicion.
[2] I.e., by allowing them advances on remaining supplies unless they gave warrants.
[3] Robert Hunt, the preacher.

free, I have learned to despise the popular verdict of the vulgar. I ever cheered up myself with a confidence in the wisdom of grave, judicious senators, and was never dismayed in all my service by any sinister event, though I bethought me of the hard beginnings which in former ages betided those worthy spirits that planted the greatest monarchies in Asia and Europe; wherein I observed rather the troubles of Moses and Aaron, with other of like history, than that venom in the mutinous brood of Cadmus, or that harmony in the sweet consent of Amphion.[1] And when with the former I had considered that even the brethren at their plantation of the Roman Empire were not free from mortal hatred and intestine garboil,[2] likewise that both the Spanish and English records are guilty of like factions, it made me more vigilant in the avoiding thereof. And I protest my greatest contention[3] was to prevent contention,[4] and my chiefest endeavor to preserve the lives of others, though with the great hazard of my own. For I never desired to enamel my name with blood.

I rejoice that my travels and dangers have done somewhat for the behoof of Jerusalem in Virginia. If it be objected as my oversight to put myself amongst such men, I can say for myself there were not any other for our consort; and I could not forsake the enterprise of opening so glorious a kingdom unto the king, wherein I shall ever be most ready to bestow the poor remainder of my days, as in any other His Highness' designs, according to my bounden duty with the utmost of my poor talent.

A discourse of Virginia per Edward Maria Wingfilld.

---

[1] Zethus and Amphion had jointly ruled Thebes in harmony. In a later generation, Oedipus' sons Eteocles and Polyneices began as joint rulers but soon fought each other for the city's throne

[2] Romulus and Remus. Garboil = wrangling? (as above).

[3] Striving.

[4] Strife.

14. Edward Maria Wingfield

Excerpt published in *Purchas His Pilgrimage*

< Purchas 1626:844

The subject is Indians. This is likely a quotation from a larger body of material now lost, and we have to thank Rev. Purchas for the tiny bit he saw fit to include in his *Pilgrimage,* both here and this on his page 946: "They speak of men two hundred years old and more, as Master Wingfield reporteth"—not quite, but on which subject see also 97–8 and 114.

My paragraphing assumes the statement "They are of modest behavior," insofar as it follows a full stop, returns to the description of the men.

MASTER WINGFIELD SAITH—They would be of good complexion if they would leave painting, which they use on their face and shoulders.

He never saw any of them gross[1] or bald. They would have beards but that they pluck away the hairs.

They have one wife, many loves, and are also Sodomites. Their elder women are cooks, barbers, and for service; the younger for dalliance. The women hang their children at their backs, in summer naked, in winter under a deerskin.

They are of modest behavior. They seldom or never brawl. In entertaining a stranger they spread a mat for him to sit down, and dance before him.

They wear their nails long to flay their deer.

They put bow and arrows into their children's hand before they are six years old.

---

[1] "Some of them are found such." (margin note in 1626 edition)

15. Peter Winne

Letter to Egerton, 26 November 1608

< **Huntington Library holograph: Jamestown Colony—Ellesmere Papers 1683;** Andrews 1934a:100/4, Wright 1946:9, Jones 1968:4, Barbour 1969:245

Here is the earliest of many such Welsh Indian reports that appear down the centuries, none of which has been substantiated, all of which today are dismissed, at the same time their existence at all is a most provocative mystery. After all, Winne did here apparently interpret Monacan. Other Welshmen were also surprised, I believe I recall, in the Carolinas, Kentucky, and the Dakota Territory on into the nineteenth century. Even William Strachey takes up the matter explicitly in his "Præmonition to the Reader" in the *History of Travel §41–577.*

MOST NOBLE KNIGHT—I was not so desirous to come into this country as I am now willing here to end my days. For I find it a far more pleasant and plentiful country than any report made mention of. Upon the river which we are seated I have gone six or seven score miles, and so far is navigable. Afterward I traveled between 50 or 60 miles by land into a country called Monacon, who owe no subjection to Powaton. This land is very high ground and fertile, being very full of very delicate springs of sweet water, the air more healthful than the place where we are seated, by reason it is not subject to such fogs and mists as we continually have.

The people of Monacon speak a far differing language from the subjects of Powaton, their pronunciation being very like Welch, so that the gentlemen in our company desired me to be their interpreter.

The commodities as yet known in this country, whereof there will be great store, is pitch, tar, soap-ashes, and some dyes, whereof we have sent examples. As for things more precious, I omit till time—which I hope will be shortly—shall make manifest proof of it.

As concerning your request of bloodhounds, I cannot learn that there is any such in this country; only the dogs which are here are a certain kind of curs like our warrener's hey-dogs[1] in England, and they keep them to hunt their land fowls, as turkeys and suchlike, for they keep nothing tame about them.

Hereafter I doubt not but to give you at large a farther relation than as yet I am able to do, and do therefore desire you to take these few lines in good part and hold me excused for the rest until fitter opportunity.

Thus commending my service to your good love with many thanks for all favors and kindnesses received from you, I do ever remain,

Your most devoted in all service,
PETER WYN

James Town in Virginia,
this XXVI of November [1608]

[endorsed:] Capt. Peter Wynne, Virginia: To the Honorable Knight, Sir John Egerton, at York House.

[1] Written "hey doggs," I am not sure what dog is meant.

16. John Smith

A Map of Virginia with a Description of the Country, the Commodities, People, Government, and Religion. Written by Captain Smith, sometimes Governor of the Country. (selections)

(at Oxford, printed by Joseph Barnes. 1612)

< Smith 1612

A True Relation had been brought out by others in 1608 while Smith was in Virginia. *A Map of Virginia* and *The Proceedings of the English Colony,* two books in one cover, were prepared and seen through the press by Smith himself in 1612 in England, three years after he had left Virginia. This time he goes to press half author, half compiler. He is the author of *A Map,* the compiler of *The Proceedings.*

Some of *A Map* is repeated in *The Proceedings.* But virtually all the text of *A Map* is duplicated in William Strachey's *History of Travel §41.* This is significant insofar as two acute observers and sojourners on the James River, but there at different times, confirm each other's information on so many points. How the two books came to be and who owes who, on the other hand, is a matter of pure speculation, to which, however, I succumb in commentary under §41. Nevertheless, an editor can hardly justify including the full text of both Smith *and* Strachey. And since the longer and fuller *History of Travel* contains the *Map* and not vice versa, Strachey's full text is given at §41 and drives out all of Smith's book except for these unique selections. Otherwise, a pregnant phrase here or there, a point made in addition—these the reader will find preserved in footnotes under the corresponding text in the *History of Travel.*

A Map is also duplicated in the Smith's *General History,* Second Book, published in 1624. In fact, the Second Book is hardly more than a second printing. The few places where it enlarges on *A Map* are included and noted here below.

So much for all that. Meanwhile, read *A Map of Virginia* and you learn to speak a new language. What a wonderful thing! What a good heart! The collection demonstrates Smith's considerable fluency in Powhatan, though it is a far from idiomatic transcription of an Algonquian language, based on what we know of other such. I include it and I include the prefatory material along with a bit under a fifth of the complete text. I identify it by the pagination in the 1612 edition.

The famous 1612 map of Virginia (opposite) first appeared in the binding of §16. It was to be reprinted many times by Smith himself and by others. It appears here with abbreviated detail. This editor has published his own reformatted version of it combined with names from the Smith/Zuñiga map.

Smith signs off with impressive salvoes at the dandies and fakes in Virginia that hardly leave the fort, but go home and slander the country, to set the stage for §17.

TO THE HAND

LEST I SHOULD WRONG any in dedicating this book to one, I have concluded it shall be particular to none. I found it only dedicated to a *hand*, and to that hand I address it. Now, for that this business is common to the world, this book may best satisfy the world, because it was penned in the land it treateth of.

If it be disliked of men, then I would recommend it to women, for being dearly bought and far-sought, it should be good for ladies. When all men rejected Christopher Collumbus, that ever-renowned Queen Izabell of Spain could pawn her jewels to supply his wants, whom all the wise men (as they thought themselves) of that age contemned. I need not say what was his worthiness, her nobleness, and their ignorance, that so scornfully did spit at his wants, seeing the whole world is enriched with his golden fortunes.

Cannot this successful example move the incredulous of this time to consider to conceive and apprehend Virginia, which might be, or breed us, a second India? Hath not England an Izabell as well as Spain? nor yet a Collumbus as well as Genua? Yes, surely it hath, whose desires are no less than was worthy Collumbus, their certainties more, their experiences no way wanting, only there wants but an Izabell, so it were not from *Spain!*

T[homas] A[bbay]

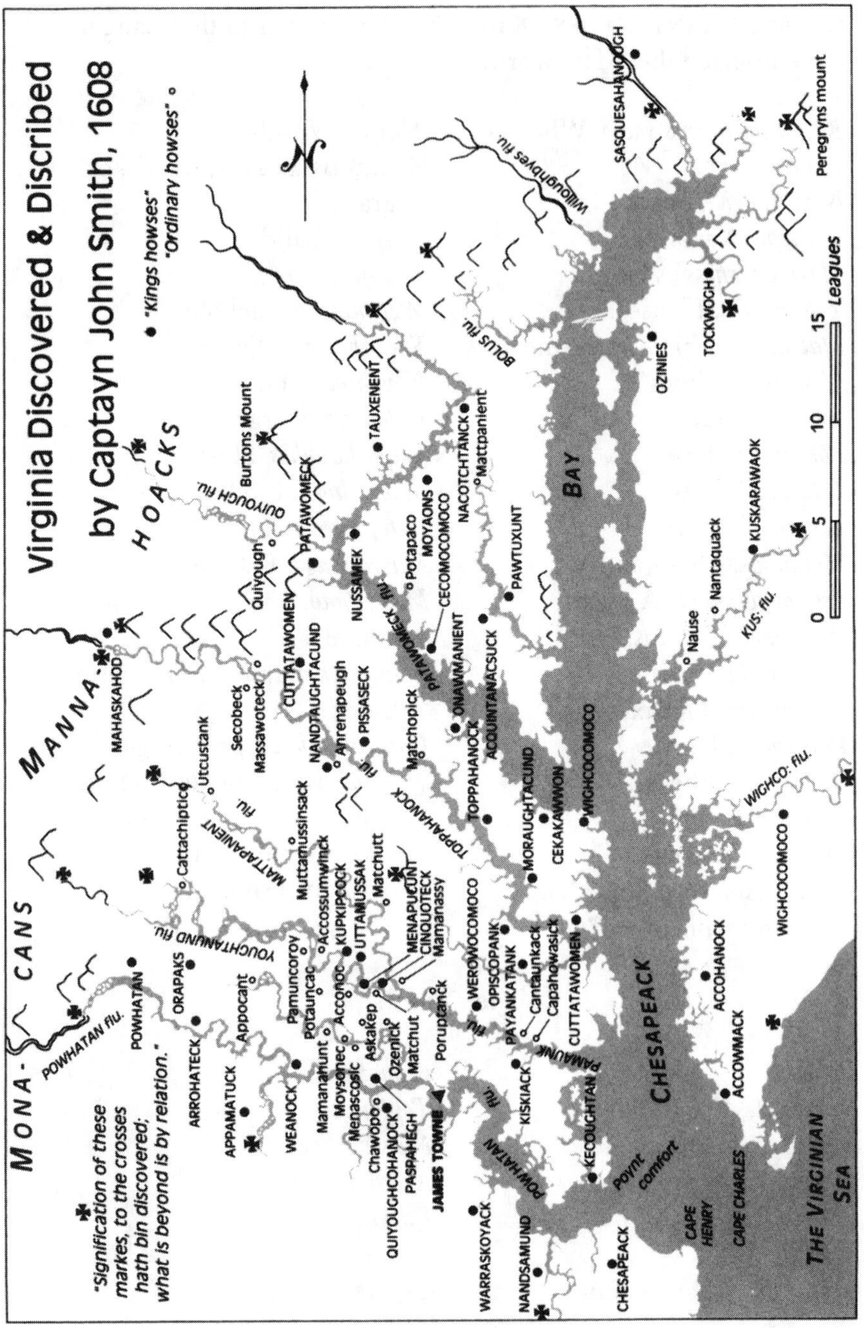
Virginia Discovered & Discribed
by Captayn John Smith, 1608
"Kings howses"
"Ordinary howses"
"Signification of these markes, to the crosses hath bin discovered; what is beyond is by relation."
MONA-CANS
MANNA-HOACKS
CHESAPEACK
BAY
THE VIRGINIAN SEA
POWHATAN flu.
YOUGHTANUND flu.
MATTAPANIENT flu.
TOPPAHANOCK flu.
PATAWOMECK flu.
QUIYOUGH flu.
BOLUS flu.
Willoughbyes flu.
KUS: flu.
WIGHCO: flu.
PAMAUNK flu.
POWHATAN flu.
Burtons Mount
Peregryns mount
SASQUESAHANOUGH
TOCKWOGH
OZINIES
KUSKARAWAOK
Nantaquack
Nause
WIGHCOCOMOCO
ACCOHANOCK
ACCOWMACK
CAPE CHARLES
CAPE HENRY
Poynt comfort
KECOUGHTAN
JAMES TOWNE
CHESAPEACK
NANDSAMUND
WARRASKOYACK
QUIYOUGHCOHANOCK
PASPAHEGH
POWHATAN
ARROHATECK
APPAMATUCK
WEANOCK
ORAPAKS
MAHASKAHOD
PATAWOMECK
TAUXENENT
NUSSAMEK
MOYAONS
NACOTCHTANCK
Mattpanient
CECOMOCOMOCO
Potapaco
PAWTUXUNT
ACQUINTANACSUCK
ONAWMANIENT
TOPPAHANOCK
MORAUGHTACUND
CEKAKAWWON
WIGHCOCOMOCO
CUTTATAWOMEN
WEROWOCOMOCO
KISKIACK
PAYANKATANK
OPISCOPANK
Cattachiptico
Utcustank
Secobeck
Massawoteck
Quiyough
CUTTATAWOMEN
NANDTAUGHTACUND
PISSASECK
Matchopick
Leagues
0
5
10
15

BECAUSE MANY DO DESIRE to know the manner of their language, I have inserted these few words.

Ka ka torawincs yowo. What call you this?
Nemarough. A man.
Crenepo. A woman.
Marowanchesso. A boy.
Yehawkans. Houses.
Matchcores. Skins, or garments.
Mockasins. Shoes.
Tussan. Beds.
Pokatawer. Fire.
Attawp. A bow.
Attonce. Arrows.
Monacookes. Swords.
Aumoughhowgh. A target.
Pawcussacks. Guns.
Tomahacks. Axes.
Tockahacks. Pickaxes.
Pamesacks. Knives.
Accowprets. Shears.
Pawpecones. Pipes.
Mattassin. Copper.
Ussawassin. Iron, brass, silver, or any white metal.
Musses. Woods.
Attasskuss. Leaves, weeds, or grass.
Chepsin. Land.
Shacquohocan. A stone.
Wepenter. A cuckold.
Suckahanna. Water.
Noughmass. Fish.
Copotone. Sturgeon.
Weghshaughes. Flesh.
Sawwehone. Blood.
Netoppew. Friends.
Marrapough. Enemies.
Maskapow. The worst of enemies.
Mawchick chammay. The best of friends.
Casacunnakack, peya quagh acquintan uttasantasough. In how many days will there come hither any more English ships?

Their numbers.

Necut. 1.
Ningh. 2.
Nuss. 3.
Yowgh. 4.
Paranske. 5.
Comotinch. 6.
Toppawoss. 7.
Nusswash. 8.
Kekatawgh. 9.
Kaskeke. [10]

They count no more but by tens as followeth—

Case, How many?
Ninghsapooeksku. 20.
Nussapooeksku. 30.
Yowghapooeksku. 40.
Parankestassapooeksku. 50.
Comatinchtassapooeksku. 60.
Nussswashtassapooeksku. 80.
Toppawousstassapooeksku. 70.
Kekataughtassapooeksku. 90.
Necuttoughtysinough. 100.
Necuttweunquaough. 1000.

Rawcosowghs. Days.
Keskowghes. Suns.
Toppquough. Nights.
Nepawweshowghs. Moons.
Pawpaxsoughes. Years.
Pummahumps. Stars.
Osies. Heavens.
Okes. Gods.
Quiyoughcosucks. Petty gods and their affinities.
Righcomoughes. Deaths.
Kekughes. Lives.
Mowchick woyawgh tawgh noeragh kaquere mecher. I am very hungry; what shall I eat?
Tawnor nehiegh Powhatan. Where dwells Powwahtan?
Mache, nehiegh yowrowgh, orapaks. Now, he dwells a great way hence at Orapaks.
Uttapitchewayne anpechitchs nehawper werowacomoco. You lie! He stay'd ever at Werowocomoco.
Kator nehiegh mattagh neer uttapitchewayne. Truly he is there; I do not lie.
Spaughtynere keragh werowance mawmarinough kekaten wawgh peyaquaugh. Run you then to the King Mawmarynough and bid him come hither.
Utteke, e peya weyack wighwhip. Get you gone, and come again quickly.
Kekaten pokahontas patiaquagh ningh tanks manotyens neer mowchick rawrenock audowgh. Bid Pokahontas bring hither two little baskets, and I will give her white beads to make her a chain.

FINIS

In the Second Book (24) Smith expands a paragraph in *A Map* that the reader will find at §41–606, 607. "Hatchets" will have been European trade hatchets of either French or English origin.

AT THE END OF THE BAY, where it is 6 or 7 miles in breadth, it divides itself into 4 branches. The best cometh northwest from among the mountains, but though canoes may go a day's journey or two up it, we could not get two miles up it with our boat for rocks. Upon it is seated the Sasquesahanocks. Near it north and by west runneth a creek a mile and a half, at the head whereof the eble [ebb] left us on shore, where we found many trees cut with hatchets. The next tide, keeping the shore to seek for some savages (for within thirty leagues sailing we saw not any, being a barren country), we went up another small river like a creek 6 or 7 mile. From thence returning we met 7 canoes of the Massowomeks, with whom we had conference by signs, for we understood one another scarce a word.

The next day we discovered the small river and people of Tockwhogh, trending eastward.

Having lost our grapnel among the rocks of Sasquesahanocks, we were then near 200 miles from home ...

In the Second Book (36) Smith expands a paragraph in *A Map* that the reader will find at §41–654.

THEY HAVE ALSO certain altar stones they call *pawcorances* ... and wildernesses, where they have had any extraordinary accident or encounter; and as you travel, at those stones they will tell you the cause why they were there erected, which from age to age they instruct their children as their best records of antiquities. Upon these they offer blood, deer suet ...

In the Second Book (38) Smith adds this sentence to the end of a paragraph in *A Map* that the reader will find at §41–618.

WE HAVE SEEN a man kneeling ... yet never cry nor complained. And he made a woman for playing the whore sit upon a great stone on her bare breech twenty-four hours, only with corn and water every three days till nine days were past. Yet he loved her exceedingly, notwithstanding there are common whores by profession.

I have counted four versions of the ritual of corn divination: three by Smith, one by Strachey. The earliest appears in *A True Relation,* then here below, then in Strachey's *History of Travel* (653–54), and lastly in the Third Book of the *General History* (237–38). Strachey claims to have taken his account from Smith but his language will be seen to differ here and there.

[31] THEY HAVE ALSO divers conjurations. One they made when Captain Smith was their prisoner (as they reported) to know if any more of his countrymen would arrive there, and what he there intended. The manner of it was thus:

First they made a fair fire in a house; about this fire set 7 priests, setting him by them; and about the fire they made a circle of meal. That done, the chief priest, attired as is expressed, began to shake his rattle, and the rest followed him in his song. At the end of the song he laid down 5 or 3 grains of wheat, and so continued counting his songs by the grains, till 3 times they encirculed the fire; then they divided the grains by certain numbers with little sticks, laying down at the end of every song a little stick. In this manner they sat 8, 10, or 12 hours without cease, with such strange stretching of their arms and violent passions and gestures as might well seem strange to him they so conjured, who but every hour expected his end. Not any meat they did eat till late in the evening they had finished this work, and then they feasted him and themselves with much mirth. But 3 or 4 days they continued this ceremony.

This is Smith's version of the Black Boys ceremony, the same described by William White §11 and William Strachey §41–655, 656. It is a matter of controversy among our reporters—including also Samuel Purchas, Henry Spelman, and John Rolfe—whether it involved ritual sacrifice.

[32] IN SOME PART OF THE COUNTRY they have yearly a sacrifice of children. Such a one was at Quiyoughcohanock, some 10 miles from

James Town, and thus performed: Fifteen of the properest young boys between 10 and 15 years of age they painted white. Having brought them forth, the people spent the forenoon in dancing and singing about them with rattles. In the afternoon they put those children to the root of a tree. By them all the men stood in a guard, everyone having a bastinado[1] in his hand, made of reeds bound together. This made a lane between them all along, through which there were appointed 5 young men [33] to fetch these children. So everyone of the five went through the guard to fetch a child, each after other by turns, the guard fearlessly beating them with their bastinadoes and they patiently enduring and receiving all, defending the children with their naked bodies from the unmerciful blows that pay them soundly, though the children escape.

All this while, the women weep and cry out very passionately, providing mats, skins, moss, and dry wood, as things fitting their children's funerals. After the children were thus past the guard, the guard tore down the tree's branches and boughs with such violence that they rent the body,[2] and made wreathes for their heads or bedecked their hair with the leaves.

What else was done with the children was not seen, but they were all cast on a heap in a valley as dead, where they made a great feast for all the company. The werowance being demanded the meaning of this sacrifice answered that the children were not all dead, but that the *oke,* or devil, did suck the blood from their left breast, [the ones] who chanced to be his by lot, till they were dead; but the rest were kept in the wilderness by the young men till nine months were expired, during which time they must not converse with any; and of these were made their priests and conjurers.

This sacrifice they held to be so necessary that if they should omit it, their *oke,* or devil, and all their other *quiyoughcosughes,* which are their other gods, would let them have no deer, turkeys, corn, nor fish; and yet besides he would make a great slaughter amongst them.

---

[1] Cudgel.

[2] Trunk.

After a book full of geographic and ethnologic matter of fact, Smith now abruptly tacks his ship and heads towards the matter and mood of the *Proceedings §17.* He manages his diatribe without using the word *gentleman,* and without naming a single name. That was all to change in the ensuing work. We are reminded here and with Wingfield §13 how close these men were to the breaking point.

[37] AND THIS IS AS MUCH as my memory can call to mind worthy of note, which I have purposely collected to satisfy my friends of the true worth and quality of Virginia. Yet some bad natures will not stick to slander the country, that will slovenly spit at all things, especially in company where they can find none to contradict them; who, though they were scarce ever 10 miles from James Town or at the most but at the Falls, yet holding it a great disgrace that **[38]** amongst so much action their actions were nothing, exclaim of *all* things, though they never adventured to know *any* thing—nor ever did anything but devour the fruits of other men's labors, being for most part of such tender educations and small experience in martial accidents—because they found not English cities, nor such fair houses, nor, at their own wishes, any of their accustomed dainties, with feather beds and down pillows, taverns and alehouses in every breathing place, neither such plenty of gold and silver and dissolute liberty as they expected; had little or no care of anything but to pamper their bellies, to fly away with our pinnaces, or procure their means to return for England. For the country was to them a misery, a ruin, a death, a hell, and their reports here and their own actions there according.

Some other there were that had yearly stipends to pass to and again for transportation, who to keep the mystery of the business in themselves, though they had neither time nor means to know much of [it] themselves, yet all men's actions or relations they so formally tuned to the temporizing time's simplicity,[1] as they could make their ignorances seem much more than all the true actors could by their experience. And those with their great words deluded the world with such strange promises as abused the business much worse than the

---

[1] A Shakespearean flourish to say, perhaps, "temporary ignorance" of those in England until others returned with more information.

rest. For the business being builded upon the foundation of their feigned experience, the planters, the money, tinne [time], and means have still miscarried. Yet they ever returning—and the planters so far absent who could contradict their excuses—which still to maintain their vainglory and estimation, from time to time they have used such diligence as made them pass for truths, though nothing more false. And that the adventurers might be thus abused, let no man wonder, for the wisest living is soonest abused by him that hath a fair tongue and a dissembling heart.

There were many in Virginia merely projecting, verbal, and idle contemplators; and those so devoted to pure idleness that, though they had lived two or three years in Virginia, lordly necessity itself could not compel them to pass the peninsula or palisadoes of James Town; and those witty spirits: What would they not affirm in the behalf of our transporters to get victual from their ships or obtain their good words in England to get their passes!

Thus from the clamors and the ignorance of false informers are sprung those disasters that sprung in Virginia; and our ingenious verbalists were no less plague to us in Virginia than the locusts to the Egyptians. For the labor of 30 of the best only preserved in Christianity by their industry the idle livers of near 200 of the rest; who living near 10 months off such natural means as the country naturally of itself afforded, notwithstanding all this and the worst fury of the savages, the extremity of sickness, mutinies, faction, ignorances, and want of victual—in all that time I lost but 7 or 8 men, yet subjected the savages to our desired obedience, and received contribution from 35 of their kings to protect and assist them against any that should assault them, in which order they continued true and faithful and as subjects to His Majesty so long after as I did govern there until I left the country. Since, how they have revolted, the country lost and again replanted, and the businesses hath succeeded from time to time, I refer you to the relations of them returned from Virginia that have been more diligent in such observations.

FINIS

17. John Smith

The General History: The Third Book—The proceedings and accidents of the English colony in Virginia, extracted from the authors following by William Simons, Doctor of Divinity

(London: Printed by I. D. and I. H. for Michael Sparkes, 1624)

< Smith 1612, Smith 1624

What Smith wrote and when is a complicated subject, insofar as he rewrote the same material again and again and again. In 1612 he "produced" and published a book with a double title: *A Map of Virginia ... whereunto is annexed the Proceedings of the English Colony.* Twelve years later he brought out his magnum opus, *The General History of Virginia, New England, and the Summer Isles* in six books. In it the Second Book is nearly a reissue of *A Map §16.* The Third Book is a revision and 30% expansion of the 1612 *Proceedings*, discarding some material while bringing in much more, including some of his most memorable passages, all garnished with heavy-treading verses from Fotherby's *Atheomastix* ("scourge of atheism").

So my editorial procedure with these two works—*The Proceedings* and the Third Book—is to combine (not conflate) the texts, making it clear always which is which. Namely, text found only in *The Proceedings* and not in the Third Book, but which is retained because it contains substance, is set off by ·dots·. This amounts to no more than a word or a phrase here and there except for the title page and front matter and several paragraphs at the end of the text that were entirely left out of the Third Book. Otherwise, portions of *The Proceedings* that are incidental or rephrased or augmented and rewritten, I silently drop. The text of the Third Book, however, I retain and give complete without a single omission, including the closing commendatory verses. The last few paragraphs of *The Proceedings* were carried by Smith over to his Fourth Book §52, but I leave them here for the continuity of the former.

The text of the title page of the Third Book is given above at the head. It names none of the "authors." The title page of *The Proceedings* (which does give the authors) appears immediately below, followed by Thomas Abbay's 1612 dedication, and the half title page (which gives most of the authors)—

all which is absent from the text of the Third Book (which gives the authors only at the end of each chapter). The complete text, therefore, of the Third Book, combined with the text of the *Proceedings,* first begins at Chapter One.

It is hard to see where Captain John Smith had a hand in the 1612 *Proceedings,*[1] but he is a contributor and overwriter to the text of the Third Book. If there he puts words in other men's mouths, in their subsequent praise of him some of them at least seem to recognize themselves in the result, e.g. the Phettiplace brothers in their commendatory verses below.

Rev. Symonds was the editor in 1612, and Barbour thinks that he was important in finding the publisher Joseph Barnes in Oxford. Apparently none could be found in London. The association of Symonds' name lent this controversial account some authority and respectability. Regardless, when the very heavily rewritten text of the Third Book appeared in the 1624 *General History,* the man credited with having "extracted [it] from the authors following" had been dead eleven years. Abbay's preface had disappeared also.

Both *The Proceedings* and the Third Book are themselves an extension, expansion, and rewrite of *A True Relation §12,* but there is enough divergence for this editor to justify retaining the shorter work at §12 as the first specimen of two, if not three, versions of events by the same author. Why did Smith keep putting served wine in new bottles? To sell books, for he lived on nothing else unless the charity of his friends.

We have hundreds of pages in this volume written by other participants, and to our dismay little of it throws more light on events. §17 is not simply one version. It is again and again the only version. Gabriel Archer (d.1609), John Sicklemore alias Ratcliffe, John Martin—all were so vilified and condemned here in print, how could they hold up their heads in public? All took issue with Smith and his "vainglory," but little survives of what they and others wrote to present another side to his account of what happened. President Wingfield's passion runs high and he says things in §13, but his case is weak and his tone often silly. Percy in his own true relation (§31) comes close to a revelation, then veers away on another tack. His account of the callow Martin at Nansemond resembles the one here.

If anything there is some support for Smith. The Virginia Company appends a list of desirables at the end of the *True and Sincere Declaration §20* that could have been written by him. Strachey says he was a great achiever and was the victim of envious factions. Hamor says that Ratcliffe was the incompetent fool Smith claims he was, and Hamor also says that

---

[1] Barbour suggests *The Proceedings* by Studley, Todkill, et al., edited by Symonds, for a time had an independent existence until joined with Capt. Smith's *A Map of Virginia* for publication in 1612.

Newport was a poor trader and gave away the store with Powhatan. Samuel Purchas, though never in Virginia, knew many who were and he accepts Smith as a foremost authority and covers him with praise. And even Sir Thomas Gates. Rev. Crashaw (703) writes that Gates told him the year preceding the arrival of Archer and company, that is, the time of Smith's presidency, had been a year of good government with the colony well supplied, all which their meddling overthrew.

But why should we doubt the captain in the first place? Snobbery because he puts too many aristocrats in their place? Jealousy because he writes more and better than men with expensive educations? Or because he writes the truth about everybody but himself? Not all braggarts are liars, but nothing comes through these pages clearer than his dread lest we read over his proud achievements too quickly. And yet, for all that, Pots and Todkill and Russell extol him loudly, and no one else in the whole Jamestown chronicle gets such adulation from anybody. His detractors were, to tell the truth, fewer among his contemporaries than among latter-day historians. And we must keep in mind his praise is sung here by contemporaries who knew he was in disfavor, broke, and out of work—the rarest sort in any age.

One reason they love him is because he had the thought and the heart to list the names of nearly every one of them with the arrival of each supply and the brave outset of each expedition.[1] Smith is proud to bring the common man onto the historical page. French and Spanish explorers named places after saints. Smith named Read's Point for a blacksmith in the boat beside him and Smith's Falls for himself.

In Chapter Eleven he decrees "who does not work shall not eat," and fortune-seeking gentlemen were put to work. It got him in more trouble than anything else he did, but the farmer's son draws our sympathy today. Americans do not like to boast about ancestors by saying they never worked. It is an attitude that may well have rubbed off on us during the slim times at James Fort, and marched from there into the Constitution (as a prohibition against titles).

For my part, I see in this man, who entitles a chapter "What happened," a simplicity and directness bespeaking a fundamental honesty, a vainglory that charms more than it deceives.

Outside of his own account, evidence of his unpopularity is indirect: He did not serve the Virginia Company again. Despite his interest in New England and his bids, neither the Plymouth Company nor those who landed at Plymouth Rock were interested in hiring his services.

He had a reputation for being difficult and he earned it. After many books he died in poverty. We call him a leader, an adventurer, an explorer, map-maker, soldier, writer, scholar, and more, but most of all he is doer of "high deeds in Hungary," a fascinating character, one larger than anybody but Powhatan. Ahead is the greatest tale of his life.

---

[1] Thomas Studley as cape merchant may have supplied the lists.

I have abstracted the following—

Table of Contents

[from the 1612 title page]

The Proceedings

of the English Colony in Virginia since their First Beginning from England in the Year of Our Lord 1606 till this Present 1612, with All their Accidents that befell them in their Journeys and Discoveries.

Also the Savages' Discourses, Orations and Relations of the Bordering Neighbors, and how they became Subject to the English,

Unfolding even the Fundamental Causes from whence have sprang so Many Miseries to the Undertakers, and Scandals to the Businesses, taken faithfully as they were Written out of the Writings of

Thomas Studley, *the First Provant-master,* Anas Todkill, Walter Russell, *Doctor of Physic,* Nathaniell Powell, William Phettyplace, Richard Wyffin, Thomas Abbay, Tho[mas] Hope, Rich[ard] Potts[1],

and the Labors of Divers Other Diligent Observers that were Residents in Virginia,
and perused and confirmed by Divers now Resident in England that were Actors in this Business.

BY W[ILLIAM] S[YMONDS]
(at Oxford. Printed by Joseph Barnes. 1612)

[1] The combined title page of *A Map* and *The Proceedings* includes most of these and adds the name Jeffra Abot.

To the Reader[1] —

Long hath the world longed but to be truly satisfied what Virginia is, with the truth of those proceedings from whence hath flown so many reports of worth, and yet few good effects of the charge,[2] which hath caused suspicion in many well-willers that desire yet but to be truly satisfied therein. If any can resolve this doubt, it is those that have lived residents in the land—not sailors or passengers, nor such mercenary contemplators that only bedeck themselves with others' plumes. This discourse is not from such, neither am I the author, for they are many whose particular discourses are signed by their names.

This solid treatise first was compiled by Richard Pots. Since, passing the hands of many to peruse, chancing into my hands, for that I know them honest men, and can partly well witness their relations true, I could do no less in charity to the world than reveal, nor in conscience but approve.

By the advice of many grave and understanding gentlemen that have pressed it, to the press it was thought fit to publish it rather in it own rude phrase than otherways, for that nothing can so purge that famous action from the infamous scandal some ignorantly have conceited as the plain simple and naked truth, for defect whereof the business is still suspected, the truth unknown, and the best deservers discouraged and neglected, some by false reports, others by conjecture; and such power hath flatt'ry to engender of those hatred and affection[3] that one is sufficient to beguile more than 500 can keep from being deceived.

But this discourse is no judge of men's manners nor catalog of their former courses, only a reporter of their actions in Virginia, not to disgrace any, accuse any, excuse any, nor flatter any; for which cause there is no wrong done but this: shortness in complaining (and so sparing in commending), as only the reader may perceive the truth for his pains, and the action purged of foul slander. It can detract from none that intendeth there to adventure their fortunes.

---

[1] From the 1612 *Proceedings.*

[2] Few returns from the money invested.

[3] Fondness.

And to speak truly of the first planters, that brake the ice and beat the path, howsoever many difficulties obscured their endeavors, he were worse than the worst of ingrates that would not spare them memory that have buried themselves in those foreign regions, from whose first adventures may spring more good blessings than are yet conceived.

So I rest thine that will read, peruse, and understand me. If you find false orthography or broken English, they are small faults in soldiers that not being able to write learnedly only strive to speak truly, and be understood without an interpreter.

T[HOMAS] ABBAY.

The Proceedings[1]

of the English Colony in Virginia,
taken faithfully out of the writings of
Thomas Studly, *Cape merchant,* Anas Todkill,
Doctor Russell, Nathaniel Powell, William Phetiplace,
and Richard Pot,
with the labors of other discreet observers,
during their residences.

[1] Half title from the 1612 *Proceedings.*

Chapter I.

IT MIGHT WELL BE THOUGHT a country so fair as Virginia is, and a people so tractable, would long ere this have been quietly possessed, to the satisfaction of the adventurers and the eternizing of the memory of those that effected it. But because all the world do see a defailment, this following treatise shall give satisfaction to all indifferent readers how the business hath been carried, where no doubt they will easily understand and answer to their question how it came to pass there was no better speed and success in those proceedings.

Captain Bartholomew Gosnoll, one of the first movers of this plantation, having many years solicited many of his friends, but found small assistance, at last prevailed with some gentlemen, as Captain John Smith, Master Edward Maria Wingfield, Master Robert Hunt, and divers others who depended[1] a year upon his projects.

But nothing could be effected till by their great charge and industry it came to be apprehended by certain of the nobility, gentry, and merchants, so that His Majesty by his letters patents gave commission for establishing councils to direct here and to govern and to execute there. To effect this was spent another year, and by that ·time· three ships were provided: one of 100 tons, another of 40, and a pinnace of 20.[2]

The transportation of the company was committed to Captain Christopher Newport, a mariner well practiced for the western parts of America. But their orders for government were put in a box not to be opened, nor the governors known, until they arrived in Virginia.

On the 19 of December, 1606, we set sail from Blackwall, but by

---

[1] Waited.

[2] The *Susan Constant, Godspeed,* and *Discovery*. The *Susan Constant* was 120 tons.

unprosperous winds were kept six weeks in the sight of England; all which time Master Hunt, our preacher, was so weak and sick that few expected his recovery. Yet, although he were but twenty miles from his habitation (the time we were in the Downs[1]), and notwithstanding the stormy weather nor the scandalous imputations of some few (little better than atheists) of the greatest rank amongst us, suggested against him, all this could never force from him so much as a *seeming* desire to leave the business, but preferred the service of God in so good a voyage before any affection to contest with his godless foes; whose disastrous designs, could they have prevailed, had even then overthrown the business, so many discontents did then arise, had he not with the water of patience and his godly exhortations, but chiefly by his true devoted examples, quenched those flames of envy and dissension.

We watered at the Canaries; we traded with the savages at Dominica; three weeks we spent in refreshing ourselves amongst these West India isles. In Gwardalupa we found a bath so hot as in it we boiled pork as well as over the fire; and at a little isle called Monica we took from the bushes with our hands near two hogsheads full of birds in three or four hours; in Mevis [Nevis], Mona, and the Virgin Isles we spent some time, where with a loathsome beast like a crocodile, called a *gwayn* [iguana], tortoises, pelicans, parrots, and fishes we daily feasted.

Gone from thence in search of Virginia, the company was not a little discomforted seeing the mariners had 3 days passed their reckoning and found no land, so that Captain Ratliffe, captain of the pinnace, rather desired to bear up the helm to return for England than make further search. But God the guider of all good actions, forcing them by an extreme storm to-hull all night,[2] did drive them by His providence to their desired port, beyond all their expectations. For never any of them had seen that coast.

The first land they made they called "Cape Henry," where anchoring, Master Wingfeild, Gosnoll, and Newport, with thirty of them recreating themselves on shore were assaulted by five savages

[1] Off the east coast of Kent. The ships had to wait for an east wind.

[2] I.e., to furl all sail and drift.

who hurt two of the English very dangerously.

That night was the box opened and the orders read in which Bartholomew Gosnoll, John Smith, Edward Wingfield, Christopher Newport, John Ratliffe, John Martin, and George Kendall were named to be the council; and to choose a president amongst them for a year who with the council should govern. Matters of moment were to be examined by a jury but determined by the major part of the council in which the president had two voices.

Until the 13 of May they sought a place to plant in. Then the council was sworn, Master Wingfield was chosen president, and an oration made why Captain Smith was not admitted of the council as the rest.

Now falleth every man to work: The council contrive the fort, the rest cut down trees to make place to pitch their tents, some provide clapboard to relade the ships, some make gardens, some nets, etc.

The savages often visited us kindly. The president's overweening jealousy would admit no exercise at arms or fortification but the boughs of trees cast together in the form of a half-moon, by the extraordinary pains and diligence of Captain Kendall.

Newport, Smith, and twenty others were sent to discover the head of the river. By divers small habitations they passed; in six days they arrived at a town called Powhatan, consisting of some twelve houses pleasantly seated on a hill, before it three fertile isles, about it many of their cornfields. The place is very pleasant and strong by nature. Of this place the prince is called Powhatan, and his people Powhatans.[1] To this place the river is navigable, but higher within a mile, by reason of the rocks and isles, there is not passage for a small boat; this they call the "Falls."

The people in all parts kindly entreated them till being returned within twenty miles of James town they gave just cause of jealousy. But had God not blessed the discoverers otherwise than those at the fort, there had then been an end of that plantation. For at the fort, where they arrived the next day, they found 17 men hurt and a boy slain by the savages. And had it not chanced a crossbar shot[2] from

---

[1] Rather his son Parahunt, called Tanxpowhatan.

[2] "A round shot, but it hath a long spike of iron cast with it, as if it did go thorough the middest of it." (Smith, *A Sea Grammar, xiv,* 67.)

the ships struck down a bough from a tree amongst them that caused them to retire, our men had all been slain, being securely all at work and their arms in dryfats.[1]

Hereupon the president was contented the fort should be palisadoed, the ordnance mounted, his men armed and exercised. For many were the assaults and ambuscadoes of the savages, and our men by their disorderly straggling were often hurt, when the savages by the nimbleness of their heels well escaped. What toil we had with so small a power to guard our workmen adays, watch all night, resist our enemies, and effect our business to relade the ships, cut down trees, and prepare the ground to plant our corn, etc. I refer to the reader's consideration. Six weeks being spent in this manner, Captain Newport, who was hired only for our transportation, was to return with the ships.

Now Captain Smith, who all this time from their departure from the Canaries was restrained as a prisoner upon the scandalous suggestions of some of the chief, envying his repute, who feigned he intended to usurp the government, murther the council, and make himself king, that his confederates were dispersed in all the three ships, and that divers of his confederates that revealed it would affirm it—for this he was committed as a prisoner.[2] Thirteen weeks he remained thus suspected; and by that time the ships should return, they pretended out of their commiserations to refer him to the council in England to receive a check,[3] rather than by particulating his designs [to] make him so odious to the world as to touch his life or utterly overthrow his reputation.

But he much scorned their charity, and publicly defied the uttermost of their cruelty, he wisely prevented their policies, though he could not suppress their envies. Yet so well he demeaned himself in this business as all the company did see his innocency and his adversaries' malice; and those suborned to accuse him accused his accusers of subornation. Many untruths were alleged against him, but being so apparently disproved begat a general hatred in the

---

[1] I.e., in storage.

[2] "The next day Captain Smith was suspected for a supposed mutiny, though never no such matter." Samuel Purchas' margin note in Percy's *Discourse §1–85n.*

[3] Reprimand.

hearts of the company against such unjust commanders that the president was adjudged to give him 200li, so that all he had was seized upon in part of satisfaction, which Smith presently returned to the store for the general use of the colony. Many were the mischiefs that daily sprung from their ignorant yet ambitious spirits. But the good doctrine and exhortation of our preacher Master Hunt reconciled them, and caused Captain Smith to be admitted of the council.

The next day all received the communion[1]; the day following, the savages voluntarily desired peace; and Captain Newport returned for England with news, leaving in Virginia 100 [colonists]—the 15 of June, 1607.

By this observe—

Good men did ne'er their country's ruin bring.
But when evil men shall injuries begin,
Not caring to corrupt and violate
The judgment seats for their own lucre's sake,
Then look, that country cannot long have peace,
Though for the present it have rest and ease.

The names of them that were the first planters, were these following:

---

[1] Many years later Smith wrote about religious services: "When I went first to Virginia I well remember we did hang an awning (which is an old sail) to three or four trees to shadow us from the sun. Our walls were rails of wood, our seats unhewed trees till we cut planks; our pulpit a bar of wood nailed to two neighboring trees. In foul weather we shifted into an old rotten tent, for we had few better, and this came by the way of adventure for new [had been supplied as new material]. This was our church till we built a homely thing like a barn set upon cratchets [forked poles], covered with rafts, sedge, and earth, so was also the walls. The best of our houses [were] of the like curiosity, but the most part far much worse workmanship that could neither well defend wind nor rain, yet we had daily common prayer morning and evening, every Sunday two sermons and every three months the holy communion (till our minister died), but our prayers daily, with an homily on Sundays. We continued two or three years after till more preachers came, and surely God did most mercifully hear us till the continual inundations of mistaking directions, factions, and numbers of unprovided libertines near consumed us all, as the Israelites in the wilderness." *(Advertisements,* 32, 33)

The Council

Master Edward Maria Wingfield
Captain Bartholomew Gosnoll
Captain John Smith
Captain John Ratliffe
Captain John Martin
Captain George Kendall

Gentlemen

Master Robert Hunt, *preacher*
Master George Percie
Anthony Gosnoll[1]
George Flower
Captain Gabriell Archer
Robert Fenton
Robert Ford
William Bruster

Edward Harrington
Dru Pickhouse
Thomas Jacob
John Brookes
Ellis Kingston
Thomas Sands
Benjamin Beast
Jehu Robinson
Thomas Mouton
Eustace Clovill
Stephen Halthrop
Kellam Throgmorton
Edward Morish
Nathaniell Powell
Edward Browne
Robert Behethland
John Penington
Jeremy Alicock

[1] Younger brother to Bartholomew and cousin to the Anthony below.

George Walker
Thomas Studley
Richard Crofts
Nicholas Houlgrave
Thomas Webbe
John Waller
John Short
William Tankard
William Smethes
Francis Snarsbrough
Richard Simons
Edward Brookes
Richard Dixon
John Martin
·George Martin·
Roger Cooke
Anthony Gosnold
Thomas Wotton, *chirurgeon*
John Stevenson

Thomas Gore
Henry Adling
Francis Midwinter
Richard Frith

Carpenters

William Laxon
Edward Pising
Thomas Emry
Robert Small

·Anas Todkill·
·John Capper·
James Read, *blacksmith*
Jonas Profit, *sailor*
Thomas Cowper, *barber*
·John Herd, *bricklayer*·
William Garret, "

Edward Brinto, *mason*
William Love, *tailor*
Nicholas Scot, *drummer*
William Wilkinson, *chirurgeon*

Laborers

John Laydon
William Cassen
George Cassen
Thomas Cassen
William Rodes
William White
Old Edward
Henry Tavin
George Goulding
John Dods
William Johnson
William Unger

Boys

Samuell Collier

Nathaniell Pecock
James Brumfield
Richard Mutton

—with divers others to the number of 100.[1]

[1] *The Proceedings* calls for 105.

Chapter II.

What happened till the first supply.

BEING THUS LEFT TO OUR FORTUNES, it fortuned that within ten days scarce ten amongst us could either go or well stand, such extreme weakness and sickness oppressed us.

And thereat none need marvel, if they consider the cause and reason, which was this: Whilest the ships stayed, our allowance was somewhat bettered by a daily proportion of biscuit which the sailors would pilfer to sell, give, or exchange with us for money, saxefras, furs, or love. But when they departed there remained neither tavern, beer house, nor place of relief but the common kettle. Had we been as free from all sins as gluttony and drunkenness, we might have been canonized for saints.

But our president would never have been admitted [a saint] for engrossing to his private [hoard] oatmeal, sack, oil, aqua vitae, beef, eggs, or whatnot, but the kettle. That indeed he allowed equally to be distributed—and that was half a pint of wheat and as much barley boiled with water for a man a day (and this having fried some 26 weeks in the ship's hold!)—contained as many worms as grains, so that we might truly call it rather so much bran than corn. Our drink was water, our lodgings castles in the air. With this lodging and diet, our extreme toil in bearing and planting palisadoes so strained and bruised us, and our continual labor in the extremity of the heat had so weakened us, as were cause sufficient to have made us as miserable in our native country or any other place in the world.

From May to September, those that escaped lived upon sturgeon and sea crabs; fifty in this time we buried. The rest, seeing the president's projects to escape these miseries in our pinnace by flight —who all this time had neither felt want nor sickness—so moved our dead spirits as we deposed him and established Ratcliffe in his place,[1] Gosnoll being dead, Kendall deposed. Smith newly recovered, Martin and Ratcliffe was by his care preserved and relieved,

---

[1] Wingfield was deposed on 10 September 1607.

and most of the soldiers recovered with the skillful diligence of Master Thomas Wotton, our chirurgeon general.

But now was all our provision spent, the sturgeon gone, all helps abandoned, each hour expecting the fury of the savages, when God the patron of all good endeavors in that desperate extremity so changed the hearts of the savages that they brought such plenty of their fruits and provision as no man wanted.

And now, where some affirmed it was ill done of the council to send forth men so badly provided, this incontradictable reason will show them plainly they are too ill advised to nourish such ill conceits. First, the fault of our going was our own. What could be thought fitting or necessary we had, but what we should find or ·what we should· want, or where we should be—we were all ignorant, and supposing to make our passage in two months, with victual to live and the advantage of the spring to work. [But] we were at sea five months, where we both spent our victual and lost the opportunity of the time and season to plant, by the unskillful presumption of our ignorant transporters that understood not at all what they undertook.[1]

[Secondly,] such actions have ever since the world's beginning been subject to such accidents; and everything of worth is found full of difficulties, but nothing so difficult as to establish a commonwealth so far remote from men and means, and where men's minds are so untoward as neither [to] do well themselves nor suffer others. But to proceed.

The new president and Martin, being little beloved, of weak judgment in dangers and less industry in peace, committed the managing of all things abroad to Captain Smith, who by his own example, good words, and fair promises set some to mow, others to bind thatch, some to build houses, others to thatch them, himself always bearing the greatest task for his own share, so that in short time he provided most of them lodgings, neglecting any for himself.

This done, seeing the savages' superfluity begin to decrease, with some of his workmen [he] shipped himself in the shallop to search the country for trade. The want of the language, knowledge to

---

[1] Smith defends the Company only to lash out at Capt. Newport.

manage his boat without sails,[1] the want of a sufficient power (knowing the multitude of the savages) [and] apparel for his men,[2] and other necessaries were infinite impediments, yet no discouragement.

Being but six or seven in company, he went down the river to Kecoughtan, where at first they scorned him as a famished man,[3] and would in derision offer him a handful of corn, a piece of bread for their swords and muskets, and suchlike proportions also for their apparel. But seeing by trade and courtesy there was nothing to be had, he made bold to try such conclusions as necessity enforced: Though contrary to his commission, [he] let fly his muskets [and] ran his boat on shore, whereat they all fled into the woods. So marching towards their houses, they might see great heaps of corn. Much ado he had to restrain his hungry soldiers from present taking of it, expecting as it hap'ned that the savages would assault them, as not long after they did with a most hideous noise. Sixty or seventy of them, some black, some red, some white, some parti-colored, came in a square order, singing and dancing out of the woods with their *okee,* which was an idol made of skins stuffed with moss, all painted and hung with chains and copper borne before them. And in this manner being well armed with clubs, targets, bows, and arrows, they charged the English, that so kindly received them with their muskets loaden with pistol shot, that down fell their god, and divers lay sprawling on the ground. The rest fled again to the woods, and ere long sent one of their *quiyoughkasoucks* to offer peace and redeem their okee. Smith told them if only six of them would come unarmed and load his boat, he would not only be their friend but restore them their okee, and give them beads, copper, and hatchets besides—which on both sides was to their contents performed. And then they brought him venison, turkeys, wildfowl, bread, and what they had, singing and dancing in sign of friendship till they departed. In his return he discovered the town and country of Warraskoyack.

---

[1] "Sailors" in *The Proceedings.*

[2] Equipment.

[3] Here to the end of the paragraph replaces (in *The Proceedings):* "Yet he so dealt with them that the next day they loaded his boat with corn; and in his return he discovered and kindly traded with the Weraskoyks. In the meantime, those at the fort so glutted the savages with their commodities as they became not regarded."

Thus God unboundless by his power
Made them thus kind would us devour.

Smith perceiving [that], notwithstanding their late misery, not any regarded but from hand to mouth—the company being well recovered,[1] [he] caused the pinnace to be provided with things fitting to get provision for the year following. But in the interim he made 3 or 4 journeys and discovered the people of Chickahamania.

Yet what he carefully provided, the rest carelessly spent. Wingfield and Kendall living in disgrace [and] seeing all things at random in the absence of Smith, [as well as] the company's dislike of their president's weakness and their small love to Martin's never-mending sickness, [the two] strengthened themselves with the sailors and other confederates to regain their former credit and authority, or at least such means aboard the pinnace, being fitted to sail as Smith had appointed for trade, to alter her course and to go for England.

Smith unexpectedly returning had the plot discovered to him. Much trouble he had to prevent it till with store of saker[2] and musket shot he forced them stay or sink in the river, which action cost the life of Captain Kendall.

These brawls are so disgustful as some will say they were better forgotten, yet all men of good judgment will conclude it were better their baseness should be manifest to the world than the business bear the scorn and shame of their excused disorders.

The president and Captain Archer not long after intended also to have abandoned the country, which project also was curbed and suppressed by Smith.

The Spaniard never more greedily desired gold than he victual, nor his soldiers more to abandon the country than he to keep it. But finding plenty of corn in the River of Chickahamania, where hundreds of savages in divers places stood with baskets expecting his coming——[3]

And now the winter approaching, the rivers became so covered with swans, geese, ducks, and cranes that we daily feasted with good

---

[1] A margin note here reads: "Amoris, a savage, his best friend, slain for loving us."

[2] A cannon.

[3] Apparently a gap in the text.

bread, Virginia peas, pumpions, and putchamins, fish, fowl, and divers sorts of wild beasts as fat as we could eat them, so that none of our tuftaffaty humorists[1] desired to go for England.

But our comedies never endured long without a tragedy: Some idle exceptions being muttered against Captain Smith for not discovering the head of Chickahamania River, and taxed by the council to be too slow in so worthy an attempt, the next voyage he proceeded so far that with much labor by cutting of trees in sunder he made his passage. But when his barge could pass no farther, he left her in a broad bay out of danger of shot, commanding none should go ashore till his return. Himself with two English and two savages went up higher in a canoe; but he was not long absent but his men went ashore, whose want of government gave both occasion and opportunity to the savages to surprise one George Cassen, whom they slew, and much failed not to have cut off the boat and all the rest.

Smith, little dreaming of that accident, being got to the marshes at the river's head twenty miles in the desert, had his two men slain,[2] as is supposed, sleeping by the canoe, whilst himself by fowling sought them victual; who finding he was beset with 200 savages, two of them he slew, still defending himself with the aid of a savage his guide, whom he bound to his arm with his garters and used him as a buckler. Yet he was shot in his thigh a little and had many arrows that stuck in his clothes, but no great hurt, till at last, ·slipping into a bogmire·, they took him prisoner.

When this news came to James town, much was their sorrow for his loss, few expecting what ensued. Six or seven weeks[3] those barbarians kept him prisoner; many strange triumphs and conjurations they made of him, yet he so demeaned[4] himself amongst them as he not only diverted them from surprising the fort but procured his own liberty, and got himself and his company such estimation amongst them that those savages admired him more than their own *quiyouckosucks.* The manner how they used and delivered him is as

---

[1] "Cranks in fancy clothes." "Charlatans dressed in tufted taffeta." (Barbour)

[2] "Jehu Robinson and Thomas Emry slain." (margin note)

[3] *The Proceedings* has "a month," which is more accurate.

[4] Behaved.

followeth:

The savages having drawn from George Cassen whither Captain Smith was gone, prosecuting that opportunity they followed him with 300 bowmen, conducted by the King of Pamaunkee, who in divisions searching the turnings of the river found Robinson and Emry by the fireside. Those they shot full of arrows and slew. Then finding the captain, as is said, that used the savage that was his guide as his shield, three of them being slain and divers other so gall'd,[1] all the rest would not come near him. Thinking thus to have returned to his boat, regarding them as he marched more than his way, [he] slipped up to the middle in an oozy creek, and his savage with him, yet durst they not come to him till being near dead with cold he threw away his arms. Then according to their composition they drew him forth and led him to the fire where his men were slain. Diligently they chafed his benumbed limbs.

He demanding for the captain, they showed him Opechankanough, King of Pamaunkee, to whom he gave a round, ivory, double compass dial. Much they marveled at the playing of the fly and needle, which they could see so plainly and yet not touch it because of the glass that covered them. But when he demonstrated by that globe-like jewel the roundness of the earth and skies, the sphere of the sun, moon, and stars, and how the sun did chase the night round about the world continually, the greatness of the land and sea, ·the qualities of our ships, shot, and powder·, the diversity of nations, variety of complexions, ·customs, and conditions·, and how we were to them antipodes, and many other suchlike matters, they all stood as amazed with admiration— ·all which he feigned to be under the command of Captain Newport, whom he termed to them his father·. Notwithstanding, within an hour after, they tied him to a tree, and as many as could stand about him prepared to shoot him. But the king holding up the compass in his hand, they all laid down their bows and arrows, and in a triumphant manner led him to Orapaks, where he was after their manner kindly feasted and well used.

Their order in conducting him was thus: Drawing themselves all in

---

[1] Harassed with shot.

file, the king in the middest had all their pieces and swords borne before him. Captain Smith was led after him by three great savages holding him fast by each arm, and on each side six went in file with their arrows nocked.

But arriving at the town, which was but only thirty or forty hunting houses made of mats, which they remove as they please as we our tents, all the women and children staring to behold him, the soldiers first all in file performed the form of a *bissone* [?] so well as could be, and on each flank officers as sergeants to see them keep their order. A good time they continued this exercise, and then cast themselves in a ring, dancing in such several postures, and singing and yelling out such hellish notes and screeches, being strangely painted, everyone his quiver of arrows, and at his back a club, on his arm a fox or an otter's skin or some such matter for his vambrace; their heads and shoulders painted red with oil and pocones mingled together, which scarlet-like color made an exceeding handsome show; his bow in his hand and the skin of a bird with her wings abroad dried tied on his head; a piece of copper, a white shell, a long feather with a small rattle growing at the tails of their snakes tied to it, or some suchlike toy—all this while Smith and the king stood in the middest guarded, as before is said. And after three dances they all departed.

Smith they conducted to a long house, where thirty or forty tall fellows did guard him. And ere long more bread and venison was brought him than would have served twenty men (I think his stomach at that time was not very good). What he left they put in baskets and tied over his head. About midnight they set the meat again before him. All this time not one of them would eat a bit with him till the next morning they brought him as much more, and then did they eat all the old and reserved the new as they had done the other—which made him think they would fat him to eat him. Yet, in this desperate estate to defend him from the cold, one Maocassater brought him his gown in requital of some beads and toys Smith had given him at his first arrival in Virginia.

Two days after, a man would have slain him—but that the guard prevented it—for the death of his son, to whom they conducted him to recover the poor man then breathing his last. Smith told them that at James town he had a water would do it if they would let him fetch it, but they would not permit that, but [rather] made all the preparations they could to assault James town, craving his advice, and for recompense he should have life, liberty, land, and women.

In part of a table book he writ his mind to them at the fort what was intended, how they should follow that direction to affright the messengers, and without fail send him such things as he writ for, and [sent] an inventory with them. The difficulty and danger he told the savages of the mines, great guns, and other engines exceedingly affrighted them, yet according to his request they went to James town in as bitter weather as could be of frost and snow, and within three days returned with an answer.

But when they came to James town, seeing men sally out as he had told them they would, they fled. Yet in the night they came again to the same place where he had told them they should receive an answer and such things as he had promised them, which they found accordingly, and with which they returned with no small expedition, to the wonder of them all that heard it that he could either divine or the paper could speak.

Then they led him to the Youghtanunds, the Mattapanients, the Payankatanks, the Nantaughtacunds, and Onawmanients upon the River of Rapahanock, and Patawomek—over all those rivers and back again by divers other several nations to the king's habitation at Pamaunkee, where they entertained him with most strange and fearful conjurations.

As if near led to hell,
Amongst the devils to dwell.

Not long after, early in a morning a great fire was made in a long house, and a mat spread on the one side as on the other. On the one they caused him to sit, and all the guard went out of the house, and presently came skipping in a great, grim fellow, all painted over with coal mingled with oil, and many snakes' and weasels' skins stuffed with moss, and all the tails tied together so as they met on the crown of his head in a tassel; and round about the tassel was as a coronet of feathers, the skins hanging round about his head, back, and shoulders, and in a manner covered his face. With a hellish voice and a rattle in his hand, with most strange gestures and pas-sions he began his invocation, and environed the fire with a circle of meal. Which done, three more such like devils came rushing in with the like antic tricks, painted half black, half red, but all their eyes were painted white, and some red strokes like mutchatos [musta-chios] along their cheeks. Round about him those fiends danced a pretty while, and then came in three more as ugly as the rest, with red eyes and white strokes over their black faces. At last they all sat down right against him, three of them on the one hand of the chief priest and three on the other. Then all with their rattles began a song, which ended, the chief priest laid down five wheat corns. Then straining his arms and hands with such violence that he sweat and his veins swelled, he began a short oration. At the conclusion they all gave a short groan, and then laid down three grains more. After that, began their song again, and then another oration, ever laying down so many corns as before till they had twice encirculed the fire. That done, they took a bunch of little sticks prepared for that purpose, continuing still their devotion, and at the end of every song and oration they laid down a stick betwixt the divisions of corn. Till night, neither he nor they did either eat or drink, and then they feasted merrily with the best provisions they could make.

Three days they used this ceremony, the meaning whereof they told him was to know if he intended them well or no. The circle of meal signified their country, the circles of corn the bounds of the sea, and the sticks his country. They imagined the world to be flat and round like a trencher, and they in the middest.

After this they brought him a bag of gunpowder which they carefully preserved till the next spring to plant as they did their corn, because they would be acquainted with the nature of that seed.

Opitchapam, the king's brother, invited him to his house where with as many platters of bread, fowl, and wild beasts as did environ him he bid him welcome. But not any of them would eat a bit with him, but put up all the remainder in baskets.

At his return to Opechancanough's, all the king's women and their children flocked about him for their parts, as a due by custom, to be merry with such fragments.

But his waking mind in hideous dreams did oft see wondrous shapes,
Of bodies strange, and huge in growth, and of stupendious makes.

At last they brought him to Meronocomoco [Werowocomoco], where was Powhatan their emperor. Here more than two hundred of those grim courtiers stood wondering at him as he had been a monster, till Powhatan and his train had put themselves in their greatest braveries. Before a fire upon a seat like a bedstead he sat covered with a great robe made of rarowcun skins, and all the tails hanging by. On either hand did sit a young wench of 16 or 18 years, and along on each side the house two rows of men, and behind them as many women, with all their heads and shoulders painted red, many of their heads bedecked with the white down of birds, but everyone with something, and a great chain of white beads about their necks.

At his entrance before the king, all the people gave a great shout. The Queen of Appamatuck was appointed to bring him water to wash his hands, and another brought him a bunch of feathers instead of a towel to dry them. Having feasted him after their best barbarous manner they could, a long consultation was held, but the conclusion was two great stones were brought before Powhatan. Then as many as could laid hands on him [Smith], dragged him to them, and thereon laid his head; and being ready with their clubs to beat out his brains, Pocahontas, the king's dearest daughter, when no entreaty could prevail, got his head in her arms and laid her own upon his to save him from death; whereat the emperor was contented he should live to make him hatchets, and her bells, beads, and copper, for they thought him as well of all occupations as themselves. For the king himself will make his own robes, shoes, bows, arrows, pots—plant, hunt, or do anything so well as the rest.

They say he bore a pleasant show,
But sure his heart was sad.
For who can pleasant be and rest
That lives in fear and dread?
And having life suspected doth
It still suspected lead.

Two days after, Powhatan, having disguised himself in the most fearfullest manner he could, caused Captain Smith to be brought forth to a great house in the woods, and there upon a mat by the fire to be left alone. Not long after, from behind a mat that divided the house was made the most dolefullest noise he ever heard. Then Powhatan more like a devil than a man, with some two hundred more as black as himself, came unto him and told him now they were friends, and presently he should go to James town to send him two great guns and a grindstone, for which he would give him the country of Capahowosick, and forever esteem him as his son Nantaquoud.

So to James town with 12 guides Powhatan sent him. That night they quarter'd in the woods, he still expecting, as he had done all this long time of his imprisonment, every hour to be put to one death or other, for all their feasting. But Almighty God by His divine providence had mollified the hearts of those stern barbarians with compassion.

The next morning betimes they came to the fort, where Smith, having used the savages with what kindness he could, he showed Rawhunt, Powhatan's trusty servant, two demi-culverins and a millstone to carry Powhatan. They found them somewhat too heavy. But when they did see him discharge them, being loaded with stones, among the boughs of a great tree loaded with icicles, the ice and branches came so tumbling down that the poor savages ran away half dead with fear. But at last we regained some conference with them, and gave them such toys and sent to Powhatan, his women, and children such presents as gave them in general full content.

Now in James Town they were all in combustion, the strongest preparing once more to run away with the pinnace ·for England,[1] which till his return could not set sail, so extreme was the weather and so great the frost·, which with the hazard of his life [and] with saker, falcon, and musket shot Smith forced now the third time to stay or sink. Some no better than they should be had plotted with the president the next day to have put him to death by the Levitical law, for the lives of Robinson and Emry, pretending the fault was his that

[1] "The 3 project to abandon the fort." (margin note)

had led them to their ends. But he quickly took such order with such lawyers that he laid them by the heels till he sent some of them prisoners for England. Now ever once in four or five days Pocahontas with her attendants brought him so much provision that saved many of their lives that else for all this had starved with hunger.

Thus from numb death our good God sent relief,
The sweet assuager of all other grief.

His relation of the plenty he had seen, especially at Werawocomoco, and of the state and bounty of Powhatan, which till that time was unknown, so revived their dead spirits, especially the love of Pocahontas, as all men's fear was abandoned.

Thus you may see what difficulties still crossed any good endeavor and the good success of the business, being thus oft brought to the very period of destruction, yet you see by what strange means God hath still delivered it. As for the insufficiency of them admitted in commission, that error could not be prevented by the electors, there being no other choice, and all ·were· strangers to each other's education, qualities, or disposition.

And if any deem it a shame to our nation to have any mention made of those enormities, let them peruse the histories of the Spaniard's discoveries and plantations, where they may see how many mutinies, ·discords·, disorders, and dissensions have accompanied them and crossed their attempts; which, being known to be particular men's offenses, doth take away the general scorn and contempt which malice, presumption, covetousness, or ignorance might ·else· produce to the scandal and reproach of those whose actions and valiant resolutions deserve a more worthy respect.

Now whether it had been better for Captain Smith to have concluded with any of those several projects to have abandoned the country with some ten or twelve of them who were called the better sort, and have left Master Hunt our preacher, Master Anthony Gosnoll—a most honest, worthy, and industrious gentleman—Master Thomas Wotton, and some 27 others of his countrymen to the fury of the savages, famine, and all manner of mischiefs and inconveniences—for they were but forty in all to keep possession of this large country—or starve himself with them for company for want of lodging, or but adventuring abroad to make them provision, or by his opposition to preserve the action and save all their lives,[1] I leave to the censure of all honest men to consider, but—

We men imagine in our jollity
That 'tis all one or good or bad to be.
But then anon we alter this again,
If happily we feel the sense of pain.
For then we're turn'd into a mourning vein.

WRITTEN BY THOMAS STUDLEY, THE FIRST CAPE MERCHANT IN VIRGINIA, ROBERT FENTON, EDWARD HARRINGTON, AND J[OHN] S[MITH].

Chapter III.

The Arrival of the First Supply with their Proceedings and the Ship's Return.

ALL THIS TIME our care was not so much to abandon the country, but[2] the treasurer and council in England were as diligent and careful to supply us. Two good ·tall· ships they sent us with near a hundred men, well furnished with all things could be imagined necessary, both for them and us, the one commanded by Captain Newport, the other by Captain Francis Nelson, an honest man and an expert mariner. But such was the leewardness of his ship that, though he was within the sight of Cape Henry, by stormy contrary winds was he forced so far to sea that the West Indies was the next land for the repair of his masts and relief of wood and water. But Newport got in and arrived at James Town not long after the redemption of Captain

---

[1] Margin note: "Of two evils the lesser was chosen."
[2] If only.

Smith, to whom the savages, as is said, every other day repaired with such provisions ·of bread, fish, turkeys, squirrels, deer, and other wild beasts· that sufficiently did serve them from hand to mouth. Part always they brought him as presents from their kings or Pocahontas. The rest he as their market clerk set the price himself how they should sell.

So he had enchanted these poor souls, being their prisoner, and now Newport, whom he called his father, arriving near as directly as he foretold, they esteemed him as an oracle; and ·by these fictions he not only saved his own life and obtained his liberty but· had them at that submission he might command them what he listed. That god that created all things they knew he adored for his god, ·whom· they would also in their discourses term "the god of Captain Smith."

Thus the Almighty was the bringer-on,
The guide, path, term—all which was God alone.

But the president and council so much envied his estimation among the savages, though we all in general equally participated with him of the good thereof, that they wrought it into the savages' understandings [that] by their great bounty in giving four times more for their commodities than Smith appointed that their greatness and authority as much exceeded his as their bounty and liberality.

Now the arrival of this first supply so overjoyed us that we could not devise too much to please the mariners. We gave them liberty to truck or trade at their pleasures. But in a short time it followed that could not be had for a pound of copper which before was sold us for an ounce. Thus ambition and sufferance cut the throat of our trade, but confirmed their opinion of the greatness of Captain Newport (wherewith Smith had possessed Powhatan), especially by the great presents Newport often sent him before he could prepare the pinnace to go and visit him, so that this great savage desired also to see him.

A great coil there was to set him forward. When he went he was accompanied with Captain Smith and Master Scrivener—a very wise, understanding gentleman, newly arrived and admitted of the council—with thirty or forty chosen men for their guard. Arriving at

Werowocomoco, Newport's conceit of this great savage bred many doubts and suspicions of treacheries, which Smith, to make appear was needless, with twenty men well appointed undertook to encounter the worst that could happen. Knowing—

All is but one and selfsame hand that thus
Both one while scourgeth and that helpeth us.

·Their names were·:

Gentlemen

Nathaniell Powell
Robert Behethland
Michell Phittiplace
William Phittiplace
Anthony Gosnoll
Richard Wyffin
John Taverner
William Dyer
Thomas Coe
Thomas Hope
Anas Todkill

These with nine others whose names I have forgotten, ·being kindly received·, coming ashore, landed amongst a many of creeks, over which they were to pass such poor bridges only made of a few cratches[1] thrust in the ooze and three or four poles laid on them, and at the end of them the like, tied together only with barks of trees, that it made them much suspect those bridges were but traps; which caused Smith to make divers savages go over first, keeping some of the chief as hostage till half his men was passed, to make a guard for himself and the rest. But finding all things well, by two or three hundred savages they were kindly conducted to their town;

Where Powhatan strained himself to the utmost of his greatness to entertain them with great shouts of joy, orations of protestations, and with the most plenty of victuals he could provide to feast them,

[1] Crotches, crutches = forked stanchions.

sitting upon his bed of mats, his pillow of leather embroidered after their rude manner with pearl and white beads, his attire a fair robe of skins as large as an Irish mantle, at his head and feet a handsome young woman. On each side his house sat twenty of his concubines, their heads and shoulders painted red, with a great chain of white beads about each of their necks; before those sat his chiefest men in like order in his arbor-like house, and [attendants with] more than forty platters of fine bread stood as a guard in two files on each side the door. Four or five hundred people made a guard behind them for our passage. And proclamation was made none upon pain of death to presume to do us any wrong or discourtesy. With many pretty discourses to renew their old acquaintance, this great king and our captain spent the time till the ebb left our barge aground. Then renewing their feasts with feats, dancing, and singing, and suchlike mirth, we quartered that night with Powhatan.

The next day, Newport came ashore and received as much content as those people could give him. A boy named Thomas Salvage was then given unto Powhatan, whom Newport called his son, for whom Powhatan gave him Namontack, his trusty servant and one of a shrewd, subtle capacity.[1] Three or four days more we spent in feasting, dancing, and trading, wherein Powhatan carried himself so proudly yet discreetly in his savage manner as made us all admire his natural gifts, considering his education. As scorning to trade as his subjects did, he bespake Newport in this manner:

"Captain Newport, it is not agreeable to my greatness in this peddling manner to trade for trifles, and I esteem you also a great

---

[1] "Amongst such as have been brought over into England from Virginia, there was one Nanawack, a youth sent over by the Lord De Laware, when he was governor there, who, coming over and living here a year or two in houses where he heard not much of religion, but saw and heard many times examples of drinking, swearing, and like evils, remained as he was, a mere pagan; but after, removed into a godly family, he was strangely altered, grew to understand the principles of religion, learned to read, delighted in the Scriptures, sermons, prayers, and other Christian duties, wonderfully bewailed the state of his countrymen, especially his brethren, and gave such testimonies of his love to the truth, that he was thought fit to be baptized; but being prevented by death, left behind such testimonies of his desire of God's favor, that it moved such godly Christians as knew him to conceive well of his condition." *The Planter's Plea*, 53–54 (1630).

werowance. Therefore lay me down all your commodities together. What I like I will take, and in recompense give you what I think fitting their value."

Captain Smith being our interpreter, regarding Newport as his father, knowing best the disposition of Powhatan, told us his intent was but only to cheat us. Yet Captain Newport, thinking to outbrave this savage in ostentation of greatness, and so to bewitch him with his bounty as to have what he listed——[1] ·But· it so hap'ned that Powhatan, having his desire, valued his corn at such a rate that I think it better cheap in Spain, for we had not four bushels for that we expected to have twenty hogsheads. This bred some unkindness between our two captains, Newport seeking to please the unsatiable desire of the savage, Smith to cause the savage to please him. But [Smith], smothering his distaste to avoid the savage's suspicion, glanced[2] in the eyes of Powhatan many trifles, who fixed his humor upon a few blue beads. A long time he importunately desired them, but Smith seemed so much the more to affect them as being composed of a most rare substance of the color of the skies, and not to be worn but by the greatest kings in the world. This made him half mad to be the owner of such strange jewels, so that, ere we departed, for a pound or two of blue beads be [he] brought over my king for 2 or 300 bushels of corn, yet parted good friends.

The like entertainment we found of Opechankanough, King of Pamaunkee, whom also he in like manner fitted at the like rates with blue beads, which grew by this means of that estimation that none durst wear any of them but their great kings, their wives, and children.

And so we returned all well to James town where this new supply,[3] being lodged with the rest, accidentally fired their quarters and so the town, which being but thatched with reeds, the fire was so fierce as it burnt their palisado's, though eight or ten yards distant, with their arms, bedding, apparel, and much private provision. Good Master Hunt our preacher lost all his library and all he had but the clothes on his back, yet none never heard him repine at his loss.

---

[1] Apparently a small gap in the text.
[2] Flashed.
[3] Of colonists.

This hap'ned in the winter in that extreme frost, 1607. Now though we had victual sufficient—I mean only of oatmeal, meal, and corn—yet the ship staying 14 weeks when she might as well have been gone in 14 days spent a great part of that, ·the beef, pork, oil, aqua vitae, fish, butter and cheese, beer·, and near all the rest that was sent to be landed. When they departed, what their discretion could spare us to make a little poor meal or two we called feasts to relish our mouths. Of each somewhat they left us, yet I must confess those that had either money, spare clothes, credit to give bills of payment, gold rings, furs, or any such commodities were ever welcome to this removing tavern. Such was our patience to obey such vile commanders and buy our own provisions at 15 times the value, suffering them [to] feast, we bearing the charge, yet must not repine, but fast, lest we should incur the censure of factious and seditious persons; and then leakage, ship rats, and other casualties occasioned them loss. But the vessels and remnants for totals[1] we were glad to receive with all our hearts to make up the account, highly commending their providence for preserving that, lest they should discourage any more to come to us.

Now for all this plenty our ordinary was but meal and water, so that this great charge little relieved our wants, whereby with the extremity of the bitter cold frost and those defects more than half of us died ·and took our deaths in that piercing winter·. I cannot deny but both Smith and Skrivener did their best to amend what was amiss, but with the president went the major part, [so] that their horns were too short.

But the worst ·mischief· was our gilded refiners with their golden promises made all men their slaves in hope of recompenses. There was no talk, no hope, no work but *dig* gold, *wash* gold, *refine* gold, *load* gold—such a bruit of GOLD that one mad fellow desired to be buried in the sands, lest they should by their art make gold of his bones! Little need there was and less reason the ship should stay, their wages run on, our victual consume 14 weeks, that the mariners might say they did help to build such a golden church that we can say the rain washed near to nothing in 14 days.

---

[1] I.e., what little remained compared to what the total had been.

Were it that Captain Smith would not applaud all those golden inventions because they admitted him not to the sight of their trials nor golden consultations, I know not. But I have heard him oft question with Captain Martin, and tell him, except he could show him a more substantial trial, he was not enamored with their "dirty" skill, breathing out these and many other passions. Never anything did more torment him than to see all necessary business neglected to fraught such a drunken ship with so much gilded dirt.

Till then we never accounted Captain Newport a refiner, who being ready to set sail for England—and we not having any use of parliaments, plays, petitions, admirals, recorders, interpreters, chronologers, courts of plea, nor justices of peace!—sent Master Wingfield and Captain Archer home with him, that had engrossed all those titles, ·for England· *to seek some place of better employment!*

O cursed gold, those hunger-starved movers,
To what misfortunes lead'st thou all those lovers!
For all the China wealth nor Indies can
Suffice the mind of an av'ricious man.

Chapter IIII.

The arrival of the Phoenix, *her return, and other accidents.*

THE AUTHORITY now consisting in ·"refining"· Captain Martin and the still-sickly president,[1] the sale of the store's commodities maintained his estate as an inheritable revenue!

The spring approaching and the ship departing, Master Scrivener and Captain Smith divided betwixt them the rebuilding James town, the repairing our palisadoes, the cutting down trees, preparing our

[1] The two leaders spent their time looking for gold and "refining" it.

fields, planting our corn, and to rebuild our church and recover our storehouse.

All men thus busy at their several labors, Master Nelson arrived with his lost *Phoenix* (lost I say, for that we all deemed him lost), landing safely all his men. So well he had managed his ill hap, causing the [West] Indian Isles to feed his company, that his victual [added] to that we had gotten, as is said before, was near after our allowance sufficient for half a year. He had not anything but he freely imparted it, which honest dealing (being a mariner) caused us admire him. We would not have wished more than he did for us.

Now to relade this ship with some good tidings, the president—not holding it stood with the dignity of his place to leave the fort—gave order to Captain Smith ·and Master Skrivener· to discover and search the commodities of the Monacans' country beyond the Falls. Sixty able men was allotted them, the which within six days Smith had so well trained to their arms and orders that they little feared with whom they should encounter. Yet so unseasonable was the time, and so opposite was Captain Martin to anything but only to fraught this ship also with his fantastical gold, as Captain Smith rather desired to relade her with cedar, which was a present dispatch, than either with dirt or the hopes and reports of an uncertain discovery which he would perform when they had less charge and more leisure.

But—

The God of heav'n, He eas'ly can
Immortalize a mortal man
With glory and with fame.
The same God ev'n as eas'ly may
Afflict a mortal man, I say,
With sorrow and with shame.

Whilst the conclusion was a-resolving, this hap'ned: Powhatan, to express his love to Newport when he departed, presented him with twenty turkeys conditionally to return him twenty swords, which immediately was sent him. Now after his departure, he presented Captain Smith with the like luggage. But not finding his humor obeyed in not sending him weapons as he desired, he caused his people with twenty devices to obtain them. At last, by ambuscadoes at our very ports they would take them perforce, surprise us at work, or any way, which was so long permitted ·that· they became so insolent there was no rule. The command from England was so strait not to offend them, as our authority bearers, keeping their houses, would rather be anything than peace-breakers.

This charitable humor prevailed till well it chanced they meddled with Captain Smith, who without farther deliberation gave them such an encounter as some he so hunted up and down the isle, some he so terrified with whipping, beating, and imprisonment as for revenge they surprised two of our foraging, disorderly soldiers, and having assembled their forces, boldly threat'ned at our ports to force Smith to redeliver seven savages which for their villainies he detained prisoners, or we were all but dead men. But to try their furies he sallied out amongst them, and in less than ·half· an hour he so hamp'red their insolencies ·that· they brought them his two men, desiring peace without any further composition for their [own seven] prisoners. Those he examined and caused them all believe by several volleys of shot [that] one of their companions was shot to death because they would not confess their intents and plotters of those villainies. And thus they all agreed in one point: They were directed only by Powhatan to obtain him our weapons to cut our own throats, with the manner where, how, and when—which we plainly found most true and apparent.

Yet he sent his messengers and his dearest daughter Pocahontas with presents to excuse him of the injuries done by some rash, untoward captains his subjects, desiring their liberties for this time, with the assurance of his love forever. After Smith had given the prisoners what correction he thought fit, [he] used them well a day or two after and then delivered them Pocahontas, for whose sake only he feigned to have saved their lives and gave them liberty.

The patient council that nothing would move to war with the savages would gladly have wrangled with Captain Smith for his cruelty. Yet none was slain, to any man's knowledge, but it brought them in such fear and obedience as his very name would sufficiently affright them, where before we had sometime peace and war twice in a day, and very seldom a week but we had some treacherous villainy or other.

The fraught of this ship being concluded to be cedar, by the diligence of the master and Captain Smith she was quickly reladed. Master Scrivener was neither idle nor slow to follow all things at the fort.

The ship being ready to set sail, ·falling to the Cedar Isle·, Captain Martin being always very sickly and unserviceable, and desirous, ·having made shift to be sick near a year—and now neither pepper, sugar, cloves, mace, nor nugmets [nutmegs], ginger, nor sweetmeats [remaining] in the country· —to enjoy the credit of his supposed art of finding the golden mine, ·at his earnest request· was most willingly admitted to return for England.

·Yet, having been there [Jamestown] but a year, and not past half a year since the ague left him, that he might say somewhat he had seen, he went twice by water to Paspahegh, a place near 7 miles from James town; but lest the dew should distemper him, was ever forced to return before night.·

·Thus much I thought fit to express, he expressly commanding me to record his journeys, I [Anas Todkill] being his man and he sometimes my master.·

For—

He hath not fill'd his lap
That still doth hold it ope.

FROM THE WRITINGS OF THOMAS STUDLEY AND ANAS TODKILL.

Their names that were landed in this supply[1]:

Mathew Scrivener, *appointed to be one of the council*

Gentlemen

Michaell Phittiplace
William Phittiplace
Ralph Morton
Richard Wyffing

[1] "1608. Sir Thomas Smith, treasurer." (margin note)

John Taverner
William Cantrell
Robert Barnes
Richard Fetherstone
George Hill
George Pretty
Nathaniell Causy
Peter Pory
Robert Cutler
Michaell Sicklemore
William Bentley
Thomas Coe
Doctor Russell
Jeffrey Abbot
Edward Gurgana
Richard Worley
Timothy Leeds
Richard Killingbeck
William Spence
Richard Prodger
Richard Pots
Richard Mullinax
William Bayley
Francis Perkins [the elder]
John Harper
George Forest
John Nichols
William Grivell

Laborers

Raymond Goodison
William Simons
John Spearman
Richard Bristow
William Perce
James Watkins
John Bouth
Christopher Rods

Richard Burket
James Burre
Nicholas Ven
Francis Perkins [the younger]
Richard Gradon
Rawland Nelstrop
Richard Savage
Thomas Savage
Richard Milmer
William May
[Master] Vere
Michaell
Bishop Wiles

Tailors

Thomas Hope
William Ward
John Powell
William Yong
William Beckwith
Larence Towtales

Apothecaries

Thomas Field
John Harford

Daniel Stallings, *jeweler*
William Dawson, *a refiner*
Abram Ransack, *a refiner*
William Johnson, *a goldsmith*
Peter Keffer, *a gunsmith*
Robert Alberton, *a perfumer*
Richard Belfield, *a goldsmith*
Post Ginnat, *a chirurgeon*
John Lewes, *a cooper*
Robert Cotton, *a tobacco pipe maker*
Richard Dole, *a blacksmith*

—and divers others to the number of 120.

Chapter V.

The Accidents that hap'ned in the Discovery of the Bay of Chisapeack

THE PRODIGALITY OF THE PRESIDENT'S STATE went so deep into our small store that Smith and Scrivener tied ·both Martin and· him and his parasites to the rules of proportion. But now Smith being to depart, the president's authority so overswayed the discretion of Master Scrivener that our store, our time, our strength, and labors were idly consumed to fulfill his fantasies.

The second of June, 1608, Smith left the fort to perform his discovery with this company:

Walter Russell, *doctor of physic*

Gentlemen

Ralfe Murton
Thomas Momford
William Cantrill
Richard Fetherston
James Burne
Michell Sicklemore

Soldiers

Jonas Profit ·*fisher*·
Anas Todkill
Robert Small
James Watkins
John Powell
James Read ·*blacksmith*·
Richard Keale ·*fishmonger*·

These being in an open barge ·of· near three tons burthen,[1] leaving the *Phoenix* at Cape Henry, they crossed the bay to the eastern shore and fell with the isles called Smith's Isles after our captain's name.

[1] "of two tons burthen" in *The Proceedings*.

The first people we saw were two grim and stout savages upon Cape Charles, with long poles like javelins headed with bone. They boldly demanded what we were and what we would, but after many circumstances they ·in time· seemed very kind, and directed us to Accomack, the habitation of their werowance, where we were kindly entreated.

This king was the comeliest proper, civil savage we encount'red. His country is a pleasant, fertile clay soil, some small creeks, good harbors for small barks but not for ships.

He told us of a strange accident lately happened him, and it was two children, being dead, some extreme passions or dreaming visions, fantasies or affection moved their parents again to revisit their dead carcasses, whose benumbed bodies reflected to the eyes of the beholders such ·pleasant·, delightful countenances as though they had regained their vital spirits. This as a miracle drew many to behold them, all which (being a great part of his people) not long after died, and but few escaped.

They spake the language of Powhatan, wherein they made such descriptions of the bay, isles, and rivers, that often did us exceeding pleasure.

Passing along the coast, searching every inlet and bay fit for harbors and habitations—seeing many isles in the midst of the bay, we bore up for them. But ere we could obtain them, such an extreme gust of wind, rain, thunder, and lightning happened that with great danger we escaped the unmerciful raging of that ocean-like water.

The highest land on the main, yet it was but low, we called Keale's Hill, and these uninhabited isles Russell's Isles.

The next day, searching them for fresh water, we could find none; the defect whereof forced us to follow the next eastern channel, which brought us to the River of Wighcocomoco.The people at first with great fury seemed to assault us, yet at last with songs and dances and much mirth became very tractable. But searching their habitations for water, we could fill but three barricoes [kegs], and that such puddle[1] that never till then we ever knew the want of good water. We digged and searched in many places, but before two days were

---

[1] Muddy like puddle water.

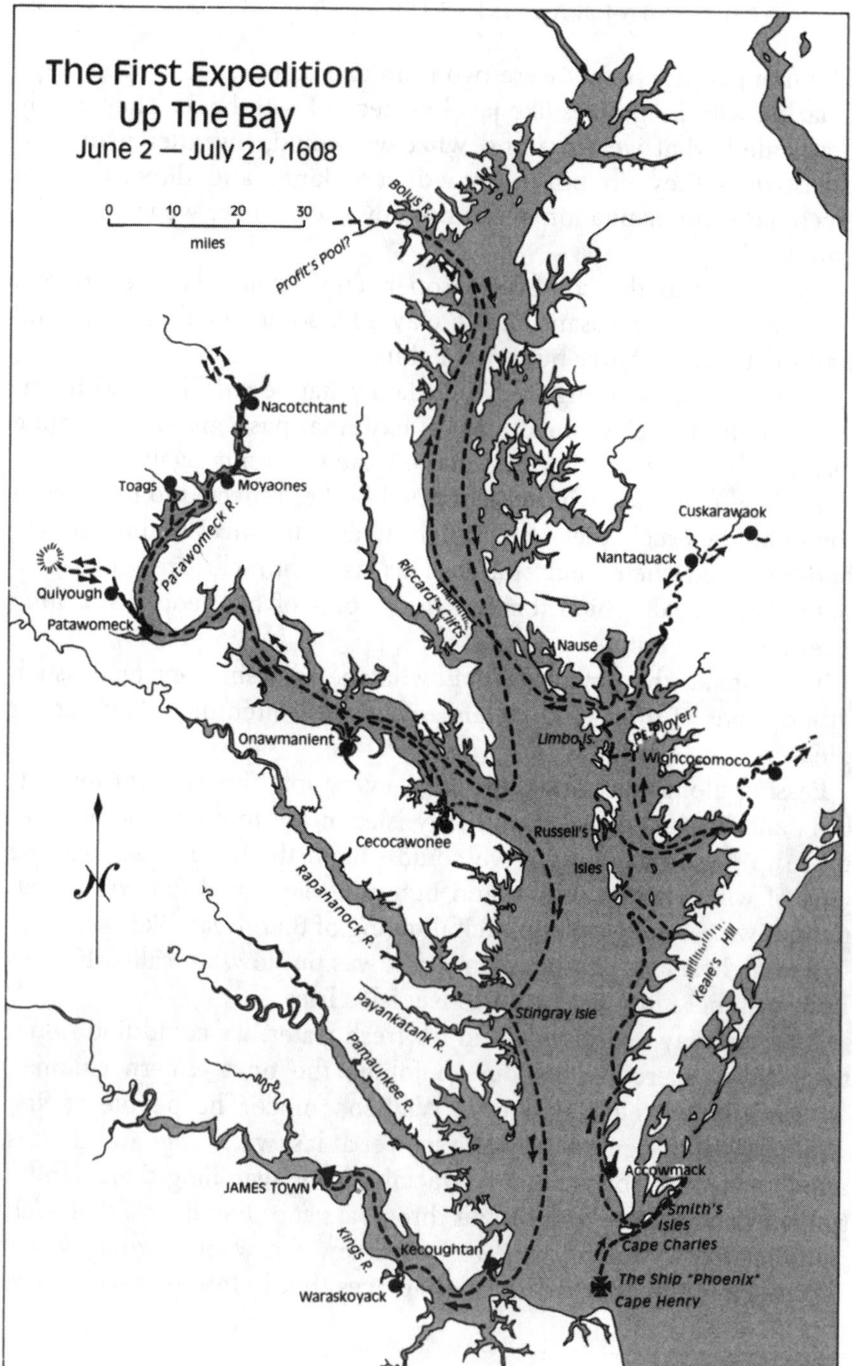
The First Expedition
Up The Bay
June 2 — July 21, 1608
0 10 20 30
miles
Bolus R.
Profit's Pool?
Nacotchtant
Toags
Moyaones
Patawomeck R.
Quiyough
Patawomeck
Riccard's Clifts
Cuskarawaok
Nantaquack
Nause
Limbo Is.
Pt. Ployer?
Wighcocomoco
Onawmanient
Cecocawonee
Russell's
Isles
Rapahanock R.
Keale's Hill
Stingray Isle
Payankatank R.
Pamaunkee R.
JAMES TOWN
Accowmack
Smith's
Isles
Cape Charles
Kings R.
Kecoughtan
Waraskoyack
The Ship "Phoenix"
Cape Henry

expired we would have refused two barricoes of gold for one of that puddle water of Wighcocomoco.

Being past these isles, which are many in number but all naught for habitation, falling with a high land upon the main, we found a great pond of fresh water, but so exceeding hot we supposed it some bath. That place we called "Point Ployer" in honor of that most honorable House of Mousay in Britain that in an extreme extremity once relieved our captain. From Wighcocomoco to this place all the coast is low broken isles of morap [?] grown a mile or two in breadth and ten or twelve in length, good to cut for hay in summer and to catch fish and fowl in winter. But the land beyond them is all covered over with wood, as is the rest of the country.

Being thus refreshed, in crossing over from the main to other isles, we discovered the wind and waters so much increased with thunder, lightning, and rain that our ·fore·mast and sail blew overboard, and such mighty waves overracked [overraked] us in that small barge that with great labor we kept her from sinking by freeing out the water. Two days we were enforced to inhabit these uninhabited isles, which for the extremity of gusts, thunder, rain, storms, and ill weather we called "Limbo."

Repairing our ·fore·sail with our shirts, we set sail for the main and fell with a pretty, convenient river on the east called Cuskarawaok.

The people ran as amazed in troops from place to place, and divers got into the tops of trees. They were not sparing of their arrows nor the greatest passion they could express of their anger. Long they shot, we still riding at an anchor without their reach, making all the signs of friendship we could. The next day they came unarmed, with everyone a basket, dancing in a ring to draw us on shore. But seeing there was nothing in them but villainy, we discharged a volley of muskets charged with pistol shot, whereat they all lay tumbling on the ground, creeping some one way, some another, into a great cluster of reeds hard by, where their companies lay in ambuscado. Towards the evening we weighed and approaching the shore, discharging five or six shot among the reeds, we landed where there lay a many of baskets and much blood, but saw not a savage. A smoke appearing on the other side the river, we rowed thither where we found two or three little houses, in each a fire. There we left some pieces of copper, beads, bells, and looking glasses, and then went into the bay. But when it was dark, we came back again. Early in the morning four savages came to us in their canoe, whom we used with such courtesy, that [they] not knowing what we were nor had done, having been in the bay a-fishing, bade us stay and ere long they would return, which they did and some twenty more with them; with whom, after a little conference, two or three thousand men, women, and children came clust'ring about us, everyone presenting us with something which a little bead would so well requite that we became such friends they would contend who should fetch us water, stay with us for hostage, conduct our men any whither, and give us the best content.

Here doth inhabit the people of Sarapinagh, Nause, Arseek, and Nantaquak, the best merchants of all other savages. They much extolled a great nation called Massawomekes, in search of whom we returned by Limbo.

This river, but only at the entrance, is very narrow and the people of small stature as them of Wighcocomoco, the land but low, yet it may prove very commodious because it is but a ridge of land betwixt the bay and the main ocean.

Finding this eastern shore shallow broken isles, and ·the main· for most part without fresh water, we passed by the Straits of Limbo for the western shore.

So broad is the bay here ·that· we could scarce perceive the great high clifts on the other side. By them we anchored that night, and called them "Riccard's Clifts."[1]

---

[1] "As they continued to sail northwards, the land from the east jutted into the bay. It narrowed so much that at one point, from the western shore towards the eastern side, it was only two leagues wide. After that they discovered coves and inlets, as well as rivers, along the western shore. Then they came upon a large freshwater river, which, where it entered the bay, was more than six fathoms deep. To the north of it there was very high land, with ravines, but without trees, cleared and like a green field and pleasant to behold. On the southern shore of this river the beach is very calm and it is covered with tiny pebbles. Farther up on the south bank of the same river appeared a delightful valley, wooded, with pleasant land, apparently fertile and suitable for stock-breeding and husbandry. This river was located in latitude 38 degrees. They named it San Pedro" (the Patuxent River). An account from the

30 leagues we sailed more northwards, not finding any inhabitants, leaving all the eastern shore, low islands but overgrown with wood, as all the coast beyond them so far as we could see. The western shore by which we sailed we found all along well watered, but very mountainous and barren, the valleys very fertile, but extreme thick of small wood so well as trees, and much frequented with wolves, bears, deer, and other wild beasts.

We passed many shallow creeks, but the first ·inlet· we found navigable for a ship we called "Bolus," for that the clay in many places under the clifts by the high-water mark did grow up in red and white knots as gum out of trees, and in some places so participated together as though they were all of one nature, excepting the color, the rest of the earth on both sides being hard sandy gravel—which made us think it bole armoniac and terra sigillata.

When we first set sail, some of our gallants doubted nothing but that our captain would make too much haste home. But having lyen [lain] in this small barge not above 12 or 14 days, oft tired at the oars, our bread spoiled with wet so much that it was rotten—yet so good were their stomachs that they could digest it—they did with continual complaints so importune him now to return as caused him bespeak them in this manner:

"Gentlemen, if you would remember the memorable history of Sir Ralph Layne, how his company importuned him to proceed in the discovery of Moratico, alleging they had yet a dog that being boiled with saxafras leaves would richly feed them in their returns, then what a shame would it be for you that have been so suspicious of my tenderness to force me return with so much provision as we have,[1] and scarce able to say where we have been nor yet heard of that we were sent to seek.[2]

"You cannot say but I have shared with you in the worst, which is past. And for what is to come—of lodging, diet, or whatsoever—I am contented you allot the worst part to myself.

"As for your fears that I will lose myself in these unknown large

---

journal of Juan Menendez Marques of the expedition under Vicente Gonzalez to the Chesapeake Bay in June 1588 (Quinn 1979e:61).

1 "A month's provision" in *The Proceedings*.

2 Quite accurate. See Lane's narrative in Quinn 1979c:298.2.

waters, or be swallowed up in some stormy gust, abandon these childish fears, for worse than is passed is not likely happen, and there is as much danger to return as to proceed.

"Regain therefore you old spirits, for return I will not (if God please) till I have seen the Massawomeks, found Patawomek, or the head of this water you conceit to be endless."

Two or 3 days we expected[1] wind and weather, whose adverse extremities added such discouragement ·to our discontents· that three or four fell ·extreme· sick, whose pitiful complaints caused us to return, leaving the bay some nine miles broad at nine and ten fadom water.

The 16 of June, we fell with the River Patowomek. Fear being gone and our men recovered, we were all content to take some pains to know the name of that seven-mile-broad river. For thirty miles' sail we could see no inhabitants.

Then we were conducted by two savages up a little bayed creek towards Onawmanient, where all the woods were laid with ambuscados to the number of three or four thousand savages,[2] so strangely painted, grimed, and disguised, shouting, yelling, and crying as so many spirits from hell could not have showed more terrible. Many bravados they made, but to appease their fury our captain prepared with as seeming a willingness as they to encounter them. But the grazing of our bullets upon the water (many being shot on purpose they might see them) with the echo of the woods so amazed them as down went their bows and arrows, and exchanging hostage, James Watkins was sent six miles up the woods to their king's habitation.

We were kindly used of those savages, of whom we understood they were commanded to betray us by the direction of Powhatan, and he so directed from the discontents at James town, because our captain did cause them stay in their country against their wills.[3]

The like encounters we found at Patowomek, Cecocawonee, and divers other places, but at Moyaones, Nacotchtant, and Toags the

[1] Waited out.

[2] "3 or 400 savages" in *The Proceedings.*

[3] Ambiguous, apparently meaning Powhatan was directed by (saw his chance from?) colonists discontent at being forced to live with Indians, likely including as well the "Dutchmen," who proved treacherous later. See 304 *passim,* 325.

people did their best to content us.

Having gone so high as we could with the boat, we met divers savages in canoes well loaden with the flesh of bears, deer, and other beasts, whereof we had part. Here we found mighty rocks growing in some places above the ground as high as the shrubby trees, and divers other solid quarries of divers tinctures. And divers places where the waters had fall'n from the high mountains they had left a tinctured, spangled scurf [layer] that made many bare places seem as gilded. Digging the ground above in the highest clifts of rocks we saw it was a clay sand so mingled with yellow spangles as if it had been half pin-dust.[1]

In our return inquiring still for this *matchqueon,* the King of Patawomeke gave us guides to conduct us up a little river called Quiyough, up which we rowed so high as we could. Leaving the boat with six shot and divers savages, he marched seven or eight mile before they came to the mine,[2] leading his hostages in a small chain they were to have for their pains, being proud so richly to be adorned.

The mine is a great rocky mountain like antimony, wherein they digged a great hole with shells and hatchets. And hard by it runneth a fair brook of crystal-like water where they wash away the dross and keep the remainder, which they put in little bags and sell it all over the country to paint their bodies, faces, or idols, which makes them look like blackmoors dusted over with silver. With so much as we could carry we returned to our boat, kindly requiting this kind king and all his kind people.

The cause of this discovery was to search this mine,[3] ·a glistering metal the savages told us they had from Patawomeck·, of which Newport did assure us that those small bags we had given him in England he had tried to hold half silver. But all we got proved of no value.

Also [we came] to search what furs (the best whereof is at

---

1 "Dust formed of the filings of brass or other metal produced in the manufacture of pins." OED

2 "The mine we found 9 or 10 miles up in the country from the river, but it proved of no value." *(The Proceedings.)* This note is new in the third printing.

3 "Antimony" (margin note in *The Proceedings).*

Cuscarawaoke where is made so much *rawranoke,* or white beads, that occasion as much dissension among the savages as gold and silver amongst Christians), and what other minerals, rivers, rocks, nations, woods, fishings, fruits, victual, and what other commodities the land afforded, and whether the bay were endless or how far it extended.

Of mines we were all ignorant, but a few beavers, otters, bears, martens, and minks, ·luswarts[1] and sables· we found, and in divers places that abundance of fish lying so thick with their heads above the water as for want of nets (our barge driving amongst them) we attempted to catch them with a frying pan, but we found it a bad instrument to catch fish with: Neither better fish, more plenty, nor more variety for small fish had any of us ever seen in any place so swimming in the water ·than in the Bay of Chesapeack·, but they are not to be caught with frying pans!

Some small cod also we did see swim close by the shore by Smith's Isles, and some as high as Riccard's Clifts, and some we have found dead upon the shore.

To express all our quarrels, treacheries, and encounters amongst those savages I should be too tedious, but, in brief, at all times we so encount'red them and curbed their insolencies that they concluded with presents to purchase peace, yet we lost not a man. At our first meeting, our captain ever observed this order: to demand their bows and arrows, swords, mantles, and furs, with some child or two for hostage, whereby we could quickly perceive when they intended any villainy.

Having finished this discovery, though our victual was near spent, he intended to see his imprisonment-acquaintances upon the River of Rapahanock, by many called Toppahanock. But our boat by reason of the ebb chancing to ground upon a many shoals lying in the entrances, we spied many fishes lurking in the reeds.[2] Our captain, sporting himself ·to catch them· by nailing them to the ground with his sword, set us all a-fishing in that manner; thus we

---

[1] Lynxes.

[2] "in the weeds on the sands." in *The Proceedings.*

took more in one hour than we could eat in a day.

But it chanced our captain taking a fish from his sword, not knowing her condition, being much of the fashion of a thornback, but ·with· a long tail like a riding rod, whereon the middest is a most poisoned sting of two or three inches long, bearded like a saw on each side, which she struck into the wrist of his arm near an inch and a half. No blood nor wound was seen, but a little blue spot. But the torment was instantly so extreme that in four hours had so swollen his hand, arm, and shoulder ·and part of his body as· we all with much sorrow concluded his funeral and prepared his grave in an island ·hard· by, as himself directed. Yet it pleased God by a precious oil Doctor Russell at the first applied to it when he sounded it with probe [that] ere night his tormenting pain was so well assuaged that he ate of the fish to his supper, which gave no less joy and content to us than ease to himself, for which we called the island "Stingray Isle" after the name of the fish.

Having neither chirurgeon nor chirurgery but that preservative oil, we presently set sails for James town; passing the mouths of Payankatank and Pamaunkee ·rivers·, the next day we safely arrived at Kecougtan.

The simple savages, seeing our captain hurt and another bloody by breaking his shin, [and] our numbers of bows, arrows, swords, ·targets·, mantles, and furs, would needs imagine we had been at wars. The truth of these accidents would not satisfy them, but impatiently ·they· importuned us to know with whom ·we fought·. Finding their aptness to believe, we failed not as a great secret to tell them anything that might affright them: what spoil we had got and made of the Massawomeks.

This rumor went faster up the river than our barge, that arrived at Waraskoyack the 20 of July, where trimming her with painted streamers and such devices as we could we made them at James town jealous of a Spanish frigate; where we all, God be thanked, safely arrived the 21 of July.

There we found the last supply were all sick, the rest—some lame, some bruised—all unable to do anything but complain of the pride and unreasonable, needless cruelty of the silly president, that had riotously consumed the store and to fulfill his follies about building him an unnecessary building for his pleasure in the woods had brought them all to that misery that, had we not arrived, they had as strangely tormented him with revenge.

But the good news of our discovery and the good hope we had by the savages' relation that our bay had stretched into the south sea or somewhat near it appeased their fury, but conditionally that Ratliffe should be deposed and that Captain Smith would take upon him the government, as by course it did belong.

Their request being effected, he substituted Master Scrivener, his dear friend, in the presidency, equally distributing those private provisions the other had engrossed; appointing more honest officers to assist Master Scrivener, who then lay exceeding sick of a calenture; and in regard of the weakness of the company and heat of the year—they being unable to work—he left them to live at ease to recover their healths, but embarked himself to finish his discovery.

WRITTEN BY WALTER RUSSELL, ANAS TODKILL, AND THOMAS MOMFORD.

Chapter VI.

The Government surrend'red to Master Scrivener. What happened the second voyage in discovering the Bay.

THE 24 OF JULY,[1] Captain Smith set forward to finish the discovery with twelve men. Their names were:

Gentlemen

Nathaniell Powell
Thomas Momford
Richard Fetherston
Michell Sicklemore
James Bourne
Anthony Bagnall, *chirurgeon*

---

[1] 20th in *The Proceedings.*

Soldiers

Jonas Profit
Anas Todkill
Edward Pising
Richard Keale
James Watkins
William Ward

The wind being contrary caused our stay two or three days at Kecoughtan. The king feasted us with much mirth. His people were persuaded we went purposely to be revenged of the Massawomeks. In the evening we fired a few rackets, which flying in the air so terrified the poor savages they supposed nothing unpossible we attempted, and desired to assist us.

The first night, we anchored at Stingray Isle; the next day, crossed Patawomek's River and hasted to the River Bolus. We went not much further before we might see the bay to divide in two heads, and arriving there we found it divided in four, all which we searched so far as we could sail them. Two of them we found inhabited,[1] but in crossing the bay ·to the other· we encount'red 7 or 8 canoes full of Massawomeks.

We, seeing them prepare to assault us, left our oars and made way with our sail to encounter them. Yet were we but five with our captain that could stand, for within 2 days after we left Kecoughtan the rest, being all of the last supply, were sick almost to death until they were seasoned to the country. Having shut them under our tarpaulin, we put their hats upon sticks by the barge's side, and betwixt two hats a man with two pieces, to make us seem many. And so we think the Indians supposed those hats to be men, for they fled with all possible speed to the shore and there stayed, staring at the sailing of our barge till we anchored right against them.

Long it was ere we could draw them to come unto us. At last they sent two of their company unarmed in a canoe; the rest all followed to second them if need required. These two, being but each presented with a bell, brought aboard all their fellows, presenting our

[1] "Uninhabited" in *The Proceedings.*

captain with venison, bear's flesh, fish, bows, arrows, clubs, targets, and bear's skins. We understood them nothing at all but by signs, whereby they signified unto us they had been at wars with the Tockwoghes, the which they confirmed by showing us their green wounds. But the night parting us, we imagined they appointed the next morning to meet, but after that we never saw them.

Ent'ring the River of Tockwogh, the savages all armed in a fleet of boats after their barbarous manner round environed us. So it chanced one of them could speak the language of Powhatan, who persuaded the rest to a friendly parley. But when they saw us furnished with the Massawomeks' weapons, and we feigning the invention of Kecoughtan to have taken them perforce, they conducted us to their palisadoed town mantled with the barks of trees, with scaffolds like mounts breasted about with breasts very formally. Their men, women, and children with dances, songs, fruits, ·fish·, furs, and what they had kindly welcomed us, spreading mats for us to sit on, stretching their best abilities to express their loves.

Many hatchets, knives, pieces of iron and brass we saw amongst them which they reported to have from the Sasquesahanocks, a mighty people and mortal enemies with the Massawomeks.

The Sasquesahanocks inhabit upon the chief spring of these four branches of the bay's head, two days' journey higher than our barge could pass for rocks. Yet we prevailed with the interpreter to take with him another interpreter to persuade the Sasquesahanocks to come visit us, for their language are different.

Three or four days we expected their return; then sixty of those giant-like people came down with presents of venison, tobacco pipes three foot in length, baskets, targets, bows, and arrows. Five of their chief werowances came boldly aboard us to cross the bay for Tockwhogh, leaving their men and canoes, the wind being so high they durst not pass.

Our order was daily to have prayer with a psalm, at which solemnity the poor savages much wond'red. Our prayers being done, a while they were busied with consultation till they had contrived their business. Then they began in a most passionate manner to hold up their hands to the sun with a most fearful song; then embracing our captain, they began to adore him in like manner; though he rebuked

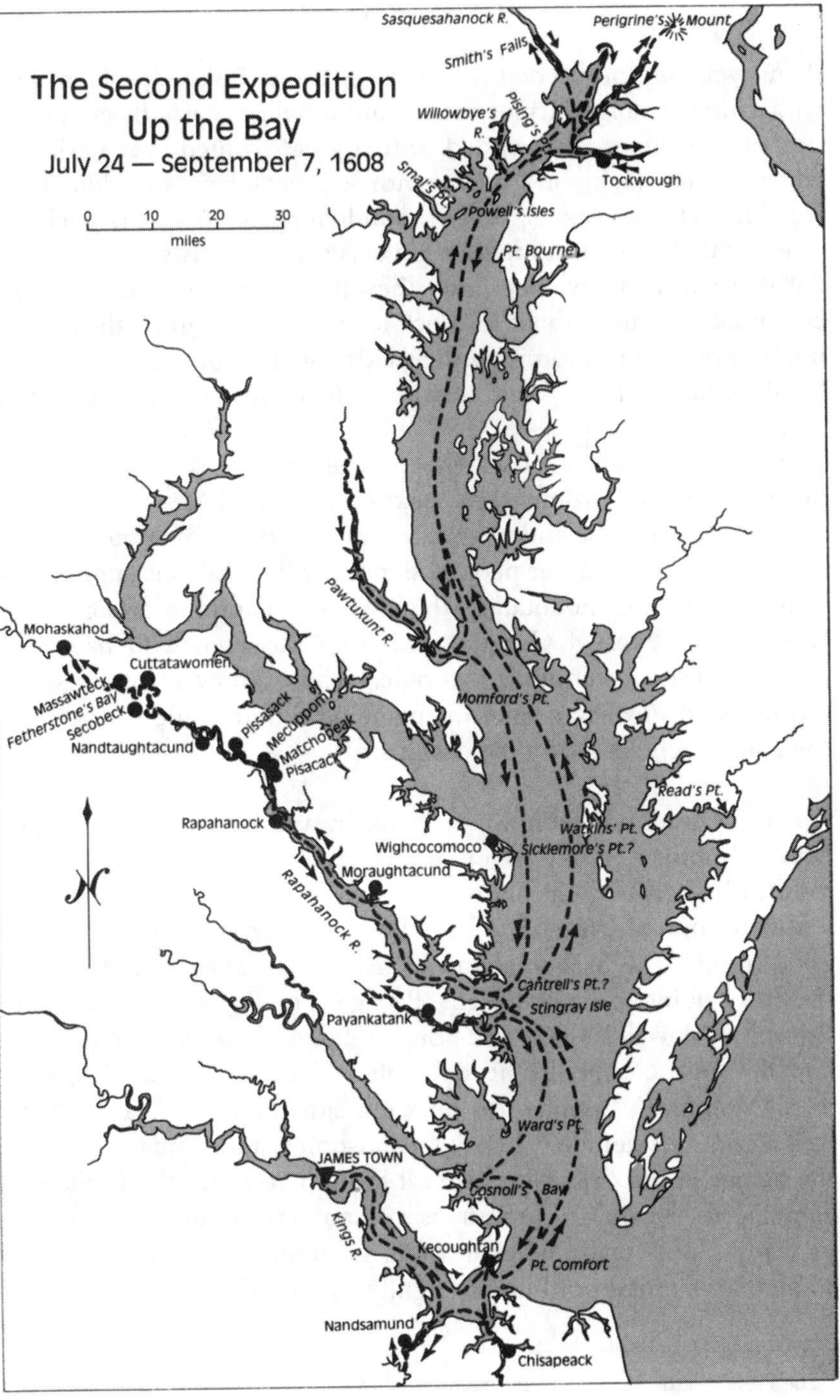
The Second Expedition
Up the Bay
July 24 — September 7, 1608
0 10 20 30
miles
Sasquesahanock R.
Perigrine's Mount
Smith's Falls
Willowbye's R.
Pising's Pt.
Smal's Pt.
Tockwough
Powell's Isles
Pt. Bourne
Pawtuxunt R.
Mohaskahod
Cuttatawomen
Massawteck
Fetherstone's Bay
Secobeck
Nandtaughtacund
Pissasack
Mecuppom
Matchopeak
Pisacack
Momford's Pt.
Read's Pt.
Rapahanock
Watkins' Pt.
Wighcocomoco
Sicklemore's Pt.?
Moraughtacund
Rapahanock R.
Cantrell's Pt.?
Stingray Isle
Payankatank
Ward's Pt.
JAMES TOWN
Cosnoll's Bay
Kings R.
Kecoughtan
Pt. Comfort
Nandsamund
Chisapeack

them, yet they proceeded till their song was finished; which done, with a most strange furious action and a hellish voice began an oration of their loves. That ended, with a great painted bear's skin they covered him; then one ready with a great chain of white beads weighing at least six or seven pound hung it about his neck; the others had 18 mantles made of divers sorts of skins sewed together. All these with many other toys they laid at his feet, stroking their ceremonious hands about his neck for his creation to be their governor and protector, promising their aids, victuals, or what they had to be his, if he would stay with them to defend and revenge them of the Massawomeks.

But we left them at Tockwhogh, ·they much· sorrowing for our departure, yet we promised the next year again to visit them.

Many descriptions and discourses they made us of Atquanachuck, Massawomek, and other people, signifying they inhabit upon a great water beyond the mountains, which we understood to be some great lake or the River of Canada, and from the French to have their hatchets and commodities by trade.[1] These know no more of the territories of Powhatan than his name, and he as little of them. But the Atquanachuks are on the ocean sea.

The highest mountain we saw northward we called "Perigrine's Mount," and a rocky river where the Massawomeks went up "Willowbyes River," in honor of the town our captain was born in and that honorable house [of] the Lord Willowby, his most honored good friend. The Sasquesahanocks' River we called "Smith's Falls"; the next point to Tockwhogh "Pising's Point"; the next it "Point Bourne." "Powell's Isles" and "Smal's Point" is by the River Bolus, and the little bay at the head "Profit's Pool." "Watkins'," Read's," and "Momford's" points are on each side Limbo; "Ward," "Cantrell," and "Sicklemore" betwixt Patawomek and Pamaunkee, after the names of the discoverers. In all those places and the furthest we came up the rivers we cut in trees so many crosses as we would, and in many places made holes in trees, wherein we writ notes, and in some places crosses of brass to signify to any [that] Englishmen had

[1] The French settled Quebec barely a month before this—July 3, 1608.

been there.

Thus having sought all the inlets and rivers worth noting, we returned to discover the River of Pawtuxunt. These people we found very tractable and more civil than any. We promised them, as also the Patawomeks, ·the next year· to revenge them of the Massawomeks, but our purposes were crossed.

In the discovery of this river some call Rapahanock (·we had much wrangling with that peevish nation. But at last they became as tractable as the rest. It is an excellent, pleasant, well inhabited, fertile, and a goodly navigable river·), we were kindly entertained by the people of Moraughtacund. Here we encountered our old friend Mosco, a lusty savage of Wighcocomoco upon the River of Patawomek.

We supposed him some Frenchman's son because he had a thick black bush beard, and the savages seldom have any at all—of which he was not a little proud to see so many of his countrymen. Wood and water he would fetch us, guide us any whither, nay, cause divers of his countrymen help us tow against wind or tide from place to place till we came to Patawomek. There he rested till we returned from the head of the river, and occasioned our conduct to the mine we supposed antimony.

And in the place [Moraughtacund] he failed not to do us all the good he could, persuading us in any case not to go to the Rapahanocks, for they would kill us for being friends with the Moraughtacunds, that but lately had stol'n three of the king's women. This we did think was but that his friends might only have our trade, so we crossed the river to the Rapahanocks.

There some 12 or 16 standing on the shore directed us a little creek where was good landing, and commodities for us in three or four canoes we saw lie there. But according to our custom we demanded to exchange a man in sign of love, which, after they had a little consulted, four or five came up to the middles to fetch our man and leave us one of them, showing we need not fear them, for they had neither clubs, bows, nor arrows. Notwithstanding, Anas Todkill, being sent on shore to see if he could discover any ambuscadoes or what they had, desired to go over the plain to fetch some wood. But they were unwilling except we would come into the creek where the boat might come close ashore. Todkill by degrees having got some two stones' throws up the plain perceived two or three hundred men, as he thought, behind the trees, so that, offering to return to the boat, the savages essayed to carry him away perforce, that he called to us we were betrayed; and by that he had spoke the word our hostage was overboard, but Watkins his keeper slew him in the water. Immediately we let fly amongst them, so that they fled and Todkill escaped. Yet they shot so fast that he fell flat on the ground ere he could recover the boat. Here the Massawomek targets stood us in good stead, for upon Mosco's words we had set them about the fore part of our boat like a forecastle, from whence we securely beat the savages from off the plain without any hurt. Yet they shot more than a thousand arrows, and then fled into the woods.

Arming ourselves with these light targets—which are made of little small sticks woven betwixt strings of their hemp and silk grass as is our cloth, but so firmly that no arrow can possibly pierce them—we rescued Todkill, who was all bloody by some of them who were shot by us that held him, but as God pleased he had no hurt. And following them up to the woods, we found some slain and in divers places much blood. It seems all their arrows were spent, for we heard no more of them. Their canoes we took. The arrows we found we broke, save them we kept for Mosco, to whom we gave the canoes for his kindness that entertained us in the best triumphing manner and warlike order in arms of conquest he could procure of the Moraughtacunds.

The rest of the day we spent in accommodating our boat: Instead of tholes we made sticks like bedstaves to which we fastened so many of our Massawomek targets that environed her as waistcloths.

The next morning we went up the river and our friend Mosco followed us along the shore, and at last desired to go with us in our boat. But as we passed by Pisacack, Matchopeak, and Mecuppom, three towns situated upon high white, clay clifts—the other side all a low plain marish, and the river there but narrow—thirty or forty of the Rapahanocks had so accommodated themselves with branches as we took them for little bushes growing among the sedge, still seeing their arrows strike the targets and dropped in the river; whereat

Mosco fell flat in the boat on his face, crying THE RAPAHANOCKS! — which presently we espied to be the bushes; which at our first volley fell down in the sedge. When we were near half a mile from them they showed themselves, dancing and singing very merrily.

The kings of Pissassack, Nandtaughtacund, and Cuttatawomen used us kindly, and all their people neglected not anything to Mosco to bring us to them.

Betwixt Secobeck and Massawteck is a small isle or two which causeth the river to be broader than ordinary. There it pleased God to take one of our company called Master Fetherstone, that all the time he had been in this country had behaved himself honestly, valiantly, and industriously, where in a little bay we called "Fetherstone's Bay" we buried him with a volley of shot. The rest, notwithstanding their ill diet and bad lodging, crowded in so small a barge in so many dangers, never resting but always tossed to and again, had all well recovered their healths.

The next day we sailed so high as our boat would float, there setting up crosses and graving our names in the trees. Our sentinel saw an arrow fall by him, though we had ranged up and down more than an hour in digging in the earth, looking of stones, herbs, and springs, not seeing where a savage could well hide himself.

Upon the alarum, by that we had recovered our arms, there was about an hundred nimble Indians skipping from tree to tree, letting fly their arrows so fast as they could. The trees here served us for barricadoes as well as they. But Mosco did us more service than we expected, for having shot away his quiver of arrows, he ran to the boat for more. The arrows of Mosco at the first made them pause upon the matter, thinking by his bruit and skipping there were many savages. About half an hour this continued; then they all vanished as suddenly as they approached. Mosco followed them so far as he could see us, till they were out of sight.

As we returned there lay a savage as dead, shot in the knee, but taking him up we found he had life; which Mosco seeing never was dog more furious against a bear than Mosco was to have beat out his brains, so we had him to our boat where our chirurgeon, who went with us to cure our captain's hurt of the stingray, so dressed this savage that within an hour after he looked somewhat cheerfully and did eat and speak.

In the meantime we contented Mosco in helping him to gather up their arrows, which were an armful, whereof he gloried not a little.

Then we desired Mosco to know what he was and what countries were beyond the mountains. The poor savage mildly answered he and all with him were of Hasinninga, where there are three kings more, like unto them, namely, the King of Stegora, the King of Tauxuntania, and the King of Shakahonea, that were come to Mohaskahod, which is only a hunting town, and the bounds betwixt the kingdom of the Mannahocks and the Nandtaughtacunds, but hard by where we were. We demanded why they came in that manner to betray us that came to them in peace and to seek their loves. He answered they heard we were a people come from under the world to take their world from them. We asked him how many worlds he did know. He replied he knew no more but that which was under the sky that covered him, which were the Powhatans, with the Monacans and the Massawomeks, that were higher up in the mountains. Then we asked him what was beyond the mountains; he answered the sun, but of anything else he knew nothing because the woods were not burnt.[1]

These and many such questions we demanded concerning the Massawomeks, the Monacans, their own country, and where were the kings of Stegora, Tauxsintania, and the rest. The Monacans he said were their neighbors and friends and did dwell as they in the hilly countries by small rivers, living upon roots and fruits, but chiefly by hunting. The Massawomeks did dwell upon a great water and had many boats and so many men that they made war with all the world. For their kings they were gone everyone a several way with their men on hunting, but those with him came thither a-fishing till they saw us. Notwithstanding, they would be all together at night at Mahaskahod.

For his relation we gave him many toys, with persuasions to go with us, and he as earnestly desired us to stay the coming of those kings that for his good usage should be friends with us, for he was brother to Hasinninga. But Mosco advised us presently to be gone,

---

[1] "They cannot travel but where the woods are burnt." (margin note)

for they were all naught, yet we told him we would not till it was night. All things we made ready to entertain what came, and Mosco was as diligent in trimming his arrows.

The night being come, we all embarked. For the river was so narrow, had it been light, the land on the one side was so high they might have done us exceeding much mischief. All this while the King of Hasinninga was seeking the rest, and had consultation a good time what to do. But by their espies seeing we were gone, it was not long before we heard their arrows dropping on every side the boat. We caused our savages to call unto them, but such a yelling and hallooing they made that they heard nothing but now and then a piece, aiming so near as we could where we heard the most voices.

More than 12 miles they followed us in this manner. Then the day appearing, we found ourselves in a broad bay out of danger of their shot, where we came to an anchor and fell to breakfast.

Not so much as speaking to them till the sun was risen, being well refreshed we untied our targets that covered us as a deck, and all showed ourselves with those shields on our arms and swords in our hands, and also our prisoner Amoroleck. A long discourse there was betwixt his countrymen and him how good we were, how well we used him, how we had a Patawomek with us loved us as his life, that would have slain him had we not preserved him, and that he should have his liberty would they be but friends, and to do us any hurt it was impossible.

Upon this they all hung their bows and quivers upon the trees. And one came swimming aboard us with a bow tied on his head, and another with a quiver of arrows, which they delivered our captain as a present. The captain, having used them so kindly as he could, told them the other three kings should do the like and then the great king of our world should be their friend, whose men we were. It was no sooner demanded but performed. So upon a low, moorish [swampy] point of land we went to the shore where those four kings came and received Amoroleck. Nothing they had but bows, arrows, tobacco bags, and pipes. What we desired none refused to give us, wondering at everything we had and heard we had done. Our pistols they took for pipes, which they much desired, but we did content them with other commodities; and so we left four or five hundred of our merry Mannahocks singing, dancing, and making merry, and set sail for Moraughtacund.

In our returns we visited all our friends, that rejoiced much at our victory against the Mannahocks, who many times had wars also with them. But now they were friends and desired we would be friends with the Rapahanocks as we were with the Mannahocks.

Our captain told them they [the Rapahanocks] had twice assaulted him that came only in love to do them good, and therefore he would now burn all their houses, destroy their corn, and forever hold them his enemies till they made him satisfaction. They desired to know what that should be. He told them they should present him the king's bow and arrows, and not offer to come armed where he was, that they should be friends with the Moraughtacunds, his friends, and give him their king's son in pledge to perform it, and then all King James his men should be their friends.

Upon this they presently sent to the Rapahanocks to meet him at the place where they first fought, where would be the kings of Nantautacund and Pissassac, which according to their promise were there so soon as we, [and] where Rapahanock presented his bow and arrows and confirmed all we desired, except his son. Having no more but him, he could not live without him, but instead of his son he would give him the three women Moraughtacund had stol'n. This was accepted, and so in three or four canoes so many as could went with us to Moraughtacund, where Mosco made them such relations and gave to his friends so many bows and arrows that they no less loved him than admired us.

The 3 women were brought our captain. To each he gave a chain of beads; and then causing Moraughtacund, Mosco, and Rapahanock stand before him, bid Rapahanock take her he loved best, and Moraughtacund choose next, and to Mosco he gave the third. Upon this, away went their canoes over the water to fetch their venison and all the provision they could. And they that wanted boats swam over the river. The dark commanded us then to rest. The next day there was of men, women, and children, as we conjectured, six or seven hundred dancing and singing, and not a bow nor arrow seen amongst them. Mosco changed his name [to] *uttasantasough,* which we interpret "stranger," for so they call us.[1] All promising ever to be our friends and to plant corn purposely for us, and we to provide hatchets, beads, and copper for them, we departed, giving them a volley of shot, and they us as loud shouts and cries as their strengths could utter.

That night we anchored in the River of Payankatank, and discovered it so high as it was navigable. But the people were most a-hunting, save a few old men, women, and children that were tending their corn, of which they promised us part when we would fetch it, as had done all the nations wherever we had yet been.

In a fair calm, rowing towards Point Comfort, we anchored in Gosnoll's Bay. But such a sudden gust surprised us in the night with thunder and rain that we never thought more to have seen James Town ·as we were half employed in freeing out water, never thinking to escape drowning·. Yet, running before the wind, we sometimes saw the land by the flashes of fire from heaven, by which light only we kept from the splitting shore, until it pleased God in that black darkness to preserve us by that light to find Point Comfort.

There refreshing ourselves, because we had only but heard of the Chisapeacks and Nandsamunds we thought it as fit to know all our neighbors near home as so many nations abroad. So setting sail for the southern shore, we sailed up a narrow river up the country of Chisapeack.

It hath a good channel, but many shoals about the entrance. By that we had sailed six or seven miles, we saw two or three little garden plots with their houses, the shores overgrown with the greatest pine and fir trees we ever saw in the country. But not seeing nor hearing any people, and the river very narrow, we returned to the great river to see if we could find any of them.

Coasting the shore towards Nandsamund, which is most oyster banks, at the mouth of that river we espied six or seven savages making their weirs, who presently fled. Ashore we went and where they wrought we threw divers toys and so departed. Far we were not gone ere they came again and began to sing and dance and recall us, and thus we began our first acquaintance. At last one of them desired

---

[1] He called himself "English" in token of friendship with them. See Hamor §51–810.

us to go to his house up that river. Into our boat voluntarily he came; the rest ran after us by the shore with all show of love that could be.

Seven or eight miles we sailed up this narrow river. At last on the western shore we saw large cornfields, in the midst a little isle, and in it was abundance of corn. The people he told us were all a-hunting, but in the isle was his house, to which he invited us with much kindness. To him, his wife, and children we gave such things as they seemed much contented them.

The others being come desired us also to go but a little higher to see their houses. Here our host left us. The rest rowed by us in a canoe till we were so far past the isle the river became very narrow. Here we desired some of them to come aboard us, whereat pausing a little they told us they would but fetch their bows and arrows and go all with us. But being ashore and thus armed, they persuaded us to go forward. But we could neither persuade them into their canoe nor into our boat. This gave us cause to provide for the worst.

Far we went not ere seven or eight canoes full of men armed appeared following us, staying to see the conclusion. Presently from each side the river came arrows so fast as two or three hundred could shoot them, whereat we returned to get the open [water]. They in the canoes let fly also as fast, but amongst them we bestowed so many shot the most of them leaped overboard and swam ashore; but two or three escaped by rowing, being against their plains. Our muskets they found shot further than their bows, for we made not twenty shot ere they all retired behind the next trees.

Being thus got out of their trap, we seized on all their canoes and moored them in the midst of the open. More than an hundred arrows stuck in our targets and about the boat, yet none hurt, only Anthony Bagnall was shot in his hat, and another in his sleeve. But seeing their multitudes and suspecting as it was that both the Nandsamunds and the Chisapeacks were together, we thought it best to ride by their canoes awhile to bethink if it were better to burn all in the isle or draw them to composition [parley] till we were provided to take all they had, which was sufficient to feed all our colony. But to burn the isle at night it was concluded.

In the interim we began to cut in pieces their canoes and they presently to lay down their bows, making signs of peace. Peace we told them we would accept, would they bring us their kings' bows and arrows with a chain of pearl and when we came again give us four hundred baskets full of corn. Otherwise we would break all their boats and burn their houses and corn and all they had.

To perform all this they alleged only the want of a canoe, so we put one adrift and bade them swim to fetch her, and till they performed their promise we would but only break their canoes. They cried to us to do no more, all should be as we would, which presently they performed: Away went their bows and arrows, and tag and rag came with their baskets. So much as we could carry we took. And so departing good friends, we returned to James Town, where we safely arrived the 7 of September, 1608.

There we found Master Scrivener and divers others well recovered, many dead, some sick, the late president[1] prisoner for mutiny, by the honest diligence of Master Scrivener the harvest gathered, but the provision in the store much spoiled with rain.

Thus was that summer[2] (when nothing wanted) consumed and spent and nothing done, such was the government of Captain Ratliffe,[3] but only this discovery; wherein to express all the dangers, accidents, and encounters this small number passed in that small barge, by the scale of proportion about three thousand miles, with such watery diet in those great waters and barbarous countries, till then to any Christian utterly unknown, I rather refer their merit to the censure of the courteous and experienced reader than I would be tedious or partial, being a party.

But to this place to come, who will adventure
with judgment's guide and reason how to enter
Finds in this world's broad sea with wind and tide
There's safer sail than anywhere beside.
But 'cause to wanton novices it is
A province full of fearfulness, I wis,
Into the great, vast deep to venture out,
Those shallow rivers let them coast about,

---

[1] Ratcliffe.

[2] "year" in *The Proceedings*.

[3] Hadn't Smith given orders to relax and recreate when he left on July 24th?

And by a small boat learn there first and mark
How they may come to make a greater bark.

Written By Anthony Bagnall, Nathanaell Powell, and Anas Todkill.

Chapter VII.

The presidency surrend'red to Captain Smith. The arrival and return of the second supply, and what happened.

THE TENTH OF SEPTEMBER, ·1608·, by the election of the council and request of the company, Captain Smith received the letters patents ·and took upon him the place of president· which till then by no means he would accept, though he was often importuned thereunto.

Now the building of Ratliffe's palace stayed as a thing needless, the church was repaired, the storehouse recovered, buildings prepared for the supplies we expected, the fort reduced to a five-square form, the order of the watch renewed, the squadrons (each setting of the watch) trained; the whole company every Saturday exercised in the plain by the west bulwark prepared for that purpose, we called "Smithfield," where sometimes more than an hundred savages would stand in an amazement to behold how a file would batter a tree where he would make them a mark to shoot at; the boats trimmed for trade—which being sent out with Lieutenant Percy in their journey encount'red the second supply, that brought them back to discover the country of Monacan.

How or why Captain Newport obtained such a private commission as not to return without [either] a lump of gold, a certainty of the South Sea, or one of the lost company sent out by Sir Walter Raleigh I know not, nor why he brought such a five-pieced barge not to bear us to that South Sea till we had borne her over the mountains, which how far they extend is yet unknown.

As for the coronation of Powhatan and his presents of basin and ewer, bed, bedstead, clothes, and such costly novelties, they had been much better well spared than so ill spent. For we had his favor much better only for a plain piece of copper till this stately kind of soliciting made him so much overvalue himself that he respected us as much as nothing at all.

As for the hiring of the Poles and Dutchmen[1] to make pitch, tar, glass, mills, and soap-ashes, when the country is replenished with people and necessaries [that] would have done well, but to send them and seventy more without victuals to work was not so well advised nor considered of as it should have been. Yet this could not have hurt us had they been 200, though then we were 130 that wanted for ourselves, for we had the savages in that decorum (their harvest being newly gathered) that we feared not to get victuals for 500.

Now was there no way to make us miserable but to neglect that time to make provision whilst it was to be had; the which [nevertheless] *was* done by direction from England to perform this strange discovery (but a more strange coronation): to lose that time, spend that victuals we had, tire and starve our men, having no means to carry victuals, munition, the hurt or sick, but on their own backs. How or by whom they were invented I know not, but Captain Newport we only accounted the author, who to effect these projects had so gilded men's hopes with great promises that both company and council concluded his resolution, for the most part.

God doth know they little knew what they did nor understood their own estates to conclude his conclusions against all the inconveniences the foreseeing president alleged.

Of this supply there was added to the council one Captain Richard Waldo and Captain Wynne, two ancient soldiers and valiant gentlemen, but yet ignorant of the business, being but newly arrived. Ratliffe was also permitted to have his voice, and Master Scrivener desirous to see strange countries, so that although Smith was president, yet the major part of the council had the authority and ruled it as they listed.

---

[1] I.e., *Deutsch,* the men were Germans.

As for clearing Smith's objections: how pitch and tar, wainscot, clapboard, glass, and soap-ashes could be provided to relade the ship, or provision got to live withal when none was in the country—and that ·which· we had [was] spent before the ship departed—to effect these projects; the answer was Captain Newport undertook to fraught the pinnace of twenty tons with corn in going and returning in his discovery, and to refraught her again from Werowocomoco of Powhatan, also promising a great proportion of victuals from the ship, inferring that Smith's propositions were only devices to hinder his journey, to effect it himself, and that the cruelty he ·Smith· had used to the savages ·in his absence· might well be the occasion to hinder these designs and seek revenge on him; for which taxation all works were left, and 120 chosen men were appointed for Newport's guard in this discovery. But Captain Smith—to make clear all those seeming suspicions, that the savages were not so desperate as was pretended by Captain Newport, and how willing (since by their authority they would have it so) he was to assist them what he could—because the coronation would consume much time, he undertook himself their message to Powhatan to entreat him to come to James Town to receive his presents.

And where Newport durst not go with less than 120, he only took with him Captain Waldo, Master Andrew Buckler, Edward Brinton, and Samuel Collier. With these four he went overland to Werawocomoco, some 12 miles. There he passed the River of Pamaunkee in a savage canoe. Powhatan being 30 miles off was presently sent for. In the meantime Pocahontas and her women[1] entertained Captain Smith in this manner:

In a fair plain field they made a fire, before which he sitting upon a mat. Suddenly amongst the woods was heard such a hideous noise and shrieking that the English betook themselves to their arms and seized on two or three old men by them, supposing Powhatan with all his power was come to surprise them. But presently Pocahontas came, willing him to kill her if any hurt were intended; and the beholders, which were men, women, and children, satisfied the captain there was no such matter. Then presently they were presented

[1] Instead of "Pocahontas and her women" *The Proceedings* has "his women."

with this antic: thirty young women came naked out of the woods, only covered behind and before with a few green leaves, their bodies all painted, some of one color, some of another (·some white, some red, some black, some parti-color·), but all differing. Their leader had a fair pair of buck's horns on her head and an otter's skin at her girdle and another at her arm, a quiver of arrows at her back, a bow and arrows in her hand; the next had in her hand a sword, another a club, another a pot stick, all horned alike, the rest everyone with their several devices. These fiends, with most hellish shouts and cries rushing from among the trees, cast themselves in a ring about the fire, singing and dancing with most excellent ill variety, oft falling into their infernal passions and ·then· solemnly again to sing and dance. Having spent near an hour in this masquerado, as they ent'red in like manner they departed.

Having reaccommodated themselves, they solemnly invited him to their lodgings, where he was no sooner within the house but all these nymphs more tormented him than ever, with crowding, pressing, and hanging about him, most tediously crying *Love you not me? Love you not me?*

This salutation ended, the feast was set, consisting of all the savage dainties they could devise: ·fruit in baskets, fish and flesh in wooden platters. Beans and peas there wanted not for 20 hogs·, some attending, others singing and dancing about them; which mirth being ended, with firebrands instead of torches they conducted him to his lodging.

Thus did they show their feats of arms, and others art in dancing.
Some other us'd their oaten pipe, and others voices chanting.

The next day came Powhatan. Smith delivered his message of the presents sent him and redelivered him Namontack he had sent for England, desiring him to come to his father Newport to accept those presents and conclude their revenge against the Monacans, whereunto this subtle savage thus replied:

"If your king have sent me presents, I also am a king and this is my land. Eight days I will stay to receive them. Your father is to come to me, not I to him nor yet to your fort, neither will I bite at such a bait.

As for the Monacans, I can revenge my own injuries, and as for Atquanachuk, where you say your brother was slain, it is a contrary way from those parts you suppose it. But [as] for any salt water beyond the mountains, the relations you have had from my people are false."

Whereupon he began to draw plots upon the ground according to his discourse of all those regions. Many other discourses they had, yet both content to give each other content in complimental courtesies; and so Captain Smith returned with this answer.

Upon this the presents were sent[1] by water, which is near an hundred miles, and the captains went by land with fifty good shot, ·which is but 12 miles, where he met with our 3 barges to transport him over·.

All being met at Werowocomoco, the next day was appointed for his coronation. Then the presents were brought him—his basin and ewer, bed and furniture set up, his scarlet cloak and apparel with much ado put on him, being persuaded by Namontack they would not hurt him. But a foul trouble there was to make him kneel to receive his crown: He neither knowing the majesty nor meaning of a crown nor bending of the knee endured so many persuasions, examples, and instructions as tired them all. At last by leaning hard on his shoulders he a little stooped, and three having the crown in their hands put it on his head,[2] when by the warning of a pistol the boats were prepared with such a volley of shot that the king start up in a horrible fear till he saw all was well. Then rememb'ring himself to congratulate their kindness, he gave his old shoes and his mantle to Captain Newport.

But perceiving his purpose was to discover the Monacans, he labored to divert his resolution, refusing to lend him either men or guides more than Namontack. And so, after some small complimental kindness on both sides, in requital of his presents he presented Newport with a heap of wheat ears that might contain some 7 or 8 bushels, and as much more we bought ·ready-dressed· in

---

[1] "Upon this, Captain Newport sent his presents by water" in *The Proceedings.*

[2] Instead of the "three" *The Proceedings* has "Newport put the crown on his head."

the town, wherewith we returned to the fort.[1]

The ship having disburdened herself of 70 persons, with the first gentlewoman and woman servant that arrived in our colony[2]—Captain Newport, with ·all the council and· 120 chosen men led by Captain Waldo, Lieutenant Percie, Captain Winne, Master West, and Master Scrivener, set forward for the discovery of Monacan, leaving the president at the fort with about 80 or 90, such as they were, to relade the ship.

Arriving at the Falls, we[3] marched by land some forty miles in two days and a half, and so returned down the same path we went. Two towns we discovered of the Monacans, called Massinacak and Mowhemenchouch. The people neither used us well nor ill, yet for our security we took one of their petty kings and led him bound to conduct us the way; and in our returns searched many places we

---

[1] Rev. Purchas in 1625 concludes: "Powhatan's coronation: So much was done to buy repentance with more cost than worship. If we seek savages we lose them; if we force them to seek us we shall find these shadows of men close at our feet. I have read more stories of them than perhaps any man, and find that a cruel mercy in awing savages to fear us is better than that merciful cruelty which by too much kindness hath made us fear them—or else by too much confidence to lose ourselves. Smith and Newport may by their examples teach the just course to be taken with such: the one breeding awe and dread without Spanish, or panic, terror, the other disgraced in seeking to grace with offices of humanity those which are graceless. Neither doth it become us to use savages with savageness, nor yet with too humane usage, but in a middle path to go and do so that they may admire and fear us as those whom God, religion, civility, and art have made so far superior, [nor] yet to abuse them (unprovoked) as hostile slaves or as mere beasts with cruel and beastly ferity whom nature hath equally made men. This breeds desperate populations, as in the Spanish Indies hath been seen, [and] that gentleness and unequal equity makes them proud and treacherous, as woeful experience hath taught in the late massacre [of 1622]. Our temperance and justice should be qualified with prudence and fortitude. Neither must we make them beasts nor yet value them as Christians, till we have made them such. And the way to make them Christian men is first to make them civil men, to file off the rust of their humanity, which as children (the like in taming wild beasts) must be done with severe gentleness and gentle severity; which may breed in them a loving awe or awful love, at least a just dread toward us, that fear may make them know us; and then the fault is ours if they see no cause to love us," and just about sums up the best thinking of the time *(Purchas His Pilgrimes,* 1778, margin note).

[2] Mistress Forest and Anne Burroughs, her maidservant.

[3] A party that did not include Smith.

supposed mines, about which we spent some time in refining, having one William Callicut, a refiner, fitted for that purpose. From that crust of earth we digged he persuaded us to believe he extracted some small quantity of silver, and not unlikely better stuff might be had for the digging.

With this poor trial being contented to leave this fair, fertile, well-watered country, and coming to the Falls, the savages feigned there were divers ships come into the bay to kill them at James Town. Trade they would not, and find their corn we could not, for they had hid it in the woods; and being thus deluded we arrived at James Town half sick, all complaining, and tired with toil, famine, and discontent to have only but discovered our gilded hopes and such fruitless certainties as Captain Smith foretold us.

But those that hunger seek to slake,
Which thus abounding wealth would rake.
Not all the gems of Ister[1] *shore*
Nor all the gold of Lydia's store
Can fill their greedy appetite,
It is a thing so infinite.

No sooner were we landed but the president dispersed so many as were able: some for glass, others for tar, pitch, and soap-ashes, leaving them with the fort to the council's oversight. But 30 of us he conducted down the river some 5 miles from James town to learn to make clapboard, cut down trees, and lie in woods.[2]

Amongst the rest he had chosen Gabriel Beadle and John Russell, the only two gallants of this last supply, and both proper gentlemen. Strange were these pleasures to their conditions, yet lodging, eating and drinking, working or playing—they but doing as the president did himself—all these things were carried so pleasantly as within a week they became masters, making it their delight to hear the trees thunder as they fell. But the axes so oft blistered their tender fingers that many times every third blow had a loud oath to drown the echo; for remedy of which sin the president devised how to have every

---

[1] The Danube.

[2] Camp out.

man's oaths numb'red, and at night for every oath to have a can of water poured down his sleeve, with which every offender was so washed, himself and all, that a man should scarce hear an oath in a week.

For he who scorns and makes but jests of cursings and his oath
He doth contemn not man but God, nor God nor man but both.

By this let no man think that the president and these gentlemen spent their times as common wood-hackers at felling of trees, or such other like labors, or that they were pressed to it as hirelings or common slaves. For what they did, after they were but once a little inured, it seemed—and some conceited it—only as a pleasure and recreation. Yet 30 or 40 of such voluntary gentlemen would do more in a day than 100 of the rest that must be press'd to it by compulsion.[1] But twenty good workmen had been better than them all.

Master Scrivener, Captain Waldo, and Captain Winne at the fort, everyone in like manner carefully regarded their charge. The president returning from amongst the woods, seeing the time consumed and no provision gotten (and the ship lay idle at a great charge and did nothing) presently embarked himself in the discovery barge, giving order to the council to send Lieutenant Percie after him with the next barge that arrived at the fort.

Two barges he had himself and 18 men. But arriving at Chickahamania, that dogged nation was too well acquainted with our wants, refusing to trade, with as much scorn and insolency as they could express. The president, perceiving it was Powhatan's policy to starve us, told them he came not so much for their corn as to revenge his imprisonment and the death of his men murthered by them, and so, landing his men and ready to charge them, they immediately fled, and presently after sent their ambassadors with corn, fish, fowl, and what they had to make their peace. Their corn being that year but bad, they complained extremely of their own wants, yet fraughted our boats with an hundred bushels of corn, and in like manner Lieutenant Percie's, that not long after ·us· arrived; and having done the best they could to content us, we parted good friends and ·within 4 or 5 days we· returned to James town.

[1] Margin note: "One gentleman better than 20 lubbers."

Though this much contented the company, that ·then· feared nothing more than starving, yet some so envied his good success that they rather desired to hazard a starving than his pains should prove so much more effectual than theirs. Some projects there were invented by Newport and Ratliffe not only to have deposed him but to have kept him out of the fort, for that being president he would leave his place and the fort without their consents, but their horns were so much too short to effect it as they themselves more narrowly escaped a greater mischief.

All this time our old tavern made as much of all them that had either money or ware as could be desired. By this time they were become so perfect on all sides—I mean the soldiers, sailors, and savages—as there was ten times more care to maintain their damnable and private trade than to provide for the colony things that were necessary.

Neither was it a small policy in Newport and the mariners to report in England we had such plenty, and bring us so many men without victuals, when they had so many private factors in the fort that, within six or seven weeks ·after the ship's return·, of two or three hundred axes, ·hatchets·, chisels, ·mattocks·, hoes, and pickaxes scarce twenty could be found; and for pike-heads, ·knives·, shot, powder, or anything they could steal from their fellows was vendible, they knew as well and as secretly how to convey them to trade with the savages for furs, baskets, *mussaneeks,*[1] young beasts, or suchlike commodities as [they did to] exchange them with the sailors for butter, cheese, beef, pork, aqua vitae, beer, biscuit, oatmeal, and oil; and then feign all was sent them from their friends. And though Virginia afforded no furs for the store, yet one master[2] in one voyage hath got so many by this indirect means as he confessed to have sold in England for 30li.

Those are the saint-seeming worthies of Virginia that have, notwithstanding, all this meat, drink, and wages. But now they begin to grow weary, their trade being both perceived and prevented. None hath been in Virginia, that hath observed anything, which knows not

---

[1] Possibly gray squirrel pelts.
[2] "Mariner" instead of "master" in *The Proceedings.*

this to be true; and yet the loss, the scorn, the misery and shame was the poor officers,[1] gentlemen, and careless governors who were all thus bought and sold, the adventurers cozened, and the action overthrown by their false excuses, informations, and directions. By this let all men judge how this business could prosper being thus abused by such pilf'ring occasions.

And had not Captain Newport cried *peccavi*,[2] the president would have discharged the ship and caused him to have stayed one year in Virginia to learn to speak of his own experience.

Master Scrivener was sent with the barges and pinnace to Werowocomoco, where he found the savages more ready to fight than trade. But his vigilancy was such as prevented their projects, and by the means of Namontack got three or four hogsheads of corn and as much *pocones,* which is a red root which then was esteemed an excellent dye.

Captain Newport, being dispatched with the trials of pitch, tar, glass, frankincense, soap-ashes, with that clapboard and wainscot that could be provided, met with Master Scrivener at Point Comfort, and so returned for England, we remaining were about two hundred ·with those he brought us·.

The Copy of a Letter sent to the Treasurer and Council of Virginia from Captain Smith, then president in Virginia.[3]

RIGHT HONORABLE, ETC.—

I received your letter, wherein you write that our minds are so set upon faction and idle conceits in dividing the country without your consents, and that we feed you but with *if*s and *and*'s, hopes and some few proofs, as if we would keep the mystery of the business to ourselves; and that we must expressly follow your instructions sent

---

[1] "Soldiers" instead of "officers" *ibid.*

[2] "My mistake." (Latin)

[3] Barbour suggests the letter was sent between the 10th September and some time in December 1608.

by Captain Newport, the charge of whose voyage amounts to near two thousand pounds; the which if we cannot defray by the ships' return, we are like to remain as banished men. To these particulars I humbly entreat your pardons if I offend you with my rude answer.

For our factions—unless you would have me run away and leave the country, I cannot prevent them, because I do make many stay that would else fly any-whither.

For the idle letter sent to my Lord of Salisbury by the president[1] and his confederates for dividing the country, etc.[2]—what it was I know not, for you saw no hand of mine to it, nor ever dreamt I of any such matter.

That we feed you with hopes, etc.—though I be no scholar, I am past a schoolboy, and I desire but to know what either you and these here do know, but that [what] I have learned to tell you by the continual hazard of my life. I have not concealed from you anything I know, but I fear some cause you to believe much more than is true.

Expressly to follow your directions by Captain Newport—though they be performed, I was directly against it. But according to our commission[3] I was content to be overruled by the major part of the council, I fear to the hazard of us all (which now is generally confessed when it is too late). Only Captain Winne and Captain Waldo I have sworn of the council, and crowned Powhatan according to your instructions.

For the charge of this voyage of two or three thousand pounds—we have not received the value of an hundred pounds! And for the quart'red boat to be borne by the soldiers over the Falls, Newport had 120 of the best men he could choose. If he had burnt her to ashes, one might have carried her in a bag; but as she is, five hundred cannot to a navigable place above the Falls.

And for him at that time to find in the South Sea a mine of gold or any of them sent by Sir Walter Raleigh—at our consultation I told them [that] was as likely as the rest. But during this "great discovery" of thirty miles (which might as well have been done by one man,

---

[1] Captain John Ratcliffe.

[2] "The 'president' referred to must have been Ratcliffe. That he may well have written to Salisbury is hinted by a later letter from him to the same effect.

[3] I.e., in accordance with our commission.

and much more for the value of a pound of copper at a seasonable time), they had the pinnace and all the boats with them but one that remained with me to serve the fort.

In their absence I followed the new-begun works of pitch and tar, glass, soap-ashes, and clapboard, whereof some small quantities we have sent you. But if you rightly consider what an infinite toil it is in Russia and Swethland, where the woods are proper for naught else, and though there be the help both of man and beast in those ancient commonwealths, which many an hundred years have used it (yet thousands of those poor people can scarce get necessaries to live but from hand to mouth), and though your factors there can buy as much in a week as will fraught you a ship, or as much as you please, you must not expect from us any such matter, which are but a many of ignorant miserable souls that are scarce able to get wherewith to live and defend ourselves against the inconstant savages, finding but here and there a tree fit for the purpose, and want all things else the Russians have.[1]

For the coronation of Powhatan—by whose advice you sent him such presents I know not, but this give me leave to tell you. I fear they will be the confusion of us all ere we hear from you again. At your ships' arrival, the savages' harvest was newly gathered, and we going to buy it, our own not being half sufficient for so great a number.

As for the two ships loading of corn Newport promised to provide us from Powhatan, he brought us but fourteen bushels, and from the Monacans nothing but the most of the men sick and near famished. From your ship we had not provision in victuals worth twenty pound, and we are more than *two hundred* to live upon this, the one half sick, the other little better.

For the sailors—I confess they daily make good cheer,[2] but our diet is a little meal and water, and not sufficient of that. Though there be fish in the sea, fouls in the air, and beasts in the woods, their bounds

---

[1] "Planting of countries is like planting of woods; for you must make account to lose almost twenty years' profit, and expect your recompense in the end: for the principal thing that hath been the destruction of most plantations has been the base and hasty drawing of profit in the first years." (Sir Francis Bacon, "Of Plantations")

[2] Live it up.

are so large, they so wild, and we so weak and ignorant we cannot much trouble them. Captain Newport we much suspect to be the author of those inventions.[1]

Now, [so] that you should know I have made you as great a discovery as he for less charge than he spendeth you every meal, I have sent you this map of the bay and rivers, with an annexed relation of the countries and nations that inhabit them, as you may see at large; also two barrels of stones, and such as I take to be good iron ore at the least—so divided as by their notes you may see in what places I found them.

The soldiers say many of your officers maintain their families out of that you send us, and that Newport hath an hundred pounds a year for carrying news.[2] For every master you have yet sent can find the way as well as he, so that an hundred pounds might be spared, which is more than we have all that help to pay him wages.

Captain Ratliffe is now called Sicklemore, a poor counterfeited imposture. I have sent you him home, lest the company should cut his throat. What he is now everyone can tell you. If he and Archer return again, they are sufficient to keep us always in factions.[3]

When you send again, I entreat you rather send but thirty carpenters, husbandmen, gardeners, fishermen, blacksmiths, masons, and diggers-up of trees' roots, well provided, than a thousand of such as we have. For except we be able both to lodge them and feed them, the most will consume with want of necessaries before they can be made good for anything.

Thus, if you please to consider this account, and of the unnecessary wages to Captain Newport, or his ships so long lingering and staying here (for notwithstanding his boasting to leave us victuals for 12 months, though we had 89 by this "discovery" lame and sick, and but a pint of corn a day for a man, we were constrained to give him three hogsheads of that to victual him homeward), or yet [whether] to send into Germany or Poland for glass-men and the rest till we be able to sustain ourselves and relieve them when they come, it were better to give five hundred pound a ton for those gross commodities

---

[1] Bad Reports.
[2] I.e., for carrying nothing but the mail.
[3] They returned in August 1609.

in Denmark than send for them hither till more necessary things be provided. For in overtoiling our weak and unskillful bodies to satisfy this desire of *present* profit, we can scarce ever recover ourselves from one supply to another.

And I humbly entreat you hereafter let us know what we should receive and not stand to the sailors' courtesy to leave us what they please, else you may charge us with what you will, but we not you with anything.

These are the causes that have kept us in Virginia from laying such a foundation that ere this might have given much better content and satisfaction. But as yet you must not look for any profitable returns.

So I humbly rest.

The names of those in this supply were these (with their proceedings and accidents):

Captain Peter Winne [and]
Captain Richard Waldo *were appointed to be of the council.*

Master Francis West, *brother to the Lord La Warre*

Gentlemen

Thomas Graves
Raleigh Chroshaw
Gabriel Beadle
John Beadle
John Russell
William Russell
John Cuderington
William Sambage
Henry Leigh
Henry Philpot
Harmon Harrison
Daniel Tucker
Henry Collins
Hugh Wolleston
John Hoult

Thomas Norton
George Yarington
George Burton
Thomas Abbay
William Dowman
Thomas Maxes
Michael Lowick
Master Hunt
Thomas Forrest
John Dauxe

Tradesmen

Thomas Phelps
John Prat
John Clarke
Jeffrey Shortridge
Dionis Oconor
Hugh Winne
David ap Hugh
Thomas Bradley
John Burras
Thomas Lavander
Henry Bell
Master Powell
David Ellis
Thomas Gibson

Laborers

Thomas Dawse
Thomas Mallard
William Tayler
Thomas Fox
Nicholas Hancock
Walker
Williams
Floud
Morley [·Morrell·?]
Rose
Scot

Hardwyn

Boys

Milman
Hilliard

—Mistress Forrest and Anne Burras her maid, eight Dutchmen and Poles, with some others to the number of seventy persons, etc.

These poor conclusions so affrighted us all with famine that the president provided for Nansamund and took with him Captain Winne and Master Scrivener, then returning from Captain Newport.[1]

These people also long denied him not only the 400 baskets of corn they promised but any trade at all, excusing themselves they had spent most they had and were commanded by Powhatan to keep that they had and not to let us come into their river—till we were constrained to begin with them perforce ·and then they would rather sell us some than we should take all·.

Upon the discharging of our muskets they all fled and shot not an arrow. The first house we came to we set on fire; which when they perceived, they desired we would make no more spoil and they would give us half they had. How they collected it I know not, but before night they loaded our three boats.

And so we returned to our quarter some four miles down the river, which was only the open woods under the lay of a hill where all the ground was covered with snow and hard frozen. The snow we digged away, and made a great fire in the place. When the ground was well dried we turned away the fire, and covering the place with a mat there we lay very warm. To keep us from the wind we made a shade of another mat. As the wind turned we turned our shade, and when the ground grew cold we removed the fire. And thus many a cold winter night have we lain in this miserable manner, yet those that most commonly went upon all those occasions were always in health, lusty and fat.

For sparing them this year, the next year they promised to plant purposely for us; and so ·loading our boats with 100 bushels, we parted friends and· we returned to James town.

---

[1] They accompanied him a ways aboard as his ship departed.

About this time there was a marriage betwixt John Laydon and Anne Burras, which was the first marriage we had in Virginia.

Long he stayed not, but fitting himself and Captain Waldo with two barges, from Chawopoweanock,[1] and all parts thereabouts all the people were fled, as being jealous of our intents, till we discovered the river and people of Apamatuck, where we found not much. That they had we equally divided ·betwixt the savages and us·, but gave them copper and such things as contented them in consideration. Master Scrivener and Lieutenant Percie went also abroad, but could find nothing.

The president, seeing the procrastinating of time was no course to live, resolved with Captain Waldo, whom he knew to be sure in time of need, to surprise Powhatan and all his provision. But the unwillingness of Captain Winne and Master Scrivener, for some private respect [that was] plotted in England to ruin Captain Smith, did their best to hinder their project.

But the president, whom no persuasions could persuade to starve, being invited by Powhatan to come unto him, and if he would send him but men to build him a house, give him a grindstone, fifty swords, some pieces, a cock and a hen, with much copper and beads, he would load his ship with corn—the president, not ignorant of his devices and subtlety, yet unwilling to neglect any opportunity, presently sent three Dutchmen and two English, having so small allowance [that] few were able to do anything to purpose, ·having no victuals to employ them, all for want thereof being idle·, knowing there needed no better a castle to effect this project ·than that house to surprise Powhatan·, took order with Captain Waldo to second him if need required; Scrivener he left his substitute; and set forth with the pinnace, two barges, and forty-six men, which only were such as voluntarily offered themselves for his journey—the which, by reason of Master Scrivener's ill success, was censured very desperate: They all knowing Smith would not return empty if it were to be had, howsoever it caused many of those that he had appointed to find excuses to stay behind.

---

[1] Two towns: Chawopo and Weanock.

Chapter VIII.

Captain Smith's Journey to Pamaunkee.

THE TWENTY-NINE OF DECEMBER, [1608], he set forward for Werowocomoco; his company were these:

In the discovery barge, himself—

Gentlemen

Robert Behethland
·Nathaniell Powell·
Nathanael Graves
John Russell
Raleigh Chrashow
Michael Sicklemore
Richard Worley

Soldiers

Anas Todkill
William Love
William Bentley
Jeffrey Shortridge
Edward Pising
William Ward

In the pinnace—

Lieutenant Percie, *brother to the Earl of Northumberland*
Master Francis West, *brother to the Lord La Warre*
William Phittiplace, *captain of the pinnace,*

Gentlemen

Michael Phittiplace
Jeffrey Abbot, *sergeant*
William Tankard
George Yarington
Jonas Profit, *master*
Robert Ford, *clerk of the council*

Soldiers

James Browne [Bourne]
Edward Brinton
George Burton
Thomas Coe
John Dods
Henry Powell

Thomas Gipson, David Ellis, Nathanael Peacock, *sailors.* John Prat, George Acrig, James Read, Nicholas Hancock, James Watkins, ·Anthony Baggly [Bagnall], *surgeon·,* Thomas Lambert, ·Edward Pising, *sergeant·,* four Dutchmen, and Richard Salvage were sent by land before to build the house for Powhatan against our arrival.

This company, being victualed but for three or four days, lodged the first night at Warraskoyack, where the president took sufficient provision. This kind king did his best to divert him from seeing Powhatan, but perceiving he could not prevail, he advised in this manner:

"Captain Smith, you shall find Powhatan to use you kindly, but trust him not; and be sure he have no opportunity to seize on your arms, for he hath sent for you only to cut your throats."

The captain thanking him for his good counsel, yet, the better to try his love, desired guides to Chawwonock, for he would send a present to that king to bind him his friend. To perform this journey was sent Master ·Michael· Sicklemore, a very valiant, honest, and a painful soldier, with him two guides and directions how to seek for the lost company of Sir Walter Raleigh's and silk grass.

Then we departed thence, the president assuring the king perpetual love, and left with him Samuel Collier, his page, to learn the language.

So this king's deeds by sacred oath adjur'd
More wary proves and circumspect, by odds
Fearing at least his double forfeiture
To offend his friends and sin against his gods.

The next night being lodged at Kecoughtan, six or seven days the extreme wind, rain, frost, and snow caused us to keep Christmas among the savages, where we were never more merry, nor fed on more plenty of good oysters, fish, flesh, wildfowl, and good bread, nor never had better fires in England than in the dry, ·warm·, smoky houses of Kecoughtan.

But departing thence, when we found no houses we were not curious [fastidious] in any weather to lie three or four nights together ·upon any shore· under the trees by a ·good· fire, as formerly is said.

An hundred forty-eight fowls the president, Anthony Bagnall, and Sergeant Pising did kill at three shoots. At Kiskiack the frost and contrary winds forced us three or four days also to suppress the insolency of those proud savages to quarter in their houses, yet guard our barge, and cause them give us what we wanted, though we were but twelve and himself.[1] Yet we never wanted shelter where we found any houses.

The 12 of January [1609], we arrived at Werowocomoco, where the river was frozen near half a mile from the shore. But to neglect no time, the president with his barge so far had approached by breaking the ice as the ebb left him amongst those oozy shoals. Yet rather than to lie there frozen to death, by his own example he taught them to march near middle deep ·more than· a flight-shot[2] through this muddy, frozen ooze. When the barge floated he appointed two or three to return her aboard the pinnace where, for want of water, in melting the ice they made fresh water, for the river there was salt. But in this march Master Russell, whom none could persuade to stay behind, being somewhat ill and exceeding heavy, so overtoiled himself as the rest had much ado ere he got ashore to regain life into his dead, benumbed spirits.

Quartering in the next houses we found, we sent to Powhatan for provision, who sent us plenty of bread, turkeys, and venison.

The next day, having feasted us after his ordinary manner, he began to ask us when we would be gone, feigning he sent not for us, neither had he any corn, and his people much less—yet for forty

---

[1] "But 12 with the president" in *The Proceedings*.

[2] Bowshot.

swords he would procure us forty baskets. The president, showing him the men there present that brought him the message and conditions, asked Powhatan how it chanced he became so forgetful. Thereat the king concluded the matter with a merry laughter, asking for our commodities. But none he liked without guns and swords, valuing a basket of corn more precious than a basket of copper, saying he could rate his corn but not the copper.[1]

Captain Smith, seeing the intent of this subtle savage, began to deal with him after this manner:

"Powhatan, though I had many courses to have made my provision, yet believing your promises to supply my wants, I neglected all to satisfy your desire. And to testify my love, I send you my men for your building, neglecting mine own. What your people had you have engrossed, forbidding them our trade; and now you think by consuming the time we shall consume for want, not having to fulfill your strange demands. As for swords and guns, I told you long ago I had none to spare. And you must know those I have can keep me from want. Yet steal or wrong you I will not, nor dissolve that friendship we have mutually promised, except you constrain me by our bad usage."

The king, having attentively list'ned to this discourse, promised that both he and his country would spare him what he could, the which within two days they should receive.

"Yet Captain Smith," saith the king, "some doubt I have of your coming hither that makes me not so kindly seek to relieve you as I would. For many do inform me your coming hither is not for trade but to invade my people and possess my country, who dare not come to bring you corn, seeing you thus armed with your men. To free us of this fear, leave aboard your weapons, for here they are needless, we being all friends and forever Powhatans."

With many such discourses they spent the day, quartering that night in the king's houses.

The next day he renewed[2] his building, which he little intended should proceed, for the Dutchmen, finding his plenty and knowing

---

[1] "eat his corn but not his copper." in *The Proceedings*.
[2] "Reviewed" *ibid.*

our want, and perceiving his preparations to surprise us, little thinking we could escape both him and famine, to obtain his favor revealed to him so much as they knew of our estates and projects, and how to prevent them. One of them being of so great a spirit, judgment, and resolution, and a hireling that was certain of his wages for his labor, and ever well used—both he and his countrymen—that the president knew not whom better to trust, and not knowing any fitter for that employment, had sent him as a spy to discover Powhatan's intent, then little doubting his honesty, nor could ever be certain of his villainy till near half a year after.

Whilst we expected the coming in of the country, we wrangled out of the king ten quarters of corn for a copper kettle, the which the president perceiving him much to affect valued it at a much greater rate, but in regard of his scarcity he [Smith] would accept it [at less] provided we should have as much more the next year or else [aid against] the country of Monacan (·the king exceeding liberal of that he had [he still had] not yielded him Monacan·); wherewith each seemed well contented, and Powhatan began to expostulate the difference of peace and war after this manner:

"Captain Smith, you may understand that I having seen the death of all my people thrice, and not anyone living of those three generations but myself—I know the difference of peace and war better than any in my country. But now I am old and ere long must die, my brethren, namely, Opitchapam, Opechancanough, and Kekataugh, [and] my two sisters and their two daughters are distinctly each other's successors: I wish their experience no less than mine, and your love to them no less than mine to you.

"But this bruit from Nansamund that you are come to destroy my country so much affrighteth all my people as they dare not visit you. What will it avail you to take that by force you may quickly[1] have by love? or to destroy them that provide you food? What can you get by war when we can hide our provisions and fly to the woods? whereby you must famish by wronging us, your friends. And why are you thus jealous of our loves, seeing us unarmed, and both do and are willing still to feed you with that you cannot get but by our

---

1 "Quietly" *ibid.*

labors?

"Think you I am so simple not to know it is better to eat good meat, lie well, and sleep quietly with my women and children, laugh and be merry with you, have copper, hatchets, or what I want, being your friend, than be forced to fly from all?—to lie cold in the woods, feed upon acorns, roots, and such trash, and be so hunted by you that I can neither rest, eat, nor sleep, but my tired men must watch, and if a twig but break, everyone crieth THERE COMETH CAPTAIN SMITH!—then must I fly I know not whither, and thus with miserable fear end my miserable life, leaving my pleasures to such youths as you, which through your rash unadvisedness may quickly as miserably end, for want of that you never know where to find.

"Let this therefore assure you of our loves, and every year our friendly trade shall furnish you with corn, and now also, if you would come in friendly manner to see us and not thus with your guns and swords as to invade your foes."

To this subtle discourse the president thus replied:

"Seeing you will not rightly conceive of our words, we strive to make you know our thoughts by our deeds. The vow I made you of my love both myself and my men have kept. As for your promise, I find it every day violated by some of your subjects. Yet, we finding your love and kindness, our custom is so far from being ungrateful that for your sake only we have curbed our thirsting desire of revenge, else had they known as well the cruelty we use to our enemies as our true love and courtesy to our friends.

"And I think your judgment sufficient to conceive as well by the adventures we have undertaken as by the advantage we have by our arms of yours that had we intended you any hurt, long ere this we could have effected it.

"Your people coming to ·me at· James Town are entertained with their bows and arrows without any exceptions, we esteeming it with you as it is with us to wear our arms as our apparel.

"As for the danger of our enemies, in such wars consist our chiefest pleasure. For your riches we have no use. As for the hiding your provision or by your flying to the woods, we shall not so unadvisedly starve as you conclude. Your friendly care in that behalf is needless, for we have a rule to find beyond your knowledge."

Many other discourses they had till at last they began to trade. But the king seeing his will would not be admitted as a law, our guard dispersed, nor our men disarmed, he (sighing) breathed his mind once more in this manner:

"Captain Smith, I never use any werowance so kindly as yourself, yet from you I receive the least kindness of any. Captain Newport gave me swords, copper, clothes, a bed, tools, or what I desired, ever taking what I offered him; and would send away his guns when I entreated him. None doth deny to lie at my feet or refuse to do what I desire, but only you; of whom I can have nothing but what you regard not, and yet you will have whatsoever you demand. Captain Newport you call father, and so you call me. But I see for all us both you will do what you list, and we must both seek to content you. But if you intend so friendly as you say, send hence your arms that I may believe you. For you see the love I bear you doth cause me thus nakedly to forget myself."

Smith, seeing this savage but trifle the time to cut his throat, procured the savages to break the ice that his boat might come to fetch his corn and him, and gave order for more men to come on shore to surprise the king, with whom also he but trifled the time till his men were landed; and to keep him from suspicion, entertained the time with this reply:

"Powhatan, you must know as I have but one God I honor but one king; and I live not here as your subject but as your friend to pleasure you with what I can. By the gifts you bestow on me you gain more than by trade. Yet would you visit me as I do you, you should know it is not our custom to sell our courtesies as a vendible commodity. Bring all your country with you for your guard, I will not dislike it as being overjealous.

"But to content you, tomorrow I will leave my arms and trust to your promise. I call you father indeed, and as a father you shall see I will love you. But the small care you have of such a child caused my men persuade me to look to myself."

By this time Powhatan—having knowledge his men were ready whilest the ice was a-breaking—with his luggage, women, and children fled, yet to avoid suspicion left two or three of the women talking with the captain whilest he secretly ran away, and his men that secretly beset the house; which being presently discovered to Captain Smith, with his pistol, sword, and target he made such a passage among these naked devils that at his first shoot they next him tumbled one over another and the rest quickly fled ·before him·, some one way, some another, so that without any hurt, only accompanied with John Russell, he obtained the *corps du guard.*

When they perceived him so well escaped and with his eighteen men[1]—for he had no more with him ashore—to the uttermost of their skill they sought excuses to dissemble the matter. And Powhatan to excuse his flight and the sudden coming of this multitude sent our captain a great bracelet and a chain of pearl by an ancient orator that bespoke us to this purpose, perceiving even then from our pinnace a barge and men departing and coming unto us:

"Captain Smith, our werowance is fled, fearing your guns, and knowing when the ice was broken there would come more men, sent these numbers but to guard his corn from stealing that might happen without your knowledge. Now though some be hurt by your misprision, yet Powhatan is your friend and so will forever continue. Now since the ice is open, he would have you send away your corn; and if you would have his company, send away also your guns, which so affrighteth his people that they dare not come to you as he promised they should."

Then having provided baskets for our men to carry our corn to the boats, they kindly offered their service to guard our arms that none should steal them. A great many they were of goodly, well-proportioned fellows as grim as devils. Yet the very sight of cocking our matches and being to let fly, a few words caused them to leave their bows and arrows to our guard, and bear down our corn on their ·own· backs. We needed not importune them to make dispatch, but our barges being left on the ooze by the ebb caused us stay till the next high water ·midnight tide·, so that we returned again to our old quarter, [and] ·spent that half night with such mirth as though we never had suspected or intended anything·.

Powhatan and his Dutchmen brusting with desire to have the head of Captain Smith (for if they could but kill him they thought all was

---

[1] "8 men" *ibid.*

theirs) neglected not any opportunity to effect his purpose. The Indians with all the merry sports they could devise spent the time till night. Then they all returned to Powhatan, who all this time was making ready his forces to surprise the house and him at supper.

Notwithstanding, the eternal all-seeing God did prevent him and by a strange means. For Pocahontas, his dearest jewel and daughter, in that dark night came through the irksome woods and told our captain great cheer should be sent us by and by. But Powhatan and all the power he could make would after come kill us all if they that brought it could not kill us with our own weapons when we were at supper. Therefore if we would live she wished us presently to be gone. Such things as she delighted in he would have given her, but with the tears running down her cheeks she said she durst not be seen to have any, for if Powhatan should know it, she were but dead, and so she ran away by herself as she came.

Within less than an hour came eight or ten lusty fellows with great platters of venison and other victual, very importunate to have us put out our matches, whose smoke made them sick, and sit down to our victual. But the captain made them taste every dish, which done he sent some of them back to Powhatan to bid him make haste for he was prepared for his coming. As for them, he knew they came to betray him at his supper, but he would prevent them and all their other intended villainies, so that they might be gone. Not long after came more messengers to see what news. Not long after them others. Thus we spent the night as vigilantly as they till it was high water, yet seemed to the savages as friendly as they to us. And that we were so desirous to give Powhatan content as he requested, we did leave him Edward Brynton to kill him fowl and the Dutchmen to finish his house, thinking at our return from Pamaunkee the frost would be gone, and then we might find a better opportunity if necessity did occasion it, little dreaming yet of the Dutchmen's treachery, whose humor well suited this verse—

Is any free that may not live as freely as he list?
Let us live so, then w'are as free and brutish as the best.

Chapter IX.

How we escaped surprising at Pamaunkee.

WE HAD no sooner set sail but Powhatan returned and sent Adam and Francis, two stout Dutchmen, to James town, who feigning to Captain Winne that all things were well, and that Captain Smith had use of their arms—wherefore they requested new, the which were given them—they told him their coming was for some extraordinary [extra] tools and shift of apparel; by which colorable excuse they obtained six or seven more to their confederacy, such expert thieves that presently furnished them with a great many swords, pike-heads, pieces, shot, powder, and suchlike. Savages they had at hand ·ready· to carry it away; and the next day they returned unsuspected, leaving their confederates to follow, and in the interim to convey them such things as they could; for which service they should live with Powhatan as his chief affected, free from those miseries that would happen the colony. Samuel, their other consort, Powhatan kept for their pledge, whose diligence had provided them three hundred of their kind of hatchets—the rest fifty swords, eight pieces, and eight pikes.

Brynton and Richard Salvage, seeing the Dutchmen so ·strangely· diligent to accommodate the savages with weapons, attempted to have gotten to James town, but they were apprehended and expected ever when to be put to death.

Within two or three days we arrived at Pamaunkee; the king as many days entertained us with feasting and much mirth. And the day ·he· appointed to begin our trade, the president, Lieutenant Percie, Master West, Master Russell, Master Behethland, Master Crashaw, Master Powell, Master Ford, and some others to the number of fifteen went up to Opechancanough's house ·near· a quarter of a mile from the river, where we found nothing but a lame fellow and a boy, and all the houses round about of all things abandoned. Not long we stayed ere the king arrived, and after him came divers of his people loaden with bows and arrows, but such pinching commodities, and those esteemed at such a value as our captain began with the king after this manner:

"Opechancanough, the great love you profess with your tongue seems mere deceit by your actions. Last year you kindly fraughted our ship, but now you have invited me to starve with hunger. You know my want, and I your plenty, of which by some means I must have part. Remember it is fit for kings to keep their promise. Here are my commodities, whereof take your choice. The rest I will proportion fit bargains for your people."

The king seemed kindly to accept his offer and the better to color his project sold us what they had to our own content, promising the next day more company better provided. The barges and pinnace being committed to the charge of Master Phetiplace, the president with his old fifteen marched up to the king's house, where we found four or five men newly arrived, each with a great basket. Not long after came the king, who with a strained cheerfulness held us with discourse what pains he had taken to keep his promise, till Master Russell brought us in news that we were all betrayed, for at least ·six or· seven hundred savages well armed had environed the house and beset the fields. The king conjecturing what Russell related, we could well perceive how the extremity of his fear bewrayed his intent; whereat some of our company seeming dismayed with the thought of such a multitude, the captain encouraged us to this effect:

"Worthy countrymen, were the mischiefs of my seeming friends no more than the danger of these *enemies,* I little cared were they as many more, if you dare do but as I.

"But this is my torment that if I escape them, our malicious council with their open-mouthed minions will make me such a 'peace-breaker' (in their opinions in England) as will break my neck. I could wish those here that make these [savages] seem saints and me an oppressor. But this is the worst of all, wherein I pray you aid me with your opinions: Should we begin with them and surprise the king? We cannot keep him and defend well ourselves. If we should each kill our man, and so proceed with all in the house, the rest will all fly. Then shall we get no more than the bodies that are slain, and so starve for victual.

"As for their fury, it is the least danger. For well you know [that] being alone assaulted with two or three hundred of them I made them by the help of God compound to save my life. And we are ·now· *sixteen* and they but seven hundred at the *most*. And assure yourselves God will so assist us that if you dare stand but to discharge your pieces, the very smoke will be sufficient to affright them. Yet howsoever, ·if there be occasion·, let us fight like men and not die like sheep. For by that means you know God hath oft delivered me, and so I trust will now.

"But first I will deal with them to bring it to pass we may fight for something and draw them to it by conditions. If you like this motion, promise me you will be valiant."

The time not permitting any argument, all vowed to execute whatsoever he attempted, or die; whereupon the captain ·approaching· in plain terms told the king this:

"I see, Opechancanough, your plot to murder me, but I fear it not. As yet your men and mine have done no harm but by our direction. Take therefore your arms. You see mine. My body shall be as naked as yours. The isle in your river is a fit place, if you be contented, and the conqueror of us two shall be lord and master over all our men.[1] ·Otherways, draw all your men into the field·. If you have not enough, take time to fetch more and bring what number you will, so everyone bring a basket of corn against all which I will stake the value in copper (you see I have but fifteen ·men·) and our game shall be the conqueror take all."

The king, being guarded with forty or fifty of his chief men, seemed kindly to appease Smith's suspicion of unkindness by a great present at the door they entreated him to receive. This was to draw him out of the door where the bait was guarded with at least two hundred men, and thirty lying under a great tree that lay thwart as a barricado, each his arrow nocked ready to shoot.

The president commanded one to go see what kind of deceit this was, and to receive the present; but he refused to do it. Yet the gentlemen and all the rest were importunate to go, but he would not permit them, being vexed at that coward, and commanded Lieutenant Percie, Master West, and the rest to make good the house, Master Powell and Master Behethland he commanded to

[1] We estimate Opechancanough was now in his sixties or seventies.

guard the door, and in such a rage snatched the king by his long lock[1] in the middest of his men, with his pistol ready bent against his breast. Thus he led the trembling king (near dead with fear) amongst all his people, who delivering the captain his vambrace, bow and arrows, all his men were easily entreated to cast down their arms, little dreaming any durst in that manner have used their king; who then to escape himself bestowed his presents in good sadness; and causing a great many of them [to] come before him unarmed, holding the king by the hair (as is said), he spake to them to this effect:

"I see, you Pamaunkees, the great desire you have to kill me; and my long suffering your injuries hath emboldened you to this presumption. The cause I have forborne your insolencies is the promise I made you before the God I serve to be your friend till you give me just cause to be your enemy. If I keep this vow, my God will keep me: You cannot hurt me. If I break it, He will destroy me. But if you shoot but one arrow to shed one drop of blood of any of my men, or steal the least of these beads or copper I spurn here before you with my foot, you shall see I will not cease revenge, if once I begin, so long as I can hear where to find one of your nation that will not deny the name of Pamaunk.

"I am not now at Rassaweak half drowned with mire where you took me prisoner. Yet then, for keeping your promise and your good usage and saving my life, I so affect you that your denials of your treachery do half persuade me to mistake myself.

"But if I be the mark you aim at, here I stand: Shoot he that dare! You promised to fraught my ship ere I departed, and so you shall or I mean to load her with your dead carcasses. Yet if as friends you will come and trade, I once more promise not to trouble you, except you give me the first occasion. And your king shall be free and be my friend, for I am not come to hurt him or any of you."

Upon this, away went their bows and arrows, and men, women, and children brought in their commodities. Two or three hours they so thronged about the president and so overwearied him as he retired himself to rest, leaving Master Behethland and Master Powell

[1] "By his vambrace" in *The Proceedings,* a forearm protector for archers.

to receive their presents.

But some savages perceiving him fast asleep and the guard somewhat carelessly dispersed—forty or fifty of their choice men, each with a club or an English sword in his hand, began to enter the house with two or three hundred others that pressed to second them. The noise and haste they made in did so shake the house they awoke him from his sleep, and being half amazed with this sudden sight, betook him straight to his sword and target. Master Chrashaw and some others charged in like manner, whereat they quickly thronged faster back than before forward. The house thus cleansed, the king and some of his ancients we kept yet with him, who with a long oration excused this intrusion.

The rest of the day was spent with much kindness, the company again renewing their presents with their best provisions, and whatsoever he gave them they seemed therewith well contented.

Now in the meanwhile since our departure this hap'ned at our fort: Master Scrivener, having received letters from England to make himself either Caesar or nothing,[1] he began to decline in his affection to Captain Smith that ever regarded him as himself, and was willing to cross the surprising of Powhatan. Some certain days[2] after the president's departure he would needs go visit the Isle of Hogs, and took with him Captain Waldo—though the president had appointed him to be ready to second his occasions—with Master Anthony Gosnoll and eight others. But so violent was the wind that extreme frozen time that the boat sunk, but where or how none doth know, ·for they were all drowned; only this was known that· the skiff was much overloaden and would scarce have lived in that extreme tempest had she been empty; but by no persuasion he could be diverted, though both Waldo and an hundred others doubted as it hap'ned.

The savages were the first that found their bodies, which so much the more encouraged them to effect their projects. To advertise the president of this heavy news none could be found would undertake it, but the journey was often refused of all in the fort until Master

---

[1] Cesare Borgia's popular motto: *Aut Cæsar aut nihil,* "either [to be] Caesar or nothing!"

[2] "9 days" in *The Proceedings,* or 9 January 1609.

Richard Wyffin undertook alone the performance thereof.

In this journey he was encount'red with many dangers and difficulties in all parts as he passed. As for that night he lodged with Powhatan, perceiving such preparation for war, not finding the president there, he did assure himself some mischief was intended. Pocahontas hid him for a time and sent them who pursued him the clean contrary way to seek him. But by her means and extraordinary bribes and much trouble, in three days' travel at length he found us in the middest of these turmoils. This unhappy news the president swore him to conceal from the company, and so dissembling his sorrow with the best countenances he could, when the night approached went safely aboard with all his soldiers, leaving Opechancanough at liberty, according to his promise, the better to have Powhatan in his return.

Now so extremely Powhatan had threat'ned the death of his men if they did not by some means kill Captain Smith that the next day they appointed all the country should come to trade unarmed, yet, unwilling to be treacherous but that they were constrained, hating fighting with him almost as ill as hanging, such fear they had of bad success.

The next morning the sun had not long appeared but the fields appeared covered with people and baskets to tempt us on shore. ·The president determined to keep aboard·, but nothing was to be had without his presence nor they would not endure the sight of a gun. When the president saw them begin to depart, being unwilling to lose such a booty, he so well contrived the pinnace and his barges with ambuscadoes as only with Lieutenant Percie, Master West, and Master Russell with their arms went on shore. Others he appointed unarmed to receive what was brought.

The savages flocked before him in heaps, and the bank serving as a trench for a retreat, he drew them fair open to his ambuscadoes. For he not being to be persuaded to go visit their king, the king, knowing the most of them unarmed, came to visit him with two or three hundred men in the form of two half-moons, and with some twenty men and many women loaden with ·great· painted baskets. But when they approached somewhat near us, their women and children fled.

For when they had environed and beset the fields in this manner, they thought their purpose sure, yet so trembled with fear as they were scarce able to nock their arrows. Smith standing with his three men ready bent, beholding them till they were within danger of our ambuscadoes, who upon the word discovered themselves (and he retired to the barge[1]), which the savages no sooner perceived than away they fled, esteeming their heels for their best advantage.

That night we sent Master Chrashaw and Master Ford to James town to Captain Winne. In the way between Werowocomoco and the fort they met four or five of the Dutchmen's confederates going to Powhatan, the which, to excuse those gentlemen's suspicion of their running to the savages, returned to the fort and there continued.

The savages, hearing our barge ·depart· [and] go down the river in the night, were so terribly afraid that we sent for more men, we having so much threat'ned their ruin and the razing of their houses, boats, and weirs ·and canoes· that the next day the king sent our captain a chain of pearl to alter his purpose and stay his men, promising—though they wanted themselves—to fraught our ship, and bring it aboard to avoid suspicion, so that five or six days after from all parts of the country within ten or twelve miles in the extreme frost and snow they brought us provision on their naked backs.

Yet notwithstanding this kindness and trade, had their art and poison been sufficient, the president with Master West and some others had been poisoned. It made them sick, but expelled itself. Wecuttanow, a stout young fellow, knowing he was suspected for bringing this present of poison, with forty or fifty of his chief companions—seeing the president but with a few men at Potauncak—so proudly braved it as though he expected to encounter a revenge; which the president perceiving in the midst of his company did not only beat but spurned him like a dog as scorning to do him any worse mischief; whereupon all of them fled into the woods, thinking they had done a great matter to have so well escaped.

And the townsmen remaining presently fraughted our barge to be rid of our companies, framing many excuses to excuse Wecuttanow,

---

[1] "And he retiring to the bank" *ibid.*

being son to their chief king but Powhatan, and told us if we would show them him that brought the poison, they would deliver him to us to punish as we pleased.

Men may think it strange there should be such a stir for a little corn, but had it been gold, with more ease we might have got it, and had it wanted, the whole colony had starved. We may be thought very patient to endure all those injuries. Yet only with fearing them we got what they had, whereas if we had taken revenge, then by their loss we should have lost ourselves.

We searched also the countries of Youghtanund and Mattapanient, where the people imparted that little they had with such complaints and tears from the eyes of women and children as he had been too cruel to have been a Christian that would not have been satisfied and moved with compassion. But had this hap'ned in October, November, and December, when that unhappy discovery of Monacan was made, and when we might have fraughted a ship of forty tons, and twice as much might have been had from the rivers of Rapahanock, Patawomek, and Pawtuxunt.

The main occasion of our thus temporizing with them was to part friends, as we did, [and] to give the less cause of suspicion to Powhatan to fly; by whom we now returned with a purpose to have surprised him and his provision; for effecting whereof when we came against the town the president sent Master Wyffin and Master Coe ashore to discover and make way for his intended project. But they found that those damned Dutchmen had caused Powhatan to abandon his new house and Werowocomoco and to carry away all his corn and provision; and the people they found so ill affected that ·had they not stood well upon their guard·, they were in great doubt how to escape with their lives.

So the president, finding his intent ·thus· frustrated and that there was nothing now to be had, and therefore an unfit time to revenge their abuses, sent Master Michael Phittiplace by land to James town, whither we sailed with all the speed we could, we having in this journey, for 25li of copper and 50li of iron and beads, enough to keep 46[1] men six weeks ·and daily feasted with bread, corn, flesh,

[1] "40 men" *ibid.*

fish, and fowl·, and every man for his reward ·and in consideration of his commodities· a month's provision extraordinary (no trade being allowed but for the store). We got near 200li weight of deer suet and delivered to the cape merchant 479 bushels of corn.[1]

Those temporizing proceedings to some may seem too charitable to such a daily daring, treacherous people; to others not pleasing that we washed not the ground with their bloods nor showed such strange inventions in mangling, murdering, ransacking, and destroying as did the Spaniards the simple bodies of such ignorant souls, nor delightful because not stufted with relations of heaps and mines of gold and silver, nor such rare commodities as the Portugals and Spaniards found in the East and West Indies, the want whereof hath begot us that were the first undertakers no less scorn and contempt than the noble conquests and valiant adventures beautified with it praise and honor. Too much I confess the world cannot attribute to their ever-memorable merit, and to clear us from the blind world's ignorant censure these few words may suffice any reasonable understanding:

It was the Spaniard's good hap to happen in those parts where were infinite numbers of people who had manured the ground with that providence ·that· it afforded victuals at all times; and time had brought them to that perfection they had the use of gold and silver and the most of such commodities as those countries afforded, so that what the Spaniard got was chiefly the spoil and pillage of those country people and not the labors of their own hands.

But had those fruitful countries been as savage, as barbarous, as ill-peopled, as little planted, labored, and manured as Virginia, their proper labors it is likely would have produced as small profit as ours. But had Virginia been peopled, planted, manured, and adorned with such store of precious jewels and rich commodities as was the Indies, then had we not gotten and done as much as by their examples might be expected from us, the world might then have traduced[2] us and our merits, and have made shame and infamy our recompense

[1] "279 bushels" *ibid.*

[2] Censured.

and reward. But we chanced in a land even as God made it, where we found only an idle, improvident, scattered people, ignorant of the knowledge of gold or silver or any commodities, and careless of anything but from hand to mouth, except baubles of no worth; nothing to encourage us but what accidentally we found nature afforded, which ere we could bring to recompense our pains, defray our charges, and satisfy our adventurers we were to discover the country, subdue the people, bring them to be tractable, civil, and industrious, and teach them trades, that the fruits of their labors might make us some recompense; or plant such colonies of our own that must first make provision how to live of themselves ere they can bring to perfection the commodities of the country, which doubtless will be as commodious for England as the West Indies for Spain, if it be rightly managed, notwithstanding all our homebred opinions that will argue the contrary, as formerly some have done against the Spaniards and Portugals.

But to conclude, against all rumor of opinion I only say this: [As] for those that the three first years began this plantation, notwithstanding all their factions, mutinies, and miseries so gently corrected and well prevented, peruse the Spanish *Decades,* the relations of Master Hackluit,[1] and tell me how many ever with such small means as a barge of 22 tons,[2] sometimes with seven, eight, or nine or but at most twelve or sixteen men, did ever discover so many fair and navigable rivers, subject so many several kings, people, and nations to obedience and contribution with so little bloodshed.

And if in the search of those countries we had hap'ned where wealth had been, we had as surely had it as obedience and contribution; but if we have overskipped it, we will not envy them that shall ·chance to· find it. Yet can we not but lament it was our ·ill· fortunes to end when we had but only learned how to begin and found the right course how to proceed.

BY RICHARD WYFFIN, WILLIAM PHITTIPLACE,
JEFFREY ABBOT, AND ANAS TODKILL.

---

[1] Peter Martyr d'Anghiera's *Decades,* Richard Hakluyt's *Principal Navigations.*
[2] Misprint for "2 tons," which in *The Proceedings.*

Chapter X.

How the savages became subject to the English.

WHEN THE SHIPS departed, all the provision of the store but that the president had gotten was so rotten with the last summer's rain and eaten with rats and worms as the hogs would scarcely eat it. Yet it was the soldiers' diet till our returns, so that we found nothing done, but our victuals spent, and the most part of our tools and a good part of our arms conveyed to the savages. But now casting up the store and finding sufficient till the next harvest, the fear of starving was abandoned; and the company divided into tens, fifteens, or as the business required. Six hours[1] each day was spent in work, the rest in pastime and merry exercises. But the untowardness of the greatest number caused the president ·to make a general assembly and then· advise as followeth:

"Countrymen, the long experience of our late miseries I hope is sufficient to persuade everyone to a present correction of himself. And think not that either my pains nor the adventurers' purses will ever maintain you in idleness and sloth.

"I speak not this to you all, for divers of you I know deserve both honor and reward better than is yet here to be had, but the greater part must be more industrious or starve. However you have been heretofore tolerated by the authority of the council from that I have often commanded you,[2] you see now that power resteth wholly in myself,[3] you must obey this now for a law that *he that will not work shall not eat,* except by sickness he be disabled. For the labors of thirty or forty honest and industrious men shall not be consumed to maintain an hundred and fifty idle loiterers.

"And though you presume the authority here is but a shadow, and that I dare not touch the lives of any but my own must answer it, the letters patents shall each week be read you, whose contents will tell you the contrary. I would wish you therefore without contempt seek

---

[1] "4 hours" in *ibid.*

[2] I.e., although the council has up to now allowed you to shirk …

[3] "Of the original councilors, Smith was the only one still surviving in Virginia." (Barbour)

to observe these orders set down. For there are now no more councilors to protect you nor curb my endeavors. Therefore he that offendeth let him assuredly expect his due punishment."

He made also a table as a public memorial of every man's deserts to encourage the good and with shame to spur on the rest to amendment. By this, many became very industrious, yet more by ·severe· punishment performed their business, for all were so tasked that there was no excuse could prevail to deceive him.

Yet the Dutchmen's consorts so closely ·still· conveyed them powder, shot, swords, and tools that though we could find the defect, we could not find by whom ·it was occasioned· till it was too late.

All this time the Dutchmen remaining with Powhatan—who kindly entertained them to instruct the savages the use of our arms—and their consorts not following them as they expected, to know the cause they sent Francis, their companion, a stout young fellow disguised like a savage, to the glass house,[1] a place in the woods near a mile from James Town, where was their rendezvous for all their unsuspected villainy.

Forty men they procured ·of Powhatan· to lie in ambuscado for Captain Smith, who no sooner heard of this Dutchman but he sent to apprehend him. But he was gone. Yet to cross his return to Powhatan, the captain presently dispatched 20 shot after him, himself returning from the glass house alone. By the way he encount'red the King of Paspahegh, a most strong, stout savage, whose persuasions not being able to persuade him to his ambush, seeing him only armed but with a falchion, attempted to have shot him. But the president prevented his shoot by grappling with him, and the savage as well prevented him for drawing his falchion, and perforce bore him into the river to have drowned him. Long they struggled in the water, ·from whence the king, perceiving two of the Poles upon the sands, would have fled·, till the president ·held him by the hair and· got such hold on his throat he had near strangled the king ·till the Poles came in·. But having drawn his falchion to cut off his head, seeing how pitifully he begged his life, he led him prisoner to James Town and put him in chains.

---

[1] A shop where glass was being made.

The Dutchman ere long was also brought in, whose villainy, though all this time it was suspected, yet he feigned such a formal excuse that for want of language Captain Winne understood him not rightly; and [as] for their dealings with Powhatan, that to save their lives they were constrained to accommodate [supply] his arms, of whom he extremely complained to have detained them perforce, and that he made this escape with the hazard of his life, and meant not to have returned but was only walking in the woods to gather walnuts. Yet for all this fair tale there was so small appearance of truth, and the plain confession of Paspahegh of his treachery, he went by the heels.[1]

·The king also he put in fetters·, Smith purposing to regain the Dutchmen by the [exchange of] saving his life. The poor savage did his best by his daily messengers to Powhatan, but all returned that the Dutchmen would not return, neither did Powhatan stay them, and to bring them fifty miles on his men's backs they were not able. Daily this king's wives, children, and people came to visit him with presents, which he liberally bestowed to make his peace, [for] much trust they had in the president's promise. But the king, finding his guard negligent, though fettered yet escaped. Captain Winne, thinking to pursue him, found such troops of savages to hinder his passage as they exchanged many volleys of shot for flights of arrows.

Captain Smith, hearing of this, in returning to the fort took two savages prisoners—called Kemps and Tussore[2]—the two most exact villains in all the country. With these he sent Captain Winne and fifty choice men and Lieutenant Percie ·that night· to have regained the king and revenged this injury, and so had done if they had followed his directions or been advised with those two villains, that would have betrayed both king and kindred for a piece of copper. But he trifling away the night, the savages the next morning by the rising of the sun braved him to come ashore to fight. A good time both sides let fly at other, but we heard of no hurt, only they took two canoes, burnt the king's house, and so returned to James town.

The president, fearing those bravadoes would but encourage the

---

[1] Was put in irons.

[2] Called Kinsock in *The Proceedings*.

savages, began again himself to try his conclusions, whereby six or seven ·savages· were slain, as many made prisoners. He burnt their houses, took their boats with all their fishing weirs, and planted some of them at James town for his own use, and now resolved not to cease till he had revenged himself of all them ·that· had injured him.

But in his journey passing by Paspahegh towards Chickahamania, the savages did their best to draw him to their ambuscadoes. But seeing him regardlessly pass their country, all showed themselves in their bravest manner. To try their valors, he could not but let fly, and ere he could land, they no sooner knew him but they threw down their arms and desired peace. Their orator was a lusty young fellow called Okaning [Ocanindge], whose worthy discourse deserveth to be rememb'red, and thus it was:

"Captain Smith, my master is here present in the company thinking it Captain Winne, and not you, [and] of him he intended to have been revenged, [you] having never offended him. If he have offended you in escaping your imprisonment, the fishes swim, the fowls fly, and the very beasts strive to escape the snare and live. Then blame not him being a man. He would entreat you remember, you being a prisoner, what pains he took to save your life. If since he hath injured you, he was compelled to it. But howsoever, you have revenged it with our too great loss.

"We perceive and well know you intend to destroy us that are here to entreat and desire your friendship, and to enjoy our houses and plant our fields, of whose fruit *you* shall participate. Otherwise, you will have the worse by our absence, for we can plant anywhere, though with more labor; and we know you cannot live if you want our harvest and that relief we bring you. If you promise us peace, we will believe you; if you proceed in revenge, we will abandon the country."

Upon these terms the president promised them peace till they did us injury, upon condition they should bring in provision. Thus all departed good friends and so continued till Smith left the country.

Arriving at James Town, complaint was made to the president that the Chickahamanians, who all this while continued trade and seemed our friends, by color thereof were the only thieves. And amongst other things a pistol being stol'n and the thief fled, there was apprehended two proper young fellows that were brothers, known to be his confederates.

Now to regain this pistol, the one was imprisoned, the other was sent to return the pistol again within twelve hours or his brother to be hanged. Yet the president pitying the poor naked savage in the dungeon sent him victual and some charcoal for a fire. Ere midnight his brother returned with the pistol, but the poor savage in the dungeon was so smothered with the smoke he had made and so piteously burnt that we found him dead. The other most lamentably bewailed his death and broke forth into such bitter agonies that the president to quiet him told him that if hereafter they would not steal, he would make him alive again, but he little thought he could be recovered. Yet we doing our best with aqua vitae and vinegar, it pleased God to restore him again to life—but so drunk and affrighted that he seemed lunatic, ·not understanding anything he spoke or heard·, the which as much tormented and grieved the other as before to see him dead; of which malady, upon promise of their good behavior, the president promised to recover him, and so caused him to be laid by a fire to sleep; who in the morning having well slept had recovered his perfect senses; and then being dressed of his burning, and each a piece of copper given them, they went away so well contented that this was spread among all the savages for a miracle that Captain Smith could make a man alive that was dead.

Another ingenuous [clever] savage of Powhatan's, having gotten a great bag of powder and the back of an armor, at Werowocomoco amongst a many of his companions, to show his extraordinary skill he did dry it on the back as he had seen the soldiers at James Town. But he dried it so long, they peeping over it to see his skill, it took fire and blew him to death and one or two more, and the rest so scorched they had little pleasure to meddle anymore with powder.

These and many other such pretty accidents so amazed and affrighted both Powhatan and all his people that from all parts with presents they desired peace, returning many stol'n things which we never demanded nor thought of. And after that, those that were taken stealing, both Powhatan and his people have sent them back to James town to receive their punishment; and all the country became absolute·ly· as free for us as for themselves.

Chapter XI.

What was done in three months having victuals. The store devoured by rats. How we lived three months off such natural fruits as the country afforded.

NOW WE so quietly followed our business that in three months we made three or four last of tar, pitch and soap-ashes,[1] produced a trial of glass, made a well in the fort of excellent sweet water, which till then was wanting, built some twenty houses, recovered our church, provided nets and weirs for fishing, and to stop the disorders of our disorderly thieves and the savages built a blockhouse in the neck of our isle, kept by a garrison to entertain the savages' trade, and none to pass nor repass—savage nor Christian—without the president's order.

Thirty or forty acres of ground we digged and planted. Of three sows in eighteen months[2] increased 60 and odd pigs, and near 500 chickings brought up themselves without having any meat given them. But the hogs were transported to Hog Isle, where also we built a blockhouse with a garrison to give us notice of any shipping; and for their exercise they made clapboard and wainscot and cut down trees ·against the ships' coming·.

We built also a fort for a retreat near a convenient river upon a high commanding hill, very hard to be assaulted, and easy to be defended.[3] But ere it was ·half· finished this defect caused a stay:

In searching our casked corn we found it half rotten and the rest so consumed with so many thousands of rats that increased so fast (but their original was from the ships[4]) as we knew not how to keep that little we had. This did drive us all to our wit's end, for there was nothing in the country but what nature afforded. Until this time

---

[1] Twelve to fourteen barrels per last.

[2] "One year" in *The Proceedings.*

[3] An earthwork known as "Smith's Fort" by Grays Creek. This and the Hog Island blockhouse were vital defensive measures in the event of a seaward attack by Spain or another European power, much expected in the early years.

[4] Rats first came to Virginia aboard English ships.

Kemps and Tassore were fettered prisoners, and ·daily wrought and· did double task and taught us how to order and plant our fields, whom now for want of victual we set at liberty. But ·so well were they used· [and] so well they liked our companies they did not desire to go from us.

And to express their loves, for 16 days' continuance the country people brought us, when least, 100 a day of squirrels, turkeys, deer, and other wild beasts.

But this want of corn occasioned the end of all our [other] works, it being work sufficient to provide victual. 60 or 80 with Ensign Laxon was sent down the river to live upon oysters, and 20 with Lieutenant Percy to try for fishing at Point Comfort; but in six weeks they would not agree once to cast out the net, he being sick and burnt sore with gunpowder. Master West with as many went up to the Falls, but nothing could be found but a few ·berries and· acorns.

Of that in ·the· store every man had their equal proportion. Till this present, by the hazard and endeavors of some thirty or forty this whole colony had ever been fed. We had more sturgeon than could be devoured by dog and man, of which the industrious by drying and pounding, mingled with caviar, sorrel, and other wholesome herbs, would make bread and good meat. Others would gather as much *tockwhogh* roots in a day as would make them bread a week, so that off those wild fruits and what we caught we lived very well in regard of such a diet.

But such was the ·most· strange condition of some 150 that had they not been forced *nolens volens*[1] perforce to gather and prepare their victual, they would all have starved or have eaten one another.

Of those wild fruits the savages often brought us, and for that the president would not fulfill the unreasonable desire of those distracted, gluttonous loiterers[2] to sell not only our kettles, hoes, tools, and iron—nay, swords, pieces, and the very ordnance and houses, might they have prevailed to have been but idle, for those savage fruits they would have had imparted all to the savages, especially for one basket of corn they heard of to be at Powhatan's,

---

[1] "Willy nilly." (Latin).
[2] "lubberly gluttons" in *The Proceedings.*

fifty miles from our fort. Though he bought near half of it to satisfy their humors, yet to have had the other half they would have sold their souls, though not sufficient to have kept them a week. Thousands were their exclamations, suggestions, and devices to force him to those base inventions to have made it an occasion to abandon the country. Want perforce constrained him to endure their exclaiming follies till he found out the author, one Dyer, a most crafty fellow and his ancient maligner, whom he worthily punished; and with the rest he argued the case in this manner:

"Fellow soldiers, I did little think any so false to report, or so many to be so simple to be persuaded that I either intend to starve you or that Powhatan at this present hath corn for himself, much less for you, or that I would not have it if I knew where it were to be had. Neither did I think any so malicious as now I see a great many. Yet it shall not so passionate me but I will do my best for my most maligner. But dream no longer of this vain hope from Powhatan, not [·nor·] that I will longer forbear to force you from your idleness and punish you if you rail. But if I find any more runners for Newfoundland with the pinnace, let him assuredly look to arrive at the gallows.

"You cannot deny but that by the hazard of my life many a time I have saved yours when, might your own wills have prevailed, you would have starved, and will do still whether I will or no.

"But I protest by that God that made me, since necessity hath not power to force you to gather for yourselves those fruits the earth doth yield, you shall not only gather for yourselves but ·for· those that are sick. As yet I never had more from the store than the worst of you; and all my English extraordinary provision that I have you shall see me divide it amongst the sick. And this savage trash you so scornfully repine at, being put in your mouths your stomachs can digest ·it· (if you would have better you should have brought it[1]); and therefore I will take a course you shall provide what is to be had. The sick shall not starve, but equally share of all our labors. And he that gathereth not every day as much as I do, the next day shall be set beyond the river and be banished from the fort as a drone till he

---

[1] A clear indication the problem is with the gentlemen and not with the rank and file, who are such precisely because they own nothing and bring nothing.

amend his conditions or starve."[1]

But some would say with Seneca—

I know those things thou say'st are true, good nurse,
But fury forceth me to follow worse.
My mind is hurried headlong up and down,
Desiring better counsel, yet finds none.

This order many murmured was very cruel, but it caused the most part so well bestir themselves that of 200, except they were drowned, there died not past seven. As for Captain Winne and Master Leigh, they were dead ere this want hap'ned, and the rest died not for want of such as preserved the rest. Many were billeted amongst the savages, whereby we knew all their passages, fields, and habitations, how to gather and use their fruits as well as themselves. For they did know we had such a commanding power at James town they durst not wrong us of a pin.

So well those poor savages used us that were thus billeted that divers of the soldiers ran away to search Kemps and Tassore, our old prisoners. Glad were these savages to have such an opportunity to testify their love unto us. For instead of entertaining them and such things as they had stolen, with all their great offers and promises they made them how to revenge their injuries upon Captain Smith, Kemps first made himself sport in showing his countrymen by them how he was used, feeding them with this law: *Who would not work must not eat*—till they were near starved indeed, continually threat'ning to beat them to death.[2] Neither could they get [anything] from him till he and his consorts brought them perforce to our captain that so well contented him and punished them, as many others that intended also to follow them were rather contented to labor at home than adventure to live idly amongst the savages, of whom there was more hope to make better Christians and good

[1] "Forever be banished from the fort and live there or starve" in *The Proceedings.*

[2] Kemps' sport then was to mimic President Smith in a display among his own people in order to discourage English freeloaders and their bribes of pilfery. But who can blame them? The tone of this whole passage is wrong. Failure of supply is a failure of leadership.

subjects than the one half of those that counterfeited themselves both. For so afraid was all those kings and the better sort of the people to displease us that some of the baser sort that we have extremely hurt and punished for their villainies would hire us we should not tell it to their kings or countrymen, who would also repunish them and yet return them to James town to content the president for a testimony of their loves.

Master Sicklemore well returned from Chawwonoke, but found little hope and less certainty of them were left by Sir Walter Raleigh. The river he saw was not great, the people few, the country most overgrown with pines, where there did grow here and there stragglingly *pemminaw,* [that] we call silk grass.[1] But by the river the ground was good and exceeding fertile.

Master Nathanael Powell and Anas Todkill were also by the Quiyoughquohanocks conducted to the Mangoags to search them there. But nothing could they learn but they were all dead. This honest, proper, good, promise-keeping king, of all the rest, did ever best affect us; and though to his false gods he was very zealous, yet he would confess our god as much exceeded his as our guns did his bow and arrows, often sending our president many presents to pray to his god for rain, or his corn would perish, for his gods were angry.

Three days' journey they conducted them through the woods into a high country towards the southwest where they saw here and there a little cornfield by some little spring or small brook, but no river they could see, the people in all respects like the rest except their language. They live most upon roots, fruits, and wild beasts, and trade with them towards the sea and the fatter countries for dried fish and corn for skins.

All this time to recover the Dutchmen and one Bentley, another fugitive, we employed one William Volday, a Switzer by birth, with pardons and promises to regain them. Little we then suspected this double villain of any villainy, who plainly taught us in the most trust was the greatest treason. For this wicked hypocrite, by the seeming hate he bore to the lewd conditions of his cursed countrymen, having this opportunity by his employment to regain them, conveyed

[1] Barbour says not so. *Pemminaw* was used to make thread.

them everything they desired to effect their projects to destroy the colony. With much devotion they expected the Spaniard, to whom they intended ·to have done· good service, or any other that would but carry them from us.

But to begin with the first opportunity, they seeing necessity thus enforced us to disperse ourselves importuned Powhatan to lend them but his forces and they would not only destroy our hogs, fire our town, and betray our pinnace, but bring to his service and subjection the most ·part· of our company.

With this plot they had acquainted many discontents, and many were agreed to their devilish practice.[1] But one Thomas Douse and Thomas Mallard—whose Christian hearts relented at such an unchristian act, voluntarily revealed it to Captain Smith, who caused them to conceal it, persuading Douse and Mallard to proceed in their confederacy only to bring the irreclaimable Dutchmen and the inconstant savages in such a manner amongst such ambuscadoes as he had prepared, that not many of them should ·ever· return from ·out· our peninsula.

But this bruit coming to the ears of the impatient multitude, they so importuned the president to cut off those Dutchmen as amongst many that offered to cut their throats before the face of Powhatan the first was Lieutenant Percy and Master John Cuderington, two gentlemen of as bold resolute spirits as could possibly be found. But the president had occasion of other employment for them, and gave way to Master Wyffin and Sergeant Jeffrey Abbot to go and stab them or shoot them. But the Dutchmen made such excuses, accusing Volday, whom they supposed had revealed their project, as Abbot would not, yet Wyffing would, perceiving it but deceit.

The king understanding of this their employment sent presently his messengers to Captain Smith to signify it was not his fault to detain them nor hinder his men from executing his command, nor did he, nor would he, maintain them or any to occasion his displeasure.

But whilst this business was in hand, ·God having seen our misery sufficient·, arrived one Captain Argall and Master Thomas Sedan, sent by Master Cornelius to truck with the colony and fish for

---

[1] This may have borne fruit earlier in the ambush laid at Onawmanient. See 260n².

sturgeon with a ship well furnished with wine ·and biscuit· and much other good provision. Though it was not sent us, our necessities was such as enforced us to take it ·at a price, but left him sufficient to return for England·.

He brought us news of a great supply and preparation for the Lord La Warre with letters that much taxed our president for his hard dealing with the savages and not returning the ships fraughted. Notwithstanding, we kept this ship till the fleet arrived. True it is Argall lost his voyage, but we revictualed him and sent him for England with a true relation of the causes of our defailments and how impossible it was to return that wealth they expected, or observe their instructions to endure the savages' insolencies, or do anything to any purpose except they would send us men and means that could produce that they so much desired. Otherwise all they did was lost and could not but come to confusion.

The villainy of Volday we still dissembled, ·but certainly he had not escaped had the president continued·. Adam upon his pardon came home, but Samuell still stayed with Powhatan, to hear further of their estates by this supply.

Now all their plots Smith so well understood they were his best advantages to secure us from any treachery [that] could be done by them or the savages—which with facility he could revenge when he would because all those countries more feared him than Powhatan, and he had such parties with all his bordering neighbors, and many of the rest for love or fear would have done anything he would have them upon any commotion, though these fugitives had done all they could to persuade Powhatan [that] King James would kill Smith for using him and his people so unkindly.

By this you may see for all those crosses, treacheries, and dissensions how he wrestled and overcame without bloodshed all that happened; also what good was done, how few died, what food the country naturally affordeth, what small cause there is men should starve or be murthered by the savages that have discretion to manage them with courage and industry. The two first years though by his adventures he had oft brought the savages to a tractable trade, yet you see how the envious authority ever crossed him and frustrated his best endeavors. But it wrought in him that experience and estimation amongst the savages as otherwise it had been impossible he had ever effected that he did. Notwithstanding the many miserable, yet generous[1] and worthy, adventures he had oft and long endured in the wide world, ·as well in some parts of Africa and America as in the most parts of Europe and Asia, by land or sea, [that] had taught him much·, yet in this case he was again to learn his lecture by experience—which with thus much ado having obtained, it was his ill chance to end when he had but only learned how to begin. And though he left those unknown difficulties made easy and familiar to his unlawful successors, who only by living in James Town presumed to know more than all the world could direct them, now though they had all his soldiers with a triple power and twice triple better means, by what they have done in his absence the world may see what they would have done in his presence, had he not prevented their indiscretions, [and] it doth justly prove what cause he had to send them for England, and that he was neither factious, mutinous, nor dishonest. But they have made it more plain since his return for England, having his absolute authority freely in their power with all the advantages and opportunity that his labors had effected. As I am sorry their actions have made it so manifest, so I am unwilling to say what reason doth compel me, but only to make apparent the truth, lest I should seem partial, reasonless, and malicious.[2]

Chapter XII.

The arrival of the third supply.

TO REDRESS those jars and ill proceedings, the Treasurer, Council, and Company of Virginia, not finding that return and profit they expected, and them engaged there not having means to subsist of

---

[1] "Gallant, courageous." (Barbour)

[2] This chapter is also unsigned in *The Proceedings.* Written by Smith?

themselves, made means to His Majesty to call in their commission and take a new in their own names, as in their own publication (1610) you may read at large.[1]

Having thus annihilated the old by virtue of a commission made to the Right Honorable Sir Thomas West, Lord de la Warre, to be general of Virginia, Sir Thomas Gates his lieutenant, Sir George Somers admiral, Sir Thomas Dale high marshal, Sir Fardinando Wainman general of the horse, and so all other offices to many other worthy gentlemen for their lives (though not any of them had ever been in Virginia except Captain Newport, who was also by patent made vice-admiral), those noble gentlemen drew in such great sums of money that they sent Sir Thomas Gates, Sir George Somers, and Captain Newport with nine ships and five hundred people—who had each of them a commission [that] who first arrived [was] to call in the old [although] without the knowledge or consent of them that had endured all those former dangers to beat the path—not any regard had at all of them.

All things being ready, because those three captains could not agree for place, it was concluded they should go all in one ship, so all their three commissions were in that ship with them called the *Sea-Venture.*

They set sail from England in May 1609. A small ketch perished at sea in a hurricano. The admiral with an hundred and fifty men [and] with the two knights and their new commission, their bills of loading with all manner of directions, and the most part of their provision, arrived not.

With the other seven ships as captains arrived Ratliffe, whose right name, as is said, was Sicklemore, Martin and Archer with Captain Wood, Captain Webbe, Captain Moone, Captain King, Captain Davis, and divers gentlemen of good means and great parentage. But the first as they had been troublesome at sea began again to mar all ashore. For though as is said they were formerly ·deposed and· sent for England, yet now returning again graced by the titles of "captains of the passengers," seeing the admiral wanting and great probability of her loss, strengthened themselves with those new companies so

[1] *A True and Sincere Declaration §20.*

·railing and· exclaiming against Captain Smith that they mortally hated him ere ever they saw him;

Who understanding by his scouts the arrival of such a fleet, little dreaming of any such supply, supposed them Spaniards. But he quickly so determined and ordered our affairs as we little feared their arrival nor the success of our encounter, nor were the savages any way negligent for the most part ·or unwilling· to aid and assist us with their best power.[1]

Had it so been, we had been happy, for we would not have trusted them but as our foes, where[as] receiving them as our countrymen and friends, they did what they could to murther our president, to surprise the store, the fort, and our lodgings, to usurp the government and make us all their servants and slaves till they could consume us and our remembrance, and rather indeed to supplant us than supply us—as master William Box, an honest gentleman in this voyage, thus relateth—

"In the tail of a hurricano we were separated from the admiral, which although it was but the remainder of that storm, there is seldom any such in England or those northern parts of Europe. Some lost their masts, some their sails blown from their yards. The seas so overraking our ships much of our provision was spoiled, our fleet separated, and our men sick, and many died, and in this miserable estate we arrived in Virginia." But in this storm—

When rattling thunder ran along the clouds
Did not the sailors poor and masters proud
A terror feel as struck with fear of God?
Did not their trembling joints then dread his rod?
Lest for foul deeds and black-mouth'd blasphemies
The rueful time be come that vengeance cries.

To a thousand mischiefs those lewd[2] captains led this lewd company, wherein were many unruly gallants packed thither by their friends to escape ill destinies; and those would dispose and

[1] The Indians hated the Spanish. Otherwise this incident is similar to Dale's reception of another supply in §31–516, 517.
[2] Good-for-nothing.

determine of the government sometimes to one, the next day to another, today the old commission must rule, tomorrow the new, the next day neither. In fine, they would rule all or ruin all. Yet in charity we must endure them thus to destroy us or by correcting their follies have brought the world's censure upon us to be guilty of their bloods. Happy had we been had they never arrived, and we forever abandoned and as we were, left to our fortunes. For on earth for the number was never more confusion or misery than their factions occasioned.

The president seeing the desire those braves had to rule, seeing how his authority was so unexpectedly changed, would willingly have left all and have returned for England. But seeing there was small hope this new commission would arrive,[1] longer he would not suffer those factious spirits to proceed. It would be too tedious, too strange, and almost incredible should I particularly relate the infinite dangers, plots, and practices he daily escaped amongst this factious crew, the chief whereof he quickly laid by the heels, till his leisure better served to do them justice. And to take away all occasions of further mischief, Master Percie had his request granted to return for England, being very sick, and Master West with an hundred and twenty of the best he could choose he sent to ·plant at· the Falls; Martin with near as many to Nandsamund, with their due proportions of all provisions according to their numbers.

Now the president's year being near expired, he made Captain Martin president (to follow the order for the election of a president every year), but he knowing his own insufficiency and the company's untowardness and little regard of him, within three hours after resigned it again to Captain Smith, and at Nandsamund thus proceeded:

The people being contributors[2] used him kindly. Yet such was his jealous fear ·and cowardice·, in the midst of their mirth he did surprise this poor naked king with his monuments, houses, and the isle he inhabited, and there fortified himself; but so apparently distracted with fear as emboldened the savages to assault him, kill his men,

---

1 The commissioners were still alive but shipwrecked on Bermuda.

2 The Nansemonds paid tribute to Jamestown.

release their king, gather and carry away ·more than· a thousand bushels of corn—he not once offering to intercept them, but sent to the president, then at the Falls, for thirty good shot, which from James Town immediately was sent him. But he so well employed them they did just nothing, but returned complaining of his tenderness,[1] yet he came away with them to James Town, leaving his company to their fortunes.

Here I cannot omit the courage of George Forrest, that had seventeen arrows sticking in him and one shot through him, yet lived six or seven days as if he had small hurt, then for want of chirurgery died.

Master West having seated his men by the Falls presently returned to revisit James Town. The president followed him to see that company seated, met him by the way, wondering at his so quick return, and found his company planted so inconsiderately in a place not only subject to the river's inundation but round environed with many intolerable inconveniences.

For remedy whereof he presently sent to Powhatan to sell him the place called Powhatan, promising to defend him against the Monacans, and these should be his conditions: with his people to resign him the fort and houses and all that country for a proportion of copper; that all stealing offenders should be sent him, there to receive their punishment; that every house as a custom should pay him a bushel of corn for an inch square of copper, and a proportion of *pocones* as a yearly tribute to King James for their protection as a duty; what else they could spare to barter at their best discretions.

But both this excellent place and those good conditions did those furies refuse, contemning both him, his kind care, and authority. So much they depended on the lord general's new commission as they regarded none. The worst they could do to show their spites they did, supposing all the Monacans' country gold, and none should come there but whom they pleased. I do more than wonder to think how only with five men he [the president] either durst or would adventure as he did, knowing how greedy they were of his blood, to land amongst them and commit to imprisonment all the chieftains of

---

[1] "Childishness" in *The Proceedings.*

those mutinies till by their multitudes being an hundred and twenty they forced him to retire. Yet in that interim he surprised one of their boats, wherewith he returned to their ship where indeed was their provision, which also he took. And well it chanced he found the mariners so tractable and constant, or there had been small possibility he had ever escaped.

·Notwithstanding·, there were divers other of better reason and experience that from their first landing, hearing the general good report of his old soldiers and seeing with their eyes his actions so well managed with discretion—as Captain Wood, Captain Webbe, Captain Moone, Captain FitzJames, Master William Powell, Master Partridge, Master White, and divers others—when they perceived the malice ·and condition· of Ratliffe, ·Martin·, and Archer, and their faction, left their companies and ever rested his faithful friends.

But the worst was that the poor savages that daily brought in their contribution to the president. That disorderly company so tormented those poor ·naked· souls by stealing their corn, robbing their gardens, beating them, breaking their houses, and keeping some prisoners[1] that they daily complained to Captain Smith he had brought them for protectors worse enemies than the Monacans themselves; which though till then for his love they had endured, they desired pardon if hereafter they defended themselves, since he would not correct them as they had long expected he would. So much they importuned him to punish their misdemeanors as they offered, if he would lead them, to fight for him against them.

But having spent nine days in seeking to reclaim them, showing them how much they did abuse themselves with these great gilded hopes of the South Sea mines, commodities, or victories they so madly conceived, then seeing nothing would prevail ·with them·, he set sail for James Town.

Thus oft we see from small green wounds and from a little grief[2]
A greater sore and sickness grows than will admit relief.
For thus themselves they did beguile and with the rest play'd thief.

---

1 "Breach of peace with the savages at the Falls." (margin note)

2 A small infection.

Now no sooner was the ship under sail but the savages assaulted those hundred and twenty in their fort. Finding some straggling abroad in the woods, they slew many and so affrighted the rest as their prisoners escaped, and they safely retired with the swords and cloaks of those they had slain.

But ere we had sailed half a league, our ship grounding gave us once more liberty to summon them to a parley, where we found them all so strangely amazed with this poor silly assault of twelve savages that they submitted themselves upon any terms to the president's mercy, who presently put by the heels six or seven of the chief offenders; the rest he seated gallantly at Powhatan in that savage fort ready built and prettily fortified with poles and barks of trees, sufficient to have defended them from all the savages in Virginia—dry houses for lodgings, and near two hundred acres[1] of ground ready to be planted; and no place we knew so strong, so pleasant and delightful in Virginia, for which we called it "Nonesuch."

The savages also he presently appeased, redelivering to either party their former losses. Thus all were friends.

New officers appointed to command and the president again ready to depart, at that instant arrived Captain West, whose gentle nature by the persuasions and compassion of those mutinous prisoners alleging they had only done this for his honor, was so much abused that to regain their old hopes new turboils[2] did arise. For they ashore, being possessed of all their victual, munition, and everything, grew to that height in their former factions as ·there· the president left them to their fortunes. They returned again to the open air at West's Fort, abandoning Nonesuch, and he to James town with his best expedition. But this hap'ned him in that journey:

Sleeping in his boat—for the ship was returned two days before—accidentally [some]one fired his powder bag, which tore the flesh from his body and thighs nine or ten inches square in a most pitiful manner. But to quench the tormenting fire frying him in his clothes, he leaped overboard into the deep river where ere they could recover him he was near drowned. In this estate without either

---

1 "And 300 acres" in *The Proceedings.*

2 Perhaps miswritten for "turmoils."

chirurgeon or chirurgery he was to go near an hundred miles.

[Smith now] arriving at James town, causing all things to be prepared for peace or wars to obtain provision—whilest those things were providing, ·Martin·, Ratliffe, Archer, and the rest of their confederates—being to come to their trials, their guilty consciences fearing a just reward for their deserts, seeing the president unable to stand, and near bereft of his senses by reason of his torment—they had plotted to have murdered him in his bed. But his heart did fail him that should have given fire to that merciless pistol. So, not finding that course to be the best, they joined together to usurp the government, thereby to escape their punishment ·and excuse themselves by accusing him·.

The president had notice of their projects, the which to withstand, though his old soldiers importuned him but permit them to take ·off· their heads that would resist his command, yet he would not suffer them, but sent for the masters of the ships and took order with them for his return for England. Seeing there was neither chirurgeon nor chirurgery in the fort to cure his hurt, and the ships to depart the next day, his commission to be suppressed he knew not why, himself and soldiers to be rewarded he knew not how, and a new commission granted they knew not to whom—the which ·so· disabled that authority he had as made them presume so oft to those mutinies ·and factions· as they did. Besides, so grievous were his wounds and so cruel his torments, few expecting he could live, nor was he able to follow his business to regain what they had lost, suppress those factions, and range the countries for provision as he intended. And well he knew in those affairs his own actions and presence was as requisite as his ·experience and· directions, which now could not be.

He went presently abroad [*sic* aboard], resolving there to appoint them governors, and to take order for the mutineers ·and their confederates·, but he could find none he thought fit for it would accept it.

In the meantime seeing him gone they persuaded Master Percy to stay—who was then to go for England—and be their president. Within less than an hour was this mutation begun and concluded. For when the company understood Smith would leave them and saw the rest in arms called presidents and councilors, divers began to fawn on those new commanders that now bent all their wits to get him resign them his commission; who after much ado and many bitter repulses that their confusion, which he told them was at their elbows, should not be attributed to him for leaving the colony without a commission (·having taken order to be free from danger of their malice·), he was not unwilling they should steal it ·from him·, but never would he *give* it to such as they. And thus—

Strange violent forces drew us on unwilling,
Reason persuading 'gainst our loves rebelling.
We saw and knew the better, ah curse accurst!
That, notwithstanding, we embrace the worst.

But had that unhappy blast not hap'ned, he would quickly have qualified the heat of those humors and factions—had the ships but once left them and us to our fortunes—and have made that provision from among the savages as we neither feared Spaniard, savage, nor famine; nor would have left Virginia nor our lawful authority but at as dear a price as we had bought it and paid for it.

What shall I say but thus we left him that in all his proceedings made justice his first guide and experience his second, even hating baseness, sloth, pride, and indignity more than any dangers, that never allowed more for himself than his soldiers with him, that upon no danger would send them where he would not lead them himself, that would never see us want what he either had or could by any means get us; that would rather want than borrow, or starve than not pay, that loved action more than words, and hated falsehood and covetousness[1] worse than death, whose adventures were our lives, and whose loss our deaths. Leaving us thus with three ships, seven boats, commodities ready to trade, the harvest newly gathered, ten weeks' provision in the store, four hundred ninety and odd persons, twenty-four pieces of ordnance, three hundred muskets, snaphances, and firelocks, shot, powder, and match sufficient, curats [cuirasses], pikes, swords, and morio[n]s[2] more than men, the savages, their language, and habitations well known to an hundred well-trained

[1] "Cozenage" in *The Proceedings.*
[2] Helmets.

and expert soldiers, nets for fishing, tools of all sorts to work, apparel to supply our wants, six mares and a horse, five or six hundred swine, as many hens and chickens, some goats, some sheep, what was brought or bred [that] there remained.

But they regarding nothing but from hand to mouth did consume that we had, took care for nothing but to perfect some colorable complaints against Captain Smith, for effecting whereof three weeks longer they stayed the ·six· ships till they could produce them. That time and charge might much better have been spent, but it suited well with the rest of their discretions.

Besides James town that was strongly palisadoed, containing some fifty or sixty houses, he left five or six other several forts and plantations. Though they were not so sumptuous as our successors expected, they were better than they provided any for us.

All this time we had but one carpenter in the country, and three others that could do little but desired to be learners; two blacksmiths, two sailors, and those we write laborers were for most part footmen and such as they that were adventurers brought to attend them or such as they could persuade to go with them that never did know what a day's work was, except the Dutchmen and Poles and some dozen other. For all the rest were poor gentlemen, tradesmen, serving men, libertines, and suchlike, ten times more fit to spoil a commonwealth than either begin one or but help to maintain one. For when neither the fear of God nor the law, nor shame, nor displeasure of their friends could rule them here, there is small hope ever to bring one in twenty of them ever to be good there.

[For] ·now[1] all those Smith had either whipped, punished, or any way disgraced had free power and liberty to say or swear anything, and from a whole armful of their examinations this was concluded:

·The mutineers at the Falls complained he caused the savages assault them, for that he would not revenge their loss—they being but 120 and he 5 men and himself; and this they proved by the oath of one he had oft whipped for perjury and pilfering. The Dutchmen that he had appointed to be stab'd for their treacheries swore he sent to poison them with ratsbane; the prudent council, that he would not

[1] This and the next six paragraphs are only found in the text of *The Proceedings*.

submit himself to their stol'n authority. Coe and Dyer that should have murdered him were highly preferred for swearing they heard one say he heard Powhatan say that he heard a man say if the king would not send that corn he had, he should not long enjoy his copper crown nor those robes he had sent him. Yet those also swore he might have had corn for tools but would not. The truth was Smith had no such engines as the king demanded, nor Powhatan any corn, yet this argued he would starve them.

·Others complained he would not let them rest in the fort (to starve!), but forced them to the oyster banks to live or starve as he lived himself. For though he had of his own private provisions sent from England sufficient, yet he gave it all away to the weak and sick, causing the most untoward by doing as he did to gather their food from the unknown parts of the rivers and woods, that they lived, though hardly, that otherways would have starved ere they would have left their beds or at most the sight of James Town to have got their own victual.

·Some prophetical spirit calculated he had the savages in such subjection he would have made himself a king by marrying Pocahontas, Powhatan's daughter.

·It is true she was the very nonpareil of his kingdom, and at most not past 13 or 14 years of age. Very oft she came to our fort with what she could get for Captain Smith, that ever loved and used all the country well, but her especially he ever much respected. And she so well requited it that when her father intended to have surprised him, she by stealth in the dark night came through the wild woods and told him of it. But her marriage could no way have entitled him by any right to the kingdom, nor was it ever suspected he had ever such a thought, or more regarded her, or any of them, than in honest reason and discretion he might. If he would he might have married her, or have done what him listed, for there was none that could have hind'red his determination.

·Some that knew not anything to say, the council instructed and advised what to swear. So diligent they were in this business that what any could remember he had ever done or said in mirth or passion, by some circumstantial oath it was applied to their fittest use, yet not past 8 or 9 could say much, and that nothing but circumstances[1] which all men did know was most false and untrue. Many got their passes by promising in England to say much against him.

·I have presumed to say this much in his behalf for that I never heard such foul slanders so certainly believed and urged for truths by many a hundred that do still not spare to spread them, say them, and swear them that I think do scarce know him though they meet him, nor have they either cause or reason but their wills or zeal to rumor or opinion. For the honorable and better sort of our Virginian adventurers, I think they understand it as I have writ it. For instead of accusing him, I have never heard any give him a better report than many of those witnesses themselves that were sent only home to testify against him·.

Notwithstanding, I confess divers amongst them had better minds and grew much more industrious than was expected. Yet ten good workmen would have done more substantial work in a day than ten of them in a week. Therefore men may rather wonder how we could do so much than use us so badly because we did no more but leave those examples to make others beware and the fruits of all we know not for whom.

But to see the justice of God upon these Dutchmen! Valdo, before spoke of, made a shift to get for England, where persuading the merchants what rich mines he had found and great service he would do them was very well rewarded and returned with the Lord La Warre. But being found a mere impostor he died most miserably.

Adam and Francis his two consorts were fled again to Powhatan to whom they promised at the arrival of my lord what wonders they would do, would he suffer them but to go to him. But the king seeing they would be gone replied, "You that would have betrayed Captain Smith to me will certainly betray me to this great lord for your peace," so caused his men to beat out their brains.

To conclude, the greatest honor that ever belonged to the greatest monarchs was the enlarging their dominions and erecting commonweals. Yet howsoever any of them have attributed to themselves "the

---

[1] "Circumstantial evidence." (Barbour)

conquerors of the world," there is more of the world never heard of them than ever any of them all had in subjection. For the Medes, Persians, and Assyrians never conquered all Asia, nor the Grecians but part of Europe and Asia. The Romans indeed had a great part of both, as well as Africa, but as for all the northern parts of Europe and Asia, the interior southern and western parts of Africa, all America and terra incognita, they were all ignorant, nor is our knowledge yet but superficial. That their beginnings, ending, and limitations were proportioned by the Almighty is most evident, but to consider of what small means many of them have begun is wonderful. For some write that even Rome herself during the reign of Romulus exceeded not the number of a thousand houses. And Carthage grew so great a potentate that at first was but encirculed in the thongs of a bull's skin, as to fight with Rome for the empire of the world. Yea, Venice at this [present] time the admiration of the earth was at first but a marish inhabited by poor fishermen. And likewise Nineveh, Thebes, Babylon, Delos, Troy, Athens, Mycenae, and Sparta grew from small beginnings to be most famous states, though now they retain little more than a naked name.

Now this our young commonwealth in Virginia as you have read once consisted but of 38 persons and in two years increased but to 200, yet by this small means so highly was approved the plantation in Virginia as how many lords with worthy knights and brave gentlemen pretended to see it, and some did, and now after the expense of fifteen years more, and such massy sums of men and money grow they disanimated? If we truly consider our proceedings with the Spaniards and the rest, we have no reason to despair, for with so small charge they never had either greater discoveries with such certain trials of more several commodities than in this short time hath been returned from Virginia, and by much less means. New England was brought out of obscurity and afforded fraught for near 200 sail of ships where there is now erected a brave plantation. For the happiness of Summer Isles, they are no less than either, and yet those have had a far less and a more difficult beginning than either Rome, Carthage, or Venice.

WRITTEN BY RICHARD POTS, CLERK OF THE COUNCIL,
·W[ILLIAM]P[HETTIPLACE]·, WILLIAM TANKARD, AND G. P.

THE[1] DAY BEFORE Captain Smith returned for England with the ships, Captain Davis arrived in a small pinnace with some sixteen proper men more. To these were added a company from James town under the command of Captain John Sickelmore, alias Ratliffe, to inhabit Point Comfort. Captain Martin and Captain West, having lost their boats and near half their men among the savages, were returned to James town. For the savages no sooner understood Smith was gone but they all revolted and did spoil and murther all they encountered.

Now we were all constrained to live only on that Smith had only for his own company, for the rest had consumed their proportions.

And now they had *twenty* presidents with all their appurtenances, ·for· Master Piercie, our new president, was so sick he could neither go nor stand.

But ere all was consumed, Captain West and Captain Sickelmore, each with a small ship [·pinnace·] and thirty or forty men well appointed, sought abroad to trade. Sickelmore, upon the confidence of Powhatan, with about thirty others as careless as himself were all slain, only Jeffrey Shortridge escaped; and Pokahontas, the king's daughter, saved a boy called Henry Spilman, that lived many years after by her means amongst the Patawomekes. Powhatan still as he found means cut off their boats [and] denied them trade, so that Captain West set sail for England.

Now we all found the loss of Captain Smith. Yea, his greatest maligners could now curse his loss. As for corn, provision, and contribution from the savages we had nothing but mortal wounds with clubs and arrows. As for our hogs, hens, goats, sheep, horse, or what lived, our commanders, officers, and savages daily consumed them. Some small proportions sometimes we tasted till all was devoured. Then swords, arms, pieces, or anything we traded with the savages, whose cruel fingers were so oft imbrued in our bloods that what by their cruelty, our governor's indiscretion, and the loss of our ships, of five hundred, within six months after Captain Smith's departure there remained not past sixty men, women, and children (most

[1] From here to 344 the text of the *General History* is from the 4th Book. I continue to set out the text of *The Proceedings* with ·points·.

miserable and poor creatures!); and those were preserved for the most part by roots, herbs, acorns, walnuts, berries, now and then a little fish. They that had starch, in these extremities made no small use of it.[1] Yea, even the very skins of our horses—nay, so great was our famine that a savage we slew and buried, the poorer sort took him up again and ate him, and so did divers one another boiled and stewed with roots and herbs. And one amongst the rest did kill his wife, powdered [salted] her, and had eaten part of her before it was known—for which he was executed, as he well deserved (now whether she was better "roasted," "boiled," or "carbonado'd" I know not, but of such a dish as *powdered wife* I never heard of!).

This was that time which still to this day we called "the starving time." It were too vile to say (and scarce to be believed) what we endured, but the occasion was ·only· our own for want of providence, industry, and government, and not the barrenness and defect of the country, as is generally supposed. For till then in three years (for the numbers [that] were landed us) we had never from England ·landed· provision sufficient for six months. Though it seemed by the bills of loading sufficient was sent us, such a glutton is the sea (and such good fellows the mariners!) we as little tasted of the great proportion sent us as they of our want and miseries, yet, notwithstanding they ever overswayed and ruled the business.[2] Though we endured all that is said, and ·3 years· chiefly lived on what this good country naturally afforded, yet ·now· had we been even in paradise itself, with these governors it would not have been much better with us. Yet there was ·some· amongst us who, had they had the government as Captain Smith appointed but that they could not maintain it, would surely have kept us from those extremities of miseries. This in ten days more would have supplanted us all with death.

But God that would not this country should be unplanted sent Sir Thomas Gates and Sir George Sommers with one hundred and fifty people most happily preserved by the Bermudas to preserve us. Strange it is to say how miraculously they were preserved in a leaking ship ·in those extreme storms and tempests in such overgrown

[1] Starch, that is, from ruffs and items of clothing.

[2] "... that, notwithstanding, ever sway'd and overruled the business" in *The Proceedings.*

seas 3 days and 3 nights by bapling [bailing] out water; and having given themselves to death, how happily when least expected that worthy captain, Sir George Somers, having lyen all that time conning the ship before those sawlowing [swallowing] waves, discovered those broken isles where how plentifully they lived with fish and flesh. What a paradise this is to inhabit, what industry they used to build their 2 ships, how happily they did transport them to James Town in Virginia, I refer you to their own printed relations·, as at large you may read in the ensuing history of those islands.[1]

The government resigned to Sir Thomas Gates, 1610.

WHEN THESE TWO noble knights did see our miseries, being but strangers in that country, and could understand no more of the cause but by ·their· conjecture of our clamors and complaints of accusing and excusing one another, they embarked us with themselves with the best means they could, and abandoning James town set sail for England; whereby you may see the event of the government of the former commanders left to themselves, although they had lived there many years, as formerly hath been spoken, who hind'red now their proceedings, Captain Smith being gone.

At noon they fell to the Isle of Hogs and the next morning to Mulberry Point, at what time they descried the longboat of the Lord la Ware, for God would not have it so abandoned. For this honorable lord, then governor of the country, met them with three ships exceedingly well furnished with all necessaries fitting, who again returned them to the abandoned James town.

OUT OF THE OBSERVATIONS OF WILLIAM SIMMONS, DOCTOR OF DIVINITY.

The government devolved to the Lord la Ware.

HIS LORDSHIP arrived the ninth of June, 1610, accompanied with Sir Ferdinando Waynman, Captain Houlcroft, Captain Lawson, ·and divers other gentlemen of sort. Sir George Somers and Captain

---

[1] In the 5th Book of the *General History*.

Argall he presently dispatcheth to require the Bermondas to furnish them with provision; Sir Thomas Gates for England to help forward their supplies; himself neglected not the best was in his power for the furtherance of the business and regaining what was lost.

·But even in the beginning of his proceedings His Lordship had such an encounter with a scurvy sickness that made him unable to wield the state of his body, much less the affairs of the colony, so that after 8 months' sickness he was forced to save his life by his return for England.

·In this time, Argall, not finding the Bermondas, having lost Sir George Somers at sea, fell on the coast of Sagadahock, where refreshing himself found a convenient fishing for cod, with a taste whereof he returned to James town; from whence the Lord De-la-ware sent him to trade in the River of Patawomecke, where finding an English boy[1] those people had preserved from the fury of Powhatan, by his acquaintance had such good usage of those kind savages that they fraughted his ship with corn, wherewith he returned to James Town, and so for England with the lord governor. Yet before his return, the adventurers had sent Sir Thomas Dale with 3 ships, men, and cattle, and all other provisions necessary for a year, all which arrived the 10 of May, 1611.

·Again, to second him with all possible expedition there was prepared for Sir Thomas Gates 6 tall ships with 300 men and 100 kine with other cattle, with munition and all manner of provision could be thought needful, and they arrived about the 1 of August next after safely at James town.

·Sir George Somers all this time was supposed lost, but thus it hap'ned: Missing the Bermondas he fell also as did Argall with Sagadahock, where being refreshed would not content himself with that repulse, but returned again in the search, and there safely arrived, but overtoiling himself on a surfeit died. And in this cedar ship built by his own directions, and partly with his own hands, that had not in her any iron but only one bolt in her keel, yet well endured thus tossed to and again in this mighty ocean till with his dead bo[dy] she arrived in England at line [fine?]; and at Whitchurch in Dorsetshire

[1] Henry Spelman.

his body by his friends was honorably buried with many volleys of shot and the rights of a soldier. And upon his tomb was bestowed this epitaph:

Hei mihi Virginia, quod tam cito praeterit aeftas,
Autumnus sequitur, saeviet inde & hyems.
At ver perpetuum nascetur, & Anglia laeta,
Decerpit flores, Floryda terra tuos.

·Alas, Virginia, summer so soon past,
Autumn succeeds and stormy winter's blast.
Yet England's joyful spring with April showers,
O Florida, shall bring thy sweetest flowers.

·Since, there was a ship fraughted with provision and 40 men, and another since then with the like number and provision to stay in the country 12 months with Captain Argall.

·The lord governor himself doth confidently determine to go with the next or, as presently as he may in his own person, with sundry other knights and gentlemen, with ships and men so far as their means will extend to furnish.

·As for all their particular actions since the return of Captain Smith, for that they have been printed from time to time and published to the world, I cease farther to trouble you with any repetition of things so well known more than are necessary, [only] to conclude the history, leaving this assurance to all posterity: How unprosperously things may succeed[1] by what changes or chances soever, the action is honorable and worthy to be approved; the defect whereof hath only been in the managing the business, which I hope now experience hath taught them to amend, or those examples may make others to beware. For the land is as good as this book doth report it.·

·FINIS·

[1] Come out.

·CAPTAIN SMITH, I return you the fruit of my labors, as Master Croshaw requested me, which I bestowed in reading the discourses and hearing the relations of such which have walked and observed the land of Virginia with you. The pains I took was great, yet did the nature of the argument and hopes I conceived of the expedition give me exceeding content. I cannot find there is anything but what they all affirm or cannot contradict: The land is good: As there is no cities, so no sons of Anak[1]; all is open for labor of a good and wise inhabitant. And my prayer shall ever be that so fair a land may be inhabited by those that profess and love the Gospel.·

·Your friend,
W[ILLIAM] S[YMONDS]·

NOW[2] SEEING there is thus much paper here to spare, that you should not be altogether cloyed with prose, such verses as my worthy friends bestowed upon New England[3] I here present you, because with honesty I can neither reject nor omit their courtesies.

IN THE DESERVED HONOR OF THE AUTHOR,
CAPTAIN JOHN SMITH, AND HIS WORK—

Damn'd envy is a sp'rit that ever haunts
Beasts (misnam'd men), cowards, or ignorants!
But only such she follows whose dear WORTH
(Maugre her malice) sets their glory forth.
If this fair overture then take not, it
Is envy's spite (dear friend) in men of wit;
Or fear, lest morsels which our mouths possess
Might fall from thence; or else 'tis sottishness.
If either (I hope neither), thee they raise.
Thy letters[4] are as letters in thy praise,
Who by their vice improve, when they reprove,

[1] I.e. giants (Numbers 13:27–28, 33)
[2] From here on the text belongs to the 3rd Book.
[3] The verses are reprinted from his *Description of New England.*
[4] I.e., "hinderers." (margin note)

Thy virtue, so in hate procure thee love.
Then on firm worth this monument I frame,
Scorning for any Smith to forge such fame.

John Davies, Heref[ordshire]

To His Worthy Captain, the Author—

That which we call the subject of all story
Is truth, which in this work of thine gives glory
To all that thou hast done. Then scorn the spite
Of envy, which doth no man's merits right.
My sword may help the rest; my pen no more
Can do but this. I've said enough before.

Your sometime soldier, J. Codrinton, now Templar.

To My Worth Friend and Cousin, Captain John Smith—

It overjoys my heart whenas thy words
Of these designs with deeds I do compare!
Here is a book such worthy truth affords
None should the due desert thereof impare,
Sith thou, the man, deserving of these ages,
Much pain hast ta'en for this our kingdom's good
In climes unknown, 'mongst Turks and savages,
T' enlarge our bounds, though with thy loss of blood.
Hence damn'd detraction!—Stand not in our way!
Envy itself will not the Truth gainsay.

N. Smith.

In the Deserved Honor of My Honest and Worthy Captain, John Smith, and His Work—

Captain and friend!—when I peruse thy book
With judgment's eyes into my heart I look,
And there I find what sometimes Albion knew:
A soldier to his country's honor true.
Some fight for wealth, and some for empty praise,
But thou alone thy country's fame to raise.
With due discretion and undaunted heart,
I oft so well have seen thee act thy part
In deepest plunge of hard extremity
As forc'd the troops of proudest foes to fly.
Though men of greater rank and less desert
Would pish away thy praise, it cannot start
From the true owner, for all good men's tongues
Shall keep the same. To them that part belongs.
If then wit, courage, and success should get
Thee fame, the Muse for that is in thy debt,
A part whereof (least able though I be)
Thus here I do disburse to honor thee.

Raleigh Crashaw.

Michael Phettiplace, William Phettiplace, and Richard Wiffing, Gentlemen and Soldiers under Captain Smith's Command: In His Deserved Honor for His Work and Worth—

Why may not we in this work have our mite
That had our share in each black day and night
When thou Virginia foil'dst, yet keptst unstain'd,
And heldst the King of Paspeheh enchain'd?
Thou all alone this savage stern didst take.

Pamaunkee's king we saw thee captive make
Among seven hundred of his stoutest men,
To murther thee and us resolved, when
Fast by the hair thou ledst this savage grim,
Thy pistol at his breast to govern him,
Which did infuse such awe in all the rest,
Sith their dread sovereign thou hadst so distress'd,
That thou and we (poor sixteen!) safe retir'd
Unto our helpless ships. Thou, thus admir'd,
Didst make proud Powhatan his subjects send
To James his Town, thy censure to attend,
And all Virginia's lords and petty kings,
Aw'd by thy virtue, crouch and presents brings
To gain thy grace—so dreaded thou hast been,
And yet a heart more mild is seldom seen,
So making valor virtue really
Who hast nought in thee counterfeit or sly,
If in the sleight be not the truest art
That makes men famoused for fair desert.
Who saith of thee this savors of vainglory
Mistakes both thee and us and this true story.
If it be ill in thee so well to do,
Then [it] is ill in us to praise thee too.
But if the first be well done, it is well
To say it doth (if so it doth) excel.
Praise is the guerdon of each dear desert,
Making the praised act the praised part
With more alacrity: Honor's spur is praise,
Without which it regardless soon decays.
And for this pains of thine we praise thee rather,
That future times may know who was the father
Of that rare work (New England) which may bring
Praise to thy God and profit to thy king.

Illustrations from *The General History*

Idoll
A Preist
C.Smith taketh the King of Pamavnkee prisoner 1608
A description of part of the adventures of Cap: Smith in Virginia
The Country wee now call Virginia beginneth at Cape Henry distant from Roanoack 60 miles, where was S.r Walter Raleigh's plantation: and because the people differ very little from them of Powhatan in any thing, I have inserted those figures in this place because of the conveniency.
steps
Howards Mountaynes
Bedfords valley
Ohanoack
Beauchamps playne
L. Salvage Rocke
Chawanok flu:
Metocaum
Catoking
Segars grove
Chisapeack
Chepanu
Heriotts Ile
Pasquenock
Mildmaids reade
C. Henry
P. Bacon
Arundells Ile
Hertfords Ile
A Scale of Leauges
1 2 3 4 5 6 7 8 9 10
history of Virginia, New England, and Somer Iles, by Robert Vaughan

18. Gabriel Archer

Letter from Jamestown, 31 August 1609

< **Purchas 1625d:1733,** Arber 1884a:xciv, Brown 1890:328, Barbour 1969:279

A brief account of the famous *hurricano*, and the arrival in Jamestown of the remnant of the fleet, published by Rev. Purchas.

Ironically the second charter, intended to strengthen government, initially provoked the worst breakdown ever during the interval between the *Blessing's* arrival in mid August with Archer and company and her departure in early October with Smith.

Meanwhile, he thinks Francis West will make a good interim president, but West soon deserted the colony. Or was he a hostage aboard a commandeered ship?

FROM WOOLWICH, the fifteenth of May, 1609, seventh sail weighed anchor and came to Plymouth the twentieth day, where Sir George Somers with two small vessels consorted with us. Here we took into the *Blessing* (being the ship wherein I went) six mares and two horses; and the fleet laid in some necessaries belonging to the action, in which business we spent time till the second of June. And then we set sail to sea, but cross'd [thwarted] by southwest winds we put into Falmouth, and there staying till the eight of June, we then gat out.

Our course was commanded to leave the Canaries one hundred leagues to the eastward at least, and to steer away directly for Virginia without touching at the West Indies, except the fleet should chance to be separated; then they were to repair to the Bermuda,[1] there to stay seven days in expectation of the admiral; and if they found him not, then to take their course to Virginia.

Now thus it happened, about six days after we lost the sight of England, one of Sir George Somers' pinnaces left our company and, as I take it, bare up for England. The rest of the ships, viz., the *Sea Adventure,* admiral, wherein was Sir Thomas Gates, Sir George Somer, and Captain Newport; the *Diamond,* vice-admiral, wherein

---

[1] Barbuda?

was Captain Ratcliffe and Captain King; the *Falcon,* rear-admiral, in which was Captain Martin and Master Nellson; the *Blessing,* wherein I and Captain Adams went; the *Unity,* wherein Captain Wood and Master Pett were; the *Lion,* wherein Captain Webb remained; and the *Swallow* of Sir George Somers', in which Captain Moone and Master Somer went; in the catch [ketch] went one Matthew Fitch master; and in the boat of Sir George Somers', called the *Virginia,* which was built in the North Colony,[1] went one Captain Davies and one Master Davies. These were the captatines [sic] and masters of our fleet.

We ran a southerly course from the Tropic of Cancer where, having the sun within six or seven degrees right over our head in July, we bore away west, so that by the fervent heat and looms[2] breezes many of our men fell sick of the calenture, and out of two ships was thrown overboard thirty-two persons. The vice-admiral was said to have the plague in her; but in the *Blessing* we had not any sick, albeit we had twenty women and children.

Upon Saint James' Day, being about one hundred and fifty leagues distant from the West Indies, in crossing the Gulf of Bahoma, there hap'ned a most terrible and vehement storm, which was a tail of the West Indian hurricano. This tempest separated all our fleet one from another, and it was so violent that men could scarce stand upon the decks, neither could any man hear another speak. Being thus divided, every man steered his own course and, as it fell out, about five or six days after the storm ceased—which endure[d] forty-four hours in extremity—the *Lion* first and, after, the *Falcon* and the *Unity* got sight of our ship, and so we lay away directly for Virginia, finding neither current nor wind opposite (as some have reported [they were], to the great charge of our council and adventurers).

The *Unity* was sore distressed when she came up with us, for of seventy landmen she had not ten sound, and all her seamen were down but only the master and his boy, with one poor sailor. But we relieved them, and we four consorting fell into the Kings River[3]

---

[1] At Sagadahoc on the coast of Maine.

[2] Light, gentle.

[3] The James River.

haply the eleventh of August. In the *Unity* were born two children at sea, but both died, being both boys.

When we came to James Town, we found a ship which had been there in the river a month before we came. This was sent out of England by our council's leave and authority to fish for sturgeon, and to go the ready way without tracing through the Torrid Zone, and she performed it. Her commander was Captain Argoll, a good mariner and a very civil gentleman, and her master, one Robert Tindall.

The people of our colony were found all in health for the most part, howbeit when Captain Argoll came in they were in such distress, for many were dispersed in the savages' towns, living upon their alms for an ounce of copper a day. And fourscore lived twenty miles from the fort and fed upon nothing but oysters eight weeks' space, having no other allowance at all. Neither were the people of the country able to relieve them if they would.[1] Whereupon Captain Newport and others have been much to blame to inform the council of such plenty of victual in this country, by which means they have been slack in this supply to give convenient content. Upon this, you that be adventurers must pardon us if you find not return of commodity so ample as you may expect, because the law of nature bids us seek sustenance first and then to labor to content you afterwards. But upon this point I shall be more large in my next letter.

After our four ships had been in harbor a few days, came in the vice-admiral, having cut her mainmast overboard, and had many of her men very sick and weak. But she could tell no news of our governor. And some three or four days after her, came in the *Swallow* with her mainmast overboard also, and had a shrewd leak; neither did she see our admiral.[2]

Now did we all lament much the absence of our governor, for contentions began to grow, and factions and partakings, etc., insomuch as the president,[3] to strengthen his authority, accorded with

---

[1] "Idleness and other vices to blame also." (margin note)

[2] "Some things, partly false rumors, partly factions, suggestions, are here left out." (margin note)

[3] Captain John Smith, whose term was due to expire on September 10th. He had already resigned in August and turned over his office to Captain Martin, who had turned it back over to him. Purchas' text has a long marginal note beginning about

the mariners and gave not any due respect to many worthy gentlemen that came in our ships. Whereupon they generally, having also my consent, chose Master West, my Lord de la War's brother, to be their governor, or president *de bene esse,*[1] in the absence of Sir Thomas Gates; or if he miscarried by sea, then to continue till we heard news from our council in England. This choice of him they made not to disturb the old president during his time but as his authority expired, then to take upon him the sole government with such assistance of the captains, as discreetest persons as the colony afforded.

Perhaps you shall have it blazoned a mutiny by such as retain old malice, but Master West, Master Percie, and all the respected gentlemen of worth in Virginia can and will testify otherwise upon their oaths. For the king's patent we ratified, but refused to be governed by the president that now is after his time was expired, and only subjected ourselves to Master West, whom we labor to have next president.[2]

I cannot certify you of much more as yet until we grow to some certain stay in this our state; but by the other ships you shall know more. So with my hearty commendations I cease.

From James Town, this last of August, 1609. [signature cut off]

[entitled:] A letter of Master Gabriel Archar touching the voyage of the fleet of ships which arrived at Virginia without Sir Thomas Gates and Sir George Summers, 1609.

---

here: *"Hinc illæ lachrymæ.* ['Thence flows the cause of the main grievance,' a line from Ben Jonson cited by Barbour that certainly renders the Latin.] Hence from the malcontents—which had been in Virginia before enemies to the president, raising now ill reports at their coming of him—arose these stirs and the following miseries [the 'starving time' of the winter of 1609–10] in which this author with almost the whole colony perished."

1 Provisionally.

2 "Despite Archer's protests, refusal to obey the elected president did constitute mutiny, regardless of the opinion of Francis West and George Percy." (Barbour)

19. John Ratcliffe, *alias* Sicklemore

Letter to Salisbury, 4 October 1609

< **Public Records Office: Colonial Office 1/1–66,** American Antiquarian 1870, Volume 10:13; Arber 1884a:xcviii; Brown 1890:334; Barbour 1969:283

History even rebukes him by denying his preferred alias. He rivals Wingfield in unpopularity. Perhaps it is only that his faction did not write its own true relations. His letter tells what is being done at Jamestown. Clearly things were drifting. The whole leadership, with commissions, had gone missing, as castaways on Bermuda. We have no paper-book of the misdemeanors Smith would have answered to, only the stout defense by colleagues in the last chapter of §17, and Strachey's observation that Smith was out of favor (unfairly) in England.

RIGHT HONORABLE—According to your gracious favor being bound, I am bold to write the truth of some late accidents befallen His Majesty's Virginia colony.

Sir Thomas Gates and Sir George Summers, Captain Newport, and 180 persons or thereabout are not yet arrived, and we much fear they are lost, and also a small pinish [pinnace]. The other ships came all in, but not together. We were thus separated by a storm.

Two ships had great loss of men by the calenture, and most of them all much weather-beaten.

At our arrival we found an English ship riding at James town and Captain Argoll, her commander.

We heard that all the council were dead but Captain Smith, the president, who reigned sole governor without assistants, and would at first admit of no council but himself. This man is sent home to answer some misdemeanors whereof I persuade me he can scarcely clear himself from great imputation of blame.

Master George Pearcye, my Lord of Northumberland's brother, is elected our president; and Master West, my Lord la war's brother, of the council with me; and Captain Martine, and some few of the best and worthiest that inhabit at James town, are assistants in their advice unto us.

Thus have we planted 100 men at the Falls, and some others upon a champion.

The president is at James town, and I am raising a fortification upon Point Comfort.

Also, we have been bold to make stay of a small ship for discovery and to procure us victuals, whereof we have exceeding much need, for the country people set no more than sufficeth each family a year. And the wood is yet so thick as the labor to prepare so much ground as would be to any purpose is more than we can afford, our number being so necessarily dispersed—so that, if I might be held worthy to advise the directors of this business, I hold it fit that there should be a sufficient supply of victuals for one year, and then to be sparing. It would less hinder the colony.

Thus fearing to be too offensive in a tedious boldness, I cease, wishing all happiness to your honor—yea, were it in the expense of my life and blood!

From James town this 4th of October, 1609.

Your Honor's in all obedience and most humble duty,
JOHN RATCLYEFFE,
so commonly called.

[endorsed:] To the Right Honorable the Earl of Salisbury, Lord High Treasurer of England, My Singular Good Lord and Master.

20. The Council of Virginia

A True and Sincere Declaration
of the purposes and ends of the plantation begun in Virginia, of the degrees which it hath received, and means by which it hath been advanced, and the resolution and conclusion of His Majesty's council of that colony for the constant and patient prosecution thereof, until by the mercies of GOD it shall retribute a fruitful harvest to the Kingdom of Heaven and this commonwealth. Set forth by the authority of the governors and councilors established for that plantation.

"A word spoken in due season is like apples of gold with pictures of silver."
(Proverbs 25:11)

"Fear is nothing else but a betraying of the succors which reason offereth."
(Wisdom 17:11)

(At London: Printed for J. Stepneth, and are to be sold at the sign of the Crane in Paul's churchyard. 1610)

< Brown 1890:339

The bulk of this volume is made up of signed material that was unpublished until modern times and long after events. Another substantial portion is matter written by people in Virginia and published by the authority and direction of the Council of Virginia—Lord Delaware's *Short Relation §34,* Hamor's *True Discourse §51,* Whitaker's *Good News §43,* as well as material published without the council's say-so, such as the writings of Smith and Purchas.

Here is another category, namely, what appears to be an unsigned eyewitness account underlying a Virginia Company promotional tract. A year after publication, Lord Delaware and the council at Jamestown call it "our own approved discourse." (§25–461). I give the full text below.

It was brought out in haste when the news the ships were missing arrived in England. But hurried or not, compare a passage in it to Robert Johnson's *Nova Britannia* which reads: "[Virginia] is inhabited with wild and savage people that live and lie up and down in troops like herds of deer in a forest. They have no law but nature ... no arts nor science." No one who met Indians and knew them wrote of them that way. Instead below we read: "For the naturals withdrew from all commerce and traffic with them, cunningly making a war upon them which they felt not who durst no otherway appear an enemy." (p. 363) This could only have been uttered by one who was *there,* a true and sincere declaration by a colonist.

The colonial enterprise required national courage and sacrifice on the order of war. And as in war, rumors of bad news infected the air until shot down in the dogfight with propaganda.[1] Survival depended on dedication, dedication depended on morale, morale depended on propaganda, and propaganda was half-truth on the way to becoming whole if only—if only wish and hope were sparks. The Virginia Company made many a promotional promise it intended to keep once the sparks lit. Few did.

The tract is a reasoned defense full of sparks well worth our examination, once we work past the list of specious commodities. It is aimed at an intelligent readership and it is pitched high. Ironically, when it hit the streets in the first half of 1610, Jamestown was in its worst throes. But reading their mail from Captain Smith (§17–290), the Council is now screening applicants for useful trades, and appends a list of desirables that does not include a single gentleman to replace the gentlemen now starving on the marsh island.

IT IS RESERVED and only proper to divine wisdom to foresee and ordain both the ends and ways of every action. In human prudence it is all can be required to propose religious and noble and feasible ends; and it can have no absolute assurance and infallibleness in the ways and means, which are contingent and various, perhaps equally reasonable, subject to unpresent circumstances, and doubtful events, which ever dignify or betray the councils from whence they were derived. And the higher the quality and nature and more removed from ordinary action—such as this is of which we discourse—the more perplexed and misty are the paths thereunto.

Upon which grounds we purpose to deliver roundly and clearly

1 "To hawk after the winged report of a vagabond rumor." *A True Declaration §27.*

our ends and ways to the hopeful plantations begun in Virginia, and to examine the truth and safety of both [in order] to redeem ourselves and so noble an action from the imputations and aspersions with which ignorant rumor, virulent envy, or impious subtlety daily calumniateth our industries and the success of it. Wherein we doubt not only to satisfy every modest and well-affected heart of this kingdom but to excite and kindle the affections of the incredulous and lazy, and to cool and assuage the curiosity of the jealous and suspicious, and to temper and convince the malignity of the false and treacherous.

The principal and main ends—out of which are easily derived, to any mean understanding, infiniteless and yet great ones—were first to preach and baptize into Christian religion and, by propagation of the Gospel, to recover out of the arms of the devil a number of poor and miserable souls wrap'd up unto death in almost invincible ignorance, [in order] to endeavor the fulfilling and accomplishment of the number of the elect, which shall be gathered from out all corners of the earth, and to add our mite to the treasury of heaven, that as we pray for the coming of the Kingdom of Glory, so to express in our actions the same desire, if God have pleased to use so weak instruments to the ripening and consummation thereof.

Secondly, to provide and build up for the public honor and safety of our gracious king and his estates—by the favor of our superiors even in that care—some small rampire[1] of our own, in this opportune and general summer of peace, by transplanting the rankness and multitude of increase in our people, of which there is left no vent but age, and [there is the] evident danger that the number and infiniteness of them will outgrow the matter whereon to work for their life and sustentation, and[2] shall one infest and become a burthen to another. But by this provision they may be seated as a bulwark of defense in a place of advantage against a stranger enemy who shall in great proportion grow rich in treasure—which was exhausted to a low estate—and may well endure an increase of his people long wasted with a continual war and dispersed uses and

---

[1] Rampart.
[2] If.

losses of them; both which cannot chose but threaten us, if we consider and compare the ends, ambitions, and practices of our neighbor countries with our own.

Lastly, the appearance and assurance of private commodity to the particular undertakers by recovering and possessing to themselves a fruitful land, whence they may furnish and provide this kingdom with all such necessities and defects under which we labor and are now enforced to buy and receive at the courtesy of other princes, under the burthen of great customs and heavy impositions, and at so high rates in traffic by reason of the great waste of them from whence they are now derived, which threatens almost an impossibility long to recover them, or at least such loss in exchange as both the kingdom and merchant will be weary of the dearness and peril.

These being the true and essential ends of this plantation, and corresponding to our first rule of religious, noble, and feasible, two of which are not questioned, the third easy and demonstrable in the second limb, when we shall examine the causes of some disaster and distemper in the ways unto them. These being admitted of, for such as we pretend them to be, and standing yet firm and safe in themselves, we hope easily to justify the first part of our undertaking, and presume to aver that in this branch there ariseth to no peaceable man any scruple or doubt to suspect the issue or to withdraw his affection and assistance or to calumniate the project or our choice of it.

In discussion and examination of the second part, which is the ways by which we hope to arrive at these ends, and in which no human reason can so provide but that many circumstances and accidents shall have as great a stroke in the event as any council shall have, we must first briefly deliver the course of this plantation from the infancy thereof; and then let us equally consider whether from so small a root it hath not had a blessed and unexpected growth. Next, we will call before us all the objections—and confess ingenuously all the errors and discouragements which seem to lie so heavy as almost to press to death this brave and hopeful action—and relieve it, we doubt not, from that which with reasonable men can at most be but a pause and no entire desertion, and restore it to the primary estate, life, and reputation.

IN THE YEAR 1606, Captain Newport, with three ships, discovered the Bay of Chessiopeock in the height of thirty-seven degrees of northerly latitude, and landed a hundred persons of sundry qualities and arts in a river falling into it; and left them under the government of a president and council, according to the authority derived from and limited by His Majesty's letters patents.

His return gave us no hope of any extraordinary consequence, yet only upon report of the navigableness of the river, pleasure, fertility, and situation of the land, to our projected ends we freshly and cheerfully sent in the next year a like number, and yet also receiving nothing new, we had courage and constancy to relieve them the third time with one hundred more; at which return, experience of error in the equality of governors, and some outrages and follies committed by them, had a little shaken so tender a body. After consultation, and advice of all the inconveniences in these three supplies, and finding them to arise out of two roots—the form of government and length and danger of the passage by the southerly course of the Indies—to encounter the first, we did resolve and obtain to renew our letters patents and to procure to ourselves such ample and large privileges and powers by which we were at liberty to reform and correct those already discovered, and to prevent such as in the future might threaten us; and so to set and furnish out, under the conduct of one able and absolute governor, a large supply of five hundred men with some number of families—of wife, children, and servants—to take fast hold and root in that land; and this resolution was with much alacrity and confidence.

And to meet the second inconvenience, we did also prepare to set out one small ship for discovery of a shorter way, and to make trial of the fishing within our bay and river.

Hitherto, until the sending of this avisal for experience and fleet for settling the government, appears no distaste nor despair. For every supply in some respect was greater than other, and that in preparation greater than them all in every respect; and must in reason hold analogy and proportion with our expectations and hopes at the disemboguing[1] of it; so that whatsoever wound or palsy this noble

[1] Discharging (on arrival).

action hath gotten, and the sickness under which it seems to faint, must needs arise out of the success[1] of these two, which we will now examine apart with all equity and clearness, and weigh whether there be any such reason to desist from the prosecution thereof, in rectified judgment, or to fall so low in our resolutions and opinions of it as rumor and ignorance doth pretend we do, or have cause to do.

For the discovery, Captain Argoll received our commission under our seal, with instruction—to avoid all danger of quarrel with the subjects of the King of Spain—not to touch upon any of his dominions actually possessed, or rightly entituled unto, and to shape his course free from the road of pirates, that hang upon all straits and skirts of lands, and to attempt a direct and clear passage by leaving the Canaries to the east, and from thence to run in a straight western course or some point near thereunto; and so to make an experience of the winds and currents which have affrighted all undertakers by the north; by which discovery there would grow to us much security and ease and all occasion of offense removed, and we should husband and save a moiety of the charge in victual and freight which was expended and lost in the southern passage.

To these ends he set sail from Portsmouth the fift day of May; and shaping his course south-southwest to the height of thirty degrees, leaving the Canaries a hundred leagues to the east, he found the winds large, and so took his course direct west, and did never turn nearer the south. And being in the longitude of the Barmudos, he found the wind a little scant upon him, yet [sufficient], so that on the thirteenth of July he recovered our harbor, and in trial found no current nor anything else which should deter us from this way.

He made his journey in nine weeks, and of that was becalmed fourteen days, whereupon he hath divers times since his return publicly avowed and undertaken to make this passage within seven weeks, and that the winds in all this course are as variable as at other places, and no apparent inconvenience in the way; so that the main end of this advice hath succeeded almost beyond our hopes.

The second, for fishing, proved so plentiful, especially of sturgeon,

---

[1] Consequence.

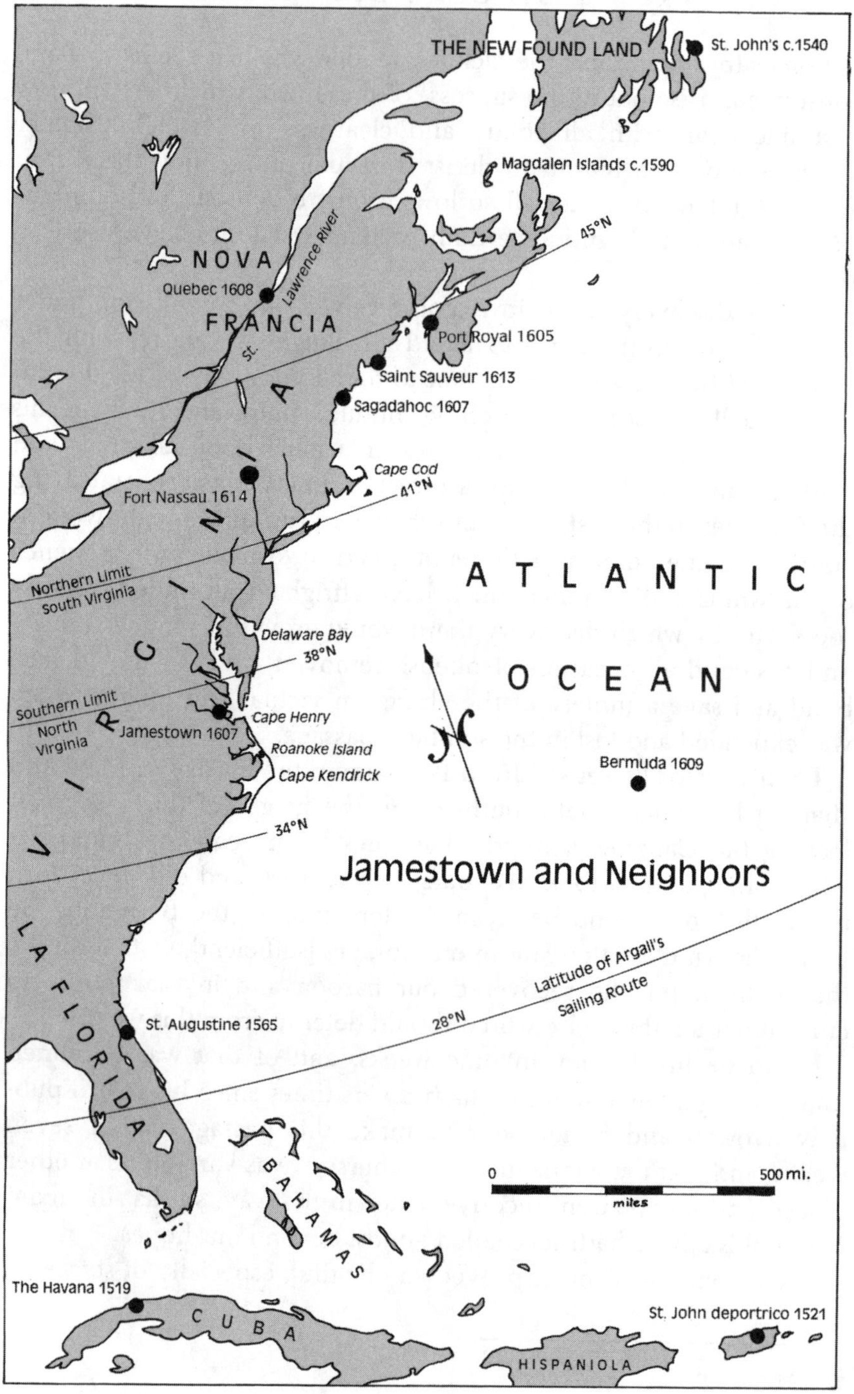
THE NEW FOUND LAND
St. John's c.1540
Magdalen Islands c.1590
45°N
NOVA
FRANCIA
Quebec 1608
St. Lawrence River
Port Royal 1605
Saint Sauveur 1613
Sagadahoc 1607
Cape Cod
Fort Nassau 1614
41°N
ATLANTIC
OCEAN
Northern Limit
South Virginia
Delaware Bay
38°N
Southern Limit
North
Virginia
Cape Henry
Jamestown 1607
Roanoke Island
Cape Kendrick
VIRGINIA
Bermuda 1609
34°N
Latitude of Argall's
Sailing Route
28°N
St. Augustine 1565
LA FLORIDA
BAHAMAS
0
500 mi.
miles
The Havana 1519
CUBA
St. John deportrico 1521
HISPANIOLA

Jamestown and Neighbors

of which sort he could have loaded many ships if he had had some man of skill to pickle and prepare it for keeping,[1] whereof he brought sufficient testimony both of the flesh and caviary, that no discreet man will question the truth of it.

So it appears clearly that from hence there can be derived no cause to suspect or desist from our first ends, but so contrary that in this project both our purposes and ways were happy and successful even to our desires. But from this ship ariseth a rumor of the necessity and distress our people were found in for want of victual of which, though the noise have exceeded the truth, yet we do confess a great part of it, but can lay aside the cause and fault from the design, truly, and home upon the misgovernment of the commanders, by dissension and ambition among themselves, and upon the idleness and bestial sloth of the common sort, who were active in nothing but adhering to factions and parts, even to their own ruin, like men almost desperate of all supply, so conscious and guilty they were to themselves of their own demerit and laziness.

But so soon as Captain Argoll arrived among them—whose presence and example gave new assurance of our cares and new life to their endeavors—by fishing only in few days, they were all recovered, grown hearty, able, and ready to undertake every action. So that if it be considered that without industry no land is sufficient to the inhabitants, and that the trade to which they trusted betrayed them to lose the opportunity of seed time, and so to rust and wear out themselves—for the naturals withdrew from all commerce and traffic with them, cunningly making a war upon them, which they felt not who durst no otherway appear an enemy[2]—and they being at division among themselves, and without warrant from hence, could not resolve to enforce that which might have preserved them, and which in such a necessity is most lawful to do, everything returning from civil propriety to natural and primary community;

Lastly, if it be rememb'red that this extremity in which they were is now relieved—which is as happy in the presage of God's future

---

[1] "He that went for that purpose died in the way." (margin note)

[2] I.e., the Indians broke off trade, hoping to starve out the colonists without a shot, carefully and cunningly avoiding violence.

blessing as in His present providence and mercy—was but an effect of that we did foresee in the first government—and for which the form was changed and the new in project, and therefore cannot be objected as any just exception to the success of this, but as a consequent considered and digested in the former—

It is then, I say, evident that in all the progress of this discovery, or anything accidental to it, there cannot be rack'd nor pressed out any confession either of error in the ends or miscarriages in the ways unto them.

To the establishment of a government such as should meet with all the revealed inconveniences, we gave our commission to an able and worthy gentleman, Sir Thomas Gates, whom we did nominate and appoint sole and absolute governor of that colony, under divers limitations and instructions expressed in writing; and with him we sent Sir George Summers, admiral, and Captain Newport, vice-admiral of Virginia, and divers other persons of rank and quality, in seven ships and two pinnaces, with several commissions sealed, successively to take place one after another, considering the mortality and uncertainty of human life, and these to be divided into several ships.

Our fleet weighed anchor from Falmouth the eight of June. The wind being fair, they shaped a course for the height of the Canaries. Within few days' sail, the governor calling a council of all the captains, masters, and pilots, it was resolved they should run southerly unto the tropic, and from thence bear away west—which error will take up all the objections of sickness, the sun being then in it, [and] was the cause of all the infection and disease of our men. At this consultation was delivered an instruction under seal to every master, with a provision what course should be taken if the fleet were separated; which was that if the winds scanted or were contrary, or that any lost sight of the admiral, they should steer away for the West Indies and make the Baruada [Barbuda], an island to the north of Dominico, and there to have their rendezvous, and to stay seven days one for another.

In this height and resolution, short of the West Indies 150 leagues, on St. James Day a terrible tempest overtook them and lasted in extremity 48 hours, which scattered the whole fleet, and wherein some of them spent their masts, and others were much distressed.

Within three days, four of the fleet met in consort, and hearing no news of their admiral, and the winds returning large for Virginia, and they wearied and beaten, it was resolved among them to bear right away for our bay—and to decline their commission—which within few days they made, and arrived in the Kings River on the eleventh of August. In this passage, fourteen degrees to the southward of Virginia, ran no current with them which should hinder or make difficult that in proposition by the northwest.

Within six days after came in one and within five another of our fleet, the masters of both having fallen upon the same counsel, by the opportunity of the wind, not to seek the Baruada but to steer away for our harbor; which doubtless the admiral himself did not observe but obeyed his own directions, and is the true or probable cause of his being cast so far into suspicion, where—perhaps bound in with wind, perhaps enforced to stay the masting or mending of somewhat in his ship torn or lost in this tempest—we doubt not but by the mercy of God he is safe, with the pinnace which attended him, and shall both, or are by this time, arrived at our colony.

Not long after these, another of our small pinnaces, yet also unaccounted for, recovered the river alone. And now seven of our fleet being in, they landed in health near four hundred persons; who being put ashore without their governor, or any order from him—all the commissioners and principal persons being aboard him—no man would acknowledge a superior nor could, from this headless and unbridled multitude, be anything expected but disorder and riot, nor any council prevent or foresee the success of these ways.

Now if we compare the disasters of this supply with the main ends, it will appear they have weakened none of them, but that they still remain safe and feasible for anything [that] ariseth in objection out of them, for that these accidents and contingencies were ever to be expected, and a resolution was to be put on at first armed against the probability of them. Who can avoid the hand of God, or dispute with Him? Is he fit to undertake any great action whose courage is shaken and dissolved with one storm? Who knows whether He that disposed of our hearts to so good beginnings be now pleased to try our constancy and perseverance, and to discern between the ends of our desires whether piety or covetousness carried us swifter? For if the first were the principal scope, hence ariseth nothing to infirm or make that impossible. But as it falleth out in business of greatest consequence, sometimes the noblest ends upon which we are most intense are furthest removed from the first steps made unto them, and must by lesser and meaner be approached.

Plantation of religion being the main and chief purpose admits many things of less and secondary consequence of necessity to be done before it. For an error or miscarriage in one of which to desist or stagger were to betray our principal end cowardly and faintly, and to draw upon ourselves just scorn and reprehension.

Whether we shall discourse out of reason or example that every action hath proportional difficulties to the greatness thereof, such as must necessarily be admitted from the first conception, and such as even in the passage dignify both the actors and the work, if with prudence they foresee all the hazards, and with patience and constancy meet and encounter them.

It must either be confessed that it was folly from the origin and first step not to have been prepared for such as these, or that it is none now not to quit it for them, but the greatest of all [folly] to say, Who would have expected this? If we cast our eye upon the Spanish conquest of the Indies, how abundant their stories are of fleets, battles, and armies lost—eighteen upon the attempt of Guiana and more than seventy in both the Indies—and yet with how indefatigable industry and prosperous fate they have pursued and vanquished all these, their many armies maintained in Europe can witness with too lamentable an experience.

If we compare the [Spanish] beginnings, they were meaner than ours, and subject to all the same and much more uncertainty. If the religion, which shall crown the success it admits no controversy nor comparison among those to whom we write.[1] If the commodities, they which we have in assurance and knowledge are of more necessity, and those in hope equally rich and abundant.

But to come home to our purpose, that which seems to dishearten or shake our first grounds in this supply ariseth from two principal

---

[1] I.e., the Church of England is superior to the Church of Rome.

sources, of which one was cause of the other.

First, the tempest, and can any man expect an answer for that?

Next, the absence of the governor, an effect of the former, for the loss of him is in suspense, and much reason of his safety against some doubt; and the hand of GOD reacheth all the Earth.

Now if these two only be the main crosses which stagger the feasibleness, consider that, of three voyages before, no man miscarried in the way, and that all other depend on these, [such] as the misgovernment of our men, their illness, their want, and the empty return of our fleet; wherein, if we recover and correct the cause, we vanquish all things consequent unto it and yet in appearance. If with these we compare the advantages which we have gotten in the shortness and security of the passage, in the intelligence of some of our nation planted by Sir Walter Raleigh yet alive within fifty mile of our fort, who can open the womb and bowels of this country—as is testified by two of our colony sent out to seek them, who, though denied by the savages speech with them, found crosses and letters, the characters and assured testimonies of Christians, newly cut in the barks of trees. If we consider the assuredness of the commodities—wines, pitch, soap-ashes, timber for all uses, iron, steel, copper, dyes, cordage, silk grass, pearl, which, though discolored and softened by fire for want of skill in the naturals to pierce them, was found in great abundance in the house of their sepultures.[1]

If we consider, I say, and compare these certainties and truths, [inasmuch] as [they are] less[er] ends to strengthen and produce our first and principal, with those casual and accidental misadventures and errors which have befallen us, before every equal and resolved heart they will vanish and become smoke and air, and not only keep upright but raise our spirits and affections, and reconcile our reasons to our desires.

If any object the difficulty of keeping that we shall possess, if this discourse could admit a disputation of it, it should easily appear that our confidence against any enemy is built upon solid and substantial reason. And to give some taste thereof: Our enemies must be either

---

[1] "With every werowan, or king, is buried all his wealth, for they believe that he that dieth richest liveth in another world happiest." (margin note)

the natives or strangers. Against the first the war would be as easy as the argument. For the second, a few men may dispute the possession of any place wherein they are fortified, where the enemy is so much a stranger as that he must discover and fight at once upon all disadvantages of straits, fords, and woods[1]; and where he can never march with horse nor with ordnance without them; nor can abide to stay many months when all his relief must be had from his ships, which cannot long supply a number competent to besiege. Neither is it possible to block us up by planting between us and the sea, the rivers being so broad, and so many outlets from them into the bay; besides the protection and privilege of subjects to so potent a king, whom any wise estate will be wary to affront or provoke.

We doubt not but by examination of what is said our first ends are yet safe and the ways unto them in no sort so difficult as should more affright and deter us now than at the first meditation of them. But if these be not sufficient to satisfy and encourage every honest affection, we will not so desist but urge the necessity of a present supply to redeem the defects and misadventures of the last; that seeing all the dangers and sicknesses have sprung from want of effecting our purpose of sending an able governor, we have concluded and resolved to set forth the Right Honor[able] the Lord de la Warr by the last of January [1610], and to give him all the liberties and privileges which we have power to derive upon him, and to furnish him with all necessaries fit for his quality, person, and the business which he shall undergo; and so by God's grace to persist until we have made perfect our good and happy beginnings.

—If these shall not yet suffice to resolution: that a baron and peer of this kingdom—whose honor nor fortune needs not any desperate medicine, one of so approved courage, temper, and experience—shall expose himself for the common good to all these hazards and pains, which we fear and safely talk of that sit idle at home, and bear a great part upon his own charge, and revive and quicken the whole by his example, constancy, and resolution;[2]

—If you have no implicit faith nor trust in us that govern this

---

[1] I.e., the enemy must explore a new terrain simultaneously while fighting in it.

[2] "As a door turneth upon his hinges, so doth a sluggard upon his bed. Prov. 26:14." (margin note)

business, to whom there must be some advantage granted in our practice and intelligence (especially in this) above ordinary persons, that we have no will nor intent to betray our poor countrymen, nor to burthen our own consciences, nor to draw so just scorn and reproach upon our reputations;

—If our knowledge and constant persuasion of the faithfulness and wholesomeness of this land, and of the recompense it shall in time bring to this kingdom and to every particular member of this plantation be of no authority;

—If this seem not to you some argument that every man returned is desirous to go back to that which they account and call their own home, and do upon their lives justify which else they willfully betray: That if the government be settled, and a supply of victual for one year sent—so that they may have a seed time and harvest before them—they will never need nor expect to charge us with more expense for anything of necessity to man's life, but they will have leisure and power to retribute with infinite advantage all the cost bestowed upon them;

If all these be yet too weak to confirm the doubtful or awake the drowsy, then let us come nearer and arise from their reasons and affections to their souls and consciences: Remember that what was at first but of conveniency and for honor is now become a case of necessity and piety. Let them consider that they have promised to adventure and not performed it; that they have encouraged and exposed many of honorable birth and, which is of more consequence, 600 of our brethren by our common mother the Church, Christians of one faith and one baptism, to a miserable and inevitable death. Let not any man flatter himself that it concerns not him. For he that forsakes whom he may safely relieve is as guilty of his death as he that can swim and forsakes himself by refusing is of his own. Let every man look inward and disperse that cloud of avarice which darkeneth his spiritual sight and he will find there that when he shall appear before the tribunal of heaven, it shall be questioned him what he hath done? Hath he fed and clothed the hungry and naked? It shall be required what he hath done for the advancement of that Gospel which hath saved him, and for the relief of His maker's image, whom he was bound to save.

O let there be a virtuous emulation between us and the Church of Rome in her own glory and treasury of good works! And let us turn all our contentions upon the common enemy of the name of CHRIST. How far hath she sent out her apostles and thorough how glorious dangers? How is it become a mark of honor to her faith to have converted nations and an obloquy cast upon us that we having the better vine should have worse dressers and husbanders of it?

If piety, honor, easiness, profit, nor conscience cannot provoke and excite—for to all these we have applied our discourse—then let us turn from hearts of stone and iron and pray unto that merciful and tender God, who is both easy and glad to be entreated, that it would please Him to bless and water these feeble beginnings, and that as He is wonderful in all his works, so to nourish this grain of seed that it may spread till all people of the earth admire the greatness and seek the shades and fruit thereof, that by so faint and weak endeavors His great councils may be brought forth, and His secret purposes to light, to our endless comforts and the infinite glory of His sacred name. AMEN.

APPENDIX—To render a more particular satisfaction and account of our care in providing—to attend the Right Honorable the Lord de la Warr in this concluded and present supply—men of most use and necessity to the foundation of a commonwealth; and to avoid both the scandal and peril of accepting idle and wicked persons, such as shame or fear compels into this action, and such as are the weeds and rankness of this land, who, being the surfeit of an able, healthy, and composed body, must needs be the poison of one so tender, feeble, and as yet unformed; and to divulge and declare to all men what kind of persons—as well for their religion and conversations as faculties, arts, and trades—we propose to accept of, we have thought it convenient to pronounce that for the first provision we will receive no man that cannot bring or render some good testimony of his religion to God, and civil manners and behavior to his neighbor with whom he hath lived.

And for the second, we have set down in a table annexed the proportion and number we will entertain in every necessary art, upon proof and assurance that every man shall be able to perform that which he doth undertake, whereby such as are requisite to us may have knowledge and preparation to offer themselves. And we shall be ready to give honest entertainment and content, and to recompense with extraordinary reward, every fit and industrious person, respectively to his pains and quality.

The Table of such as are required to this Plantation—

Four honest and learned ministers.
2 Surgeons.
2 Druggists.
10 Ironmen for the furnace and hammer.
2 Armorers.
2 Gun-founders.
6 Blacksmiths.
10 Sawyers.
6 Carpenters.
6 Shipwrights.
6 Gardeners.
4 Turners.
4 Brickmakers.
2 Tile-makers.
10 Fishermen.
6 Fowlers.
4 Sturgeon dressers and preservers of the caviary.
2 Saltmakers.
6 Coopers.
2 Collar-makers for draft [animals].
2 Plow-wrights.
4 Ropemakers.
6 Vinedressers.
2 Press-makers.
2 Joiners.
2 Soap-ash men.
4 Pitch boilers.
2 Mineral men.
2 Planters of sugar cane.
2 Silk-dressers.
2 Pearl-drillers.
2 Bakers.
2 Brewers.
2 Colliers.

FINIS

21. Richard Rich[1]

News from Virginia.
The lost flock triumphant, with the happy arrival of that famous and worthy knight, Sir Thomas Gates, and the well-reputed and valiant captain, Mr. Christopher Newporte, and others, into England. With the manner of their distress in the Island of Devils (otherwise called Bermoothawes), where they remained 42 weeks, and builded two pinnaces in which they returned unto Virginia. by R. Rich, gent., one of the voyage.

(London: Printed by Edw. Allde, and are to be sold by John Wright at Christchurch door. 1610.)

< **Rich 1610 [1976],** Neill 1878:29, Brown 1890:420

We do not know if this is Robert or Richard Rich. It is the gruff voice of a hard soldier but who is no mercenary when it comes to rhyming. This was one of the first accounts of the shipwreck and of the little dog that brought down feral hogs to feed the castaways on Bermuda, a canine paradise. Rich reports a population of 400 in Virginia, a number the company of Lord Delaware augments in June 1610.

The vagrants brought to the colony he says are doing well in their new home. The call goes out to the common man: Let the immigrants come—the poor who want to work. They will have pay, house and garden, plus a share in profits. There is much news and information here.

If the meter does not impress us, the rosy promises do. The Virginia Company was brimming with good intentions. America fulfilled every one of them.

---

[1] Robert Rich according to Brown, Richard Rich according to Barbour.

TO THE READER—

Reader, how to style thee I know not, perhaps learned, perhaps unlearned; happily captious,[1] happily envious. Indeed, what or how to term thee I know not, only as I began I will proceed.

Reader, thou dost peradventure imagine that I am mercenary in this business and write for money, as your modern poets use—hired by some of those ever-to-be-admired adventurers to flatter the world. No—I disclaim it! I have known the voyage, pass'd the danger, seen that honorable work of Virginia, and, I thank God, am arriv'd here to tell thee what I have seen, done, and pass'd. If thou wilt believe me, so; if not, so too; for I cannot force thee but to thy own liking. I am a soldier, blunt and plain, and so is the phrase of my news; and I protest it is true. If thou ask why I put it in verse, I prithee know it was only to feed mine own humor. I must confess that had I not debar'd myself of that large scope which to the writing of prose is allowed, I should have much eas'd myself and given thee better content.[2] But I entreat thee to take this as it is, and before many days expire I will promise thee the same work more at large.[3]

I did fear prevention[4] by some of your writers, if they should have gotten but some part of the news by the tail, and therefore, though it be rude, let it pass with thy liking, and in so doing I shall like well of thee. But however, I have not long to stay. If thou wilt be unnatural to thy countryman, thou mayest. I must not lose my patrimony. I am for Virginia again, and so I will bid thee heartily farewell with an honest verse:

As I came hither to see my native land,
to waft me back lend me thy gentle hand—

Thy loving countryman, R. R.

---

[1] *Happily captious* means "perhaps quick to find fault."

[2] Con*tent*, satisfaction.

[3] "I am inclined to think that this 'work more at large,' of which no copy is now known, was entered for publication August 16, 1611." (Brown) Also on that date at Stationers' Hall John Wright, bookseller, entered for publication "A ballad called the last news from Virginia, being an encouragement to all others to follow that noble enterprise."

[4] To be scooped as news.

News from Virginia

Of the happy arrival of that famous and worthy knight, Sir Thomas Gates, and well-reputed and valiant Captain Newport, into England.

IT IS no idle, fabulous tale,
  nor is it feigned news,
For Truth herself is here arriv'd,
  because you should not muse.
With her both Gates and Newport come,
  to tell report doth lie
Which did divulge unto the world
  that they at sea did die.

'Tis true that eleven months and more
  these gallant worthy wights
Was in the ship *Sea Venture* nam'd
  deprived Virginia's sight.
And bravely did they glide the main
  till Neptune 'gan to frown,
As if a courser proudly back'd
  would throw his rider down.

The seas did rage, the winds did blow,
  distressed were they then.
Their ship did leak, her tacklings break,
  in danger were her men.
But heaven was pilot in this storm,
  and to an island near,
Bermoothawes call'd, conducted then,
  which did abate their fear.

But yet these worthies forced were,
oppress'd with weather again,
To run their ship between two rocks,
where she doth still remain;
And then on shore the island came,
Inhabited by hogs.
Some fowl and tortoises there were.
They only had one dog

To kill these swine to yield them food,
that little had to eat.
Their store was spent, and all things scant,
Alas!—they wanted meat.
A thousand hogs that dog did kill
their hunger to sustain,
And with such food did in that isle
two and forty weeks remain;

And there two gallant pinnaces
did build of cedar tree:
The brave *Deliverance* one was call'd
of seventy ton was she,
The other *Patience* had to name,
her burthen thirty ton.
Two only of their men which there
pale death did overcome.

And for the loss of those two souls,
which were accounted dear,
A son and daughter then was born
and were baptized there.
The two and forty weeks being past,
they hois'd sail and away;
Their ships with hogs well freighted were,
their hearts with mickle joy;

And so unto Virginia came,
where these brave soldiers find
The Englishmen oppress'd with grief
and discontent in mind.
They seem'd distracted and forlorn
for those two worthies' loss,
Yet at their home return they joy'd.
Among'st them some were cross,

And in the mid'st of discontent
came noble Delaware.
He heard the griefs on either part,
and set them free from care:
He comforts them and cheers their hearts,
that they abound with [j]oy;
He feeds them full, and feeds their souls
with God's word every day.

A discreet council he creates
of men of worthy fame:
That noble Gates lieutenant was
the admiral had to name,
The worthy Sir George Somers, knight,
and others of command,
Master Georg Pearcy, which is brother
unto Northumberland,

Sir Fardinando Wayneman, knight,
and others of good fame,
That noble Lord his company
which to Virginia came,
And landed there his number was
one hundred seventy; then
Add to the rest, and they make full
four hundred able men.

Where they unto their labor fall
    as men that mean to thrive,
Let's pray that heaven may bless them all
    and keep them long alive:
Those men that vagrants liv'd with us
    have there deserved well.
Their governor writes in their praise,
    as divers letters tell.[1]

And to th' adventurers thus he writes,
    Be not dismayed at all,
For scandal cannot do us wrong,
    God will not let us fall.
Let England know our willingness,
    for that our work is good;
We hope to plant a nation
    where none before hath stood.

To glorify the Lord 'tis done,
    and to no other end.
He that would cross so good a work
    to God can be no friend.
There is no fear of hunger here,
    for corn much store here grows,
Much fish the gallant rivers yield—
    'tis truth without suppose.

Great store of fowl, of venison,
    of grapes and mulberries,
Of chestnuts, walnuts, and suchlike,
    of fruits and strawberries
There is indeed no want at all.
    But some, condition'd ill,
That wish the work should not go on,
    with words do seem to kill.

[1] Already Emma Lazarus' sentiments had reached America.

And for an instance of their store,
  the noble Delaware
Hath for a present hither sent
  to testify his care
In managing so good a work,
  two gallant ships, by name
The *Blessing* and the *Hercules,*
  well fraught, and in the same

Two ships are these commodities:
  Furs, sturgeon, caviar,
Black walnut tree, and some deal boards—
  With such they laden are—
Some pearl, some wainscot and clapboards,
  With some sassafras wood,
And iron promis'd, for 'tis true
  their mines are very good.

Then maugre[1] scandal, false report,
  or any opposition,
Th' adventurers do thus divulge
  to men of good condition
That he that wants shall have relief,
  be he of honest mind—
Apparel, coin, or anything
  —to such they will be kind,

To such as to Virginia
  do purpose to repair.
And when that they shall thither come,
  each man shall have his share:
Day wages for the laborer,
  and for his more content
A house and garden plot shall have.
  Besides 'tis further meant

[1] Despite.

That every man shall have a part
and not thereof denied
Of general profit, as if that he
twelve pounds ten shillings paid.[1]
And he that in Virginia
shall copper coin receive
For hire or commodities,
and will the country leave,

Upon delivery of such coin
unto the governor,
Shall by exchange at his return
be by their treasurer
Paid him in London at first sight,
no man shall cause to grieve.
For 'tis their general will and wish
that every man shall live.

The number of adventurers
that are for this plantation
Are full eight hundred worthy men,
some noble, all of fashion,
Good, discreet, their work is good;
And as they have begun
May heaven assist them in their work!
—And thus our news is done.

FINIS

[1] The price of one share in the Virginia Company.

LIBRARY OF VIRGINIA

SIR THOMAS GATES

22. William Strachey

A True Reportory of the wrack and redemption of Sir Thomas Gates, knight, upon and from the Islands of the Bermudas; his coming to Virginia, and the estate of that colony then, and after under the government of the Lord La Warre. July 15, 1610. Written by William Strachy, esquire.

< **Purchas 1625d:1734**

Strachey's letter to an excellent noble lady is the finest writing of our collection. It begins like an ordinary travelogue cum diary until suddenly we are in the vortex of a hurricane and the mountains of the sea. The pace of this terrifying story from then on is in the hands of a master.

But this is non-fiction. The long anticlimax in Bermuda and Virginia represents Strachey's fine workmanship when he applies himself unself-consciously, but only here and there returns to the first height. Instead it is the well-drawn and frank truth about the fate of the castaways and the conditions they found on arrival in the colony. The Council decided to suppress publication. They selected what they could use and put it in *A True Declaration §27.*

No one today knows the identity of the excellent lady who received a letter of 25,000 words. Culliford (1965:188) suggests Dame Sara Smythe, wife of Sir Thomas Smythe, treasurer of the Virginia Company, but mentions also Lady Elizabeth Howard, wife of Theophilus Howard, Lord Howard of Walden, who seems likelier, all in all.

Strachey thought of himself as a man of letters and he moved in London literary circles. He was close friends with John Donne and Thomas Campion, wrote a dedicatory verse to Jonson's *Sejanus*, and he owned stock in the Blackfriars Theater. Here doubtless he either knew William Shakespeare or shared friends. It would not be surprising for Shakespeare to be familiar with something written by Strachey, but the poet was also close to several prominent "liberals" in the Virginia Company, notably Southampton and Sandys, who were holding Strachey's letter in safekeeping. By either route, the manuscript was read by Shakespeare and became a source and source of inspiration for *The Tempest. The Tempest* was published in 1623. *The*

True Reportory was published by Purchas in his *Pilgrims* two years later, when he gave it its title and put it in book format.[1] The Bermuda and Virginia portions are of equal length.

I have abstracted the following—

Table of Contents

---

[1] Unless this was done by Hakluyt, who, it seems, made the MS over to Purchas.

A True Reportory

I.

A most dreadful tempest, the manifold deaths[1] *whereof are here to the life described – Their wrack on Bermuda, and the description of those islands.*

EXCELLENT LADY—

KNOW THAT upon Friday late in the evening[2] we brake ground out of the sound of Plymouth, our whole fleet then consisting of seven good ships and two pinnaces, all which from the said second of June unto the twenty-three of July kept in friendly consort together, not a whole watch at any time losing the sight each of other. Our course when we came about the height of between 26 and 27 degrees we declined to the northward, and according to our governor's instructions altered the trade and ordinary way used heretofore by Dominico and Mevis [Nevis] in the West Indies, and found the wind to this course indeed as friendly as, in the judgment of all seamen, it is upon a more direct line, and by Sir George Summers, our admiral, had been likewise in former time sailed—being a gentleman of approved assuredness and ready knowledge in seafaring actions, having often carried command and chief charge in many ships royal of Her Majesty's, and in sundry voyages made many defeats and attempts in the time of the Spaniard's quarreling with us upon the islands and Indies, etc.

We had followed this course so long as now we were within seven

[1] There are no deaths.
[2] "1 June 1609." (margin note).

or eight days at the most, by Captain Newport's reckoning, of making Cape Henry upon the coast of Virginia, when on Saint James his day, July 24, being Monday, preparing for no less all the black night before—the clouds gathering thick upon us, and the winds singing and whistling most unusually, which made us to cast off our pinnace, towing the same until then astern—a dreadful storm and hideous began to blow from out the northeast, which swelling and roaring, as it were, by fits, some hours with more violence than others, at length did beat all light from heaven, which like an hell of darkness turned black upon us, so much the more fuller of horror, as in such cases horror and fear use to overrun the troubled and overmastered senses of all, which, taken up with amazement, the ears lay so sensible to the terrible cries and murmurs of the winds and distraction of our company, as who was most armed and best prepared was not a little shaken. For surely (noble lady) as death comes not so sudden nor apparent, so he comes not so elvish and painful to men, especially even then in health and perfect habitudes of body, as at sea; who comes at no time so welcome but our frailty (so weak is the hold of hope in miserable demonstrations of danger) it makes guilty of many contrary changes and conflicts. For indeed death is accompanied at no time nor place with circumstances every way so uncapable of particularities of goodness and inward comforts as at sea. For it is most true there ariseth commonly no such unmerciful tempest, compound of so many contrary and diverse nations,[1] but that it worketh upon the whole frame of the body, and most loathsomely affecteth all the powers thereof. And the manner of the sickness it lays upon the body, being so unsufferable, gives not the mind any free and quiet time to use her judgment and empire. Which made the poet say,

Hostium uxores puerique caecos
sentiant motus orientis Haedi &
aequoris nigri fremitum & trementes
verbere ripas.[2]

[1] Quantities of things.

[2] "May our enemies' wives and children feel the blind motions of rising [Haedus], and the roaring of the black sea and the shore quaking with the blow." (Latin:

For four and twenty hours the storm in a restless tumult had blown so exceedingly as we could not apprehend in our imaginations any possibility of greater violence. Yet did we still find it not only more terrible but more constant, fury added to fury, and one storm urging a second more outrageous than the former, whether it so wrought upon our fears or indeed met with new forces.

Sometimes strikes[1] in our ship amongst women and passengers not used to such hurly and discomforts made us look one upon the other with troubled hearts and panting bosoms, our clamors drown'd in the winds, and the winds in thunder. Prayers might well be in the heart and lips, but drowned in the outcries of the officers, nothing heard that could give comfort, nothing seen that might encourage hope. It is impossible for me, had I the voice of Stentor, and expression of as many tongues as his throat of voices, to express the outcries and miseries, not languishing but wasting his spirits and art, constant to his own principles, but not prevailing.[2]

Our sails, wound up, lay without their use. And if at any time we bore but a hullock, or half forecourse,[3] to guide her before the sea, six and sometimes eight men were not enough to hold the whipstaff in the steerage and the tiller below in the gunner room, by which may be imagined the strength of the storm in which the sea swelled above the clouds and gave battle unto heaven.

It could not be said to rain. The waters like whole rivers did flood in the air. And this I did still observe that whereas upon the land when a storm hath poured itself forth once in drifts of rain, the wind, as beaten down and vanquished therewith, not long after endureth. Here the glut of water, as if throttling the wind erewhile, was no sooner a little emptied and qualified but instantly the winds, as having gotten their mouths now free and at liberty, spake more loud, and grew more tumultuous and malignant. What shall I say?—Winds and seas were as mad as fury and rage could make them. For

---

Horace, *Carmina* 3.27.21, where he says "orientis Austri" the south wind, but uses "orientis Haedi" at *Car.* 3.1.28. Haedus is one of the Kids of the star Capella.)

[1] Sea water slopping below from decks awash.

[2] I.e., it would have taken more than the voice of Stentor, who had the voice of fifty men, to exhort courage here. The allusion is to the *Iliad.*

[3] A single storm sail on the foremast to help her run.

mine own part, I had been in some storms before, as well upon the coast of Barbary and Algier in the Levant, and once more distressful in the Adriatic Gulf, in a bottom of Candy,[1] so as I may well say, *Ego quid sit ater Adriae novi sinus & quid albus peccet Iapex.*[2] Yet all that I had ever suffered gathered together might not hold comparison with this. There was not a moment in which the sudden splitting or instant oversetting of the ship was not expected.

Howbeit this was not all. It pleased God to bring a greater affliction yet upon us, for in the beginning of the storm we had received likewise a mighty leak, and the ship in every joint almost having spewed out her oakum before we were aware (a casualty more desperate than any other that a voyage by sea draweth with it) was grown five foot suddenly deep with water above her ballast, and we almost drowned within whilest we sat looking when to perish from above. This imparting no less terror than danger ran through the whole ship with much fright and amazement, startled and turned the blood, and took down the braves of the most hardy mariner of them all, insomuch as he that before happily felt not the sorrow of others now began to sorrow for himself when he saw such a pond of water so suddenly broken in, and which he knew could not without present avoiding but instantly sink him, so as joining only for his own sake, not yet worth the saving in the public safety.

There might be seen master, master's mate, boatswain, quartermaster, coopers, carpenters, and who not with candles in their hands, creeping along the ribs viewing the sides, searching every corner, and listening in every place, if they could hear the water run. Many a weeping leak was this way found and hastily stop'd, and at length one in the gunner room made up with I know not how many pieces of beef. But all was to no purpose: The leak (if it were but one) which drunk in our greatest seas and took in our destruction fastest could not then be found, nor ever was, by any labor, counsel, or search. The waters still increasing, and the pumps going, which at length choked with bringing up whole and continual biscuit—and indeed all we had, ten thousand weight—it was conceived as most likely that

[1] A ship of Crete.

[2] "I know what the black gulf of the Adriatic is like, and the mischief of the white west-nor'wester." (Latin: Horace, *Carmina* 3.27.19)

the leak might be sprung in the bread room, whereupon the carpenter went down and rip'd up all the room, but could not find it so.

I am not able to give unto Your Ladyship every man's thought in this perplexity to which we were now brought; but to me this leakage appeared as a wound given to men that were before dead. The Lord knoweth I had as little hope as desire of life in the storm, and in this it went beyond my will because beyond my reason why we should labor to preserve life. Yet we did, either because so dear are a few ling'ring hours of life in all mankind or that our Christian knowledges taught us how much we owed to the rites of nature, as bound not to be false to ourselves, or to neglect the means of our own preservation, the most despairful things amongst men being matters of no wonder nor moment with Him who is the rich fountain and admirable essence of all mercy.

Our governor, upon the Tuesday morning (at what time by such who had been below in the hold the leak was first discovered) had caused the whole company—about one hundred and forty, besides women—to be equally divided into three parts, and opening the ship in three places: under the forecastle, in the waist, and hard by the bittake[1]—appointed each man where to attend; and thereunto every man came duly upon his watch, took the bucket or pump for one hour, and rested another. Then men might be seen to labor (I may well say) for life, and the better sort, even our governor and admiral themselves, not refusing their turn, and to spell each the other to give example to other. The common sort stripped naked as men in galleys the easier both to hold out, and to shrink from under the salt water, which continually leapt in among them, kept their eyes waking and their thoughts and hands working, with tired bodies and wasted spirits, three days and four nights destitute of outward comfort and desperate of any deliverance, testifying how mutually willing they were yet by labor to keep each other from drowning, albeit each one drowned whilest he labored.

Once, so huge a sea brake upon the poop and quarter upon us as it covered our ship from stern to stem. Like a garment or a vast cloud, it filled her brim full for a while within from the hatches up to the

[1] Binnacle.

spar deck. This source or confluence of water was so violent as it rush'd and carried the helm-man from the helm, and wrested the whipstaff out of his hand, which so flew from side to side that when he would have seized the same again, it so tossed him from starboard to larboard as it was God's mercy it had not split him. It so beat him from his hold, and so bruised him, as a fresh man, hazarding in by chance, fell fair with it, and by main strength bearing somewhat up, made good his place, and with much clamor encouraged and called upon others, who gave her now up rent in pieces and absolutely lost.

Our governor was at this time below at the capstan, both by his speech and authority heartening every man unto his labor. It struck him from the place where he sat and groveled him, and all us about him on our faces, beating together with our breaths all thoughts from our bosoms else than that we were now sinking. For my part, I thought her already in the bottom of the sea; and I have heard him say, wading out of the flood thereof, all his ambition was but to climb up above hatches to die in *aperto coelo,*[1] and in the company of his old friends. It so stun'd the ship in her full pace that she stirred no more than if she had been caught in a net or than as if the fabulous remora had stuck to her forecastle.[2] Yet, without bearing one inch of sail, even then she was making her way nine or ten leagues in a watch. One thing, it is not without his wonder whether it were the fear of death in so great a storm or that it pleased God to be gracious unto us: There was not a passenger, gentleman or other, after he began to stir and labor but was able to relieve his fellow and make good his course. And it is most true such as in all their lifetimes had never done hours' work before (their minds now helping their bodies) were able twice forty-eight hours together to toil with the best.

During all this time, the heavens look'd so black upon us that it was not possible the elevation of the Pole might be observed, nor a star by night, not sunbeam by day was to be seen. Only upon the Thursday night, Sir George Summers, being upon the watch, had an apparition of a little round light like a faint star, trembling and

---

[1] "Under the open sky." (Latin)

[2] "Remora is fabled to be a small fish able to withstand a ship in her course." (margin note)

streaming along with a sparkling blaze half the height upon the mainmast, and shooting sometimes from shroud to shroud, tempting to settle as it were upon any of the four shrouds. And for three or four hours together, or rather more, half the night it kept with us, running sometimes along the main yard to the very end, and then returning; at which Sir George Summers called divers about him and showed them the same, who observed it with much wonder and carefulness. But upon a sudden, towards the morning watch, they lost the sight of it and knew not what way it made.

The superstitious seamen make many constructions of this sea fire, which nevertheless is usual in storms. The same it may be which the Grecians were wont in the Mediterranean to call "Castor and Pollux," of which, if one only appeared without the other, they took it for an evil sign of great tempest. The Italians, and such who lie open to the Adriatic and Tyrrhene Sea, call it a "sacred body" *(corpo sancto)*. The Spaniards call it Saint Elmo, and have an authentic and miraculous legend for it. Be it what it will, we laid other foundations of safety or ruin than in the rising or falling of it. Could it have served us now miraculously to have taken our height by, it might have strucken amazement and a reverence in our devotions, according to the due of a miracle. But it did not light us any whit the more to our known way, who ran now as do hoodwinked men at all adventures, sometimes north and northeast, then north and by west, and in an instant again varying two or three points, and sometimes half the compass.

East and by south we steered away, as much as we could to bear upright, which was no small carefulness nor pain to do, albeit we much unrigged our ship, threw overboard much luggage, many a trunk and chest (in which I suffered no mean loss), and staved many a butt of beer, hogsheads of oil, cider, wine, and vinegar, and heaved away all our ordnance on the starboard side, and had now purposed to have cut down the mainmast the more to lighten her, for we were much spent, and our men so weary as their strengths together failed them with their hearts, having travailed now from Tuesday till Friday morning, day and night, without either sleep or food. For the leakage taking up all the hold, we could neither come by beer nor fresh water; fire we could keep none in the cookroom to dress any meat, and carefulness, grief, and our turn at the pump or bucket were sufficient to hold sleep from our eyes.

And surely, madam, it is most true there was not any hour (a matter of admiration) all these days in which we freed not twelve hundred barricoes of water, the least whereof contained six gallons, and some eight, besides three deep pumps continually going, two beneath at the capstan and the other above in the half deck, and at each pump four thousand strokes at the least in a watch, so as I may well say every four hours we quitted one hundred tons of water. And from Tuesday noon till Friday noon, we bailed and pumped two thousand ton, and yet, do what we could, when our ship held least in her (after Tuesday night second watch) she bore ten foot deep, at which stay our extreme working kept her one [for] eight glasses, forbearance whereof had instantly sunk us. And it being now Friday, the fourth morning, it wanted little but that there had been a general determination to have shut up hatches, and commending our sinful souls to God, committed the ship to the mercy of the sea. Surely that night we must have done it, and that night had we then perished.

But see the goodness and sweet introduction of better hope by our merciful God given unto us: Sir George Summers, when no man dreamed of such happiness, had discovered and cried LAND! Indeed the morning, now three quarters spent, had won a little clearness from the days before, and it being better surveyed, the very trees were seen to move with the wind upon the shore side. Whereupon our governor commanded the helm-man to bear up. The boatswain sounding at the first found it thirteen fathom, and when we stood a little in, seven fathom; and presently heaving his lead the third time had ground at four fathom. And by this we had got her within a mile under the southeast point of the land, where we had somewhat smooth water. But having no hope to save her by coming to an anchor in the same, we were enforced to run her ashore as near the land as we could, which brought us within three quarters of a mile offshore; and by the mercy of God unto us, making out our boats, we had ere night brought all our men, women, and children, about the number of one hundred and fifty, safe into the island.

We found it to be the dangerous and dreaded island, or rather islands, of the Bermuda, whereof let me give Your Ladyship a brief description before I proceed to my narration; and that the rather, because they be so terrible to all that ever touched on them, and such tempests, thunders, and other fearful objects are seen and heard about them that they be called commonly "the Devil's Islands," and are feared and avoided of all sea travelers alive above any other place in the world. Yet it pleased our merciful God to make even this hideous and hated place both the place of our safety and means of our deliverance.

And hereby also I hope to deliver the world from a foul and general error: it being counted of most that they can be no habitation for men, but rather given over to devils and wicked spirits; whereas indeed we find them now by experience to be as habitable and commodious as most countries of the same climate and situation, insomuch as if the entrance into them were as easy as the place itself is contenting, it had long ere this been inhabited as well as other islands. Thus shall we make it appear that truth is the daughter of time, and that men ought not to deny everything which is not subject to their own sense.

The Bermudas be broken islands, five hundred of them in manner of an archipelagus (at least if you may call them all "islands" that lie how little soever into the sea and by themselves) of small compass, some larger yet than other, as time and the sea hath won from them and eaten his passage through, and all now lying in the figure of a croissant, within the circuit of six or seven leagues at the most, albeit at first it is said of them that they were thirteen or fourteen leagues and more in longitude, as I have heard. For no greater distance is it from the northwest point to Gates his Bay as by this map Your Ladyship may see, in which Sir George Summers, who coasted in his boat about them all, took great care to express the same exactly and full, and made his draft perfect for all good occasions,[1] and the benefit of such who either in distress might be brought upon them or make sail this way.

It should seem by the testimony of Gonzalus Ferdinandus Oviedus, in his book entituled *The Summary* or *Abridgment* of his

---

[1] "Sir George Summers' diligent survey: his draft which we have not. M. Norgate hath since published an exact map." (margin note)

General History of the West Indies, written to the Emperor Charles the Fift, that they have been indeed of greater compass (and I easily believe it) than they are now, who thus saith, "In the year 1515, when I came first to inform Your Majesty of the state of the things in India, and was the year following in Flanders, in the time of your most fortunate success in these your kingdoms of Aragony and Castile; whereas at that voyage I sailed above the Island Bermudas, otherwise called Gorza, being the farthest of all the islands that are yet found at this day in the world, and arriving there at the depth of eight yards[1] of water, and distant from the land as far as the shot of a piece of ordnance, I determined to send some of the ship to land, as well to make search of such things as were there as also to leave in the island certain hogs for increase. But the time not serving my purpose by reason of contrary wind, I could bring my ships no nearer—the island being twelve leagues in length and sixteen in breadth, and about thirty in circuit, lying in the thirty-three degrees of the north side." Thus far he.

True it is the main island, or greatest of them now, may be some sixteen miles in length east-northeast and west-southwest, the longest part of it, standing in thirty-two degrees and twenty minutes, in which is a great bay on the north side in the northwest end, and many broken islands in that sound, or bay, and a little round island at the southwest end. As occasions were offered, so we gave titles and names to certain places.

These islands are often afflicted and rent with tempests—great strokes of thunder, lightning, and rain in the extremity of violence—which (and it may well be) hath so sund'red and torn down the rocks, and whirried whole quarters of islands into the main sea some six, some seven leagues, and is like in time to swallow them all, so as

---

[1] "Or *fadams braccia.* In his *Gen. Hist.* II, 2, ch. 9, he reciteth the same history. More particularly he saith it hath two names: *Garza,* of the ship which first discovered it being so called, and *Bermudez* of the captain of that ship, named John Bermudes. Note that he placeth it more to the north than that which is by ours inhabited, and say sometime they see it, sometime not, as they pass. The Spaniards (as I have heard) which were wracked there in Captain Butler's time were of opinion that ours are not the Bermudas. Yea, some of ours affirm they have seen such an island to the north of ours, and have offered to discover it. *Sub judice lis est; veritas temporis filia* ['The case is pending; truth is the daughter of time']." (margin note)

even in that distance from the shore there is no small danger of them and with them, of the storms continually raging from them, which once in the full and change commonly of every moon (winter or summer) keep their unchangeable round, and rather thunder than blow from every corner about them, sometimes forty-eight hours together; especially if the circle which the philosophers call "halo" were (in our being there) seen about the moon at any season, which bow indeed appeared there often and would be of a mighty compass and breadth. I have not observed it anywhere one quarter so great. Especially about the twentieth of March, I saw the greatest, when followed upon the eve's eve of the Annunciation of Our Lady the mightiest blast of lightning and most terrible rap of thunder that ever astonied mortal men, I think. In August, September, and until the end of October, we had very hot and pleasant weather, only (as I say) thunder, lightning, and many scattering showers of rain, which would pass swiftly over, and yet fall with such force and darkness for the time as if it would never be clear again. We wanted not any; and of rain more in summer than in winter.

And in the beginning of December we had great store of hail, the sharp winds blowing northerly, but it continued not. And to say truth, it is wintry or summer weather there according as those north and northwest winds blow. Much taste of this kind of winter we had, for those cold winds would suddenly alter the air. But when there was no breath of wind to bring the moist air out of the seas from the north and northwest, we were rather weary of the heat than pinched with extremity of cold. Yet the three winter months—December, January, and February—the winds kept in those cold corners, and indeed then it was heavy and melancholy being there. Nor were the winds more rough in March than in the foresaid months, and yet even then would the birds breed. I think they bred there most months in the year. In September and at Christmas I saw young birds, and in February, at which time the mornings are there, as in May in England, fresh and sharp.

Well may the Spaniards and these Biscany pilots, with all their traders into the Indies, pass by these islands as afraid (either bound out or homewards) of their very meridian, and leave the fishing for the pearl (which some say, and I believe well, is as good there as in any of their other Indian islands, and whereof we had some trial) to such as will adventure for them. The seas about them are so full of breaches as with those dangers they may well be said to be the strongest situate in the world. I have often heard Sir George Summers and Captain Newport say how they have not been by any chance or discovery upon their like. It is impossible without great and perfect knowledge and search first made of them to bring in a bauble boat[1] so much as of ten ton without apparent ruin, albeit within there are many fair harbors for the greatest English ship. Yea, the argosies of Venice may ride there with water enough, and safe landlock'd. There is one only side that admits so much as hope of safety by many a league, on which (as before described) it pleased God to bring us. We had not come one man of us else ashore, as the weather was. They have been ever therefore left desolate and not inhabited.

The soil of the whole island is one and the same, the mould dark, red, sandy, dry, and uncapable, I believe, of any of our commodities or fruits. Sir George Summers, in the beginning of August, squared out a garden by the quarter—the quarter being set down before a goodly bay upon which our governor did first leap ashore, and therefore called it (as aforesaid) Gates his Bay, which opened into the east, and into which the sea did ebb and flow according to their tides—and sowed muskmelons, peas, onions, radish, lettuce, and many English seeds and kitchen herbs, all which in some ten days did appear above ground. But whether by the small birds, of which there be many kinds, or by flies—worms I never saw any, nor any venomous thing as toad or snake, or any creeping beast hurtful, only some spiders which, as many affirm, are signs of great store of gold. But they were long and slender-leg spiders, and whether venomous or no I know not. I believe not since we should still find them amongst our linen in our chests and drinking cans; but we never received any danger from them. A kind of me[lo]lontha, or black beetle, there was which bruised gave a savor like many sweet and

[1] A small boat, a toy of a boat.

strong gums punned[1] together—whether, I say, hind'red by these or by the condition or vice of the soil, they came to no proof nor thrived.

It is like enough that the commodities of the other western islands would prosper there, as vines, lemons, oranges, and sugar canes. Our governor made trial of the latter, and buried some two or three in the garden mould, which were reserved in the wrack amongst many which we carried to plant here in Virginia; and they began to grow, but the hogs breaking in both rooted them up and ate them.

There is not through the whole islands either champion ground, valleys, or fresh rivers.

They are full of shaws [copses] of goodly cedar, fairer than ours here of Virginia, the berries whereof our men seething, straining, and letting stand some three or four days made a kind of pleasant drink. These berries are of the same bigness and color of corinths [currants], full of little stones, and very restringent or hard building. Peter Martin saith that at Alexandria in Egypt there is a kind of cedar which the Jews dwelling there affirm to be the cedars of Libanus, which bear old fruit and new all the year, being a kind of apple which taste like prunes. But then neither those there in the Bermudas nor ours here in Virginia are of that happy kind.

Likewise there grow great store of palm trees, not the right Indian palms, such as in Saint John Port-Rico are called *cocos,* and are there full of small fruits like almonds of the bigness of the grains in pomegranates, nor of those kind of palms which bears dates, but a kind of simerons, or wild palms, in growth, fashion, leaves, and branches resembling those true palms. For the tree is high and straight, sappy and spongeous, unfirm for any use, no branches but in the uppermost part thereof, and in the top grow leaves about the head of it, the most inmost part whereof they call *palmetto,* and it is the heart and pith of the same trunk, so white and thin as it will peel off into pleats as smooth and delicate as white satin into twenty folds, in which a man may write as in paper, where they spread and fall downward about the tree like an overblown rose or saffron flower not early gathered. So broad are the leaves as an Italian *umbrello.* A man may

[1] Pounded.

well defend his whole body under one of them from the greatest storm rain that falls. For they being stiff and smooth, as if so many flags were knit together, the rain easily slideth off. We oftentimes found growing to these leaves many silkworms, involved therein like those small worms which Acosta writeth of, which grew in the leaves of the tunal tree, of which being dried the Indians make their cochineal, so precious and merchantable. With these leaves we thatched our cabins, and roasting the palmetto, or soft top thereof, they had a taste like fried melons. And being sod they ate like cabbages, but not so offensively thankful to the stomach. Many an ancient burgher was therefore heaved at, and fell not for his place but for his head. For our common people, whose bellies never had ears, made it no breach of charity in their hot bloods and tall stomachs to murder thousands of them. They bear a kind of berry black and round, as big as a damson, which about December were ripe and luscious. Being scalded whilest they are green, they eat like bullaces. These trees shed their leaves in the winter months, as withered or burnt with the cold blasts of the north wind, especially those that grow to the seaward; and in March there burgeon new in their room fresh and tender.

Other kinds of high and sweet-smelling woods there be, and divers colors: black, yellow, and red, and one which bears a round blue berry, much eaten by our own people, of a styptic quality and rough taste on the tongue, like a sloe, to stay or bind the flux, which the often eating of the luscious palm berry would bring them into. For the nature of sweet things is to cleanse and dissolve.

A kind of peas, of the bigness and shape of a Catherine pear, we found growing upon the rocks, full of many sharp subtle pricks as a thistle, which we therefore called "the prickle pear," the outside green, but being opened, of a deep murrey, full of juice like a mulberry, and just of the same substance and taste; we both ate them raw and baked.

Sure it is that there are no rivers nor running springs of fresh water to be found upon any of them. When we came first, we digged and found certain gushings and soft bubblings, which being either in bottoms or on the side of hanging ground were only fed with rain water, which nevertheless soon sinketh into the earth and vanisheth away, or emptieth itself out of sight into the sea, without any channel above or upon the superficies of the earth. For according as their rains fell, we had our wells and pits, which we digged, either half full or absolute exhausted and dry, howbeit some low bottoms which the continual descent from the hills filled full, and in those flats could have no passage away, we found to continue as fishing ponds or standing pools, continually summer and winter full of fresh water.

The shore and bays round about, when we landed first, afforded great store of fish, and that of divers kinds and good. But it should seem that our fires, which we maintained on the shore's side, drave them from us, so as we were in some want until we had made a flat bottom gondol[a] of cedar with which we put off farther into the sea, and then daily hooked great store of many kinds, as excellent angelfish, salmon, peal,[1] bonitos, stingray, cavally,[2] snappers, hogfish, sharks, dogfish, pilchards, mullets, and rockfish, of which be divers kinds. And of these our governor dried and salted and, barreling them up, brought to sea five hundred. For he had procured salt to be made with some brine, which happily was preserved, and once having made a little quantity, he kept three or four pots boiling, and two or three men attending nothing else in an house some little distance from his bay, set up on purpose for the same work.

Likewise in Furbusher's Building Bay we had a large seine, or trammel net, which our governor caused to be made of the deer toils which we were to carry to Virginia, by drawing the masts more straight and narrow with rope yarn, and which reached from one side of the dock to the other, with which, I may boldly say, we have taken five thousand of small and great fish at one hale, as pilchards, breams, mullets, rockfish, etc., and other kinds for which we have no names. We have taken also from under the broken rocks crayfishes oftentimes greater than any of our best English lobsters; and likewise abundance of crabs, oysters, and whelks. True it is for fish in every cove and creek we found snaules [snails?] and schools in that abundance as, I think, no island in the world may have greater store or better fish. For they, sucking of the very water which descendeth

[1] A small salmon.

[2] Horse mackerel

from the high hills mingled with juice and verdor of the palms, cedars, and other sweet woods—which likewise make the herbs, roots, and weeds sweet which grow about the banks—become thereby both fat and wholesome, as must those fish needs be gross, slimy, and corrupt the blood which feed in fens, marishes, ditches, muddy pools, and near unto places where much filth is daily cast forth.

Unscaled fishes, such as Junius calleth *molles pisces,* as trenche[r]s, eel, or lampreys, and such feculent and dangerous snakes, we never saw any, nor may any river be envenomed with them (I pray God) where I come.

I forbear to speak what a sort of whales we have seen hard aboard the shore, followed sometime by the swordfish and the thresher, the sport whereof was not unpleasant: the swordfish with his sharp and needle fin pricking him into the belly when he would sink and fall into the sea; and when he startled upward from his wounds, the thresher with his large fins like flails beating him above water. The examples whereof gives us (saith Oviedus) to understand that in the selfsame peril and danger do men live in this mortal life wherein is no certain security, neither in high estate nor low.[1]

Fowl there is great store, small birds, sparrows fat and plump like a bunting, bigger than ours, robins of divers colors green and yellow, ordinary and familiar in our cabins, and other of less sort; white and gray heronshews, bitterns, teal, snites, crows, and hawks, of which in March we found divers aeries, [and] goshawks and tassels [tercels], oxenbirds,[2] cormorants, baldcoots, moorhens, owls, and bats in great store. And upon New Year's Day in the morning, our governor being walked forth with another gentleman, Master James Swift, each of them with their pieces killed a wild swan in a great sea water bay, or pond, in our island. A kind of web-footed fowl there is, of the bigness of an English green plover, or sea mew, which all the summer we saw not, and in the darkest nights of November and December (for in the night they only feed) they would come forth, but not fly far from home, and hovering in the air and over the sea,

---

[1] Cf. Percy's *Discourse §1–86.* Both our reporters write like eyewitnesses to something, but the reference here to Oviedus is suspicious as the real source.

[2] A double plural for oxbird. Perhaps a sandpiper.

made a strange hollow and harsh howling.[1] Their color is inclining to russet, with white bellies, as are likewise the long feathers of their wings russet and white. These gather themselves together and breed in those islands which are high, and so far alone into the sea that the wild hogs cannot swim over them; and there in the ground they have their burrows, like conies in a warren, and so brought in the loose mould, though not so deep; which birds with a light bough in a dark night, as in our lowbelling,[2] we caught. I have been at the taking of three hundred in an hour, and we might have laden our boats. Our men found a pretty way to take them, which was by standing on the rocks or sands by the seaside, and holloing, laughing, and making the strangest outcry that possibly they could, with the noise whereof the birds would come flocking to that place, and settle upon the very arms and head of him that so cried, and still creep nearer and nearer, answering the noise themselves; by which our men would weigh them with their hand, and which weighed heaviest they took for the best and let the others alone; and so our men would take twenty dozen in two hours of the chiefest of them; and they were a good and well-relished fowl, fat and full as a partridge. In January we had great store of their eggs, which are as great as an hen's egg, and so fashioned and white-shelled, and have no difference in yolk nor white from an hen's egg. There are thousands of these birds, and two or three islands full of their burrows, whither at any time in two hours' warning we could send our cockboat and bring home as many as would serve the whole company; which birds, for their blindness (for they see weakly in the day) and for their cry and hooting, we called the "sea owl." They will bite cruelly with their crooked bills.

We had knowledge that there were wild hogs upon the island at first by our own swine preserved from the wrack and brought to shore. For they straying into the woods, an huge wild boar followed down to our quarter, which at night was watched and taken in this sort: One of Sir George Summers' men went and lay among the swine. When the boar being come and groveled by the sows, he put over his hand and rubbed the side gently of the boar, which then lay

---

[1] This is a most beautiful sentence.

[2] The lowbell was rung to stupefy the birds who were then netted.

still, by which means he fast'ned a rope with a sliding knot to the hinder leg, and so took him, and after him in this sort two or three more.

But in the end (a little business over), our people would go a-hunting with our ship dog, and sometimes bring home thirty, sometimes fifty boars, sows, and pigs in a week alive. For the dog would fasten on them and hold whilest the huntsmen made in. And there be thousands of them in the islands, and at that time of the year—in August, September, October, and November—they were well fed with berries that dropped from the cedars and the palms. And in our quarter we made sties for them, and gathering of these berries served them twice a day, by which means we kept them in good plight. And when there was any fret of weather (for upon every increase of wind the billow would be so great as it was no putting out with our gondol, or canoe) that we could not fish nor take tortoises, then we killed our hogs. But in February, when the palm berries began to be scant or dry, and the cedar berries failed two months sooner, true it is the hogs grew poor. And being taken so, we could not raise them to be better, for besides those berries we had nothing wherewith to frank them. But even then the tortoises came in again, of which we daily both turned up great store, finding them on land as also sculling after them in our boat, struck them with an iron goad and sod, baked, and roasted them.

The tortoise is reasonable toothsome, some say wholesome meat. I am sure our company liked the meat of them very well. And one tortoise would go further amongst them than three hogs. One turtle, for so we called them, feasted well a dozen messes, appointing six to every mess. It is such a kind of meat as a man can neither absolutely call fish nor flesh, keeping most what in the water, and feeding upon sea grass like a heifer in the bottom of the coves and bays, and laying their eggs (of which we should find five hundred at a time in the opening of a she-turtle) in the sand by the shore side, and so covering them close, leave them to the hatching of the sun, like the manatee at Saint Dominique which made the Spanish friars, at their first arrival, make some scruple to eat them on a Friday because in color and taste the flesh is like to morsels of veal. Concerning the laying of their eggs and hatching of their young, Peter Martyr writeth thus in his *Decades of the Ocean:* At such time as the heat of nature moveth them to generation, they came forth of the sea, and making a deep pit in the sand, they lay three or four hundred eggs therein. When they have thus emptied their bag of conception, they put as much of the same again into the pit as may satisfy to cover the eggs, and so resort again unto the sea, nothing careful of their succession. At the day appointed of nature to the procreation of these creatures, there creepeth out a multitude of tortoises as it were pismires out of an anthill, and this only by the heat of the sun, without any help of their parents. Their eggs are as big as geese eggs; and themselves grown to perfection, bigger than great round targets.

II.

Actions and occurrents whiles they continued in the islands – Ravens sent for Virginia – Divers mutinies – Paine executed – Two pinnaces built.

SO SOON as we were a little settled after our landing, with all the conveniency we might, and as the place and our many wants would give us leave, we made up our longboat (as Your Ladyship hath heard) in fashion of a pinnace, fitting her with a little deck made of the hatches of our ruin'd ship, so close that no water could go in her, gave her sails and oars; and entreating with our master's mate, Henry Ravens, who was supposed a sufficient pilot, we found him easily won to make over therewith as a bark of aviso[1] for Virginia; which being in the height of thirty-seven degrees, five degrees from the island which we were, might be some one hundred and forty leagues from us, or thereabouts (reckoning to every degree that lies northeast and westerly twenty-eight English leagues)[2]; who, the

[1] Advice-boat, intelligencer.
[2] At Bermuda a degree of longitude is 60 miles. Cape Henry is 700 miles away.

twenty-eight of August being Monday, with six sailors and our cape merchant, Thomas Whittingham, departed from us out of Gates his Bay, but to our much wonder returned again upon the Wednesday night after, having attempted to have got clear of the island from the north-northeast to the southwest, but could not, as little water as she drew (which might not be above twenty inches), for shoals and breaches; so as he was fain to go out from Summers' Creeks and the same way we came in on the south-southeast of the islands; and from thence we [he?] made to sea the Friday after the first of September, promising if he lived and arrived safe there to return unto us the next new moon with the pinnace belonging to the colony there. According unto which, instructions were directed unto the new lieutenant governor and council from our governor here, for which the islands were appointed carefully to be watched, and fires prepared as beacons to have directed and wafted him in. But two moons were wasted upon the promontory before mentioned, and gave many a long and wished look round about the horizon from the northeast to the southwest, but in vain, discovering nothing all the while, which way soever we turned our eye, but air and sea.

You may please, excellent lady, to know the reason which moved our governor to dispatch this longboat was the care which he took for the estate of the colony in this his enforced absence. For by a long-practiced experience, foreseeing and fearing what innovation and tumult might happily arise amongst the younger and ambitious spirits of the new companies to arrive in Virginia, now coming with him along in this same fleet, he framed his letters to the colony, and by a particular commission confirmed Captain Peter Win his lieutenant governor, with an assistance of six councilors, writing withal to divers and such gentlemen of quality and knowledge of virtue and to such lovers of goodness in this cause whom he knew, entreating them by giving examples in themselves of duty and obedience to assist likewise the said lieutenant governor against such as should attempt the innovating of the person (now named by him) or form of government, which in some articles he did likewise prescribe unto them; and had fair hopes all should go well if these his letters might arrive there, until such time as either some ship there (which he fairly believed) might be moved presently to adventure for him or that it should please the right honorable the lords and the rest of His Majesty's council in England to address thither the right honorable the Lord Lawar (one of more eminency and worthiness), as the project was before his coming forth, whilest by their honorable favors a charitable consideration in like manner might be taken of our estates to redeem us from hence; for which purpose likewise our governor directed a particular letter to the council in England, and sent it to the foresaid Captain Peter Winne, his now-to-be-chosen lieutenant governor, by him to be dispatched (which is the first) from thence into England.

In his absence, Sir George Summers coasted the islands, and drew the former plat of them, and daily fished and hunted for our whole company until the seven and twentieth of November, when then well perceiving that we were not likely to hear from Virginia, and conceiving how the pinnace which Richard Frubbusher was a-building would not be of burthen sufficient to transport all our men from thence into Virginia, especially considering the season of the year wherein we were likely to put off, he consulted with our governor that if he might have two carpenters (for we had four, such as they were) and twenty men over with him into the main island, he would quickly frame up another little bark to second ours, for the better fitting and conveyance of our people. Our governor, with many thanks as the cause required, cherishing this so careful and religious consideration in him, and whose experience likewise was somewhat in these affairs, granted him all things suitable to his desire and to the furthering of the work; who therefore had made ready for him all such tools and instruments as our own use required not. And for him were drawn forth twenty of the ablest and stoutest of the company, and the best of our men to hew and square timber, when himself then with daily pains and labor wrought upon a small vessel which was soon ready as ours—at which we leave him awhile busied, and return to ourselves.

In the mean space did one Frubbusher, born at Gravesend, and at his coming forth now dwelling at Lime House, a painful and well-experienced shipwright and skillful workman, labor the building of a little pinnace, for the furtherance of which the governor dispensed with no travail of his body, nor forbare any care or study of mind, persuading as much and more an ill-qualified parcel of people by his own performance than by authority, thereby to hold them at their work, namely to fell, carry, and saw cedar fit for the carpenter's purpose. For what was so mean whereto he would not himself set his hand, being therefore up early and down late? Yet nevertheless were they hardly drawn to it, as the tortoise to the enchantment, as the proverb is. But his own presence and hand being set to every mean labor and employed so readily to every office made our people at length more diligent and willing to be called thereunto where they should see him before they came—in which we may observe how much example prevails above precepts, and how readier men are to be led by eyes than ears.

And sure it was happy for us, who had now run this fortune and were fallen into the bottom of this misery, that we both had our governor with us, and one so solicitous and careful, whose both example, as I said, and authority could lay shame and command upon our people. Else, I am persuaded, we had most of us finished our days there, so willing were the major part of the common sort, especially when they found such a plenty of victuals, to settle a foundation of ever inhabiting there, as well appeared by many practices of theirs, and perhaps of some of the better sort.

Lo, what are our affections and passions if not rightly squared? How irreligious and irregular they express us!—not perhaps so ill as we would be, but yet as we are: Some dangerous and secret discontents nourished amongst us had like to have been the parents of bloody issues and mischiefs. They began first in the seamen, who in time had fastened onto them, by false baits, many of our landmen likewise, and some of whom, for opinion of their religion, was carried an extraordinary and good respect. The angles wherewith chiefly they thus hooked in these disquieted pools were how that in Virginia nothing but wretchedness and labor must be expected, with many wants, and a churlish entreaty, there being [there] neither that fish, flesh, nor fowl which here—without wasting on the one part or watching on theirs, or any threat'ning and air of authority—at ease and pleasure might be enjoyed; and since both in the one and the other place they were, for the time, to lose the fruition both of their friends and country, as good and better were it for them to repose and seat them where they should have the least outward wants the while.

This thus preached and published each to other, though by such who never had been more onward towards Virginia than before this voyage a sculler could happily row him (and what hath a more adamantive power to draw unto it the consent and attraction of the idle, untoward, and wretched number of the many than liberty and fullness of sensuality?) begat such a murmur and such a discontent and disunion of hearts and hands from this labor and forwarding the means of redeeming us from hence as each one wrought with his mate how to divorce him from the same.

And first, and it was the first of September, a conspiracy was discovered, of which six were found principals, who had promised each unto the other not to set their hands to any travail or endeavor which might expedite or forward this pinnace. And each of these had severally, according to appointment, sought his opportunity to draw the smith and one of our carpenters, Nicholas Bennit, who made much profession of Scripture (a mutinous and dissembling impostor!), the captain and one of the chief persuaders of others who afterwards brake from the society of the colony and like outlaws retired into the woods to make a settlement and habitation there on their party, with whom they purposed to leave our quarter and possess another island by themselves. But this happily found out, they were condemned to the same punishment which they would have chosen—but without smith or carpenter!—and to an island far by itself they were carried and there left. Their names were John Want—the chief of them, an Essex man of Newport by Saffron Walden,[1] both seditious and a sectary in points of religion, in his own prayers much devout and frequent, but hardly drawn to the public, insomuch as being suspected by our minister for a Brownist, he was often compelled to the common liturgy and form of prayer—[and] the rest of the confederates were Christopher Carter, Francis Pearepoint, William Brian, William Martin, Richard Knowles.

---

[1] Strachey's own home town, Newport being five miles away down the London road. Gayley thinks this detail proves that Strachey is writing to the Lady Howard, who was also of this neighborhood.

But soon they missed comfort, who were far removed from our store. Besides, the society of their acquaintance had wrought in some of them, if not a loathsomeness of their offense, yet a sorrow that their complement was not more full, and therefore a weariness of their being thus untimely prescribed[1]; insomuch as many humble petitions were sent unto our governor fraught full of their seeming sorrow and repentance and earnest vows to redeem the former trespass with example of duties in them all to the common cause and general business; upon which our governor, not easy to admit any accusation, and hard to remit an offense, but at all times sorry in the punishment of him in whom may appear either shame or contrition, was easily content to reacknowledge them again.

Yet could not this be any warning to others who more subtly began to shake the foundation of our quiet safety. And therein did one Stephen Hopkins commence the first act or overture, a fellow who had much knowledge in the Scriptures and could reason well therein, whom our minister therefore chose to be his clerk to read the psalms and chapters upon Sundays at the assembly of the congregation under him; who in January the twenty-four [1610] brake with one Samuel Sharpe and Humfrey Reede—who presently discovered it to the governor—and alleged substantial arguments both civil and divine (the Scripture falsely quoted!) that it was no breach of honesty, conscience, nor religion to decline from the obedience of the governor, or refuse to go any further led by his authority, except it so pleased themselves, since the authority ceased when the wrack was committed, and with it they were all then freed from the government of any man; and for a matter of conscience it was not unknown to the meanest how much we were therein bound each one to provide for himself and his own family. For which were two apparent reasons to stay them even in this place: first, abundance by God's providence of all manner of good food; next, some hope in reasonable time, when they might grow weary of the place, to build a small bark with the skill and help of the aforesaid Nicholas Bennit, whom they insinuated to them—albeit he was now absent from his quarter and working in the main island with Sir George Summers

[1] Confined.

upon his pinnace—to be of the conspiracy, that so might get clear from hence at their own pleasures; [that] when in Virginia, the first would be assuredly wanting, and they might well fear to be detained in that country by the authority of the commander thereof, and their whole life to serve the turns of the adventurers with their travails and labors.

This being thus laid, and by such a one who had gotten an opinion, as I before rememb'red, of religion (when it was declared by those two accusers), not knowing what further ground it had or complices, it pleased the governor to let this his factious offense to have a public affront and contestation by these two witnesses before the whole company, who at the tolling of a bell assemble[d] before a *corps du guard,* where the prisoner was brought forth in manacles, and both accused and suffered to make at large to every particular his answer, which was only full of sorrow and tears, pleading simplicity[1] and denial. But he being only found at this time both the captain and the follower of this mutiny, and generally held worthy to satisfy the punishment of his offense with the sacrifice of his life, our governor passed the sentence of a martial court upon him, such as belongs to mutiny and rebellion. But so penitent he was, and made so much moan, alleging the ruin of his wife and children in this his trespass, as it wrought in the hearts of all the better sort of the company, who therefore with humble entreaties and earnest supplications went unto our governor, whom they besought, as likewise did Captain Newport and myself, and never left him until we had got his pardon.[2]

In these dangers and devilish disquiets, whilest the Almighty God wrought for us and sent us, miraculously delivered from the calamities of the sea, all blessings upon the shore to content and bind us to gratefulness, thus enraged amongst ourselves to the destruction each of other, into what a mischief and misery had we been given up had we not had a governor with his authority to have suppressed the

---

1 Ignorance.

2 Eleven years later Hopkins found himself with his wife and children cast up on another rock, namely, the one at Plymouth, with Brewster and Carver. We can see here for ourselves why it was so important to get him and others like him to sign the Mayflower Compact.

same? Yet was there a worse practice, faction, and conjuration afoot, deadly and bloody, in which the life of our governor with many others were threat'ned, and could not but miscarry in his fall. But such is ever the will of God, who in the execution of His judgments breaketh the firebrands upon the head of him who first kindleth them!

There were who conceived that our governor indeed neither durst nor had authority to put in execution or pass the act of justice upon anyone, how treacherous or impious soever, their own opinions so much deceiving them for the unlawfulness of any act which they would execute, daring to justify among themselves that if they should be apprehended before the performance, they should happily suffer as martyrs. They persevered therefore not only to draw unto them such a number and associates as they could work into the abandoning of our governor and to the inhabiting of this island, they had now purposed [also] to have made a surprise of the storehouse, and to have forced from thence what was therein either of meal, cloth, cables, arms, sails, oars, or what else it pleased God that we had recovered from the wrack, and was to serve our general necessity and use, either for the relief of us while we stayed here, or for the carrying of us from this place again, when our pinnace should have been furnished.

But as all giddy and lawless attempts have always something of imperfection,[1] and that as well by the property of the action, which holdeth of disobedience and rebellion (both full of fear), as through the ignorance of the devisers themselves; so in this, besides those defects, there were some of the association who, not strong enough fortified in their own conceits, brake from the plot itself and before the time was ripe for the execution thereof discovered the whole order and every agent and actor thereof; who nevertheless were not suddenly apprehended by reason the confederates were divided and separated in place, some with us, and the chief with Sir George Summers in his island and indeed all his whole company, but good watch passed upon them, every man from thenceforth commanded

[1] "Evil, as it hath a deficient cause, so, in and before the effects, defects are found." (margin note)

to wear his weapon, without which before we freely walked from quarter to quarter and conversed among ourselves, and every man advised to stand upon his guard, his own life not being in safety whilest his next neighbor was not to be trusted.

The sentinels and nightwarders doubled, the passages of both the quarters were carefully observed, by which means nothing was further attempted until a gentleman amongst them, one Henry Paine, the thirteenth of March—full of mischief and every hour preparing something or other, stealing swords, adzes, axes, hatchets, saws, augers, planes, mallets, etc. to make good his own bad end—his watch night coming about, and being called by the captain of the same to be upon the guard, did not only give his said commander evil language but struck at him, doubled his blows, and when he was not suffered to close with him, went off the guard, scoffing at the double diligence and attendance of the watch appointed by the governor for much purpose, as he said. Upon which the watch telling him if the governor should understand of this his insolency, it might turn him to much blame, and happily be as much as his life were worth, the said Paine replied with a settled and bitter violence, and in such unreverent terms as I should offend the modest ear too much to express it in his own phrase, but the contents were how that the governor had no authority of that quality to justify upon anyone, how mean soever in the colony, an action of that nature, and therefore let the governor (said he) kiss, etc. Which words being with the omitted additions brought the next day unto every common and public discourse, at length they were delivered over to the governor, who examining well the fact—the transgression so much the more exemplary and odious as being in a dangerous time, in a confederate, and the success of the same wish'dly[1] listened after—with a doubtful conceit what might be the issue of so notorious a boldness and impudency, calling the said Paine before him and the whole company, where, being soon convinced both by the witness of the commander, and many which were upon the watch with him, our governor, who had now the eyes of the whole colony fixed upon him, condemned him to be instantly hanged; and the ladder being

[1] Intently.

ready, after he had made many confessions, he earnestly desired, being a gentleman, that he might be shot to death; and towards the evening he had his desire, the sun and his life setting together.

But for the other which were with Sir George, upon the Sunday following, the bark being now in good forwardness and ready to launch in short time from that place, as we supposed, to meet ours at a pond of fresh water where they were both to be moored until such time as, being fully tackled, the wind should serve fair for our putting to sea together, being the eighteenth of March, hearing of Payne's death, and fearing he had appeached them,[1] and discovered the attempt—who, poor gentleman, therein in so bad a cause was too secret and constant to his own faith engaged unto them, and as little needed as urged thereunto, though somewhat was voluntarily delivered by him—by a mutual consent forsook their labor and Sir George Summers, and like outlaws betook them to the wild woods.

Whether mere rage and greediness after some little pearl, as it was thought, wherewith they conceived they should forever enrich themselves, and saw how to obtain the same easily in this place, or whether the desire forever to inhabit here, or what other secret else moved them thereunto, true it is they sent an audacious and formal petition to our governor, subscribed with all their names and seals, not only entreating him that they might stay here but with great art importuned him that he would perform other conditions with them, and not waive nor evade from some of his own promises, as, namely, to furnish each of them with two suits of apparel and contribute meal ratably for one whole year, so much among them as they had weekly now, which was one pound and an half a week, for such had been our proportion for nine months.

Our governor answered this their petition, writing to Sir George Summers to this effect, that true it was at their first arrival upon this island, when it was feared how our means would not extend to the making of a vessel capable and large enough to transport all our countrymen at once—indeed out of his Christian consideration mourning for such his countrymen who, coming under his command, he foresaw that for a while he was like enough to leave here

[1] Named them in an accusation.

behind, compelled by tyranny of necessity—his purpose was not yet to forsake them so as given up like savages, but to leave them all things fitting to defend them from want and wretchedness—as much at least as lay in his power to spare from the present use and perhaps *necessity* of others whose fortunes should be to be transported with him—for one whole year or more, if so long by any casualty the ships which he would send unto them might be stayed before their arrival, so many hazards accompanying the sea; but withal entreated Sir George to remember unto his company, if by any means he could learn where they were, how he had vowed unto him that if either his own means, his authority in Virginia, or love with his friends in England could dispatch for them sooner, how far it was from him to let them remain abandoned and neglected without their redemption so long; and then proceeded, requesting Sir George Summers again to signify unto them, since now our own pinnace did arise to that burthen and that it would sufficiently transport them all, beside the necessity of any other bark; and yet, that since his bark was now ready too, that those consultations, howsoever charitable and most passionate in themselves, might determine as taken away thereby, and therefore that he should now be pleased to advise them well how unanswerable this grant or consent of his should be, first, to His Majesty for so many of his subjects, next, to the adventurers, and lastly, what an imputation and infamy it might be to both their own proper reputations and honors, having each of them authority in their places to compel the adversant and irregular multitude at any time to what should be obedient and honest; which, if they should not execute, the blame would not lie upon the people (at all times wavering and insolent) but upon themselves, so weak and unworthy in their command—and moreover entreated him[1] by any secret practice to apprehend them, since that the obstinate and precipitate many were no more in such a condition and state to be favored than the murmuring and mutiny of such rebellious and turbulent humorists who had not conscience nor knowledge to draw in the yoke of goodness—and in the business for which they were sent out of England, for which likewise at the expense and charge of the

[1] I.e., Gates entreated Somers.

adventurers they were to him committed; and that the meanest in the whole fleet stood the Company in no less than twenty pounds for his own personal transportation and things necessary to accompany him; and therefore lovingly conjured Sir George, by the worthiness of his heretofore well-maintained reputation, and by the powers of his own judgment, and by the virtue of that ancient love and friendship which had these many years been settled between them, to do his best to give this revolted company, if he could send unto them, the consideration of these particulars, and so work with them, if he might, that by fair means (the mutiny reconciled) they would at length survey their own errors, which he would be as ready upon their rend'ring and coming into pardon as he did now pity them, assuring them in general and particular that whatsoever they had sinisterly committed or practiced hitherto against the laws of duty and honesty should not in any sort be imputed against them; in which good office Sir George Summers did so nobly work and heartily labor as he brought most of them in, and indeed all but Christopher Carter and Robert Waters, who by no means would anymore come amongst Sir George's men, hearing that Sir George had commanded his men indeed (since they would not be entreated by fair means) to surprise them, if they could, by any device or force; from which time they grew so cautelous and wary for their own ill as at our coming away we were fain to leave them behind. That Waters was a sailor who at his first landing upon the island (as after you shall hear) killed another fellow sailor of his, the body of the murthered and murtherer so dwelling, as prescribed now, together.[1]

During our time of abode upon these islands, we had daily every Sunday two sermons preached by our minister,[2] besides every morning and evening at the ringing of a bell we repaired all to public prayer, at what time the names of our whole company were called

---

[1] "Waters and Carter stand out and are left behind." (margin note) Edward Waters reached Virginia in 1617 on a mission to obtain hogs, but settled at Blunt Point on the lower James, and with his wife was carried off by the Warraskoyacks during the massacre of March 1622. They stole a canoe, recrossed the river, and escaped with their lives.

[2] "Religious exercises performed by Master Bucke." (margin note)

by bill, and such as were wanting were duly punished.

The contents for the most part of all our preacher's sermons were especially of thankfulness and unity, etc.

It pleased God also to give us opportunity to perform all the other offices and rites of our Christian profession in this island, as marriage, for the six and twentieth of November [1609] we had one of Sir George Summers his men, his cook named Thomas Powell, who married a maidservant of one Mistress Horton, whose name was Elizabeth Persons; and upon Christmas Eve, as also once before, the first of October.

Our minister preached a godly sermon, which being ended, he celebrated a communion, at the partaking whereof our governor was and the greatest part of our company. And the eleventh of February [1610], we had the child of one John Rofe [Rolfe] christened, a daughter, to which Captain Newport and myself were witnesses, and the aforesaid Mistress Horton, and we named it Bermuda; as also the five and twentieth of March, the wife of one Edward Eason, being delivered the week before of a boy, had him then christened, to which Captain Newport and myself and Master James Swift were godfathers, and we named it Bermudas.

Likewise we buried five of our company: Jeffery Briars, Richard Lewis, William Hitchman, and my goddaughter Bermuda Rolfe, and one untimely Edward Samuell, a sailor, being villainously killed by the foresaid Robert Waters, a sailor likewise, with a shovel, who strake him therewith under the lift of the ear, for which he was apprehended and appointed to be hanged the next day, the fact being done in the twilight. But being bound fast to a tree all night with many ropes, and a guard of five or six to attend him, his fellow sailors, watching the advantage of the sentinels sleeping, in despite and disdain that justice should be showed upon a sailor and that one of their crew should be an example to others, not taking into consideration the unmanliness of the murther nor the horror of the sin, they cut his bands and conveyed him into the woods, where they fed him nightly and closely, who afterward, by the mediation of Sir George Summers, upon many conditions had his trial respited by our governor.

We had brought our pinnace so forward by this time as the eight and twentieth of August we having laid her keel; the six and twentieth of February we now began to caulk: Old cables we had preserved unto us which afforded oakum enough; and one barrel of pitch and another of tar we likewise saved, which served our use some little way upon the bilge. We breamed her otherwise with lime made of whelk shells, and an hard white stone which we burned in a kiln, slaked with fresh water, and tempered with tortoise's oil.[1] The thirtieth of March, being Friday, we towed her out in the morning spring tide from the wharf where she was built, buoying her with four cask in her run only, which opened into the northwest, and into which, when the breeze stood north and by west with any stiff gale, and upon the spring tides, the sea would increase with that violence (especially twice it did so) as at the first time—before our governor had caused a solid causey of an hundred load of stone to be brought from the hills and neighbor rocks, and round about her ribs from stem to stem, where it made a pointed balk, and thereby brake the violence of the flow and billow—it endangered her overthrow and ruin, being green, as it were, upon the stocks. With much difficulty, diligence, and labor, we saved her at the first, all her bases, shores, and piles, which underset her, being almost carried from her, which was the second of January, when her knees were not set to, nor one joint firm.[2]

We launched her unrigged to carry her to a little round island lying west-northwest, and close aboard to the backside of our island, both nearer the ponds and wells of some fresh water, as also from thence to make our way to the sea the better, the channel being there sufficient and deep enough to lead her forth when her masts, sails, and all her trim should be about her. She was forty foot by the keel and nineteen foot broad at the beam, six foot floor; her rake forward was fourteen foot; her rake aft from the top of her post, which was twelve foot long, was three foot; she was eight foot deep under her beam; between her decks she was four foot and an half, with a rising of half a foot more under her forecastle of purpose to scour the deck with small shot, if at any time we should be boarded by the enemy.

---

[1] To "bream" means to "sweep" a ship's bottom of growth and fouling, but here Strachey seems to mean that they painted their new hull.

[2] The passage mixes the accounts of her building and launching.

She had a fall of eighteen inches aft to make her steerage and her great cabin the more large; her steerage was five foot long and six foot high, with a close gallery right aft, with a window on each side and two right aft. The most part of her timber was cedar, which we found to be bad for shipping for that it is wondrous false inward and, besides, it is so spalt or brickle that it will make no good planks. Her beams were all oak of our ruin ship, and some planks in her bow of oak, and all the rest as is aforesaid. When she began to swim upon her launching, our governor called her the *Deliverance;* and she might be some eighty tons of burthen.

Before we quitted our old quarter, and dislodged to the fresh water with our pinnace, our governor set up in Sir George Summers' garden a fair mnemosynon,[1] in figure of a cross made of some of the timber of our ruined ship, which was screwed in with strong and great trunnels to a mighty cedar, which grew in the middest of the said garden, and whose top and upper branches he caused to be lopped, that the violence of the wind and weather might have the less power over her.

In the middest of the cross, our governor fastened the picture of His Majesty in a piece of silver of twelve pence, and on each side of the cross he set an inscription graven in copper in the Latin and English to this purpose:

> "In memory of our great deliverance, both from a mighty storm and leak, we have set up this to the honor of God. It is the spoil of an English ship of three hundred ton, called the *Sea Venture,* bound with seven ships more, from which the storm divided us, to Virginia, or Nova Britannia, in America. In it were two knights, Sir Thomas Gates, knight, governor of the English forces and colony there; and Sir George Summers, knight, admiral of the seas. Her captain was Christopher Newport; passengers and mariners she had beside (which came all safe to land) one hundred and fifty. We were forced to run her ashore, by reason of her leak, under a point that bore southeast from the northern point of the island, which we discovered first the eight and twentieth of July, 1609."

About the last of April, Sir George Summers launched his pinnace, and brought her from his building bay in the main island into the

---

[1] Memorial.

channel where ours did ride. And she was by the keel nine and twenty foot; at the beam fifteen foot and an half; at the luff[1] fourteen; at the transom nine; and she was eight foot deep, and drew six foot water; and he called her the *Patience.*

III.

Their departure from Bermuda and arrival in Virginia – Miseries there – Departure and return upon the Lord La Warre's arriving – James Town described.

FROM THIS TIME we only awaited a favorable westerly wind to carry us forth, which longer than usual now kept at the east and southeast, the way which we were to go. The tenth of May early, Sir George Summers and Captain Newport went off with their longboats, and with two canoas buoyed the channel which we were to lead it out in, and which was no broader from shoals on the one side and rocks on the other than about three times the length of our pinnace. About ten of the clock, that day being Thursday, we set sail an easy gale, the wind at south, and by reason no more wind blew, we were fain to tow her with our longboat. Yet neither with the help of that were we able to fit our buoys, but even when we came just upon them we struck a rock on the starboard side, over which the buoy rid; and had it not been a soft rock, by which means she bore it before her and crushed it to pieces, God knows we might have been like enough to have returned anew and dwelt there after ten months of carefulness and great labor a longer time.

But God was more merciful unto us: When she struck upon the rock, the cockswain, one Walsingham, being in the boat, with a quick spirit, when we were all amazed, and our hearts failed [...] and so by God's goodness we led it out at three fadom, and three fadom

---

[1] "The fullest and broadest part of a ship's bow, where the sides begin to curve in towards the stem." (OED)

and a half water. The wind served us easily all that day and the next, when (God be ever praised for it) to the no little joy of us all we got clear of the islands; after which, holding a southerly course, for seven days we had the wind sometimes fair and sometimes scarce and contrary, in which time we lost Sir George Summers twice, albeit we still spared him our main topsail, and sometimes our forecourse too.[1]

The seventeenth of May, we saw change of water, and had much rubbish swim by our ship side, whereby we knew we were not far from land. The eighteenth about midnight, we sounded with the dipsing lead and found thirty-seven fadom. The nineteenth in the morning, we sounded and had nineteen and an half fadom, stony and sandy ground. The twentieth about midnight, we had a marvelous sweet smell from the shore, as from the coast of Spain short of the Straits, strong and pleasant, which did not a little glad us. In the morning by daybreak, so soon as one might well see from the foretop, one of the sailors descried land. About an hour after, I went up and might discover two hummocks to the southward, from which northward all along lay the land which we were to coast to Cape Henrie. About seven of the clock, we cast forth an anchor because the tide by reason of the freshet that set into the bay make a strong ebb there, and the wind was but easy; so as not being able to stem the tide, we purposed to lie at an anchor until the next flood. But the wind coming southwest a loom gale[2] about eleven, we set sail again, and having got over the bar, bore in for the cape.

This is the famous Chesipiacke Bay, which we have called, in honor of our young prince, Cape Henrie, over against which within the bay lieth another headland which we called, in honor of our princely Duke of York, Cape Charles; and these lie northeast and by east, and southwest and by west, and they may be distant each from the other in breadth seven leagues, between which the sea runs in as broad as between Queenborough and Leigh.[3] Indeed, it is a goodly bay and a fairer not easily to be found.

The one and twentieth, being Monday in the morning, we came

---

[1] I.e., they furled these sails hoping the slower *Patience* would catch up.

[2] Gentle breeze.

[3] The mouth of the Thames is five to six miles wide. The Virginia capes stand eleven miles apart.

up within two miles of Point Comfort, when the captain of the fort discharged a warning piece at us; whereupon we came to an anchor, and sent off our longboat to the fort to certify who we were. By reason of the shoals which lie on the south side, this fort easily commands the mouth of the river, albeit it is as broad as between Greenwich and the Isle of Dogs.[1]

True it is such who talked with our men from the shore delivered how safely all our ships the last year (excepting only the admiral and the little pinnace in which one Michael Philes commanded, of some twenty ton, which we towed astern till the storm blew) arrived; and how our people, well increased, had therefore builded this fort; only we could not learn anything of our longboat sent from the Bermudas but what we gathered by the Indians themselves, especially from Powhatan, who would tell our men of such a boat landed in one of his rivers, and would describe the people and make much scoffing sport thereat; by which we have gathered that it is most likely how it arrived upon our coast and, not meeting with our river, were taken at some time or other at some advantage by the savages, and so cut off.

When our skiff came up again, the good news of our ships' and men's arrival the last year did not a little glad our governor, who went soon ashore and as soon (contrary to all our fair hopes) had new unexpected, uncomfortable, and heavy news of a worse condition of our people above at James Town.

Upon Point Comfort our men did the last year (as you have heard) raise a little fortification; which since hath been better perfected, and is likely to prove a strong fort, and is now kept by Captain James Davies with forty men, and hath to name Algernoone Fort, so called by Captain George Percy, whom we found at our arrival president of the colony, and at this time likewise in the fort.

When we got into the point, which was the one and twentieth of May, being Monday about noon, where riding before an Indian town called Kecoughton, a mighty storm of thunder, lightning, and rain gave us a shrewd and fearful welcome.

---

[1] I.e., three miles downstream from London Bridge where the Thames is 500 yards across.

From hence in two days—only by the help of tides, no wind stirring—we plied it sadly up the river, and the three and twentieth of May, we cast anchor before James Town, where we landed, and our much grieved governor, first visiting the church, caused the bell to be rung, at which all such as were able to come forth of their houses repaired to church, where our minister, Master Bucke, made a zealous and sorrowful prayer, finding all things so contrary to our expectations, so full of misery and misgovernment. After service, our governor caused me to read his commission, and Captain Percie, then president, delivered up unto him his commission, the old patent, and the council seal.

Viewing the fort, we found the palisadoes torn down, the ports open, the gates from off the hinges, and empty houses, which [the] owners' death had taken from them, rent up and burnt, rather than the dwellers would step into the woods a stone's cast off from them to fetch other firewood. And it is true the Indian killed as fast without, if our men stirred but beyond the bounds of their blockhouse, as famine and pestilence did within, with many more particularities of their sufferances brought upon them by their own disorders the last year than I have heart to express.

In this desolation and misery our governor found the condition and state of the colony and, which added more to his grief, no hope how to amend it or save his own company and those yet remaining alive from falling into the like necessities. For we had brought from the Bermudas no greater store of provision (fearing no such accidents possible to befall the colony here) than might well serve one hundred and fifty for a sea voyage; and it was not possible at this time of the year to amend it by any help from the Indian. For besides that they at their best have little more than from hand to mouth, it was now likewise but their seed time and all their corn scarce put into the ground. Nor was there at the fort, as they whom we found related unto us, any means to take fish, neither sufficient seine nor other convenient net; and yet, if there had, there was not one eye of sturgeon yet come into the river.

All which considered, it pleased our governor to make a speech unto the company, giving them to understand that what provision he had they should equally share with him, and if he should find it not possible and easy to supply them with something from the country by the endeavors of his able men, he would make ready and transport them all into their native country, accommodating them the best that he could, at which there was a general acclamation and shout of joy on both sides, for even our own men began to be disheartened and faint when they saw this misery amongst the others, and no less threat'ned unto themselves. In the meanwhile, our governor published certain orders and instructions, which he enjoined them strictly to observe, the time that he should stay amongst them, which being written out fair were set up upon a post in the church for everyone to take notice of.[1]

If I should be examined from whence and by what occasion all these disasters and afflictions descended upon our people, I can only refer you (honored lady) to the book which the adventurers have sent hither entituled *Advertisements unto the Colony in Virginia*, wherein the ground and causes are favorably abridged from whence these miserable effects have been produced, not excusing likewise the form of government of some error, which was not powerful enough among so heady a multitude, especially as those who arrived here in the supply sent the last year with us, with whom the better authority and government, now changed into an absolute command, came along, and had been as happily established, had it pleased God that we with them had reached our wished harbor.

Unto such calamity can sloth, riot, and vanity bring the most settled and plentiful estate. Indeed (right noble lady), no story can remember unto us more woes and anguishes than these people thus governed have both suffered and pull'd upon their own heads. And yet true it is some of them whose voices and command might not be heard may easily be absolved from the guilt hereof, as standing untouched and upright in their innocencies, whilest the privy factionaries shall never find time nor darkness to wipe away or cover their ignoble and irreligious practices, who, it may be, lay all the discredits

---

[1] *Laws Divine, Moral,* etc. written out by Strachey himself and published in his lifetime, epitomized in the Introduction, 27.

and imputations the while upon the country.

But under pardon let me speak freely to them: Let them remember that if riot and sloth should both meet in anyone of their best families in a country most stored with abundance and plenty in England—continual wasting, no husbandry, the old store still spent on, no order for new provisions—what better could befall unto the inhabitants, landlords, and tenants of that corner than necessarily following cleanness of teeth, famine, and death? Is it not the sentence and doom of the wise man? "Yet a little sleep, a little slumber, and a little folding of the hands to sleep: So thy poverty cometh as one that traveleth by the way, and thy necessity like an armed man."[1] And with this idleness, when something was in store, all wasteful courses exercised to the heighth, and the headless multitude, some neither of quality nor religion, not employed to the end for which they were sent hither, no, not compelled, since in themselves unwilling to sow corn for their own bellies, nor to put a root, herb, etc. for their own particular good in their gardens or elsewhere—I say in this neglect and sensual surfeit, all things suffered to run on, to lie sick and languish, must it be expected that health, plenty, and all the goodness of a well-ordered state of necessity for all this to flow in this country?

You have a right and noble heart, worthy lady; be judge of the truth herein. Then suffer it not be concluded unto you, nor believe, I beseech you, that the wants and wretchedness which they have endured ascend out of the poverty and vileness of the country, whether be respected the land or rivers, the one and the other, having not only promised but poured enough in their veins to convince[2] them in such calumnies, and to quit those common calamities which, as the shadow accompanies the body, the precedent neglects touched at, if truly followed, and wrought upon. What England may boast of, having the fair hand of husbandry to manure and dress it, God and nature have favorably bestowed upon this country; and as it hath given unto it, both by situation, height,[3] and soil, all those (past hopes) assurances which follow our well-planted native country and

---

[1] Proverbs 6:11–12.

[2] Convict.

[3] Latitude, implying climate.

others lying under the same influence. If as ours the country and soil might be improved and drawn forth, so hath it endowed it, as is most certain, with many more which England fetcheth far unto her from elsewhere. For first we have experience and even our eyes' witness, how young soever we are to the country, that no country yieldeth goodlier corn nor more manifold increase. Large fields we have as prospects of the same, and not far from our palisado. Besides, we have thousands of goodly vines in every hedge and bosk[1] running along the ground, which yield a plentiful grape in their kind. Let me appeal then to knowledge, if these natural vines were planted, dressed, and ordered by skillful vignerons, whether we might not make a perfect grape and fruitful vintage in short time.

And we have made trial of our own English seeds, kitchen herbs, and roots, and find them to prosper as speedily as in England.

Only let me truly acknowledge they are not [but?] an hundred or two of deboist[2] hands, drop'd forth by year after year, with penury and leisure, ill provided for before they come and worse to be governed when they are here, men of such distempered bodies and infected minds, whom no examples daily before their eyes, either of goodness or punishment, can deter from their habitual impieties, or terrify from a shameful death—that must be the *carpenters* and *workmen* in this so glorious a-building!

Then let no rumor of the poverty of the country—as if in the womb thereof there lay not those elemental seeds which could produce as many fair births of plenty and increase and better hopes than any land under the heaven to which the sun is no nearer a neighbor—I say, let no imposture rumor nor any fame of some one or a few more changeable actions, interposing by the way or at home, wave [off] any man's fair purposes hitherward or wrest them to a declining and falling off from the business.

I will acknowledge, dear lady, I have seen much propenseness already towards the unity and general[3] endeavors. How contentedly do such as labor with us go forth when men of rank and quality assist and set on their labors! I have seen it, and I protest it; I have heard

[1] Thicket.
[2] Debauched.
[3] Collective.

the inferior people with alacrity of spirit profess that they should never refuse to do their best in the practice of their sciences and knowledges when such worthy and noble gentlemen go in and out before them, and not only so but, as the occasion shall be offered, no less help them with their hand than defend them with their sword.

And it is to be understood that such as labor are not yet so taxed but that easily they perform the same, and ever by ten of the clock have done their morning's work. At what time they have their allowances set out ready for them, and until it be three of the clock again, they take their own pleasure. And afterwards with the sun set, their day's labor is finished. In all which courses, if the business be continued, I doubt nothing with God's favor towards us but to see it in time a country, an haven, and a staple,[1] fitted for such a trade as shall advance assureder increase both to the adventurers and free burghers thereof than any trade in Christendom or than that—even in her early days when Michael Cavacco the Greek did first discover it to our English factor in Poland—which extends itself now from Calpe and Avila to the bottom of Sidon, and so wide as Alexandria and all the ports and havens north and south through the Arches[2] to Chio, Smyrna, Troy, the Hellespont, and up to Pompey's Pillar, which as a Pharos, or watchtower, stands upon the wondrous opening into the Euxine Sea.[3]

From the three and twentieth of May unto the seventh of June, our governor attempted and made trial of all the ways that both his own judgment could prompt him in and the advice of Captain George Percy and those gentlemen whom he found of the council when he came in, as of others whom he caused to deliver their knowledges concerning the state and condition of the country. But after much debating, it could not appear how possibly they might preserve themselves—reserving that little which we brought from the Bermudas in our ships, and was upon all occasions to stand good by us—ten days from starving.

---

[1] Hub of commerce.
[2] The Greek Archipelago.
[3] The Black Sea. A lighthouse built by the Roman consul Pompey that marked the northern entrance to the Bosporus.

For besides that the Indians were of themselves poor, they were forbidden likewise by their subtle King Powhatan at all to trade with us; and not only so but to endanger and assault any boat upon the river or straggler out of the fort by land, by which not long before our arrival our people had a large boat cut off and divers of our men killed, even within command of our blockhouse, as likewise they shot two of our people to death after we had been four and five days come in. And yet would they dare then to enter our ports and truck with us, as they counterfeited underhand, when indeed they came but as spies to discover our strength, trucking with us upon such hard conditions that our governor might very well see their subtlety, and therefore neither could well endure nor would continue it. And I may truly say beside, so had our men abased, and to such a contempt had they brought, the value of our copper that a piece which would have bought a bushel of their corn in former time would not now buy a little cade, or basket, of a pottle.[1]

And for this misgovernment chiefly our colony is much bound to the mariners, who never yet in any voyage hither but have made a prey of our poor people in want, insomuch as unless they might advance four or five for one, how assured soever of the payments of their bills of exchange, they would not spare them a dust of corn nor a pint of beer to give unto them the least comfort or relief, although that beer purloined and stol'n perhaps either from some particular supply or from the general store, so uncharitable a parcel of people they be and ill conditioned. I myself have heard the master of a ship say even upon the arrival of this fleet with the lord governor and captain general, when the said master was treated with for such commodities as he brought to sell, that unless he might have an East Indian increase, four for one, all charges cleared, he would not part with a can of beer! Besides, to do us more villainy and mischief, they would send off their longboats full by night, and well guarded make out to the neighbor villages and towns and there, contrary to the articles of the fort, which now pronounce death for a trespass of that quality, truck with the Indians giving for their trifles otter skins, beavers, *rokoone* furs, bears skins, etc., so large a quantity and

[1] Half a dry gallon.

measure of copper as when the truck master for the colony in the daytime offered trade, the Indians would laugh and scorn the same, telling what bargains they met withal by night from our *mangot quintons,* so calling our great ships, by which means the market with them forestalled thus by these dishonest men, I may boldly say they have been a consequent cause this last year to the death and starving of many a worthy spirit.

But I hope to see a true amendment and reformation as well of those as of divers other intolerable abuses thrust upon the colony by these shameless people, as also for the transportation of such provisions and supplies as are sent hither and come under the charge of pursers—a parcel, fragment, and odd ends of fellows, dependencies to the others—a better course thought upon; of which supplies, never yet came into the store or to the parties unto whom such supplies were sent, by relation hitherto, a moiety or third part.

For the speedy redress of this, being so sovereign a point, I understand how the lord governor and captain general hath advised unto the council that there may be no more provisions at all delivered unto pursers but hath entreated to have the provision thus ordered. He would have a commissary general of the victuals to be appointed who, receiving the store for the colony by indenture from the treasurer, and victualers in England, may keep a just account what the gross amounteth unto, and what is transported every voyage, in several kinds, as of bread, meat, beer, wine, etc., which said commissary shall deliver over the same to the master of every ship, and take an indenture from the said master of what he hath in charge and what he is to deliver to the treasurer of the store in Virginia; of which, if any be wanting, he the said master shall make it good out of his own entertainment. Otherwise the pursers, stewards, coopers, and quartermasters will be sure still not only to give themselves and their friends double allowances, but think it all well gotten that they can purloin and steal away.

Besides that the Indian thus evil entreated us, the river, which were wont before this time of the year to be plentiful of sturgeon, had not now a fish to be seen in it. And albeit we labored and haul'd our net twenty times day and night, yet we took not so much as would content half the fishermen. Our governor therefore sent away his longboat to coast the river downward as far as Point Comfort, and from thence to Cape Henry and Cape Charles and all within the bay, which after a seven nights' trial and travail returned without any fruits of their labors, scarce getting so much fish as served their own company.

And to take anything from the Indian by force we never used nor willingly ever will. And though they had well deserved it, yet it was not now time, for they did, as I said before, but then *set* their corn, and at their best they had but from hand to mouth; so as what now remained—such as we found in the fort—had we stay'd but four days, had doubtless been the most part of them starved. For their best relief was only mushrooms and some herbs, which sod together made but a thin and unsavory broth, and swelled them much.

The pity hereof moved our governor to draw forth such provision as he had brought, proportioning a measure equally to everyone alike. But then our governor began to examine how long this his store would hold out and found it, husbanded to the best advantage, not possible to serve longer than sixteen days, after which nothing was to be possibly supposed out of the country, as before remem-b'red, nor remained there then any means to transport him else-where. Whereupon he then ent'red into the consultation with Sir George Summers and Captain Newport, calling unto the same the gentlemen and council of the former government, entreating both the one and the other to advise with him what was best to be done. The provision which they both had aboard, himself and Sir George Summers, was examined and delivered, how it, being rack'd to the uttermost, extended not above as I said sixteen days, after two cakes a day. The gentlemen of the town, who knew better of the country, could not give him any hope or ways how to improve it from the Indian. It soon then appeared most fit, by a general approbation, that to preserve and save all from starving, there could be no readier course thought on than to abandon the country, and accommodating themselves the best that they might in the present pinnaces then in the road, namely in the *Discovery* and the *Virginia,* and in the two brought from and builded at the Bermudas, the *Deliverance* and the *Patience,* with all speed convenient to make for the New found Land, where, being the fishing time, they might meet with many English ships into which happily they might disperse most of the company.

This consultation taking effect, our governor having caused to be carried aboard all the arms and all the best things in the store which might to the adventurers make some commodity upon the sale thereof at home, and burying our ordnances before the fort gate, which looked into the river, the seventh of June, having appointed to every pinnace likewise his complement and number, also delivered thereunto a proportionable rate of provision, he commanded every man at the beating of the drum to repair aboard. And because he would preserve the town (albeit now to be quitted) unburned, which some intemperate and malicious people threat'ned, his own company he caused to be last ashore, and was himself the last of them, when about noon giving a farewell, with a peal of small shot, we set sail, and that night with the tide fell down to an island in the river, which our people have called Hog Island; and the morning tide brought us to another island, which we have called Mulberry Island, where lying at an anchor in the afternoon stemming the tide, we discovered a longboat making towards us from Point Comfort. Much descant[1] we made thereof; about an hour it came up, by which, to our no little joys we had intelligence of the honorable my Lord La Warr his arrival before Algarnoone Fort, the sixt of June, at what time, true it is, His Lordship, having understood of our governor's resolution to depart the country, with all expedition caused his skiff to be manned and in it dispatched his letters by Captain Edward Bruster (who commandeth His Lordship's company) to our governor, which preventing us before the aforesaid Mulberry Island, the eight of June aforesaid. Upon the receipt of His Honor's letters, our governor bore up the helm with the wind coming easterly, and that night, the wind so favorable, relanded all his men at the fort again, before which, the tenth of June, being Sunday, His Lordship had likewise brought his ships, and in the afternoon came ashore with Sir Ferdinando Weinman, and all His Lordship's followers.

Here (worthy lady) let me have a little your pardon. For having now a better heart than when I first landed, I will briefly describe

[1] Discussion.

unto you the situation and form of our fort. When Captain Newport in his first voyage did not like to inhabit upon so open a road as Cape Henry nor Point Comfort, he plied it up to the river, still looking out for the most apt and securest place, as well for his company to sit down in as which might give the least cause of offense or distaste, in his judgment, to the inhabitants.

At length, after much and weary search, with their barge coasting still before—as Virgil writeth Aeneas did, arriving in the region of Italy called Latium, upon the banks of the River Tiber—in the country of a werowance talled [called] Wowinchapuncke, a ditionary[1] to Powhatan, within this fair river of Paspiheigh, which we have called the Kings River, a country least inhabited by the Indian, as they all the way observed, and threescore miles and better up the fresh channel from Cape Henry, they had sight of an extended plain and spot of earth which thrust out into the depth and middest of the channel, making a kind of Chersonesus, or peninsula, for it was fastened only to the land with a slender neck no broader than a man may well quait a tile shard,[2] and no inhabitants by seven or six miles near it. The trumpets sounding, the admiral struck sail, and before the same the rest of the fleet came to an anchor and here, as the best yet offered unto their view—supposed so much the more convenient by how much with their small company they were like enough the better to assure it—to lose no further time, the colony disembarked, and every man brought his particular store and furniture together with the general provision ashore; for the safety of which, as likewise for their own security, ease, and better accommodating, a certain canton and quantity of that little half island of ground was measured, which they began to fortify, and thereon in the name of God to raise a fortress with the ablest and speediest means they could; which fort, growing since to more perfection, is now at this present in this manner:

A low level of ground about half an acre—or so much as Queen Dido might buy of King Hyarbas [Iarbus], which she compassed about with the thongs cut out of one bull hide, and therein built her

---

[1] Subject.

[2] Quoit a tile shard = throw it like a discus.

castle of Byrza—on the north side of the river, is cast almost into the form of a triangle, and so palisadoed. The south side next the river, howbeit extended in a line, or curtain, sixscore foot more in length than the other two by reason the advantage of the ground doth so require, contains one hundred and forty yards, the west and east sides a hundred only. At every angle, or corner, where the lines meet, a bulwark, or watchtower, is raised, and in each bulwark a piece of ordnance or two well mounted. To every side, a proportioned distance from the palisado, is a settled street of houses that runs along so as each line of the angle hath his street. In the middest is a marketplace, a storehouse, and a *corps du guard,* as likewise a pretty chapel, though at this time when we came in as ruined and unfrequented; but the lord governor and captain general hath given order for the repairing of it, and at this instant many hands are about it. It is in length threescore foot, in breadth twenty-four, and shall have a chancel in it of cedar and a communion table of the black walnut, and all the pews of cedar with fair broad windows to shut and open, as the weather shall occasion, of the same wood, a pulpit of the same with a font hewn hollow like a canoa, with two bells at the west end. It is so cast as it be very light within and the lord governor and captain general doth cause it to be kept passing sweet and trimmed up with divers flowers, with a sexton belonging to it; and in it every Sunday we have sermons twice a day, and every Thursday a sermon, having true preachers, which take their weekly turns; and every morning at the ringing of a bell, about ten of the clock, each man addresseth himself to prayers, and so at four of the clock before supper. Every Sunday, when the lord governor and captain general goeth to church, he is accompanied with all the councilors, captains, other officers, and all the gentlemen, and with a guard of halberdiers in His Lordship's livery (fair red cloaks) to the number of fifty, both on each side and behind him; and being in the church, His Lordship hath his seat in the choir in a green velvet chair with a cloth, with a velvet cushion spread on a table before him, on which he kneeleth; and on each side sit the council, captains, and officers, each in their place; and when he returneth home again, he is waited on to his house in the same manner.

And thus enclosed, as I said, round with a palisado of planks and strong posts, four foot deep in the ground, of young oaks, walnuts, etc., the fort is called, in honor of His Majesty's name, James Town. The principal gate from the town through the palisado opens to the river, as at each bulwark there is a gate likewise to go forth, and at every gate a demi-culverin,[1] and so in the marketplace. The houses first raised were all burnt by a casualty of fire the beginning of the second year of their seat, and in the second voyage of Captain Newport—which since have been better rebuilded, though as yet in no great uniformity, either for the fashion or beauty of the street.

A delicate-wrought fine kind of mat the Indians make, with which, as they can be trucked for or snatched up, our people do dress their chambers and inward rooms, which make their houses so much the more handsome. The houses have wide and large country chimneys in the which is to be supposed, in such plenty of wood, what fires are maintained. And they have found the way to cover their houses now as the Indians, with barks of trees as durable and as good proof against storms and winter weather as the best tile, defending likewise the piercing sunbeams of summer, and keeping the inner lodgings cool enough, which before in sultry weather would be like stoves whilest they were, as at first, pargeted and plastered with bitumen or tough clay.

And thus armed for the injury of changing times and seasons of the year, we hold ourselves well apaid, though wanting arras hangings, tapestry, and gilded Venetian cordovan, or more spruce household garniture, and wanton city ornaments, rememb'ring the old epigraph:

We dwell not here to build us bowers,
And halls for pleasure and good cheer,
But halls we build for us and ours,
To dwell in them whilst we live here.

True it is, I may not excuse this our fort, or James Town, as yet seated in somewhat an unwholesome and sickly air, by reason it is in a marish ground, low, flat to the river, and hath no fresh water springs serving the town but what we drew from a well six or seven

---

[1] A cannon.

fathom deep, fed by the brackish river oozing into it; from whence I verily believe the chief causes have proceeded of many diseases and sicknesses which have happened to our people, who are indeed strangely afflicted with fluxes and agues; and every particular season, by the relation of the old inhabitants, hath his particular infirmity too; all which, if it had been our fortunes to have seated upon some hill accommodated with fresh springs and clear air, as do the natives of the country, we might have, I believe, well escaped.

And some experience we have to persuade ourselves that it may be so. For of four hundred and odd men which were seated at the Falls the last year when the fleet came in with fresh and young able spirits, under the government of Captain Francis West, and of one hundred to the seawards on the south side of our river in the country of the Nansamundes, under the charge of Captain John Martin, there did not so much as one man miscarry, and but very few or none fall sick; whereas at James Town, the same time and the same months, one hundred sick'ned and half the number died. Howbeit, as we condemn not Kent in England for a small town called Plumsted continually assaulting the dwellers there, especially newcomers, with agues and fevers, no more let us lay scandal and imputation upon the country of Virginia because the little quarter wherein we are set down, unadvisedly so chosed, appears to be unwholesome and subject to many ill airs, which accompany the like marish places.

IIII.

The Lord La Warre's beginnings and proceedings in James Town – Sir Thomas Gates sent into England – His and the Company's testimony of Virginia and cause of the late miseries.

UPON His Lordship's landing at the south gate of the palisado, which looks into the river, our governor caused his company in arms to stand in order and make a guard. It pleased him that I should bear his colors for that time. His Lordship landing fell upon his knees and before us all made a long and silent prayer to himself, and after marched up into the town, where at the gate I bowed with the colors, and let them fall at His Lordship's feet, who passed on into the chapel, where he heard a sermon by Master Bucke, our governor's preacher; and after that, caused a gentleman, one of his own followers, Master Anthony Scot, his ancient, to read his commission, which entituled him lord governor and captain general, during his life, of the colony and plantation in Virginia (Sir Thomas Gates, our governor hitherto, being now styled therein lieutenant general).

After the reading of His Lordship's commission, Sir Thomas Gates rend'red up unto His Lordship his own commission, both patents and the council seal. After which, the lord governor and captain general delivered some few words unto the company, laying many blames upon them for many vanities and their idleness, earnestly wishing that he might no more find it so, lest he should be compelled to draw the sword of justice to cut off such delinquents, which he had much rather, he protested, draw in their defense to protect them from injuries; heartening them with the knowledge of what store of provisions he had brought for them, viz., sufficient to serve four hundred men for one whole year.

The twelfth of June, being Tuesday, the lord governor and captain general did constitute and give places of office and charge to divers captains and gentlemen, and elected unto him a council, unto whom he did administer an oath mixed with the oath of allegiance and supremacy to His Majesty; which oath likewise he caused to be administ'red the next day after to every particular member of the colony—of faith, assistance, and secrecy. The council which he elected were Sir Thomas Gates, knight, lieutenant general; Sir George Summers, knight, admiral; Captain George Percy, esquire, and in the fort captain of fifty; Sir Ferdinando Weinman, knight, master of the ordnance; Captain Christopher Newport, vice-admiral; William Strachei, esquire, secretary and recorder.

As likewise the lord governor and captain general nominated Captain John Martin master of the battery works for steel and iron, and Captain George Webb sergeant major of the fort; and especial captains over companies were these appointed: Captain Edward Bruster, who hath the command of His Honor's own company; Captain Thomas Lawson, Captain Thomas Holecroft, Captain Samuell Argoll, Captain George Yardley, who commandeth the lieutenant general's company. Divers other officers were likewise made, as Master Ralph Hamor and Master Browne clerks of the council, and Master Daniell Tucker and Master Robert Wilde clerks of the store, etc.

The first business which the lord governor and captain general (after the settling of these officers) thought upon was to advise with his council for the obtaining of such provisions of victuals for store and quality as the country afforded. It did not appear that any kind of flesh, deer, or what else of that kind could be recovered from the Indian, or to be sought in the country by the travail or search of his people; and the old dwellers in the fort, together with the Indians not to friend, who had the last winter destroyed and killed up all the hogs, insomuch as of five or six hundred (as it is supposed) there was not one left alive; nor an hen nor chick in the fort; and our horses and mares they had eaten with the first; and the provision which the lord governor and captain general had brought, concerning any kind of flesh, was little or nothing, in respect it was not dreamt of by the adventurers in England that the swine were destroyed.

In council therefore the thirteenth of June, it pleased Sir George Summers, knight, admiral, to propose a voyage which for the better relief and good of the colony he would perform into the Bermudas, from whence he would fetch six months' provision of flesh and fish and some live hogs to store our colony again; and had a commission given unto him the fifteenth of June, 1610, who in his own Bermuda pinnace, the *Patience,* consorted with Captain Samuell Argoll in the *Discovery,* whom the lord governor and captain general made of the council before his departure, the nineteenth of June, fell with the tide from before our town and, the twenty-two, left the bay, or Cape Henry, astern.

And likewise, because at the lord governor and captain general's first coming there was found in our own river no store of fish, after many trials the lord governor and captain general dispatched in the *Virginia* with instructions, the seventeenth of June, 1610, Robert Tyndall, master of the *De la Warre,* to fish unto, all along, and between Cape Henry and Cape Charles, within the bay; who the last of the said month returned unto us again, but as ill speeding as the former, whom our governor (now lieutenant general) had addressed thither before for the same purpose. Nor was the lord governor and captain general in the meanwhile idle at the fort, but every day and night he caused the nets to be hauled, sometimes a dozen times one after another. But it pleased not God so to bless our labors that we did at any time take one quarter so much as would give unto our people one pound at a meal apiece, by which we might have better husbanded our peas and oatmeal, notwithstanding the great store we now saw daily in our river. But let the blame of this lie where it is, both upon our nets and the unskillfulness of our men to lay them.

The sixth of July, Sir Thomas Gates, lieutenant general, coming down to Point Comfort, the north wind blowing rough he found had forced the longboat belonging to Algernoone Fort to the other shore upon Nansamund side, somewhat short of Weroscoick, which to recover again, one of the lieutenant general's men, Humfrey Blunt, in an old canoe made over. But the wind driving him upon the strand, certain Indians watching the occasion seized the poor fellow and led him up into the woods and sacrificed him. It did not a little trouble the lieutenant governor, who since his first landing in the country, how justly soever provoked, would not by any means be wrought to a violent proceeding against them, for all the practices of villainy with which they daily endangered our men, thinking it possible[1] by a more tractable course to win them to a better condition. But now, being startled by this, he well perceived how little a fair and noble entreaty works upon a barbarous disposition, and therefore in some measure purposed to be revenged.

The ninth of July, he prepared his forces, and early in the morning set upon a town of theirs, some four miles from Algernoone Fort, called Kecoughtan, and had soon taken it without loss or hurt of any of his men. The governor[2] and his women fled (the young King Powhatan's son not being there), but left his poor baggage and treasure to the spoil of our soldiers, which was only a few baskets of old wheat and some other of peas and beans, a little tobacco, and some few women's girdles of silk of the grass silk, not without art and much neatness finely wrought, of which I have sent divers into England (being at the taking of the town), and would have sent Your Ladyship some of them, had they been a present so worthy.

We purposed to set a Frenchman here a-work to plant vines, which grew naturally in great plenty. Some few cornfields it hath, and the corn in good forwardness, and we despair not but to be able, if our men stand in health, to make it good against the Indian.

The continual practices of the subtle King Powhatan doth not meanly awaken all the powers and workings of virtue and knowledge in our lord governor and captain general, how to prevent not only his mischiefs but to draw him upon some better terms and acknowledgment of our forces and spirits, both able and daring to quit him in any valiant and martial course whatsoever he shall dare to run with us, which he doth yet scarcely believe. For this therefore—since first and that so lately he hath set on his people to attempt us with private conspiracies and actual violence, into the one drawing his neighbor confederates and under-princes, and by the other working the loss and death of divers of our men, and by such their loss seizing their arms, swords, pieces, etc., of which he hath

---

[1] "*Ad Graecas kalendas!* ['When hell freezes over!'] Can a leopard change his spots? Can a savage remaining a savage be civil? Were not we ourselves made and not born civil in our progenitors' days? And were not Cæsar's Britons as brutish as Virginians? The Roman swords were best teachers of civility to this and other countries near us." (margin note)

[2] I.e., the werowance.

gathered into his store a great quantity and number, by intelligence above two hundred swords, besides axes and poleaxes, chisels, hoes to pare and cleanse their ground, with an infinite treasure of copper —our lord governor and captain general sent two gentlemen with an embassy unto him, letting him to understand of his practices and outrage hitherto used toward our people, not only abroad but at our fort also; yet flattering him withal how the lord governor and captain general did not suppose that these mischiefs were contrived by him or with his knowledge, but conceived them rather to be the acts of his worst and unruly people; His Lordship therefore now complaining unto him required that he, being so great and wise a king, would give an universal order to his subjects that it might be no more so, lest the lord governor and captain general should be compelled by defending him and his to offend him, which he would be loath to do. Withal he willed the messengers to demand of him, the said Powhatan, that he would either punish or send unto His Lordship such of his people whom Powhatan knew well not long before had assaulted our men at the blockhouse and but newly killed four of them; as also to demand of Powhatan, willing him to return unto the English fort both such men as he detained of ours, and such arms as he had of theirs in his possession, and those conditions performed, he willed them to assure unto Powhatan that then their great werowance, the lord governor and captain general, would hold fair quarter and enter friendship with him as a friend to King James and his subjects. But refusing to submit to these demands, the lord governor and captain general gave in charge to the messengers so sent to signify unto Powhatan that His Lordship would by all means public and private seek to recover from him such of the English as he had, being subjects to his king and master, unto whom even Powhatan himself had formerly vowed not only friendship but homage, receiving from His Majesty therefore many gifts, and upon his knees a crown and scepter, with other ornaments, the symbols of civil state and Christian sovereignty, thereby obliging himself to offices of duty to His Majesty; unto all which Powhatan returned no other answer but that either we should depart his country or confine ourselves to James Town only, without searching further up into his land or rivers, or otherwise he would give in command to his people to kill us, and do unto us all the mischief which they at their pleasure could and we feared, withal forewarning the said messengers not to return anymore unto him unless they brought him a coach and three horses, for he had understood by the Indians which were in England how such was the state of great werowances and lords in England to ride and visit other great men.

After this, divers times and daily he sent sometimes two, sometimes three, unto our fort to understand our strength, and to observe our watch and guard, and how our people stood in health, and what numbers were arrived with this new weroance, which being soon perceived, our lord governor and captain general forewarned such his spies upon their own peril to resort no more unto our fort. Howbeit, they would daily press into our blockhouse and come up to our palisado gates, supposing the government as well now as fantastical and negligent in the former times, the whilest some quarter of a mile short of the blockhouse the greatest number of them would make assault and lie in ambush about our glass house, whither divers times indeed our men would make out either to gather strawberries or to fetch fresh water; anyone of which so straggled, if they could with conveniency they would assault and charge with their bows and arrows, in which manner they killed many of our men. Two of which being Paspaheans (who were ever our deadliest enemies) and not to be reconciled, at length being apprehended, and one of them a notable villain who had attempted upon many in our fort, the lord governor caused them to be manacled and convented before him and his council, where it was determined that he that had done so much mischief should have his right hand struck off, sending him away withal with a message to Powhatan that unless he would yet return such Englishmen as he detained, together with all such their arms, as before spoken of, that not only the other now prisoner should die, but all such of his savages as the lord governor and captain general could by any means surprise should run the same course. As likewise the lord governor and captain general would fire all his neighbor cornfields, towns, and villages, and that suddenly, if Powhatan sent not to contract with him the sooner.

What this will work with him we know not as yet, for this was but the day before our ships were now falling to Point Comfort, and so to set sail for England; which ships, riding before Weroscoick to take in their freight of cedar, clapboard, black walnut, and iron ore, took prisoners likewise the chief king of Weroscoick, called Sasenticum, with his son Kainta, and one of his chief men. And the fifteenth day of July, in the *Blessing,* Captain Adams brought them to Point Comfort, where at that time, as well to take his leave of the Lieutenant General Sir Thomas Gates, now bound for England as to dispatch the ships, the lord governor and captain general had pitched his tent in Algernoone Fort.

The king's son, Kainta, the lord governor and captain general hath sent now into England until the ships arrive here again the next spring, dismissing the old werowance and the other with all terms of kindness and friendship, promising further designs to be effected by him, to which he hath bound himself, by divers savage ceremonies and admirations.

And thus (right noble lady) once more this famous business, as recreated and dipped anew into life and spirit, hath raised it (I hope) from infamy, and shall redeem the stains and losses under which she hath suffered since her first conception. Your Graces still accompany the least appearance of her, and vouchsafe her to be limned out with the beauty which we will beg and borrow from the fair lips. Nor fear you that she will return blushes to your cheeks for praising her, since (more than most excellent lady) like yourself (were all tongues dumb and envious) she will praise herself in her most silence. May she once be but seen, or but her shadow lively by a skillful workman set out indeed, which here (bungerly as I am) I have presumed (though defacing it) in these papers to present unto Your Ladyship.

After Sir Thomas Gates his arrival, a book called *A True Declaration of Virginia* [§27] was published by the Company, out of which I have here inserted this their public testimony of the causes of the former evils, and Sir Thomas Gates his report upon oath of Virginia.

THE GROUND OF ALL THOSE MISERIES was the permissive providence of God, who in the forementioned violent storm separated the head from the body, all the vital powers of regiment being exiled with Sir Thomas Gates in those infortunate yet fortunate islands. The broken remainder of those supplies[1] made a greater shipwrack in the continent of Virginia by the tempest of dissension: Every man, overvaluing his own worth, would be a commander; every man, underprizing another's value, denied to be commanded.

The next fountain of woes was secure[2] negligence and improvidence, when every man sharked for his present booty, but was altogether careless of succeeding penury. Now I demand whether Sicilia or Sardinia (sometimes the barns of Rome) could hope for increase without manuring? A colony is therefore denominated because they should be *coloni,* "the tillers of the earth," and stewards of fertility. Our mutinous loiterers would not sow with providence, and therefore they reaped the fruits of too-dear bought repentance.

An incredible example of their idleness is the report of Sir Thomas Gates, who affirmeth that after his first coming thither he hath seen some of them eat their fish raw rather than they would go a stone's cast to fetch wood and dress it. *Dei laboribus omnia vendunt,* "God sells us all things for our labor," when Adam himself might not live in Paradise without dressing the garden.

Unto idleness you many join treasons wrought by those unhallowed creatures that forsook the colony, and exposed their desolate brethren to extreme misery. You shall know that eight and twenty or thirty of the company were appointed in the ship called the *Swallow* to truck for corn with the Indians. And having obtained a great quantity by trading, the most seditious of them conspired together, persuaded some, and enforced others to this barbarous project: They stole away the ship, they made a league amongst themselves to be professed pirates, with dreams of mountains of gold and happy robberies. Thus, at one instant, they wronged the hopes and subverted the cares of the colony who, depending upon their return, forslowed to look out for further provision; they created the Indians our implacable enemies by some violence they had offered; they carried away the best ship, which should have been a refuge in extremities; they weakened our forces by subtraction of their arms

[1] I.e., the supply ships that survived the storm and arrived.
[2] Surely.

and succors.

These are that scum of men that sailing in their piracy, that being pinched with famine and penury after their wild roving upon the sea, when all their lawless hopes failed, some remained with other pirates they met upon the sea, the others resolved to return for England, [and] bound themselves by mutual oath to agree all in one report to discredit the land, to deplore the famine, and to protest that this their coming away proceeded from desperate necessity! These are they that roared out the tragical history of the man eating of his dead wife in Virginia, when the master of this ship willingly confessed before forty witnesses that at their coming away they left three months' victuals and all the cattle living in the fort! Sometimes they reported that they saw this horrible action, sometimes that Captain Davies said so, sometimes that one Beadle, the lieutenant of Captain Davies, did relate it, varying this report into diversity of false colors which hold no likeness and proportion. But to clear all doubts, Sir Thomas Gates thus relateth the tragedy: "There was one of the company who mortally hated his wife, and therefore secretly killed her, then cut her in pieces, and hid her in divers parts of his house; when the woman was missing, the man suspected, his house searched, and parts of her mangled body were discovered. To excuse himself he said that his wife died, that he hid her to satisfy his hunger, and that he fed daily upon her. Upon this, his house was again searched, where they found a good quantity of meal, oatmeal, beans, and peas. He thereupon was arraigned, confessed the murder, and was burned for his horrible villainy."

Now shall the scandalous reports of a viperous generation preponderate the testimonies of so worthy leaders? Shall their venomous tongues blast the reputation of an ancient and worthy peer[1] who, upon the ocular certainty of future blessings, hath protested in his letters that he will sacrifice himself for his country in this service, if he may be seconded; and if the Company do give it over, he will yet lay all his fortunes upon the prosecution of the plantation?

Unto treasons you may join covetousness in the mariners, who for their private lucre partly embezzled the provisions, partly prevented

---

1 "Lord La Warr." (Strachey's margin note)

our trade with the Indians, making the matches in the night, and forestalling our market in the day; whereby the Virginians were glutted with our trifles and enhanced the prices of their corn and victual, that copper, which before would have provided a bushel, would not now obtain so much as a pottle.[1]

Join unto these another evil: There is great store of fish in the river, especially of sturgeon, but our men provided no more of them than for present necessity, not barreling up any store against that season the sturgeon returned to the sea. And not to dissemble their folly, they suffered fourteen nets (which was all they had) to rot and spoil which by orderly drying and mending might have been preserved. But being lost, all help of fishing perished.

The state of the colony by these accidents began to find a sensible[2] declining; which Powhatan as a greedy vulture observing, and boiling with desire of revenge, he invited Captain Ratcliffe and about thirty others to trade for corn. And under the color of fairest friendship, he brought them within the compass of his ambush whereby they were cruelly murthered and massacred. For upon confidence of his fidelity, they went one and one into several houses, which caused their several destructions, when if but any six had remained together, they would have been a bulwark for the general preservation.

After this, Powhatan in the night cut off some of our boats; he drave away all the deer into the farther part of the country; he and his people destroyed our hogs to the number of about six hundred; he sent one of his Indians to trade with us, but laid secret ambushes in the woods, that if one or two dropped out of the fort alone, they were endangered.

Cast up the reckoning together: want of government, store of idleness, their expectations frustrated by the traito[r]s, their market spoiled by the mariners, our nets broken, the deer chased, our boats lost, our hogs killed, our trade with the Indians forbidden, some of our men fled, some murthered, and most by drinking of the brackish water of James Fort weakened and endangered, famine and sickness by all these means increased—here at home the monies came in so

---

[1] A sixteenfold devaluation!

[2] Noticeable.

slowly, that the Lord Laware could not be dispatched till the colony was worn and spent with difficulties. Above all, having neither ruler nor preacher, they neither feared God nor man, which provoked the wrath of the Lord of Hosts, and pulled down His judgments upon them. *Discite justitiam moniti.*[1]

The Council of Virginia, finding the smallness of that return which they hoped should have defrayed the charge of a new supply, ent'red into a deep consultation, and propounded amongst themselves whether it were fit to enter into a new contribution or in time to send for home the Lord La-ware and to abandon the action. They resolved to send for Sir Thomas Gates, who being come, they adjured him to deal plainly with them, and to make a true relation of those things which were presently to be had, or hereafter to be hoped for, in Virginia.

Sir Thomas Gates, with a solemn and sacred oath, replied that all things before reported were true—that the country yielded abundance of wood, as oak, wainscot, walnut trees, bay trees, ash, sarsafrase, liveoak green all the year, cedar and fir, which are the materials of soap-ashes and potashes, of oils of walnuts, and bays, of pitch and tar, of clapboards, pipe-staves, masts, and excellent boards of forty, fifty, and sixty length and three foot breath, when one fir tree is able to make the mainmast of the greatest ship in England. He avouched that there are incredible variety of sweet woods, especially of the balsamum tree which distilleth a precious gum; that there are innumerable white mulberry trees which in so warm a climate may cherish and feed millions of silkworms, and return us in a very short time as great a plenty of silk as is vented into the whole world from all the parts of Italy; that there are divers sorts of minerals, especially of iron ore lying upon the ground for ten miles circuit, of which we have made a trial at home that it maketh as good iron as any is in Europe; that a kind of hemp, or flax, and silk grass do grow there naturally, which will afford stuff for all manner of excellent cordage; that the river swarmeth with all manner of sturgeon, the land aboundeth with vines, the woods do harbor exceeding store of

[1] "Having been warned, learn justice!" (Latin)

beavers, foxes, and squirrels, the waters do nourish a great increase of otters, all which are covered with precious furs; that there are in present discovered dyes and drugs of sundry qualities; that the oranges which have been planted did prosper in the winter, which is an infallible argument that lemons, sugar canes, almonds, rice, anise seed, and all other commodities which we have from the Straits[1] may be supplied to us in our own country and by our own industry; that the corn yieldeth a terrible increase more than ours; and lastly that it is one of the goodliest countries under the sun, interveined with five main rivers, and promising as rich entrails as any kingdom of the earth to whom the sun is no nearer a neighbor.

---

[1] The Mediterranean via the Straits of Gibraltar.

LIBRARY OF VIRGINIA

SIR GEORGE SOMERS

23. George Somers

Letter to Salisbury, 15 June 1610

< **State Papers Colonial: James I, 1–84,** Brown 1890:400

Frobisher rescued the whole complement of the *Dennis* when she sank in the ice off Baffin Island in the summer of 1578. Otherwise Admiral Somers' achievement surpasses all seamanship. He got everybody safely ashore inside the Bermudian reef. But if that wasn't enough, instead of becoming another "lost colony," he got them all off again in jury-built vessels, and completed the year-old voyage in safety. Unfortunately their destination was Jamestown at its lowest ebb.

The last statement in his report is prophetic of his approaching death upon his return to those beautiful islands to be named for him.

RIGHT HONORABLE—May it please your good honor to be advertised that sithence our departure out of England in going to Virginia, about some 100 leagues from the Bermooda we were taken with a very great storm, or hurricane, which sund'red all the fleet, and on St. James' eve, being the 23 of July, we had such a leak in our ship, insomuch that there was in her 9 feet of water before we knew of anything. We pumped with ii pumps and bailed in iii or iiii hour places with certain barricoes, and then we kept 100 men always working night and day from the 23 of until the 28 of the same July, being Friday; at which time we saw the Island of Bermooda, where our ship lieth upon a rock a quarter of a mile distant from the shore, where we saved all our lives and afterwards saved much of our goods, but all our bread was wet and lost.

We continued in this island from the 28 of July [1609] until the 10 of May [1610], in which time we built ii small barks to carry our people to Virginia, which in number were 140 men and women at the coming to the island.

We departed from the Bermooda the 13 of May, and arrived in Virginia the 23 of the same month. And coming to Cape Henrie, the captain there told us of the famine that was in James Town, whereupon we hastened up and found it true. For they had eaten all the quick things that were there, and some of them had eaten snakes or adders. But by the industry of our governor in the Bermooda there was saved [? blotted ink] a little meal—for our allowance would not extend to above one pound and a half for a man a week, and [on] this with fish we lived—and this allowance 9 months our governor, Sir Thomas Gates, did allow them as we had, with some pork, and recovered all saving iii that did die and were past recovery before our coming.

We consulted together what course were best to be taken, for our means would not continue above 14 days. We thought good to take into our iiii pinnaces as much of the munition as we could, and took in all the people; and were going down the river, but by the way we met with the Lord Laware and lord governor, which made our hearts very glad, and we presently returned up to James Town. And there we found no savages, for they were afraid to come thither, for they did not trade with our men these many months. The truth is they had nothing to trade withal but mulberries.

Now we are in a good hope to plant and ab[ide] there, for here is a good course taken and a greater care than ever there was. I am going to the Bermooda for fish and hog with ii small pinnaces, and am in a good opinion to be back again before the Indians do gather their harvest. The Bermooda is the most plentiful place that ever I came to for fish, hogs, and fowl.

—Thus wishing all health with the increase of honor, do humbly take my leave.

From Virginia the xvth of June, 1610.

Your Honor's to command,
GEORGE SOMERS.

From James Town in Virginia.
I have sent Your Honor a brief of the Island of Bermooda [lost].
Sir George Sommers to My Lord, from Virginia. 15 June 1610.

[endorsed:] To the Right Honorable the Earl of Salisbury, Lord Treasurer of England, give these.

24. Francis Maguel

Report of what Francisco Maguel, an Irishman, learned in the state of Virginia during the eight months that he was there, July 1, 1610

(translated from the Spanish by Maximilian Schele de Vere)

< Simancas Archive 2587–98, **Brown 1890:393,** Barbour 1969:151

This is a translation of the Spanish translation of a lost English original. It was an enclosure in a letter from Don Alonso de Velasco, the Spanish ambassador in London, to the King of Spain (30 September 1610). It is an Irish spy's deposition taken by another Irishman who calls himself the archbishop of an Irish town near Galway, then under English control. Maguel was serving his country. The Protestant Orange arrived in Ulster in 1607. The Irish and the Powhatan were undergoing simultaneous invasion from the same vanguard.

As a spy Maguel may have used an alias in Virginia. Whether his name here was Maguel or Magill or Maguire and similar, it does not appear on any of Captain John Smith's lists of arrivals.

His report contains many overeager falsehoods and exaggerations. There were no mines and little proof of ore anywhere, let alone diamonds. Almonds do not grow in Virginia. West India ("La India occidental") is a mystery, but Maguel's description of the chain of forts the English will build on the way to the "South Sea" sounds like it is inspired by Ralph Lane's account of 1585–86.

The Spanish *real* will equal sixpence.

Bracketed *italic* is retained from Schele de Vere. Bracketed roman is taken from the Barbour translation.

About the voyage he made and the direction the English took at first in order to discover Virginia

1. From England they sail for Santo Domingo [Dominica], from there to Mevis, and from Mevis to San Nicolas, and from there to Puerto Rico. From Puerto Rico they took their route directly towards Virginia, sailing sixteen days towards the northwest till they discover

a Cape of Virginia which the English call San Nicolas,[1] which in the opinion of said narrator is about six hundred leagues distant from Puerto Rico.

And all this seacoast is low land like La Florida, and is free from any danger; and all along there close to the shore there are ten or twelve fathoms *[?]*[2] deep water, and is very convenient for anchoring there. And in all that space there is a sandy beach, or a sand bank, eight leagues out from the seashore, which is covered to the depth of sixteen or eighteen fathoms. This bank begins close to La Florida and continues all the way towards the mountains until it comes to unite with another bank of Terranova *[Newfoundland]*. There is navigation between this bank and the firm land for some hundred and fifty leagues, on account of the great current which the water has on the other side of said bank. Between this bank and the land there is a tide which runs from south-southeast to north-northwest.

From Cape San Nicolas to Cape Comfort it is eight leagues. This Cape Comfort is an island which lies at the mouth of a great river on which the English live. This river lies under 37½ degrees. In order to enter this river the vessels that come up have to pass very close to said island, where they find ten fathoms of water. And half a league inside of this island in the river there is a large and ample bay with twelve fathoms of water, and in it all the ships of England might lie at anchor. The English had determined to erect a fort on this island so as to defend the entrance to that river, but the narrator does not know whether it has ever been finished.

Twenty leagues up from this island, or this mouth of the river, the English built a well-entrenched fort, standing on a point which goes out from the land into the river; and the English determined to cut this point so that the water should surround them on all sides. And in this fort they put twenty pieces of artillery, and afterwards they sent there from England much more artillery.

This river will be little more than a league wide in most parts, and where it is least deep it still has three fathoms of water when the tide

---

[1] Cape Henry.

[2] The *braza,* the Spanish fathom, is slightly under six feet.

is low, and in other parts it has ten or twelve fathoms. From this fort, which the English call James Fort, the river flows towards the west for twenty leagues more, where the English penetrated in a few pinnaces, taking with them some of the natives of the country to show them the way.

Of the commodities which the English find in that country and of its climate

2. In this country are found many mines of iron and of copper and others [mines], which they took to England. And the English do not wish it to be known what kind of mines there are until they are first well fortified in Virginia. And of these mines the narrator brought a sample to England which weighed eighty pounds, and in it he found the weight of three reales of gold, of five in silver, and of four pounds in copper.

There are many large pearls in that country and a great quantity of coral, and in the mountains they find a few stones which look very much like diamants [diamonds].

And in order to discover more such mines and to examine [purify] the products, the King of England sent many skilled workmen who understand it, and also other laborers in all the mechanic arts to live there.

There are found there many varieties of dye stuff, which are sold in England at forty *reales* a pound. The English make a very great quantity of soap-ashes, which they send home to their country. There are in those rivers great numbers of salmons *[sallos]* and other fish,[1] and such a quantity of codfish and as good as in Newfoundland. There is in that country an infinite supply of deer, peacock [turkeys], swans, and every kind of fowl. There grow in that country wild many forest grapes, of which the English make a wine that resembles much the wine of Alicante, according to the opinion of the narrator, who has tasted both. There is also a great quantity of *[hanas]*,[2] chickpeas,

---

[1] Barbour has "salmon, sole, and other fish."
[2] "Beans" in Barbour.

maize, almonds, [wal]nuts and chestnuts, and above all much flax which grows wild without any cultivation. They have a great abundance of peltry for very rich furs, especially sable martens, and the king has houses full of them, they being his treasure. The English draw from there many drugs and things necessary for pharmacy.

The land lies very pleasantly and level, and is very fertile with many large rivers; the air is healthy and the temperature about the same as in Spain, although the winters are somewhat colder.

Of the emperor and the natives of the country

3. The emperor of Virginia has sixteen kings under his dominion. He and all his subjects deal peaceably with the English and attend a market which the English hold daily near the fort, and bring to them there the commodities of the country to exchange them for many little trifles which the English give them, as knives, glass, mirrors, little bells, etc. The natives of this country are a robust, well-disposed race, and generally go about dressed in very well-tanned deerskins, as they understand very well how to prepare them. Their arms are bows and arrows.

The emperor sends every year some men by land to West India and to Newfoundland and other countries, to bring him news of what is going on there. And these messengers report that those who are in West India treat the natives very badly and as slaves, and the English tell them that those people are Spaniards, who are very cruel and evil disposed.

The English have some boys there among these people to learn their language, which they already know, at least some of them, perfectly. The emperor sent one of his sons to England, where they treated him well and returned him once more to his own country, from which the said emperor and his people derived great contentment through the account which he gave of the kind reception and treatment he received in England.

The English sent the emperor a crown of shining copper and many copper vessels and silk dresses for himself and for his wives and children. This narrator returned to England in the same vessel with the said son of the emperor.[1]

There they worship the devil, whom they consider their god, and say that he often speaks to them, appearing in human form. The emperor and his sons promised the English that they would give up their religion and believe in the god of the English, and on account of the great familiarity [friendliness] which they show, it seems that they would be easily converted.

Of the designs and intentions of the English against His Catholic Majesty, as the said narrator learned when he was in Virginia

4. In the first place the natives of Virginia assure the English that they can easily take them to the South Sea by three routes: The first route on which they will take them is by land from the head of that river on which the English have a fort to the South Sea, as the natives affirm *[is ten days' march]*. The second route is because in a day's march and a half from the head of that river inland there is another river so long that it falls into the South Sea. The third route is that twelve leagues from the mouth of this river where the English are towards the northwest there are four other rivers, to which there came *[went?]* one of those English captains in a pinnace,[2] who says that one of these rivers is of great importance; and the natives affirm that fourteen leagues farther on from these four rivers towards the northwest there is another great river which flows very far into the country until it meets another large river which flows to the South Sea.

The English desire nothing else so much as to make themselves masters of the South Sea in order to secure their share of the riches of the Indies and to cut off the trade of the King of Spain, and to seek new worlds for themselves. With a view to this end (to make themselves masters of the South Sea), they have determined to erect

[1] "Namontack, to whom the Irishman evidently alludes, sailed for England with Captain Newport, April 10 and arrived there May 21, 1608. He returned to Virginia with Newport about July and arrived there about the last of September 1608." (Brown)

[2] Either Smith or Argall.

a fort at the end of every day's march of these ten days' march which lie between the head of their river and the South Sea, to secure themselves on this route; and two other forts on that day's march and a half which lie between the two rivers. This they hope to accomplish in a short time because they do not intend to fortify them very strongly, but only so much as would suffice to defend themselves against these savages. Likewise, for this aforesaid purpose the King of England has sent out many carpenters of his kingdom who are to build ships and boats for those seas and rivers, for which they have there the very greatest facilities, since they have there a great abundance of the best timber that can be found for shipbuilding, and their land abounds in pitch, rosin, and tar [turpentine]. Besides there grows wild there much hemp of which they mean to make cables and ropes for their ships, and having as they do have all these facilities for shipbuilding, and with them, as before mentioned, so many iron mines (to work which, as well as to work other metals they have already erected there some machinery [mills], it will be very easy to them to build many ships. And according to themselves (as the narrator heard) if they once have twenty or thirty thousand effective Englishmen settled there, they will be able to do much injury to the King of Spain, much more than France and England can do.

The English are much encouraged to make this march to the South Sea by the report of the natives of Virginia that on the other side of Virginia, close to the South Sea, there is a country, the inhabitants of which wear wide silk dresses for their clothing, and bright colored buskins, that they have much gold and that ships are in the habit of coming to that country who deal with the natives and get from them both silk and gold. As a proof of this the Virginians showed the English a few knives and other things which they had gotten from those who came in these aforesaid ships, and the English believe these vessels must be Spanish.

Item: The English in that country have among themselves proclaimed and sworn (allegiance to) the King of England as King of Virginia. And the anxiety they feel that the secrets of this country shall not become known, is so great that they have issued orders prohibiting anyone from taking letters with him beyond the frontiers, and also from sending any, especially to private individuals, without their being first seen and read by the governor. For the same reason they have tried in that fort of theirs at Jamestown an English captain, a Catholic, called Captain Tindol [George Kendall], because they knew that he had tried to get to Spain, in order to reveal to His Majesty all about this country and many plans of the English which he knew, but which the narrator does not know.

And in conclusion of this it must be observed that now, since they have fully discovered this country, they no longer follow the first route and sailing course, which they took by Puerto Rico when they were about to discover Virginia, but that from England they take their course much more towards the north so as not to fall in with Spanish ships, and also to make the voyage in less time. The same narrator affirms that he returned from Virginia to England in 31 days[1] because in coming back the voyage is much shorter than in going out.

And in proof of the truth of all that has been stated within, the said narrator promises and binds himself to go in person to serve His Catholic Majesty, by showing to the eye all that he says, if His Majesty should be pleased to employ him in this service.

I, DON FRAY FLORENCIO CONRYO, Archbishop of Tuam, certify that the said Irishman, the narrator, Francisco Miguel, has sworn in my presence that he has either seen himself or heard said or done all that is herein contained, and among the best people of the English, when he was in Virginia, and that all he has said in his own language is here faithfully translated into the Spanish language, and for the truth of it he signed it at Madrid, July the first, 1610.

FRAY FLORENCIO CONRYO
Archbishop of Tuam.

---

[1] Barbour reads "21 days" but says the number is absurd.

25. The Governor and Council in Virginia

Letter to the Virginia Company of London, 7 July 1610

< **British Library, Harleian MS 7009–58,** Brown 1890:402

Lord Delaware and company expand on matter in his letter to Salisbury, recording the dramatic days of 7–8 June 1610 when Jamestown was abandoned, Virginia was not, and the settlement was restored. I recall years ago seeing in a simple, standard early 19th-century primary school history that Virginia was "founded by Lord Delaware in 1610." He explains and defends Gates's decision to abort, and why now it is just as good a decision to resettle, meanwhile going over some of the same ground found at the end of William Strachey's *True Reportory §22.*

London suppliers read about how rich the soil was and assumed the colonists could or should farm their own food.

The right margin of the manuscript is often torn away, hence the gaps and restorations by both this editor and Alexander Brown.

RIGHT HONORABLE AND THE REST OF OUR VERY LOVING FRIENDS—We are not ignorant how divers perplex'd and jealous eyes may look out and keep more than friendly espial over this our passive[1] and misconceived business, and now more especially, haply, than at any other time, in these our early days; and after the aspersion of so many slanderous and wandering discourses, which have been scattered by malignant and ill-disposed people against it; for which we have conceived it essential, with the birth of the work itself, to give up unto your noble knowledges the truth of the state of the same, and of some consequences most material following it since it took protection and fostering from us.

You shall please then to know how the first of April, 1610, in the good ship the *De la Warr,* admiral, accompanied with the *Blissing* of Plymouth, vice-admiral, and the *Hercules* of Rye, rear-admiral, we

[1] Arduous.

weighed from the Cowes, getting out of the Needles, and with a favorable passage holding consort, the 12 day we fell with the Treseras [Terceira in the Azores], and recovered that evening within three leagues the westermost part of St. George's Island [São Jorge], where we lay that night becalmed. But the next morning with the sunrise did the wind likewise rise west and west by south, a rough and loud gale, at what time the master of the rear-admiral told me of a road fit for that wind at Gratiosa, whereupon I willed him to go before and I would follow, and so we stood for that road. But it was my fortune to lead in it, where we came to an anchor, at forty fathom, when it blew so much wind presently that our anchor came home, and we were forced to sea again. The same time the *Blissing* was compel'd to cut her cable at half, for in the weighing of it the pale of her capstan brake and dangerously hurt 12 of our men. The *Hercules* was likewise forced from the road and brake her anchor. Yet the next day we met all together again. The 15, we lost sight of the *Hercules,* between the Treceras and Gratiosa, and we saw her no more until the 6 of June, at what time we made land to the southward of our harbor, the Chesiopiock Bay, where running in towards the shore, steering away nor'west, before noon we made Cape Henry, bearing nor'west and by west; and that night came to an anchor under the cape, where we went ashore as well to refresh ourselves as to fish, and to set up a cross upon the point, if haply the *Hercules* might arrive there, to signify our coming in. Whilest we were a-fishing, divers Indians came down from the woods unto us, and with fair entreaty on both sides I gave unto them of such fish as we took, which was good store and was not unwelcome unto them, for indeed at this time of the year they live poor, their corn being but newly put into the ground and their old store spent. Oysters and crabs and such fish as they take in their weirs is their best relief. As we were returning aboard again, our master descried a sail close by the point at Cape Henry, whereupon I commanded him to bear up the helm, and we gave it chase, when within an hour or a little more, to our no little [joy], made her to be the *Hercules,* our rear-admiral, whom we had now [? lost] ... weeks and odd days; and this night (all praise be to God for it) came all to an anchor,[1] from whence the captain of the fort, C[aptain] James Davies, repaired unto us and soon had unfolded a strange [rela]tion of a double quality, mixed both with joy and sorrow. He let us to un[der]stand first (because thereof I first inquired) of the arrival of Sir Thomas Gates and Sir George Sumers in 2 pinnaces, with all their company safe from the Barmudas, the 21 of May, about some fortnight before our now coming in, whom, he told us, were now up our river at James Town. I was heartily glad to hear the happiness of this news, but it was seasoned with a following discourse, compound of so many miseries and calamities, and those in such horrid changes and divers forms, as no story, I believe, ever presented the wrath and curse of the Eternal Offended Majesty in a greater measure. I understood moreover, by reason I saw the *Virginia* to lie then in road before the point, rig'd and prepared to set sail out of the river, how that Sir Thomas Gates and Sir George Sumers were within a tide or two coming down again, purposing to abandon the country whilest they had means yet left to transport them and the whole company to New found land.

For most true it is the strange and unexpected condition and … in which Sir Thomas Gates found the colony gave him to underst[and] never was there more need of all the powers of judgment, and … knowing and long-exercised virtue than now to be awak … calling upon him to save such whom he found so fe … as in redeeming himself and his again from falling into the [like calami]ties. For besides that he found the fort unfurnished and that … and many casualties of so large an account and number … as he expected, and knew came along the last year, trained in … fleet with himself; so likewise found he as empty and unfurnished a s … entering the town, it appeared rather as the ruins of some ancient [for]tification than that any people living might now inhabit it. The palisadoes he found torn down, the ports open, the gates from off the h … hinges, the church ruined and unfrequented, empty houses whose owners untimely death had taken newly from them, rent up and burnt, the living not hable, as they pretended, to step into the woods to gather other firewood; and, it is true, the *Indian as fast killing without as the*

---

[1] "Under Point Comfort." (margin note)

famine and pestilence within.[1] Only the blockhouse, somewhat regarded,[2] was the safety of the remainder that lived, which yet could not have preserved them now many days longer from the watching, subtle, and offended Indian, who, it is most certain, knew all this their weakness and forbare too timely to assault the fort or hazard themselves in a fruitless war on such whom they were assured in short time would of themselves perish, and being provoked, their desperate condition might draw forth to a valiant defense. Yet were they so ready and prepared that such whom they found of our men straggled single beyond the bounds, at any time, of the blockhouse, they would fiercely charge, for all their pieces,[3] as they did 2 of our people not many days before Sir Thomas Gates was come in, and 2 likewise they killed after his arrival 4 or 5 days.

But that which added most to his sorrow, and not a little startled him, was the impossibility which he conceived (and conceived truly) how to amend any one whit of this. His forces were not of hability to revenge upon the Indian, nor his own supply now brought from the Bermudas sufficient to relieve his people, for he had brought no greater store of provision, as not jealous that any such disaster could have befall'n the colony, than might well serve 150 for a sea voyage; and at this time of the year neither by force, had his power been sufficient, nor trade might they have amended these wants by any help from the Indian. Nor was there any means in the fort to take fish, for there was neither a sufficient seine to be found nor any other convenient nets, and, to say true, if there had, yet was there not any of sturgeon come into the river.

All these considered, he then entered into consultation with Sir George Sumers and Captain Newporte, calling unto the same the gentlemen and council of the former government, entreating both the one and the other to advise with him what was to be done. The provision which they both had aboard, both Sir George Sumers and Captain Newporte, was examined and delivered how it being rack'd to the uttermost extended not to above 16 days after 2 cakes a day. The gentlemen of the town who knew better of the country could

---

[1] Original emphasis.
[2] Looked after.
[3] I.e., despite the fact the Englishmen venturing out had firearms.

not give them any hope or ways how to recover ought from the Indian. It soon then appeared most fit, by a general approbation, that, to preserve and save all from starving, there could be no readier course thought on than to abandon the country; and accommodating themselves the best that they might in the present pinnaces then in the road, as namely in the *Discovery* and the *Virginia,* in the 2 brought from and builded at the Bermudas, the one called the *Deliveraunce,* of about 70 ton, and the other the *Patience,* of 30 ton, with all speed convenient to make for the New found land where, it being then fishing time, they might meet with many English ships into which happily they might disperse most of the company.

This consultation taking effect the 7th of June, Sir Thomas Gates, having appointed to every pinnace his complement and number, and delivered likewise thereinto a proportionable rate of provision, caused every man to repair aboard. And because he would preserve the town, albeit now to be quitted, unburned, which some intemperate and malicious people threatened, his own company he caused likewise to be last ashore, and was himself the last of them when about noon, giving a farewell with a peal of small shot, he set sail and that night with the tide fell down to an island in the river which our people have called Hog Island. And the next morning the tide brought them to another island which they have called Mulberry Island, at what time they discovered my longboat. For I, having understood of the resolution by the aforesaid pinnace, which was some 4 or 5 days come away before to prepare those at Point Comfort, with all expedition I caused the same to be man'd, and in it, with the news of our arrival, dispatched my letters by Captain Edward Brewister to Sir Thomas Gates, which, meeting to[gether] ... before the aforesaid Mulberry Island, the 8 of June aforesaid ... upon the receipt of our letters, Sir Thomas Gates bore up the h[elm] again, and that night (the wind favorable) relanded all his m[en] at the fort; before which, the 10 of June, being Sunday, I brought my ship and in the afternoon went ashore where, after a sermon made by Mr. Buck, Sir Thomas Gates his preacher, I caused my commission to be read, upon which Sir Thomas Gates delivered up unto me his own commission, both patents, and the council seal. And then I delivered some few words unto the company, laying some blames upon them for many vanities and their idleness, earnestly wishing that I might no more find it so lest I should be compel'd to draw the sword in justice to cut off such delinquents which I had much rather draw in their defense to protect from enemies, heartening them with the knowledge of what store of provisions I had brought for them. And after not finding as yet in the town a convenient house, I repaired aboard again where, the 12 of June, I did constitute and give places of office and charge to divers captains and gentlemen, a[nd] elected unto me a council unto whom I administered an oath of faith, assistance, and secrecy. Their names were these:

Sir Thomas Gates, knight, lieutenant general
Sir George Sumers, knight, admiral
Captain George Percey, esquire
Sir Ferdinando Wenman, knight, m[aster of ordnance]
Captain Christopher Newport
William Strachey, esquire, secr[etary and recorder].

As likewise I nominated Captain John Martin master of the b[attery] works for steel and iron, and Captain George Webb sergeant [major] of the fort, and Mr. Daniell Tucker and Mr. Robert Wild clerks of the store.

Our first care was to advise with our council for the obtaining of such provisions of victuals for store and [of] quality as the country afforded for our people. It did not appear unto us that any kind of flesh, deer, or what else of that kind could be recovered from the Indian, or to be sought in the country by us. And our people together with the Indians not to friend had the last winter destroyed and kill'd up all our hogs,[1] insomuch as of five or six hundred, as it is supposed, there was not above one sow that we can hear of left alive; not a hen nor chick in the fort*; and our horses and mares they had eaten with the first*[2]; and the provision which we had brought concerning any kind of flesh was little or nothing.

Whereupon it pleased Sir George Sumers to propose a voyage which, for the better relief and good of the colony, he would perform

[1] It is hard to believe anybody, including the Indians, ever killed *all* the hogs in the Southside of Virginia.
[2] Original emphasis.

into the Bermudas; which lying in the height of 32 degrees and 20 minutes, 5 degrees from our bay, may be some seve[n] score leagues from us, or thereabouts, reckoning to every degree that lies nor'west and westerly 28 English leagues. And from thence he would fetch 6 months' provision of flesh and fish, and some live hog[s], of which those islands—by their own report, however, most dangerous to fall with—are marvelous full and well stored.

Whereupon, well approving and applauding a motion relishing of so fair hopes and much goodness, we gave him a commission the 15 of June, who in his own Bermuda pinnace, the *Patience,* accompanied with Captain Samuell Argall in the *Discovery,* whom we sware of our council before his departure, the 19 of June fell with the tide from before our town, whom we have ever since accompanied with our hearty prayers for his happy and safe return.

And likewise, because at our first coming we found in our own river no store of fish after many trials, we dispatched with instructions, the 17 of June, Robert Tindall, master of the *De la warr,* to fish unto, all along, and between Cape Henry and Cape Charles within the bay, who the last of the same returned unto us again; but met with so small a quantity and store of fish as he scarce took so much as served the company that he carried forth with him.

Nor were we in the meanwhile idle at the fort, but every day and night we haled our net sometimes a dozen times one after another. But it pleased not God so to bless our labors that we should at any time take one quarter so much as would give unto our people one pound at a meal apiece, by which we might have better husbanded and spared our peas and oatmeal, notwithstanding the great store we now saw daily in our river.

Thus much in brief concerning our voyage hither, our meeting with Sir Thomas Gates here, and our joint cares and endeavors since our arrival. Nor shall we be failing on our part to do the uttermost that we may for the happy structure and raising again of this too much stooped and dejected employment.

It rests that I should now truly deliver unto ye, Right Honorable and the rest of our good friends, somewhat our opinion, or rather better judgment, which hath observed many things and those objected clear to reason most beneficial concerning this country. And first, we have experience and our own eyes' witness, how young soever we are to this place, that no country yieldeth goodlier corn or more manifold increase. Large fields we have as prospects hourly before us of the same, and those not many miles from our quarter, some whereof, true it is, to quit[1] the mischievous Indian, and irreconcilable for his late injuries and murthering of our men, our purpose is to be masters of ere long, and to thresh it out on the floors of our barns when the time shall serve.

Next, in every bosk and common hedge, and not far from our palisado gates, we have thousands of goodly vines running along and leaning to every tree which yield a plentiful grape in their kind. Let me appeal then to knowledge: If these natural vines were planted, dressed, and ordered by skillful vignerons, whether we might not make a perfect grape and fruitful vintage in short time?

Lastly, we have made trial of our own English seeds, kitchen herbs, and roots, and find them no sooner put into the ground than to prosper as speedily and after the same quality as in England.

Only let me truly acknowledge they are not an hundred or two of deboisht[2] hands, drop'd forth by year after year, with penury and leisure, ill provided for before they come and worse governed when they are here, men of such distempered bodies and infected minds, whom no examples daily before their eyes either of goodness or punishment can deter from their habitual impieties or terrify from a shameful death, that must be the carpenters and workers in this so glorious a building. But, to delude and mock the business no longer, as a necessary quantity of provision for a year at least must be carefully sent with men, so likewise must there be the same care for men of quality, and painstaking men of arts and practices, chosen out and sent into the business. And such are in due time now promised [and] set down in the schedule at the end of our own approved discourse, which we have entituled *A True and Sincere Declaration of the Purpose and End of our Plantation begun in Virginia, etc.* [§20]

And these two, such men and such provision, are like enough to make good the ends of the employment in all the ways both for

---

[1] Requite.
[2] Debauched.

r[epu]tation, search, and discovery of the country, and the hope of the South Sea, as also to return by all ships sent hither many commodities well known to be here, if means be to prepare them.

Whereupon give me leave, I beseech ye, further to make inference that since it hath been well thought on by ye to provide for the government by changing the authority into an absolute command (indeed ... virtual advancement to these like businesses and m ... company us) of a noble and well instructed lieut[enant] ... of an industrious admiral, and other knights and gen[tlemen], and officers, each in their several place of quality and emplo[yment], if the other two, as I have said, be taken into due account ... valued as the sinews (as indeed they be) of this action, without w[hich] it cannot possible have any fair subsisting, however men have belied both it and themselves heretofore, then let no rumor of the poverty of the country—as if in the womb thereof there lay not those elemental seeds which could produce as many goodly births of plenty and increase, yea, and of better hopes as of any land under the heavens unto whom the sun is no nearer a neighbor—I say, let no imposture, rumor then, nor any fame of some one or a few more chanceable actions interposing by the way or at home, wave [away] any man's fair purposes hitherward or wrest them to a declining and falling-off from the business.

For let them be assured, as of the truth itself, these premises considered, look what the country can afford, which may by the quantity of our men be safely and conveniently explored, searched, and made practice of. Those things shall not be omitted for our part, nor will be by the lieutenant general to be commanded; nor are our commands received (as in former times) with unwillingness or falseness, either in our people's going forth or in execution, being for each one in his place, whether commander, overseer, or laborer.[1]

---

[1] A full and difficult passage. Read, "We shall omit none of these things, but rather shall do them at the command of the lieutenant general; nor will discipline again lapse into malingering and insubordination as when men are ordered to do things in details or on patrol without regard to their rank, whether commander, etc." This last clause must refer to John Smith the Autocrat compelling gentlemen to do manual labor, a surmise only strengthened by the next paragraph. Smith had returned to England in October 1609.

For the causes of those idle and resty untowardness' being by the authority and unity of our government removed, all hands hourly already set to it; and he that knew not the way to goodness himself before, but cherish'd singularity and faction, now can beat out a path himself of industry and goodness for others to tread in. Such, may I well say, is the power of exemplar virtue. Nor would I have it conceived that we would exclude[1] altogether gentlemen and such whose breeding never knew what a day's labor meant, for even to such this country, I doubt not, but will give likewise excellent satisfaction, especially to the better and staid spirits. For he amongst us that cannot dig, use the square, nor practice the ax and chisel, yet he shall find how to employ the force of knowledge, the exercise of council, and the operation and power of his best breeding and quality.

And thus, Right Honorable and the rest of our very good friends, assuring ye of our resolution to tarry God's mercy towards us in continuing for our part this plantation, I only will entreat ye to stand favorable unto us for a new supply in such matters of the twofold physic which both the souls and bodies of our poor people here stand much in need of; the specialties[2] belonging to the one the physicians themselves, whom I hope you will be careful to send unto us, will bring along with them; the particularities[3] of the other we have sent herein enclosed, delivered unto us by Mr. Doctor Boone, whose care and industry for the preservation of our men's lives, assaulted with strange fluxes and agues, we have just cause to commend unto your noble favors. Nor let it, I beseech ye, be passed over as a motion slight and of no moment to furnish us with these things, so much importuning the strength and health of our people, since we have true experience how many men's lives these physic helps have preserved since our coming in, God so blessing the practice and diligence of our doctor, whose store is now grown thereby to so low an ebb as we have not above 3 weeks' physical provisions, if our men continue still thus visited with the sicknesses of the country, of the which every season hath his particular infirmity

---

[1] Deny immigration to.
[2] Medical training.
[3] Prescription of drugs.

reigning in it, as we have it related unto us by the old inhabitants, and since our own arrival have had cause to fear it to be true, who have had 150 at a time much afflicted and, I am persuaded, had lost the greatest part of them if we had not brought these helps with us.

And so concluding your farther troubles with this only remembrance that we have, with the advice of our council, conceived it most fit to detain yet awhile, for all good occasions, the good ship the *De la ware,* to which we hope ye will be no whit gainsaying, we cease with unnecessary relations to provoke ye any farther.

July 7th, 1610. James Town.

THOMAS LAWARRE
THOMAS GATES
FARDINANDO WENMAN
GEORGE PERCY
WILLIAM STRACHEY

26. Thomas West, Lord Delaware

Letter to Salisbury, rec'd September 1610

< **State Papers Colonial, James I, 1/22–86,** Brown 1890:413, Virginia Magazine 14:379

This information is more fully dealt with in §25. However, he gives the number of passengers in his fleet, and interesting details about the crossing, such as taking Argall's route along 28°N; and another very important detail, namely, that when Gates abandoned Jamestown, he intended to wait ten days at Point Comfort for Delaware's arrival before setting out for Newfoundland. Fate, then, did not depend upon a single day.

MAY IT PLEASE YOUR GOOD LORDSHIP—Since I departed from Your Lordship, I have met with very much comfort. Yet, mingled with as many lamentable accidents as ever your ears have been filled withal, and because Sir Thomas Gattes, who is the bearer hereof, was the first that found our men in misery, I will leave that relation to him, as being best able to inform, and only touch briefly what myself can testify.

The first of April, I departed the Cowes in the Isle of Wight with 3 good ships, and in them an 150 persons to land as planters in Virginia.

The 12 of April, I made land, it being the Tracera Island [Terceira in the Azores]. That night the wind came in contrary and it blew hard the next day, that we were forced to seek out a road unknown unto our best mariners, and we fared accordingly. For 2 of my ships lost their anchors and spoiled divers of their men in seeking to weigh them, and the anchor of my own ship came home, so that I was forced to sea again so soon as my anchor was down. The 15 day, I lost sight of my rear-admiral and I continued beating up and down with the wind contrary to meet with our lost ship, but could not be so happy. The [wind] continued still contrary, so that I was forced to run to the southward to the height of 28 degrees of northerly latitude, and until the 27 of April I had no wind to carry me forward on my course.

But then the wind came fairer and I went before the wind till I came near the coast of Virginia, so that time, if it had not scanted, I had recovered the place in less than 8 weeks. But I lay beating upon the coast, that it was near ten weeks before I made the land. For it was the 5 of June before I saw land, and that night I came to an anchor at Cape Henrye, having the *Blessing* wherein was Sir Fardinando Wenman in my company.

The next day, the wind being contrary, I was fain to take the opportunity of the tide to turn up the river; and a little after noon I descried a sail coming in at the point, and then I presently bow up with her. And when I came to make what she was, I found her to be my own consort that had been missing near 8 weeks.

The 6 of June, I came to an anchor under Cape Comfort, where I met with much cold comfort as, if it had not been accompanied with the most happy news of Sir Thomas Gattes his arrival, it had been sufficient to have broke my heart and to have made me altogether unable to have done my king or country any service. Sir Thomas Gattes likewise being in despair of any present supply had prepared himself and all his company for England and meant to quit the country. Upon which advertisement I presently sent my skiff away to give him notice of my arrival, which news I knew would alter that resolution of his. Myself with all possible speed followed after, and met him coming down the river, having shipped the whole company and colony in two small pinnaces with a determination to stay some ten days at Cape Comfort to expect our coming, and otherwise so to go for England, having but 30 days' victuals left him and his hungry company.

So upon the tenth of June, I landed at James' Town, being a very noisome and unwholesome place occasioned much by the mortality and idleness of our own people. So the next day, I set the sailors a-work to unlade ships and the landmen some to cleanse the town, some to make coal for our forges; I sent fishermen out to provide fish for our men, to save other provision, but they had but ill success. Likewise I dispatched Sir George Sommers back again to the Barmudas, the good old gentleman out of his love and zeal not motioning, but most cheerfully and resolutely undertaking to perform so dangerous a voyage and, if it please God he do safely return, he will store us with hog's flesh and fish enough to serve the whole colony this winter.

Thus by God's ass[istance] I will go forwards employing my best endeavors in settling and managing these affairs, although they were never so weak and so far out of order as now I found them. I make no question, if God restore me to health and give me a blessing to my labors, I s[hall] very shortly in some measure recompense the great care and charge the Company hath been at, and return something valuable unto the adventurers, who have so w[ell?] began and constantly seconded these but as yet unfortunate proceedings. I make no question but Your Lordship will be a favorer and a furtherer herein unto us and make it your own cause, since it is undertaken for God's glory and our country's good, to both of which you have been so zealious and so faithful a professor.

Assuring Your Lordship you shall ever find me ready to execute all your commandments and to do you all the faithful service that lieth in my power.

Virginia, about July 1610.

[endorsed:] Lord De La Ware to My Lord from Virginia.
Received in September 1610.

[endorsed:] To the Right Honorable my most worthy and special friend, the Earl of Salisbury, lord high treasurer of England, give these.

27. The Council of Virginia

A True Declaration
of the estate of the colony in Virginia, with a confutation of such scandalous reports as have tended to the disgrace of so worthy an enterprise. Published by advice and direction of the Council of Virginia. (selections)

(London: Printed for William Barret, and are to be sold at the Black Bear in Paul's churchyard. 1610)

< The Council of Virginia 1610, **Force 1836a:4/3**

Published by the Council of Virginia. If the *True and Sincere Declaration* §20 was issued to respond to the bad news that Gates and Somers were lost, here the *True Declaration* follows it to announce the good news of their safe arrival in Virginia.

When not quoting Latin and citing Scripture, and giving us a sweep of historical perspective, it is a worthy sequel to the former publication and borrows verbatim from Lord Delaware's letters and Strachey's *True Repertory §22,* to name the principal locations. Hence it demonstrates that much promotional literature was selected and adapted from writings by people in Virginia. Furthermore, some of this matter was adapted and reprinted in Smith's *General History,* Fourth Book §52, where it is attributed to a William Box, who was at Jamestown with Lord Delaware.

Along with a defense of the man, the quoted material, which is here given complete, is invaluable for being all but *the only words we have of Sir Thomas Gates,* Virginia's first governor. There are isolated statements in other communications, such as Chamberlain's letter to Carlton (12 May 1612): "Sir Thomas Gates has come back from Virginia and states that this plantation will collapse if no supplies are being sent. There are wonderful commodities 'if we could have the patience and would be at the cost to bring them to perfection.'" And more at the end of §22, pp. 442–43.

Brown (1890: 428) gives the publication date 8 November 1610.

I have comfortably excerpted 3500 words out of an 11,000 total.

HINC AUCUPARI VERBA RUMORIS VAGI, "to hawk after the winged report of a vagabond rumor." But judgment is a Salomon in his throne, able by the spirit of wisdom to discern betwixt contesting truth and falsehood.

The compiler of this relation endeavoreth to wash away those spots which foul mouths, to justify their own disloyalty, have cast upon so fruitful, so fertile, and so excellent a country—wherein he professeth that he will relate nothing concerning Virginia but what he hath from the secrets of the judicial Council of Virginia, from the letters of the Lord La Ware, from the mouth of Sir Thomas Gates, whose wisdoms, he conceiveth, are not so shallow as easily to be deceived of others, nor consciences so wretched as by pretenses to deceive others.

The admiral of France, among all the fears and discouragements of civil wars, never gave over the project of plantation in Florida.

Black envy and pale fear being not able to produce any arguments why that should be lawful for France which is in us unlawful, that which to Rome was possible to us is impossible, that which to others is honorable and profitable in us should be traduced as incommodious, base, and contemptible [namely, the project of plantation in Virginia].

To preach the Gospel to a nation conquered, and to set their souls at liberty when we have brought their bodies to slavery, it may be a matter sacred in the preachers, but I know not how justifiable in the rulers, who for their mere ambition do set upon it the gloss of religion. Let the divines of Salamanca discuss that question how the possessor of the West Indies first destroyed and then instructed.

[It is honorable profit if we] by way of merchandising and trade do buy of them the pearls of earth and sell to them the pearls of heaven.

It is not unlawful that we possess part of their [the native people's] land and dwell with them and defend ourselves from them—partly because there is no other moderate and mix'd course to bring them to conversion but by daily conversation where they may see the life and learn the language each of other; partly because there is no trust to the fidelity of human beasts except a man will make a league with lions, bears, and crocodiles; partly because there is room sufficient in the land ... for them and us, the extent of an hundred miles being scarce peopled with 2000 inhabitants; partly because they have violated the law of nations and used our ambassadors as Ammon did the servants of David. If in him it were a just cause to war against the Ammonites, it is lawful in us to secure ourselves against the infidels;

But chiefly because Paspehay, one of their kings, sold unto us for copper land to inherit and inhabit. Powhatan, their chief king, received voluntarily a crown and a scepter, with a full acknowledgment of duty and submission;

Principally when Captain Newport was with Powhatan at Warow a comaco, he desired him to come from James town as a place unwholesome, and to take possession of another whole kingdom which he gave unto him.

[As for the Pope's authority to divide the world's colonies between Spain and Portugal to the exclusion of other nations]

Petrarch recordeth a memorable history of Santius, brother to the King of Spain, who was elected general against the Saracens of Egypt; and coming to Rome for that purpose, the Bishop of Rome made it to be proclaimed in the consistory that he bestowed the kingdom of Egypt upon Santius. Santius understanding this favor by his interpreter commanded to proclaim the Pope "Great Caliph of Baldacho," perfuming the son of pride with his own smoke—the Pope having no more power to make Santius a king than Santius had power to make the Pope a caliph.

[Concerning the 1609 voyage and shipwreck on Bermuda]

Sir Thomas Gates supposeth himself accused publicly and in print of a treble defect—first, that he ran so far southerly and into the tropic that the heat caused the infection in the ships; secondly, that he gave a sealed direction that if they were separated by any storm that they should make for the Baruada [Barbuda] in the West Indies, which direction himself following, it caused his shipwrack, but the other ships upon better judgment declining these instruction arrived safely in Virginia; thirdly, that he carried in one bottom all the principal commissioners who should successively have governed the colony. Against all which imputations he maketh this just apology:

First, he confesseth that a little before they came unto the Canaries, that he ent'red into consultation with Sir George Summers, Captain Newport, and the other of chief regard in the fleet, wherein it was resolved by an uniformity of consent to run southerly into the tropic, which they did till they came to the height of four and twenty [degrees north latitude]. But he denieth that this course was any cause of infection, for in the *Falcon,* the *Blessing,* the *Lion*—and in the admiral wherein were one hundred and fifty souls—there was not one sick of the pestilence nor other disease. In the other two ships the infection was somewhat hot, but they shipped the same from London.

To the second he affirmeth that he first gave them sealed instructions (not to be opened till a time of storm) which directed them to the Baruada. But after, when they came to the height of four and twenty, he countermanded those directions by word of mouth and assigned them that if they were scattered that they should make with all speed for Virginia, which himself, esteeming the price of time unvaluable, would have executed had not the violent leak of the ship hind'red him, so that the other ships' safe arrival in Virginia proceeded originally from his advice and authority.

To the third he briefly signifieth that no other commissioners were in his ship but such as for especial reasons were precisely and peremptorily appointed by the Council of Virginia. And thus you see that Tacitus wisely observed two great enemies of great actions—*ignorantiam veri & invidiam,* "the ignorance of truth and the emulation of virtue."

[As for the time shipwrecked on Bermuda]

The islands on which they fell were the Bermudos, a place hardly accessible through the environing rocks and dangers notwithstanding, they were forced to run their ship on shore, which through God's providence fell betwixt two rocks that caused her to stand firm and not immediately to be broken; God continuing His mercy unto them, that with their longboats they transported to land before night all their company—men, women, and children to the number of one hundred and fifty, [and] they carried to shore all the provision of unspent and unspoiled victuals, all their furniture and tackling of the ship, leaving nothing but bared ribs as a prey unto the ocean.

These islands of the Bermudos have ever been accounted as an enchanted pile of rocks and a desert inhabitation for devils, but all the fairies of the rocks were but flocks of birds, and all the devils that haunted the woods were but herds of swine.

[Beginning a discussion of Virginia's agricultural resources, quoting apparently Gates]

"They use to put their wheat into the ground, five corns in one spit of earth, and two beans with them; which wheat corns, multiplying into divers stalks, grow up twelve or fourteen foot high, yielding some four, five, or six ears on every stalk; and in every ear some five hundred, some six hundred, some seven hundred corns. The two beans run upon the stalks of the wheat as our garden peas upon sticks, which multiply to a wondrous increase. I cannot let slip[1] a great secret," saith the author, "whereof I will avouch no more than with my hands and eyes I have handled and seen, and whereof to my great comfort I have often tasted: The wheat being sown thick, some stalks bear ears of corn and some like siences[2] in trees bear none. But in those barren stalks there is as much juice as in some sugar cane, of so delicate a taste as no fruit in England is comparable to it; out of which Sir Ralph Lane conceived that we may extract sugar in great quantity." But Sir Thomas Gates affirmeth that our men do make cordial drink thereof to their great comfort.

The beasts of the country, as deer, red and fallow, do answer in multitude (people for people considered) to our proportion of oxen, which appeareth by these experiences. First, the people of the country are appareled in the skins of these beasts. Next, hard by the fort, two hundred in one herd have been usually observed. Further, our

---

[1] Omit.

[2] Old form of "scions."

men have seen 4000 of these skins piled up in one wardrobe of Powhaton. Lastly, infinite store have been presented to Captain Newport upon sundry occurrents, such a plenty of cattle as all the Spaniards found not in the whole kingdom of Mexico when all their presents were but hens and guinea cocks and the bread of maize and cently[?].

The rivers from August or September till February are covered with flocks of wildfowl ... (to use the words of Sir Thomas Gates) "in such abundance as are not in all the world to be equaled."

[As for the wholesomeness of Virginia's climate]

In that country flesh will receive salt and continue unputrefied (which it will not in the West Indies) when the most delicate of all flowers grow there as familiarly as in the fields of Portingale, where the woods are replenished with more sweet barks and odors than they are in the pleasantest places of Florida. How is it possible that such a virgin and temperate air should work such contrary effects but because our fort [at Jamestown] that lieth as a semi-island is most part environed with an ebbing and flowing salt water, the ooze of which sendeth forth an unwholesome and contagious vapor?

To close up this part with Sir Thomas Gates his experiment [experience], he professeth that in a fortnight's space he recovered the health of most of them by moderate labor, whose sickness was bred in them by intemperate idleness.

[In England returnees full of slander] are they that roared out the tragical history of the man eating of his dead wife in Virginia, when the master of this ship willingly confessed before 40 witnesses that at their coming away they left three months' victuals, and all the cattle living in the fort. Sometimes they reported that they saw this horrible action, sometimes that Captain Davies said so, sometimes that one Beadle, the lieutenant of Captain Davies, did relate it, varying this report into diversity of false colors which hold no likeness and proportion. But to clear all doubts, Sir Thomas Gates thus relateth the tragedy:

"There was one of the company who mortally hated his wife and therefore secretly killed her, then cut her in pieces and hid her in divers parts of his house. When the woman was missing, the man suspected, his house searched, and parts of her mangled body were discovered, to excuse himself he said that his wife died, that he hid her to satisfy his hunger, and that he fed daily upon her. Upon this his house was again searched, where they found a good quantity of meal, oatmeal, beans, and peas. He thereupon was arraigned, confessed the murder, and was burned for his horrible villainy."

He that shall turn up his eye and behold the spangled canopy of heaven shall but cast down his eye and consider the embroidered carpet of the earth, and withal shall mark how the heavens hear the earth, the earth hear the corn and oil, and they relieve the necessities of man that man will acknowledge God's infinite providence. But he that shall further observe how God inclineth all casual events to work the necessary help of his saints, must needs adore the Lord's infinite goodness. Never had any people more just cause to cast themselves at the footstool of God and to reverence His mercy than our distressed colony! For if God had not sent Sir Thomas Gates from the Bermudos within four days, they had all been famished. If God had not directed the heart of that worthy knight to save the fort from fire at their shipping, they had been destitute of a present harbor and succor. If they had abandoned the fort any longer time and had not so soon returned, questionless the Indians would have destroyed the fort, which had been the means of our safety among them, and a terror unto them. If they had set sail sooner and had launched into the vast ocean, who could have promised that they should have encountered the fleet of the Lord La-ware?—especially when they made for the New-found land, a course contrary to our navy's approaching. If the Lord La-ware had not brought with him a year's provision, what comfort could those souls have received to have been relanded to a second destruction?

Brachium Domini, this was the arm of the Lord of Hosts! who would have His people to pass the Red Sea and wilderness, and then to possess the land of Canaan. It was divinely spoken of[1] heathen

[1] By.

Socrates, *"Si Deus sit solicitus pro te, cur tu tibi sis solicitus?"* If God for man be careful, why should man be over distrustful?

[The colony during the governorship of Lord Delaware has good housing]

The houses which are built are as warm and defensible against wind and weather as if they were tiled and slated, being covered above with strong boards and matted round within according to the fashion of the Indians.

The lord governor [Delaware] hath built two new forts [Henry and Charles at Kecoughtan] ... upon a pleasant hill and near a little rivulet which we call Southampton River. They stand in a wholesome air, having plenty of springs of sweet water. They command a great circuit of ground containing wood, pasture, and meadow; with apt places for vines, corn, and gardens—in which forts it is resolved that all those that come out of England shall be at their first landing quartered, that the wearisomeness of the sea may be refreshed in this pleasing part of the country.

The merchants know that the commodity of soap- and potashes are very scant in Prussia, that they are brought three hundred miles by land ... But in Virginia they may have them without carriage by land or custom because five navigable rivers do lead up five several ways into the bowels of the whole country. As therefore the like rivers are the cause of the riches of Holland, so will these be to us a wondrous cause of saving of expenses. The merchant knoweth that through the troubles in Poland and Muscovy, whose eternal wars are like the antipathy of the dragon and elephants, all their traffic for masts, deals,[1] pitch, tar, flax, hemp, and cordage are every day more and more endangered, and the woods of those countries are almost exhausted—all which are to be had in Virginia with far less charge and far more safety. Lastly, the merchant knoweth that for our commodities in the St[r]aits,[2] as sweet wines, oranges, lemons, anise

[1] Sawn lumber.

[2] The Mediterranean.

seeds, etc., that we stand at the devotion of politic princes and states, who for their proper utility devise all courses to grind our merchants, all pretenses to confiscate their goods, and to draw from us all marrow of gain by their inquisitive inventions, when in Virginia a few years' labor by planting and husbandry will furnish all our defects with honor and security, especially since the Frenchmen who are with the lord governor do confidently promise that within two years we may expect a plentiful vintage.

Let any wisdom give a solid reason why his purpose should be changed when those grounds which gave life to his first purpose are not changed.

Hannibal by too much wisdom lost opportunity to have sacked Rome. Charles the Eighth of France by temporizing lost the Kingdom of Naples and the government of Florence. Henry the Seventh by too much overwariness lost the riches of the golden Indies. Occasion is precious but when it is occasion. Some of our neighbors would join in the action if they might be joint inheritors in the plantation, which is an evident proof that Virginia shall no sooner be quitted by us than it will be reinhabited by them—a dishonor of that nature that will eternally blemish our nation as though we were like the furious Pyrrhus or impetuous Swissers who in a brunt can conquer anything, but with wisdom can maintain nothing.

He is overblind that doth not see what an inundation of people doth overflow this little island. [A problem that the compiler sees to have some very ugly remedies and only one handsome one: colonies.]

It was a fit emblem that painted Death standing upon the shores of France, Germany, and Spain, and looking over into England, intimating unto us that so long as we are lords of the narrow seas, Death stands on the other shores and only can *look* upon us. But if our wooden walls were ruinated, Death would soon make a bridge to come over and devour our nation.

When therefore our mills of iron and excess of building have already turned our greatest woods into pasture and champion within these few years, neither the scattered forests of England nor the diminished groves of Ireland will supply the defect of our navy, when in Virginia there is nothing wanting ...

Let any man resolve why the Council of Virginia do now most earnestly continue their adventures, why those that were eyewitnesses of the former supposed "miseries" do voluntarily return with joy and comfort, why those noble and worthy personages do offer to make the action good upon the hazard of their lives and fortunes, and why Sir Thomas Gates longeth and hasteneth to go thither again, and the Lord La-ware desireth so earnestly to stay there. Are not all these things as dear to them as to any other of the adventurers? Have not their hopes the same wings? their fears the same fetters? their estates the same rocks? their lives and souls greater gulfs of peril and despair? And yet neither the embracements of their wives nor indulgence to their babes nor the neglect of their domestic fortunes nor banishment from their native soil nor any experimented dangers[1] have broken their noble resolution.

[1] Dangers they have experienced.

28. George Yeardley

Letter to Peyton, 18 November 1610

< Kingsbury 1906c:29

The man who in less than eight years became Virginia's best governor tells us Virginia's resources are abundant and can be plowed to the surface with enough men, capital, and provisions to see it through the beginning. And this would have already been well along if there had been good government the first three years. Governor Delaware plans an expedition above the Falls to look for gold and silver and a route to the South Sea. It is hoped in addition that the newly discovered Delaware Bay will provide a route to the interior.

Sir Henry Peyton was collector of customs in Plymouth. "He followed the long wars in the Netherlands." (Brown) He was a member of the household of Henry, Prince of Wales.

HONORABLE SIR—Upon the return of the last fleet of ships, which brought my Lord La Warr, our lord governor and captain general, into this country, I did not forbear to challenge your noble patience with reading unworthy and fruitless lines; and although at this present I am little or nothing better furnished with any matter of value, either for discovery of mines or ought else worth your knowledge, yet when I consider your many and noble favors towards me (which when I forget to acknowledge let me forever be put out of your remembrance) I thought good to write something, if but thereby to preserve my humble service in your honored memory.

For the present state and condition of this country, it wants only supports, round and free supplies both of men and monies, to make good the main and profitable ends of a most happy plantation.

Concerning the country and the soil thereof, we find it fertile and full of increase, bringing forth goodly corn, many kind of fruits, natural vines, and quickly rend'ring us our own country seeds and roots, which we bury therein, as prosperous and unchangeable for taste and quantity as England itself. For these commodities of pitch and tar, soap-ashes, wood, iron, etc., most true it is, noble sir, that there they be most plentifully to be returned home, if so be it the means and skillful workmen, together with fit provisions for those laborers—until the color may quit some of these charges by planting their own vines, sowing their own corn, and brooding their own cattle, kine, swine, goats, etc., which would shortly be, and had been ere this, had the government been carefully and honestly established and carried here these 3 years past—may be provided and sent over to work in those businesses.

For the opening and finding out of silver or gold, we have now probable intelligence to be brought unto; for which cause our lord governor hath gathered together most of his choicest men, and intendeth a voyage forthwith up unto a famous fall, or cataract of waters, where leaving his pinnaces and boats safe riding he purposeth to lead us up into the land called the Monocane 2 or 3 days' journey; where at the foot of certain mountains he meaneth to build a fort, and there to winter some of his people, who shall every day dig at those mines; and though they prove not according to our expectation, yet we have lost nothing but our labor, with this advantage nevertheless that we shall have a redoubt and some of our men in it, against the next spring when his lordship intendeth to march that way something more southerly for the finding out the South Sea.

We have some hope also by a westerly trade thorough a fair and goodly bay lying in the height of 382,[1] some 30 leagues from our own bay, newly discovered since his lordship's coming hither, from whence we promise ourselves many commodities both of fish from the bay, for our color,[2] and from the tractable Indians of that place, of whom we have made already some trial, both corn, furs, etc.

And, honorable sir, I have by these few yet troublesome lines given you the account and truth of what we know and purpose concerning this His Majesty's country and new kingdom. As further passages herein material and worthy your knowledge shall occur and

---

[1] Delaware Bay at 38°20'N.

[2] As it appears to us.

be off'red unto us, I will presume to address them unto you.

Ever vowing myself in the utmost of my endeavors to do you service, I kiss your honored hand.

In Virginia, dated at James Town this xviii[th] of November, 1610,

At your commandment,
GEORGE YARDLY

[endorsed:] To the Honorable Sir Henry Peyton, knight, at his house in the Blackfriars, or elsewhere: Leave these. London.

29. Henry Spelman

Relation of Virginia, 1609

< **Hunnewell 1872,** Arber 1884a:ci, Brown 1890:483 *in part.*

The manuscript was brought to light in the 19th century only to get lost again in the 20th! James Hunnewell tells us of the faltering steps after its discovery to put it in print, culminating in his own arrangement at the "world-renowned" Chiswick Press in 1872 for fifty impressions. Brown and Arber do not make clear whether their texts are based on this or the manuscript.

Hunnewell in his own long introduction never tells us what the bracketed material in the Chiswick edition represents in the manuscript. So Alexander Brown tells us,"[Spelman] has corrected his MS by marking out the words in italics and writing instead the words in brackets." However, Brown's text goes down only to the section "Of Their Service to Their Gods." Edward Arber gives the full text without stating his, Hunnewell's, purpose for italics, but it is apparently the reverse of Brown: to indicate Spelman's *insertions.*

Unbracketed *italics* are my own indications for exotic words, the normal practice. My bracketed roman supplies a missing conjunction or two.

The parallel passage results apparently from Spelman's having made a revision but not a clean copy. Hunnewell here tells us something: "Another version of this passage is given in the last leaf of the manuscript, which may be the original draft." This is the material in my right column.

He was a troubled teenager, packed off to Virginia for good or ill. He launches into his account like a fist to the jaw. As to the altercation at the Falls, *The Proceedings §17* supports Smith, Percy's *True Relation §31* supports Spelman. We only know that soon both Smith and West were gone—Smith as a sick and injured man sent home, and Francis West, commandeering a ship loaded with corn (the *Swallow?),* deserted the colony just prior to the "starving time" (he came back in the spring with his brother Lord Delaware).

Spelman lived with the Indians two years. He learned the language fluently, and his observations on native culture can be accepted as those of not just an eyewitness but an insider, albeit an immature one at the time. His most controversial assertion is that the Patawomeck sacrificed children. We hear the same claim from William White in connection with the black boys ceremony §11, and we hear it denied by John Rolfe.

He tells us that widows had a life interest in their houses; that Indians had laws, but does not tell us how they determined guilt. The gruesome execution reminds us of Europe of those days. The spectacle made a terrifying example. Spelman's Indian society was a stratified patriarchy that practiced polygamy, and had an exchange based on copper. His mention of football reminds us that so soon America was taking shape. See also Strachey's *History §41–641.*

This charming, intimate Indian portrait makes us understand why so many colonists were running away to them. And how utterly impossible it is for us members of modern urban mega-states to understand what it must feel like to live in a sovereign village going to war with stones against another sovereign village. What a pity it breaks off.

BEING IN DISPLEASURE of my friends, and desirous to see other countries: After *[some weeks]* three months' sail we come with prosperous winds in sight of Virginia, where a storm suddenly arising severed our *[ship]* fleet—which was of x sail—every ship from other, putting us all in great danger for vii or viii days together. But the storm then ceasing, our ship, called the *Unity,* came the next morning safely to an anchor at Cape Henry, the—— day of October, 1609, where we found three other of our fleet; and about a sennight after, three more came thither also. The residue *[still remained],* amongst which was Sir Thomas Gates and Sir George Summers, knights, *[who]* were not *[being]* heard of many months after our arrival.

From Cape Henry we sailed up the River of Powáhtan, and within 4 or 5 days arrived at James town, where we were joyfully welcomed by our countrymen, being at that time about 80 persons under the government of Captain Smith, the president.

Having here unladed our goods, and bestowed some sennight or fortnight in viewing of the country, I was carried by Captain Smith, our president, to the Falls, to the Little Powhatan where, unknown to me, he sold me to him for a town called Powhatan.[1] And leaving me with him, the Little Powhatann, he made known to Captain Weste how he had bought a town for them to dwell in *[whereupon Captain Weste growing angry, because he had bestowed cost to begin a town in another place, Captain Smith etc.]* desiring that Captain West would come and settle himself there. But Captain Weste, having bestowed cost to begin a town in another place, misliked it; and unkindness

[1] To learn the language. A standard procedure. cf. 168, Thomas Savage.

thereupon arising between them, Captain Smith at that time *[saying]* replied little, *[yet]* but afterward *[wrought]* conspired with the Pohawtan to kill Captain Weste; which plot took but small effect. For in the *[interim]* meantime Captain Smith was apprehended and sent aboard for England; myself having been now about vii or viii days with the Little Powhatan, who, though he made very much of me, giving me such things as he had to win me to live with him, *[when]* yet I desired to see our English, and therefore made signs unto him to give me leave to go to our ship to fetch such things as I left behind me, which he agreed unto, and setting himself down, he clap'd his hand on the ground in token he would stay there till I returned. But I staying somewhat too long, at my coming *[back]* to the place where I left him, I found him departed. Whereupon I went back to our ship, being still in the Falls, and sailed with them to James town; where not being long there before one Thomas Savage, with 4 or 5 Indians, came from the Great Powhatan with venison to Captain Percye, who now was president. After the delivery thereof—and that he must return—he was loith[1] to go without some of his countrymen went with him. Whereupon I was appointed to go, which I the more willingly did by reason that victuals were scarce with us, carrying with me some copper and a hatchet *[with me]*, which I had gotten. *[And]* coming to the Great Powetan, I presented to him such things as I had, which he took, using me very kindly *[setting this Savage and me at his own table mess]*. And after I had been with him about 3 weeks, he sent me back to our English, bidding me tell them that if they would bring their ship and some copper, he would

fraught her back with corn; which I having reported to our English, and returning their answer to the king, he before their coming laid plots to take them, which in some sort he effected. For xxvi or vii they killed, which came towards land in their	fraught her back corn; which I having reported to our English, and returning their answer to the Powhatan, Captain Ratclyff came with a ship with xxiiii or xxv men to Orohpikes; and leaving his ship there, came by barge with sixteen men to the

[1] Loath.

longboat, and shot many arrows into the ship; which our men perceiving, and fearing the worst, weighed anchor and returned.

Powhatan to Powmunkey, where he very courteously in show received them by sending them bread and venison; in reward whereof Captain Ratclyff sent him copper and beads and suchlike.

Then Powhatan appointed Captain Ratclyff a house for him and his men to lie in during the time that they should *[traff]* traffic, not far from his own but above half a mile from the barge. And himself in the evening coming to the *[their]* house slenderly accompanied welcomed him thither; and *[after Captain Rat]* returned, leaving the Dutchman, Savage, and myself behind him.

The next day, the Powhatan with a company of savages came to Captain Ratcliff, and carried our English to their storehouse, where their corn was, to traffic with them: giving them pieces of copper and beads and other things according to the proportion of the baskets of corn which they brought. But the Indians dealing deceitfully by pulling or bearing up the bottom of their baskets with their hands, so that the less corn might *[serve to]* fill them, the Englishmen taking exceptions against it, and a discontentment rising upon it, the king *[conveyed himself and]* departed, taking me and the Dutchman with him [and] his wives hence.

Now while this business was in *[doing]* action, the Powhatan sends me and one Samwell, a Dutchman, to a town about xvi miles off, called Yawtanoone, willing us there to stay *[till]* for him.

And presently a great number Indians, that lay lurking in the woods and corn about, began with an oulis and whoopubb. And whilest our Englishmen were in haste carrying their corn to their ships, the Indians that were hidden in the corn shot the men as they passed by them, and so killed them all, saving one William Russell and one other who, being acquainted with the country, escaped to James town by land.

At his coming thither, we understood how all things had passed by Thomas Savage, as before is related. The king in show made still much of us, yet his mind was much declined from us, which made us fear the worst.

And having now been with him about 24 or 25 weeks, it hap'ned that the King *[of Pasptan]* of Patomeck came to visit the Great Powetan; where being awhile with him, he showed such kindness to Savage, Samuell, and myself as we determined to go away with him.

When the day of his departure was come, we did as we agreed. And having gone a mile or two on the way, Savage feigned some excuse of stay, and unknown to us went back to the Powetan and acquainted him with our *[fleeing]* departing with the Patowomeck. The Powetan presently sends after us, commanding our return, which we *[not believing]* refusing went still on our way. And those that were sent went still on with us till one of them, finding opportunity, on a sunden struck Samuell with an ax and killed him; which I seeing ran away from among the company, they after me, the king and his men after them; who overtake them held them; till I shifted for myself and got to the Patomecke's country.

With this King Patomecke I lived a year and more, at a town of his called Pasptanzie, until such time as an worthy gentleman named Captain Argall arrived at a town call'd Nacottawtanke[1]—but by our English call'd Camocacocke—where he understood that there was an English boy named Harry. He desiring to hear further of me came up the river; which the king of Patomeck hearing sent me to him; and I going back again brought the king to *[him]* the ship, where Captain Argall gave the king *[some]* copper for me, *[and he]* which he received. Thus was I set *[free]* at liberty and brought into England.

Of their service to their gods.

TO GIVE some satisfaction to my friends and contentment unto others which wish well to this viage *[voyage]*, and are desirous to hear the fashions of that country, I have set down as well as I can what I observed in the time I was among them.

And therefore first, concerning their gods, you must understand that for the most part they worship the devil, which the conjurers, who are their priests, can make appear unto them at their pleasure. Yet, nevertheless, in every country they have a several image whom they call their god, as with the Great Pawetan. He hath an image called *cakeres* which most commonly standeth at Yaughtawnoone *[in one of the king's houses]* or at Oropikes[2] in a house for that purpose. And with him are set all the king's goods and presents that are sent him, as the corn. But the beads and crown or bed which the king of England sent him are in the god's house at Oropikes. And in their houses are all the king ancestors and kindred commonly buried *[commonly]*. In the Patomeck's country they have another god whom the call Quioquascacke; and unto their images they offer beads and copper, if at any time they want rain or have too much. And though they observe no day to worship their god but upon necessity, yet once in the year their priests, which are their conjurers, with the *[people]* men, women, and children, do go into the woods, where their priests makes a great circle of fire in the which, after many

---

[1] "Xatauahane" (margin note)

[2] "Caukewis Manato. Taukinge souke Quiauasack." (margin note)

observances in their conjurations, they make offer of 2 or 3 children to be given to their god, if he will appear unto them, and show his mind whom he *[will have]* desire. Upon which offering, they hear a noise out of the circle nominating such as he will have, whom presently they take, binding them hand and foot, and cast them into the circle of the fire. For be it the king's son, he must be given if once named by their god. After the bodies which are offered are consumed in the fire, and their ceremonies performed, the men depart merrily, the women weeping.

Of the country of Virginia.

THE COUNTRY is full of wood *[and]* in some parts, and water they have plentiful. They have marish ground, and small fields for corn, and other grounds whereon their deer, goats, and stags feedeth. There be in this country lions, bears, wolves, foxes, musk cats, hares, flying squirrels[1] and other squirrels being all gray like conies, great store of fowl (only peacocks and common hens wanting), fish in abundance whereon they live most part of the summertime. They have a kind of wheat call'd *locataunce,* and peas and beans, great store of walnuts growing in every place. They have no orchard fruits; only two kind of plums, the one a sweet and luscious plum, long and thick, in form and likeness of a nut palm, the other resembling a medlar, but somewhat sweeter, yet not eatable till they be rotten as ours are.

Of their towns & buildings.

PLACES OF HABITATION they have but few, for the greatest town have not above 20 or 30 houses in it. Their building are made like an oven with a little hole to come in at, but more spacious within, having a hole in the middest of the house for smoke to go out at. The king's houses are both broader and longer than the rest, having many dark windings and turnings before any come where the king is. But in that time when they go a-hunting, the women goes to a place

---

1 "Called *assapameek.*" (margin note)

appointed before to build houses for their husbands to lie in at night, carrying mats with them to cover their houses withal. And as the men goes further a-hunting, the women *[goes before]* follows to make houses, always carrying their mats with them. Their manner of their hunting is this: *[Where]* they meet some 2 or 300 together, and having their bows and arrows, and everyone with a fire *[sti]* stick in their hand, they beset a great thicket round about. Which done, everyone set fire on the rank grass, *[and]* which the deer seeing fleeth from the fire. And the men, coming in by a little and little, encloseth their game in a narrow room, so as with their bows and arrows they kill them at their pleasure, taking their skins, which is the greatest thing they desire, and some flesh for their provision.

Their manner of marrying.

THE CUSTOM of the country is to have many wives, and to buy them, so that he which have most copper and beads may have most wives. For if he taketh liking of any woman, he makes love to her, and seeketh to her father or kinsfolk to set what price he must pay for her; which being on[c]e agreed on, the kindred meet and make good cheer. And when the sum agreed on be paid, she shall be delivered to him for his wife.

The ceremony is thus: The parents brings their daughter between them (if her parents be dead, then some of her kinsfolk, or whom it pleaseth the king to appoint). For the man goes not unto any place to be married, but the woman is brought to him where he dwelleth. At her coming to him, her father or chief friends joins the hands together; and then the father or chief friend of the man bringeth a long string of beads, and measuring his arm's length thereof, doth break it over the hands of those that are to be married, while their hands be joined together; and gives it unto the woman's father or him that brings her. And so with much mirth and feasting they go together.

When the king of the country will have any wives, he acquaints his chief men with his purpose, who sends *[for]* into all parts of the country for the fairest and comeliest maids, out of which the king taketh his choice, given their parents what he pleaseth.

If any of the king's wives have once a child by him, he *[never lieth with her more]* keeps her no longer, but puts her from him, giving her sufficient copper and beads to maintain her and the child while it is young; and then [it] is taken from her and maintained by the king*['s charge]*, it now being lawful for her, being thus put away, to marry with any other.

The king Poetan, having many wives, when he goeth a-hunting, or to visit another king under him (for he goeth not out of his own country) he leaveth them with two old men who have the charge on them till his return.

It was my hap to be left at one of the King's Pasptanse's[1] houses when he went to visit another king. And two of his wives were there also. After the king's departure, one of them would go visit her father —*[whose]* her name was Paupauwiske—and seeing me, willed me to go with her, and to take her child and carry him thither in *[his]* my arms, being a *[long]* day's journey from the place where we dwelt; *[but]* which I refusing, she struck me 3 or 4 blows; but I being loith to bear too much, got to her and pull'd her down, giving her some blows again; which the other of the king's wives perceiving, they both fell on me beating me so as I thought they had lam'd me.

Afterward, when the king came home, in their presence I acquainted him how they had used me. The king without further delay took up a *couwascohocan*, which is a kind of paring iron, and struck at one of them with such violence as he fell'd her to the ground, in manner dead. I seeing that fled to a neighbor's house for fear of the king's displeasure. But his wife, coming again to herself, somewhat appeased his anger, so as understanding where I was by his brother, he sent me his young child to still, for none could quiet him so well as myself. And about midnight he sent for him again.

The next day morning, the king was early up, and came to the house where I was. Loith I was to see him; yet being come to him, instead of his anger I found him kind to me, asking me how I did, and whether I was afraid of him last night, because I ran away from him and hid myself. I being by his speeches somewhat bolder asked him for his queen. He answered all was well and that I should go home with him, telling me he loved me and none *[should]* should

---

1 "This Pasptanse was brother to Patoomsk." (margin note)

hurt me. I though loith went with him where, at my coming, the queen looked but discontentedly on me. But hoping on the king's promise, I cared the less for others' frowns, knowing well that the king made the more of me in hope I should help him to some copper, if at any time our English came into those parts, which I often had promised him to do, and which was by Captain Argoll bountifully performed.

How the[y] name their Children.

AFTER THE MOTHER is delivered of her child, within some few days after, the kinsfolk and neighbors, being entreated thereunto, comes unto the house where, being assembled, the father takes the child in his arms and declares that his name shall be. As he then calls him, so his name is. Which done, the rest of the day is spent in feasting and dancing.

Their Manner of visiting the Sick, with the Fashion of their Burial if they die.

WHEN ANY BE SICK among them, their priests comes unto the party, whom he layeth on the ground upon a mat. And having a bowl of water set between him and the sick party, and a rattle by it, the priest, kneeling by the sick man's side, dips his hand into the bowl, which taking up full of water, he sups into his mouth, spouting it out again upon his own arms and breast. Then takes he the rattle, and with one hand shakes that, and with the other he beats his breast, making a great noise; which having done he easily riseth (as loith to wake the sick body), first with one leg, then with the other. And being now got up, he leisurely goeth about the sick man, shaking his rattle very *[easily]* softly over all his body. And with his hand he stroketh the grieved parts of the sick. Then doth he besprinkle him with water, mumbling certain words over him; and so for that time leave him.

But if he be wounded, after these ceremonies done unto him, he with a little flintstone gasheth the wound, making it to run and bleed; which he setting his mouth unto it sucks out, and then applies a certain root beaten to powder unto the sore.

If he dies his burial is thus: There is a scaffold built about 3 or 4 yards high from the ground, and the dead body wrapped in a mat is brought to the place where, when he is laid thereon, the kinsfolk falls a-weeping and make great sorrow. And instead of a dole for him—the poorer people being got together—some of his kinsfolk flings beads among them, making them to scramble for them, so that many times divers do break their arms and legs, being pressed by the company. This finished, they go to the party's house, where they have meat given them; which being eaten, all the rest of the day they spend in singing and dancing, using then as much mirth as before sorrow. Moreover, if any of the kindreds' bodies which have been laid on the scaffold be so consumed as nothing is left but bones, they take those bones from the scaffold, and putting them into a new mat, hangs them in their houses, where they continue while their house falleth, and then they are buried in the ruins of the house. What goods the party leaveth is divided among his wives and children. But his house he giveth to the wife he liketh best for life; after her death, unto what child he most loveth.

The Justice and Government.

CONCERNING THEIR LAWS, my years and understanding made me the less to look after, because I thought that infidels were lawless. Yet when I saw some put to death, I asked the cause of their offense. For in the time I was with the Patomecke I saw 5 executed: 4 for murther of a child, id est, the mother and two other that did the fact with her, and a 4 for concealing it as he passed by (being bribed to hold his peace); and one for robbing a traveler of copper and beads. For to steal their neighbor's corn or copper is death; or to lie one with another's wife is death, if he be taken in the manner.

The Manner of Execution.

THOSE THAT BE CONVICTED of capital offenses are brough[t] into a plain place before the king's house, when then he lay—which was at

Pomunkeye, the chiefest house he hath—where one or two appointed by the king did bind them hand and foot; which being done, a great fire was made. Then came the officer to those that should die, and with a shell cut off their long lock, which they wear on the left side of their head, and hangeth that on a bow before the king's house. Then those for murther were beaten with staves till their bones were broken, and being alive were flung into the fire. The other for robbing was knock'd on the head, and being dead his body was burnt.

The manner of setting their corn with the gathering and dressing.

THEY MAKE most commonly a place about their houses to set their corn, which, if there be much wood in that place, the[y] cut down the great trees some half a yard above the ground. And the smaller they burn at the root, pulling a good part of bark from them to make them die. And in this place they dig many holes which, before the English brought them scavels and spades, they used to make with a crooked piece of wood, being scraped on both sides in fashion of a gardener's paring iron.

They put into these holes ordinarily 4 or 5 kernels of their wheat and 2 beans like French beans, which, when the wheat do grow up, having a straw as big as a cane reed, the beans run up thereon like our hops on poles. The ear of the wheat is of great bigness in length and compass, and yet, for all the greatness of it, every stalk hath most commonly some four or five ears on it. Their corn is set and gathered about the time we use. But their manner of their gathering is as we do our *[aplse]* apples: first in a hand baskets *[putti]* emptying them as they are filled into other bigger baskets, whereof some are made of the barks of trees, some of hemp which naturally groweth there, and some of the straw whereon the wheat groweth.

Now after the gathering, they lay it upon mats a good thickness in the sun to dry. And every night they make a great pile of it, covering it over with mats to defend it from the dew; *[which]* and when it is sufficiently weathered, they pile it up in their houses, daily as occasion serveth wringing the ears in pieces between their hands; and so rubbing out their corn do put it to a great basket which taketh up the best part of some of their houses. And all this is chiefly the women's work. For the men do only hunt to get skins in winter, and do tew, or dress, them in summer.

But though now out of order, yet let me not altogether forget the setting of the king's corn, for which a day is appointed wherein great part of the country people meet, who with such diligence worketh as for the most part all the king's corn is set on a day. After which setting, the king takes the crown which the King of England sent him, being brought him by two men, and sets it on his head. Which done, the people goeth about the corn in manner backwards—for they going before, and the king following. Their faces are always toward the king, expecting when he should fling some beads among them, which his custom is at that time to do, making those which had wrought to scramble for them. But to some he favors he bids those that carry his beads to call such and such unto him, unto whom he giveth beads into their hand. And this is the greatest courtesy he doth his people.

When his corn is ripe, the country people comes to him again and gathers, dries, and rubs out all his corn for him, which is laid in houses appointed for that purpose.

The setting at meat.

THEY SET ON MATS round about the house, the men by themselves and the women by theirselves. The women bring to everyone a dish of meat. For the better sort never eats together in one dish. When he hath eaten what he will, or that which was given him—for he looks for no *[meat]* second course—he sets down his dish by him and mumbleth certain words to himself in manner of *[a saying grace]* giving thanks. If any left, the women gather it up and either keeps it till the next meal or gives it to the poorer sort, if any be there.

The differences among them.

THE KING IS NOT KNOW by any difference from other of the *[better]* chief sort in the country but only when he comes to any of their houses they present him with copper beads or victual, and show much reverence to him.

The priest are shaven on the right side of their head, close to the skull, only a little lock left at the ear. And some of these have beards. But the common people have no beards at all. For they pull away their hairs as fast as it grows. And they also cut the hairs on the right side of their head, that it might not hinder them by flapping about their bowstring when they draw it to shoot. But on the other side they let it grow, and have a long lock hanging down their shoulder.

The armor and weapon with discipline in war.

AS FOR armor or discipline in war, they have not any. The weapons they use for offense are bows and arrows, with a weapon like a hammer, and their *tomahaucks;* for defense which are shields made of the bark of a tree, and hanged on their left shoulder to cover that side as they stand forth to shoot.

They never fight in open fields, but always either among reed or behind trees, taking their opportunity to shoot at their enemies. And till they can nock another arrow, they make the trees their defense.

In the time that I was there, I saw a battle fought between the Patomeck and the Masomeck. Their place where they fought was a marish ground full of reed, being in the country of the Patomecke. The people of Masomeck were brought thither in canoes, which is a kind of boat they have made in the form of an hog's trough, but somewhat more hollowed in.

On both sides they scatter themselves some little distant one from the other. Then take they their bows and arrows, and having made ready to shoot, they softly steal toward their enemies, sometime squatting down and prying if they can spy any to shoot at, whom, if at any time he so hurteth that he cannot flee, they make haste to him to knock him on the head. And they that kill most of their enemies are held the chiefest men among them.

Drums and trumpets they have none. But when they will gather themselves together they have a kind of howling, or hubbabub, so differing in sound one from the other as both part may very easily be distinguished. There was no greater slaughter of neither side. But the

Massomecks, having shot away most of their arrows, and wanting victual, *[was]* were glad to retire.

The pastimes.

WHEN THEY MEET at feasts or otherwise, they use sports much like to ours here in England, as their dancing, which is like our Derbyshire hornpipe: a man first and then a woman, and so through them all, hanging all in a round. There is one which stand in the middest with a pipe and a rattle with which, when he begins to make a noise, all the rest jiggets about, wrying their necks and stamping on the ground.

They use, beside, football play, which women and young boys do much play at, the men never. They make their goals as ours, only they never fight nor pull one another down.

The men play with a little ball, letting it fall out of their hand, and striketh it with the top of his foot. And he that can strike the ball furthest wins that they play for.

30. Henry Spelman

Excerpt published in *Purchas His Pilgrimage*

< **Purchas** 1613:641, 1614:767, 1617:954, **1626:842**

Rev. Purchas is here quoting Spelman in a digression on the religion of the Patawomecks that has the same source as that so beautifully recounted by Strachey at §41–658ff.

I MAY ALSO here insert the ridiculous conceits which some Virginians hold concerning their First Original, as I have heard from the relation of an English youth[1] which lived long amongst the savages: that a hare came into their country and made the first men, and after preserved them from a great serpent; and when two other hares came thither, that hare for their entertainment killed a deer, which was then the only deer that was, and strewing the hairs of that deer hide, every hair proved a deer.

He said they worshipped towards a certain hoop or sphere doubled across, which was set upon an heap of stones in their houses.

They had a house without the town for the women in the time of their natural sickness to keep in, where no men might come.

[1] "Captain Argol's boy. His name is Henry Spilman." (margin note)

31. George Percy

A True Relation
of the proceedings and occurrents of moment which have hap'ned in Virginia from the time Sir Thomas Gates was shipwrack'd upon the Bermudes, anno 1609, until my departure out of the country, which was in anno Domini 1612

< **Elkins 106, The Free Library of Philadelphia MSS;** Tyler's Quarterly Magazine (1922) 3:259

Percy's disparaging remarks in his address must be aimed at Captain John Smith and the 1624 publication of the *General History,* and are a good indicator of when he wrote this. If Smith provoked his quill, those of us waiting for the goods on the notorious captain are nearly disappointed. His account of the quarrel at the Falls and Smith's injury, events he did not witness, is puzzling and crudely gloating. Smith mentions that Percy was also incapacitated by a gunpowder accident, namely, at Point Comfort where he sent him to fish §17–320. But until the arrival of Gates, Smith was the only *legally constituted head of government* at Jamestown, whether or not he was popular with the new faction.

Instead of telling all about the Captain, *A True Relation* confirms Percy's own ineptitude. He is wellborn, honest, intelligent, and thoroughly dense. Is he unaware of the horrendous self-indictment as governor in admitting Kecoughtan was well supplied while Jamestown went through the infamous "starving time"? He can't understand Don Diego's revenge, but appears to question the justice of Argall's action to destroy the French settlement of Saint Sauveur in Maine.

This reads like a recollection without notes. The writing is spare, without the "eloquent style or phrase" of his *Discourse §1.* I find it a piece of grimness relieved by sheer horror.

LIBRARY OF VIRGINIA

CAPTAIN GEORGE PERCY

A TRUE RELATION

TO THE RIGHT HONORABLE THE LORD PERCY,

MY LORD—This relation I have here sent Your Lordship is for two respects: the one to show how much I honor you and desire to do you service, the other in regard that many untruths concerning these proceedings have been formerly published, wherein the author hath not spared to appropriate many deserts to himself which he never performed, and stuffed his relations with so many falsities and malicious detractions, not only of this part and time which I have selected to treat of but of former occurrents also, so that I could not contain myself but express the truth unto Your Lordship concerning these affairs.

And all which I aim at is to manifest myself in all my actions both now and always to be

Your Lordship's humble and faithful servant,
G[EORGE] P[ERCY]

IF WE TRULY consider the diversity of miseries, mutinies, and famishments which have attended upon discoveries and plantations in these our modern times, we shall not find our plantation in Virginia to have suffered alone. Ladoniere had his share thereof in Florida, next neighbor unto Virginia, where his soldiers did fall into mutinies, and in the end were almost all starved for want of food.

The Spaniard's plantation in the River of Plate and the Straits of Magellan suffered also insomuch that, having eaten up all their horses to sustain themselves withal, mutinies did arise and grow amongst them for the which the general, Diego Mendosa, caused some of them to be executed, extremity of hunger enforcing others secretly in the night to cut down their dead fellows from off the gallows and bury them in their hungry bowels.

The plantation in Carthagena was also lamentable that [for] want of wholesome food wherewith for to maintain life were enforced to eat toads, snakes, and suchlike venomous worms, such is the sharpness of hunger.

To this purpose many other examples might be recited, but the relation itself being brief, I have no intent to be tedious, but to deliver the truth briefly and plainly, the which I doubt not but will rather like than loathe the reader. Nor do I purpose to use any eloquent style or phrase, the which indeed in me is wanting, but to deliver that truly which myself and many others have had bitter experience of.

Many other woes and miseries have hap'ned unto our colony in Virginia, both before and since that time, which now I do intend to treat of, having selected this part from the rest for two respects: first, in regard I was most frequent and acquainted with these proceedings, being most part of the time president and governor; next, in respect the least part hereof hath not been formerly published.

In the year of our Lord 1609, Sir Thomas Gates and Sir George Somers, accompanied with divers gentlemen, soldiers, and seamen, in nine good ships, did begin their voyage for Virginia, the two knights being in the admiral, whereof Christopher Newport was captain; and having sailed with prosperous winds many leagues, at length did fall upon the Bermudes where, meeting with a violent storm, the admiral, wherein the two knights were embarked, suff'red wrack; nevertheless, hoising out[1] their boat, safely landed the 2 knights and the rest of that company upon the Bermudes, of whom I will forbear to treat of further until their arrival in Virginia.

The other 8 ships shortly after arrived in Virginia, where the passengers being no sooner well landed but presently a dissension did grow between them and Captain Smithe, then president. But after some debate all was quieted and pacified. Yet Captain Smithe, fearing the worst, and that the seamen and that faction might grow too strong and be a means to depose him off his government, so juggled with[2] them by the way of feastings, expense of much powder, and other unnecessary triumphs,[3] that much was spent to no other purpose but to insinuate with his reconciled enemies, and for his own vainglory, for the which we all after suff'red; and that which was intolerable, did give leave unto the seamen to carry away what victuals and other necessaries they would, doing the same more safely in regard the contents[4] thereof was in the admiral which was

---

[1] Launching.
[2] Cozened.
[3] Pomp.
[4] Compensation.

cast away.

Not long after, Captain Smithe sent Captain Martin and myself with threescore people to go for Nansemunde, Captain Martin's lieutenant leading most of the men overland, and we two with the rest followed them by water. Where being arrived, we inquired of the Indians of our men. But they according to their subtleties would not acquaint us therewith. Whereupon I requested Captain Martin that I might go ashore to discover the truth, to the which he would not condescend. Nevertheless, the night being stormy and wet, I went on land with my company, where I found our men by good fires in safety, whereof I advertised Captain Martin the next morning; who presently with his company did come ashore unto us where, after some consultation held, we sent 2 messengers to the King of Nancemonde to barter with him for an island right opposite against the main we were upon, for copper hatches[1] and other commodities. But our messengers staying longer than we expected, we feared that which after hap'ned.

So Captain Martin did appoint with half of our men to take the island perforce. And being upon the way, we espied a canoe wherein we were persuaded our messengers to be. But they, perceiving us, returned back from whence they came, and we never set eye upon our messengers after, but understood from the Indians themselves that they were sacrificed, and that their brains were cut and scraped out of their heads with mussel shells. Being landed and acquainted with their treachery, we beat the savages out of the island, burned their houses, ransacked their temples, took down the corpse' of their dead kings from off their tombs, and carried away their pearls, copper, and bracelets wherewith they do decore their kings' funerals.

In the meantime, the savages upon the main did fall into dissension with Captain Martin, who seized the king's son and one other Indian, and brought them bound unto the island where I was, when a ship boy taking up a pistol, accidentally, not meaning any harm, the pistol suddenly fired and shot the savage prisoner into the breast. And thereupon, what with his passion and fear, he broke the cords

[1] Hatchets.

asunder wherewith he was tied, and did swim over unto the main with his wound bleeding.

And there being great store of maize upon the main, I counseled Captain Martin to take possession thereof, the which he refused, pretending that he would not put his men into hazard and danger. So, having seen Captain Martin well settled, I returned with Captain Nellson to James Town again, according to appointment.

Shortly after, Captain Smithe sent Captain Francis West with one hundreth and forty men up to the Falls with six months' victuals to inhabit there. Where being reasonable well settled, divers of his men straggled from their fort, some of them coming home wounded, others never returned to bring any tidings but were cut off and slain by the savages; so that in small process of time Captain Smithe did take his journey up to the Falls to understand how things were there ordered; when presently, after his coming thither, a great division did grow amongst them. Captain Smithe, perceiving both his authority and person neglected, incensed and animated the savages against Captain West and his company, reporting unto them that our men had no more powder left them than would serve for one volley of shot. And so Captain Smithe returning to James Town again, found to have too much powder about him, the which being in his pocket, where the spark of a match lighted, very shrewdly burned him.

And coming in that case to James Town, captains Rattliefe, Archer, and Martin practiced against him and deposed him off his government: Smithe being an ambitious, unworthy, and vainglorious fellow, attempting to take all men's authorities from them. For both Ratliefe, Archer, and Martin, being formerly of the council, Smithe would rule all and engross all authority into his own hands, although indeed there was no other certain appointed government than Sir Thomas Gates had commission for, who was then in the Bermudes, only a yearly presidentship to govern by the advice of the council. But Smithe, aiming at a sovereign rule without the assistance of the council, was justly deprived of all.

The place of government being void, the three busy instruments in the plantation preferred the same unto me, the which at first I refused in regard of my sickness. But by their importunity, promising to undergo the chiefest offices and burthen of government for me until I were recovered, at length I accepted thereof, and then was Smithe presently sent for England.

After I had been president some fourteen days, I sent Captain Rattliefe to Point Comfort for to build a fort there, the which I did for two respects: the one for the plenty of the place for fishing, the other for the commodious discovery of any shipping which should come upon the coast. And for the honor of Your Lordship's name and house, I named the same "Algernown's Fort."

Not long after, Captain Martin, whom I left at the island,[1] did come to James town pretending some occasions of business. But indeed his own safety moved him thereunto, fearing to be surprised by the Indians, who had made divers excursions against him, so that having left Lieutenant Sicklemore to command in his absence, amongst whose company shortly after did grow a dangerous mutiny insomuch that divers of his men, to the number of seventeen, did take away a boat from him perforce, and went therein to Kekowhaton, pretending they would trade there for victuals. But they were served according to their deserts, for not any of them were heard of after, and in all likelihood were cut off and slain by the savages. And within few days after, Lieutenant Sickelmore and divers others were found also slain, with their mouths stopped full of bread, being done as it seemeth in contempt and scorn that others might expect the like when they should come to seek for bread and relief amongst them.

Baldivia [Valdivia], a Spanish general, being served somewhat answerable hereunto in Chile in the West Indies, who being surprised by the Indians, enforced him to drink up a certain quantity of melted gold, using these words unto him: "Now glut thyself with gold, Baldivia!"—having there sought for gold as Sickelmore did here for food; and all the rest of Sickelmor's company which were living returned to us to James town to feed upon the poor store we had left us.

Also within a short time after, Captain Weste did come down to us

[1] In the Nansemond River.

from the Falls, having lost eleven men and a boat at Arsetecke, besides those men he lost at the Falls.

So our number at James Town increasing and our store decreasing —for in charity we could not deny them to participate with us— whereupon I appointed Captain Tucker to calculate and cast up our store; the which, at a poor allowance of half a can of meal for a man a day, amounted unto three months' provision. Yet Captain Tucker by his industry and care caused the same to hold out four months.

But having no expectation of relief to come in so short a time, I sent Captain Ratliefe to Powhatan to procure victuals and corn by the way of commerce and trade, the which the subtle old fox at first made good semblance of, although his intent was otherways, only waiting a fitting time for their destruction, as after plainly appeared. The which was partly occasioned by Captain Ratliefe's credulity, for having Powhatan's son and daughter aboard his pinnace, [he] freely suff'red them to depart again on shore, whom if he had detained, might have been a sufficient pledge for his safety. And after, not keeping a proper and fitting court of guard but suff'ring his men by two and three and small numbers in a company to straggle into the savages' houses, when the sly old king espied a fitting time, cut them all off, only surprised Captain Ratliefe alive, who he caused to be bound unto a tree naked with a fire before, and by women his flesh was scraped from his bones with mussel shells and, before his face, thrown into the fire; and so for want of circumspection miserably perished.

In the meantime, Captain William Phetiplace remained in the pinnace with some few men, and was divers times assaulted by the Indians; but after divers conflicts with them, with the loss of some of his men, hardly escaped and at length arrived at James Town only with sixteen men, the remainder of fifty Captain Ratliefe hath charge of at his going forth. And so he related unto us the tragedy of Captain Ratlife, not bringing any relief with them either for themselves or us.

Upon which defeat, I sent Captain James Davis to Algernone Fort to command there in Captain Ratliefe's place. And Captain Weste I sent to Potoamack with about thirty-six men to trade for maize and grain, where he in short time loaded his pinnace sufficiently, yet used some harsh and cruel dealing by cutting off two of the savages' heads and other extremities. And coming by Algernown's Fort, Captain Davis did call unto them, acquainting them with our great wants, exhorting them to make all the speed they could to relieve us, upon which report Captain Weste, by the persuasion, or rather by the enforcement, of his company, hoised up sails and shaped their course directly for England, and left us in that extreme misery and want.

Now all of us at James Town beginning to feel that sharp prick of hunger, which no man truly describe but he which hath tasted the bitterness thereof. A world of miseries ensued, as the sequel will express unto you, insomuch that some, to satisfy their hunger, have robbed the store, for the which I caused them to be executed. Then having fed upon horses and other beasts as long as they lasted, we were glad to make shift with vermin, as dogs, cats, rats, and mice. All was fish that came to net to satisfy cruel hunger, as to eat boots, shoes, or any other leather some could come by. And those being spent and devoured, some were enforced to search the woods and to feed upon serpents and snakes and to dig the earth for wild and unknown roots, where many of our men were cut off and slain by the savages. And now famine beginning to look ghastly and pale in every face that nothing was spared to maintain life and to do those things which seem incredible, as to dig up dead corpse out of graves and to eat them, and some have licked up the blood which hath fallen from their weak fellows. And amongst the rest, this was most lamentable that one of our[s], Collines, murdered his wife, ripped the child out of her womb and threw it into the river, and after chopped the mother in pieces and salted her for his food. The same not being discovered before he had eaten part thereof, for the which cruel and unhuman fact I adjudged him to be executed, the acknowledgment of the deed being enforced from him by torture, having hung by the thumbs with weights at his feet a quarter of an hour, before he would confess the same.

Upon these calamities, having one boat and a canoe left us, our boat did accidentally break loose and did drive four miles down the river before she was espied. Whereupon Captain Martin appointing some to follow her, the which being neglected, and acquainting me therewith, I stepped out of my house with my sword drawn, and what with my threats and their fears, happy was he could ship himself into the canoe first. And so our boat that night was again recovered. Yet wanting more boats for fishing and other needful occasions, Captain Daniell Tucker by his great industry and pains builded a large boat with his own hands, the which was some help and a little relief unto us, and did keep us from killing one of another.

To eat, many of our men this starving time did run away unto the savages, whom we never heard of after.

By this time being reasonable well recovered of my sickness, I did undertake a journey unto Algernown's Fort both to understand how things were there ordered as also to have been revenged of the savages at Kekowhatan who had treacherously slain divers of our men. Our people I found in good case and well liking, having concealed their plenty from us above at James Town, being so well stored that the crab fishes wherewith they had fed their hogs would have been a great relief unto us and saved many of our lives. But their intent was for to have kept some of the better sort alive and with their two pinnaces to have returned for England, not regarding our miseries and wants at all, wherewith I taxed Captain Davis and told him that I had a full intent to bring half of our men from James Town to be there relieved, and after to return them back again and bring the rest to be sustained there also. And if all this would not serve to save our men's lives, I purposed to bring them all unto Algernown's Fort, telling Captain Davis that another town or fort might be erected and builded, but men's lives once lost could never be recovered.

Our miseries now being at the highest, and intending, as I formerly related unto you, to remove some of our men to Algernown's Fort the very next tide, we espied two pinnaces coming into the bay, not knowing as yet what they were, but keeping a court of guard and watch all that night. The next morning we espied a boat coming off from one of the pinnaces; so, standing upon our guard, we hailed them, and understood that Sir Thomas Gates and Sir George Somers were come in these pinnaces, which by their great industry they had builded in the Burmudes with the remainder of their wrack'd ship and other wood they found in the country—upon which news we received no small joy, requesting them in the boat to come ashore, the which they refused, and returned aboard again. For Sir Thomas Gates, having no knowledge of any fort to be builded there, was doubtful whether we were friends or no. But being possessed of the truth, he and Sir George Somers with divers others did come ashore at Algernowne's Fort, and the next tide went up to James Town where they might read a lecture of misery in our people's faces, and perceive the scarcity of victuals, and understand the malice of the savages who knowing our weakness had divers times assaulted us without the fort, finding of five hundreth men we had only left about sixty, the rest being either starved through famine or cut off by the savages, and those which were living were so maugre [meager] and lean that it was lamentable to behold them.

For many through extreme hunger have run out of their naked beds, being so lean that they looked like anatomies[1] crying out WE ARE STARVED! WE ARE STARVED! Others going to bed, as we imagined, in health were found dead the next morning. And amongst the rest one thing hap'ned which was very remarkable, wherein God showed His just judgment. For one Hughe Pryse, being pinched with extreme famine, in a furious distracted mood did come openly into the marketplace blaspheming, exclaiming, and crying out that there was no God, alleging that if there were a God He would not suffer His creatures, whom He had made and framed, to endure those miseries, and to perish for want of food and sustenance. But it appeared the same day that the Almighty was displeased with him. For going that afternoon with a butcher, a corpulent fat man, into the woods to seek for some relief, both of them were slain by the savages. And after being found, God's indignation was showed upon Pryse's corpse, which was rent in pieces with wolves or other wild beasts, and his bowels torn out of his body, being a lean, spare man; and the fat butcher, not lying above six yards from him, was found altogether untouched, only by the savages' arrows whereby he received his death.

---

[1] A corpse shriveled to a skeleton.

These miseries considered, it was resolved upon by Sir Thomas Gates and the whole colony with all speed to return for England. Whereupon most of our men were set to work, some to make pitch and tar for trimming of our ships, others to bake bread, and few or none not employed in one occasion or another, so that in a small space of time four pinnaces were fitted and made ready, all preparing to go aboard. And if Sir Thomas Gates had not labored with our men, they had set the town on fire, using these or the like words unto them: "My masters, let the town stand. We know not but that as honest men as ourselves may come and inhabit here."

Then all of us embarking ourselves: Sir Thomas Gates in the *Deliverance* with his company, Sir George Somers in the *Patience,* myself in the *Discovery,* and Captain Davis in the *Virginia*—all of us sailing down the river with a full intent to have proceeded upon our voyage for England, when suddenly we espied a boat making towards us wherein we found to be Captain Bruster sent from my Lord La Ware, who was come unto us with many gentlemen of quality, and three hundreth men, besides great store of victuals, munition, and other provision; whereupon we all returned to James Town again, where my lord shortly after landed and set all things in good order, selecting a council and making captains over fifty men apiece.

Then Sir Thomas Gates, being desirous for to be revenged upon the Indians at Kekowhatan, did go thither by water with a certain number of men. And amongst the rest a taborer with him being landed, he caused the taborer to play and dance thereby to allure the Indians to come unto him, the which prevailed; and then espying a fitting opportunity, fell in upon them, put five to the sword, wounded many others, some of them being after found in the woods with such extraordinary large and mortal wounds that it seemed strange they could fly so far. The rest of the savages he put to flight. And so possessing himself of the town and the fertile ground thereunto adjacent, having well ordered all things, he left his Lieutenant Earely to command his company, and then returned to James Town again, and shortly after did take his voyage for England. My lord general about this time sent Captain Howldcrofte to build a fort in the woods near unto Kekowhatan. The which being finished, my lord named the same "Charles Fort," in honor of our King's Majesty that now is.[1]

Also my lord sent Sir George Somers and Captain Argoll in two ships into the Bermudes to make provision of hogs and fish for us. Sir George arrived there where shortly after he died. His men, making good profit of ambergris and other commodities, returned for England. But Captain Argoll, failing of the place, fell to the northward, where he hap'ned upon some fish; the which having salted and dried, returned therewith to us to James Town again.

Sir Ferdinando Wayman about this time died, whose death was much lamented, being both an honest and valiant gentleman.

My lord general, not forgetting old Powhatan's subtle treachery, sent a messenger unto him to demand certain arms and divers men which we supposed might be living in his country. But he returned no other than proud and disdainful answers. Whereupon my lord, being much incensed, caused a commission to be drawn wherein he appointed me chief commander over seventy men, and sent me to take revenge upon the Paspaheans and Chiconamians. And so, shipping myself and my soldiers in two boats, I departed from James Town the 9th of August, 1610, and the same night landed within three miles of Paspaha's town. Then drawing my soldiers into battalio,[2] placing a captain or lieutenant at every file, we marched towards the town, having an Indian guide with me named Kempes, whom the provost marshal led in a handlock. This subtle savage was leading us out of the way; the which I misdoubting bastinaded him with my truncheon, and threat'ned to cut off his head. Whereupon the slave altered his course and brought us the right way near unto the town, so that then I commanded every leader to draw away his file before me to beset the savages' houses that none might escape, with a charge not to give the alarum until I were come up unto them with the colors. At my coming I appointed Captain William Weste to give the alarum, the which he performed by shooting off a pistol.

And then we fell in upon them, put some fifteen or sixteen to the

---

[1] An indication of when this was written: Charles I became king in 1625.

[2] Battalia, battle array.

sword, and almost all the rest to flight. Whereupon I caused my drum to beat, and drew all my soldiers to the colors. My lieutenant, bringing with him the queen and her children and one Indian prisoners, for the which I taxed him because he had spared them, his answer was that, having them now in my custody, I might do with them what I pleased. Upon the same I caused the Indian's head to be cut off; and then dispersed my files, appointing my soldiers to burn their houses and to cut down their corn growing about the town. And after, we marched with the queen and her children to our boats again where, being no sooner well shipped, my soldiers did begin to murmur because the queen and her children were spared. So upon the same a council being called, it was agreed upon to put the children to death, the which was effected by throwing them overboard and shooting out their brains in the water. Yet, for all this cruelty, the soldiers were not well pleased, and I had much to do to save the queen's life for that time.

Then sailing some two miles down the river, I sent Captain Davis ashore with most of my soldiers, myself being wearied before, and for my own part but an easy foot man. Captain Davis at his landing was affronted by some Indians, who spared not to send their arrows amongst our men. But within a short time he put them to flight, and landed without further opposition; marching about fourteen miles into the country, cut down their corn, burned their houses, temples, and idols, and amongst the rest a spacious temple, clean and neatly kept, a thing strange and seldom seen amongst the Indians in those parts; so having performed all the spoil he could, returned aboard to me again, and then we sailed down the river to James Town.

My lord general, not being well, did lie a-shipboard, to whom we rowed; he being joyful of our safe return, yet seemed to be discontent because the queen was spared, as Captain Davis told me, and that it was my lord's pleasure that we should see her dispatched (the way he thought best—to burn her). To the first I replied that having seen so much bloodshed that day, now in my cold blood I desired to see no more; and for to burn her I did not hold it fitting, but either by shot or sword to give her a quicker dispatch. So turning myself from Captain Davis, he did take the queen with two soldiers ashore, and in the woods put her to the sword. And although Captain Davis told me it was my lord's direction, I am persuaded to the contrary.

Not long after our return to James Town, Captain Argoll was sent with the like commission against the Wariscoyans. The savages, being warned by their neighbors' harms, were very vigilant and careful, and all of them fled and escaped, so that Captain Argoll could have [no] other revenge than by cutting down their corn, burning their houses, and suchlike. The which being performed, he returned to James Town again.

The savages, still continuing their malice against us, sent some as spies to our fort, who being apprehended, my lord caused one to have his hand cut off, and so sent unto his fellows to give them warning for attempting the like.

About this time there was a conspiracy plotting amongst some of our men which wrought in iron mines to run away with a bark. The same being discovered, my lord for an example adjudged one of them by marshal law to be executed. The execution proving strange and seldom heard of, I thought not to omit. For the party being thrown off the lather, what with the swinge and weight of his body, the rope did break, and he fell upon the ground. And in regard of the accident my lord pardoned him, although it nothing availed him, having received his death with the gird[1] of the rope and extremity of the fall, so that within 2 days after he died.

My lord, intending to search for minerals and to make further proof of the iron mines, sent divers men in a bark up to the Falls. And going by Apoamatake, they were called ashore by the savages; and being to fill their barricoes with water,[2] were easily thereunto induced, and after enticed by the savages up to their houses, pretending to feast them. But our men, forgetting their subtleties, like greedy fools accepted thereof, more esteeming of a little food than their own lives and safety. For when the Indians had them in their houses, and found a fitting time when they least dreaded any danger, did fall upon them, slew divers, and wounded all the rest, who within two days after also died; only Dowse the taborer, who flying to their

---

[1] Jerk.
[2] The river at Jamestown is brackish. Appamatuck is the beginning of fresh water.

boat was hardly pursued. But gaining the same, he made a virtue of necessity, using the rudder instead of a target to keep their arrows out of his body, and so sculling off by little and little got out of their reach and freed himself.

The savages be not so simple as many imagine who be not acquainted with their subtleties. For they had not forgotten how their neighbors at Kekowhatan were allured and defeated by Sir Thomas Gates when he had the same taborer with him.

Presently after, Captain Bruster was sent up to the Falls with a certain number of men to attend there for my lord's coming, who purposed to proceed in the search of minerals. In his journey he had divers encounters and skirmishes with the Indians, at length arriving at the Falls, where my lord did shortly after come unto him, leaving the charge and command of James Town with me.

Now my lord being at the Falls, and winter coming on, he caused a fort to be builded there both for their defense and shelter, and named the same "Laware's Fort," intending to have reposed himself there all the winter, and to have proceeded upon the discovery of minerals the next spring—where for a time we will leave him, and return to our proceedings at James Town again.

The government whereof being left to me, Paspahe with a small troop of Indians in show did come unto our blockhouse, thinking by some policy either to have surprised the same or some of our men. The which coming to my hearing, I presently sent Captain Powell, then my ancient, with a certain number of men to surprise Paspahe alive, if possible they could. For the same would have been to good purpose if it could have been effected. Whereupon our men drawing near unto him where he stood upon the end of a bank, when presently Mr. John Waller stepped unto him and caught hold of him, and gave the watchword for the rest to come to assist him. The which the savages perceiving, divers of them appeared which before were not seen, sending their arrows freely amongst our men. The which Captain Powell seeing did apprehend that there was small hope to bring in Paspahe alive, for he struggled mainly, whereupon he thrust him twice through the body with his sword. And for all that, the stout Indian lived and was carried away upon rafters by the savages. And Lieutenant Puttocke, encountering with one of the savages hand to fist, grappled with him and stabbed him to death with his poniard.

My lord general all this time remaining at the Falls, where neither sickness nor scarcity was wanting, had divers encounters with the Indians, some of his men being slain, among the rest his kinsman, Captain William Weste; and Captain Bruster narrowly escaped.

And now my lord growing very sick, he was enforced to alter his former determination, and to return to James town again, where his sickness nothing abated but rather increased, so that for the recovery of his health he did take his voyage for the bath at Mevis in the West Indies. But the winds not favoring them, they were enforced to shape their course directly for England—my lord having left and appointed me deputy governor in his absence, to execute marshal law or any other power and authority as absolute as himself.

After my lord's departure, the Indians did fall to their wonted practices again, coming one evening late, and called at our blockhouse. The which when I understood, I presently sent to Lieutenant Puttocke, who commanded there, that he should by no means stir out of the blockhouse, but to keep an exceeding careful guard and watches. And to strengthen him, I sent him more men to double his guard, again expressly giving him charge that he should not go out of the blockhouse upon any terms whatsoever, promising him that the next morning I would send him a convenient number of men to discover what they were and of what strength which had so called them.

But Lieutenant Puttocke, being called again early the next morning before our watch was discharged in the fort, contrary to my command, and most unadvisedly, did go out of the blockhouse with the small number of men he had, showing more valor than will, more fury than judgment. And some few Indians being in show, he followed them without apprehension of that which ensued. For the savages still retiring, he followed them until they brought him into their ambuscado where, being five or six hundreth of savages, let fly their arrows as thick as hail amongst our handful of men, and defeated and cut them all off in a moment, the arrows which they had shot being so many in number that the ground thereabouts was almost covered with them.

Upon which defeat the savages did so acclamate, shout, and halloo in triumph of their gained victory that the echo thereof made both the air and woods to ring. The which filling our ears in the fort, presently with all speed I sent Lieutenant Abbott with fifty men to assist Puttocke, not knowing directly what had befallen them, although we feared that which had already hap'ned. Nevertheless Lieutenant Abbott encount'red with the savages; they then changing their note, crying PASPAHE! PASPAHE!—thereby importing as much as that they had revenged his wrongs. At length Abbott put the Indians to flight, recovered the dead bodies of our men, whom he brought to our fort, where they were buried.

Upon this disaster I sent a messenger unto Algernown's Fort, supposing my Lord Laware had been no further on his voyage, to have informed him hereof. But the messenger lost his labor, my lord being before departed.

In short time after, Captain Addames did come into our bay in a shipped [sic] called the *Blessing,* with fresh supply both of men and victuals, giving us notice that Sir Thomas Dale was to come shortly after with a greater supply.

The which proved true, for, within two months after, he arrived in Virginia, and brought with him three hundreth men, besides great store of armor, munition, victuals, and other provision. And being landed, he ordained new laws, set down good articles which were well observed, all our men being set to work: some to plant, some to sow corn, and others to build boats and houses, most men employed in one thing or another.

All things in time being well settled and ordered, Sir Thomas Dale made preparation and went against the Nancemondies with a hundreth men in armor, where he had divers encounters and skirmishes with the savages, both by land and water, divers of his company being wounded. Amongst the rest, Captain Francis Weste was shot into the thigh and Captain Martin into the arm, Sir Thomas Dale himself narrowly escaping, for an arrow lit just upon the edge, or brim, of his headpiece, the which, if it had fallen a thought lower, might have shot him into the brains and endangered his life.

In these conflicts many Indians being also slain and wounded, and not being acquainted nor accustomed to encounter with men in armor, much wondered thereat, especially that they did not see any of our men fall as they had done in other conflicts. Whereupon they did fall into their exorcisms, conjurations, and charms, throwing fire up into the skies, running up and down with rattles, and making many diabolical gestures with many necromantic[1] spells and incantations, imaging[2] thereby to cause rain to fall from the clouds to extinguish and put out our men's matches and to wet and spoil their powder. But neither the devil whom they adore nor all their sorceries did anything avail them. For our men cut down their corn, burned their houses and, besides those which they had slain, brought some of them prisoners to our fort.

Sir Thomas Dale, making more invasions and excursions upon the savages, had many conflicts with them. And one thing amongst the rest was very remarkable, the which may be supposed to have been occasioned by the savages' sorceries and charms. For Sir Thomas Dale, with some of the better sort sitting in an Indian's house, a fantasy possessed them that they imagined the savages were set upon them, each man taking one another for an Indian, and so did fall pell-mell one upon another, beating one another down and breaking one of another's heads, that much mischief might have been done but that it pleased God the fantasy was taken away whereby they had been deluded, and every man understood his error.

About this time, a Spanish caravel arrived upon the coast, and did come into the bay without command of shot.[3] Three principal of the Spaniards coming ashore in their boat not fur off Algernown's Fort, the which Captain Davis espying laid in ambush for them, they not knowing of any fort to be there, and so surprised them—the chiefest of them being one Diego Malinos, a commander of some fort or hold in the West Indies, the other Antonio Pereos, his companion, the third a pilot who went under the name and habit of a Spaniard, but was after found and discovered to be Englishman,[4] his name being Limbrecke, having lived many years amongst the Spaniards,

---

[1] Written "nigramantcke."

[2] Imagining.

[3] I.e., out of range of shore batteries.

[4] John Clark, the English pilot at Fort Algernon, knew him and identified him.

and reputed to be a good pilot. After the surprising of these three, the boat wherein they did come put from the shore. The men, therein being questioned, pretended to seek for one of the King of Spain's ships loaden with munition, bound for the West Indies, requesting Captain Davis to let them have a pilot to bring their ship into the harbor, the which was granted; but having the pilot no sooner aboard, hoised up their sails and carried the pilot quite away with them, leaving the three which were surprised in his stead behind them, who were thereupon brought to James Town and sent as prisoners aboard several ships.

And shortly after, Sir Thomas Dale sent myself, Captain Newport, and Mr. Stracy [Strachey], secretary to the colony, to examine them. And so accusing them to have come for spies, they utterly denied the same; but still urging them, therewith Antonio Pereos answered that we had no cause at all to fear anything this year, but what might happen the next he could not tell. And as it after appeared their intent was as evil as we imagined, for the Spanish ambassador shortly after gained a commission from the King's Majesty King James that we should send the principal, Diego Malinos, into England, the which with all speed was effected, Captain Martin being his conduct. Don Diego stayed not long in England, but was sent home, where he was made general of six tall ships, in all likelihood, and, as we were after certainly informed, set out of purpose to supplant us. But having been at sea about a month, a mutiny did grow amongst them insomuch that one of Diego's company stabbed him to death. Whereupon their course was altered and their former determination ceased.

Antonio Pereos, he died before in Virginia; and Sir Thomas Dale at his going for England did take our hispaniolated Englishman Limbrecke with him. And according to some private commission, when he did come within sight of the English shore, he caused him to be hanged up at the yard's arm, as afterwards it was truly reported.

Before Sir Thomas Dale's departure, Captain Davis at Algernown's Fort espied nine ships upon the coast. Supposing them to be Spanish, and sending notice thereof to Sir Thomas Dale, he presently sent Captain Bruster and Lieutenant Abbott with forty men to discover what they were. And they not returning according to Sir

Thomas' expectation, he feared that they were either surprised or defeated. Whereupon he drew all his forces into form and order ready for encounter, calling a council to resolve whether it were best to meet with them aboard our ships or for to maintain the fort. My opinion I delivered to Sir Thomas Dale and the rest: that it was doubtful whether our men would stand unto it ashore and abide the brunt, but a-shipboard of necessity they must, for *there* was no running away.

So making preparation to go aboard, Captain Bruster and Lieutenant Abbott returned, and brought us certain news that it was Sir Thomas Gates' fleet, who was come now to be governor; and arrived there that evening with a fresh supply both of men and provision.

Having unladen the ships and ordered other necessary occasions, Sir Thomas Gates appointed Sir Thomas Dale their marshal of the colony, as it was agreed upon in England, to pass up into the country near unto the Falls with about two hundreth men to inhabit there, Captain Bruster leading most of his men overland, and himself and a small company going by water. Captain Bruster in his march was divers times assaulted and encountered by the savages being sent from Powhatan, having for their leader one Munetute, commonly called amongst us "Jack of the Feathers," by reason that he used to come into the field all covered over with feathers and swan's wings fastened unto his shoulders as though he meant to fly.

Captain Bruster coming to the place appointed, where Sir Thomas Dale did also meet with him, and after divers encounter and skirmishes with the savages, gained a convenient place for fortification, where presently they did begin to build a fort; and Sir Thomas Dale named the same "Henericus Fort," in honor of Prince Henry. The savages were not idle all this time but hind'red their designs as much as they could, shooting arrows into the fort, wherewith divers of our men were wounded and others endangered. And some having employment without the fort did come short home and were slain by the savages.

Sir Thomas Dale having almost finished the fort and settled a plantation in that part, divers of his men, being idle and not willing to take pains, did run away unto the Indians. Many of them being taken again Sir Thomas in a most severe manner caused to be executed: Some he appointed to be hanged, some burned, some to be broken upon wheels, others to be staked, and some to be shot to death. All these extreme and cruel tortures he used and inflicted upon them to terrify the rest for attempting the like; and some which robbed the store, he caused them to be bound fast unto trees and so starved them to death.

So leaving Sir Thomas busily employed in finishing the fort and settling their habitations, let us return to James Town again, where our governor, Sir Thomas Gates, was resident, only by the way south a little at Algernowne's Fort, the which was accidentially burned down to the ground, except Captain Davis' house and the storehouse. Whereupon Captain Davis, fearing to receive some displeasure and to be removed from thence, the same being the most plentifullest place for food, he used such expedition in the rebuilding of the same again that it is almost incredible.

Divers Indians used to come to our fort at James Town bringing victuals with them, but indeed did rather come as spies than any good affection they did bear unto us. Some of them Sir Thomas Gates caused to be apprehended and executed for a terror to the rest, to cause them to desist from their subtle practices.

Thus having related unto Your Lordship the true proceedings in Virginia from Sir Thomas Gates' shipwrack upon the Bermudes until my departure out of the country, which was the 22th April, 1612, the which day I set sail in a ship named the *Tryall,* and having by computation sailed about 200 leagues with a reasonable good wind and fair weather, upon a sudden a great storm did arise insomuch that the mizzenmast did spring with the violence of the winds. And lying in the great cabin where the mizzen stood, I was thereby much endangered and in peril of my life, for the same with great force did grate upon my cabin, and narrowly missed me. And a barrel full with beer being in the cabin, the mizzen struck the same to pieces, that all the beer did run about the cabin.

The storm ceasing and our mizzen amended, we recovered Flores, Corves, and St. Michells,[1] not touching at any of these islands, but

---

[1] The Azores: Flores, Corvo, São Miguel.

shaped our course northward where, falling becalmed, our danger was greater than the former for fear of famine and want of food, having but a poor small quantity of fresh water, and that was so stencheous that only washing my hands therewith I could not endure the scent thereof. Our greatest store of food was peas, and those were so corrupted, moldy, rotten, worm-eaten that there was no substance left in them but being stirred would crumble into dust, so that for want of food we were like to perish.

But God looking mercifully upon us, when we least expected to see our native country again we happily met with a ship of London bound for Newfoundland, one Baker being master thereof, who relieved us with beef, fish, bread, beer, and tobacco, which greatly comforted us and saved our lives. For it was above thirty days after before we made land, which was Ireland. So after a long and dangerous voyage, we did fall with the land and put into Crookhaven, where we remained some fourteen days, in which time we refreshed ourselves, and revictualed our ship; and then set sail again, and within eight days after arrived in England, and anchored in Dover road, where we did meet with Sir Samuell Argall, bound for New England to displant the French colony there. The which, as I after heard, he valiantly performed; but how just the cause was I refer the same to a judicious censure.

So staying some few days at Dover to accompany Sir Samuell, I took post-horse, and from thence rode to London.

FINIS

32. Thomas Dale

Letter to the Council of Virginia, 25 May 1611

< **British Library: Bodleian Library additional MSS 21/993–190,** Neill 1885:77, Brown 1890:488

Let us never lose sight of the sternness of Dale's faith and the severity of his passion. He is a career officer and hard-forged veteran of the Dutch Wars. He prefers solutions to accommodations, and his were probably determined before he arrived. Characteristically his farming project around Fort Henry is a military operation under captains. May we guess the result?—not much card playing but not much corn either.

He reports the dilapidation at Jamestown, careful always to avoid direct criticism of Governor Percy, whom he relieves.

RIGHT HONORABLE AND THE REST OF OUR NOBLE FRIENDS—After I had left the Land's End the 17th of March, with so happy success (by the permission of the Divine Goodness) and with so fair winds was our whole journey accompanied as within one month, namely, the 29th of April, we had, in friendly consort, all our whole fleet together, reached Dominico—a passage which I could heartily wish might not be declined by those our English fleet which should at any time make into Virginia, probable enough, as may appear by this our trial, to be most speedy and, I am right well assured, most convenient for our people's refreshing and preservation of our cattle. The first may be made good by reason of a continual easterly wind from the Canaries to the West Indies, the second by restitution of our sick people unto health by the helps of fresh air, diet, and the baths. For true it is, we being undershipped of tonnage,[1] and pest'red by that means, that our goods filled up the orlage [hold?], having no room for our men to be accommodated, but crowded together their own airs and the uncleanliness both of the ship, dogs, etc., gave some infection amongst us, and was the cause of the loss of well near a

[1] The ships were overloaded.

dozen men. I could earnestly wish therefore that you will be pleased to advise the undertakers concerning this point, that the like inconvenience may be avoided in the future.

The 12th of May, we seized our bay, and the same night with a favorable southeast gale (all praise be to God for it) we came to an anchor before Algernoone fort at Point Comfort, where to our no small comfort again we discov'red the *Hercules* even then preparing to take the advantage of the present tide to set sail for England. We had no sooner saluted the fort, and that us, and were come to an anchor, but Captain Adams came aboard us in his longboat, who gave me to understand both of his Lordship's departure for Mevis [Nevis] in the West Indies some ten days before his coming in—as by his Lordship's letters he shall further understand thereof—as of Captain Pearcye's being at the fort, who, together with some of the present council, had come down thither to give Captain Adams his discharge.

It was not full two hours before myself and Captain Newport went ashore, where we had related unto us the full circumstance of many things and the condition of the present colony.

In this fort we found, besides Captain Davies his company, the most of Sir Thomas Gates his company there living quartered as well, by reason they were not of competency in numbers to take in again the two forts of Kecoughtan and to supply James Town and Algernoune Fort both, as also because at all times this place yieldeth the better relief by means of the fishing than James Town.

I found many omissions of necessary duties which would have indeed advanced the end which we have now proposed concerning the perpetual subsistence of the colony. But a plantation being not the full and utmost intention resolved on or so advised from home, but rather they search after those mines which Faldoe the Helvetian had given intelligence of in England, and which his Lordship was entreated unto by the committee's letters (which I have since seen) to make exploration of, was the cause of those omissions. Howbeit I found how careful his Lordship hath been in what either his forces or his own ability of body hath enabled him unto. And well I perceive his zeal, how it is enflamed to this right noble work.

According, therefore, as his Lordship left in direction for me—if I should come in before his return—with a commission likewise to govern as his deputy in the interim, my first labor was to repossess me of the two last years' erected forts upon Southampton River—Fort Henry and Fort Charles.

The second day therefore after my arrival, I went and viewed the forts and ground for corn; and finding the palisadoes yet most standing about those forts, and the ground, though somewhat later in the year to be sowed, with some little pains to be cleared, I drew all my new men ashore; and taking some of the rest of both companies, quartered as aforesaid in Algernoune Fort—whilest I employed our carpenters to build cabins and cottages for the present—we on all hands fell to digging and cleaning the ground and setting of corn; and in four or five days we had set more ground about Fort Henry than Sir Thomas Gates found set by the Indians in the year before.

After I had forwarded this work—because I conceived it necessary as well to look into the present state of James Town and what might be fit to be accomplished there, before my search further up for a convenient new seat to raise a principal town according to my directions, as also to unlade our provisions into our magazines, of which I know some of our ill-conditioned ships required the more speed, as likewise careful to set some hands likewise on work for the lading of these ships with all conveniency and speed for their return—I left the charge of corn setting about Charles Fort under the command and care of the captains which I now had brought, leaving therefore still on shore with them all my new company, constituting Captain James Davis tax-master [taskmaster] of the whole three forts; who having instructions given from myself should appoint each captain of the fort what to command his officers and his people to execute, who weekly therefore (I did so order it) that they should give account to Captain Davis and Captain Davis to me.

These thus settled and everyone busy at his task and day's labor, the 19 [of May], I came before James Town, being Sunday in the afternoon, where I landed and first preparing to the church (the company thither assembled), Mr. Poole gave us a sermon. After that, Mr. Starchy did openly read that commission which his Lordship had left with him for me, Captain Percy surrend'ring up his, it being accordingly so to expire.

I found here likewise no corn set, some few seeds put into a private garden or two, but the cattle, cows, goats, swine, poultry, etc. to be well and carefully on all hands preserved, and all in good plight and liking.

The next day, I called into consultation such whom I found here made of the council by his lordship, where were proposed many businesses necessary, and almost every one essential, which indeed required much labor and many hands as, namely, the reparation of the falling church, and so of the storehouse, a stable for our horses, a munition house, a powder house, a new well for the amending of the most unwholesome waters which the old afforded, brick to be made, a sturgeon house—which the late curer you sent by the *Hercules* much complaineth of, his work otherwise impossible to come to good, and indeed he dresseth the same sturgeon perfect and well—a blockhouse to be raised on the north side of our back river to prevent the Indians from killing our cattle, a house to be set up to lodge our cattle in the winter, and hay to be appointed in his due time to be made, a smith's forge to be perfected, cask for our sturgeon to be made, and besides private gardens for each man, common gardens for hemp and flax and such and other seeds, and lastly a bridge[1] to land our goods dry and safe upon, for most of which I took present order.

And [I] appointed first for the church Captain Edward Breuster with his ging, and for the stable Captain Lawson with his ging. Captain Newport undertook the bridge with his mariners. All the sawyers I set on work, who duly ply their task. And thus when these are done the others shall be set upon.

In the meanwhile we now of necessity are enforced to ply the unlading of our ships, to which we call other hands not employed; and I myself likewise [am] somewhat busied two or three days to dispatch Captain Adams with all speed with these our letters of aviso, who the 21 was present with us at the council—where we positively determined, with God's grace, after the corn's setting at the two princes'

---

[1] Wharf.

forts, to go up unto the falls-ward to search and advise upon a seat for a new town, with 200 men, where we will set down and build houses as fast as we may, resolving to leave at s—— [?] of James Town some fifty men with a sufficient commander for the preservation of our breeders.

Likewise at that council, it being then debated how hopeful the trade for a while would be unto the northward rivers, especially that of Pattomack for corn after harvest, I did forbid all manner of trading with the Indians lest our commodities should grow every day with them more vile and cheap by their plenty, and being politicly conveyed by Pawhaton unto those northern people; who being our access thither again—as in this last winter was Captain Argoll in the discovery—might forestall our trucking.

Likewise the 21, I went into Paspehaighe's old town, because it was related unto me to be good ground to sow corn in, purposing to set there some hemp and flax. But surveying it, I found it too much rough-weeded and overgrown with shrubs and bushes, which now being green and high would not be so readily cleansed this year for any service.

The 22, I made divers proclamations which I caused to be set up for the public view, one for the preservation of our cattle amongst ourselves, another for the valuation of provisions amongst the mariners, the copy of which I have sent and leave to your noble considerations, everyone here thinking those rates very easy and reasonable.

Let me entreat you that we may have both a vice-admiral and hired mariners to be all times resident here. The benefit will quickly make good the charge as well by a trade of furs, to be obtained with the savages in the northern rivers, to be returned home, as also to furnish us here with corn and fish. The want of such men at this time whom we might trust with our pinnaces leaves us destitute this season of so great a quantity of fish as not far from our own bay would sufficiently satisfy the whole colony for a whole year.

Our want likewise of able chirurgeons is not a little: Be pleased to advise the committees for us in this point.

And thus having nothing else at this present to be further unnecessary troublesome, I humbly take my leave, in all offices and travails to the advancement of your hopeful colony vowing me, ever unto the same and your honorable command

A constant and perpetual servant,
THOMAS DALE.

Virginea, James Town, the 25th of May, 1611.

[endorsed:] To the President and Council of the Company of Adventurers and Planters in Virginia.

33. Thomas West, Lord Delaware

Letter to Salisbury, 22 June 1611

< **State Papers Domestic, James I, 64/63,** Brown 1890:476, Virginia Magazine 14:382

The incapacitated governor and captain general has now returned to England in despair of recovering his health in Virginia. He promises to "proceed in the business" by returning as soon as possible, and promises an immediate and full report of his actions, which became *A Short Relation §34.*

MAY IT PLEASE YOUR LORDSHIP—I would gladly have waited on Your Lordship the last night as soon as I came to town, but I understood from Sir Walter Cope that your advice was otherwise, [and rather] first to have a care of my health, then to attend His Majesty, and afterward Your Lordship.

For my health, I thank God I find myself perfectly recovered though something weak in regard of my long sickness. Ever since my first arrival at the islands I have recovered daily—and arrived at Fiall [Fayal in the Azores] the 18th of April or thereabouts—so that I dare boldly say that I have no touch of my disease remaining on me; and if Your Lordship shall think it fit, I would presently attend His

Majesty.

This long and painful sickness of mine hath no whit discouraged me to proceed with the business I have undertaken, if it be now prosecuted as it is begun; neither had my return hither been so sudden if the winds had favored mine intention for the West Indies at my departure from Virginia. For I dare boldly say there was never more hope than at this present, and when it shall please Your Lordship I doubt not but to give you full satisfaction to every doubt or scandal that lieth upon that country, fearing nothing less than an honorable and profitable end of all if now it be not let fall.

Thus attending Your Lordship's further advice, I humbly take my leave this 22th of June 1611.

Your Lordship's Servant to command,
THOMAS LAWARRE.

[endorsed:] To the Right Honorable My very good Lord, the Earl of Salisbury, Lord High Treasurer of England give this.

34. Thomas West, Lord Delaware

A Short Relation made by the Lord De-La-Warre to the lords and others of the Council of Virginea, touching his unexpected return home, and afterwards delivered to the General Assembly of the said Company at a court holden the twenty-five of June 1611. Published by authority of the said Council.

< Delaware 1611, **Whittingham 1858,** Brown 1890:477

Virginia's lord governor and captain general had some explaining to do when he unexpectedly returned to England after only a year in the colony. His choice of George Percy as interim governor was at this stage not an assuring one. His response, therefore, requires several persuasive skills. His whole reason was personal illness: "a hot and violent ague." He was dying in Virginia. He took a nautical ambulance to healthier parts. Recovery has been slow. Meanwhile Virginia (fear not) remains full of promise and potential: Gates and Dale are going out with more livestock, Argall has opened up Indian trade and found a new fishing bank, ground is ready for corn, and so forth. The Company had no choice but to see it printed.

He had reestablished the colony and put in a good year of administration, but he never went back. He died on the way seven years later.

MY LORDS, ETC.—Being now by accident returned from my charge at Virginea contrary either to my own desire or other men's expectations, who spare not to censure me in point of duty, and to discourse and question the reason, though they apprehend not the true cause of my return, I am forced, out of a willingness to satisfy every man, to deliver unto Your Lordships and the rest of this assembly briefly but truly in what state I have lived ever since my arrival to the colony; what hath been the just occasion of my sudden departure thence; and in what terms I have left the same—the rather because I perceive that, since my coming into England, such a

LIBRARY OF VIRGINIA

THOMAS WEST, BARON DELAWARE

coldness and irresolution is bred in many of the adventurers that some of them seek to withdraw those payments which they have subscribed towards the charge of the plantation, and by which that action must be supported and maintained, making this my return the color of their needless backwardness and unjust protraction.

Which, that you may the better understand, I must inform Your Lordships that presently after my arrival in James Town I was welcomed by a hot and violent ague, which held me a time, till by the advice of my physician, Doctor Laurence Bohun, by bloodletting I was recovered, as in my first letters by Sir Thomas Gates I have informed you. That disease had not long left me till, within three weeks after I had gotten a little strength, I began to be distempered with other grievous sicknesses which successively and severally assailed me. For besides a relapse into the former disease, which with much more violence held me more than a month and brought me to great weakness, the flux surprised me and kept me many days; then the cramp assaulted my weak body with strong pains; and afterwards the gout, with which I had heretofore been sometime troubled, afflicted me in such sort that, making my body through weakness unable to stir or to use any manner of exercise, drew upon me the disease called the scurvy; which though in others it be a sickness of slothfulness yet was in me an effect of weakness which never left me till I was upon the point to leave the world.

These several maladies and calamities I am the more desirous to particularize unto Your Lordships, although they were [all] too notorious to the whole colony, lest any man should misdeem that under the general name and common excuse of sickness I went about to cloak either sloth or fear or any other base apprehension unworthy the high and general charge which you had entrusted to my fidelity.

In these extremities I resolved to consult my friends who, finding nature spent in me and my body almost consumed, my pains likewise daily increasing, gave me advice to prefer a hopeful recovery before an assured ruin; which must necessarily had ensued had I lived but twenty days longer in Virginia, wanting at that instant both food and physic fit to remedy such extraordinary diseases and restore that strength so desperately decayed.

Whereupon, after a long consultation held, I resolved by general consent and persuasion to ship myself for Mevis [Nevis], an island in the West Indies famous for wholesome baths, there to try what help the heavenly providence would afford me by the benefit of the hot bath.

But GOD, who guideth all things according to His good will and pleasure, so provided that after we had sailed an hundred leagues we met with southerly winds which forced me to change my purpose, my body being altogether unable to endure the tediousness of a long voyage, and so [to] stern my course for the Western Islands, which I no sooner recovered than I found help for my health and my sickness assuaged by means of fresh diet, and especially of oranges and lemons, an undoubted remedy and medicine for that disease which lastly and so long had afflicted me.

Which ease as soon as I found, I resolved, although my body remained still feeble and weak, to return back to my charge in Virginia again. But I was advised not to hazard myself before I had perfectly recovered my strength, which by counsel I was persuaded to seek in the natural air of my country, and so I came for England; in which accident I doubt not but men of reason and of judgment will imagine there would more danger and prejudice have hap'ned by my death there than I hope can do by my return.

In the next place, I am to give account in what estate I left the colony for government in my absence. It may please Your Lordships therefore to understand that upon my departure thence I made choice of Captain George Pearcie, a gentleman of honor and resolution, and of no small experience in that place, to remain deputy governor until the coming of the marshal, Sir Thomas Dale, whose commission was likewise to be determined upon the arrival of Sir Thomas Gates, according to the intent and order of Your Lordships and the council here.

The number of men I left there were upward of two hundred, the most in health and provided of at least ten months' victuals in their storehouse, which is daily issued unto them, besides other helps in the country lately found out by Captain Argoll by trading with petty kings in those parts—who for a small return of a piece of iron, copper, etc. have consented to truck great quantities of corn, and willingly embrace the intercourse of traffic, showing unto our people certain signs of amity and affection.

And for the better strengthening and securing of the colony in the time of my weakness there, I took order for the building of three several forts, two of which are seated near Point Comfort, to which adjoineth a large circuit of ground, open and fit for corn. The third fort is at the Falls upon an island environed also with corn ground. These are not all manned, for I wanted the commodity of boats, having but two and one barge in all the country, which hath been cause that our fishing hath been in some sort hindered for want of those provisions, which easily will be remedied when we can gain sufficient men to be employed about those businesses, which in Virginia I found not. But since meeting with Sir Thomas Gates at the Cowes near Portsmouth, to whom I gave a particular account of all my proceedings and of the present estate of the colony as I left it, I understood those wants are supplied in his fleet.

The country is wonderful fertile and very rich, and makes good whatsoever heretofore hath been reported of it. The cattle already there are much increased and thrive exceedingly with the pasture of that country. The kine all this last winter, though the ground was covered most with snow and the season sharp, lived without other feeding than the grass they found, with which they prospered well, and many of them ready to fall with calf. Milk being a great nourishment and refreshing to our people, serving also in occasion as well for physic as for food; so that it is no way to be doubted but when it shall please God that Sir Thomas Dale and Sir Thomas Gates shall arrive in Virginia with their extraordinary supply of one hundred kine and two hundred swine, besides store of all manner of other provisions, for the sustenance and maintenance of the colony, there will appear that success in the action as shall give no man cause of distrust that hath already adventured, but encourage every good mind to further so worthy a work, as will redound both to the glory of GOD, to the credit of our nation, and to the comfort of all those that have been instruments in the furthering of it.

The last discovery, during my continual sickness, was by Captain Argoll who hath found a trade with Patamack, a king as great as Powhatan, who still remains our enemy, though not able to do us hurt. This is in a goodly river called Patomack, upon the borders whereof there are grown the goodliest trees for masts that may be found elsewhere in the world; hemp better than English, growing wild in abundance; mines of antimony and lead without our bay to the northward.

There is also found an excellent fishing bank for cod and ling as good as can be eaten and of a kind that will keep a whole year in ship's hold with little care, a trial whereof I now have brought over with me. Other islands there are upon our coasts that do promise rich merchandise and will further exceedingly the establishing of the plantation by supply of many helps and will speedily afford a return of many worthy commodities.

I have left much ground in part manured to receive corn, having caused it the last winter to be sowed for roots, with which our people were greatly relieved.

There are many vines planted in divers places, and do prosper well. There is no want of anything if the action can be upheld with constancy and resolution.

Lastly, concerning myself and my course: Though the world may imagine that this country and climate will—by that which I have suffered beyond any other of that plantation—ill agree with the state of my body, yet I am so far from shrinking or giving over this honorable enterprise as that I am willing and ready to lay all I am worth upon the adventure of the action, rather than so honorable a work should fail; and to return with all the convenient expedition I may, beseeching Your Lordships and the rest not only to excuse my former wants, happened by the Almighty Hand, but to second my resolutions with your friendly endeavors, that both the state may receive honor [and] yourselves profit and future comfort, by being employed, though but as a weak instrument, in so great an action.

And thus having plainly, truly, and briefly delivered the cause of my return, with the state of our affairs as we now stand, I hope every worthy and indifferent hearer will, by comparing my present resolution of return with the necessity of my coming home, rest satisfied with this true and short declaration.

FINIS

35. The Shipmates of Don Diego de Molina

Report of the Voyage to the Indies as far as Virginia, which the large sloop made by order of His Majesty, in behalf of the Alcalde Don Diego de Molino, the Ensign Marco Antonio Perez, and in their company Francisco Lembri, English, pilot of the navy

(Translated from the Spanish by Maximilian Schele de Vere)

< Simancas Archive 2588–81, **Brown 1890:511**

This is a document enclosed in a letter from the Duke of Lerma to the Secretary Antonio de Aroztegui, dated 13 November 1611. It is an unattributed statement of the Spanish council of war concerning the incident at Point Comfort in June 1611. It is the official Spanish account, derived apparently from what was given in deposition in Havana by the master, mariner, and pilot of the Spanish sloop. The whole affair is a cruel fluke. Two men were to die and two more to languish five years in prison—while their nations were at peace!

The Clark portion is another version and another translation of §36, John Clark's June 23rd deposition.

SAID SLOOP left Lisbon April 13th, 1611, with the persons mentioned above and a master, a pilot, and 13 sailors, sailing by the Havana, which was reached on May 24. And they handed to Don Gaspar Ruyz de Pereda, governor of that island [Cuba], Your Majesty's [Philip III, King of Spain] dispatches which the said Don Diego and the Ensign Marco Antonio Perez brought; and in obedience to His Majesty's orders, said governor dispatched the *caravela,* consenting, however, to their wish that they might not be named commanders of a squadron, so as not to add to the suspicions about this plan [which was, as squadron commanders in fact, to use the sloop and caravel to search the coast of "La Florida," the whole coast from Newfoundland to Key West, for whereabouts of the Spanish ship *Plantation,* of 300 tons, which had been carrying a cargo of ammunition out of Cartagena (in Colombia) and had lost her rudder and broken a mast and had fallen out of convoy, running in to the coast somewhere north of St. Augustine].

DON GASPAR RUIZ DE PEREDA.

WITH THIS ORDER, and the sloop and four seamen for it, which Don Gaspar [the Governor of Cuba] gave them, they left *la Havana* on June 2d, [sailing] towards the channel, and landed at St. Augustine ... on the 8th of May. And having been there 8 days, their purpose was not discovered or even suspected.

[They then proceed searching along the coast northward, taking soundings, noting the direction of the coastline, and arrive at the Cape of Trafalgar (Hatteras)]

From Trafalgar to Virginia the coast runs to the north quarter to northwest. The distance may be about 45 leagues, and here you can go hugging the coast at the distance of an arquebus shot from the land, because there are always 7 to 10 fathoms, and there is no shallow at all till you come to the point of the Bay of Virginia [Cape Henry], where there is a shallow before you come to the entrance which stretches out into the sea less than half a league.

This point of the bay on the south side is at 37°10′ north latitude; and although they did not think of making a regular ship's course, it is certain that from St. Augustine ..., which is at 30° close measure, to Virginia it may be by sea in a straight line perhaps 170 leagues, and following the coast perhaps 200 leagues. The *caravela* having reached this aforesaid bay of Virginia, which is called the Bay of Xacan, they found it to be very large.

Here Don Diego said was the country they were in search of. Sailing up in the center of the bay and sounding, they found that it had at the mouth 15 fathoms, and in the middle and higher up 10 to 4. Here they found a ship lying at anchor close to a point where there was an earthwork, like trenches,[1] and they heard a gun being fired from that direction. But it was not known whether there was a ball

[1] Fort Algernon on the site of Fortress Monroe.

fired, but that Don Diego ordered another gun to be fired in reply, but without a ball.

They sent for the sloop, into which went [Don Diego de Molina himself], Marco Antonio, the pilot Lembri, and the master of the caravela, with 8 or 9 other men armed with muskets and ammunition; and made them pull them on shore because, as he [Don Diego] said, he was quite certain that this was the ship they were looking for.[1] Before landing, however, they discovered near the fortification some 60 or 70 men, and upon their coming to shore these disappeared.

One of the sailors having told him that it would be better to get away from that place to the leeward, because he did not think well of those people, Don Diego said no one should say a word or he would break his head. Coming then on shore he [Don Diego] ordered the master to remain in the sloop with the crew, and that he should not come on shore unless he himself should first come and order him to do so, calling "Pedro." And although he should come if he spoke this name, he should not trust anyone.

The master, wondering very much at this, replied to him, regretting very much that he should not wish him to come on shore with him. Only Don Diego, Marco Antonio, and Francisco Lembri did go on shore with their guns, which was a resolution springing from his great courage and because everyone insisted upon him, that to him belonged the risk and the danger.[2] One sailor, seeing the footsteps which there were in the soil, said they were made by English or Flemish shoes. And then Don Diego replied again that they should keep quiet and say nothing to him, because there were no enemies who would do them harm, and began to walk over the sand.

The sloop having pushed off from land, they saw some 50 men come out of a creek in 3 or 4 detachments, apparently Englishmen and Flemish men, who took the three and, depriving them of their arms, carried them to the fort.

An hour afterwards, there came some 20 of them back again and called to the sloop to come ashore; and the master replied that he

---

[1] The disabled galleon *Plantation.*

[2] I.e., the rest agreed with the sailor that Don Diego was walking into a trap.

would do so if his captain [Don Diego, according to instructions] came, to which they replied that that was not possible. Some of these men remained there and others went away [and returned] bringing Francisco Lembri, and saying that he had come on shore, although he did not speak a word. And seeing that he did not come forward, they made the said Lembri tell them [aboard the sloop], as he did very sadly, striking with his hand outward and crossing his arms, declaring and making them understand that he was a prisoner.

Then the master caused one of the crew to go on shore swimming to see if he could learn anything of the three. But they did not permit him to speak to him [Lembri], standing there surrounded by a guard of ten men with their helmets and their arquebusses, the matches all ready.

Soon there came 7 or 8 Englishmen, and one of them asked for the master; and the sailor replied to him that he was in the sloop and that if he wished to speak to him, he would take him there—and thus he did on his shoulders. Being on board he told the master that he was a pilot and meant to put the caravela close to the fort, and that he [the master] should go on shore with 4 other companions, where they would be very well treated. To this he [the master] replied that they should show him his captain [Don Diego], whom they had in their power, that thereupon he would go on shore. To this he said that that was not possible, and the master said that on his side also it would not be possible for him to go on shore, and ordered the sloop to be rowed to the caravela; which when he [the English pilot] saw, he intended to throw himself into the sea. But 3 men seizing him prevented him, and when be began to cry aloud they shut up his mouth, so that he should not be heard on shore, and put him on board the caravela for good security.

On the next day, the master resolved to embark in the sloop with 12 men, with their muskets and the English pilot, to see if they could not for him exchange our men. They came close to the land and discovered on the shore the same men as the day before. These concealed themselves in a creek, with the expectation that they would thus be tempted to land and then be caught. But whilst preparing for this, they stopped at the swell of the sea, a stone's throw from land. And the English, seeing their caution, came down to the shore, calling with their cloak, and bringing Francisco Lembri there they made him say again to the master of the caravela that he should come on shore and that they would then consider what was most suitable to be done (as he did not wish to come nor give up the Englishman, if they did not first set free Don Diego and send him back).

The aforesaid Englishman tried again to throw himself into the sea, but was prevented by the great care that was taken of him. He said that it was not right to keep him in bonds as he was the chief pilot of the English in that bay and the coast of Xacan; with whom then the master agreed that he should make his captain come there and speak to him and negotiate with him for his exchange for the three, which he had in his power, and that in all this he was to be alone and without guards. Having said this, and the captain (of the English) having come with 20 musketeers, he was not willing to bring any one of the three. When the master learned this, he made the Englishman tell the captain that unless he [the captain] determined to surrender Don Diego and his companions, that he [the master] would fight him. Having heard this, he [the captain] replied from the shore with great anger that they might go to the devil. At this time it was seen that they took away Francisco Lembri with much violence and that from behind the English captain he made signs that they should push out to sea, crossing his arms and hastening [them] to get away.

Thus they returned to the caravela, and discovering that a small vessel was coming out from within the river which falls in on the right hand, they resolved to be off to sea and to return to the Havana —where they arrived on July 20th, without anything of importance having occurred or befallen them on the way, with all the people they took out except Don Diego de Molino, Marco Antonio Perez, and Francisco Lembri, who remained in the power of the English.

They promptly reported to the governor all that had happened to them during the voyage, and delivered up the English pilot whom they brought with them.

He was ordered to be put in a safe place where he could not communicate with anyone. Having examined him on the 23rd of said month and taken his deposition, with the aid as interpreter of

John *Lak*, an Englishman who was a prisoner in that city, with the usual solemnities and formalities he declared that his name was John *Clerique* [Clark], an Englishman by nation, a native of London, and of the same religion as his king; that his duty is to act as pilot, and his age is 35 years; that he sailed from the port of London in the month of March of this year [1611], taking the route for the Xacan, since that is the name of Virginia, on the coast of Florida, with three ships, one of 300 tons in which he came himself, and the others of 150 and 90.

They went as far as Dominica of the Leeward Islands, and took on water in stormy weather, from which they went to reconnoiter Puerto Rico; and from thence they took the route and sailed northwest, and the first land which they made was 12 leagues to the west of the harbor of Virginia; whilst at other times they are not apt to come to Dominica to make water. For unless they fall below 22°, they make their voyage steering W or E N W, without touching land or making the Leeward Islands,[1] as the coast of Virginia is clear for 40 leagues, the current running up from east-northeast to west-southwest, with 60 fathoms water, and at 30 leagues 50 fathoms, at 20 leagues 36 fathoms, at 10 leagues 18 fathoms, and at 5 leagues 15 fathoms, and within the five leagues from the land the least water that there is 5 fathoms to 4; and in the proper entrance of the bay the depth is from 12 to 14 fathoms; and on the south side of the harbor there is a shallow which has not more than one fathom or one and a half; and on the north side of it in the real opening of the bay there are, close to the point [Cape Charles? Point Comfort?], 10 or 12 fathoms of water, and from one point of the harbor [Hampton Roads] to the other from 8 to 5 fathoms; and inside a very good anchoring place for ships under shelter from all winds. Within the bay itself there are five rivers which flow in different directions,[2] and of 4 of them he has no knowledge of what they are. At the mouth of this said bay there are four earthworks towards the northern side, all on one bank. And the first fort is at the mouth of that river, which consists of stockades and posts without stone or brick, and contains 7

[1] Confusing compass points, but this is the route Argall found to the north of the West Indies. The passage is clearer in Clark's *Declaration §36.*

[2] I.e., tidal.

pieces of artillery, two of 35 *quintales,* and the others of 30, 20, and 18, and all of iron—where 50 persons are present, counting men, women, and boys, of which 40 are fit to carry arms.

The second fort stands at two thirds of a league from the first, and the third at a musket shot [from the second],[1] and both of them with their supply of pieces of artillery for defense against the Indians.

The principal settlement is the fourth fort,[2] which is 20 leagues up the river from the first fort, and in it there are 16 pieces of artillery of—— iron, and is surrounded with palisades like the others. The houses of the colonists are of wood.

As high up as where large ships come, and along the bank of the river where the depth is least, there are three and a half fathoms of water. This changes sometimes with inundations. High and low tide are of half a fathom. The tides go up the river 30 leagues above the town, which must be, in all, 50 leagues from the entrance to the harbor.

But you cannot travel by land along that bank (river); and from the end of it to the South Sea it may be 16 to 18 days' journey, according to what has been understood from the native Indians. He [Clark] has never heard that any pirates should have come to this harbor or these rivers from anywhere; and says that there may be a thousand persons in all the said settlements, and in the forts some 600 fit for carrying arms, and the others all women, children, and old people.

The trade for the present does not go beyond some provisions, clothes, and other things which they have brought here for said people, and in return they carry wood for barrels and vessels and sasifrage [sassafras].

They have brought to this colony 100 cows, 200 pigs, 100 goats, and 17 horses and mares; and he hears there is a gold mine, for which cause the king has given permission to them to sail from England to these parts.

The government of which was in charge of a brother of *Nortomberlan*, appointed for himself, who has been succeeded by Don Thomas *Del* by order of the King of England, who recently came over to said

---

[1] Forts Algernon, Henry, and Charles.

[2] Jamestown.

government in the 3 ships of which mention has been made.

[He says] that for August they expected four more ships with some people and a large quantity of cattle, and all under the charge of Don Thomas Gates.

[He says] that the people who go out there are outcasts and live by piracy; that the aforesaid narrator has only been this one time in those parts, coasts, and ports, where at present there remain six ships in the before-mentioned river: the 3 to which he has referred, two others of 70 and of 50 tons, which were built two years ago in la Bermuda—for the purpose of bringing from there to Virginia, in the spring, 150 persons who had been wrecked there in a ship which was of 200 tons, that went in charge of Captain Nioporte, [and] that the blacksmiths and carpenters which they carried took advantage of [salvaged] the wreck to provide the two said vessels, which they were building, with iron and pitch—and one boat of 12 or 13 tons which was built in said Virginia; where there is also now building a galley of 25 benches, which will not be finished so soon, as they had but little to begin with and only a few workmen.

The colony of Virginia had a beginning now about five years ago, where there is no intercourse with the Indians, because at one time it is war, at another time it is peace. They go about dressed in deer-skins and with their bows and arrows, which are the weapons they use. The soil produces no other fruit but maize and nuts, but very far inland there is much game, and fine fishing is found more or less there.

Mines of gold and silver have been looked for and this still goes on, but none have yet been found. The Indians bring them none of those metals.

As to the manner in which our people took him [Clark] and carried him to the Havana, he reports that—a [Spanish] caravela having come to Virginia—one boat of theirs went towards the land with some men, of whom three jumped on shore, two Spaniards and an Englishman [Lembri] (whom he knew and saw two years ago in Malaga, who was pilot of the fleet commanded by Don Luis Fajardo).

They carried the 3 men to the fort, with the aid of the soldiers who came out on the shore, with the captain of the aforesaid fort, who is called Davis. And they ate with them and told him that he should go with three or four others to put the caravela in the port; and that thus he went to the sloop, to which a sailor carried him on his shoulders; and when they had him inside, they did not let him out again, but carried him to the caravela; and on the following day, they made him go once more in the boat, together with the master of the caravela and other sailors, and they went towards the land in order to speak with the English and negotiate the return of each one to his own people. By means of a boy, who served as interpreter, they replied that until they had given an account to the governor of that country, who was in the colony, they could not.

And as the people of the caravela thought that one of the vessels which were in the harbor might come out, they did not want to wait longer and thus they came away.

[Other Spanish officials soon reexamined the mariners and reinterrogated Clark, finding to their satisfaction that accounts remained consistent, at which point they decided to detain Clark in prison at Havana "without any communication with anyone, and especially of his own nation, which could not be done in Spain," if they transported him there; then proceeded to notify King James' ambassador.]

36. John Clark

Declaration of the Englishman in Virginia [23 July] 1611

(translated from the Spanish by Irene A. Wright)

< Seville A. G. I. 147/15–16, **Wright 1920:470** (with original), Quinn 1979e: 154

A translation of the Spanish translation, this is material not written by Clark but given by him in deposition under coercive interrogation in Havana immediately following his abduction. Similarly the *Confession §42,* given ahead. The whole sad Point Comfort incident is of small significance in the history of the world, only that those involved reveal interesting details about the colony.

We have several accounts: three by Clark, one by the unnamed master of the Spanish vessel, and an unsigned report in "the voyage to the Indies as far as Virginia" (the most detailed, appending another copy of Clark's deposition), an account by George Percy in his *True Relation §31,* and a brief mention with brooding reflections in §38, Dale's letter to Salisbury of 17 August 1611 (Dale was very worried about Spain). They agree well enough, so that there is little need to summarize or compare them. All are included here. De Molina must have given his own version; we do not have it. We do have a brief and most revealing account by Smith in his *General History,* 4th Book (119, not given at §52), that is quoted in part by Purchas. Neither of these sources, however, is an eyewitness. Here is Smith's:

> About this time it chanced a Spanish ship beat too near and again before Point Comfort, and at last sent ashore their boat, as desirous of a pilot. Captain James Davis, the governor, immediately gave them one, but he was no sooner in the boat but away they went with him, leaving three of their companions behind them.
>
> This sudden accident occasioned some distrust and a strict examination of those three thus left, yet with as good usage as our estate could afford them. They only confessed having lost their admiral; accident had forced them into those parts, and two of them were captains, and in chief authority in the fleet. Thus they lived till one of them was found to be an Englishman, and had been Spaniards' pilot for England in '88; and having here induced some malcontents to believe his projects to run away with a small bark, which was apprehended, some executed, and he expecting but the hangman's courtesy, directly confessed that two or three Spanish

ships was at sea purposely to discover the estate of the colony, but their commission was not to be opened till they arrived in the Bay, so that of anything more he was utterly ignorant. One of the Spaniards at last died, the other was sent for England, but this reprieved till Sir Thomas Dale hanged him at sea in his voyage homeward; the English pilot they carried for Spain, whom after a long time imprisonment with much suit was returned for England.

Also aboard with Dale had been "Pocahontas, the king's daughter, and Master Rolfe, her husband," landing 12 June 1616 at Plymouth.

Clark under orders had gone aboard the Spanish sloop in order to bring it under Point Comfort, a tricky anchorage for which a pilot was needed.

Most of his information is frank and true, but there are some patriotic lies: There are only three forts, not four (the second version says three). And it is quite possible to march overland up the Peninsula of Virginia, as Gen. McClellan and the Army of the Potomac did in 1862. Or was that the question? He surely exaggerates the population and the number of effectives able to bear arms.[1] The mountain of gold rumor may have been rife at Jamestown as a leftover from the gold fever days of 1607.

What about pirates? Clark denies their presence only to say a few statements further in both versions of his deposition that the colonists are "abandoned people who ... live by piracy." This hints at a rough interrogation.

Clark's identification of Lembri as an Englishman was fatal. Lembri was adjudged a traitor—whether or not he tried to escape, whether or not he was a spy in addition—and met his end. The community of ship's pilots was intimately small.

The Spanish master's account adds a detail saying they were looking for the wreck of the ship *Plantation* to salvage her guns.

THAT HE IS CALLED JUAN CLERG, and is a native of London, a pilot, thirty-five years of age, and that he is of the religion of his king; and in the month of March of this year sailed from the port of the said city for Virginia with three ships, the one of 300 tons, another of 150, and another of 90, and that the course they took was for Dominica and Niebes, where they took in water; and from there, sighting Porto Rico, they took their course to the north, and the first land they discovered was twelve leagues to the west of the port of Virginia; and

---

[1] *The New Life of Virginea* in May 1612 claimed "Our colony consisteth now of seven hundred men at least." (Force, 13) At most, surely.

that at other times they are not accustomed to go to Dominica to get water, but sail for 22 degrees, steering to the west [and] west-northwest without sighting land or making the Windward Islands; and that the coast is clear, and at forty leagues running from the southeast to the west-southwest there are sixty fathoms, at thirty leagues fifty, at twenty leagues thirty-six, at ten leagues eighteen, and at five leagues fifteen fathoms, and five leagues off the land the least water there is from five to four fathoms; and in the mouth itself of the bay there are from twelve to fourteen fathoms, and along the south shore of the harbor is a shoal which has not more than one fathom to a fathom and a half of water, and on the north side of it, in the mouth itself of the bay alongside the harbor there are ten or twelve fathoms of water; and from one point of the harbor to the other there are from eight to five fathoms of water, and within there is a good roadstead for ships, well sheltered from all winds; and within the bay itself there are five rivers flowing in different directions; and of four of these he has no knowledge as to what kind they are.

That at the mouth of the said harbor in one of these rivers there are four fortifications on the north side, all on one bank; and that the first fort is at the mouth of the river, where there are fifty persons settled, men and women, of whom forty are fit to bear arms; and that the fort is of palisades and timber, without stone or brick, and has seven pieces of artillery, two of them of about thirty-five hundred-weight and the rest of thirty, twenty, and eighteen, and all cast iron; and that the second fort is two thirds of a league from there, and another at a distance of one musket-shot, and the fourth at another musket-shot,[1] each having one cast-iron piece for defense against the Indians; and the principal settlement, where there is another fortification, is twenty leagues up the river from the first fort, and in it there are sixteen pieces, and it is also surrounded by palisades, and the houses of the settlement are all wood and the cannon of cast iron like the rest, and ships of deep draft go up to the said settlement.

That where there is least water in the channel of the river there are three fathoms and one half of water, but that this changes sometimes

[1] There were three forts, in order east to west, Algernon, Charles, and Henry.

with the freshes, although the difference between flood and ebb is not more than half a fathom, and that barges go thirty leagues farther up from the town, that is, fifty from the mouth of the harbor.

That it is not possible to journey by land along the river bank; and that from the uppermost part of the river to the South Sea would be sixteen or eighteen days' journey, as they have understood from the native Indians; and that he does not know that pirates or ships from any region gather in the said port and river; and that in all the settlements and fortifications there are about 1000 persons, 600 of them fit to bear arms, and the rest women, boys, and old men.

That he does not know that there is any further trade with England than that some provisions and clothing and other things have been brought for the people that are settled there; and on the return voyage they go back laden with wood for hogsheads and for ships, and sassafras wood, and that also they have brought over 100 cows, 200 pigs, 100 goats, and 17 mares and horses; and that he understands that there is a certain gold mine which is the cause why his king gives permission to sail from England to those parts, although up to the present time they have not found any gold or silver, though they have sought for it, nor do the Indians bring any of it, and he denied that he had confessed to the master that pieces of gold were found.

That that land has been governed by a brother of the Conde Nontonborlan, named Perse, who brought his government to an end at the coming of a knight who is called Don Tomas, who was in the three ships in which the deponent made his voyage, and who governs by the order of the King of England.

That in August of this year they expect four ships with some people and a quantity of cattle, under command of Don Tomas Guies, and that those who sail to these regions and gather there are abandoned people, who are accustomed to live by piracy.

That he has been only once in Virginia, and that at present there were six ships there, and the three that went with him, and of the other three two were made in Bermuda, where one from England came ashore in a storm, with more than 150 persons, and among them some officials; and taking the iron, pitch, and what else was necessary, they made them two years ago, the one of seventy tons and the other of twenty-five, and that the last of the said vessels was a barge of about twelve or thirteen tons, made in the said Virginia, where they were also making a galley of twenty-five benches, but that it would not be finished very soon because of having little that is prepared and not having the necessary men; and that it is five years since they began to settle that land, and that all those who are there or go to it are English.

That the Indians of that land are sometimes at peace and other times at war, and go clothed in deerskins and with their bows and arrows, which are *gusamar* [?], and that the produce they gather is maize and walnuts; and up in the land there are many deer and the cattle that they have taken from England; and as to fisheries, at times there is abundance and at others very little.

And as to the manner in which they took him, he declares that a caravel having come to the said harbor of Virginia, a boat came ashore from it with some men, of whom three landed, two Spaniards and an Englishman, the last of whom this deponent knew, because two years ago he saw him in the city of Malaga serving as a pilot in the armada of Don Luis Faxardo; and that the soldiers who went down to the shore with the captain of the fort, who is called David, took all three; and they all ate together; and then they ordered the deponent with three or four others to go and bring the caravel into the port; and he went to the shallop, and one of the mariners put him into the boat, carrying him on his shoulders; and when they saw him in it they would not let him go, but carried him on board the caravel, where they kept him all night; and in the morning they set him in a boat together with the master of the caravel and other men, and went to the land to speak with the English and to ask them for their three men, which they did, saying that they would give them the deponent in return for these; to which they replied that until they should have given account to the governor of that land, who was at the settlement, they could not do anything; and the master and the people of the caravel, seeing this, feared that the ships which were in the port might do them some harm, and being unwilling to wait longer went away to Havana, taking him with them.

Declaration of the master, pilot, mariner.

THAT WHEN THEY SAILED from the port of Havana, which was one day after Corpus Christi, Don Diego de Molina, who had command of the caravel, told them that they were going to seek the artillery of a ship which had been lost on the coast of Florida, and that they should sail in that direction; which they did, and came to the port of San Agustín of those provinces, where they remained with the governor five days; and from there they sailed on the 15th or 16th of June, and took their course up along the said coast sounding, until they came to 37 degrees, where they found a great bay; and that Don Diego de Molina said that this was the place which they were to seek; and that having entered and sounded the bay up to the middle of it, they found that at the entrance it has fifteen fathoms, and then from ten to four; and that they saw that there was a ship anchored near a point where there was a fort like an entrenchment; and near it they went ashore in a shallop; and Don Diego de Molina and the ensign Marco Antonio Perez, and the English pilot [Francis Lembri] they had taken with them, a spy *[confidente]* married in Lisbon, jumped ashore, having their muskets; and Don Diego ordered the master, this deponent, to put to sea with all the people, and that they should not come to land nor disembark in any manner unless they should so signal to them; and that being in sight of what went on, they saw some fifty men, English or Flemish as it appeared to them, come out in three or four squads from a cove; and they seized them and took away their arms and took them to a fort; and an hour later twenty Englishmen returned in three squads, and called to the master, this deponent, and requested him to come to land; and he said to them to first bring back his captain, and the English replied that it was not possible; and while this was going on, others came with the English spy [Lembri] whom they had taken, and seeing that the master would not come to land, they told the latter that he should call him, assuring him that they would not do him damage, but that he should be regaled; but that although to comply with their orders he [Lembri] did it, yet by some signs and by his sad countenance he gave him to understand that he was taken prisoner, and that consequently he should go away; and thereupon [this deponent] ordered a sailor to swim ashore and try to learn something concerning the captain, but they would not let him speak with the English spy; and then eight others came, and one of them said he wished to speak to the master, and the sailor undertook to carry him out upon his shoulders, and did so; and when they had come to the caravel, he tried to persuade the master to come to land; and he not only would not do it, but seeing that they would not bring back his captain and the other two companions, he put out to sea with the Englishman; and although the latter tried to escape from the caravel, they detained him and brought him to Havana, and on the voyage they asked him certain things; and among other things he said that a hundred leagues up into the land there was a mountain from which they obtained pieces of gold.

37. Reverend Alexander Whitaker

Letter to the Reverend William Crashaw, 9 August 1611

< **British Library: Bodleian Library additional MSS 21/993–193, Ashmolean MSS 1147–219,** Richmond Standard (newspaper) 4 Feby 1882, Brown 1890:497

Who can deny Whitaker was fascinated with the rich and vigorous paganism of America? He was an educated man, and it is a rare MA who does not have a general curiosity about exotic ways. But he is a Protestant clergyman, and he surely saw it as his job to know his adversary, namely, the *quiyoughcosoughs,* or native priests, who played his opposites in the fresh landscape. Far from dismissing them as superstitious "witch doctors," the man of God recognizes the man of Satan as nearly his equal, and that sorcery too can move mountains.

He says that it was God's purpose to lay riches in the New World sufficient to lure the bringers of Christianity. Hmm. Whitaker's letter is a new preacher's first report home.

GOOD MR. CRASHAW—You heard by my last two letters[1] how prosperous a journey I had hither, and must now again send you word how God hath continued His goodness towards me and preserved me safe hitherto with great hope of good success to our purposes.

It is needless that I should write unto you of every particular of our doings, for I suppose it would be unsavory to the conceit of a scholar and your heavenly meditations to hear what corn we have set, what boats we have built, etc. But I will acquaint you with one thing which may be worthy your consideration and wherein I desire to know your opinion.

Our governor, Sir Thomas Dale, pretended an expedition to a place called the Falls. 7 or 8 days before his going, the king of the Indians, Powhaton, by his messengers forbid him those quarters and demanded of them 2 Indian prisoners which he had taken from them. Otherwise he threatened to destroy us after strange manner.

First, he said he would make us drunk and then kill us, and for a more solemnity gave us six or seven days' respite. Sir Thomas was very merry at this message, and returned them with the like answer.

Shortly after, without any deliverance of the prisoners, he went armed to the Falls, where one night, our men being at prayers in the court of guard, a strange noise was heard coming out of the corn towards the trenches of our men like an Indian *hup hup!* with an *oho oho!* Some say that they saw one like an Indian leap over the fire and run into the corn with the same noise, at the which all our men were confusedly amazed. They could speak nothing but *oho oho,* and all generally taking the wrong end of their arms began the Thebans' war against Cadmus.[2] But thanks be to God this alarum lasted not above half a quarter of an hour and no harm was done, excepting 2 or 3 which were knock'd down without any further harm. For suddenly, as men awaked out of a dream, they began to search for their

1 "These letters, which have not been found, were probably sent by Captain Adams, May 25, 1611." (Brown)

2 In Greek myth, Athena ordered Cadmus to sow the teeth of the slain serpent of the Castalian Spring. At once, armed men sprang up from the soil clashing their weapons. Cadmus tossed a stone among them and they began fighting until only five were left alive.

supposed enemies, but, finding none, remained ever after very quiet.

Another accident fell out in a march up Nansamund River. As our men passed by one of their towns, there issued out of the shore a mad crew dancing like antics, or our morris dancers, before whom there went a *quiockosite,* or their priest, [who] tossed smoke and flame out of a thing like a censer. An Indian, by name Munchumps, amongst our men, seeing this dance, told us that there would be very much rain presently, and indeed there was forthwith exceeding thunder and lightning and much rain within 5 miles, and so further off, but not so much there as made their powder dank.

Many such casualties[1] happen, as that the principal amongst them, being bound with strong irons and kept with great watch, have escaped from us without our knowledge or prevention.

All which things make me think that there be great witches among them, and they very familiar with the devil. I should more admire Virginea with these inhabitants if I did not remember that Egypt was exceeding fruitful, that Canaan flowed with milk and honey before Israel did overrun it, and that Sodom was like the garden of God in the days of Lot. Only I think that the Lord hath spared this people and enriched the bowels of the country with the riches and beauty of nature, that we wanting them might in the search of them communicate the most excellent merchandise and treasure of the Gospel with them.

God hath heretofore most horribly plagued our countrymen with famine, death, the sword, etc., for the sins of our men were intolerable. I marvel more that God did not sweep them away all at once than that in such manner He did punish them. Yet He in the middest of His anger rememb'red mercy, and minding now, as we hope, to fulfill His purpose and set up the kingdom of His Son on these parts, [He] most miraculously withstood many times the purposes of our men who were returning home, and now again with far more successive proceedings and better hopes doth preserve us here.

As for me, God hath dealt mercifully with me beyond my friends' opinion and my own hopes. My coming hither hath been prosperous and my continuance here hath been answerable. I think I have

---

[1] Accidents.

fared better for your prayers and the rest. If there be any young godly and learned ministers whom the Church of England hath not, or refuseth, to set a-work, send them hither. Our harvest is forward and great here for want of such. Young men are fittest for this country, and we have no need either of ceremonies or bad lives. Discretion with learning, zeal with knowledge would do much good.

I have much more to write, but now can no more besides my prayers to God for a blessing upon our labors.

Farewell, your loving friend,
ALLEXANDER WHITAKER.

James Town in Virginea, this 9th of August, 1611.

38. Thomas Dale

Letter to Salisbury, 17 August 1611

< **State Papers Colonial, James I, 1/26–94,** Brown 1890:501

Governor Dale has assessed the situation and here is his grand proposal: He will secure the Peninsula with five strongholds and 2000 colonists, promising they will be self-sufficient in six months if fully supplied till then. He even has a plan for recruiting them from among those in the next nine months sentenced to death in England. On the whole, he says, they will prove superior to what is picked up "peradventure" off the streets. Perhaps, but the figure means that annually one Englishman in every 1500 was getting hanged. And yet this is a piece of insight: Then as now many a first-time perpetrator of the highest crime, ironically, was not otherwise a criminal.

The last item, the Spanish caravel affair, actually touches on Dale's deepest fears about Virginia's security.

RIGHT HONORABLE—I know right well how covetous, if not jealous, your full and absolute meditations are over and concerning this so pious, so heroic enterprise, in these days not employing any state in Christendom with a like work parallel to it, whether be admitted the access of honor, bounties of nature, enlargement of temporary respects, or the honor of God and enlargement of His kingdom, insomuch as it is well observed that you lend no busy thought so much welcome and grace as what brings tales and restless discourse of the constitution thereof. And it is out of this, thrice-honored Lord, that I presume to give up somewhat of her praises, who since my coming into this country have taken pains to inform myself of it, even concerning those mixed conditions and secondary ways by which she may meet us with the more favor, knowing it to be true that the same conditions are to be required in this country—habitable air, temperate and wholesome the breeders of the land and rivers, and benefits of the earth for corn and fruit, etc.—which other countries deliver unto the subsisting and being of mankind, and both of the one and all of these under this kind I have approved,[1] and may uprightly testify, insomuch as there are not those fears and slanders to be laid out upon the commodities or clime or soil of this country which ignorance or malice have poisoned the general opinion with.

I do find here many kind of beasts, fish, and fowl, goodly corn, and a greater quantity than may easily win belief, vines, and these with hable means[2] soon to return a certain and plentiful vintage. For our ordinary well-known commodities I may not deny but that here are their materials, though here no hands to gather and work them unto our advantage.

It is only in the power, excellent Lord, of so true a lover of God and your country—and of so free an offerer unto so languishing and forsaken a holy action—as Your Honor is to advance this work unto her proper heighth and send such laborers thereunto as may take off the films of ignorance and simplicity which veil the eyes of these poor wretches from looking upon their own beauty which, if the divine goodness by your potent means should make them see what a work had you wrought into them and unto yourself, no age would be ever silent of it. And indeed, right worthy to be most famous Lord, so largely hath already your exchequer opened unto her being as but for your bounty she had not long since been at all,[3] and then not now to make complaint by me of her weak being.

In that she hath hitherto no better thrived, but still every year, after fresh and new additions of men and monies, declined rather and stooped under many disasters almost past reparation, hath been because the true grounds which should have advanced her have not been hitherto so faithfully followed as faithfully and maturely advised. Howbeit I can lay no blame upon the will and desires of the interchangeable undertakers, but upon the want of those great disbursements which at one time and at first must fix and settle her, for I confess it an enterprise of charge.

Yet now at length let me boldly affirm it unto Your Lordship—and

---

[1] Avouched.

[2] With proper cultivation.

[3] "From this it seems that Salisbury had rescued the colony from destruction or abandonment." (Brown)

laying for the same my life to pawn if I perform it not—that with the expense of so much money as now at once disbursed to furnish hither 2000 men to be here by the beginning of next April [1612], I would in the space of two years (my number still made good) render this whole country unto His Majesty, settle a colony here secure for themselves and ready to answer all her ends and expectations. For by the several plantations and seats which I would make I should so overmaster the subtle, mischievous Great Powhatan that I should leave him either no room in his country to harbor in or draw him to a firm association with ourselves. And he being brought to this shift of fortune to seek a stranger country or to accept of a well-liked condition of life with us, how would it strike upon the neighbor savages confining him—who in all probability of reason may be won then unto our own conditions?

And that it may be thus wrought, I humbly beseech Your Lordship to pardon my weakness, if unto your habler judgment I presume to present the means thus unto Your Honor.

All the tract of land which lieth between our river, which we call the King's River, and that whereupon Powhatan dwelleth, which may be in some places twenty miles over, and from Point Comfort up to the Falls extendeth in length some 150 miles, is all in the command and containeth the principallest seats of Powhatan, which I would thus secure unto us and, by having them, of necessity be commanders of the opposite, south shore.

At Point Comfort I would first fortify to secure us above, and hold open the mouth of our river to let shipping into us; and where the two princes' forts there are at Kecoughtan, fashion and lay out a spacious and commodious town for a chief commander, where is already 2 or 3000 acres of cleared ground to set corn; and plant vines —and vines grow naturally there in great abundance.

Withal this place is apt for fishing, as likewise there grows our best silk grass.

Some 15 miles from hence at a place called Kiskaick, somewhat short of Powhatan's chief town, called Worowocomaco upon the north side of the river, should my second plantation be, for that would make good the inland and assure us likewise of Pamunkie River.

My third should hold as it doth at James town.

My fourth should be at Arsahattacks, 80[1] miles up our river from James Town, where I have surveyed a convenient strong, healthy, and sweet seat to plant a new town in, according as I had in my instructions upon my departure there to build,[2] from whence might be no more remove of the principal seat; and in that form to build, as might accommodate the inhabitants, and become the title and name which it hath pleased the lords already to appoint for it.

A fifth I could advise to be ten[3] miles above this, to command the head of the river, and the many fruitful islands in the same; these divisions, like nurseries, sending out smaller settlements, upon some places yet of moment, would work my former promise concerning the full possession of Powhatan's country, and this country of itself would afford many excellent seats for many a thousand householder.

And believe it, right noble Lord, without these forces to make good these several seats, the having whereof not only secures our lives from the subtle Indian but brings us in plenty of wherewith to feed our lives, to clothe our bodies, and to explore the hidden and unknown commodities of the whole country, it shall be in vain to strive any longer to settle a handful of wretched and untoward people here, and great expectations to be placed over their labors, with waking and jealous eyes, expecting the return of such retributions and benefits, secret commodities and riches, which is as impossible for them to get either into their possession or knowledge as it is to poise and weigh the mountains.

I have seen, right excellent Lord, a spacious and fruitful circuit of ground even from Point Comfort up to the Falls, upon many seats both upon the one and the other shore, and in all places within the lower country find that plenty of corn which our Company adventurers in England hardly believe can be here at all. And at the Falls, I cannot only testify of corn but of all probabilities of mines, when our time shall serve, which may not be yet, and where I gathered many scattered pieces of crystal.

---

1 "Fifty" crossed out.

2 "So the city of Henricus was planned in England about March 1611." (Brown)

3 "Forty" crossed out.

I am not ignorant, noble Lord, how cold the devotions of men take this great work, and some former slanders yet upon it, not removed, deter many a meaner man far from his personal adventure hither, howbeit I am right well assured if we once had here the number of 2000 men, as aforesaid, I should in little time even satisfy the worst and widest assertion of him who most maligns it or flies from it.

For the two plantations, the one at Arsahatacks, the other at the head of the Falls upon the main, of Tanx Powhatan's land, do so nearly neighbor all the chief and only variety and change of towns and houses belonging to the Great Powhatan as either he would join friendship with us or will leave then to our possession [of] his country, and thereby leave us in security. Upon them we might nourish our own breeders, and hunt and fowl upon the land, and fish in the rivers, and plant our corn and vines boldly and with safety, by which means we should no more lament us of want or scarcity of any provision, and only the not having of sufficient of provision—and, in these, good kinds likewise—hath been and is yet the greatest enemy unto the speedy peopling of the colony.

And upon the arrival of those 2000 men, may they be here before the next April, though sent at two several times, if but sent hither furnished with six months' provision of corn, I would never after charge the Company for any commodity or supply in that kind again for them so long as they stay'd in the country.

And sithence, noble Lord, I know well, the colony standing in such conditions and state as it doth, how hard it is to procure so many men in so short time, I have, under Your Lordship's pardon, conceived that if it will please His Majesty to banish hither all offenders condemned betwixt this and then[1] to die out of common gaols, and likewise so continue that grant for 3 years unto the colony (and thus doth the Spaniard people his Indies), it would be a ready way to furnish us with men—and not always with the worst kind of men either for birth, spirits, or body—and such who would be right glad so to escape a just sentence to make this their new country and plant and inhabit therein with all diligence, cheerfulness, and

[1] Between August 1611 and April 1612.

comfort; whereas now such is the universal disposition throughout our whole little colony, as by reason of some present want of our English provisions, as every man almost laments himself of being here and murmurs at his present state—though haply he would not better it in England—not taking unto them so much patience until some few years have accomplish'd the fullness of our better store by the growth and increase of our cattle, planting and tilling of our corn and vines. And indeed, right noble Lord, our discontented company makes good that old saying, *Jejunus exercitus non habet aures.*[1]

Nor can I conceive how such people as we are enforced to bring over hither by peradventure, and gathering them up in such riotous, lazy, and infected places, can entertain themselves with other thoughts or put on other behavior than what accompanies such disord'red persons, so profane, so riotous, so full of mutiny and treasonable intendments—as I am well to witness in a parcel of 300 which I brought with me, of which well may I say not many give testimony beside their names that they are Christians—besides of such diseased and crazed bodies as, the sea hither and this clime here but a little searching them, render them so unhable, faint, and desperate of recovery as of 300 not threescore may be called forth or employed upon any labor or service.

Thus, my right noble Lord, I have presumed to appeal you from your grave and serious affairs to peruse a tedious story of the condition wherein your colony both ever heretofore and now for the present remaineth. Some means likewise I have presumed, as I conceive it, to offer unto Your Lordship how it may be truly recovered and prosper with greater comfort both to the adventurers at home and to us here.

Unto all which, if it shall be pleasing unto Your Lordship still to vouchsafe your powerful and honorable furtherance, you shall much bind us the poor planters forever to continue our prayers which we make daily for the access of all honor and happiness unto Your Lordship, and in few years should His Majesty possess another kingdom as goodly as what the sun can look upon to which his gold-

---

[1] "A hungry army listens to no one." (Latin)

creating power is no nearer a neighbor; and thus both it and my unworthy services humbly commending unto Your Lordship, ceasing to be unnecessary troublesome, I humbly kiss Your Lordship's hand.

August 17th, 1611. Virginia, James Town.

One advertisement[1] I am loth to omit unto Your Lordship who may be pleased to understand how this summer a Spanish carvel [caravel] came into our river fitted with a shallop necessary and proper to discover freshets, rivers, and creeks,[2] where she, anchoring at the mouth of our bay upon Point Comfort, sent three Spaniards ashore unto the fort there placed demanding a pilot to bring their said carvel into our river. What may be the danger of this unto us, who are here so few, so weak, and unfortified, since they have by this means sufficiently instructed themselves concerning our just height and seat, and know the ready way unto us both by this discoverer and by the help likewise of our own pilot, I refer me to your own honorable knowledge.

[margin note:] The captain of the fort sent him a pilot, and the carvel made out of our bay, leaving the 3 Spaniards ashore, who I have now here prisoners.

Your Lordship's humble servant,
THOMAS DALE.

39. George Percy

Letter to Northumberland, 17 August 1611

< **Northumberland Papers, Alnwick MSS, 9-23/6,** Neill 1885:84, Brown 1890:500. It is worth noting that even among the gullies and tree stumps of Virginia the governor has to put on the dog and receive fashionable comers in high style.

---

[1] "Probably the main advertisement. The three Spaniards were Molina, Perez, and Lymbry. The English pilot was Captain Clark." (Brown)

[2] Freshets are streams; creeks are small tidal coves and estuaries.

RIGHT HONORABLE—I am not ignorant and cannot therefore [be] unmindful in what I may to satisfy Your Lordship for your manifold and continual courtesies, which I daily and at the reproach of every shipping do abundantly taste of; and I must acknowledge freely that this last year hath not been a little chargeable into Your Honor who I hope will continue so noble and honorable opinion of me as you shall not think anything prodigally by me wasted or spent which tendeth to my no little advancement.

True [as] it is the place which I hold in this colony (the store affording no other means than a pound of meal a day and a little oatmeal) cannot be defrayed with small expense, it standing upon my reputation, being governor of James Town, to keep a continual and daily table for gentlemen of fashion about me, my request unto Your Lordship at this present is to entreat Your Honor to be highly pleased to discharge a bill of my hand made to Mr. Nellson, and likewise a bill of eight pounds unto Mr. Pindle Burie of London, merchant, and I shall ever be in all humble duty bound unto Your Lordship.

And thus wishing all honor and happiness to accompany you in this world, and eternal bliss in the other to come, I cease to be further unnecessary troublesome unto Your Lordship, ever vowing myself and the uttermost of my services in all duty unto Your Honor, and rest

Your Lordship's loving brother,
GEORGE PERCY.

Virginia, James Town, August 17, 1611.

[endorsed:] To the Right Honorable My singular good Lord and Brother, the Earl of Northumberland.

40. Robert Johnson

The New Life of Virginea: Declaring the former success and present estate of that plantation, being the second part of [the tract] Nova Britannia. (selections) [1 May 1612]

< Force 1836a, 4:12 & 13

This is a Virginia Company publication that calls itself a sequel to *Nova Britannia* (1609). There our author exhorted the English race to outgrow the island and embrace destiny in America: convert and civilize Indians, exploit resources, clear farms in land richer than at home, dig mines, build ships, set womenfolk spinning silk. England must not refuse twice the opportunity of wealth and empire that was lost when Henry VII turned away Bartholomew Columbus.

The New Life is signed by a man who claims never to have been in America. It reads that way until we get to the selections below.

Robert Johnson the alderman, a member of the grocer's guild and a man of high position in London's mercantile establishment, was quite active in all the overseas companies, including the Virginia Company, throughout our era. He was the king's candidate to replace Sir Edwin Sandys as treasurer in 1620; he was a strong supporter of Sir Thomas Smythe, to whom *The New Life* is dedicated. In 1623 we will find him writing a defense of Smythe's treasuryship of the Virginia Company, including the policies of Gates and Dale, to which §57 and §58 were formed to respond. "He had a house at Bow, and Capt. John Bargrave says 'the idea of taking away of the patent from the Virginia Company was hatched at Alderman Johnson's house at Bow at the king's being there.'" (Brown 1890).

His plan here is simply a windy presentation of the colony's proud accomplishments, flourishing present, and future promise, helping himself to 8100 words. Our selections come out of a few middle pages.

Much support for Virginia was from investors who wanted quick returns. Marshal Dale, cited below, believes in America's long-term, not only as an English commonwealth, rich in natural endowments, but as a great nation in its own right. He was looking ahead to Canada and to the United States, both of which had now been born.

BUT IF ANYTHING otherwise than well betide me in this business, let me commend unto your carefulness the pursuit and dignity of this business, than which your purses and endeavors will never open nor travel in a more acceptable and meritorious enterprise: Take four of the best kingdoms in Christendom and put them all together, they may no way compare with this country either for commodities or goodness of soil.

And next is a description of the new upriver settlement of Henrico. We hear nothing about the Dale's harsh disciplinary measures or of the terrible shortages of food and materiel Dale himself reports in §47. The promise of hemp and flax came to nothing: There were not enough workers; what workers there were could not compete with European shops; tobacco soon carried all before.

The source of this information may be the marshal but I would rather credit Governor Gates.

YOU SHALL KNOW that our colony consisteth now of seven hundred men at least, of sundry arts and professions, some more or less. They stand in health and few sick at the ships' coming thence; having left the fort at Cape Henry fortified and kept by Captain Davies, and the keeping of James town to that noble and well-deserving gentleman, Master George Percie.

The colony is removed up the river fourscore miles further beyond James town to a place of higher ground, strong and defensible by nature—a good air, wholesome and clear (unlike the marish seat at James town) with fresh and plenty of water springs, much fair and open grounds freed from woods, and wood enough at hand.

Being thus invited, here they pitch: the spade men fell to digging, the brick men burnt their bricks, the company cut down wood, the carpenters fell to squaring out, the sawyers to sawing, the soldier to fortifying, and every man to somewhat. And to answer the first objection for wholesome lodging, here they have built competent and decent houses (the first storey all of bricks) that every man may have his lodging and dwelling place apart by himself, with a sufficient quantity of ground allotted thereto for his orchard and garden to plant at his pleasure, and for his own use. Here they were building also an hospital with fourscore lodgings (and beds already sent to furnish them) for the sick and lame, with keepers to attend them for their comfort and recovery. And as for their clothing, first of woolen (whereof they have least need because the country is very warm) it is and must be always supplied from hence, to the benefit of English clothing. But for linen, which they shall most need, without doubt by small and easy industry there may amount a great increase from thence to furnish by way of merchandise for England, not only by planting hemp and flax, which that climate maketh far surpassing ours both in growth and goodness, but by a newfound stuff of a certain sedge or water flag (revealed unto them by an Indian) which groweth there naturally in endless abundance, and with little pains of boiling, it being gathered yieldeth great quantity of sundry sorts of skeins of good strength and length, some like silk, and some a coarser sort as hemp. Whereof the last ships brought hither for a trial about two hundred pound weight, which being put to trial here (as many can witness which have seen it) will make cordage, linen, and fine stuffs both for strength and beauty, such as no use nor service can find the like of any other kind.

And for the last and main objection of food, it cannot be denied by anyone of reason but with their now diligent planting and sowing of corn, whereof they have two harvests in a summer, the plentiful fishing there, the store of fowls and fruits of the earth, their present provision sent from hence at every shipping, together with the speedy increase of those sundry sorts of tame poultry, conies, goats, swine, and kine landed there above a year ago with Sir Thomas Dale, and since again by Sir Thomas Gates, that this objection too, this main objection of wanting food, is utterly removed, so that I cannot see, nor any man else can judge in truth, but that ill and odious wound of Virginea, which settled so deep a scar in the minds of many, in [is] so sufficiently recovered as it may now encourage not such alone (as heretofore) which cannot live at home nor lay their bones to labor but those of honest minds and better sort which get their bread but meanly here may seek to mend it there. Captain Samuel Argoll, a gentleman of good service, is ready with two ships!

41. William Strachey

The History of Travel into Virginia Britannia: The First Book of the First Decade

< **Bodleian Library: Ashmole 1758, folios 1–102,** Major 1849, Wright & Freund 1953

Secretary Strachey is the best and the worst of our collection. Many disparage his *History* because it borrows wholesale, yet he admits it on the title page (Percy MS) and this was in his day an acceptable, forthright way to make books. So they disparage it for being uneven, hasty, rambling, and so on. Strachey was a man of prodigious literary talents. The simplest plausible way to explain his failure is to say he was a born fiction writer in the golden age of poetry and drama and philosophy (Spenser, Shakespeare, Bacon). So he wrote terrible poems and pretty good non-fiction. He knew a good sentence from a bad one, but it is only when he has a chance to describe a scene or a character that we see a flash. When the rest of the time he is warming over the ideas of Eden, Hakluyt, Raleigh, and Smith he is but adequate.

Here, of course, we get both. His record of the conversations on religion and the hereafter during Christmas at Matchipongo is the best of the collection, but also about the best page of writing one will ever encounter, and it was while reading it aloud one evening that I determined to produce this volume. By contrast, his labored "Præmonition," immediately ahead, is slow going, even though in fairness it has the subject all down and rewards patience. One can learn *why* England was in America.

Strachey began writing in 1609 and finished what we have in 1612. *The History* then lay unpublished 237 years, but well preserved in three manuscripts: the Apsley, in the Bodleian Library at Oxford; the Percy, at Princeton University; the Bacon/Sloan, in the British Library. They tally closely enough not to concern us, though they naturally have different dedicatories. The Percy and Apsley have several engravings by DeBry of the Indians of Roanoke (the Percy with Strachey's captions and coloring) and Capt. John Smith's 1612 map of Virginia. The Apsley and Bacon/Sloan append the famous "Dictionary of the Indian Language."

The manuscripts take their names from the people he submitted them to, who turned him down as patrons.

The Hakluyt Society published the Bacon/Sloan MS in 1849, R. H. Major editor. Notes I cite from there are followed by (Major) in parenthesis.

The Hakluyt Society next published the Percy MS in 1953, Louis B. Wright and Virginia Freund editors. Footnotes from there are followed by (Wright & Freund) in parenthesis. Citations of the Percy MS are all based on the Wright and Freund transcription.

My text is the Apsley, so named for Sir Allen Apsley (c.1569–1630), knighted in 1605, who was provisioner of the navy by 1610. Brown thinks he was presented with our manuscript in late 1612. It has none of the underlined minuscule so striking and so tedious in the Percy manuscript.

Dr. Culliford, his biographer, has tracked down Strachey's sources and borrowings. I will not try to enumerate them except to note the three in our collection: Percy's *Discourse §1,* White's *Excerpt §11,* and above all Smith's *A Map of Virginia §16* (Second Book of the *General History).*

In fact Strachey has all but repeated the whole of Smith's book, so much so that this editor cannot justify printing both works under one cover. Smith and Strachey are our only contributors who aimed to produce a comprehensive account of England in America. In the works at hand, Strachey arrived secondest with the mostest. That is, I let Strachey drive out Smith because *The History* contains *A Map* but *A Map* makes up only a third of *The History.* What little it does not is given in footnotes to *The History* or retained at §16.

Did Strachey plagiarize? Plagiarism is literary theft. Strachey copies much. He copies much and he acknowledges many of his sources, including Smith. But did he copy *A Map?* After putting the two works side by side and studying them quite closely, I am not sure. Their duplication may well be the result of using a common source now lost, namely, relations, letters, and reports either in the records of the Virginia Company or in the private hands of acquaintances connected to it. I suspect the credit for the inventory of plants and animals should go to Dr. Boone and assistants. Strachey's information is often more detailed and knowledgeable. Smith writes in *A Map,* "There is also some elm, some black walnut tree[s], and some ash. Of ash and elm they make soap-ashes. If the trees be very great, the ashes will be good and melt to hard lumps; but if they be small, it will be but powder and not so good as the other." (*General History* 25) One would hardly expect this to be Smith's area of expertise, but Strachey (685) has, "There is also elm and ash of which are made soap-ashes. If the trees be very great, the ashes will be very good and melt to hard lumps, being carefully burned. But if they be small and suff'red to partake too much of the smoke, they will be but powder, nothing so good as the other, beside they will be very foul and black." This is hardly copied from Smith at all, let alone plagiarized.

The geographic information certainly derives much of it from Smith's explorations, but Christopher Newport and Samuel Argall also filed reports (now lost), and I am inclined to think that when distance estimates are good they can be attributed to anybody but the great captain. When Strachey discusses Indians (so much of our text) he always mentions Smith as a source when the information comes from what we know is Smith's experience, such as the meeting with the Sasquesahanock werowances and the corn divination at Werowocomoco. But this suggests that the rest of the Indian material the two writers share, containing minute and lengthy descriptions, comes from someone who had a notebook, not a French pistol. It is easier to imagine Strachey as the note-taker, but there should have been many other Jamestown notebooks and even a few still surviving from the Roanoke Colony. In fact, doesn't Hamor tell us (837) Powhatan himself had a notebook?

Hence I will go no further in such speculation in the hope that it suggests in regard to our two most magnificent contributors that we need not praise one to the other's cost. Their literary efforts overlap. Smith was a man of tremendous energy, resource, and conviction. He climbed the slope of publishing his fame and renown. Strachey tried and fell. In the end, they both died poor and alone.

The reader, historian, student should bear in mind above all that Strachey's Virginia "plagiarism," if we must call it that, including even the DeBry engravings,[1] is important to us as a *confirmation* of these sources by another eyewitness.

His plan included three books. He wrote all or most of two. The first book, reproduced here, deals with Jamestown. The second book, omitted here, deals with Roanoke and Sagadahoc. A third element, the dictionary of the Powhatan language, I also omit. He tells us the *Laws divine, moral, and martial* is also part of this work.

The History is not a history. It is a description of the land and the native people. Strachey worked very hard writing his "Præmonition." Too hard. It is a *mega biblion.* Its Latin and Biblical quotes, here and throughout the text, add little more than tail fins and hood ornaments to writing otherwise fairly lean and swift.[2] He was at pains to defend the moral basis of colonization and England's claim on our coasts. International law and human rights did not begin with the UN Charter.

His essay behind him, Strachey begins a geography in Caput One where he tries to coin the terms "Virginia" for the coastal plain and "Britannia" for the Piedmont and beyond. He makes the statement that North and South Virginia are divided at the James River. This is contrary to the first charter, that puts it no further south than 38°, but accounts for the "Popham/Salisbury" designations used by others for the north and south banks, and may reflect a usage that grew out of the second charter.

He says the Indians "are not conceived" to have lived below the falls on

---

[1] Granted that these engravings were in circulation and easily obtainable, as they still are, the free and unqualified use of them by both Smith and Strachey convinces me the Virginia and Carolina Algonquian were a cultural continuum.

[2] E.g. his peppering of Greek and Latin words as special terms, such as *popanon,* which is a general term for cake in Ancient Greek.

the coastal plain for more than 300 years. Ethnologists dispute this by a couple of centuries longer if he means to say the people of the southern Algonquian culture, that is, the Powhatan people.

In Caput Two he gives us the same Indian geography we find in Smith, and both accounts mention the extermination of the Payankatank ordered by Powhatan, with fresh scalps on view at Werowocomoco.

Caput Three begins with the Biblical theory of human origin and dispersal, tells of the flaying of George Cassen, and proceeds to give us the best (verbal) portrait of Powhatan we possess. He mentions Kemps and Mechumps as his main informants on many topics, but doubtless he visited Orapax or Werowocomoco and saw Powhatan with his own eyes. All the same, there is little reason to believe Strachey ranged much beyond the fort while in Virginia, and when he did he tells us he was in the company of Governor Dale. *The History of Travel* hardly travels, but here in Caput Three if anywhere he earns his reputation as a rambler.

Caput Four, the catalog of werowances, is the most valuable part of the book for historians. It is the only caput without duplications of *A Map.* We meet the unforgettable Dame Oholasc, along with Tsenacomacah in panoply, with a little history. It reads like an intelligence report that burgeoned with vivid personal knowledge.

In Caput Seven, Strachey urges the destruction of the native priesthood as a necessary step to assimilating Indians into English society. Free him of the feeders of his superstition, show him the superiority of English culture and religion, coax him into the money economy with quitrents and, Strachey tells us confidently, like all men the Powhatan Indian will abandon his native ways and choose civilization. If this sounds crazy, what else is it but McNamara's pacification program for Vietnam? Nonetheless, Strachey has a lot of company when he makes it plain that English colonization policy very much includes Indians *in situ* as future citizens. Attitudes soon changed for two reasons: the massacre of 1622 and the assurance with the passing of time that Protestantism was going to survive in plentiful numbers in Europe. In 1612, Protestants were losing on most fronts to the Counter Reformation even as, by the way, the Chesapeake region was in retreat from the Massawomecks—the Iroquois.

The mock battle at Mattapanient, described in Caput Eight, and found also in Smith, reads very much like something lifted out of George Percy. It is typical of his style that we are left wondering if this was a game or a fight or both.

I have abstracted the following—

Table of Contents

"Their danses which they use att their hyghe feastes"

Plate XVIII, engraved by Theodor DeBry, in Thomas Harriot's *A Briefe and True Report of the New Found Land of Virginia* (1590), based on a watercolor by John White, Governor of Roanoke. It makes up the fourth leaf of Strachey's Apsley/Bodleian manuscript.

The First Book of the First Decade

containing

The History of Travel into Virginia Britannia,

expressing together with the conditions, manners, and qualities of the inhabitants, the cosmography and commodities of the country; obtained and gathered by William Strachey, *gent., three years thither employed secretary unto the State and of Council with* the Right Honorable the Lord La Warre, *His Majesty's Lord Governor and Captain General for the Colony.*

Alget qui non ardet.

W[ILLIAM] ST[RACHEY]

TO THE RIGHT WORTHY AND NOBLE GENT[LEMAN] COVETOUS OF ALL KNOWLEDGE, SIR ALLEN APSLEY, KNIGHT, PURVEYOR FOR HIS MAJESTY'S NAVY ROYAL.

WORTHY SIR—It is common, if not natural, to worldings, where things succeed not according to the heat of their large expectations, not only to fall from their resolutions in a business—how well weighed soever in counsels or full of fame, honor, or goodness—and first grounds, but to quarrel all means that gave heart (almost connivance) to the setting on, so testy is the insatiate passion and that immeasurable hope which will needs convert itself into deluding assurance. As low hillocks (such are surely men) covered with snow let the least sun or wind give them up naked, though no worse than they were, yet the mountainous imagination, not satisfied, turns into such a laughter as madmen take up, an unkindly and bastard laughter, little different from madness itself.

I confess I would ever be free from the fury of such, yet what I can speak of goodness I must not be ashamed nor fear, and all good angels deceive me, if any aviso in that return the reader distraction, or me a chiding. And can my voice be exalted in any tune more full of piety and happiness than in the business for Virginia?—which was once a thing so full of expectance, and that not above three years since, as not a year of a Roman jubilee, no, nor the ethnic Queen of Ephesus, can be said to have been followed with more heat and zeal. The discourse and visitation of it took up all meetings, times, terms, all degrees, all purses, and such throngs and concourse of personal undertakers as the air seemed not to have more lights than that holy cause inflamed spirits to partake with it. Almost every religious subject that stood sound indeed at the core within to loyalty and to the possession of the present faith brought his freewill off 'ring, and professed then to throw his bread upon those waters.

However, alas, now in these times the back and worse face of Janus with the repining eye and tongue of slander hath been turn'd upon it, when yet it transcends the reach of such who both will and do understand it, what rubbish interposition should so strangely change her former conceived felicity? Or why the plenulune and fullness of her hopes should suffer under so many petulant new fears and false friends?

I will counsel no man in the ways of the world, but where my reason may tell me that I may advise of profit, since interposing hazards may meet—there being no permanent or real happiness under the sun—and then may I be well assured of hasty and sinister judgment censured a party to the least loss, though no competitor in any gain; only yet let me dare to publish to anyone that hath adventured in this sprightly and pious action, especially to such who have assumed it for their ravish'd love to fair virtue that the former ends and first motives to the undertaking stand yet as apparent and profitable as at first—whether be respected a nation to bless with knowledge, a fruitful and pleasant country to seat and settle the swarms of our rank multitudes, who taste in this our own clime nothing but of idleness, profaneness, and want; or whether be respected a secure and necessary retreat for our many ships when the insolent enemy of those seas shall at any time quarrel us, or whether be respected the commodities and materials for shipping, so much exhausted, and so dearly obtained from the easterly countries, as flax for cordage, pitch and tar, pine and fir for mastage, etc.; or whether be respected the hopes of the upland country amongest the mountains, we conceive of many sorts of minerals, finding already in the surface and upper crust the spar of good proof and worthy the expense of trial; or lastly, whether be respected that more than likelihood of the discovery that way westerly [of] the great and hopeful descent into the Mar del Zur, or South Sea, of which the late discourse, published in print by an able and understanding gentleman of quality, of the nor'west passage gives so clear and undoubted testimony.

But, worthy Sir, I do forget myself to open a book unto your knowledge which is full of love and understanding of the true ends of this great action, yet so it may be that these gathered observations thus bungled, bound up, and to your view alone intended by me may fall into such hands as may put some doubts—which even this entrance may resolve them in, and so beget towards the further reading hereof a better opinion. Be it only your honor to pardon me the appealing of you from your more serious affairs to the perusal of these unfirm and scattered collections, since, if I have offended, the nobleness and bounty of your fair disposition, expressed even in my knowledge to many of my best friends, makes me presume that I cannot in any action which hath relish of virtue and goodness too much challenge or provoke your patience.

And so, not striving to be unnecessarily troublesome, I wish unto you the just accomplishment of your own virtuous desires,

by him who is truly to you devoted,
WILLIAM STRACHEY

Ecclesiae et Reipub[licae][1]:

Wild as they are, accept them. So were we.
    To make them civil will our honor be.
And if good works be the effects of minds
    That like good angels be, let our designs,
As we are *Angli*, make us angels too:
    No better work can church or statesman do.

[1] "For church and state." (Latin) The verse is about Indians.

A Præmonition to the Reader.

Wherein, as the foundation to all the succeeding business, is derived down to our times the ancient right and claim which we made to this part of America; and therein both the objections answered, and doubts clearly satisfied, of such who, through malice or ignorance, either have, or may hereafter, call the lawfulness of the proceeding hereof in question.

THE MANY MOUTHS of ignorance and slander, which are ever too apt to let fall the venom of their worst and most depraving envies upon the best and most sacred works, and so not afraid to blast both this enterprise and the devoutest laborers therein, wrings from me the necessity of this imperfect defense, whom yet I have observ'd more in clamor (methought) than at any time in force, to cry out still upon it, calling it an unnational and unlawful undertaking, when let [it] be but observed (I pray) and soon will appear their malice and petulancy to speak, as also what a distance there is truly set between the business and their knowledge.

For in a clear judgment if any such attaint lay upon the act, neither the general peace of the time might suffer it to go forth with such liberty nor the honor of such who have set it forward [and] importune it of His Majesty; nor would the consciences (it is known right well) of the chief commanders for the execution and actual part thereof—let custom have taken away however that quickness from the chargers' own unsensible and seared heart—hazard the last and setting hours of their days in traitorous or ignoble prosecutions; it being the pious and only end both intended by His Majesty, by the honorable council for the business, by the lord general, lieutenant general, marshal, and suchlike eminent officers called forth for the dignity of so great a cause, together with the general adventurers, with all carefulness principally to endeavor the conversion of the natives to the knowledge and worship of the true God and the world's redeemer Christ Jesus.

How rotten and unsound then, both to His Majesty and the present faith (is it to be feared) may [they] be at the core within that dare (except it be as I said out of ignorance, yet cannot that excuse a factious and pragmatic tongue) quarrel and traduce the proceedings of a whole state, and to which the royal authority by letters made patents, both in Her Majesty's time, of famous memory, and now likewise, hath been five times concurrent. May it be supposed anyone but lukewarm in Christian charity would be parcel guilty herein? or make it questionable whether should be attempted a work of this piety upon a barbarous nation?

Let the busy knowledge (to say no more) of such a one be shrewdly suspected and blemished. May any lover of his country? No, it is to be feared that he borroweth but a counterfeit face from Janus to turn to the penal edict, or to his prince, if such be his grace.

But however, let them both know the grounds of goodness are not laid so weak in well-weighed counsels that the clamor of a centurion or two can disturb Numa Pompilius kneeling at the altar. Let them give it up in rumor or, more subtly, cry out that our enemies at Seville or Lishborne [Lisbon], at Dominica or Mevis [Nevis], or at the Havana, are up in arms for us—we can yet go on in the justifiableness of our cause, making only Pompilius' answer, "And we do sacrifice."[1] Will it please the reader to favor me a little?

Two sorts especially I must conceive of, untoward (to style them no worse) and ill-disposed in their wisdoms, [that] stand much offended with this business, and have devised against it many slanders and calumnies: the mere ignorant (not only in *scientia scientiae*, as the Schoolman says, but including grossness and simplicity in any knowledge) and the mere opposite, in *scientia conscientiae*, in religion. I would to God the latter were not more dangerous by how much *celeberrima per loca vadet*,[2] and can speak amiss out of the corrupt seeds of goodness, and perhaps so speaking be heard!

And these both say how the undertaking cannot be lawful. Why? —because the King of Spain hath a primer interest into the country.

---

[1] Plutarch's point was that the *piety* of Pompilius could not be interrupted, no matter what the emergency.

[2] "He wanders through the most crowded places." (Latin: Horace, *Ep.* 1.17.28) Strachey denounces "ignorant" and "irreligious" detractors.

Next, it cannot be honest in itself. Why?—because injurious to the naturals; and which connected together, it must then necessarily follow (say they) that it can be no other than a travail of flat impiety and displeasing before God—indeed no mean objections to stumble shallow home wits who, whilst they look lazily and broadly on it, are presented with an ugly face. But if by a more respective direction we will examine how these particularities may lie together, we shall find another model and an air of that dignity and truth which aspires to a clean contrary comeliness.

For the King of Spain, he hath no more title nor color of title to this place, which we by our industry and expenses have only made ours (as for the Pope's donative of all America unto him, that is sufficiently elsewhere answered in a discourse already published by a most worthy undertaker), than hath any Christian prince, or than we or any other prince may have to his Mexico and Peru or any dominions else of any free state or kingdom, how near soever the West Indies and Florida may join thereunto and lie under the same portion of heaven. With as great bravery may we lay claim to all the islands which the Seigniory of Venice now holds in the Levant seas because Cyprus was once ours by the conquest of Richard Cœur de Lion, and confines with theirs—than which what more infirm and ridiculous pretense could be framed? And yet is the King of Spain's argument to our interest in Virginia just in this mood and figure.

No prince may lay claim to any more amongst these new discoveries (and so it was heretofore, a just distinction being therefore kept between the King of Castile and Portugal) than what his people have discovered, took actual possession of, and passed over to his right. And no otherwise from Columbus doth the King of Spain hold his strength and dominions to this day in his golden Indies, and no otherwise from Soto, his *adelantado,* concerning our neighbor Florida.

And so we allow him, without any one inch of intrusion, both his longitude and latitude in this New World—we keeping from Cape Florida nor'ward to Cape Briton [Breton] the lands, countries, and territories of this part of America, or Nova Britannia, being carefully laid out of purpose to avoid offense into certain bounds and regions: Beginning from the point of land called Cape Comfort and so holding all along the seacoast to the nor'ward[1] 200 miles; and from the point of the said Cape Comfort all along the seacoast to the so'ward 300 miles; and so only all that space and circuit of land lying from the seacoasts of these precincts, not coming near any land in his actual possession, but rather diverting from it many a league. And yet holds he neither any chargeable forces to dispute [for] his right upon the main nor keeps colonies (except in Florida at St. Augustine only), nor reckons of the same, but that it is at his best pleasure.

But what now concerning this point (for the more clearing of it to such who stumble thereat) if we should say that our right to the West Indies themselves (since they will needs awaken us with pretense of title) is as firm, proper, and far more ancient than the Spaniard's, and before the royal spirited Lady Isabella Princess of Castile laid her jewels to pawn to Luis of St. Angello, the king her husband's secretary, to forward the design, and to prevent our King Henry the 7th, who was both offered and accepted Columbus' offer, and ent'red into capitulations with his brother Bartholomew about them, anno 1489?

Sure we shall not want some pregnant likelihoods, and those not only by our simple discoveries but by our planting and inhabiting them with the people of our own nation 400 years before Columbus had notice of them by the Biscan pilot[2]—who, when he dwelt in the islands of Madeira, arrived with a weather-beaten caravel, and dying in his house bequeathed (as they say) to Columbus his card of the description of such new lands as he had found.

True it is the first ships that Columbus carried thither were but in anno 1492, which is now since 120 years, when let any man be but pleased to look into the learned and industrious antiquities of Mr. Camden (the carefulness and truth of whose searches he that will undervalue or slander shall be much out of love with the labors of all good men and powers of virtue), and he remembers us of Madoc, the son of Owen Gwyneth, Prince of North Wales, in the year 1170, which may be 439 years since, who, leaving the land in contention between his two brethren, Howell and David, prepared certain ships

---

[1] "Within the Chesapeake Bay six leagues, which bay the Spaniards in their cartes call Santa Maria." (margin note in Percy MS)

[2] A figure of legend.

with men and munition, and after many unknown lands and strange discoveries made (sailing within the Atlantic Sea) a southwardly course, yet still into the west, at last settled in the West Indies, as his own relation suffers construction,[1] which he made in his return for new supplies the second and third time, which he transported and after that was heard no more of; and late observations taken in these times may confirm the probability hereof, as first in Acuramill (so writing Frauncis Lopez de Gomera) the natives, when they were first found, had their crosses in their chapels and in dedicated groves, in gardens, by woods, springs, and fountains, which they did honor and fall down before, thereto saying their usual prayers, which must make ill[ustr]ation that Christians had been there before the coming of the Spaniard; and no ecclesiastical history commends unto us, since Solomon's voyage to Ophir ceased, nor any records of other antiquities since the fabulous drowning by Deucalion's flood or burning by Phaëthon or since the sinking of the Atlantic islands,[2] [a discovery] more ancient or before the voyage of Madoc.

Lastly, the language of the Indians admitting much and many words, both of places and names of many creatures, which have the accents and Welch significations,[3] and are yet retained both by the Indian *crollos* (Spaniards born there) and mulattoes.

But this is material and punctual to our hypothesis: King Henry the 7th gave his letters patents anno 1495 unto John Cabot, a Venetian endenized his subject and dwelling within the Blackfriars, and to his 3 sons, who discovered for the king the north parts of America to Meta Incognita; and annexed to the Crown of England all that great tract of land stretching from the Cape of Florida unto those parts main and islands which we call the New-found Land, some of which were not before known to Columbus nor afterwards to Nicuesa, Colmenaris, nor Vasquez Nunnez [de Balboa], nor any of the Castilians; the draft of which voyage is yet to be seen in His Majesty's privy gallery in his palace at Westminster. But the tumults (say they who wrote of those times) then and preparations for wars in Scotland took away the seconding of that enterprise, yet no whit take

---

[1] I.e., allows the interpretation.
[2] I.e., from the time of deep antiquity lost in myth.
[3] See Peter Winne §15–203.

away (I hope) our title more than the King of Spain may lose his to those parts covered with the same heavens which he neither fortifies nor planteth to this day.

So as we may conclude then at least that as Christopher Columbus discovered the islands and continent of the West Indies for Spain, John and Sebastian Cabot made discovery no less of the rest from Florida nor'ward to the behoof of England, being supported by the regal authority and set forth at the charge and expense of King Henry 7th.

And we hope that they will leave unto us the same way and propriety, both to go unto our own and hold it by, as we give them. And if they will do so—and all laws of nations will assist us herein—how unjust and partial shall that subject be, and how ill a servant in the court of his own prince, that will dare to give from him and his country the right and honor of both, gained with the expense of the public purse and with the travails and lives of the industrious subject? As well may such a traitor lay the crown of His Majesty upon the Spaniard's head as appropriate unto him his titles, his territories, and possessions, since so indistinguishable. And such relatives are the prince and his principalities as he is said no longer to be a king that is deprived and is every way denied the title of his kingdoms.

And if this argument be in force (he will say) only where countries lie near and approximate each to other, let me then ask this question: What kingdoms (I pray you) and provinces lie more disjoined and scattered (as some families that agree best when they are farthest each from other!) than the King of Spain's?—insomuch as it is only that which holds him to this day from not being reckoned among the 5 great monarchs of the world. Let not man therefore be traduced by the accounts which false-hearted subjects—more jealous of a foreign prince's pride than zealous of His Majesty's royalties and joyous in the felicity of his government—have heretofore made audit to him of, here being raised to the view, though a short, yet a clear prospect of our right.

Her Majesty of famous memory so well understood her princely right herein, derived down from her heroic grandfather to herself, as she granted many large patents and gracious commissions to divers gentlemen of birth and quality to inhabit those parts and to keep her title quick and panting still therein, as first to Sir Humfry Gilbert, whom the light first forsook before he would forsake his hopes and journeys thither; and afterward to the sometime much honored Sir W[alter] R[aleigh], knight, to whom and to his heirs, in the 26 year of her reign, she confirmed at Westminster a large grant from 33 to 40 degrees of latitude, exemplified with many immunities and privileges; who thereupon sent first thither Captain Amadas and Captain Barlow, 1584; which Amadas, in memory of himself, entitled a bay at Roanoak to this day called Bay Amadas. And after them he sent a fleet of 7 sails, anno 1585, commanded by Sir R[ichard] Greenvile, who at Wococon likewise, more to the so'ward from Roanoak, gave name to a port which yet retains the name of Port Greenvile; who left a colony of 100 in the said island of Roanoak, which remained there one whole year under the charge of Sir Raph Lane, general of the same, and which were afterward brought from thence—by the neglect of due supplies growing into some wants—by Sir Francis Drake in his return homewards from the sacking of St. Domingo, Carthagena, and St. Augustine.

Yet after this did Sir W. R. continue a third and fourth voyage, which had their misfortunes and, anno 1587, sent a second colony of 150 under the command of Captain White and 12 assistants, unto whom he gave a charter and incorporated them by the name of "Governor and Assistants of the City Raleigh in Virginia"—all which likewise miscarried by the wretchedness of unskillful instruments, abusing therein Sir W. R., who, falling upon other practices and which those time[s] afforded, after the said White had been in England the second time and was refurnished out with things needful for the colony, endeavoring nothing less than the relief of the poor planters who afterward, as you shall read in this following discourse, came therefore to a miserable and untimely destiny.[1]

And this fatal period had Sir W. R. his good purposes and great charges, all which I have the more largely extracted that it may the more expressively appear how this is no new enterprise, nor taken in hand now by a generality (which, true it is, before Sir W. R. his attainder, without his leave we might not make intrusion upon the

[1] In his second book, not included here.

title being only in him) to offer cause of quarrel or offense to a peaceful confederate or Christian neighbor prince—a purpose so far from the undertakers, council, or body politic to whom the charter is granted by His Majesty as they shall wrest with too much strained applications the endeavors of such honorable and religious personages who would raise their country and the fame of their sovereign equal with others who have enlarged their powers and their titles by the like means; and to avow unto the world that if the Spaniard shall attempt us at any time with ill measure, offering either to make surreption of our ships by the way thither or to break into our plantations with acts of hostility—as most despitefully did Pedro Melendes,[1] their admiral, into the French colony 44 years since in Nova Francia, who razed their fort and hung up the common soldiers (Landonnier, the general, being strangely escaped) and wrought over them disdainful inscriptions in Spanish importing, "I do not this as unto Frenchmen, but as unto *Lutherans!*"—which Spanish cruelty was yet in the winding up as bloodily revenged again by Dominique de Gourgnes of Bourdeaux, who not long after arriving there trussed up the selfsame Spaniards upon the boughs of the same trees whereon they hung the French, with these words: "I do not this as unto Spaniards, but as unto *tyrants and murtherers!*"—now we are set down here, have [how] unjustly they shall proceed herein, and how much they shall lay themselves and their faiths upon the construction of all nations, and haply to our revenge, which cannot strike weakly which strikes with the sword of justice, in all quarrels the good success of the same ever depending upon the innocency of the cause.

Secondly, where they say it is unhonest in itself because injurious to the naturals, it being the fulfilling of the perpetual rule of justice, *suum cuique tribuere,*[2] how unfit soever that *suum* be for the possessor—indeed it carries some show of the right and we culpable whilst we do labor in the contrary. As Xenophon said, instructing the young Cyrus, when the prince, being walked out one day into the fields and

---

[1] Referring to the French Fort Caroline on the St. Johns River. The upshot was the immediate founding of St. Augustine by the Spanish in 1565.
[2] "To give each his own." (Latin)

had spied two boys coming towards him: a great boy covered with a short and scant coat and a little boy clad in a large train'd, wide, and long gown—Cyrus strip'd them both and shifted them, by the exchange so making a better proportion, as he thought, of fitness for either. But (I say) his learned tutor told him how he had not done well herein, since everyone was to be master of his own, however it might appear a matter of much inequality and the owner unworthy of so large a measure of fortune.[1]

That mind is to be loved well that will not leave doubting until it hath found out the truth. But it must then be *veritatem quaerere, non insidias struere.*[2] Indeed this were a sufficient argument in such a commonweal which, governed with the well-ordered powers of philosophy and all natural knowledges, wanted not neither the supernal light. But the grounds of *both* these (who knows not?) do we go to lay amongest a simple and barbarous people.

Yet, had they of themselves the first, that is, the practice of all moral policies and offices of virtue as perfect, peremptory, and exact as the unbelieving Grecians and infidelious Romans had, yet since we as true Christians know that the world never was, nor must be, only and alone governed by morality—and our charity suffers for them until we have derived unto them the true knowledge indeed which is the worship of the true God and their and our blessed redeemer Christ Jesus—this can be no absolute instance of the right to tie us, appear it never so upright and full of humanity. For sometimes, and to the bettering of mankind, the divine politic law itself (we see) doth put on change, and bindeth not *semper, et in omne,*[3] as in the cases of theft and adultery, etc.

Let me ask this question: Do we not go in a business that must result greater effects, and strive within us beyond the powers and

---

[1] The young Cyrus had only suggested approving a swap already made by the larger boy, but "at that my teacher whacked me and said that when I was to judge a *good fit* I should so decide, but when the question is who should *own* the cloak, he told me, one must look into the justice of ownership by forceful seizure versus ownership by having something made for you and buying it." Xenophon's *Cyropedia,* I, iii, 17.

[2] Argument "to seek the truth, not set ambushes" like Sophists and lawyers. (Latin)

[3] "Always and in every instance." (Latin)

prescriptions of morality? No man must deny it that will not hoodwink his knowledge from the end and aim at least to which we let go all our travails. Yet shall we no whit advance our early and first prosecutions against those moral duties neither, but like the best prescribers of those rules themselves in the learned and last monarchies, and with the lovers of them now, we will manly proceed and exactly observe the same even in this work, so as the best Christian shall not be aggrieved to hear of our proceedings when they shall read of the same in *our* "decades,"[1] most true it is, we knowing that the offices of humanity can help much in the forwarding hereof.

Then, if our actions must relish all of piety, not excluding neither any one particular help of courtesy and manliness, how religious and manly both is it to communicate with these simple and innocent people?—unless perhaps you will say that it is altogether unlawful to intercommune and traffic with savages and infidels, so bringing to the test the rich and necessary trades into Turkey and the East Indies—kneeling when we kneel, and lifting up their hands and eyes when we pray, not so docible as willing to receive our customs—herein like raced and unblotted tables apt to receive what form soever shall be first drawn thereon, and who have less faith in religion which may be the more probably shaken by how much they have less power either of reason or of arms to defend it than the Turk hath; and with whom to hold discourse of their religion carrieth not (at least) that challenge and stepping into danger as it doth amongest other barbarous nations—especially with the Turks, with whom we hold such interchangeable courtesies, who suffer not their divine law given them in their *musaph [mishaf]*, or Alcaron, by their false prophet Mahomet, and which makes them, as they say, the true Mussulman before the Persian, to be subject to the disputation of any Christian upon pain of a sure death—where amongest these a more easy passage lies open to wound the illusions of Satan, and to gain a poor innocent to partake in our knowledges.

We take heaven by violence, saith the Evangelist.[2] I am sure it is

---

[1] Recalling Richard Eden's translation of Peter Martyr's *The Decades of the Newe Worlde* (1555). Strachey's *History* was projected to be in "decades," books of ten chapters.
[2] Matthew 11:12.

given to men of fervent charity *et operantibus* (and good works), albeit they be not *concausae,* yet are they *consectaria* (as the Schoolman saith) of our faith[1]; though not *causa regnandi,* yet are they *via ad regnum*[2]; though they justify not before God, yet do they glorify God in his servants.

And what more meritorious work can there be than to labor in God's cause (let the world however brand it for folly) and work them to be His whose image they bear, and participate with us of reason, carrying in their nostrils more than the spirit of life, the breath of beasts, which how should we then pity and take religious compassion of? And compassion, saith Guicciardini, debates not causes and reasons, but proceeds to relief; for which the duty of a good man is said to be compounded of these two things: the glory of his Creator and the love of his neighbor. And who is our neighbor? demandeth our Saviour. He that (as in an inn) quartereth next lodging and door unto us? No, sure, for albeit in the old law the elected few accounted every Jew his neighbor only, yet, since the time of grace, we are taught to acknowledge *every* man that bears the impression of God's stamp to be not only our neighbor but to be our brother, how far distinguished and removed by seas or lands soever from us. And in that style do far-disjoined princes salute each the other. And indeed it is the general office of manking [mankind] not only to wish good but to bring it to pass for one of the like creation.

Now what greater good can we derive unto them than the knowledge of the true and ever-living God? And what doth more directly and rarely minister that effect than society and to join with them in friendship?—since we daily see amongest ourselves the profane and the most disordered (might I not say almost barbarous?), by keeping [our] company, doth light upon something the while which stumbles him in his haste and makes him often take a pause be[fore] he proceeds, either shame or compunction striving within him.

Nor is this without some plea of reason, for like doth in time fasten and work into like, as fire worketh wood altogether into fire. And as the eye, if it be opposed and presented to any sensible object that

---

[1] I.e., not things that promote faith but result from it. St. Thomas Aquinas.
[2] I.e., though not bringing about the Kingdom, they are a way towards it.

excelleth, will lose his proper and natural function, so, by conversing, the time or reverence and awe of the better company, or some particular advantage, circumstance, or other may object[1] that to the most sensual, which may strike his proud heart so as he may find somewhat to be amazed at about which, whilst his imaginations busy themselves, they may beget further discourse and arguments of more and more goodness.

Oh, let heavy things tend to their center! Let light and airy spirits salute heaven and fly up to the circumference! That great and famous instrument of publishing the Gospel and knowledge of Christ Jesus: Christopher Columbus, as also Vesputius Americus—who five years after Columbus arrived here gave this whole country and immeasurable continent (which is and may well be called the New World for his greatness, reaching from the one pole to the other, being divided by the Straits of Magelane where it endeth under 52 degrees on the south side of the Equinoctial Line) his own name—may teach us what progress to make even in this glorious enterprise. The first of these opened the way to the Spaniard, who since hath fill'd both islands and main with the form of their worship to God (I leave to say how officious and superstitious); and the other, as inflamed to do some notable Christian act, answered the other (a "health" yet unpledg'd by us, unless we will now set to it). Let the examples of these move us to advance (now opportunity is offered) our profession and faith, as catholic and more purged from self-inventions. Have we either less means, fainter spirits, or a charity more cold, or a religion more shameful and afraid to dilate itself? Or is it a lawful work in them and not in us, that it is authorized unto them even by the warrant of the church? Here [is] Pope Alexander the 6th in his bull and donation to the kings of Castile and their successors, [omitted Latin original, followed by Strachey's translation] which is:

> We greatly commending this your godly and laudable purpose in our Lord, and desirous to have the same brought to a due end, and the name of our Saviour to be known in those parts, do exhort you in our

[1] Present.

> Lord and by the receiving of your holy baptism, whereby you are bound to apostolical obedience, and earnestly require you by the bowels of mercy of our Lord Jesus Christ, that when you intend for the zeal of the Catholic faith to prosecute the said expedition to reduce the people of the foresaid lands and islands to the Christian religion, you shall spare no labors at any time or be deterred with any perils, conceiving firm hope and assurance that the Omnipotent God will give good success to your godly attempts.

It is read that Themistocles, hearing of the great victory that Miltiades had obtained on the Plain of Marathon, said that that report would not let him take any rest. And Julius Caesar wept at the sight of Alexander's image who had at the years of 24 obtained the name of "Great," and cried out, "Am not I miserable that have done nothing worthy of memory, and yet this prince at these years hath executed so many notable things?" Shall these for the smoke of momentary glory break out thus passionately and forward? And shall not we for the glory of our God be as affectionate and ambitious? Shall we now when we know most the effects and perfection of goodness (as the sun, when he is highest in the zodiac moveth slowest) be dullest in our solstice and supremest height? The glorious Saint Augustine in his first book, *De Concord: Evang.*, cap. 32, goeth so far concerning the spreading abroad and teaching of our Saviour crucified, not only to the right but to the left hand, as it is in the 54 of Esau, as he there amply discourseth how the Gospel should be published abroad not only by those who sincerely with true and perfect charity assume the function of preachers but also by those that declare it tending to temporal ends. And surely many powerful and divine arguments might be extracted for this place, which he there at large prosecuteth, which would confirm and speak satisfaction to the most sensual. If so, why, then, besides these divine alleged motives [and] politic and rational respects, even common trade and hope of profit might make us forward to be adventurers.

Our country of Virginia hath no want of many merchandises—which we in England accomplish in Denmark, Norway, Prussia, Poland, etc., [and] fetch far and buy dear—which advance much and assured increase with less exchange of our own, with as few hazards by sea, and which would maintain as frequent and goodly a navy as what runs the Levant stage. And those [merchandises] by divers treaties, both in Latin and English, private and public, have been in their particular names and values oftentimes expressed, especially [in] that which hath been published by that true lover of virtue and great learned professor of all arts and knowledges, Mr. Harriotts, who lived there in the time of the first colony, spake the Indian language, search'd the country, and made many proofs of the richness of the soil and commodities thereof.

Besides, many planters from thence, and right worthy merchants and those well known to be men of much belief and credit, have witnessed as much to the world in these latter times, if men will give them stowage and welcome in their good opinions, and set aside their own overweenings and singularity to entertain a truth.

And out of those great plenties and havings, which God hath lent them to be His stewards here, [may they] be pleased to hear themselves entreated to spare but a little little portion to the raising and building up of a *sanctum sanctorum,* a "holy house" and a sanctuary to His blessed name among infidels—placing those therein on whom it hath now pleased Him both to be sufficiently revenged for their forefathers' ingratitude and treasons, and to descend in mercy to lighten [them] that sat in darkness and in the shadow of death, and to direct their feet in the way of peace.

But perhaps there be those who will grant that what they have read in those discourses delivered to the world may be true, but, will they say, What open and actual injury shall we do to the poor and innocent inhabitants to intrude upon them? I must ask them again: In which shall we offer them injury for proffering them trade or the knowledge of Christ? From one of these two or both the injury must proceed.

Why, what injury can it be to people of any nation for Christians to come unto their ports, havens, or territories, when the law of nations, which is the law of God and man, doth privilege all men to do so?—which admits it lawful to trade with any manner of people, insomuch as no man is to take upon him, that knows anything, the defense of the savages in this point, since the savages themselves may not impugn or forbid the same in respect of common fellowship and community betwixt man and man. Albeit I will not deny but that the savages may without peradventure be ignorant of as much and, alas, more graces beside and particularities of humanity, the reason whereof being because, poor souls, they know not the good which they stand in need of. But we that are Christians *do* know how this law, enriching all kingdoms, gives privileges to ambassadors, keeps the seas common and safe, lays open ports and havens, and allows free scales and liberal access for whosoever that will import unto them such commodities as their countries have and they want, or export from them some of their plenty (duties and customs provincial observed).

If this be so for the first, concerning the other, it may fully be answered with this demand: Shall it not follow, if traffic be thus justifiable which intends nothing but transitory profit and increase of temporal and worldly goods, shall not planting the Christian faith be much more? Yes, by how much the divine good (not subject to change, and under no alteration) excels, takes an account, and surveys and surpasseth all things, and all our actions are to bend their intentions thitherward—and what way soever we make, yet miserable and wretched he whose every line he draws, every act and thought, do not close and meet in the center of that!

Alas, would we but truly examine all and the best of things which the round eye of the sun looks upon, what is the travail for all the pomp, the treasure, the pleasure, and whatsoever belongeth to this life compared to the riches of the soul?—the excellency whereof, if there were no other proof to confirm it, is sufficiently set forth by the rich ransom that was paid for it, even the precious blood of Jesus Christ.

Oh, our dull ignorance, depraved wills, or imperfection of reason, or all three—how do ye transport us who, when we should labor [for] a wane and diminution of the most imposture, the most false and yet eye-pleasing objects of our carnal senses, not so much as making out after the least of them in poor Indian canoas, how their godly representations beguile us that we neglect all good things and like English lords pursue these on the stream of delight in swift barges; when let us hear the end of all and the sum of all happiness (saith St.

John, chapter 7, verse 3), and that is to know one only true God and Jesus Christ whom He hath sent; who, being the ever-blessed and only wisdom of the Father, gives amongst other commandments to His Apostles this: "Go and baptize all nations." *Universa enim propter semetipsum operatus est Dominus* (Prov. 16)[1]—this word and particle all infallibly and mathematically concluding then, even these poor savages.

"But yet it is injurious to the natural inhabitants," still say ours. Wherefore? "It is because it is" (now indeed a most doughty and martial reason!) "a great piece of injury to bring them" (to invert our English proverb) "out of the warm sun into God's blessing"—to bring them from bodily wants, confusion, misery, and these outward anguishes to the knowledge of a better practice and improving of those benefits, to a more and ever-during advantage, and to a civiler use, which God hath given unto them, but involved and hid in the bowels and womb of their land to them barren and unprofitable because unknown. Nay, to exalt, as I may say, mere privation to the highest degree of perfection by bringing their wretched souls, like Cerberus from hell, from the chains of Satan to the arms and bosom of their Saviour—here is a most impious piece of injury!

Let me remember what Mr. Symondes, preacher of St. Saviour's, saith in this behalf: "It is as much," saith he, "as if a father should be said to offer violence to his child when he beats him to bring him to goodness." Had not this violence and this injury been off'red unto us by the Romans—as the warlike Scots did likewise the same in Caledonia unto the Picts—even by Julius Caesar himself, then by the Emperor Claudius, who was therefore called "Britannicus," and his captains, Aulus Plautius and Vespasian, who took in the Isle of Wight, and lastly by the first lieutenant sent hither, Ostorius Scapula (as writes Tacitus in *The Life of Agricola),* who reduced the conquered parts of our barbarous island into provinces and established in them colonies of old soldiers, building castles and towns, and in every corner teaching us even to know the powerful discourse of divine reason (which makes us only men and distinguisheth us from beasts, amongest whom we lived as naked and as beastly as they), we might

[1] "The Lord works out everything for his own ends." (Latin) Prov. 16:4 (NIV).

yet have lived overgrown satyrs, rude and untut'red, wand'ring in the woods, dwelling in caves, and hunting for our dinners as the wild beasts in the forests for their prey, prostituting our daughters to strangers, sacrificing our children to our idols—nay, *eating* our own children as did the Scots in those days, as reciteth Thomas Cogan, bachelor of physic, in his book *De Sanitate,* chapter 137 (printed 1189, and dedicated to the Earl of Hertford), in which place he bringeth in St. Hierom himself by way of prosopopeia, affirming so much upon his knowledge. His words there alleged are these: "What shall I say," saith St.Hierom, "of other nations, since that when I was a boy I saw in France Scots, a people of Britannia, roast man's flesh; and when they found in the forests herds of swine, beasts, and cattle, they would cut off the buttocks of the boys which kept them, and also the women's paps, and took that to be the most dainty and delicate meat." And as the reverend Beda reports, before the Britons were converted to the Gospel, murthering whole troops of men to accompany and serve their friends' dying in the other life, as they did to the sundry *zemes*[1] in the West Indies at what time Columbus arrived there, and as they did in Peru and Mexico at what time Ferdinando Cortez reduced them to Christianity, and as the *quiyoughquisocks,* or "priests," do to the idols of the savages here—albeit I hope they will not long do so if by a gentle and fair entreaty we may win them to be willing to hear and learn of us and our preachers the more civil use of every particular in which they now too rudely and beastly do amiss.

All the injury that we purpose unto them is but the amendment of these horrible heathenishness and the reduction of them to the aforesaid manly duties; and to the knowledge, which the Romans could not give us, of that God who must save both them and us, and who bought us alike with a dear sufferance and precious measure of mercy.

For the apter enabling of ourselves unto which so heavenly an enterprise, who will think it an unlawful act to fortify and strengthen ourselves as nature requires with the best helps? and by sitting down with guards and forces about us in the waste and vast unhabited

[1] Idols.

grounds of their[s], amongest a world of which not one foot of a thousand do they either use or know how to turn to any benefit, and therefore lies so great a circuit vain and idle before them.

Nor is this any injury unto them, from whom we will not forcibly take of their provision and labors, nor make rape of what they cleanse and manure, but prepare and break up new grounds, and thereby open unto them likewise a new way of thrift or husbandry. For as a righteous man, according to Solomon, ought to regard the life of his beast, so surely Christian men should not show themselves like wolves to devour, who cannot forget that every soul which God hath sealed for himself he hath done it with the print of charity and compassion. And therefore even every foot of land which we shall take unto our use we will bargain and buy of them for copper, hatchets, and suchlike commodities (for which they will even sell themselves, and with which they will purchase double that quantity from their neighbors!). And thus we will commune and entreat with them, truck and barter our commodities for theirs, and theirs for ours (of which they seem more fain) in all love and friendship—until for our good purposes towards them we shall find them practice violence or treason against us, as they have done to our other colony at Roanoak, when then I would gladly know of such who presume to know all things whether we may stand upon our own innocency or no, or hold it a scruple in humanity, or any of charity, to prevent our own throats from the cutting, to draw our swords *et vim vi repellere.*[1]

Planting, saith Sir George Pecham,[2] writing an apology in the like cause, may well be divided into two sorts: When Christians by the good liking and willing assent of the savages are admitted by them to quiet possession; and when Christians, being inhumanly repulsed, do seek to attain and maintain the right for which they come, in regard of establishment of Christian religion. Either of them may be lawfully exercised. For whatsoever God by the ministration of nature hath created on earth was at the beginning common among men. May it not then be lawful now to attempt the possession of such lands as are void of Christian inhabitants, for Christ's sake?

---

[1] "And meet force with force." (Latin)

[2] Sir George Peckham, *A True Reporte of the Late Discoveries* (1583).

"Hark, hark: The earth is the Lord's, and all that is therein."

"And all the world he will call and provoke, even from the east, and so forth to the west."

As it is in the 50 Psalm where David prophesieth how God will call all nations by the Gospel, and in the 12 verse, "For all is mine that in the world doth dwell." And who shall bar Him from His possession? In the second book of Esdras, the 6 chapter, 14 verse,[1] says the prophet, "And besides this Adam whom thou madest lord over all the works which thou hadst created, of him come we all." And in the New Testament, Paul, calling himself the apostle of the Gentiles, in the 11 of the Romans, 32 verse, saith that "God hath shut up all in unbelief, that He might have mercy on all." Yet in another place of the same Epistle he saith, "And how shall they call on Him in whom they have not believed? And how shall they believe in Him on whom they have not heard?" And therefore he concludeth, "Oh, how beautiful are the feet of them which bring glad tidings of peace and bring glad tidings of good things!" And in the third of Sophonias, "The children of my dispersed" (so he calleth the Apostles) "shall bring me presents from beyond the banks of Ethiopia."—besides omitting the peregrination of Paul and the travels of Barnabas into so many strange countries, islands, and kingdoms of the Gentiles, laboring in this office and reducing so many cities of theirs to knowledge of Christ crucified—in Graecia [Greece], in Pisidia, Pamphylia, Perga, Attalia, in Asia, and [in] Syria insomuch as Antioch was come to be called at length the "New City" and "Jerusalem of the Gentiles"; as also omitting the vision which Peter saw in Joppa of a vessel, as it had been a great sheet let down from heaven by the 4 corners, in which were four-footed beasts of the earth, wild beasts, creeping things, and fowls of the heaven, with the voice which accompanied it saying, "Arise (Peter), slay, and eat"; and this done 3 times, forbidding him to account those things polluted or unclean, meaning the Gentiles which God had sanctified and made holy—and which is worth all observation, and to be bound to the palms of

---

[1] Verse 54. One of the Apocryphal books.

our hands, and to be written upon the lintels and brow-posts of all our doors for the encouragement and comfort of us who are impress'd in this service. It is one of our daily petitions which we are taught by our blessed Saviour when we pray; and of that quality, as when we have first entreated grace, to esteem, value, and honor God according as He ought to be, both in words and works, as also in our holy and Christian conversation. For so much signifieth "Hallowed be thy name." We presently add, "Thy kingdom come," which implieth that it would please the great and merciful God that His sacred word might have a powerful passage throughout the world, yea, in such sort that all nations might be reduced to the kingdom of grace and made partakers of their redemption. Nor must we imagine that this is now to be done by miracle, for which it is thus foresaid by Esay [Isaiah] in his 66 chapter, "Those which shall escape out of Israel shall go far off to Tharsis and to remote islands where they shall convert many nations unto the Lord." And therefore is Christ called "the salvation of nations" (Genesis 4, Esay 7), there being no other name under heaven unto men whereby to be saved, but only this of Christ's (Acts 4).

And in the Old Testament we shall read when strange and great nations would not submit to the yoke of this knowledge of the everlasting God by fair entreaty they were *ferro et flammis*[1] compel'd thereunto. In Joshua and the Judges plentiful instances adhere to the making of this good. There is to be seen how Moses, Joshua, and Gideon would send spies and discoverers for the like purposes (*Misit igitur Josue filius Nun de Setim duos viros exploratores in abscondito, et dixit eis, "Ite et considerate terram urbemque Jerico."* Jos. 2)[2] into kingdoms, nations, and provinces, and thereafter besieged their towns and strongholds; and when the Gentiles would not call for mercy they would lay waste and burn their chief cities. So fell Jericho and so was Ai surprised, the inhabitants slain, and their king hanged up. Read the 12 chapter and you shall find a catalog of 31 kings and great princes of the heathen put to the edge of the sword, whilst the Gibeonites, entreating by ambassadors, were taken into protection

---

[1] "By iron and flames," i.e., fire and sword. (Latin)

[2] "And Joshua the son of Nun sent … two men to spy secretly, saying, 'Go view the land, even Jericho.'" (Latin) Jos. 2:1.

and admitted into the colony of the Israelites, and yet made their servants and fetch-waters.

And thus these few and unskillful scenes—but scenes of truth!—brought to this act, they shall suffice to beget a settled opinion of goodness and of the right of this business in any who hath heretofore doubted, appealing to impartial judgments whether the King of Spain hath priority of title to this part of America before the English; nay, whether he hath *any* color of title by this at all; or whether this enterprise be an unchristian act of injury to the naturals; and if neither, whether their *epiphonema*[1] deserves just shout and applause who declare it unlawful and an unnational business and to God displeasing.

FINIS

[omitted here is a folio containing Capt. John Smith's 1612 map of Virginia. See page 207]

[1] Animadversion.

Caput 1.

The cosmography, description, and division of Virginia Britannia, etc.

VIRGINIA BRITANNIA is a country in America that lieth between the degrees of 30 and 44 of the north latitude, the bounds whereof may well be thus laid: On the east runneth the great ocean, or main Atlantic Sea; on the south lieth Florida; on the north, Nova Francia; as for the west, thereof the limits are unknown, only it is supposed there may be found the descent into the South Sea, by the Spaniards called Mar del Zur, so meeting with that doubtful Nor'west Passage which leads into the east to China, Cathay, Gyapan, the Moluccas, etc., now imagined to be discovered by our countryman Hudson, and therefore, for the more certainty thereof, the search anew this present year[1] undertaken by Captain Button, Captain Nelson, and Captain [Ingram]; albeit there be who affirm that if there should be a third land-locked sea which hath no intercourse at all with the ocean (like the Mare Caspium, and the Mare Mortuum in Palestina) it lieth upon the nor'west of America.[2]

It is a spacious and ample tract of land. From north to south upon a right line it may be 700 miles; from east to west in the narrowest place supposed some 300 miles, and in other places 1000—a sufficient space and ground enough to satisfy the most covetous and wide affection of him who frames to himself any other end than the only true one of this plantation.

Of all this country in due place we purpose to speak, though more particularly of that part which was begun to be planted by the

[1] "Anno 1612." (Percy MS)

[2] The Percy MS on this page includes two paragraphs mentioning Drake's Nova Albion and Frobisher and the Strait of Anian (Bering Strait) and some rumors.

English in the year of our Lord God 1606, and which may lie under the degrees of 37, 38, and 39, and which part divided may well suffer with Germany the appellation of the "high" and "low" country—our residence, towns, and forts for the present comprehended and lying in the "low" country from the mouth of the Chesapeak Bay up to the head of the rivers, all which I call "Virginia," as the high land above the Falls, as yet [un]discovered, being the main continent, I call "Britannia." Nor do I hold this partition less proper or more impertinent unto this kingdom than England, Scotland, and Wales is to Great Brittany, or Aquitania, Celtica, and Belgia to France, or to Spain Portugal, Castile, and Aragon.

Concerning the high land, little can we say as yet because thereof little have we discovered, only some Indians' relations and some few days' marches into the Monocan country of our own have instructed us thus far.

This high land, or Britannia, then say we is the main and firm continent which extendeth we wot not how far beyond that cataract, or fall of water, which the Indians call Paquacowng, from whence one day's journey into the Monocan country our elder planters at their first coming proclaimed His Majesty king of the country at Mohominge, a neighbor village, and set up a cross there with His Majesty's name inscribed thereon—the said Falls being 150 miles up from the mouth of the bay, and where the current there at his head falleth with an easy descent 3 or 4 fathom down into the low country.

From the Falls our men have heretofore marched as the river led about 40 or 50 miles, and found the high land woody, little champion, with rising hills rocky and mountainous, and so all along from the north by a southwest line, insomuch as the more southward the further off from the bay are those mountains from which fall certain brooks which after come to 5 principal navigable rivers. These run from the nor'west into the southeast, and so into the west side of the bay, as hasting to empty themselves into the bay to pay their tribute to the ocean.

The mountains here at the head are of divers natures, for the rocks are of a composition like millstones, some of a blue metalline color, some of marble, etc.; and many pieces of scattered crystal we find as thrown down by water from the mountains. For in winter these mountains are covered with much snow, and when it dissolveth the waters fall with such violence that they cause great inundations in the narrow valleys, which yet is scarce perceived being once in the rivers. These waters wash from the rocks such glistering tinctures that the ground in some places seemeth as gilded where both the rocks and the earth are so splendant to behold that very good judgments would perhaps be persuaded they contained more than probabilities. Sure it is that some minerals have been there found.

This high land is in all likelihoods a pleasant tract and the mould fruitful, especially what may lie to the so'ward, where at Peccarecanick[1] and Ochanahoen, by the relation of Machumps, the people have houses built with stone walls and one story above another—so taught them by those English who escaped the slaughter at Roanoack at what time this our colony under the conduct of Captain Newport landed within the Chesapeack Bay—and where the people breed up tame turkeys about their houses and take apes in the mountains [?], and where at Ritanoe the weroane Eyanoco preserved 7 of the English alive—four men, two boys, and one young maid, who escaped and fled up the River of Chaonoke—to beat his copper, of which he hath certain mines at the said Ritanoe, as also at Pannawaick are said to be store of salt stones.

Poketawes, which the West Indians, our neighbors, call *maize,* their kind of wheat, is here said to be in more plenty than below. And the low country fruits grow here.[2] It is supposed that the low land hath more fish and fowl, and the high land more number of beasts. The people differ not much in nature, habit, or condition, only they are more daring upon us. And before we erected our forts among them, there was ever enmity and open wars between the high and low

---

[1] "Peccarecanick between 35 and 36 de[grees] of the Line, and in her warm valleys may be planted sugar canes, oranges, lemons, and all sorts of southren fruits, and whatsoever, the south—Spain, Italy, Barbary, Greece, Judea, and Syria—bring forth, being answerable to the same height." (margin note in Percy MS) Height is latitude, in this case that of North Carolina.

[2] "Likewise silk of the grass and habundance of the dyeing root." "Copper so plentiful as the metal is said to be taken out of the stone without furnace, fire, blast, or aditament." (margin note in Percy MS)

country, going by the names of Monocans and Powhatans.

To the nor'ward of the Falls and bending to the nor'east lieth the skirt of this high land country, from whence the aforesaid 5 great navigable rivers take their heads, which run through the low land (as is before mentioned) into the Chesapeak Bay. This quarter is altogether unknown to us as yet, only herein are seated, say the Indians, those people whom Powhatan calls the Bocootawwonaukes, who (he saith) do likewise melt copper and other metals, how true we must leave to further discovery.

To the nor'ward again of this, in the height of 44 [degrees], lieth the country called Pamaquid, the kingdom wherein our western colony upon the River of Sachadehock was sometime planted,[1] which is a high land and no less fruitful than these other parts, save only the extremity of the winter's coldness makes it less pleasant. Yet did our men in their ill-builded and bleak cottages endure one whole winter there without any great loss or danger; nor is it more cold than the winter in Scotland; and therefore, though that colony be now discontinued, yet is not that the reason, but rather the death of the honorable gentleman, Sir John Popham, knight, late lord chief justice, chief patron of the same.

Now concerning the low land, or "Virginia," which bordereth west and nor'west upon the Falls and the country of the Monacans, and north upon the Bocootawwonaukes, east upon the sea, and south upon Florida, it may well enough be divided into "South Virginia" and "North Virginia," the Chesapeak Bay and Powhatan River parting these two.[2]

The cape of this bay on the south side we call Cape Henry in honor of our most royal prince, where the land shows white hilly sand like unto the Downs, and all along the shore grow great plenty of pines and firs.

The north foreland of this bay, which the Indians term Accowmack, we call Cape Charles in honor of our princely Duke of York. Within these lies our country, and only by the mouth of this goodly

[1] "Pamaquid in the height of 44." (margin note in Percy MS)

[2] The border between "north" and "south" Virginia as set out in the charters was not at all here but much further north. At any rate, once Capt. John Smith coined the name "New England," the terms disappeared.

bay the entrance thereunto.

South Virginia is a very low, sandy soil, without rocks or any stones at all. It is thick set with woods of divers kinds, and in all things resembleth North Virginia, excepted the lowness of the land and want of stones. It hath divers rivers in it, but none navigable, to our knowledge. It hath many islands which lie into the sea before the firm land, but the water is not deep for shipping between them and the main. It is said to have of the same silk whereof the *Chynoes* [Chinese] make their damask, called by the Portugals *soue del cherua* [?],[1] in great abundance, and sundry apothecary drugs which are now found likewise as frequent in our north part. It is a fruitful country and not much subject to cold. In this country it was that Sir Walter Raleigh planted his two colonies in the islands aforesaid, called Roanoak.

No part of this south country is supposed to be under Powhatan, but under an absolute weroance as powerful and great as Powhatan. It shall not fall in here so well at large to particulate the bounds, estate, customs, and commodities of this south part, since it shall be exemplified in his due place in the second book of this decade, and it is already set forth and expressed to public view both in English and Latin by Theodorus de Bry and Mr. Hariotts, who was a planter there one whole year, albeit I must acknowledge the coherence of both the countries is such as the relation of the one may suffice to give understanding of the condition and quality of both.

North Virginia lieth on the north side of Powhatan, or the first river within the Chesapeak Bay (which [river] we have called the Kings River), up to the Falls, and from thence by the skirt of the high land, by the heads of the rivers, even to our main sea, upon the northern shore of the which said Kings River (as London upon the Thames) are seated as yet our principal towns and forts—which are in chief commanded by their Great King Powhatan are comprehended under the denomination of Tsenacommacoh, of which we may the more by experience speak, it being the place wherein our abode and habitation hath now well near six years consisted.

The summer here is hot as in Spain, the winter cold as in France or

---

[1] See p. 23.

England; the heat of summer is in June, July, and August, but commonly the cool breezes assuage the vehemency of the heat. The chief of winter is half December, January, February, and half March.

The temperature of this country doth well agree with the English constitutions, being sometimes seasoned in the same, which hath appeared unto us by this that albeit by many occasions ill lodging at the first (the poorer on the bare ground and the best in such miserable cottages at the best as through which the fervent piercing heat of the sun—which there, it is true, is the first cause creating such summer fevers amongest them—found never resistance), hard fare, and their own judgments and safeties instructing them to work hard in the faint time of summer the better to be accommodated and fitted for the winter, they have fallen sick; yet have they recovered again by very small means without help of fresh diet or comfort of wholesome physic, there being at the first but few physic helps or skillful surgeons who knew how to apply the right medicine in a new country or to search the quality and constitution of the patient and his distemper, or that knew how to counsel when to let blood or not, or in necessity to use a lance in that office at all.

In the year 1607 was an extraordinary frost in most of Europe, and this frost was found as extreme in Virginia. But the next year following, and so ever since hitherto, for 8 or 10 days of ill weather we have commonly 14 days of fair and summery weather.

The winds here are variable. From the so'west come the greatest gusts, with thunder and heat. The nor'west wind is commonly cool, and bringeth fair weather with it. From the north is the greatest cold, and from the east and southeast (as from the Bermudas) fogs and rains. Sometimes there are great droughts, other times much rain. Yet we see not but that all the variety of needful fruits and vegetables which we transport from hence and plant there thrive and prosper well, of which husbandry and thrift we have made many experiments, and they stand us now in no little use, having plenty of them. Here is not that seed or herb which our country here by manuring and culture brings forth but do likewise there grow quickly and to no changeable taste from their nature, nay, to better than in England, as parsnips, carrots, turnips, pumpions, melons, cucumbers, and many of our English garden seeds, parsley, endive, succory, etc.

There have been brought from the West Indies the plants of orange trees which put into the ground carelessly and neglected have yet prospered; as also the vines of France, tobacco seed from Trinidado, cotton wool, and potatoes we have committed to the trial of the soil and they yearly come to good pass. The roots of the delicious Indian pina[1] set in a sandy place thrived and continued life without respect had of it until the cold winter and the weeds choked it. Yet is this fruit said to be so dainty, nice, and of that nature that no art or industry hath been found out hitherto that could preserve it in any climate but in the West Indy islands only. For the likelihood of growing of sugar canes we have some probable hopes by reason of the greatness and sweetness of the stalk of the country wheat and the soil being aromatical, as I may speak by the saxafras, galbanum, Mechoacan (otherwise called *rhubarbum album*), of which Doctor Bohun[2] made trial in cold and moist bodies for the purging [of] phlegm and superfluous matter, as also a white bole, which Dr. Bohun calls *terra alba virginiensis*, both aromatical and cordial, and diaphoretic in pestilent and malignant fevers, and some other drugs. It can be but some little time industriously spent to make trial of this so rich commodity.

The vesture of the earth in most places doth manifestly prove the nature of the soil to be lusty and very rich. The color of the earth we find in most places resembleth bole armoniac [armeniac], fuller's earth, marl, and that earth which we suppose of the like quality with the Lemnian terra sigillata, so priceful and merchantable in Turkey; as likewise there is a clay which the Indians call *assesqueth*, whereof they make their tobacco pipes, which is more smooth and fine than I have elsewhere seen any. But generally the earth upon the upper crust is a black, fat mould; next under that is a gray, sandy marl, under which in divers places is a red sand and in other places a hard clay, in some places a fat, slimy clay. But the best ground is known

---

[1] Pineapple.

[2] Here is likely another credit. I am inclined to believe Dr. Bohun is the real source of the bulk of Strachey's and Smith's natural histories. Not a word survives in his name, but who else was out there day after day testing and observing? Bohun must have been Thomas Harriot's man on the spot.

by the burthen which it beareth, as by the greatness of trees or abundance of weeds, etc.

This part is not mountainous; we sometime meet with pleasant plains, small, rising hills and fertile valleys, one crossing another, and all watered conveniently with brooks and springs. By the rivers are many plain marishes containing some 20, some 100, some 200 acres, some more, some less. Other plains there are few, but only where the savages inhabit, but all overgrown with trees and woods, being a plain wilderness as God first ordained it.

All the low land of South and North Virginia is conjectured to have been gained naturally out of the sea, for the sea, through his impetuous and vast revolution (who knows not?) swaying upon every coast, in some places wins and in other places loseth. And we find within the shores of our rivers whole banks of oysters and scallops which lie unopened and thick together as if there had been their natural bed before the sea left them.[1] Likewise the fashion of the earth is in small, rising mounts which may well be supposed that the violence of the wind hath caused by driving the light sand together. Moreover the mould and sward of the earth is not two foot deep all along near the sea, and that which is comes only by the grass and leaves of trees and such rubbish rotting upon it in continuance of time. For in digging but a fathom or two we commonly find quicksand.

Again, under the crust of the surface we find not any stones nor rocks except near the high land—nay, in most places to so'ward not so much as a pebble stone, which must proceed through want of time that no duration hath there been wrought. Besides, the water ebbs and flows well-nigh unto the heads of all the rivers (I mean to the Falls unto the high land), and the natives which now people with us on this side beneath the said Falls are conceived not to have inhabited here below much more in 300 years; by all which we cannot but truly conjecture that the upland country is a fair and goodly country, more sweet and wholesome in respect of air and more rich in soil and freighted with better commodities, and those more necessary, besides the assurance of minerals, concerning which

[1] Fossils.

we do already hear the Indians talk both of alum mines and copper to the so'ward, where hath been sufficient time for digestion—all which we must submit to more clear discoveries.

Caput 2.

Description of the five principal rivers within the Chesipiock Bay that is between Cape Henry and Cape Charles, and of the inhabitants thereof.

ON THE WEST SIDE OF THE BAY we said were 5 fair and delightful navigable rivers, of which we will now proceed to report. The first of these rivers, and the next to the mouth of the bay, hath his course from the west and by north. The name of this river we call the Kings River, they call Powhatan, according to the name of a principal country that lieth upon the head of it. The mouth of this river is near three miles in breadth, yet do the shoals force the channel so near the land that a saker will overshoot it at pointblank. This river hath a channel for 140 miles, of depth betwixt 7 and 15 fathom, holding in breadth for the most part 2 or 3 miles, and in which are many isles both great and small. It falleth from rocks far west in a country inhabited by a nation as aforesaid that they call Monocan. But where it cometh into our discovery it is Powhatan. In the furthest place that hath been diligently observed are falls, rocks, shoals, etc., which makes it past navigation any higher, albeit 40 miles above the said Falls it hath 2 branches, or other rivers, that fall into it. The head of the northermost comes from certain steep mountains that are said to be impassable. The head of the other comes from high hills afar off within the land, from the tops of which hills the people say they see another sea, and that the water is there salt; and the journey to this sea from the Falls by their account should be about 10 days, allowing according unto a march some 14 or 16 miles a day.

In the running downward, the river is enriched with many goodly brooks, which are maintained by an infinite number of small rundles and pleasant springs, that disperse themselves for best service as do the veins of a man's body.

From the south side there falls into this river first the pleasant river of Appamatuck; next more to the east are the two rivers of Quiyoughcohanock; a little further is a bay wherein falleth 3 or 4 pretty brooks and creeks that half entrench the inhabitants of Warraskoyack; then the river of Nandsamund, and lastly the brook of Chesapeak.

From the north side is the river of Chickahamania, the back river of James-Town, another by the Cedar Isle, wherein are great store of goodly oysters; then a convenient harborough for crayes, frigates or fisher boats of Kecoughtan,[1] the which by-rill so conveniently turneth itself into bays, coves, and creeks that the place is made very pleasant thereby to inhabit, the cornfields being circled therein in manner as so many peninsulas.

The most of these by-rivers are inhabited by several nations, or rather families, taking their names from those rivers, and wherein a several governor, or weroance, commandeth.

The first, and next the river's mouth, are the Kecoughtans, then the Paspaheghes, the Arrahatecks, and the place called Powhatan. On the south side of this river are the Appamatucks, the Quiyoughcohanocks, the Warraskoyacks, the Nandsamunds, the Chesapeacks. Of this last place the bay beareth his name.

Fourteen miles nor'ward from the River Powhatan is the River Pamunck, which we call the Princes River, navigable 60 or 70 miles with ships of good burthen, but with ketches and small barks 30 or 40 miles further at the ordinary flowing of the salt water. It divideth itself at Cinquoteck into 2 gallant branches. On the south branch inhabit the people of Youghtamund, on the north branch Mattapanient. On the north side of this river is Werowocomoco, where their great king inhabited when we came first into the country. 10 or 12 miles lower on the south side of this river is Kiskiack. These as also Appamatuck, Orapaks, Arrahatack, and Powhatan are their

---

[1] The kind of small craft that today tie up in the Hampton River.

great king's inheritance, chief alliance, and inhabitance.

Upon Youghtamund is the seat of Powhatan's 3 brethren, whom we learn are successively to govern after Powhatan in the same dominions which Powhatan by right of birth, as the elder brother, now holds. The rest of the countries under his command are, as they report, his conquests.

Before we come to the third river that falleth from the mountains, there is another river which taketh not his birth or head so high, but is only some 30 miles navigable, and issueth from out the riffs and breaches from the inland. The river is called Payankatank[1]; the inhabitants whereof are but few, not now above 40 or 50, and are the remain of the conquered Kecoughtans whom he transported thither.

For in the year 1608, Powhatan surprised the natural inhabitants of Payankatank, his neighbors and subjects. The occasion was to us unknown, but the manner was thus performed: First he sent divers of his men to lodge amongest them one night, pretending a general hunt, who were to give the alarum unto an ambuscado of a greater company within the woods; who upon the sign given at the hour appointed environed all the houses and fell to the execution. 24 men they kill'd outright, the rest escaping by fortune and their swift footmanship. And the long hair of the one side of their heads with the skin razed off with shells or reeds they brought away to Powhatan. They surprised also the women and children and the weroance, all whom they presented to Powhatan. The locks of hair with their skins they hanged on a line between two trees; and of these Powhatan made ostentation as of a great triumph at Werowocomoco not long after, showing them to such the English as came unto him at his appointment to trade with him for corn, thinking to have terrified them with this spectacle, and in the middest of their amazement to have seized them. But God be praised, it wrought not fear but courage in our people, and awaked their discretions to stand upon their guard the more cautelously; and by that means they came off again from him, contrary to his purpose.

And let me truly say how they never killed man of ours but by our men's own folly and indiscretion, suff'ring themselves to be beguiled

---

[1] "The Payankatanck, or Sydney River" (margin note in Percy MS).

and enticed up into their houses without their arms; when then indeed they have fallen upon them and knock'd out their brains or stuck them full of arrows (no force) for their credulity. But of so many men which the common report out of ignorance gives out here to have been slain by those Indians, I would but know if they can name me *three men* that they ever killed of ours in skirmish, fort, or field but by this kind of subtlety in them and weakness in ours, and whom the sword of justice would have cut off, had they escaped the Indian, for adventuring so amongest them, either against discipline and the charge given them or indeed against common sense and duty unto their own lives.

The third navigable river by the naturals of old was called Opiscatumeck, of late Toppahanock, and we the Queens River. This is navigable some 130 miles. At the top of it inhabit the people called Mannahoacks amongest the mountains, but they are above the place described in Captain Smith's map. Upon this river on the north side are seated a people called Cuttatawomen with 30 fighting men; higher on the river are the Moraughtacunds with 80 able men; beyond them Toppahanock with 100 men; far above is another Cuttatawomen with 20 men; on the south far within the river is Nandtaughtacund having 150 men. This river also as the two former hath her burthen extraordinary both of fish and fowl.

The fourth river is called Patawomeck, and we call Elizabeth River, and is 6 or 7 miles in breadth. It is navigable 120 miles, and fed as the rest with many sweet rivers and springs which fall from the bordering hills. Many of them are planted and yield no less plenty and variety of fruit than the other rivers. It exceedeth with abundance of fish, and is inhabited on both sides: First on the south side at the very entrance is Wighcocomoco, and which hath some 130 fighting men; beyond that is Cekakawwon with 30 men; then Onawmanient with 100 men; then Patawomeck with 160 able men. Here doth the river divide itself into 3 or 4 convenient rivers; the greatest of the least is called Quiyough, trending nor'west. But the river itself turneth nor'east and is still a navigable stream. On the western side of this bought is Tauxenent with 40 able men; on the north side of this river is Cecomocomoco with 40 men; somewhat farther is Potapoco with 20 men; in the east part of the bought of the river is Pamacocack with 60 men; after, Moyoones with 100 men; and lastly Nacothtanck with 80 able men. The river 10 miles above this place maketh his passage down a low pleasant valley overshadowed in many places with high rocky mountains, from whence distill innumerable sweet and pleasant springs.

Within this river, Captain Samuell Argoll in a small river, which the Indians call Oquiho, anno 1610, trading in a bark called the *Discovery* for corn with the great king of Patawomeck, from him obtained well near 400 bushels of wheat, peas, and beans, beside many kinds of furs, for 9^{li} of copper, 4 bunches of beads, 8 dozen of hatchets, five dozen of knives, iiii bunches of bells, one dozen of scissors—all not much more worth than 40 shillings English; as also from the said king's brother, I-Opassous, king of a place called Pastanzo, [he] recovered an English boy called Henry Spilman, who had lived amongest them one whole year and despaired of ever seeing his native country, his father's house (for he was descended of a gentle family), or Christians anymore. Likewise here Captain Argoll found a mine of antimony, which seldom goes unaccompanied with quicksilver, as also a kind of heavy black sand upon the banks, which being washed weighed massy with lead.

The fift river is called Pawtuxunt,[1] and is of a less proportion than the rest, but the channel is 16 or 18 fathom deep in some places. Here are infinite schools of divers kinds of fish more than elsewhere. Upon this river dwell the people called Acquintanacsuck, Pawtuxunt, and Mattapanient. 200 men was the greatest strength that could be there perceived by our discoverers, but they inhabit together and not so dispersed as the rest. These of all other were found the most civil to give entertainment, and therefore from them we received great courtesy and much good cheer.

Thirty leagues nor'ward is a river not inhabited[2] yet navigable. By reason of the red earth or clay resembling bole armoniac, the discoverers call'd it "Bolus."

At the end of the bay, where it is 6 or 7 miles in breadth, there fall into it 4 small rivers, 3 of them issuing from divers bogs environed

---

1 "Pawtuxunt, or Dukes River" (margin note in Percy MS).

2 "Bolus, or Mountgomery River" (margin note in Percy MS). Likely the Patapsco.

with divers mountains. There is one that cometh due north, 3 or 4 days journey from the head of the Bay and falls from rocks and mountains. Upon this river inhabit a people called the Sasquesahanougs. They are seated 2 days higher than was passage for the discoverers' barge, howbeit 60 of the Sasquesahanougs came to the discoverers with skins, bows, arrows, targets, swords, beads, and tobacco pipes for presents. Such great and well proportion'd men are seldom seen, for they seemed like giants to the English—yea, and to the neighbors—yet seemed of an honest and simple disposition, with much ado restrained from adoring the discoverers as gods. These are the most strange people of all those countries, both in language and attire. For their language yet may well beseem their proportions, sounding from them as it were a great voice in a vault or cave as an echo.

Their attire is the skins of bears and wolves. Some have cassocks made of bears' hides and skins that a man's neck goeth through the skin's neck, and the ears of the bear are fastened to his shoulders behind, the nose and teeth hanging down his breast, and at the end of the nose hangs a bear's paw; the half-sleeves coming to the elbow were the necks of bears, and the arms through the mouth with paws hanging at their noses. One had the head of a wolf hanging in a chain for a jewel, his tobacco pipe three quarters of a yard long, prettily carved with a bird, a deer, or some such device at the great end, sufficient to beat out the brains of a horse. Likewise their bows and arrows and clubs are suitable to their greatness.

These are scarce known to Powhatan. They can make well near 600 able and mighty men, and are palisado'd in their towns to defend them from the Massawomecks, their mortal enemies.

Five of these chief weroances came aboard the discoverers and crossed the bay with them in their barge. The picture of the greatest of them is here portrayed—

[blank half page][1]

---

[1] Surely the Susquehannock warrior depicted on the right of Smith's map of Virginia was intended.

—the calf of whose leg was 3 quarters of a yard about, and all the rest of his limbs so answerable to that proportion that he seemed the goodliest man they ever beheld. His hair the one side was long, the other shorn close with a ridge over his crown like a coxcomb. His arrows were 5 quarters long, headed with flints or splinters of stones in form like a heart, an inch broad and an inch and a half or more long. These he wore in a wolf's skin at his back for his quiver, his bow in the one hand and his club in the other.

On the east side the bay is the River of Tockwough,[1] and upon it a people that can make 100 men, seated some 7 miles within the river, where they have a fort very well palisado'd and mantled with the bark of trees.

Next unto them are the Ozinies with 60 men. More to the south of that east side of the bay is the River of Rapahanock, near unto which is the River of Kuscarawoak, upon which is seated a people with 200 men. After that is the River of Wighcocomaco, and on it a people with 100 men. The people of these rivers are of little stature and of another language from the rest, and very rude.

But they on the River of Accohanock with 40 men and they of Accowmack with 80 men do equalize any of the territories of Powhatan, and speak his language, who over all those doth rule as king.

Southward they went to some parts of Chawonock and the Mangoaugs to search them there left by Sir Walter Raleigh, which parts to the town of Chesapeacks hath formerly been discovered by Master Harriots and Sir Raph Lane.

Amongst those people are thus many several nations of sundry languages which environ Powhatan's territories: The Chawonocks, the Mangoaugs, the Monacans, the Mannahocks, the Sasquesahanougs, the Acquanachuks, the Tockwoughs, and the Kuscarawaoks.

Of all these not anyone understandeth another but by interpreters, their several habitations are more plainly described by the annexed map, set forth by Captain Smith.[2] Of whose pains taken herein I leave to the censure of the reader to judge. Sure I am there will not

[1] "Tockwough, or Howard River" (margin note in Percy MS)

[2] Omitted here. The 1612 Smith map is given with abbreviated detail on 207.

return from thence in haste anyone who hath been more industrious [than Captain John Smith], or who hath had—Captain George Percy excepted—greater experience amongest them, however misconstruction may traduce him here at home where is not easily seen the mixed sufferances both of body and mind which is there daily and with no few hazards and hearty griefs undergone.

The map will likewise present to the eye the way of the mountains and current of the rivers, with their several turnings, bays, shoals, isles, inlets, and creeks, the breadth of the waters, the distances of places, and suchlike; in which map observe this that as far as you see the little crosses, either rivers, mountains, or other places, have been discovered. The rest was had by information of the savages and are set down according to their instructions.[1]

Likewise from the north point of our bay, which (as aforesaid) the Indians call Accowmack and we Cape Charles, hath the coast all along been discovered even to the river of Sachadehock. For Captain Argoll in his return from the search of the Bermudas, anno 1610, after he had lost Sir George Somers the 28 of July in a dangerous fog, well beaten to and fro, fell with the main, standing for Cape Cod, and made good from 44 degrees what Captain Bartilmew Gosnoll and Captain Waymouth wanted in their discoveries, observing all along the coast and drawing the plots thereof, as he steered homewards unto our bay; and divers times went ashore off 'ring acquaintance and trade unto the people; and in the latitude of 39 discovered another goodly bay into which fell many tails of fair and large rivers, and which might make promise of some westerly passage, the cape-land whereof in 38½ [degrees] he called "Cape la Warr"[2]; from which not far off lay a fair bank into the sea, as upon the New-found Land, where he hauled excellent fish[3] and of such a kind as will keep a whole year in ship's hold with little care, a trial

---

[1] This note copied from Smith's *Map of Virginia* contains a piece of the captain's modesty: A cross is at the falls of the James despite the overland trek of Newport and company without Smith to Massinacack, which is shown by a stippled line along the north bank. The crosses represent what Smith *has seen with his own eyes.*

[2] Delaware Bay and Cape May.

[3] "Both halibut, cod, and ling, of which he brought an assay and taste of 200 couple into the colony—an excellent fish." (margin note)

whereof His Lordship likewise brought with him into England. And upon the shores in divers places he killed great store of seals.

Concerning the falling with our own coast, it is true that there cannot be a bolder shore to come in withal in any country in the world. For first, before we come in sight of it, 30 leagues [at sea] we smell a sweet savor, as is usually from off Cape Vincent, the south cape of Spain, if the wind come from the shore, besides we have change of water and sounding at 25 fathom 20 leagues off.

The coast of South Virginia from Cape Henry lieth south and north next hand some 7 leagues, where there goeth in a river, as is nearest guessed, by the Chawanokes and Mangoauges, but is not navigable far.[1] All along this coast for 7 leagues we have 7 and 8 fathom water within one league of the shore. Not far more to the southward of this inlet river is a cape of an island called Croatoan, which cape is that which we call the South Cape of Virginia,[2] beyond which cape southwardly the coast is held to be somewhat dangerous. To the so'west and no'west of this cape, or Croaton, lie certain small islands, as before rememb'red, that from [front] the coast of the main. But the sea between the main and them is not for any shipping to pass. Into this shallow sea there fall divers fresh rivers from the main, which the savages have described unto us, and plenty of people thereon.[3]

If we come in with the Chesapeak Bay open, our soundings are from 15 fathom to 5; but if we hit the channel we have no less than 7 or 8 fathom. So it is all over bold enough, having neither ledges of rocks, no bars, no sandy shelves, but the bottom even and plain.

Our two capes—Cape Henry and Cape Charles—do lie no'east and by east, and so'west and by west, and they be distant each from other in breadth (where the sea runs in between both lands, so making our bay an only entrance into our country) as broad as may be between Queenborough and Leigh.[4]

When we come in with Cape Henry we have 6, 7, and 8 fathom to

---

[1] Albemarle Sound.

[2] Cape Hatteras.

[3] Pamlico Sound.

[4] Hardly. The mouth of the Thames here is five miles wide; the Virginia capes stand eleven miles apart.

the point at the bottom of the bay and mouth of the Kings River, into which all ships that will enter must borrow so much of the shore as to come within less than musket shot of the point, by reason of the shoals lying upon the southern shore, by which may be observed how convenient and necessary a point this is for a substantial fortification to be raised to secure all the other forts and towns upon this river from what enemies soever.

Caput 3.

From whence and how it may be conjectured that these people first descended into these parts of America. The description of the Emperor Powhatan.

IT WERE NOT perhaps too curious a thing to demand how these people might come first and from whom and whence to inhabit these so far remote westerly parts of the world, having no intercourse with Africa, Asia, nor Europe, and considering the whole world so many years (by all knowledge received) was supposed to be only contained and circumscribed in the discovered and known traveled bounds of those three, according to that old conclusion in the schools: *Quicquid praeter Africam et Europam est, Asia est*, "Whatsoever land doth neither appertain unto Africa nor to Europe is part of Asia"; as also to question how it should be that they, if descended from the people of the first creation, should maintain so general and gross a defection from the true knowledge of God with one kind, as it were, of rude and savage life, customs, manners, and religion; it being to be granted that with us infallibly they had one and the same descent and beginning from the universal deluge in the scattering of Noah his children and nephews with their families as little colonies, some to one, some to other borders of the earth to dwell; as in Egypt (so writing Berosus) Esenius and his household took up their inhabitation; in Libya and Cyrene, Tritames; and in all the rest of Africa, Japetus Priscus; Attalaas in East Asia; Ganges with some of

Gomerus Gallus' children in Arabia-Felix within the confines of Sabaea, called the "frankincense bearer"; Canaan in Damascus unto the utmost bounds of Palestine.

But it is observed that Cham and his family were the only far travelers and stragglers into divers and unknown countries, searching, exploring, and sitting down in the same. As also it is said of his family that what country soever the children of Cham happened to possess, there began both the ignorance of true godliness and a kind of bondage and slavery to be taxed one upon another, and that no inhabited countries cast forth greater multitudes to range and stray into divers remote regions than that part of Arabia in which Cham himself—constrained to fly with wife and children by reason of the mocking that he had done to his father—took into possession. So great a misery (saith Boem of Auba) brought to mankind the unsatisfied wand'ring of that one man, for first from him the ignorance of the true worship of God took beginning, the inventions of heathenism, and adoration of false gods and the devil. For he himself, not applying him to learn from his father the knowledge and prescribed worship of the eternal God, the God of his fathers, yet by a fearful or superstitious instinct of nature carried to ascribe unto some supernatural power a kind of honor and reverence, [and] not devout to know the essence and quality of that power, [he] taught his successors new and divided manner of gods, sacrifices, and ceremonies; and which he might the easier impress into the children, by reason they were carried with him so young away from the elders, not instructed nor seasoned first in their true customs and religion, insomuch as then we may conclude that from Cham and his took birth and beginning the first universal confusion and diversity which ensued afterwards throughout the whole world, especially in divine and sacred matters; whilst it is said again of the children of Sem and Japhet how they, being taught by their elders, and content with their own limits and confines, not traveling beyond them into new countries as the other, retained still until the coming of the Messias the only knowledge of the eternal and never-changeable truth.

By all which it is very probable likewise that both in the travels and idolatry of the family of Cham this portion of the world, westward from Africa upon the Atlantic Sea, became both peopled and instructed in the form of profane worship and of an unknown deity. Nor is it to be wond'red at where the abused truth of religion is suff'red to perish if men in their own inventions and lives become so gross and barbarous as by reading the process of this history will hardly be perceived what difference may be between them and brute beasts, sometimes worshiping brute beasts, nay, things more vile, and abhorring the inbred motions of nature itself, with such headlong and bloody ceremonies of will and act.

But how the vagabond race of Cham might descend into this new world without furniture (as may be questioned) of shipping and means to tempt the seas, together how this great continent, divided from the other three, should become stored with beasts and some fowl of one and the same kind with the other parts, especially with lions, bears, deer, wolves, and suchlike as from the first creation took beginning in their kind, and after the general flood were not anew created, nor have their being or generation as some other *ex putredine et sole,* "by corruption and heat," let me refer the reader to the search of Acosta in his—— book, chapter——[1] of his moral and natural history of the West Indies, who hath so officiously labored herein as he should but bring owls to Athens who should study for more strained or new authority concerning the same.

Thus much then may in brief be said and allowed concerning their original, or first, beginning in general, and which may well reach even down unto the particular inhabitants of this particular region by us discovered, who cannot be any other than parcel of the same and first mankind.

Concerning themselves more especially and their division as we find them in these provinces where we are, we may well say how this tract or portion of land, which we call Virginia Britannia, by the inhabitants as aforesaid Tsenacommacah, is govern'd in chief by a great king, by them called by sundry names according to his divers places, qualities, or honors by himself obtained amongest them either for his valor, his government, or some suchlike goodness, which they use to admire and commend to succeeding times, with memorable titles; and so commonly they of greatest merit amongest

---

[1] José de Acosta, *Historia natural y moral de las Indias* (1590), translated in 1604.

them aspire to many names.

The great emperor at this time amongest them we commonly call Powhatan, for by that name true it is he was made known unto us when we arrived in the country first. And so indeed he was generally called when he was a young man, as taking his denomination from the country Powhatan wherein he was born, which is above at the Falls, as before mentioned, right over against the islands at the head of our river; and which place, or birthright, of his he sold, anno 1609, about September, unto Captain Francis West, our lord general's brother, who therefore erected there a fort, calling it "West's Fort," and sat himself down there with one hundred and twenty English. The inhabitants themselves, especially his frontier neighbor princes, call him still Powhatan; his own people sometimes call him Ottaniack, sometime Mamanatowick, which last signifies "great king"; but his proper right name which they salute him with (himself in presence) is Wahunsenacawh; the greatness and bounds of whose empire by reason of his powerfulness and ambition in his youth hath larger limits than ever had any of his predecessors in former times. For he seems to command, south and north, from the Mangoages and Chawonoaks, bordering upon Roanoak and the old Virginia, to Tockwogh—a town palisado'd, standing at the north end of our bay in 40 degrees or thereabouts—southwest to Anueg—not expressed in the map,[1] whose houses are built as ours, 10 days' journey distant from us, from whence those weroances send unto him of their commodities, as Weionock (a servant in whom Powhatan reposed much trust) would tell our elder planters and could repeat many words of their language, which he had learned amongest them in his employment thither for his king, and whence he often returned full of presents to Powhatan.[2]

He hath divers seats or houses. His chief when we came into the

[1] Smith's 1612 map shows no Anueg (nor does the Smith/Zuñiga map).

[2] "—and westward he commands to Monahassanugh, which stands at the foot of the mountains from Chesapeak, or the mouth of our bay, 200 miles—nor'west to the borders of Massawomeck and Bocootawwonough; nor'east and by east to Accohanock, Accowmack, and some other petty nations lying on the east side of our bay." (Percy MS)

country was upon Pamunky River, on the north side, or Pembrook side, called Werowocomaco, which by interpretation signifies "king's house"; howbeit not liking to neighbor so near us—that house being within some 15 or 16 miles [of] where he saw we purposed to hold ourselves, and from whence in 6 or 7 hours we were able to visit him—he removed and ever since hath most what kept at a place in the deserts called Orapaks, at the top of the river Chickahamania, between Youghtamund and Powhatan.

He is a goodly old man, not yet shrinking, though well beaten with many cold and stormy winters, in which he hath been patient of many necessities and attempts of his fortune to make his name and family great. He is supposed to be little less than 80 years old (I dare not say how much more others say he is); of a tall stature and clean limbs, of a sad aspect, round [and] fat visaged, with gray hairs, but plain and thin hanging upon his broad shoulders, some few hairs upon his chin and so on his upper lip. He hath been a strong and able savage, sinewy, active, and of a daring spirit, vigilant, ambitious, subtle to enlarge his dominions. For but the countries Powhatan, Arrohateck, Appamatuck, Pamunky, Youghtamund, and Mattapanient, which are said to come unto him by inheritance, all the rest of the territories before named and expressed in the map, and which are all adjoining to that river whereon we are seated, they report (as is likewise before rememb'red) to have been either by force subdued unto him or through fear yielded. Cruel he hath been and quarrelous as well with his own weroances for trifles, and that to strike a terror and awe into them of his power and condition, as also with his neighbors in his younger days, though now delighted in security and pleasure; and therefore stands upon reasonable conditions of peace with all the great and absolute weroances about him, and is likewise more quietly settled amongest his own.

Watchful he is over us and keeps good espial upon our proceedings, concerning which he hath his sentinels that at what time soever any of our boats, pinnaces, or ships come in, fall down, or make up the river give the alarum and take it quickly the one from the other until it reach and come even to the court, or hunting house, wheresoever he and his *cronoccoes* (1) "councilors and priests" are. And then he calls to advise, and gives out directions what is to be done, as more fearing than harmed at any time with the danger and mischief which he saith we intend unto him by taking away his land from him, and conspiring to surprise him, which we never yet imagined nor attempted. And yet, albeit the concept of as much strongly possesseth him, he doth often send unto us to temporize with us, awaiting perhaps but a fit opportunity, inflamed by his furious and bloody priests, to offer us a taste of the same cup which he made our poor countrymen drink of at Roanoak; not yet seeming willing to hold any open quarrel or hostility with us, but in all advantages which he sometimes takes against our credulous and beguiled people, he hath it always so carried as, upon our complaint to him, it is rather laid upon some of his worst and unruly people, of which he tells us even our King James, commanding so many divers men, must have some irregular and unruly; or else upon some of his petty weroances whom peradventure we have attempted (saith he) with offenses of the like nature, than that it is any act of *his,* or done by *his* command, or according to *his* will, often flattering us that he will take order that it shall be no more so, but that the *tassantesses,* that is, the "strangers," King James his people, and his people shall be all one, brothers and friends.

And thus he served us at what time he wrought the Chikahamines (a nation as we have learned before the coming in of us so far from being his subjects as they were ever his enemies) into a hatred of us, [they] being a mighty people and our neighbors,[1] and us into suspicion of them, by urging them to betray such of our men as traded with them for corn; three whereof it is true they slew without cause or offense given, and had done as much for them rest had not their own fear and cowardice withheld them. And this he wholly laid upon them, excusing himself unto us by their number and unruliness. Yea, so far he will go herein sometime that when some of his people have done us wrong—and by his provoking too—he will not fail underhand after the fact to tell us the authors of our wrong, giving us leave and bidding us revenge us upon them, of such subtle understanding and politic carriage is he.

[1] "within some 10 or 12 miles of Jamestown." (Percy MS). The rest of the paragraph is somewhat fuller there also.

In all his ancient inheritances he hath houses built after their manner, and at every house provision for his entertainment according to the time. About his person ordinarily attendeth a guard of 40 or 50 of the tallest men his country do afford. Every night upon the 4 quarters of his house are 4 sentinels drawn forth, each standing from other a flight shot, and at every half hour one from the *corps du guard* doth hollo, unto whom every sentinel returns answer round from his stand. If any fail, an officer is presently sent forth that beateth him extremely.

The word *weroance,* which we call and conster for a king, is a common word whereby they call all commanders, for they have but few words in their language and but few occasions to use any officers more than one commander, which commonly they call weroance.

It is strange to see with what great fear and adoration all these people do obey this Powhatan, for at his feet they present whatsoever he commandeth, and at the least frown of his brow their greatest will tremble. It may be because he is very terrible and inexorable in punishing such as offend him. For example, he caused certain malefactors—at what time Captain Smith was prisoner with them, and to the sight whereof Captain Smith for some purpose was brought—to be bound hand and foot, when certain officers appointed thereunto, having from many fires gathered great store of burning coals round in the form of a cockpit, and in the midst they cast the offenders to broil to death. Sometimes he causeth the heads of them that offend to be laid upon the altar, or sacrificing stone, and one or two with clubs beat out their brains. When he would punish any notorious enemy or trespasser he causeth him to be tied unto a tree, and with mussel shells or reeds the executioner cutteth off his joints one after another, ever casting what is cut off into the fire. Then doth he proceed with shells and reeds to case the skin from his head and face, after which they rip up his belly, tear out his bowels, and so burn him with the tree and all. Thus themselves reported that they executed an Englishman, one George Cawson, whom the women enticed up from the barge unto their houses at a place called Appocant. Howbeit his ordinary correction is to have an offender whom he will only punish and not put to death to be beaten with cudgels as the Turks do. We have seen a man kneeling on his knees and at Powhatan's command two men have beat him on the bare skin till the skin hath been all bollen [swollen] and blistered, and all on a gore blood, and till he hath fallen senseless in a sound [swoon], and yet never cried, complained, nor seemed to ask pardon, for that they seldom do.

And sure it is to be wond'red at how such a barbarous and uncivil prince should take into him (adorned and set forth with no greater ornament and munificence) a form and ostentation of such majesty as he expresseth, which oftentimes strikes awe and sufficient wonder into our people presenting themselves before him. But such is (I believe) the impression of the divine nature. And howsoever these as other heathens forsaken by the true light have not that portion of the knowing, blessed Christian spirit, yet I am persuaded there is an infused kind of divineness, and extraordinary—appointed that it shall be so by the King of Kings—to such who are his immediate instruments on earth, how wretched soever otherwise under the course of misbelief and infidelity,[1] as it is in the psalm, *Dixi vos sicut Dii estis*[2]—to govern and dwell in the eyes and countenances of princes, somewhat may this catagraph, or portraiture, following serve to express the presentment of this Great King Powhatan.

[blank half page][3]

According to the order and custom of sensual heathenism in the allowance of polygamy, he may have as many women as he will, and

---

[1] "There's such divinity doth hedge a king." (HAMLET 4.5.122) Powhatan was simply overwhelming, and Strachey is struggling to discover how a naked heathen can project such presence when, for example, King James in all his Christian, courtly pomp is so little and drab. Strachey likely met Powhatan in company with either Gates or Dale, since his traveling seems to be to the extent he accompanied his bosses. Apparently the emperor cut a splendid figure compared to them too.

[2] "I have said ye are gods." (Latin) Psalm 82:6.

[3] No illustration was included in Strachey's manuscript. An artist and engraver would have been hired once the MS found a patron. The only thing we know of at this time even remotely approaching a likeness of Powhatan is the crude engraving on Capt. John Smith's map of Virginia. And there, in fact, we see him surrounded by his women, as described below. Strachey may have had in mind nothing more than using this.

hath (as is supposed) many one more than one hundred, all which he doth not keep as the Turk in one *saraglia,* or house, but hath an appointed number which reside still in every their several places, amongst whom when he lieth on his bed one sitteth on his head and another at his feet. But when he sitteth at meat, or in presenting himself to any strangers, one sitteth on his right hand and another on his left, as is here expressed.

[blank half page][1]

Of his women there are said to be about some dozen at this present in whose company he takes more delight than in the rest, being for the most part very young women. And these commonly remove with him from house to house either in his time of hunting or visitation of his several houses. I obtained their names from one Kempes, an Indian who died the last year of the scurvy at James Town after he had dwelt with us almost one whole year, much made of by our lord general; and who could speak a pretty deal of our English, and came orderly to church every day to prayers, and observed with us the keeping of the Sabbath both by ceasing from labor and repairing to church. The names of the women I have not thought altogether amiss to set down as he gave them unto me and as they stood foremost in his king's affection. For they observe certain degrees of greatness according to the nearness they stand in their prince's love and amorous entertainment.

Winganuske	Attossocomisk	Ortoughnoiske
Ashetoiske	Ponnoiske	Oweroughwough
Amopotoiske	Appomosiscut	Ottermiske
Ottopomtacke	Appimmonoiske	Memeoughquiske

He was reported by the said Kemps—as also by the Indian Machumps, who was sometime in England and comes to and fro amongst us as he dares and as Powhatan gives him leave, for it is not otherwise safe for him, no more than it was for one Amarice who

[1] See note above.

had his brains knock'd out for selling but a basket of corn and lying in the English fort 2 or 3 days without Powhatan's leave—I say they often reported unto us that Powhatan had then living 20 sons and 20 daughters beside a young one by Winganuske, Machumps his sister and a great darling of the king's, and besides young Pocohunta, a daughter of his using sometimes to our fort in times past, now married to a private captain called Kocoum some two years since.

As he is weary of his women he bestoweth them on those that best deserve them at his hands. When he dineth or suppeth, one of his women before and after meat bringeth him water in a wooden platter to wash his hands, another waiting with a bunch of feathers to wipe them instead of a towel, and the feathers, when he hath wiped, are washed and dried again.

A mile from Orapaks in a thicket of wood he hath a principal house in which he keepeth his kind of treasure, as skins, copper, pearl, and beads, which he storeth up against the time of his death and burial. Here is also his store of red paint for ointment, and bows and arrows. This house is 50 or 60 yards in length, frequented only by priests; at the four corners of this house stand 4 images, not as Atlantes or Telamones, supporters to bear up pillars, posts, or somewhat else in the stately building, nor as in the ancient times the images and pedigrees of the whole stock or family were wont to be set in porches, or the first entrance into houses, with a porter of special trust, who had the charge of keeping and looking unto them, called *atrienses;* but these are merely set as careful sentinels (forsooth) to defend and protect the house, for so they believe of them. One is like a dragon, another like a bear, the third like a leopard, and the fourth a giant-like man, all made evil-favored enough according to their best workmanship.

Caput 4.

A catalog of the several petty weroaunces, or princes, under the government of Powhaton, their names now at this present, and what forces they are able to raise for the wars.

THE GREAT KING POWHATAN hath divided his country into many provinces, or shires, as it were, and over every one placed a several absolute commander, or weroance, to him contributory, to govern the people there to inhabit. And his petty weroances in all may be in number about 3 or 4 and thirty, all which have their precincts and bounds proper and commodiously appointed out, that no one intrude upon the other of several forces. And for the ground wherein each one soweth his corn, plants his *apoke* and garden fruits, he tithes to the great king of all the commodities growing in the same, or of what else his shire brings forth appertaining to the land or rivers—corn, beasts, pearl, fowl, fish, hides, furs, copper, beads—by what means soever obtained, a peremptory rate set down as shall be mentioned in the 6th chapter. Nor have I thought it altogether amiss to remember here and offer to consideration for all after occasions a cathalog of the several weroances' names, with the denomination of the particular shire, as aforesaid, wherein they govern, together with what forces for the present they are able to send unto the wars:

UPON POWHATAN, OR THE KINGS, RIVER ARE SEATED AS FOLLOWETH:

1. Parahunt, one of Powhant's sons, whom we therefore call *Tanxpowhatan,* which is as much [as] to say "little Powhatan"; and is weroance of the country which hath his own name called Powhatan, lying (as is before mentioned) close under the Falls bordering the Monacans; and he may at the present be furnished with 50 fighting and ready men.
2. Ashuaquid, weroance of Arahateck—60 men.
3. Coquonasum, weroance of Appamatuck—100 men.

4. Opussoquonuske,[1] sister to Coquonasum, a *weroancqua* [werowansqua], or "queen," of a little *mussaran,* or "small village," of Appamatuck, not unlike an ancient *episcata villatica* [?]—and she was of power to have spared upon command some 20 able fighting men, howbeit her town we burnt and killed some of her people (herself miscarrying with small shot in pursuit in the woods in winter, 1610) for a treacherous massacre which she practiced upon 14 of our men, whom she caused her people to invite up into her town to feast and make merry, entreating our men beforehand to leave their arms in their boat because they said how their women would be afraid else of their pieces.

5. Kaquothocum, weroance of Weanock—100 men.

6. Ohoroquoh, another petty weroance in the province of Weanock called Cecocomake, upon a by-river to the southward of Weanock—50 men.

7. Oholasc, queen of Coiacohhanauke, which [town] we commonly though corruptly call Tapahanock, and is the same which Captain Smith in his map calls Quiyoughcohanock, on the south shore, or Salisbury side; whose son being yet young shall be by Powhatan's appointment weroance of the said Quiyoughcohanock; his name is Tatahcoope. The weroance Pepiscunimah, whom by construction as well the Indians as we call "Pipisco," was sometime possessed in right of this part as by birth and possession descended the true and lawful weroance of the same. But upon a displeasure which Powhatan conceived against him, in that the said Pipisco—and that not many years since—had stolen away a chief woman from Opechankeno, one of Powhatan's brothers, he was departed from that regiment [kingship], and the foresaid Tatacoope, a supposed son of Powhatan's by this said Queen Oholasc, [was] made weroance; who being yet young, as is said, is for the most part in the government of Chopoke at Chawopo, one of Pipiscoe's brothers. Yet is Pipisco suff'red to retain in this his country a little small *kaason,* or "village," upon the rivage of the stream with some few people about him, keeping the said woman still, whom he makes his best beloved. And she travels with him upon any remove in hunting time or in his

[1] "Opossunoquonuske" in the Percy MS.

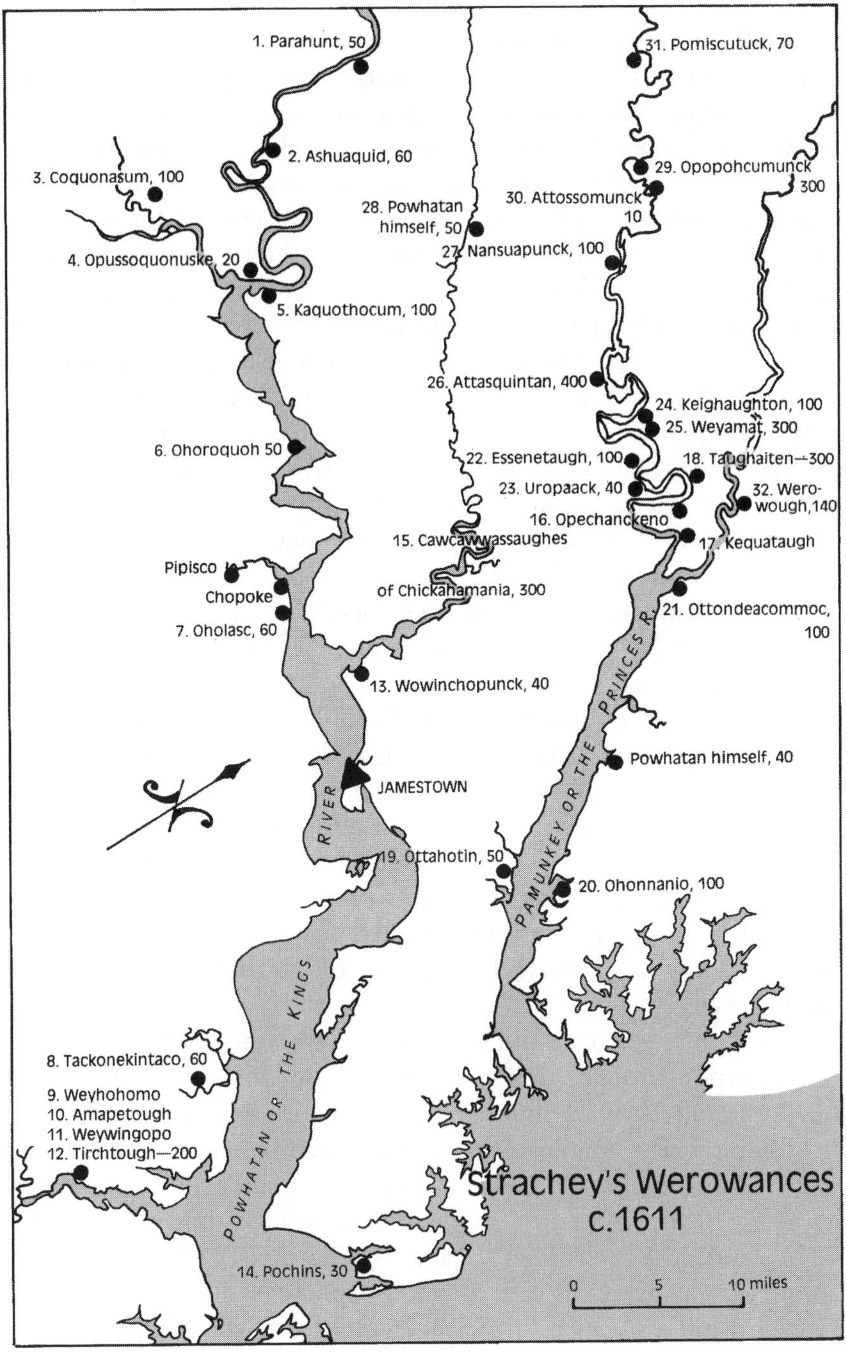
1. Parahunt, 50
2. Ashuaquid, 60
3. Coquonasum, 100
4. Opussoquonuske, 20
5. Kaquothocum, 100
6. Ohoroquoh 50
Pipisco
Chopoke
7. Oholasc, 60
8. Tackonekintaco, 60
9. Weyhohomo
10. Amapetough
11. Weywingopo
12. Tirchtough—200
13. Wowinchopunck, 40
14. Pochins, 30
15. Cawcawwassaughes
of Chickahamania, 300
16. Opechanckeno
17. Kequataugh
18. Taughaiten—300
19. Ottahotin, 50
20. Ohonnanio, 100
21. Ottondeacommoc, 100
22. Essenetaugh, 100
23. Uropaack, 40
24. Keighaughton, 100
25. Weyamat, 300
26. Attasquintan, 400
27. Nansuapunck, 100
28. Powhatan himself, 50
29. Opopohcumunck 300
30. Attossomunck 10
31. Pomiscutuck, 70
32. Wero-wough,140
Powhatan himself, 40
JAMESTOWN
POWHATAN OR THE KINGS RIVER
PAMUNKEY OR THE PRINCES R.
Strachey's Werowances
c.1611
0 5 10 miles

visitation of us, by which means twice or thrice in a summer she hath come unto our town. Nor is so handsome a savage woman as I have seen amongest them, yet with a kind of pride can take upon her a show of greatness. For we have seen her forbear to come out of her *quintan,* or "boat," through the water, as the other both maids and married women usually do, unless she were carried forth between two of her servants. I was once early at her house (it being summer-time) when she was laid without doors under the shadow of a broad-leav'd tree upon a pallet of osiers spread over with 4 or 5 fine gray mats, herself covered with a fair white dress'd deerskin or two. And when she rose she had a maid who fetch'd her a frontal of white coral, and pendants of great but imperfect colored and worse drilled pearls, which she put into her ears, and a chain of long links of copper *tapaantaminais,* and which came twice or thrice double about her neck, and they account a jolly ornament. And sure thus attired with some variety of feathers and flowers stuck in their hairs, they seem as debonair, quaint, and well pleased as, I wis, a daughter of the House of Austria behung with all her jewels. Likewise her maid fetch'd her a mantel, which they call *puttawus,* which is like a side cloak, made of blue feathers so artificially and thick sewed together that it shows like a deep purple satin and is very smooth and sleek. And after she brought her water for her hands, and then a branch or two of fresh green ashen leaves as for a tower [towel] to dry them. I offend in this digression the willinger since these were ceremonies which I did little look for, carrying so much presentment of civility, and which are not ordinarily performed to any other amongest them. And the Quiyoughcohanocks may be able to make for the wars 60 fighting men.

8. Tackonekintaco, an old weroance of Warrascoyack, whom Captain Newport brought prisoner with his son Tangoit about 1610 to our lord general, lying then at Point Comfort, and whom again His Lordship released upon promises and a solemn contract made by the old man to exchange with His Lordship, after he should have gathered in his harvest in August following, 500 bushels of wheat, beans, and peas for copper, beads, and hatchets; and for the better color carrying away his son, he left a nephew, as he said, of his with His Lordship as a pawn, or hostage, until the performance. Howbeit

the imposture nephew, privy beforehand to the falsehood of the old man, watched his opportunity, leapt overboard one night, being kept in the *De la warr,* and to be more sure of him at that time fettered both legs together and a sea gown upon him. Yet he adventured to get clear by swimming, and either to recover the south shore or to sink in the attempt. Which of either was his fortune we know not, only if he miscarried we never found his body nor gown. And the Indians of Warraskoiack would oftentimes afterwards mock us and call to us for him, and at length make a great laughter and tell us he was come home. How true or false is no great matter. But indeed the old king after that time refused to perform the former bargain, for which His Lordship, to give them to understand how he would not be so dealt withal, sent forth 2 companies the—— of—— : His Lordship's own company under the command of Captain Brewster, and some seamen under Captain Argoll, who fell upon two towns of his and burnt them to the ground with all their goodly furniture of mats and dishes, wooden pots and platters. For of this sort is all their goodly *epitrapezia,* or vessels belonging to their use for the table or what else. And these Warraskoyocks may make 60 men.

9. Weyhohomo, a great weroance of Nansamund.

10. Amapetough, another less weroance of Nansamund.

11. Weywingopo, a third weroance of Nansamund.

12. Tirchtough, a fourth weroance of Nansamund. And these four together may make of sturdy and bold savages 200.

13. Wowinchopunck, weroance of Paspahegh, whom the 9 of February 1610, whilst he with a company of his people were attempting some practice upon our old blockhouse at James town, and had been for the same skulking about there some 2 or 3 days and nights, Captain George Percey, governor of the town, sent forth Ensign Powell and Ensign Waller to make surprise of him, if they could possible, and bring him alive into the town. But they not finding him at any such advantage, yet loth to lose him or let him escape altogether, set upon him—he being one of the mightiest and strongest savages that Powhatan had under him, and was therefore one of his champions, and one who had killed treacherously many of our men as he could beguile them, or as he at any time found them by chance single in the woods strayed beyond the command of the blockhouse

—and Powell running upon him thrust him twice though the body with an arming sword, howbeit his people came in so fast and shot their arrows so thick as our men being unarmed in their doublet and hose only, and without pieces, were fain to retire whilst the Indians recovered the weroance's body and carried it away with a mighty quickness and speed of foot, and with a horrible yell and howling. Howbeit the lieutenant of the blockhouse, one Puttock, followed hard and overreached one of the *cronockoes,* or "chief men," and closing with him overthrew him and with his dagger sent him to accompany his master in the other world.[1] And the Paspaheighes may make in number for the wars 40.

14. Pochins, one of Powhatan's sons at Kecoughtan, and was the young weroance there at the same time when Sir Thomas Gates, lieutenant general, took possession of it. It is an ample and fair country indeed, an admirable portion of land comparatively high, wholesome, and fruitful, the seat sometimes of a thousand Indians and three hundred Indian houses, and those Indians, as it may appear, better husbands [farmers] than in any part else that we have observed; which is the reason that so much ground is there cleared and open, enough with little labor already prepared to receive corn or make vineyards of two or three thousand acres, and where beside we find many fruit trees, a kind of gooseberry, cherries and other plums, the *maricock* apple, and many pretty copses, or bosks, as it were, of mulberry trees; and is indeed a delicate and necessary seat for a city, or chief fortification, being so near (within 3 miles by water) the mouth of our bay; and is well appointed a fit seat for one of our chief commanders, since Point Comfort being (out of our dispute) to be fortified to secure our towns above, to keep open the mouth of our river by which our shipping may be let in. It will require the faith and judgment of a worthy commander to be there always present, besides there will be good fishing. And upon one of the capes may be placed a garrison to attend the furnaces and boiling pots for the making of salt, which without question there as in the Bermudas may be made for all occasions to serve the colony and the fishing voyages for the same. Likewise upon Point Comfort a great quantity of one

---

[1] cf. Percy's version, §31–512, 513.

kind of silk grass grows there, as yet disorderly, which having the ground prepared and fitted for it would retribute a commodity worthy the pains, if not going beyond the expectation of the good which is hoped of it. Our lord general and lieutenant general have erected there 2 forts as is before rememb'red, the one called Fort Henry, the other Charles Fort, as the river which runs in and serves both His Lordship hath called Southampton River. Upon the death of an old weroance of this place some 15 or 16 years since, being too powerful neighbors to side the great Powhatan, it is said Powhatan taking the advantage subtly stepped in and conquered the people, killing the chief and most of them. And the reserved he transported over the river, craftily changing their seat and quartering them amongst his own people, until now at length the remain of those living have with much suit obtained of him Payankatank, which he not long since (as you have heard likewise) dispeopled. They might have made of able men for the wars 30.

15. Upon the River of Chickahamania, some 8 or 12 miles from James town, which falls from the north side unto our Kings River, are the Chechaham*in*ias, being a warlike and free people, albeit they pay certain duties to Powhatan, and for copper will be waged to serve and help him in his wars; yet they will not admit of any weroance from him to govern over them, but suffer themselves to be regulated and guided by their priests with the assistance of their elders, whom they call *cawcawwassaughes*—and they may make 300 men.

UPON PAMUNKEY, OR THE PRINCES RIVER:

16. Opechanckeno 17. Kequataugh 18. Taughaiten—all three Powhatan's brethren and are the *triumviri,* as it were, or "3 kings," of a country called Opechanckeno upon the head of Pamunkey River, and these may make 300 men.

19. Ottahotin, weroance of Kiskiack—50.

At Werowocomoco Powhatan himself hath a principal residence, and there may be of able men 40.

20. Ohonnanio, weroance of Cantaunkack—100.
21. Ottondeacommoc, wer. of Mummapacun—100.
22. Essenetaugh, wer. of Pataunck—100.
23. Uropaack, wer. of Ochahannauke—40.
24. Keighaughton, wer. of Cassapecock—100.
25. Weyamat, wero. of Kaposepock—300.
26. Attasquintan, wer. of Pamareke—400.
27. Nansuapunck, wero. of Shamapa—100.
28. At Orapaks, Powhatan himself commands with 50.
29. Opopohcumunck, wero. of Chepeco—300.
30. Attossomunck, a tanx weroance of Paraconos—10.
31. Pomiscutuck, weroance of Youghtamund—70.
32. Werowough, wero. of Mattapanient—140.

And thus it may appear how they are a people who have their several divisions, provinces, and princes to live in and to command over, and do differ likewise as amongest Christians both in stature, language, and condition, some being great people, as the Sasquesahanoughes, some very little, as the Wighcocomocos, some speaking likewise more articulate and plain, and some more inward and hollow, as is before rememb'red, some courteous and more civil, others cruel and bloody, Powhatan having large territories and many petty kings under him; as some have fewer.

Caput 5.

Of the color, fashion, and form of the people. Of their painting and anointing their bodies. Their dispositions, etc.

THEY ARE GENERALLY OF COLOR BROWN, or rather tawny, which they cast themselves into with a kind of arsenic stone like red patise or orpiment, or rather red-tempered ointments of earth and the juice of certed [certain] scruzed[1] roots, when they come unto certain years. And this they do, keeping themselves still so smudged and besmeared, either for the custom of the country or the better to defend them, since they go most what naked, from the stinging of mosquitoes—kinds of flies or biting gnats such as the Greeks called *scynipes,* as yet in great swarms within the Arches[2]—and which here breed abundantly among the marish whorts and fenberries.[3] And of the same hue are their women, howbeit it is supposed neither of them naturally born so discolored, for Captain Smith living sometime amongst them affirmeth how they are from the womb indifferent white, but as the men so do the women dye and disguise themselves into this tawny color, esteeming it the best beauty to be nearest such a kind of murrey as a sodden quince is of, to liken it to the nearest color I can, for which they daily anoint both face and bodies all over with such a kind of fucus, or unguent, as can cast them into that stain—as is said of the Greek women how they colored their faces with certain roots called *brenthina,* and as the Britons dyed themselves red with woad. Howbeit he or she that hath obtained the perfectest art in the tempering of this color with any better kind of earth, herb, or root preserves it not yet so secret and precious unto herself as do our great ladies their oil of talcum or other painting white and red, but they friendly communicate the secret and teach it one another. After their anointing, which is daily, they dry them in the sun, and thereby make their skins, beside the color, more black

---

[1] Squeezed.

[2] The archipelagoes of the Aegean.

[3] Cranberries.

and spotted, which the sun kissing oft and hard adds to their painting the more rough and rugged.

Their heads and shoulders they paint oftentimes, and those red with the root *pochone* brayed to powder mixed with oil of the walnut or bear's grease. This they hold in summer doth check the heat and in winter arms them in some measure against the cold. Many other forms of paintings they use, but he is the most gallant who is the most monstrous and ugly to behold.

Their hair is black, gross, long, and thick. The men have no beards. Their noses are broad, flat, and full at the end; great big lips and wide mouths, yet nothing so unsightly as the Moors. They are generally tall of stature and straight, of comely proportion. And the women have handsome limbs, slender arms, and pretty hands; and when they sing they have a delightful and pleasant tang in their voices.

For their apparel they are sometimes covered with the skins of wild beasts, which in winter are dressed with the hair, but in summer without. The better sort use large mantles of deerskins not much differing from the Irish *falings,* some embroidered with white beads, some with copper, other painted after their manner. But the common sort have scarce wherewithal to cover their nakedness, but stick long-bladed grass, the leaves of trees, or suchlike under broad baldrics of leather, which covers them behind and before.

The better sort of women cover them for the most part all over with skin mantles finely dress'd, shagged and fringed at the skirt, carved and colored, with some pretty work or the proportion of beasts, fowl, tortoises, or other suchlike imagery, as shall best please or express the fancy of the wearer. Their younger women go not shadowed amongst their own company until they be nigh 11 or 12 returns of the leaf old—for so they account and bring about the year, calling the fall of the leaf *taquitock*—nor are they much ashamed thereof, and therefore would the before-rememb'red Pochahuntas, a well-featured but wanton young girl, Powhatan's daughter, sometimes resorting to our fort, of the age then of 11 or 12 years, get the boys forth with her into the marketplace and make them wheel falling on their hands, turning their heels upwards, whom she would follow and wheel so herself naked as she was all the fort over. But being past once 12 years, they put on a kind of *semicinctum* leath'ren apron, as do our artificers or handicraftsmen, before their bellies and are very shamefast to be seen bare. We have seen some use mantles made both of turkey feathers and other fowl so prettily wrought and woven with threads that nothing could be discerned but the feathers, which were exceeding [warm] and very handsome. *Nuda mulier erat pulchra,* saith Plautus, *quam purpurata pulchrior?*[1]—indeed the ornament of that sex, who receive an addition of delicacy by their garments. True it is sometimes in cold weather, or when they go a-hunting or seeking the fruits of the woods, or gathering bents for their mats, both men and women to defend them from the bushes and shrubs put on a kind of leather breeches and stockings, all fastened together made of deerskins, which they tie and wrap about the loins after the fashion of the Turk's or Irish trouses.

They adorn themselves most with copper beads and painting. Of the men there be some who will paint their bodies black and some yellow, and being oiled over they will stick therein the soft down of sundry colored birds: of blue birds, white heronshews, and the feathers of the carnation bird, which they call *ashhowcutteis*—as if so many varieties of laces were stitched to their skins, which makes a wondrous show. The men being angry and prepared to fight paint and cross their foreheads, cheeks, and the right side of their heads diversly either with terra sigillata or with their root *pochone.*

The women have their arms, breasts, thighs, shoulders, and faces cunningly embroidered with divers works for [from] pouncing or searing their skins with a kind of instrument heated in the fire. They figure therein flowers and fruits of sundry lively kinds, as also snakes, serpents, efts, etc. And this they do by dropping upon the seared flesh sundry colors which rub'd into the stamp will never be taken away again because it will not only be dried into the flesh but grow therein.

The men shave their hair on the right side very close, keeping a ridge commonly on the top or crown like a coxcomb, for their women with two shells will grate away the hair into any fashion they please. On the left side they wear their hair at full length with a lock

[1] "A pretty woman will be [erit] prettier naked than dressed in purple." (Latin: his *Mostellaria* 289, where the statement is not a question.)

of an ell long, which they anoint often with walnut oil, whereby it is very sleek and shines like a raven's wing. Sometimes they tie up their lock with an artificial and well-labored knot—just in the same fashion as I have seen the *carrazzaies* of Scio and Pera[1]—stuck with many colored gewgaws, as the cast head or brow-antle of a deer, the hand of their enemy dried, croisettes of bright and shining copper like the new moon. Many wear the whole skin of a hawk stuffed with the wings abroad, and buzzards' or other fowls' whole wings. And to the feathers they will fasten a little rattle about the bigness of a the [sic] chape of a rapier, which they take from the tail of a snake, and sometimes divers kinds of shells hanging loose by small purfleets[2] or threads, that being shaken as they move they might make a certain murmuring, or whistling noise, by gathering wind, in which they seem to take great jollity and hold it a kind of bravery.[3]

Their ears they bore with wide holes commonly two or three, and in the same they do hang chains of stained pearl, bracelets of white bone, or shreds of copper beaten thin and bright and wound up hollow, and with a great pride certain fowls' legs, eagles, hawks, turkeys, etc., with beasts' claws, bears, *arrahacounes*, squirrels, etc. The claws thrust through they let hang upon the cheek to the full view. And some of their men there be who will wear in these holes a small green and yellow-colored, live snake near half a yard in length, which crawling and lapping himself about his neck oftentimes familiarly he suffers to kiss his lips. Others wear a dead rat tied by the tail, and suchlike conundrums.

The women are in themselves so modest as in the time of their sickness they have great care to be seen abroad,[4] at what time they go apart and keep from the men in a several room, which they have for themselves as a kind of *gynaeceum*[5]; nor will the men at such a time press into the nursery where they are.

The men are very strong, of able bodies and full of agility, accustoming themselves to endure hardness, to lie in the woods under a

---

[1] "Girls," that is, of etc. in the Aegean.
[2] Purfles, borders.
[3] Finery.
[4] Modern English would say "great care *not* to be seen."
[5] "Women's quarters" (Greek).

tree by a small fire in the worst of winter in frost and snow, or in the weeds and grass as in ambuscado to accomplish their purposes in the summer.

They are inconstant in everything but what fear constraineth them to keep—crafty, timorous, quick of apprehension, ingenious enough in their own works as may testify their weirs in which they take their fish, which are certain enclosures made of reeds and framed in the fashion of a labyrinth, or maze, set a fathom deep in the water with divers chambers or beds, out of which the entangled fish cannot return or get out being once in, well may a great one by chance break the reeds and so escape. Otherwise he remains a prey to the fisherman the next low water, which they fish with a net tied at the end of a pole. As likewise may speak for them their nets, their artificial dressing of leather, their cordage which they make of their natural hemp and flax, together with their cunning dressing of that, and preserving the whole year great litches, or bundles, of the same to be used upon any occasion; and of their girdles which they make of silk grass, much like St. Francis' cordon[1]; their cloaks of feathers, their bows and bowstrings, their arrows, their crownets which their weroances wear, and their queen's *fasciae crinales* [2] (borders, or frontals, of white beads, coral, and copper); especially their boats, which they call *quintans* and are very shapeful, made of one piece of timber like the ancient *monoxylum navigium*[3]; their mats and all their household implements and suchlike.

Some of them are of disposition fearful (as I said) and not easily wrought therefore to trust us or come unto our forts. Others again of them are so bold and audacious as they dare come into our forts, truck and trade with us, and look us in the face crying "All friends!" when they have but new done us a mischief and when they intend presently again if it lie in their power to do the like. They are generally covetous of our commodities, as copper, white beads for their women, hatchets, of which we make them poor ones of iron,

---

1 "The girdle used by the monks of the Franciscan order is of twisted cord, and knotted." (Major)

2 Hair bands. (Wright & Freund)

3 "Single-log vessel" (Greco-Latin) found at all times the world over. Why didn't the English build them?

hoes to pare their corn ground, knives, and suchlike.

They are soon moved to anger, and so malicious that they seldom forget an injury. They are very thievish and will as closely as they can convey anything away from us, howbeit they seldom steal one from another, lest their conjurers should reveal it, and so they be pursued and punished. That they are thus feared it is certain; nor let any man doubt but that the devil cannot reveal an offense actually committed.

Caput 6.

Of their houses, exercises, fowling, hunting, and fishing. Of their entertainment of strangers, and their music.

ALTHOUGH THE COUNTRY PEOPLE be very barbarous, yet have they amongst them such government as that their magistrates for good commanding and their people for due subjection and obeying excel many places that would be counted civil. The form of their commonwealth, by what hath been already delivered, you may well gather to be a monarchal government, where one as emperor ruleth over many kings. Their chief ruler likewise for the present you have heard before how named and from whence, as also you have heard the number of his weroances, their forces, and his own description. You shall now understand how his kingdom descendeth not to his sons nor children but first to his brethren, whereof he hath (as you have heard) three; and after their decease to his sisters: first to the eldest sister, then to the rest, and after them to the heirs male and female of the eldest sister—but never to the heirs of the male.

[Neither] he nor any of his people understand how to express their minds by any kinds of letters to write and read in barks of trees or any other kind of way, which necessity or invention might have instructed them in, as do other barbarians and some even in these new discoveries. Nor have they positive laws; only the law whereby he ruleth is custom. Yet when he pleaseth his will is a law and must be obeyed, not only as a king but as half a god, his people esteem him so. His inferior kings are tied likewise to rule by like customs, and have permitted them power of life and death over their people as their command in that nature.

Their habitations, or towns, are for the most part by the rivers or not far distant from fresh springs, commonly upon the rise of a hill, that they may overlook the river and take every small thing into view which stirs upon the same. Their houses are not many in one town, and those that are stand dissite and scattered, without form of a street, far and wide asunder.

As for their houses, who knoweth one of them knoweth them all, even the chief king's house itself, for they be all alike builded one to another: They are like garden arbors, at best like our shepherd's cottages, made yet handsomely enough, though without strength or gains [mortises?], [and] of such young plants as they can pluck up, bow, and make the green tops meet together in fashion like a round roof, which they thatch with mats thrown over. The walls are made with barks of trees, but then those be principal houses, for so many barks which go to the making up of a house are long time of purchasing. In the midst of the house there is a louver out of which the smoke issueth, the fire being kept right under. Every house commonly hath two doors, one before and a postern; the doors be hung with mats, never locked nor bolted, but only those mats be to turn up or let fall at pleasure. And their houses are commonly so placed under covert of trees that the violence of foul weather, snow or rain cannot assault them, nor the sun in summer annoy them. And the roof being covered, as I say, the wind is easily kept out, insomuch as they are as warm as stoves, albeit very smoky. Windows they have none, but the light comes in at the door and at the louver. For should they have broad and open windows in the quarters of their houses, they knew not well how upon any occasion to make them close and to let in the light too, for glass they know not—though the country wants not salsodiac enough to make glass of, and of which we have made some store in a goodly house set up for the same purpose, with all offices and furnaces thereto belonging, a little without the island where James town stands—nor have they linen cloth, albeit they want not neither naturally the materials for that, paper, or suchlike to dip in oil to convey in as a diaphanic body the light, or to keep out the weather.

By their houses they have sometimes a scene, or high stage, raised like a scaffold, of small spelts,[1] reeds, or dried osiers, covered with mats, which both gives a shadow and is a shelter, and serves for such a covered place where men used in old time to sit and talk for recreation and pleasure, which they called *praestega,*[2] and where on a loft of hurdles they lay forth their corn and fish to dry. They eat, sleep, and dress their meat all under one roof and in one chamber, as it were.

Round about the house on both sides are their bedsteads, which are thick short posts stak'd into the ground, a foot high and somewhat more, and for the sides small poles laid along with a hurdle of reeds cast over, whereon they roll down a fine white mat or two as for a bed when they go to sleep, and the which they roll up again in the morning when they rise, as we do our pallets. And upon these round about the house they lie, heads and points one by the other, especially making a fire before them in the midst of the house, as they do usually every night. And some one of them by agreement maintains the fire for all that night long. Some of them when they lie down to sleep cover them with mats, some with skins, and some lie stark naked on the ground from six to twenty in a house, as do the Irish.

About their houses they have commonly square plots of cleared ground which serve them for gardens, some 100, some 200 foot square, wherein they sow their tobacco, pumpions, and a fruit like unto a muskmillion (but less and worse) which they call *macocks;* gourds and suchlike, which fruits increase exceedingly and ripen in the beginning of July and continue until September. They plant also the field apple, the *maracock*—a wild fruit like a kind of pomegranate, which increaseth infinitely and ripens in August, continuing unto the end of October when all the other fruits be gathered. But they sow neither herb, flower, nor any other kind of fruit.

---

[1] A thin piece of wood.

[2] "Porch roof" (Greco-Latin).

They neither do impale for deer nor breed cattle, nor bring up tame poultry, albeit they have great store of turkeys; nor keep birds, squirrels, nor tame partridges, swan, duck, nor geese. In March and April they live much upon their weirs and feed on fish, turkeys, and squirrels, and then, as also sometimes in May, they plant their fields and set their corn, and live after those months most off acrons, walnuts, chestnuts, *chechinquamins,* and fish. But to mend their diet, some disperse themselves in small companies and live upon such beasts as they can kill with their bow and arrows, [and] upon crabs, oysters, land tortoises, strawberries, mulberries, and suchlike. In June, July, and August they feed upon the roots of *tockohow* berries, groundnuts, fish, and green wheat,[1] and sometime upon a kind of serpent, or great snake, of which our people likewise use to eat.

It is strange to see how their bodies alter with their diet: Even as the deer and wild beasts they seem fat and lean, strong and weak. Powhatan and some others that are provident roast their fish and flesh upon hurdles and reserve of the same until the scarce times. Commonly their fish and flesh they boil either very tenderly or broil it long on hurdles over the fire; or else after the Spanish fashion putting it on a spit they turn first the one side, then the other, till it be as dry as their jerkin beef in the West Indies; and so they may keep it a month or more without putrefying. The broth of fish or flesh they sup up as ordinarily as they eat the meat.

Their corn they eat in the ears green [or] roasted; and sometimes bruised in a mortar of wood with a like pestle they lap it in rolls within the leaves of the corn, and so boil it for a dainty. They also reserve that corn late planted, that will not ripe, by roasting it in hot ashes, the which in winter, being boiled with beans, they esteem for a rare dish, calling it *Pausarowmena.* Their old wheat they first steep a night in hot water, and in the morning, pounding it in a mortar, they use a small basket for the bolter or searser[2]; and when they have sifted forth the finest they pound again the great, and so separating it by dashing their hand in the basket, receive the flour in a platter of wood; which blending with water, they make into flat broad cakes

[1] Corn on the cob.
[2] Sifter and sieve.

much like the sacrificing bread which the Grecians off'red to their gods, called *popanum*, and these they call *appones;* which covering with ashes till they be baked, as was the ancient *escharites panis*[1] raked within the embers; and then washing them in fair water, they let dry with their own heat, or else boil them with water, eating the broth with the bread, which they call *ponepope.*[2] The grouts and broken pieces of the corn remaining they likewise reserve, and by fanning away the bran, or husks, in a platter or in the wind, they let boil in an earthen pot three or four hours, and thereof make a strange thick pottage which they call *usketehamun*, and is their kind of furmentry [frumenty], and indeed is like our ptisan (husked barley sodden in water). It may be not much unlike that homely *ius nigrum* which the Lacedemonians used to eat, and which Dionysius could not abide to taste of, albeit he bought a cook from thence only to make him that broth, for which the cook told him he must have a Lacedemonian stomach indeed to eat of the Lacedemonian diet.[3] And some of them more thrifty than cleanly do burn the core of the ear to powder, which they call *punguough,* mingling that in their meal, but it never tasted well in bread or broth.

Their drink is as the Turk's—clear water. For albeit they have grapes, and those good store, yet they have not fall'n upon the use of them nor advised how to press them into wine. Pears and apples they have none to make cider or perry of, nor honey to make meath, nor licorice to seethe in their water. They call all things that have a spicy taste *wassacan*, which leaves a supposition that they may have some kind of spice trees, though not perhaps such as elsewhere.

The men bestow their times in fishing, hunting, wars, and such man-like exercises without the doors, scorning to be seen in any effeminate labor, which is the cause that the women be very painful and the men often idle.

Their fishing is much in boats; these they call *quintans,* as the West Indians call their canoas. They make them with one tree by burning and scraping away the coals with stones and shells till they have

---

[1] "Hearth bread" (Greco-Latin).
[2] Written "ponap" in Smith's *Map.*
[3] "The black broth or soup made of hare's blood and entrails, favored by the Spartans." (Wright & Freund)

made them in form of a trough. Some of them are an ell deep and 40 or 50 foot in length; and some will transport 40 men, but the most ordinary are smaller and will ferry 10 or 20 with some luggage over their broadest rivers. Instead of oars they use paddles and sticks with which they will row faster than we in our barges.

They have nets for fishing, for the quantity as formally braided and meshed as ours; and these are made of barks of certain trees, deer sinews, for [or?] a kind of grass which they call *pemmenaw*, of which their women between their hands and thighs spin a thread very even and readily. And this thread serveth for many uses, as about their housing, their mantles of feathers, and their trouses; and they make also with it lines for angles.

Their angles are long, small rods, at the end whereof they have a clift to the which the line is fastened; and at the line they hang a hook made either of a bone grated (as they nock their arrows) in the form of a crooked pin or fishhook, or of the splinter of a bone; and with a thread of the line they tie on the bait. They use also long arrows tied in a line, wherewith they shoot at fish in the rivers. Those of Accowmack use staves like unto javelins headed with bone. With these they dart fish swimming in the water. They have also many artificial weirs (before described) in which they take abundance of fish.

In the time of their huntings they leave their habitations and gather themselves into companies as do the Tartars, and go to the most desert places with their families, where they pass the time with hunting and fowling up towards the mountains by the heads of their rivers, where indeed there is plenty of game. For betwixt the rivers the land is not so large below that therein breed sufficient to give them all content, considering especially how at all times and seasons they destroy them. It may seem a marvel how they can so directly pass and wander in these deserts, sometimes three or four days' journeys, meeting with no habitations, and by reason of the woods not having sight of the sun whereby to direct them how to coast it.

Their hunting houses are not so labored, substantial, nor artificial as their other, but are like our soldiers' cabins: the frame set up in 2 or 3 hours, cast overhead with mats, which the women bear after them as they carry likewise corn, acrons, mortars, and all bag and baggage to use when they come to the place where they purpose for the time to hunt.

In the time of hunting every man will strive to do his best to show his fortune and dexterity, for by their excelling therein they obtain the favor of the women.

At their hunting in the deserts they are commonly two or three hundred together. With the sun rising, they call up one another and go forth searching after the herd, which when they have found they environ and circle with many fires; and betwixt the fires they place themselves, and there take up their stands, making the most terrible noise that they can. The deer being thus feared by the fires and their voices betake them to their heels, whom they chase so long within that circle that many times they kill 6, 8, 10, or 15 in a morning. They use also to drive them into some narrow point of land, when they find that advantage, and so force them into the river where with their boats they have ambuscadoes to kill them.

When they have shot a deer by land, they follow him like bloodhounds by the blood and strain, and oftentimes so take him.

Hares, partridges, turkeys—fat and lean, young and old, in eggs, in breeding time, or however—they devour, at no time sparing any that they can catch in their power.

One savage hunting alone useth the skin of a deer slit on the one side and so put upon his arm through the neck, in that sort that the hand comes to the head which is stuffed, and the horns, head, eyes, ears, and every part as artificially counterfeited as they can devise. Thus shrouding his body in the skin, by stalking he approacheth the deer, creeping on the ground from one tree to another. If the deer chance to find fault or stand at gaze, he turneth the head with his hand to the best advantage to win his shoot[1]; having shot him he chaseth him by his blood and strain till he get him.

In these hunting and fishing exercises they take extreme pains. Yet they being their ordinary labors from their infancy, they place them amongest their sports and pleasures, and are very proud to be expert therein. For thereby (as before remembʼred) they win the loves of

---

[1] Smith has: "He turneth the head with his hand to his best advantage to seem like a deer also, gazing and licking himself."

their women, who will be the sooner contented to live with such a man, by the readiness and fortune of whose bow and diligence such provision they perceive they are likely to be fed with well, especially of fish and flesh, as the place wherein they are to dwell can afford. For indeed they be all of them huge eaters, as of whom we may say with Plautus, *Noctes diesque estur,*[1] for which we ourselves do give unto every Indian that labors with us in our forts double allowance of one of our own men; and these active hunters by their continual ranging and travel do know all the advantages and places most frequented and best stored with deer or other beasts, fish, fowl, roots, fruits, and berries.

A kind of exercise they have often amongest them much like that which our boys call bandy in English, and may be an ancient game as it seemeth in Virgil. For when Aeneas came into Italy, at his marriage with Lavinia, King Latinus' daughter, it is said the Trojans taught the Latins skipping and frisking at the ball. Likewise they have the exercise of football, in which yet they only forcibly encounter with the foot to carry the ball the one from the other, and spurn it to the goal with a kind of dexterity and swift footmanship which is the honor of it. But they never strike up one another's heels as we do, not accounting that praiseworthy to purchase a goal by such an advantage.[2]

Dice play, cards, or lots they know not, howbeit they use a game upon rushes much like primero, wherein they card and discard and lay a stake to, and so win and lose. They will play at this for their bows and arrows, their copper, beads, hatchets, and their leather coats.

If any great commander arrive at the habitation of a weroance, they spread a mat, as the Turks do a carpet, for him to sit upon. Upon another right opposite they sit themselves. Then do they all with a tunable voice of shouting bid him welcome. After this do two or more of their chief men make several orations, testifying their love, which they do with such vehemency and so earnestness of passion that they sweat till they drop, and are so out of breath that they

---

[1] "He eats night and day." (Latin: his *Mostellaria* 235)

[2] cf. Spelman §29–495.

can scarce speak, insomuch as a stranger would take them to be exceeding angry or stark mad.

After this verbal entertainment, they cause such victual as they have or can provide to be brought forth, with which they feast him fully and freely. And at night they bring him to the lodging appointed for him, whither upon their departure they send a young woman fresh painted red with *pochone* and oil, to be his bedfellow.

The void time between their sleep and meat they commonly bestow in reveling, dancing, and singing, and in their kind of music, and have sundry instruments for the same: They have a kind of cane on which they pipe as on a recorder and are like the Greek pipes which they called *bombices,* being hardly to be sounded without great straining of the breath, upon which they observe certain rude tunes. But their chief instruments are rattles made of small gourds or pumpion shells. Of these they have bass, tenor, countertenor, mean, and treble. These mingled with their voices, sometimes 20 or 30 together, make such a terrible howling as would rather affright than give pleasure to any man.

They have likewise their *erotica carmina,* or amorous ditties, in their language, some numerous [humorous?] and some not, which they will sing tunable enough. They have contrived a kind of angry song against us in their homely rhymes, which concludeth with a kind of petition unto their Okeus and to all the host of their idols, to plague the *tassantasses,* for so they call us, and their posterities; as likewise another scornful song they made of us the last year at the Falls in manner of triumph at what time they killed Captain William West, our lord general's nephew, and two or three more, and took one Simon Skore, a sailor, and one Cob, a boy, prisoners. That song goes thus:

Matanerew shashashewaw erawango, pechecoma,
Whe Tassantassa, inoshashaw yehockan pocosack
whe, whe, yah, ha ha, ne he, wittowa, wittowa.
Matanerew, shashashewaw erawango pechecoma
Capt. Newport *inoshasha neir inhoc nantian matassan*
whe whe yah ha ha, etc.
Matanerew shashashewaw erowango pechecoma

Thom. Newport *inoshasha neir inhoc nantian monocock*
whe whe etc.
Matanerew shashashewaw erawango pechecoma
Pechen Simon *moshasha nirigon nantian Tamahauck.*
whe whe, etc.

Which may signify how that they killed us for all our *poccasacks,* that is, our "guns," and for all Captain Newport brought them copper, and could hurt Thomas Newport—a boy indeed whose name is Thomas Savadge, whom Captain Newport leaving with Powhatan to learn the language, at what time he presented the said Powhatan with a copper crown and other gifts from His Majesty, said he was his son—for all his *monacock,* that is, his "bright sword," and how they could take Symon (for they seldom add our surname) prisoner for all his *tamahauke,* that is his "hatchet," adding as for a burthen unto their song what lamentation our people made when they killed him, namely, how they would cry *whe whe,* etc., which they mock'd us for and cried again to us *Yah ha ha, tewittawa tewittawa.* For it is true they never bemoan themselves nor cry out giving up so much as a groan for any death, how cruel soever and full of torment.

As for their dancing, the sport seems unto them and the use almost as frequent and necessary as their meat and drink, in which they consume much time and for which they appoint many and often meetings, and have therefore, as it were, set orgies or festivals for the same pastime, as have yet at this day the merry Greeks within the Arches. At our colony's first sitting down amongst them, when any of our people repaired unto their towns the Indians would not think they had expressed their welcome unto them sufficient enough until they had showed them a dance, the manner of which is thus: One of them standeth by with some fur or leather thing in his left hand, upon which he beats with his right, and sings withal as if he began the choir and kept unto the rest their just time, when upon a certain stroke or word, as upon his cue or time to come in, one riseth up and begins the dance; after he hath danced awhile steps forth another as if he came in just upon his rest; and in this order all of them so many as there be one after another, who then dance an equal distance from each other in a ring shooting [shouting], howling, and stamping their feet against the ground with such force and pain that they sweat again, and with all variety of mimic tricks and distorted faces, making so confused a yell and noise as so many frantic and disquieted bacchanals. And sure they will keep stroke just with their feet to the time he gives, and just one with another, but with the hands, head, face, and body everyone hath a several gesture as who have seen the dervishes in their holy dances in the moschas [mosques] upon Wednesdays and Fridays in Turkey may resemble these unto them. You shall find the manner expressed in the figure in the second decade, chapter——.[1]

Every weroance knoweth his own meres and limits to fish, fowl, or hunt in, as before said, but they hold all of their great weroance Powhatan, unto whom they pay 8 parts of 10 tribute of all the commodities which their country yieldeth, as of wheat, peas, beans—8 measures of ten (and these measured out in little cades, or baskets, which the great king appoints), as of the dyeing roots—8 measures of 10; of all sorts of skins and furs—8 of ten; and so he robs the people in effect of all they have,[2] even to the deerskin wherewith they cover them from cold, insomuch as they dare not dress it and put it on until he have seen it and refused it. For what he commandeth they dare not disobey in the least thing.

---

[1] Strachey must have had nothing more in mind than to reproduce the DeBry engraving on 568, which is part of his MS inter-leaved following the Apsley dedication.

[2] "So well observed by Sir W[alter] R[aleigh]." (margin note in Percy MS)

Caput 7.

Of their religion, priests, temples, altars, sacrifices, and of their opinion concerning the immortality of the soul.

THERE IS AS YET IN VIRGINIA no place discovered to be so savage or simple in which the inhabitants have not a religion and the use of bow and arrows. All things they conceive able to do them hurt beyond their prevention they adore with their kind of divine worship, as the fire, water, lightning, thunder, our ordnance, pieces, horses, etc. But their chief god they worship is no other indeed than the devil, whom they make presentments of and shadow under the form of an idol, which they entitle Okeus, and whom they worship as the Romans did their hurtful god Vejovis, more for fear of harm than for hope of any good. They say they have conference with him, and fashion themselves in their disguisements as near to his shape as they can imagine.

In every territory of a weroance is a temple and a priest, peradventure 2 or 3. Yet happy doth that weroance account himself who can detain with him a *quiyoughquisock* of the best: grave, lucky, well instructed in their mysteries, and beloved of their god. And such a one is no less honored than was Diana's priests at Ephesus, for whom they have their more private temples with oratories and chancels therein according as is the dignity and reverence of the quiyoughquisock, which the weroance will be at charge to build upon purpose, sometime 20 foot broad and a hundred in length, fashioned arbor-wise after their building, having commonly the door opening into the east, and at the west end a spence, or chancel, separated from the body of the temple with hollow windings and pillars, whereon stand divers black images fashioned to the shoulders, with their faces looking down the church, and where within their weroances upon a kind of bier of reeds lie buried. And under them, apart in a vault low in the ground as a more secret thing, veiled with a mat, sits their Okeus—an image ill-favoredly carved, all black, dressed with chains of pearl, the presentment and figure of that god (say the priests unto the laity, and who religiously believe what the priests say), which doth them all the harm they suffer, be it in their bodies or goods, within doors or abroad. And true it is many of them are divers times (especially offenders) shrewdly scratched as they walk alone in the woods: It may well be by the subtle spirit, the malicious enemy to mankind, whom therefore to pacify and work to do them good (at least no harm) the priests tell them they must do these and these sacrifices unto, of these and these things, and thus and thus often, by which means not only their own children but strangers are sometimes sacrificed unto him; whilst the great god (the priests tell them) who governs all the world and makes the sun to shine, creating the moon and stars his companions, great powers, and which dwell with him, and by whose virtues and influences the under-earth is tempered and brings forth her fruits according to her seasons—they calling Ahone, the good and peaceable god—requires no such duties nor needs be sacrificed unto, for he intendeth all good unto them, and will do no harm, only the displeased Okeus, looking into all men's actions and examining the same according to the severe scale of justice, punisheth them with sicknesses, beats them, and strikes their ripe corn with blastings, storms, and thunderclaps, stirs up war, and makes their women false unto them. Such is the misery and thralldom under which Satan hath bound these wretched miscreants.

Indeed their priests, being the ministers of Satan, who is very likely or visibly conversant amongst them,[1] fear and tremble lest the knowledge of God and of our Saviour Jesus Christ should be taught in those parts, [and] do now with the more vehemency persuade the people to hold on their wonted ceremonies, and every year to sacrifice still their own children to the ancient god of their fathers and, it is supposed, gain double oblations this way, by reason they do at all times so absolutely govern and direct the weroances, or lords, of countries in all their actions. And this custom he hath politically maintained and doth yet universally, a few places excepted, over all the Indies: In Florida they sacrifice the first born male child; in Mexico they forbear their own and offer up such prisoners as they take in the wars, whom they torture with a most barbarous cruelty.

---

[1] "Sir W[alter] R[aleigh] obser: and advi:" (margin note in Percy MS)

That the devil hath obtained the use of the like offering in many other parts of America, Acosta hath observed and related in his moral and natural history of the West Indies—the same honor the devil obtained from all antiquity in effect, even from the Israelites and their borderers, from the Carthaginians, Persians, and the first planters of Italy, and other nations. To have suff'red still therefore, methinks, these priests of Baal or Beelzebub were greatly offensive to the majesty of God, as most perilous for the English to inhabit within those parts. For these quiyoughquisocks, or prophets, be they that persuade their weroances to resist our settlement, and tell them how much their Okeus will be offended with them, and that he will not be appeased with a sacrifice of a thousand, nay, *a hecatomb,* of their children, if they permit a nation despising the ancient religion of their forefathers to inhabit among them, since their own have hitherto preserved them and given them victory over their enemies from age to age.

It is true that hitherto our colony hath consisted, as it were, but of a handful of men, and not stored with desired victuals fit for such eaters as the English are, nor until anno 1610 hath it been the best governed to undertake this service to God. But now the commodities of our own country being thither in some good quantity transported, and those there thriving and growing daily into good increase—as kine, goats, swine, horses, mares, etc.—and the first ragged government now likewise prudently changed into an absolute command, and over the same many learned and judicious gentlemen of His Majesty's council as a body politic resident in England, and they also enlightened from the supreme understanding of His Majesty's Privy Council, and the lord general now to go again is a very worthy, valiant nobleman, and well instructed in the business, who hath Sir Thomas Gates, lieutenant general (whose commendation lieth in his name), [and] Sir Thomas Dale, marshal, both there at this present, informing themselves of the country and people, both excellent old soldiers and well knowing all circumstances of war and advantages of ground—it cannot be doubted but that all things shall be so foreseen that the best courses shall be taken and the surreption of these priests more seriously thought on than heretofore; and by whose apprehension will be wrought the safety of such our people as shall be employed herein for His Majesty's honor and the enlargement of his dominion, for whose sake God will prosper all our lawful and Christian attempts.

Yet no Spanish intention shall be entertained by us neither hereby to root out the naturals, as the Spaniards have done in Hispaniola and other parts, but only to take from them these *seducers,* until when they will never know God nor obey the king's majesty, and by which means we shall by degrees change their barbarous natures, make them ashamed the sooner of their savage nakedness, inform them of the true God and of the way to their salvation, and finally teach them obedience to the king's majesty and to his governor in those parts declaring in the attempt thereof—unto the several weroances, and making the common people likewise to understand—how that His Majesty hath been acquainted that the men, women, and children of the first plantation at Roanoak were by practice and commandment of Powhatan (he himself persuaded thereunto by his priests) miserably slaughtered without any offense given him either by those first planted, who 20 and odd years had peaceably lived and intermix'd with those savages, and were out of his territory, or by those who now are come to inhabit some part of his desert lands and to trade with him for some commodities of ours which he and his people stand in want of, notwithstanding. Because His Majesty is of all the world the most just and the most merciful prince, he hath given order that Powhatan himself with his weroances and all the people shall be spared and revenge taken only upon his quiyoughquisocks, by whose advice and persuasions was exercised that bloody cruelty; and only how that Powhatan himself and the weroances must depend on His Majesty, both acknowledging him for their superior lord—and whereunto the inferior weronces sure will most willingly condescend when it shall be told them that whereas Powhatan doth at his pleasure despoil them both of their lives and goods without yielding them any reason, or alleging or proving any just cause against them, they shall for hereafter be delivered from his tyranny and shall enjoy freely the fruits of their own territories; so shall they the fish and the fowl thereof, of which the most rare and delicate of the one and the best and wholesomest of the other are now forbidden them and reserved and preserved to

Powhatan; and that they shall be freed likewise from delivering up their children for sacrifice, and the poor women's songs of lamentation converted into rejoicings, the true God and his governor King James commanding that the children of men be preserved and not slaughtered without offense given, as the devil and his quiyoughquisocks have ordained; against which satanical invention may it please His Majesty to make an ordinance that the fathers of those children and all that consent to the sacrifices hereafter shall be put to death as traitors to God and His Majesty, as also when they shall understand how the tribute which they shall pay unto His Majesty shall be far less than that which Powhatan exacteth from them, who robs them, as you have heard, of all they have.

But after such time as they shall submit themselves to the king's majesty and consent to pay him a tribute to be agreed upon, Powhatan shall lay no more his exactions upon them, but they shall freely enjoy all they can gather and have a peaceable and frank trade with the English for the commodities they can make of their own, exchanging them for ours; and that the English will take of their poorest into their families, as their better sort shall by patents and proclamations hold their lands as free burghers and citizens with the English and subjects to King James, who will give them justice and defend them against all their enemies, whereas now they live in miserable slavery and have no assurance either of their lives or of their goods.

And indeed these double and mixed commodities will arise, namely, the English garrisons shall not only be provided of corn and their storehouses of merchandise but the naturals, being thus constrained to pay duly this their tribute, will cleanse double as much ground as they do, whereby the country will not only be made the more passable both for horse and foot but the people themselves, who are now for the most part of the year idle and do little else than sharpen their arrows against the English, shall find by their gathering together of their several sorts of tribute somewhat to entertain themselves withal. And although peradventure this may seem a burthen at the first, until they have acquainted themselves with another kind of life and perceive themselves indeed to become thereby the more civil, as likewise to enjoy the rest of their own more freely than under

Powhatan, they will find themselves in far better estate than now they are. For the caciques, or commanders, of Indian towns in Peru, whom the Virginians call weroances, although they pay unto the King of Spain great tribute, yet because they make exchange with the Spaniard for what remains they do not only keep great hospitality and are rich in their furniture, horses, and cattle but as Captain Ellis avows, who lived amongest them some few years, their diet is served to them in silver vessels and many of them have natural Spaniards that attend them in their houses; when on the other side the Spaniards were not able to make the twentieth part of profit which they now do but by the help of those captives—for they furnish out of their several territories not so few as fifty thousand people to work in the mines of Patasi [Potosí], who after so many months' travail are returned into their countries, and 50,000 others by another company of caciques provided to supply them. In New Spain they do the like, for the natural people gather all the *scutchinella* [cochineal] which the Spaniards have, and require no more for a week's labor than so much money as will buy them a pot of wine to drink drunk the Saturday night.

In Guiana, thirty of the people with their canoa will be hired for one hatchet to row where they are commanded for a whole month, and sell a hundredweight of good biscuit for a three-penny knife. And if our copper had been well ordered in Virginia, as may be hereafter, I am assured that less than one crown will serve to entertain the labor of a whole household for 10 days.

And surely all this being delivered in fit terms by some perfect interpreter, and to men that are capable enough of understanding, it may beget a fair conceit in them of us and our proceedings and leave them well satisfied, and indeed be it believed that when so just an occasion shall offer these priests of Asmodias, or the devil, into the hands of the lord general, a better time than that will not be found to perform the same acceptable service to God that Jehu King of Israel did when he assembled all the priests of Baal and slew them to the last man in their own temple.

Of this may every vulgar sense be well assured that seeing these monsters do offer up unto the devil their own children and being hardened against all compassion natural and divine enforce their own mothers to deliver them to the executioner with their own hands, they will easily condescend unto and assist the destruction and extirpation of all strangers knowing or acknowledging the true God.

Within the chancel of the temple by the Okeus are the cenotaphies, or the monuments, of their kings, whose bodies, so soon as they be dead, they embowel. And scraping the flesh from off the bones, they dry the same upon hurdles into ashes, which they put into little pots like the ancient urns. The anatomy of the bones[1] they bind together, or case up, in leather, hanging bracelets or chains of copper, beads, pearl, and suchlike as they used to wear about most of their joints and neck, and so repose the body upon a little scaffold as upon a tomb, laying by the dead body's feet all his riches in several baskets, his *apooke* and pipe, and any one toy which in his life he held most dear in his fancy. Their inwards they stuff with pearl, copper, beads, and such trash sewed in a skin, which they overlap again very carefully in white skins, one or two, and the bodies thus dressed lastly they roll in mats, as for winding sheets, and so lay them orderly one by one, as they die in their turns, upon an arch standing, as aforesaid, for the tomb. And these are all the ceremonies we yet can learn that they give unto their dead. We hear of no sweet oils or ointments that they use to dress or chest[2] their dead bodies with, albeit they want not of the precious rosin running out of the great cedar, wherewith in the old time they used to embalm dead bodies, washing them in the oil and liquor thereof. Only to the priests the care of these temples and holy interments are committed, and these temples are to them as solitary *asceteria*,[3] colleges, or ministers [minsters], to exercise themselves in contemplation, for they are seldom out of them, and therefore often lie in them and maintain continual fire in the same upon a hearth somewhat near to the east end.

For their ordinary burials they dig a deep hole in the earth with sharp stakes, and the corpse, being lapped in skins and mats with their jewels, they lay them upon sticks in the ground, and so cover

---

1 The bones all disconnected.

2 Put in a coffin.

3 "Hermitage," "monastery" (Ecclesiastic Greek).

them with earth. The burial ended, the women being painted all their faces with black coal and oil do sit 24 hours in their houses mourning and lamenting by turns, with such yelling and howling as may express their great passions.

Their principal temple, or place of superstition, is at Uttamussack at Pamunky, near unto which town within the woods is a chief holy house proper to Powhatan upon the top of certain red sandy hills; and it is accompanied with 2 other 60 foot in length, filled with images of their kings and devils and tombs of their predecessors. This place they count so holy as that none but the priests and kings dare come therein. In this, as the Grecian necromancers in their psychomanty did use to call up spirits, either the priests have conference and consult indeed with the devil and receive verbal answers. And so saith Acosta he spake to the *boity,* or "chaplains," of the West Indies in their *guacas,* or "oratories." Or at least these conjurers make the simple laity so to believe, who therefore (so much are the people at the priests' devotion) are ready to execute anything, how desperate soever which they shall command.

The savages dare not go up the river in boats by it but that they solemnly cast some piece of copper, white beads, or *pocones* into the river for fear their Okeus should be offended and revenged of them. In this place commonly are resident 7 priests, the chief differing from the rest in his ornament, whilst the inferior priests can hardly be known from the common people, save that they had not—it may be *may* not have—so many holes in their ears to hang their jewels at. The ornaments of the chief priest was upon his shoulders: a middle-sized cloak of feathers, much like the old sacrificing garment which Isodorus calls *casiola,* and the burlet,[1] or attire of his head, was thus made: Some 12 or 16 or more snakes' sloughs, or skins, were stuffed with moss, and of weasels and other vermin were skins perhaps as many. All these were tied by the tails, so as all their tails met in the top of the head like a great tassel; and round about the tassel was circled a crownet, as it were, of feathers, the skins hanging round about his head, neck, and shoulders, and in a manner covering his face. The faces of all their priests are painted as ugly as they can

[1] Coif or hood.

devise. In their hands they carry everyone his rattle for the most part as a symbol of his place and profession, some bass, some smaller. Their devotion is most in songs, which the chief priest begins and the rest follow him. Sometimes he makes invocation with broken sentences by starts and strange passions, and at every pause the rest of the priests give a short groan.

We have not yet hitherto perceived that any solemn *fasti* or *feriae praecidaniae, vigilli,*[1] or any one day more holy than other is amongst them, but only in some great distress of want, fear of enemies, times of triumph, and gathering together their fruits the whole country—men, women, and children—come together to their solemnities. The manner of which solemn devotion is sometimes to make a great fire in the house or fields, and all to sing and dance about it in a ring, like to many fairies, with rattles and shouts 4 or 5 hours together, sometimes fashioning themselves in two companies, keeping a great circuit, one company danceth one way and the other the contrary, all very finely painted—certain men going before with either of them a rattle, other following in the midst, and the rest of the train of both wings in order 4 and 4, and in the rear certain of the chiefest young men with long switches in their hands to keep them in their places; after all which follows the governor, or weroance, himself in a more slow or solemn measure, stopping and dancing, and all singing very tunable.

They have also divers conjurations. One they made at what time they had taken Captain Smith prisoner to know, as they reported, if any more of his countrymen would arrive there, and what they intended. The manner of it Captain Smith observed to be as followeth: First, so soon as day was shut in, they kindled a fair great fire in a low house, about which assembled seven priests, taking Captain Smith by the hand and appointing him his seat. About the fire they made a kind of enchanted circle of meal. That done, the chief priest, attired as is expressed, gravely began to sing and shake his rattle, solemnly rounding and marching about the fire. The rest followed him silently until his song was done, which [whereupon] they all shut up with a groan. At the end of the first song the chief

[1] Festivals, holidays, vigils.

priest laid down certain grains of wheat, and so continued howling and invoking their Okeus to stand firm and powerful unto them, in divers varieties of songs still counting the songs by the grains, until they had circled the fire 3 times. Then they divided the grains by certain numbers with little sticks, all the while uttering some impious thing unto themselves, oftentimes looking upon Captain Smith. In this manner they continued 10 or 12 hours without any other ceremonies or intermission, with such violent stretching of their arms and various passions, gestures, and symptoms as might well seem strange to him before whom they so conjured, and who every hour expected to be the host and end of their sacrifice. Not any meat did they eat until it was very late and the night far spent. About the rising of the morning star they seemed to have finished their work of darkness, and then drew forth such provision as was in the said house and feasted themselves and him with much mirth. Three or four days they continued these elvish ceremonies.

Now beside these manners of conjurations, thus within doors (as we read) the augurers in old times of the like superstition did ascend or go up into certain towers or high places called therefore *auguracula* to divine of matters. So do they go forth and either upon some rock standing alone or upon some desolate promontory top, or else into the midst of thick and solitary woods, they call out upon their Okeus and importune their other quiyoughcosughes with most impetious [impetuous] and interminate clamors and howling, and with such pains and strained actions as the neighbor places echo again of the same, and themselves are all in a sweat and overwearied.[1]

They have also certain altar stones which they call *pawcorances,* but those stand from their temples, some by their houses, others in the woods and wilderness. Upon these they offer blood, deer suet, and tobacco, and that when they return safe from the wars, luckily from hunting, and upon many other occasions.

We understand they give great reverence to the sun, for which both at his early rising and late sitting they couch themselves down and lift up their hands and eyes; and at certain times make a round circle on the ground with tobacco, into which they reverently enter

---

[1] cf. §12–164 and §17–240.

and murmur certain unhallowed words with many a deformed gesture.

They have also another kind of sorcery which they use in storms, a kind of *botanomantia* with herbs.[1] When the waters are rough in the rivers and seacoasts, their conjurers run to the watersides, or passing in their quintans, [and] after many hellish outcries and invocations they cast *whesican,* tobacco, copper, *pocones,* or such trash into the water to pacify that god whom they thing [think] to be very angry in those storms.

Before their dinners and suppers—as Heliodorus remembers the Egyptians were wont to do when they sat to meat or at candle light—the better sort will do a kind of sacrifice, taking the first bit and casting it into the fire, and to it repeat certain words. I have heard Machumps at Sir Thomas Dale's table once or twice upon our request repeat the said grace, as it were, howbeit I forgot to take it from him in writing.

In some part of the country they have yearly a sacrifice of children. Such a one was at Quyyoughcohanock, some ten miles from James town, as also at Kecoughtan, which Captain Georg Percy was at and observed. The manner of it was 15 of the properest young boys between 10 and 15 years of age the[y] painted white, [and] having brought them forth, the people spent the forenoon in dancing and singing about them with rattles. In the afternoon they solemnly led those children to a certain tree appointed for the same purpose, at the root whereof round about they made the children to sit down; and by them stood the most and the ablest of the men, and some of them the fathers of the children, as a watchful guard, everyone having a bastinado in his hand of reeds.

And these opened a lane between all along through which were appointed 5 young men to fetch those children. And accordingly every one of the 5 took his turn and passed through the guards to fetch a child, the guard fiercely beating them the while with their bastinadoes, and showing much anger and displeasure to have the children so ravish'd from them, all which the young men patiently

[1] Botanomancy would be divination by plants.

endured, receiving the blows and defending the children with their naked bodies from the unmerciful strokes that paid them soundly, though the children escaped. All the while sat the mothers and kinswomen afar off looking on, weeping and crying out very passionately, and some in pretty waymenting tunes singing, as it were, their dirge or funeral song, provided with mats, skins, moss, and dry wood by them as things fitting their children's funerals.

After the children were thus forcibly taken from the guard, the guard, possessed, as it were, with a violent fury, ent'red upon the tree and tore it down boughs and branches with such a terrible fierceness and strength that they rent the very body of it and shivered it in a hundred pieces; whereof some of them made them garlands for their heads, and some stuck of the branches and leaves in their hair, wreathing them in the same, and so went up and down as mourners with heavy and sad downcast looks.

What else was done with the children might not be seen by our people further than that they were all cast on a heap in a valley where was made a great and solemn feast for all the company, at the going whereunto, the night now approaching, the Indians desired our people that they would withdraw themselves and leave them to their further proceedings, the which they did; only some of the weroances being demanded the meaning of this sacrifice made answer that the children did not all of them suffer death, but that the Okeus did suck the blood from the left breast of that child whose chance it was to be his by lot, till he were dead, and the remain were kept in the wilderness by the said young men till 9 months were expired, during which time they must not converse with any; and of these were made their priests and conjurers, to be instructed by tradition from the elder priests. These sacrifices, or *catharmata*,[1] they hold to be so necessary that if they should omit them they suppose their Okeus and all the other quioughcosughes, which are their other gods, would let them have no deer, turkeys, corn, nor fish, and yet beside he would make a great slaughter amongst them insomuch as if ever the ancient superstitious times feared the devil's *postularia*

---

[1] "Purifications" (Greek).

fulgura[1]—lightning that signified religion of sacrifices and voices to be neglected—these people are dreadfully afflicted with the terror of the like, insomuch as I may truly say therefore the like thunder and lightning is seldom again either seen or heard in Europe as is here.

Concerning the immortality of the soul, they suppose that the common people shall not live after death. But they think that their weroances and priests indeed, whom they esteem also half quioughcosughes, when their bodies are laid in the earth, that that which is within shall go beyond the mountains and travel as far as where the sun sets into most pleasant fields, grounds, and pastures, where it shall do no labor, but stuck finely with feathers and painted with oil and *pocones* rest in all peace and quiet, and eat delicious fruits, and have store of copper, beads, and hatchets, sing, dance, and have all variety of delights and merriments, till that wax old there as the body did on earth, and then it shall dissolve and die and come into a woman's womb again and so be anew born unto the world—not unlike the heathen Pythagoras his opinion and fable of metempsychosis.

Nor is this opinion more ridiculous or savage than was the Epicure's long since in time too of morality, who taught that the soul of man, as of brute beasts, was nothing else but life, or the vital power, arising of the temperature and perfection of the body, and therefore died and extinguished together with the body, the soul so being a mere quality in the body. And when the body was to dissolve, the soul must likewise become nothing.

Nor is it more heathenous than our ath[e]ists, who would even out of Scripture profanely conclude no immortality of the soul to be, wresting that of Solomon who saith, "The condition of men and beasts are even as one," not acknowledging their impious reasoning by fallacies, concluding that which is in some respects so, to be simply so, as because their bodies die alike, therefore the soul of man

---

[1] "The rendering here given by Strachey ... is evidently from Festus, though his quaint diction would mislead the reader as to the intention of the words. Festus gives the following definition of the term: '*Fulgura quae votorum aut sacrificiorum spretam religionem designant.*'" (Major) Which translates: "Lightning bolts that signify prayers or sacrifices *despicably performed*."

must perish too.

But alas, well may these poor heathen be pitied and pardoned until they shall be taught better, neither born under grace nor of the seed of promise, when such as profess themselves in their great places to be our Saviour Christ's *chief vicars* here upon earth dare be far more dissolute, as it is written of Paul the Third, Pope of Rome, when he was breathing out his soul and ready to die [and] said that now at length he should try and know three things whereof in his whole time he much doubted, viz., first, whether there was a God; secondly, whether souls were immortal; and lastly, whether there was any hell. And Stephanus upon Herodotus remembers us what Pope Leo the 10 answered Cardinal Bembo that alleged some part of the Gospel unto him, "Lord Cardinal, what a wealth this fable of Jesus Christ hath gotten us!" I say therefore it may well seem less strange if among these infidels both the knowledge of our Saviour be questioned and the immortality of the soul not rightly understood, howbeit to divert them from this blindness many of our people have used their best endeavors, chiefly with Pepiscuminah, weroance of Quiyoughcohanock, whose apprehension and good disposition towards us hath hitherto much exceeded any in those countries, with whom, though as yet we have not prevailed to forsake his false gods, yet this he was won to say: that he believed our god as much exceeded theirs as our guns did their bow and arrows; and many times upon our people's first coming into the country did send to the president at James Town men with presents, entreating him to pray to his god for rain, for his gods would not send him any. And in this lamentable ignorance do these poor souls live.

I will conclude these points with opinion of the Indians of Patawomeck River the last year, 1610, about Christmas, when Captain Argoll was there trading with Iopassus, the great king's brother. After many days of acquaintance with him, as the pinnace rode before the town Matchipongo—Iopassus coming aboard and sitting (the weather being very cold) by the fire upon a hearth in the hold with the captain—one of our men was reading of a Bible, to which the Indian gave an attent ear, and looked with a very wish'd[1] eye upon him, as if he desired to understand what he read; whereupon the captain took the book and turned to the picture of the creation of the world in the beginning of the book and caused a boy, one Spilman,[2] who had lived a whole year with this Indian king and spake his language, to show it unto him and to interpret it in his language, which the boy did, and which the king seemed to like well of. Howbeit he bade the boy tell the captain, if he would hear, he would tell him the manner of *their* beginning, which was a pretty fabulous tale indeed.

"We have," said he, "5 gods in all. Our chief god appears often unto us in the likeness of a mighty Great Hare; the other 4 have no visible shape, but are indeed the 4 winds which keep the 4 corners of the earth." And then with his hand he seemed to quarter out the situation of the world. "Our god who takes upon him this shape of a hare conceived with himself how to people this great world, and with what kind of creatures. And it is true," said he, "that at length he devised and made divers men and women, and made provision for them to be kept up yet for a while in a great bag." Now there were certain spirits, which he described to be like great giants, which came to the Hare's dwelling place (being towards the rising of the sun), and had perseverance of the men and women which he had put into that great bag. And they would have had them to eat, but the godlike Hare reproved those cannibal spirits and drove them away.

Now if the boy had asked him of what he made those men and women, and what those spirits more particularly had been, and so had proceeded in some order, they should have made it hang together the better. But the boy was unwilling to question him so many things lest he should offend him, only the old man went on and said how that godlike Hare made the water and the fish therein, and the land and a great deer which should feed upon the land, at which assembled the other 4 gods, envious hereat, from the east, the west, from the north and south, and with hunting poles kill'd this deer, dress'd him, and after they had feasted with him, departed again east,

---

[1] Curious.

[2] Who has left us his own version of this myth at §30–496.

"THE CREATION OF THE WORLD"
from Robert Barker's 1607 edition of the Geneva Bible

west, north, and south; at which the other god, in despite for this their malice to him, took all the hairs of the slain deer and spread them upon the earth and with many powerful words and charms, whereby every hair became a deer. And then he opened the great bag wherein the men and the women were, and placed them upon the earth, a man and a woman in one country and a man and a woman in another country. And so the world took his first beginning of mankind.

The captain bade the boy ask him what he thought became of them after their death, to which he answered somewhat like as is expressed before of the inhabitants about us, how that after they are dead here they go up to the top of a high tree; and there they espy a fair plain, broad pathway, on both sides whereof doth grow all manner of pleasant fruits, as mulberries, strawberries, plums, etc. In this pleasant path they run toward the rising of the sun, where the godlike Hare's house is, and in the midway they come to a house where a woman goddess doth dwell, who hath always her doors open for hospitality, and hath at all times ready-dress'd green *uskatahomen* and *pokahichary*—which is green corn bruised and boiled, and walnuts beaten small, then washed from the shells with a quantity of water, which makes a kind of milk and which they esteem an extraordinary dainty dish—together with all manner of pleasant fruits in a readiness to entertain all such as do travel to the Great Hare's house. And when they are well refreshed, they run in this pleasant path to the rising of the sun, where they find their forefathers living in great pleasure in a goodly field, where they do nothing but dance and sing and feed on delicious fruits with that Great Hare, who is their great god. And when they have lived there until they be stark old men, they say they die there likewise by turns and come into the world again.

Concerning further of their religion we have not yet learned, nor indeed shall we ever know all the certainty either of these their unhallowed mysteries or of their further orders and policies until we can make surprise of some of their quiyoughquisocks.

Caput 8.

The manner of their wars. Drums.
Their surgery in curing their wounds.
Their weapons of offense, etc.

WHEN THEY INTEND ANY WARS, the weroances usually advise with their priests, or conjurers, [and] their allies and best trusted counselors and friends. But commonly the priests have the resulting voice, and determine therefore their resolutions. Either a weroance or some lusty fellow is appointed captain over a nation or regiment to be led forth. And when the[y] would press a number of soldiers to be ready by a day, an officer is dispatch'd away, who coming into the towns or otherwise meeting such whom he hath order to warn, he strikes them over the back a sound blow with a bastinado, and bids them be ready to serve the great king, and tells them the rendezvous from whence they dare not at the time appointed be absent.

They seldom make wars for lands or goods, but for women and children, and principally for revenge, so vindicative and jealous they be to be made a derision of and to be insulted upon by an enemy.

There be at this time certain prophecies afoot amongest the people inhabiting about us of which Powhatan is not meanly jealous and careful to divert the construction and danger, which his priests continually put him in fear of. Not long since it was that his priests told him how that from the Chesapeack Bay a nation should arise which should dissolve and give end to his empire, for which not many years since, perplex'd with this devilish oracle and divers understanding thereof, according to the ancient and gentile [pagan] custom he destroyed and put to sword all such who might lie under any doubtful construction of the said prophecy, as all the inhabitants, the weroance, and his subjects of that province. And so remain all the Chessiopeians at this day and for this cause extinct.

Some of the inhabitants again have not spared to give us to understand how they have a second prophecy likewise amongst them that twice they should give overthrow and dishearten the attempters and such strangers as should invade their territories or labor to settle a plantation amongst them, but the third time they themselves should fall into their subjection and under their conquest. And sure in the observation of our settlement and the manner thereof hitherto, we may well suppose that this their apprehension may fully touch at us. I leave to express the particulars unto another place, albeit let me say here strange whispers indeed, and secret, at this hour run among these people and possess them with amazement what may be the issue of these strange preparations landed in their coasts and yearly supplied with fresher troops. Every news and blast of rumor strikes them, to which they open their ears wide and keep their eyes waking with good espial upon everything that stirs: The noise of our drums, of our shrill trumpets and great ordnance terrifies them, so as they startle at the report of them, how far soever from the reach of danger. Suspicions have bred strange fears amongst them, and those fears create as strange constructions.

And those constructions therefore beget strong watch and guard, especially about their great king, who thrusts forth trusty scouts and careful sentinels, as before mentioned, which reach even from his own court down almost to our palisado gates, which answer one another duly. Many things whilst they observe us are suff'red amiss amongst themselves, who were wont to be so servilely fearful to trespass against their customs, as it was a chief point of their religion not to break in any. And all this and more than this is thus with them, whilst [neither] the great tyrant himself nor his priests are now confident in their wonted courses.

Judge all men whether these may not be forerunners of an alteration of the devil's empire here! I hope they be. Nay, I dare prognosticate that they usher accidents and that we shall effect them. The Divine Power assist us in this work which begun for heavenly ends may have as heavenly a period!

Powhatan had many enemies, especially in the westerly countries, before we made our forts and habitations so near the Falls. But now the general cause hath united them, and the poor power of their malice they contend to pour upon us. Beyond the mountains and at the heads of the rivers upon the head of the Powhatans, are the Monacans, whose chief habitation is at Rassawek, unto whom the

Mowhemenchughes, the Massinnacacks, the Monahassanughes, and other nations pay tribute. And the Monacans, as I said, have been deadly enemies ever unto Powhatan, and may easily be joined friendship with by us to be so again until when we shall ever have Powhatan at these proud and insolent terms at which he now stands.

And therefore it was most considerately and directly advised by one of good place and great knowledge, and [one] by long experience trained in the managing of business of this nature, when Sir Thomas Gates went over sole governor, May 1609, that we should endeavor what all invaders and planters seek out, namely, to know and entertain the bordering enemy of that nation whom we shall be forced by our sitting down amongst them out of many off'red occasions to offend and constrain. For who can be ignorant, saith he, that there was never any invasion, conquest, or far-off plantation that had success without some party[1] in the place itself or near it? Witness all the conquests made in these our own parts of the world and all that the Spaniards have performed in America [and] it cannot but appear to all men of judgment essentially necessary for our colony to get knowledge or make friendship as conveniently as it may with as many of the weroances which border and make war with Powhatan as it can, against whom, or against whose people, if we should find cause now or hereafter to use violence, there is no man among themselves so savage or not capable of so much sense but that he will approve our cause when he shall be made to understand that Powhatan hath slaughtered so many of our nation without offense given, and such as were seated far from him, and in the territory of those weroances which did in no sort depend on him or acknowledge him.[2]

But it hath been Powhatan's great care to keep us by all means from the acquaintance of those nations that border and confront him. For besides his knowledge how easily and willingly his enemies will be drawn upon him by the least countenance and encouragement

---

[1] Ally.

[2] Here and above Strachey assumes that Powhatan, at the first landing of the English in 1607, exterminated the Chesapeakes because white survivors of the Roanoke Colony were living among them. This may be so but has, of course, no historical corroboration. The Lost Colony remains lost down to this day. See also p. 24.

from us, he doth by keeping us from trading with them monopolize all the copper brought into Virginia by the English. And whereas the English are now content to receive in exchange a few measures of corn for a great deal of that metal, valuing it according to the extreme price it bears with them, not to the estimation it hath with us,[1] Powhatan doth again vent some small quantity thereof to his neighbor nations for *100 times the value,* reserving notwithstanding for himself a plentiful quantity to levy men withal when he shall find cause to use them against us. For the before-rememb'red weroance of Paspahegh did once wage 14 or 15 weroances to assist him in the attempt upon the fort of James Town for one copper plate promised to each weroance.

Beyond the springs of the river of Toppahanock (the second from Powhatan) is a people called Mannahoacks. To these are contributary the Tanxsnitanians, the Shachaconias, the Outpankas, the Tegoneas, the Whonkentias, the Stegaras, the Hassningas, and divers others, all confederates with the Monacans, though many of them different in language, and very barbarous, living for the most part upon wild beasts and fruits; and have likewise assisted the Monacans in times past against Powhatan, and may also by us be dealt withal and taken into friendship as opportunity and means shall afford.

Beyond the mountains from whence is the head of the River Patawomeck do inhabit the Massawomecks, Powhatan's yet mortal enemies, upon a great salt water, which by all likelihoods may either be some part of Caneda, some great lake, or some inlet of some sea that may fall into the West Ocean, or Mar del Zur. These Massawomecks are a great nation and very populous, for the inhabitants of the heads of all those rivers, especially the Patawomecks, the Pawtuxunts, the Sasquesahanoughes, [and] the Tockwoghes are continually harrowed and frighted by them—of whose cruelty the said people generally complained, and were very importunate with Captain Smith and his company in the time of their discovery to free them from those tormentors; to which purpose they off'red food, conduct, assistance, and continual subjection, which were motives

---

[1] The illicit free market was running smoothly. Read, "Valuing copper *not* according to the extreme *high* price it bears with them, but to the *lower* estimation which it hath with us."

sufficient for Captain Smith to promise to return with sufficient forces to constrain the said Massawomecks. But there were in the colony at that time such factions and base envies as malice in some, in some ignorance, and cowardice in others made that opportunity to be lost.

Seven boats full of these Massawomecks the discoverers (before mentioned) encount'red at the head of the bay, whose targets, baskets, swords, tobacco pipes, platters, bows and arrows, and everything showed they much exceeded them of our parts. And their dexterity in their small boats, made of the barks of trees, sewed together and well luted with gum and rosin of the pine tree argueth that they are seated upon some great water. Of these likewise it may please the lord general again to inform himself as circumstances and occasion shall serve to turn against Powhatan.

I grant that such the new inhabitants who now people [the site of the village of] Chesapeak—the old extinguished, as you have heard, upon the conceit of a prophecy—together with the weroances of Nansamund, Warraskoyack, and Weanock, are now at peace with him, howbeit they may peradventure be drawn from him for some round rewards and a plentifully promise of copper, thus much and not unnecessarily I digressed.

Their weapons for offense are bows and arrows and wooden swords; for defense, targets. Their bows are of some young plant, either of the locust tree or of a wych [elm], which they bring to the form of ours by the scraping of a shell, and give them strings of a stag's gut or thong of a deer's hide twisted. Their arrows are made some of straight young sprigs which they head with bone two or three inches long; and these they use to shoot at squirrels and all king [kind] of fowl. Another sort of arrows they use made of reeds. These are pieced with wood, headed with splinters of crystal or some sharp stone, with the spurs of a turkey cock or the bill of some bird, feathered with a turkey's feather which, with a knife made with the splinter of a reed, which he will make as sharp as a surgeon's gammot, he cuts him into form; and with which knife also he will joint a deer or any beast, shape his sandals, buskins, mantle, etc. To make the notch of his arrow he hath the tooth of a beaver set in a stick, wherewith he grateth it by degrees. His arrowhead he quickly maketh with a little bone, which he ever weareth at his bracer—and his bracer is commonly of some beast's skin, either of the wolf, badger, or black fox, etc.—of any splint of a stone or piece of a deer's bone, of an oyster shell, or of crystal in the form of a heart barb'd and jagged; and these they glue to the end of their arrows, with the sinews of deer and the tops of deer's horn boiled into a jelly of which they make a glue that will not dissolve in cold water.

40 yards will they shoot level or very near the mark, and 120 is their best at random.

Their swords be made of a kind of heavy wood which they have, much like such wooden instruments as our Englishwomen swingle their flax withal, and which they call *monococks*, as the savages in Dariena in the West Indies call their *macanas*, and be alike made. But oftentimes they use for swords the horn of a deer put through a piece of wood in form of a pickax. Some use a long stone sharpened at both ends, thrust through a handle of wood in the same manner; and these last they were wont to use instead of hatchets to fell a tree or cut any massy thing in sunder. But now by trucking with us they have thousands of our iron hatchets, such as they be.

Targets they have, though not many nor everywhere. But those they have are made of the barks of trees, round and thick enough to keep out an arrow.

For their drums they have a great deep platter of wood, the mouth whereof covering with a skin at each corner, they tie a walnut, which meeting on the backside near the bottom, with a small cord they twitch them together until they be so taught and stiff as they may beat upon them as do we upon a drum—and they yield a reasonable rattling sound.

Their chief attempts are by stratagems, surprises, and treacheries. Yet the weroances, women, or children they put not to death, but keep them captives. They have a method in war, and for a pleasure Powhatan would needs have it showed once to our people; and it was in this manner performed at Mattapanient:

Having painted and disguised themselves in the fairest manner[1]

[1] Surely "fiercest manner" as Smith has it.

they could devise, they divided themselves into two companies, well near 100 in a company. The one company they called "Monacans," the other "Powhatans." Either army had their captain. These as enemies took their stands a musket-shot one from another, [and] ranking themselves 15 abreast, and each rank from other 4 or 5 yards, not in file but in the opening betwixt their files, so as the rear should shoot as conveniently as the front. Having thus pitched their field, from either part went a messenger with conditions that whosoever were vanquished, such as escaped—upon their submission or coming in, though two days after—should live, but their wives and children should be prize for the conquerors. The messengers were no sooner returned but they approached in their orders: On each flank a sergeant, and in the rear an officer for lieutenant, all duly keeping their ranks, yet leaping and singing after their customed tune which they use only in wars. Upon the first flight of arrows they gave such horrible shouts and screeches as so many infernal hellhounds. When they had spent their arrows, they joined together prettily, charging and retiring, every rank seconding other. As they got advantage, they catched their enemies by the hair of the head and down he came that was taken. His enemy with a wooden sword seemed[1] to beat out his brains, and still they crept to the rear to maintain the skirmish. The Monacans decreasing, the Powhatans charged them in form of a half-moon. They, unwilling to be enclosed, fled all in a troop to their ambuscadoes, on whom they led them very cunningly. The Monacans dispers'd themselves among the fresh men, whereupon the Powhatans retired with all speed to their seconds; which the Monacans seeing took that advantage to retire again to their own battle; and so each returned to their own quarter. All their action, voices, and gestures, both in charging and retiring, were so strained to the height of their quality and nature that the strangeness thereof made it seem very delightful.

Concerning a green wound caused either by the stroke of an ax or sword or such sharp thing, they have present remedy for of the juice of certain herbs. Howbeit a compound wound, as the surgeons call it,

---

[1] Pretended.

where beside the opening and cutting of the flesh any rupture is or bone broken, such as our small shot make upon them, they know not easily how to cure and therefore languish in the misery of the pain thereof. Old ulcers likewise and putrefied hurts are seldom seen cured amongst them. Howbeit to scarify a swelling or make incision they have a kind of instrument of some splinted stone.

Every spring they make themselves sick with drinking the juice of a root which they call *wighsacan,* and water, whereof they take so great a quantity that it purgeth them in a very violent manner, so that in 3 or 4 days after they scarce recover their former health.

Sometimes they are sore troubled with dropsies, swellings, aches, and suchlike diseases, by reason of their uncleanness and foul feeding; for cure whereof they build a stove in the form of a dove house with mats so close that a few coals therein covered with a pot will make the patient sweat extremely.

For swellings also they use small pieces of touchwood in the form of cloves, which pricking on the grief they burn close to the flesh, and from thence draw the corruption with their mouth.

They have many professed physicians who with their charms and rattles with an infernal rout of words and actions will seem to suck their inward grief from their navels or their affected places. But concerning our surgeons they are generally so conceited of them that they believe that their plasters will heal any hurt.

Caput 9.

Of their economic and household affairs. The manner of obtaining their wives, and their wives' duties.

THEY EXPRESS THEIR LOVES TO SUCH WOMEN as they would make choice to live withal by presenting them with the fruits of their labors, as by fowl, fish, or wild beasts, which by their huntings, their bows and arrows, by weirs or otherwise they obtain; which they bring unto the young woman, as also of such summer fruits and berries which their travel abroad hath made them know readily where to gather, and those of the best kind in their season.

If the young maiden become once to be *sororians virgo*[1] and live under parents, the parents must allow of the suitor. And for their good wills the wooer promiseth that the daughter shall not want of such provisions nor of deerskins fitly dress'd for to wear; besides he promiseth to do his endeavor to procure her beads, pearl, and copper, and for handsel gives her before them something as a kind of *arra sponsalitia,* token of betrothing, or contract of a further amity and acquaintance to be continued between them. And so after as the liking grows, and as soon as he hath provided her a house (if he have none before) and some platters, mortars, and mats, he takes her home. And the weroances after this manner may have as many as they can obtain, howbeit all the rest whom they take after their first choice are, as it were, mercenary—hired but by covenant and condition for a time, a year or so after which they may put them away. But if they keep them longer than the time appointed, they must ever keep them, how deformed, diseased, or unaccompanable soever they may prove.

They are people most voluptuous, yet are the women very careful not to be suspected of dishonesty without the leave of their husbands. But he giving his consent, they are like Virgil's *scrantiae,* and may embrace the acquaintance of any stranger for nothing, and it is accounted no offense. And incredible it is with what heat both sexes of them are given over to those intemperances, and the men to preposterous Venus,[2] for which they are full of their own country diseases (the pox) very young; for cure of which yet they have both means of their own and sufficient skill, applying certain herbs and bruised roots which do presently ease and in time cure, and which kind of medicines—— calleth—— *medicamenta,*[3] having, beside the saxafras, one herb, as it is supposed, which in short time quencheth and mortifieth the malignant poison of that foul disease.

The women are said to be easily delivered of child, yet do they

---

[1] "Pubescent girl," *sororians* referring to the "swelling" of the breasts. (Latin)

[2] Immoderate sexual desire.

[3] Wright & Freund suggest "medicines Paracelsus calleth *sedativa medicamenta.*"

love children very dearly. To make the children hardy, in the coldest mornings they wash them in the rivers, and by paintings and ointments so tan their skins that after a year or two no weather will hurt them. As also to practice their children in the use of their bows and arrows, their mothers do not give them their breakfast in a morning before they have hit a mark which [s]he appoints them to shoot at. And commonly so cunning they will have them as throwing up in the air a piece of moss or some such light thing, the boy must with his arrow meet it in the fall and hit it or else he shall not have his breakfast.

Both men, women, and children have their several names, at first according to the several humor of their parents. And for the men-children at first, when they are young, their mothers give them a name, calling them by some affectionate title, or perhaps observing their promising inclination give it accordingly. And so the Great King Powhatan called a young daughter of his Pochahuntas, which may signify "little wanton," howbeit she was rightly called Amonute. At more ripe years, when they become able to travel into the woods and to go forth a-hunting, fowling, and fishing with their fathers, the father gives them another name as he finds him apt and of spirit to prove toward and valiant or otherwise, changing the mother's [name], which yet in the family is not so soon forgotten. And if so be it by agility, strength, or any extraordinary strain of wit, [or] he performs any remarkable or valorous exploit in open act of arms or by stratagem, especially in the time of extremity in the wars for the public, or common, state upon the enemy, the king taking notice of the same doth then not only in open view and solemnly reward him with some present of copper or chain of pearl and beads, but doth then likewise—and which they take for the most eminent and supreme favor—give him a name answerable to the attempt, not much differing herein from the ancient warlike encouragement and order of the Romans to a well-deserving and gallant young spirit.

The men fish, hunt, fowl, go to the wars, make the weirs, boats, and suchlike manly exercises and all labors abroad; the women as the weaker sort be put to the easier works: to sow their corn, to weed and cleanse the same of the orobanche, dodder, and chokeweed, and suchlike, which else would wind about the corn and hinder the growth of it. For by reason of the rankness and lustiness of the ground, such weeds spring up very easily and thick and if not pluck'd away, the corn would prosper so much the worse, for which they keep the hillocks of their corn and the passage between—for they set their wheat as we do our hops an equal distance one hill from another—as neat and clean as we do our garden beds. Likewise the women plant and attend the gardens, dress the meat brought home, and make their broths and *pockerehicory* drinks, make mats and baskets, pound their wheat, make their break [bread], prepare their vessels, bear all kinds of burthens, and suchlike; and to which the children set their hands, helping their mothers.

There are notes to be taken by which may be discerned a married woman from a maid: The maids have the forepart of their heads and sides shaven close, the hinder part very long, which they wind prettily and embroider with plaits, letting it hang so to the full length, shaven, as the Irish, by a dish.[1]

The women have a great care to maintain and keep firelight still within their houses. And if at any time it go out, they take it for an evil sign. But if it be out, they kindle it again presently by chafing a dry pointed stick in a hole of a little square piece of wood that firing itself will so fire moss, leaves, or any suchlike thing, that is apt quickly to burn.

They make themselves sometimes candles of the fattest splinters of the pine or fir tree, which will give a good clear light and burn strongly, though the matter will soon consume, for which they have many slivers ready cut out a foot long, some shorter, to be ready to light a second as soon as the first goes out. And in Shropshire between the lordships of Oswestry and Ellesmere the like lights they use at this day of the fir tree, of which it is said there be infinite taken daily out of the earth in a marish ground, and supposed to have lyen in the moist earth ever since the general floods, the chips whereof they use instead of candles in poor houses, so fat is the wood as is the

[1] The Percy MS between "full length" and "shaven" has, "The married women wear their hair all of a length shaven," etc.

smell also strong and sweet.

Their corn and indeed their copper, hatchets, hoes, beads, pearl, and most things with them of value, according to their own estimation, they hide one from the knowledge of another in the ground within the woods, and so keep them all the year or until they have fit use for them, as the Romans did their money and treasure in certain cellars called therefore, as Pliny remembers, *favissae.* And when they take them forth they scarce make their women privy to the storehouse.

They are much desirous of our commodities, and therefore when any of our boats arrive before their towns they will come down unto us and suffer us to come up unto their houses, and demand after copper, white beads, hoes to pare their cornfields, and hatchets, for which they will give us of such things as they have in exchange, as deerskins, furs of the wildcat, black fox, beaver, otter, *arrachoune,* etc., fowl, fish, deer, or bear-[?][1] skins, tried deer's suet made up handsomely in cakes, their country corn, peas, beans, and suchlike. And indeed, to say truth, their victual is their chief riches.

We have observed how when they would affirm anything by much earnestness and truth they use to bind it by a kind of oath, either by the life of the great king or by pointing up to the sun and clapping the right hand upon the heart. And sometimes they have been understood to swear by the manes of their dead father.

If they will express that we and they will be or are all one friends or brothers, as their word is, they will join the indices, or two forefingers, together of either hand, as the Indians of Nova Francia, or else clasping their fingers within ours they will say so, and so close joined and near we are unto their loves.

The reason why each chief patron of a family, especially weroances, are desirous and indeed strive for many wives is because they would have many children who may, if chance be, fight for them when they are old, as also then feed and maintain them. Yet sure for the number of people inhabiting these parts this country hath not

[1] I am unable to read the second element in this compound: "-shck" "-thck"?

appeared so populous here to us as elsewhere in the West Indies, and perhaps their ignorance in not finding out yet the use of many things necessary and beneficial to nature, which their country yet plentifully and naturally affords, their often wars for women, in which many hundreds perish, and their immoderate use and multiplicity of women—and those often full of foul diseases—leave this country not so well stocked as other parts of the main and as the islands have been found to be by the Spaniards. Besides (under correction) and it may be a problem in philosophy whether variety of women be a furtherer or hinderer of many births, it being clear in these countries where, as I said, so many penuries for want of knowledge yet be amongst the people that the tired body cannot have these sensual helps, as the Turks [have], to hold up the immoderate desires. Many women dividing the body and the strength thereof make it generally unfit to the office of increase, rather than otherwise. And so may the common people especially, for the most part for this reason likewise, be not so long lived here as elsewhere, even[1] amongst savages where greater moderation is used, and where they keep a stricter ceremony in the kind of marriages, and have not as many women as they can buy or win by force and violence from the enemies.

Caput 10.

The native commodities of the country and sustenance which it yields for the life of man, as of the fruits, herbs, roots; trees for use and ornament; beasts, fowl, fish; metals, pearls, etc.

THAT IT MAY YET FURTHER APPEAR how this country is not so naked of commodity nor wretched of provision fit for the sustenance of mankind as some ignorantly imagine and others have falsely reported, I will in this chapter propose, for the testimony of the truth

[1] Precisely.

whereof I may appeal to many hundreds which may convince the relation of a discourse only for form or assentation delivered.

Nor let any man suppose that materials of so goodly a navy as may be there framed—for planks, masts, pitch and tar, soap-ashes, turpentine, iron, cordage; mulberry trees for silk, and another kind of silk of the grass; saxafras and other aromatical drugs, gums, oil, and dyes are of no value or not worthy the exposure of a colony for secondary and politic ends to be established there, since Muscovia and Polonia do yearly receive many thousands for pitch, tar, soap-ashes, rosin, flax, cordage, sturgeon, masts, yards, wainscot, furs,[1] glass, and suchlike; also Sweathland [Sweden] receives much from us for iron and copper; France in the like manner for wine, canvas, and salt; Spain as much for iron, steel, figs, raisins, and sacks; Italy for silks and velvets consumes our chief commodities; Holland maintains itself by fishing and trading at our own doors. All these temporize[2] with others for necessity, but all as uncertain as peace and war, besides the charge, travel, and danger in transporting them by seas, lands, storms, and pirates.

Then how much may Virginia have the prerogative for the benefit of our land, whenas within one hundred miles all these are to be had, either ready provided by nature or else to be prepared, were there but industrious men to labor, so as then here is a place: a nurse for soldiers, a practice for mariners, a trade for merchants, a reward for the good, and that which is most of all: a business most acceptable to God to bring poor infidels to His knowledge. And albeit our ships, some will object, now returning from thence yearly come freighted home only yet with certain precious woods, it is to be rememb'red how that from Hispaniola, Cuba, and Portricco the Spaniards in their yearly [early] days of possessing the Indies made returns a long time of the like, as of cassia, fistola, ebony, guacum, lignum vitae, etc., until they found out the mines, as may we, we doubt nothing in the heart and bosom of ours, when we shall be enabled truly to dissect it, finding such appearances now in the suburbs of it, as it were, the which to time, the true revealer of great things, I submit; or rather to

[1] Or perhaps "firs."
[2] Negotiate.

Him from whom, if our unthankfulness deprive us not of the blessing, we may expect a prosperous and assured compensation and satisfaction to wipe off all scars *et in assem satisfacere*[1] all the charges and disbursements which have hitherto gone out for it. Albeit such is the business as it should awake all charitable Christians to follow it according to the goodness of the *cause* and not according to the greatness of profit and commodity. Let Mammon perish with his gold, that hath no other but such stubble merely to enkindle the flame of his zeal unto so holy a work!

The natives have here a kind of wheat which they call *poketawes,* as the West Indians call the same *maize.* The form of it is of a man's tooth somewhat thicker, for the preparing of the ground for which they use this manner: They bruise the bark of those trees which they will take away near the root; then do they scorch the roots with fire that they grow no more; the next year with a crooked piece of wood they beat up the trees by the roots, and in their moulds they plant their corn. The manner is thus:

They make a hole in the earth with a stick, and into it they put 3 or 5 grains of wheat and one or 3 of beans. These holes they make 4 or 5 foot one from another, for the corn being set close together one stalk would choke else the growth of another and so render both unprofitable. Their women and children do continually keep the ground with weeding. And when the corn is grown middle high they hill it about like a hop-yard, and the stalk will grow a man's height or rather more from the ground, and every stalk commonly beareth two ears, some 3, many but one, and some none.

Every ear ordinarily hath betwixt 300 and 600 grains, and the ear grows with a great hose, or pill [peel], about it and above it. The stalk being green hath a sweet juice in it somewhat like a sugar cane, which is the cause that when they gather their corn green they suck the stalks. For as we gather green peas so do they their corn being green, which excelleth their old.

Peas they have which the natives call *assentemmens* and are the same which in Italy they call *fagioli.*

---

[1] "To satisfy to the penny." (Latin)

Their beans are little like a French bean, and are the same which the Turks call *garnances;* and these kind of pulse they much esteem for dainties.

By their dwellings are some great mulberry trees, and these in some part of the country are found growing naturally in pretty groves. There was an essay made to make silk, and surely the worms prospered excellently well until the master workman fell sick, during which time they were eaten with rats. And this will be a commodity not meanly profitable, now it is seriously considered of and order taken that it shall be duly followed.

In some places we find chestnuts whose wild fruit I may well say equalize the best in France, Spain, Germany, Italy, or those so commended in the Black Sea by Constantinople, of all which I have eaten.

They have a small fruit growing in little trees, husked like a chestnut, but the fruit most like a very small acron. This they call *chechinquamins,* and these with chestnuts they boil 4 or 5 hours, of which they make both broth and bread for their chief men or at their greatest feasts.

They have cherries much like a damozin [damson], but for their taste and color we call them cherries. And a plum there is somewhat fairer than a cherry, of the same relish, than which are seldom a better eaten.

They have a berry much like our gooseberries in greatness, color, and taste. These they call *rawcomenes,* and they do eat them raw or boiled.

In the wat'ry valleys groweth a berry which they call *ocoughtanamins,*[1] very much like unto capers. These they gather and dry in the heat of the sun. And when they will eat them they boil them near half a day, for otherwise they differ not much from poison.

Mattoume groweth as our bents [rushes] do in meadows. The seed is not much unlike to rye, though much smaller. This they use for a dainty bread butt'red with deer's suet.

They have a plum which they call *pessemmins,* like to a medlar in

[1] Chokecherries?

England, but of a deep tawny color. They grow on a most high tree. When they are not fully ripe they are harsh and choky and fur a man's mouth like alum, howbeit being taken fully ripe it is a reasonable pleasant fruit, somewhat luscious. I have seen our people put them into their baked and sodden puddings. There be [those] whose taste allows them to be as precious as the English apricock. I confess it is a good kind of horse plum.

Here is a cherry-red fruit both within and without as I have seen the like in the Bermudas, which we call the prickle-pear. In the Indies they are well known to every common mariner. They bear a broad, thick, spongeous leaf full of kernels. They be like the pomegranate. The taste of this pear is very pleasant and the juice cold and fresh like the water in the West Indian nut called *cocus*. The juice is sharp and penetrable like deal-wine [Rhenish?], prescribed powerful against the stone.

Here is a fruit by the naturals called a *maracock;* this groweth generally low and creepeth in a manner amongst the corn, albeit I have seen it planted in a garden within our fort at James-town to spread and rise as high as the pale. It is of the bigness of a queen-apple, and hath many azurine, or blue, kernels like as a pomegranate, and it bloometh a most sweet and delicate flower, and it is a good summer cooling fruit, and in every field where the Indians plant their corn be cartloads of them.

The *macokos* is of the form of our pumpions; I must confess nothing so good; 'tis of a more waterish taste. The inhabitants seethe a kind of million [melon] which they put into their walnut milk and so make a kind of toothsome meat.

In April, May, and June are great store of strawberries, raspices, hurts, etc., and many herbs in the springtime are commonly dispersed throughout the woods, good for broths and salads, as violets, purslane, sorrel, and roses in their season etc., besides many we used whose names we know not.

It would easily raise a well-stayed judgment into wonder, as Sir Thomas Dale hath writ sometimes unto His Majesty's council here for Virginia, to behold the goodly vines burthening every neighbor bush and climbing the tops of highest trees, and those full of clusters of grapes in their kind, how overdreeped and shadowed soever from the sun and though never pruned or manured. I dare say it that we have eaten there as full and luscious a grape as in the villages between Paris and Amiens. And I have drunk often of the rathe wine which Doctor Bohune and other of our people have made full as good as your French-British wine. XX [twenty] gallons at a time have been sometimes made without any other help than by crushing the grape with the hand, which letting to settle 5 or 6 days hath in the drawing forth proved strong and heady. Unto what perfection might not these be brought by the art and industry of many skillful vignerons, being thus naturally good? And how material and principal a commodity this may prove either for the benefit of such who shall inhabit there or to be returned over hither, especially where we may have pipe-staves to make our cask of so cheap and at hand, I refer it to indifferent judgments.

Many roots the Indians have here likewise for food. The chief they call *tockawhough,* and it groweth like a flag in low muddy freshes. In one day a savage will gather sufficient for a week. These roots are much of the greatness and taste of potatoes. They use to rake up a great number of them in old leaves[1] and fern, and then cover all with earth or sand in the manner of a coal pit. On each side they continue a great fire a day and a night before they dare eat it. Raw it is no better than poison, and being roasted, except it be tender and the heat abated, or sliced and dried in the sun, mixed with sorrel and meal, or suchlike, it will prickle and torment the throat extremely. And yet, in summer they use this ordinarily for bread.

They have another root which they call *vighsacan [wighsacan,* likely milkweed]. As the other feedeth the body, so this cureth their hurts and diseases. It is a small root which they bruise and apply to the wound.

Pocones is a small root that groweth in the mountains, which being dried and beaten into powder turneth red. And this they use for swellings, aches, anointing their joints, painting their heads and garments with it, for which they account it very precious and of much worth.

---

[1] Smith has "oak leaves."

Musquaspenne is a root of the bigness of a finger, and as red as blood. In drying, it will wither almost to nothing. With this they use to paint their mats, targets, and suchlike.

There is here great store of tobacco, which the savages call *apooke,* howbeit it is not of the best kind. It is but poor and weak and of a biting taste; it grows not fully a yard above ground, bearing a little yellow flower like to henbane; the leaves are short and thick, somewhat round at the upper end, whereas the best tobacco, of Trinidado and the Oronoque, is large, sharp, and growing 2 or 3 yards from the ground, bearing a flower of the breadth of our bellflowers in England. The savages here dry the leaves of this apooke over the fire and sometimes in the sun, and crumble it into powder—stalks, leaves, and all—taking the same in pipes of earth, which very ingeniously they can make. We observe that those Indians which have one, two, or more women take much, but such who have as yet no appropriate woman take little or none at all.

Here is also pellitory of Spain and divers other simples which our apothecaries have gathered and found to be good and medicinable.

In the low marishes grow plots of onions, containing an acre of ground or more in many places, but they are small like chibols or scallions, not past the bigness of the top of one's thumb. They eat well sod or otherwise in salad or in bak'd meats. Our people find good and wholesome relish in them, howbeit the inhabitants cannot abide to eat of them. And these onions, they do for the most part appear in the last season of the year, for it is to be understood how the Indians divide the year into 5 seasons: the winter which they call *papanow,* the spring *cattapeuk,* the summer *cohattayough,* the earing of their corn *nepenough,* the harvest and fall of the leaf *taquitock.*

They have divers beasts fit for provision. The chief are deer, both red and fallow—great store in the country towards the heads of the rivers, though not so many amongst the rivers. In our island about James-Town or [are] some few, nothing differing from ours in England but that of some of them the antlets of their horns are not so many. Our people have seen 200, 100, and 50 in a herd.

There is a beast they call *aroughcoune,* much like a badger, tailed like a fox, and of a mingle black and grayish color, and which useth to live on trees as squirrels do, excellent meat. We kill often of them, the greatest number yet we obtain by trade.

Squirrels they have and those in great plenty are very good meat. Some are near as great as our smallest sort of wild rabbits, some blackish or black and white like those which are here called silver-haired, but the most are gray.

A smaller beast they have which the Indians call *assapanick,* not passing so big as a rat, but we call them "flying squirrels" because spreading their legs from whence to either shoulder runs a flap, or fin, much like a bat's wing, and so stretching the largeness of their skins, they have been seen to make a pretty flight from one tree to another sometimes 30 or 40 yards.

An *opussum* is a beast as big as a pretty beagle. Of gray color, it hath a head like a swine, ears, feet, and tail like a rat. She carries her young ones under her belly in a piece of her own skin like as in a bag, which she can open and shut to let them out or take them in as she pleaseth, and doth therein lodge, carry, and suckle her young, and eats in taste like a pig.

Muscascus is a beast black in color, proportioned like a water rat. He hath a cod within him which yieldeth a strong scent like unto musk. It is good meat if the cod be taken out, otherwise the flesh will taste most strong and rank of the musk; so will the broth wherein it is sod.

Hares they have some few about James Town, but both in the islands and main up at the Falls, and below about Fort Henry and Charles Fort, great store, howbeit they are no bigger than our conies.

Bears there be many towards the seacoast, which the Indians hunt most greedily, for indeed they love them above all other their flesh, and therefore hardly sell any of them unto us unless upon large proffers of copper, beads, and hatchets. We have eaten of them and they are very toothsome, sweet venison, as good to be eaten as the flesh of a calf of two years old, howbeit they are very little in comparison of those of Muscovia and Tartaria.

The beaver there is as big as an ordinary water dog, but his legs exceeding short, her forefeet like a dog's, his hinder-feet like a swan's, his tail somewhat like the form of a racket, bare without hair, which to eat the savages esteem a great delicate.

Otters there be many, which, as the beavers, the Indians take with gins and snares, and esteem the skins great ornaments.

And of all these beasts they use to feed when they catch them.

Lions I will not positively affirm that the country hath, since our people never yet saw any, howbeit in their discoveries to the Mangoags they did light once upon two skins which by all the judgments in the fort were supposed to be lions' skins; and this last year, myself being at the Falls with Sir Thomas Dale, I found in an Indian house certain claws tied up in a string, which I brought away and into England, and they are assured unto me to be lion's claws.

There is also a beast which the Indians call *vetchumquoyes* in the form of a wildcat.

Their foxes are like our silver-haired conies, of a small proportion and not smelling so rank like those in England.

The dogs of the country are like their wolves and cannot bark but howl, and are not unlike those ancient dogs called *cracutae* which were said to be engend'red of a wolf and a bitch, and are like the Turkish jackals keeping about the graves of the dead in the common *polyandrium,* or place of sepulture.

Their wolves are not much bigger than our English foxes.

Martens, polecats, weasels, and monkeys[1] we know they have because we have seen many of their skins, though very seldom any of them alive. But one thing is worth the observing: We could never perceive[2] that their flies, serpents, or other vermin were any way pernicious, when in the south parts of America they are always dangerous and often deadly.

Likewise as they have fruits and beasts, so have they fowl, and that great store. Of birds the eagle is the greatest devourer, and many of them there. There be divers sort of hawks, spar[row]hawks, lannerets, goshawks, falcons, and ospreys. I brought home from thence this year myself a falcon and a tassel [tercel], the one sent by Sir Thomas Dale to His Highness the Prince and the other was presented to the Earl of Salisbury—fair ones, what the proof of them may be I have not learned. They prey most upon fish.

---

[1] Smith has "minks."

[2] Smith has, "We could never perceive their vermin destroy our hens, eggs, nor chickens ... nor their flies, etc."

Turkeys there be great store wild in the woods like pheasants in England, 40 in a company, as big as our tame here, and it is an excellent fowl, and so passing good meat as I may well say it is the best of any kind of flesh which I have ever yet eaten there.

Partridges there are little bigger than our quails. I have known of our men to have killed them with their small shot sometime from off a tree, 5 or 6 at a shoot.

Cranes white and gray, herns [herons] both gray and white, ouzels, or blackbirds, with red shoulders, thrushes and divers sorts of small birds, some carnation, some blue, and some other strange kinds to us unknown by name.

In winter there are great plenty of swans, geese, brants, duck, widgeon, dotterel, oxeyes, mallard, teal, sheldrakes, and divers diving fowls, and of all these sorts that abundance, as I dare avow it, no country in the world may have more!

Parakitoes[1] I have seen many in the winter and known divers killed, yet be they a fowl most swift of wing. Their wings and breasts are of a greenish color with forked tails; their heads some crimson, some yellow, some orange tawny, very beautiful. Some of our colony who have seen of the East Indian parrots affirm how they are like to that kind, which hath given us somewhat the more hope of the nearness of the South Sea. These parrots by all probability like enough to come from some of the countries upon that sea.

A kind of wood pigeon we see in the wintertime and of them such numbers as I should draw from our homelings here (such who have seen peradventure scarce one more than in the market!) the credit of my relation concerning all the other in question if I should express what extended flocks and how many thousands in one flock I have seen in one day, wond'ring, I must confess, at their flight when like so many thickened clouds they having fed to the nor'ward in the daytime return again more southwardly towards night to their roost. But there be many hundred witnesses who may convince this report if herein it testifieth an untruth.

To the natural commodities which the country hath of fruits, beasts, and fowl, we may also add the no mean commodity of fish, of

---

[1] The Carolina parakeet, now hunted to extinction.

which in March and April are great shoals of herrings.

Sturgeon great store, commonly in May, if the year be forward. I have been at the taking of some before Algernoone Fort and in Southampton River in midst of March. And they remain with us June, July, and August and in that plenty as before expressed in the—— chapter.

Shads great store of a yard long, and for sweetness and fatness a reasonable good fish. He is only full of small bones like our barbels in England.

Grampus, porpoise, seals, stingrays, brets, mullets, white salmons, trouts, soles, plaice, conyfish, rockfish, eels, lampreys, catfish, perch of three sorts, shrimps, crayfishes, cockles, mussels, and more such needless to name—all good fish.

There is the garfish, some of which are a yard long, small and round like an eel and as big as a man's leg, having a long snout full of sharp teeth.

Oysters there be in whole banks and beds, and those of the best. I have seen some 13 inches long. The savages use to boil oysters and mussels together; and with the broth they make a good spoon meat thickened with the flour of their wheat. And it is a great thrift and husbandry with them to hang the oysters upon strings, being shal'd, and dried in the smoke, thereby to preserve them all the year.

There be two sorts of sea crabs and the one our people call a king crab, and they are taken in shoal waters from off the shore a dozen at a time hanging one upon another's tail. They are of a foot in length and half a foot in breadth, having many legs and a long tail. The Indians seldom eat of this kind.

There is a kind of shellfish of the proportion of a cockle but far greater. It hath a smooth shell, not ragged as our cockles. 'Tis good meat though somewhat tough.

Tortoises here such as in the Bermudas I have seen about the entrance of our bay, but we have not taken of them. But of the land tortoises we take and eat daily, the difference between which is nothing in shape but in color and bigness: Those of the land are gray with a long tail; those of the sea have black shells speckled with yellow, the bodies great in compass like a target.

But the most strange fish is a small one so like the picture of St.

George's dragon as possibly can be except the legs and wings; and the toad fish which will swell till it be like to burst when it cometh into the air.

Thus it appeareth that this country affordeth many excellent vegetables and living creatures, yet I must say true of grass for the present, there is little or none but what groweth in low marishes. For all the country is overshadowed with trees whose droppings continually turneth grass to weeds, by reason of the rankness of the ground which would soon be amended by good husbandry.

Howbeit woods it hath great, beautiful, fruitful, pleasant, and profitable, the grounds clean under them at least passable both for horse and foot. The oak here for stature and timber may compare with any, being so tall and straight that they will bear—— [s]quare of good timber for 20 yards long. Of this wood there is 2 or 3 several kinds, the acrons of one kind, whose bark is more white than the other, is somewhat sweetish; which being boiled half a day in several waters at last affords a sweet oil which they call *monohominy*. They keep it in gourds to anoint their heads and joints. The fruit they eat made in bread or otherwise.

There is also elm and ash of which are made soap-ashes. If the trees be very great, the ashes will be very good and melt to hard lumps, being carefully burned. But if they be small and suff'red to partake too much of the smoke, they will be but powder, nothing so good as the other, beside they will be very foul and black.

Of walnuts there be three kinds: The black walnut, which is returned home yearly by all shipping from thence, and yields good profit, for it is well bought up to make wainscot, tables, cupboards, chairs, and stools—of a delicate grain and color like ebony and not subject to the worm. The fruit of this is little; it is thin-shelled and the kernel bitter. Another kind there is which bears a great fruit with a hard shell and the meat very sweet, and of these the Indians make oil to drop[1] their joints and smear their bodies with, which do make them supple and nimble.

The third sort is as this last exceeding hard shelled and hath a

[1] Sprinkle.

passing sweet kernel. This last kind the Indians beat into pieces with stones, and putting them shells and all into mortars, mingling water with them, wooden pestles pound them so long together until they make a kind of milk, or oily liquor, which they call *powcohicora.*

There is a kind of wood which we call cypress because both the wood, the fruit, and leaf did most resemble it; and of these trees there are some near 3 fathom about at the root, very straight and 50, 60, or 80 foot without a branch.

The cedars for savor and color may compare with those of Lebanon, the climate of the one and the other differing little.

Of saxafras there is plenty enough, the roots whereof not many years since were sold for 20^{s} a lb. and better. And if order may yet be taken that overmuch quantity be not returned, and that which shall be brought be kept in one hand, all Europe may be served thereof at good rates. The cedars and saxafras yield a kind of gum in a small proportion of themselves. There have been conclusions tried to extract it out of the wood, but nature afforded greater quantity than art could produce.

There are pines infinite, especially by the seacoast, and many other sorts, the use of which are commodious for shipping, pipe-staves, clapboard, yards, and masts for shipping. And those here are so fair and large as a ship of 300 ton burthen called the *Starre*, sent thither the last year [and] upon purpose fitted and prepared with scupper holes to take in masts, was not able to stow 40 of fourscore unless they should have cut them shorter, which is a commodity rightly understood of such moment for this kingdom—all the easterly countries from whence we have heretofore had them so impoverished and wasted as they are not able to furnish His Majesty's navy (witness how hardly were obtained those which we had last from thence, and those upon His Majesty's private and particular letter to the King of Denmark)—as were enough, it may be boldly said, to make good the whole charge of our plantation!

By the dwellings of the savages are bay trees, wild roses, and a kind of low tree which bears a cod like to the peas, but nothing so big—we take it to be locust.

Crabtrees there be, but the fruit small and bitter. Howbeit being graffed upon, soon might we have of our own apples of any kind, pears, and what else.

Besides these fruit trees there is a white poplar and another tree like unto it that yieldeth a very clear and odoriferous gum like turpentine, which I have heard Doctor Bohoune and some of our surgeons there say may well be reckoned a kind of balsam, and will heal a green wound.

There groweth in the island of James Town a small tree of leaves, arms, and fruit like the myrtle tree. The fruit thereof hath a taste with the myrtle, but much more binding. These trees grow in great plenty round about a standing pond of fresh water in the midst of the island, the pill, or rind, whereof is of great force against inveterate dysenterical fluxes, of which Doctor Bohoune made open experiment in many of our men laboring with such diseases, and therefore wisheth all such physicians as shall go thither to make use thereof.

For minerals we will promise nothing but the hope, of which, seeing the low ground yields many fair shows, the mountains cannot be doubted but that in them many sorts will be found. And our people in their first discovery into the Monocan country discovered 2 mines, the one within 6 miles of the head of the Falls, which takes the name of Namantack, the finder of it, which is conceived will be worth the exploring and with little charge; the other lies in the midway between 2 towns of Monocan, the nearest called Mowhemniche, the furthest Massinnacack, distant one from another 14 miles, of whose goodness there is no great doubt, since the spar only taken no further than 2 or 3 foot into the earth affords metal worth the labor.

And concerning a silver mine not far from the same place, an Helvetian, one William Henrick Faldoe, assured our lord general, and therefore made his provision for the search thereof; and having been in England, made earnest suit unto our treasurer and His Majesty's council here resident for Virginia, with whom he contracted and ent'red into conditions for one year and a half for the full performance of this work. But His Lordship being not at that time enabled with sufficient company to make good that search by raising forts and planting so far into the country, which only must have secured the workmen, it hath pleased God since that time that the said Helvetian hath died of a burning fever and with him the knowledge of that mine which in his lifetime he would not be drawn to reveal unto anyone else of the colony.

And there is extant an old plot which His Lordship hath showed me wherein by a Portugal our seat is laid out and in the same two silver mines pricked down.

And at the head of the said Falls the Indians there inhabiting tip their arrows with crystal, and we find many pieces scattered in the grit and sand of the same, where likewise on Pembrook side Sir Thomas Dale hath mentioned in his letters to the lords of the council of a goodly iron mine. And Captain Newport hath brought home of that metal so sufficient a trial as there hath been made 16 or 17 ton of iron so good as the East Indian merchants bought it of the Virginian Company, preferring it before any other iron of what country soever.

And for copper, the hills to the nor'west have that store, as the people themselves, rememb'red in the first chapter called the Bocootawwonaukes, are said to part the solid metal from the stone without fire, bellows, or additament, and beat it into plates, the like whereof is hardly found in any other part of the world. Likewise Captain Argoll, as his lordship bears record in his printed narration, in the River Patawomeck found a mine of antimony, which, as aforesaid, never dwells single but holds assured league with quicksilver; as likewise a mine of lead. And we hear the Indians make many particular descriptions of alum mines to the southward.

Lastly, that the lakes have pearls it cannot be doubted, for we ourselves have seen many chains and bracelets worn by the people, and we have found plenty of them in the sepulchers of their kings, though discolored by burning the oysters in the fire and deformed by the gross boring.

And thus to conclude, we may well say how these poor people have many moral goods, such as are *per accidens* plentiful enough amongest them, and as much, poor souls, as they come short of those *bona moralia* which are *per se.* For the country (who sees not by what hath been said?) is not so barren, ill-destined, and wretched under an unhappy constellation, but that it hath even beside necessary helps and commodities for life apparent proofs of many natural riches, and which are all *bona fortunae.* Again, they are healthy enough, which is *bonum corporis.* Nor is nature a stepdame unto them concerning their *aptas membrorum compositiones.* Only, God wot, I must grant the *bonum morale,* as aforesaid, which is *per se,* they have not *in medio* which is *in virtute.* And then how can they ever obtain it *in ultimo,* which is *in faelicitate?*—to teach them both which is the end of our planting amongst them, to let them know what virtue and goodness is and the reward of both; to teach them religion and the crown of the righteous; to acquaint them with grace that they may participate with glory, which God grant in mercy unto them.

FINIS LIB[RI] 1.

42. John Clark

Confession of the English Pilot of Virginia, 18 February 1613

[translated from the Spanish by Irene A. Wright]

< A. G. I. 147–5–17, **Wright 1920:476** (with original), Quinn 1979e:156

Clark has been a captive over a year and a half. More information is now persuaded out of him in Spain. We get a picture of the downriver forts, the size of Jamestown, and other matters. Clark had hardly felt threatened by the Indians—some friendly, some not, but not many of either.

It is noteworthy how well his account of the Point Comfort incident tallies with the others. But contrast his report of forts and garrisons and ordnance with de Molina's airy dismissal of the military effectiveness of same.

Clark changes some of his testimony from Havana §36. He claims to be three years older and a Catholic. He says nothing about gold, nothing about pirates among the colonists, and says that a thousand men there can bear arms—a patriotic exaggeration in wholesale.

IN THE CITY OF MADRID on the 18th day of the month of February of 1613, the Señor Licenciado Don Francisco de Texada, of His Majesty's Royal Council of the Indies, and of his Council for War in the Indies, for certain purposes touching the service of His Majesty, caused to be brought before him a man, English by nation, who was in the custody of Captain Don Alonso Flores by order of the said war council, and in the presence of me the present scribe, His Worship took and received this man's oath in form of law, and he gave it well and completely; and having been sworn the following questions were asked him—

Being asked how he was called, he said that he is called Juan Clarque.

Being asked of what place he was an inhabitant and native, he said that he is an inhabitant of the city of London in England.

Being asked if he is a Roman Catholic, he said yes.

CONFESSION

Being asked what office and profession he has, he said a pilot, and that for four years he has followed that office, though before this he was in a way of knowing it, because for four years he had sailed in different parts of the world.

Being asked when he made the voyage to Virginia, and with whom, and for what purposes, and how he was brought to the city of Havana, he said that in the previous year of 1611, at the beginning of March, he set sail from the port of London in a ship of 300 tons, in which he went as pilot, together with two other ships, the one of 150 tons and the other of 90, in which went 300 men of war in addition to the mariners, and 600 barrels of flour and 50 of powder and some boxes of arquebusses, the whole dispatched on account of the merchants of London for Virginia, [and] as general of which went Don Thomas Diel, who was to live there, as in fact he remained, as governor of Virginia; and they spent upon that voyage two months and one half; and the course they took was that from England they were sailing to the southwest until they came into the latitude of the Canary Islands, which was at 28 degrees; and from there they sailed west-southwest to the latitude of Dominica in 14½ degrees, where they took in water and stayed two days; and from there they sailed north-northwest to the island of Niebes, where they remained four days refreshing the people, because they had some men sick; and from there northwest-quarter-north to the Passage, up which they went until they made the coast of Virginia between the Cape of Deception and Cape Henry; and that the reason for steering north-west-quarter-north and north-northwest several times was because of the currents which pushed them to the northeast and the variation of the needle, which they warned him to be 7 and 8 degrees; and from there they sailed north-northwest until they were off Cape Henry, which is one of the capes between which one enters into the bay, into which they entered, and proceeded to go up within the river to a point which in English they call Punt Confort, which in Castilian means "point of consolation"; and there they put the people ashore; and the mariners took the three ships up the river to the principal place, which they call Jacobus, where they anchored, because the ships could not go up beyond the said port, though ships of 40 or 50 tons, which draw two yards and one half of water, can go up 30 leagues;

and that this deponent being in company with the English, because he had come from that principal place to bring a barge with flour, of that which he brought in the ships, for the provision of the English who garrison the forts at Point Comfort, there came a longboat in which were twelve or thirteen men, of whom three landed; and the captain of the fort having gone to them with a squad of soldiers asked the three men—one of whom this deponent knew that he was an Englishman and a pilot because of having seen him in a house when Don Luis Faxardo went to burn the galleons of Tunis—why they came there, and they replied to seek a ship of the King of Spain which had been lost on that coast; and the captain told him that he would have to give account to his governor of their coming, who was then at the principal place called Jacobus, twenty leagues from there, and so he did in a barge. And he said to one of the three that in order that the caravel should not be lost in the bay where it had anchored, they should bring it up into the river and to Point Comfort, where it would be safe; and he having replied that whoever was left in her would not know how to do it, and that they should give him a pilot for that purpose, the captain ordered this deponent to take the same longboat in which the three had come and go on board the said caravel, and so he did; and on his coming to her, the master said that he would not sail in unless they brought back to her those who were missing; and as [the English captain] would not give them up, though on another day the longboat returned for them, the said caravel without waiting longer sailed away with this deponent to Havana, leaving the three in the power of the English.

Being asked what roadsteads and of what quality, and what forts and of what sort, there are from the bay up to the said city of Jacobus, he said that the bay is seven or eight leagues wide and with good soundings, although ships have not security or shelter in it, and so go in until they shelter themselves behind Point Comfort, as he did, where there is room for thirty ships up to 800 tons to anchor; for although when the wind is north[1] some sea is felt in there, it is not a

[1] Apparently when the wind blows northward (a south wind), where there is a five mile fetch across Hampton Roads.

matter of much importance. And on that same point there is a fort beside the shore where seven pieces of artillery are mounted, each of about thirty hundredweight, placed alongside the water in such a way that, since the entrance is narrow and the channel is not more than a musket-shot broad, ships cannot enter or anchor without the artillery doing them damage; and in that fort there are fifty soldiers of ordinary garrison; and half a league from it there are two other small fortifications, each having one piece of artillery of ten or twelve hundredweight, to guard the cornfields from the Indians; and that these forts and the first one on the point are fortified with stout palisades well joined together.

Being asked how many houses there were in the said place called Jacobus, and of what sort, and what soldiers and what artillery, he said that there are about 100 wooden houses, and in them and in the other places that he has mentioned about a thousand men capable of bearing arms, what with traders and soldiers and laborers, and thirty women; and that the place is fortified with palisades in the form mentioned, and probably has about sixteen pieces of artillery, ten heavy and the other smaller, the heavy pieces of about forty or fifty hundredweight, and the others of about sixteen or seventeen; and that he does not know that there is any other settlement besides that; and that of the Indians some are friendly and some are not, and that it appears to him that there is no great number of either sort; and that what up to the present time he has seen taken from that region to England by way of merchandise is timber for making different things, and sassafras; and what they bring from England are provisions of flour and other things, and munitions, and cattle of different sorts, which do well.

Being asked if he knows that they have found any mines of silver, he said that he does not know.

Being asked if he knows the reasons why the English have settled that country, and for how long at that place, he said that he understands that they have been settled at the place for six years, and that the reasons are to acquire land and build ships; and that he does not know the result, beyond the fact that they are in such a situation that in fifteen days at most they can reach the Windward Islands.[1]

Being asked how long it takes to sail from Virginia to England, he said a month, and that he has understood that the voyage is good; and that sometimes they sail east-quarter-northeast until they make the islands of Flores, but that it is possible for them not to make them on their way to England, though it is better and safe navigation to make the islands; and that for Spain, sailing east, they make the islands of Fayal or Tercera, whence the ordinary course is taken.

Being asked how many times he had been in Virginia, and for how long, and what ships he found there [besides] that in which he was, he said that he has made no other voyage than that which he has mentioned, and that he was there forty days before he was taken, and that he found there a ship of 150 tons about to sail for England with timber and sassafras.

Being asked what he believes the English will have done to the three persons who were left in their power, he says that he considers it certain that they will not be ill-treated, because the English do not ill-treat prisoners.

Being asked if he has learned subsequently that there is in this court any news respecting them, he said that an Englishman who lives in the Calle Mayor of this town told this deponent that an acquaintance of his told him that he had talked in England with the English pilot who went with Don Diego Molina,[2] and he was one of the three who was left in Virginia.

Being asked his age, he said that he was forty years old. And he signed this with his name, and declared that what he has said in this his answer and declaration is the truth, under obligation of the said oath which he has taken. And His Worship has added his rubric.

JOHN CLARK.

I, Damian de Carrion y Bricuela, was present.

[1] This played into Spanish fears of Jamestown as a harbor for corsairs.

[2] False. By Dale's order Lembri was hanged from the yardarm once they sighted England.

43. Reverend Alexander Whitaker

Good News from Virginia

< **Whitaker 1613 [1937]**

Here is a wonderful sermon on liberality, preached west to east across the Atlantic by the minister at Henrico. Virginia in 1612 is God's Cause, manifest in having been three times saved by coincidence (coincidence customarily considered as a miracle revealing divine will). Hence the Reverend Master Whitaker assures us the lessons of the Bible on charity now oblige the English nation to be forthcoming with support in any form commensurate with a giver's resources, even if only prayers, in securing both God's kingdom and England's colony.

The sermon is prefaced by Rev. Crashaw's lecture, which is nearly as long. Crashaw was never in Virginia but furnishes an intimate introduction to the preacher and a complementary appeal for support for his colony. He seems to have functioned as a canon missioner for Virginia, but had no such title that I can determine.

Is Protestantism to be put to shame, they wonder, beside the worldwide Roman Catholic missionary effort and the national dedication pouring forth from the Iberian kingdoms? In 1613, Protestantism is on the retreat on all European fronts and barely planted in the New World.

Meanwhile both preachers tell us a great deal about Virginia. The land is so fertile and so virgin, the future is obvious, only the timetable is in question.

And about Whitaker. He rejects monkish, mendicant Catholicism, yet he has given up everything he owns to be a missionary. He believes in the good work of charity, hence is no Puritan, yet he insists good works must come from a pure heart. We confront a scholar in all three Classical languages who speaks plainly; who says he has little space, only to give us, I think, an exhaustive expostulation of the grandest lesson of the Bible. He is a master of argument with a minimum of rhetoric, well traveled in books and yet quite happy to be where he is right in the middle of North America. He complains he is out of shape and loves the chance to get outdoors and do some physical labor. Most of our texts are best read initially with some speed. Not so Whitaker. This is *spoken* delivery and formal argument, and should be read slowly with moving lips.

Good News was carried straight to the printer and published under the auspices of the Virginia Company, who were all too glad to do so. It seems curious to me, however, that Whitaker gives no concrete details about the Christian mission in Virginia, which surely would have made a direct appeal to those who listened to sermons in England. Or if he was preaching only to his own congregation, Crashaw should then have done so somewhere in his length. Instead he adds a William Strachey-style appendix about raccoons, flying squirrels, and possums (leaving off that effete *o*-), and doesn't tell us nearly enough about the *quiokosoughs.* Alas, of all the fascinating reports (and sermons) he must have written, all that survives is this, §37, and §51–848, from this kind-hearted man.

His skill, aside from the brilliant finish of his composition, is in his balance. His beauty is in the sincerity of his Christian passion, that goes far beyond the mundane promotional needs of those who saw fit to put him before the public. For example, he considers feeding the poor to be more pleasing in the sight of the Lord than contributing towards "buildings" such as the Pope's and the archbishop's cathedrals, not to mention Sir Thomas Gates' ships, forts, and settlements. And his lesson is so fully developed, launching from five points like a symphonic theme, we are not sure at the recap whether we should devote our relief to the beggars, widows, afflicted, and orphans of England or the short-shrifted clapboard splitters of Henrico. Meanwhile, the opportunities afforded the latter in the Virginia forest for whoring and dicing can only intrigue us today.

John the Baptist says if one has two cloaks it is enough to give one. But Christ commends the poor widow for giving all, namely her two mites. In order to avoid discouraging everybody, Whitaker calls for only "one cloak." But then he calls just as fervently for our mighty prayers. Perhaps he believes prayer most of all will prosper Virginia.

Whitaker would prompt our charity, and yet he is hard put to discriminate between Virginia charity as an investment in the "present" fortunes of the London Company versus an investment in God's grace. God's promise is valid, and He rewards those who are charitable, but in due season. A Christian does not give away two mites in order to earn back four, but to earn infinity and eternity. We must give from faith, he says, and not from "covetousness." And yet if we give, the London Company, the Virginia *action,* clearly will also succeed and pay off.

But no, we possess nothing but the charity of God, and we act merely as stewards and dispensers in common out of the divine commissary. We have everything and we own nothing. In the great cafeteria line of humanity, why should one plate-holder be served and another denied, especially the one who is so hungry?

Virginia will languish and stall, says Whitaker, until Christian hearts open Christian purses on *Christian* impulses. The challenge will be taken up by this generation or the next, or the next. Whitaker's argument steers around difficulties since he is a deft helmsman. But he was right in essence. Virginia required more than a little money and a little planning. There was the whirlwind: Protestant zeal and English nationalism stirred the masses with a sense of glorious mission and destiny.

My quotation marks have been problematical. Crashaw's and Whitaker's English-language Bible was doubtless the Geneva Bible of 1560, which varies a bit from the King James, but neither did they write, I think, with a book on their knee. If their citations are close, I put them in quotes. Occasionally their references are off, *pace.*

Biblical references in parenthesis have moved from the margins of the original.

Good News from Virginia

sent to the Council and Company of Virginia
resident in England
from Alexander Whitaker,
the Minister of Henrico in Virginia,
wherein also is
a Narration of the Present State of that country and our colonies there, perused and published by direction from that council, and a preface prefixed of some matters touching that plantation very requisite to be made known.

(At London, imprinted by Felix Kyngston for William Welby, and are to be sold at his Shop in Paul's Churchyard at the sign of the swan, 1613)

[Crashaw's Epistle Dedicatory:]

TO THE RIGHT HONORABLE, MY VERY GOOD LORD, RAPH LORD VRE [EURE], LORD PRESIDENT OF WALES: Continuance and Increase of All Honor and Happiness from Christ Jesus!

RIGHT HONORABLE—Amongst the many discouragements that have attended this glorious business of the Virginian plantation, none hath been so frequent and so forcible as the calumnies and slanders raised upon our colonies and the country itself. These being devised by the devil, and set abroach by idle and base companions, are blown abroad by Papists, players,[1] and suchlike, till they have filled the

[1] Stage satirists, violent then as now.

vulgar ears. And having once ent'red, then they run like wildfire from man to man. For as wildfire hardly finds a house which is not matter combustible, so these idle tales hardly meet a man who gives not passage at the least if not credit to them. Whereupon the devil and his associates of all sorts hold and practice this rule as a sure maxim: Speak anything, some will believe it[1]; be it never so false, some will entertain it. Truth and innocency shall never so wipe it off but something will stick behind.

Our only comfort is, next to the assurance of God's acceptation of the work, that men of honorable minds and ingenuous dispositions, and all that are godly wise, will check and control these idle and slanderous surmises as they meet with them. And for their better assistance, encouragement, and direction in so doing, our council and governors hold it needful to make known to the world such relations and informations as we receive from thence from men of judgment and experience and of approved faithfulness and integrity. And therefore, though this ensuing treatise, written by Master Whitaker, one of our ministers in Virginia, was spoken there and sent hither rather for the private use and encouragement of such whose purses here or persons there were engaged in the action than with any intent to make it public, yet for the reasons aforesaid it was held fit after mature consideration to divulge it, that so the naked and plain truth may give a just affront to the cunning and colored falsehoods devised by the enemies of this plantation.

And because the man was once so well known to me (as he is still and ever shall be beloved of me), I was desired by them that may command me to peruse the original itself; and for that I had as they probably thought some knowledge of his hand to consider whether truly or suspiciously it bore his name, and if I found cause of the least suspicion, to reject it; but if by true and infallible tokens to be his hand, then to give some testimony to the world of a truth so evident.

Two points therefore I perceive needful to be made known, which I desire all men to take notice of from me, who have peculiar reason to know them both so well as few or no other can. First, who the

---

[1] Margin note: "*Calumniare audacter, aliquid haeret.*" (a Latin rendering)

author is, and then whether this come undoubtedly from him or no.

The author is MASTER ALEXANDER WHITAKER, preacher to the colony at Henrico, under the government of the valorous and worthy knight, Sir Thomas Dale, with whom also he went. He was son to that reverend, renowned Doctor Whitaker; a master of arts of five or six years' standing in Cambridge; was seated in the north country, where he was well approved by the greatest and beloved of his people, and had competent allowance to his good liking, and was in as good possibility of better living as any of his time. He had also some means of his own left him by his parents.

All which notwithstanding, he merely of himself, for ought I know, entertained a purpose of going to Virginia to assist that Christian plantation in the function of a preacher of the Gospel. And having after many distractions and combats with himself (as he told me) settled his resolution that God called him thither, and therefore he would go, he accordingly made it good—notwithstanding the earnest dissuasions of many his nearest friends, and the great discouragements which he daily heard of touching the business and country itself—and arrived there with Sir Thomas Dale by a very speedy and safe passage (scarce of eight weeks long) in May 1611, from whence he hath since then written many comfortable letters, both to the council and committees, and his private friends; and of late, after he had been there a year and more, hath sent us this little treatise which as I know assuredly to come from him and to be a great part of it written and all of it subscribed with his own hand. So I daresay if he had thought we would have published it, he would otherwise have adorned it. For I know, and so do others that know him, he is able to have written it in Latin or in Greek, and so to have decked it both for phrase and style and other ornaments of learning and language as might show him no unworthy son of so worthy a father. And I daresay if he live, be it in England or Virginia, he will in due time manifest to the world by true and good evidence that God hath made him heir as of divers of the holy virtues so of a good part of the learning of his renowned father. And the more liberal am I in giving him his due the further he is off from me, and by that means can be the less sensible of it.

Nor speak I this so much for his sake (though I love him above many, and know it above any other), whose own deeds will sufficiently approve him, as for the truth which is so much suppressed, and that Christian plantation so much disparaged in this base world. For are they not so impudent as to say, Who go thither but base and bankrupt persons and who have no means of their own? or else such as are persuaded and wrought upon to go? And when they come there are they not starved, and do they not die like dogs?

But how false this is in respect of the country, the narration interlaced in this discourse from him that lives there will declare. And how slanderous the other is to the persons, I shall in some sort make it appear.

I therefore hereby let all men know (and malice itself shall never disprove it) that a scholar, a graduate, a preacher, wellborn and friended in England, not in debt nor disgrace, but competently provided for, and liked and beloved where he lived, not in want, but (for a scholar and as these days be) rich in possession and more in possibility, of himself, without any persuasion but God's and his own heart, did voluntarily leave his warm nest and, to the wonder of his kindred and amazement of them that knew him, undertook this hard but in my judgment heroical resolution to go to Virginia and help to bear the name of God unto the Gentiles.

Men may muse at it, some may laugh, and others wonder at it. But will you know the reason? God will be glorified in His own works, and what He hath determined to do He will find means to bring to pass for the perfecting therefore of this blessed work. He hath stirred up able and worthy men to undertake the manning and managing of it. Magistracy and ministery are the strength and sinews, nay, the very life and being of a Christian body politic. Therefore, seeing without these all-emptying of purses here and ventering [venturing] of persons thither is to no purpose, God in His wisdom provided, and in His mercy provoked, godly and able men to furnish both these functions. And such as might at home have lived in places of honor and command, or in fashion competent and convenient to their conditions.

And this, Right Honorable, is one of the four arguments and, as it were, plain demonstrations that have convinced me to believe that assuredly God Himself is the founder and favorer of this plantation.

And I will crave leave of Your Lordship to put them down, because I am of mind that the want either of knowledge or consideration hereof hath been and is the cause of the error and misprision of the world touching this business, and do think that if men did ruminate and advisedly consider of these particulars, they would reprove themselves for their former thoughts, and say plainly *digitus Dei est hic.*[1]

1 The marvelous and indeed miraculous deliverance of our worthy governors, Sir Thomas Gates, lieutenant general, and Sir George Somers, admiral, with all their company of some hundred and fifty persons, upon the feared and abhorred islands of the Barmudaes, without loss of *one person,* when the same hour nothing was before their eyes but imminent and inevitable death. As never ship came there that perished not, so never was it heard of that any ship wrack'd there but with the death of all or most of the people, save only this of ours. Oh, how the world should have rung of it ere this, if a far less deliverance had happened to any of the Jesuitical plantations! And surely the Council of Virginia do wrong themselves and the business—nay, they must give me leave to tell them they obscure the Glory of God if they take not order that a full, complete, and plain narration of that whole action, both danger and deliverance, be published to the world.

2 The full discovery, by means of their former deliverance, of those Barmuda Islands, which hitherto have been held in the world as inaccessible, so not habitable, but so fearful, hideous, and hateful as it seemed a place abandoned of God and man, and given up to the devil's power and possession, and to be of all known places in the world a very hell upon earth rather than a place for men to dwell in. But those honorable gentlemen, being by the Heavenly Pilot preserved upon them where all men else perished, living there almost a year till they had made themselves two little ships of cedar, found it so goodly, so rich, so plentiful, so healthy, and so temperate a country as in so long a time scarce three died of 150; insomuch as hardly could they get their men away when they departed.

These islands, being then discovered and since possessed and

[1] "This is the hand of God." (Latin)

planted by us, are found a habitation of such safety and security, having no enemy within nor any to be feared without (because the entrance is so difficult), and of such plenty of all things for life and of so good temper for health, and fraught with so many rich commodities for satisfaction of the adventurers, as for the present they be even as a new life and a seminary to Virginia, and for the future times, it is likely, will prove a matter of greater consequence than most men think of, and of more worth than any islands or continent discovered in our age.

3 The special and most fatherly providence of God over this action in upholding it when man had forsaken it, and giving it life again when man had left it for dead. For had not Sir Thomas Gates and Sir George Somers come into Virginia from the Barmudaes even when they did, the poor colony—which during that year of their absence by enduring the misery of misgovernment had fallen into all extremity of distress—had been gone away, and our plantation possessed by the savages. And, which was much more miraculous, when they being come in and in all about 240 persons, and in such extreme misery and famine as the honorable commander was even forced to yield to that which others moved (but himself had rather have died than done)—namely, to put themselves to the sea to come for England and quit the country—and when this (full sore against his heart) was put in execution and every man aboard, their ordnance and armor buried, and not an English soul left in James Town, and, giving by their peal of shot their last and woeful farewell to that pleasant land, were now with sorrowful hearts going down the river, behold!—the Hand of Heaven from above at the very instant sent in the Right Honorable La-war to meet them even at the river's mouth with provision and comforts of all kind; who if he had stayed but two tides longer had come into Virginia and not found *one Englishman.* Whereupon they all with as much joy returned as with sorrow they had come away, and making, as it were, a new entry and possession, took up their ordnance and their armor, and the next day received their honorable lord general with all joy and applause. And from that day by God's blessing, they never wanting government, they never wanted bread for him that would take pains and do his duty.

GOOD NEWS FROM VIRGINIA

If ever the hand of God appeared in action of man, it was here most evident. For when man had forsaken this business, God took it in hand; and when men said, Now hath all the earth cast off the care of this plantation, the Hand of Heaven hath taken hold of it. God therefore be glorified in His own work.

But it will be here said by such as are strangers or enemies to this business [that] if this country be so rich and plentiful, and your commanders so wise and provident as you pretend, how could it be that they being there and not hindered by war nor invasions should fall into such extremities of want as to be fain to quit the country and come for England, or else there to starve for want of food?

Indeed, Right Honorable, this objection is of such moment as though I am unwilling to be large, yet must I needs spend some lines in giving answer, which shall be such I hope as shall give satisfaction to the indifferent, and stop the mouths of the malignant.

Let therefore the Christian and courteous reader be pleased to know that when the two forenamed commanders in the great ship called the *Sea Venture* were lost, and yet saved upon the Barmudaes, their fleet consisting of six or seven ships more, and fraught with almost four hundred men, landed, after a long and terrible tempest, in Virginia; where so many men wanting their governors, and being too many to be commanded by the colony they found there before them, fell first into factions, and at last into plain distractions. And so one year of misgovernment overthrew that body, which till then had prospered and by good government was brought to so good a state as at their landing they had corn sufficient in store, a harvest in the ground, good store of living cattle, and had the savages in good correspondency. But this one—yea, our want of government—the most disastrous accident that ever befell that business, brought all to nothing, for it hindered the building of houses and planting of corn. Nay, it burnt up the houses and consumed the provisions, so that of good store of poultry it left not one alive, and of six hundred living swine not three; and which was worse consumed our men, and which was worst of all it lost us the savages, which since hath cost many a man his blood, and to this day is not recovered.

All this while were the commanders and their company in the Barmudaes, where no man dreamed of them, but all the world held them dead men. And being there where none could hear from them, nor they from any others, after almost a year's absence, they got out of the rocks in the two ships themselves there made, and going for Virginia they landed there in the beginning of May [1610], where expecting to find a full and well-planted colony of six or seven hundred men, well stored with corn and cattle—in assurance whereof they had carried no live hogs with them from the Barmudaes, nor other provisions more than for a month's voyage, which they might have done in as great abundance as they could have carried—they contrariwise found a poor colony of not an hundred men, who had endured all miseries and more than ever we heard of—all the live cattle, corn, and other provisions spent, and the savages their deadly enemies; at which meeting, though there was joy to see them who had been held so long in the bottom of the sea, yet their sweet congratulation was sharply sauced when it was known they had no provision of their own (the savages sought their lives), [and] the earth could yield none where none had been planted. And if it had, yet in May the old being spent, the new is not ready. All which considered, it soon appeared there was no human help left on earth but with all speed to hasten for England for new provisions, which motion, though so harsh to the honorable commander, as he had rather there have starved, yet being carried by voices, he would not overrule. And so having buried their armor and ordnance, they went away as we heard before.

All this to be true I know well. And if any man ask how I know it, for their satisfaction I answer I have it from the faithful relation of that religious, valorous and prudent gentleman, SIR THOMAS GATES, then and yet our lieutenant general, who being himself in his own person a doer of much, a sufferer of more, and an eyewitness of the whole, hath since related this and much more unto me, face to face. And all that know him know him for such a man as well deserves to be believed.

All which then being true, as is also well known to many my betters, then let any reasonable man judge (especially if he be experienced in such affairs) if there were not a necessary cause of their coming away, and yet neither fault in the governor nor want in the country.

[4] My fourth and last argument is the stirring up of so many honorable and worthy persons of all conditions to disburse so freely and so willingly such fair sums of money, and some of them even a good part of their estate, and that without any certain or apparent hope of speedy profit. This to do willingly and voluntarily, and without assurance of gain, cannot be but the working of God to some higher end than ordinary. And if it be said there be some that wish their money in their purses, it may be so, but for one so base-thoughted man I daresay we have many that wish a great deal more *out* of their purses, conditionally this happy business may take good effect. And this, though it be much, yet in my judgment is but little to this that followeth: that God should vouchsafe to stir up such able and worthy men for the functions both of magistracy and ministery, who upon very uncertain hope of profit, and most certain danger of life itself, should put themselves into this business, and voluntarily undergo the danger of sea and all the miseries and difficulties that necessarily and undoubtedly attend a new plantation.

To have done this upon pressure or by calling of superiors or command of a state had been little. To have done it upon safe and fair terms and without danger had been no great matter. To have done it upon expectation and assurance of high rewards and present profit had been nothing. But to do it voluntarily, upon sight of danger present and certain, but of gain future and contingent, seeing it is contrary to the course of reason, and cannot proceed from folly or madness, they being wise men, nor from humor and rashness, being staid men, nor from malcontentedness, being men that lived in good respect at home, nor in the conceit of meriting, being not Papists but of sound religion, it must therefore needs proceed from the extraordinary motion of God's spirit. For if any, out of ignorance or malice, do object they had nothing to do at home, it is false and frivolous. False, for they were men employed; frivolous, for many more had less to do than they, yet would not go.

As for those that think they wanted in England, do they not see how in disgracing the persons they honor the country? For if they went from England to Virginia because they were in want, and voluntarily stay there still, then it follows that Virginia is able to supply the wants of England. But how idle and slanderous that imputation is may easily appear if we take a view of the persons themselves. And to begin with the magistrates and commanders, what noble man is there in England, what colonel or captain in the Low Countries, but knows and will acknowledge that the Right Honorable the Lord La-war, and the right worthy knights, Sir Thomas Gates, Sir Thomas Dale, and Sir George Somers, be persons of honor, estimation, and good respect, and had both means and employment at home of their own?

But to speak of them and other religious gentlemen and captains who voluntarily left their easy, pleasant, and wealthy lives in England, and betook themselves to this voyage, I will leave it to some who are better able to do it, according to their desert and worth. I will contain myself within my element, and speak of them of my own function, and amongst them of those two especially, MASTER GLOVER and MASTER WHITAKER, because they went by my knowledge, but not by my procurement. For I testify it for truth they moved me that they might go, not I them that they would go. Master Glover, an ancient master of arts in Cambridge, an approved preacher in Bedford and Huntingdonshire, reverenced and respected, and never wanting a competent stipend, yet of himself (I know not how nor why) made known his desire to go to Virginia to a reverend preacher in Huntingdon,[1] and procuring his letters to me, upon my answer, came up, being a man I had never seen before; and so being well liked of the council, and conditions being tendered him to his content, he went away with Sir Thomas Gates in June 1611; but, being in years and of a weak constitution, endured not the sea and sickness of the country so well as younger and stronger bodies. And so after zealous and faithful performance of his ministerial duty whilest he was able, he gave his soul to Christ Jesus, under whose banner he went to fight, and for whose glorious name's sake he undertook the danger, more worthy to be accounted a true confessor of Christ than hundreds that are canonized in the Pope's martyrologe.

Master Whitaker—a man born, brought up, qualitied, and qualified, settled and provided for, as you heard before, of whom I have

---

[1] "Master Beard." (margin note)

spoken the more because he was of long time so well known to me—though he lived as well and in as good case and credit as most young men in our church, yet voluntarily, and not suddenly, but after serious deliberation, overcoming, as himself said, many inward temptations and outward discouragements and dissuasions, removed himself from a good stipend of value and certainty,[1] and put himself into this dangerous voyage, where now he diligently preacheth and catechizeth, and thereby, and by other ministerial duties, public and private—and otherwise also, for he is otherways qualitied—he performs daily and diligent service acceptable to God and comfortable to our people, over whom he is pastor, and from whence, as a token of his love and duty to the council and adventurers and as a testimony of the good liking he conceives of the country by these almost two years' experience, he hath sent us this plain but pithy and godly exhortation, interlaced with narrations of many particulars touching the country, climate, and commodities worthy to be known of all, especially coming from one of his place and profession, and of so good experience in the matter he writes of.

There is also, besides it may be some others whom I know not, MASTER BUCKE, an able and painful preacher, of whom I can say the less because he was of Oxford and unknown to me, but of whom I have heard Sir Thomas Gates give a good and worthy testimony. And he came to the council and to this employment with the commendation of a right reverend prelate.[2] But no matter, though I say nothing of him, seeing I doubt not he will shortly give notice to the world what he is, and what the country of Virginia is, and what hope there is of that plantation, for the service whereof he hazarded his dearest life. And the rather do I expect it from him because he is a man now of long experience, having been there so long a time, and was himself in person in the danger and deliverance at the Barmudaes. So that now, for the conclusion, we see to our comfort the God of Heaven found us out and made us ready to our hands, able and fit men for the ministerial function in this plantation—all of them graduates, allowed preachers, single men, having no pastoral

---

1 "About forty pound a year in a cheap country." (margin note)
2 "Doctor [Thomas] Ravis, lord bishop of London." (margin note)

cures nor charge of children, and as it were every way fitted for that work.

And because God would more grace this business and honor His own work, He provided us such men as wanted neither living nor liberty of preaching at home. More in my judgment have they to answer for who, wanting both, will not only not go themselves but disparage and deprave them that go. Hereafter, when all is settled [i]n peace and plenty, what marvel if many and greater than they be willing to go? But in the infancy of this plantation to put their lives into their hands, and under the assurance of so many dangers and difficulties to devote themselves unto it, was certainly a holy and heroical resolution, and proceeded undoubtedly from the blessed spirit of Christ Jesus, who for this cause appeared, that He might dissolve the works of the devil (1 John 3:7). And though Satan visibly and palpably reigns there more than in any other known place of the world, yet be of courage, blessed brethren: God will tread Satan under your feet shortly (Rom. 16), and the ages to come will eternize your names as the "Apostles of Virginia."

And thus, Right Honorable, you have the reasons that have satisfied my conscience that this work is of God, and will therefore stand, though man should unfaithfully forsake it. And I doubt not but if many others did know them and consider of them, they would certainly change their minds and say with me doubtless here is the finger of God. As for the continual calumnies and daily slanders raised of the place, plantation, and persons that are in it—and the jests of profane players and other sycophants, and the flouts and mocks of some who by their age and profession should be no mockers (for as for the rest, who can expect any better figs from thistles, or any sweeter grapes from such pricking thorns?)—for all those, I say, and all other discouragements and depravements of like nature, I profess I like the business the better, and have more hope of God's blessing upon it, even of that God whose wisdom is but foolishness with worldly men, and whose ways are hid from carnal eyes.

And these reasons, I confess, have so far prevailed with me as this plantation shall ever have a portion of my poor estate, and my best prayers and my personal pains—and presence also if God had not provided them fitter men for such a work.

There is but one thing more, that an indifferent reader may probably stumble at, which I will briefly and easily remove. It may be very well, will some say, that these honorable persons, godly preachers, and valorous gentlemen, out of their good minds or desire to see foreign countries, might put themselves for once into this work. But do they hold on or are they there still? And how many of them having once been there will go again? Or being there, would they not full gladly be at home again if they could?

Indeed, such base words are given out by some, but they be either ignorant or malicious, and how can ignorance or malice speak the truth? Ignorance cannot, though it would, and malice will not though it can. But will Your Lordship and all men know the truth? Be pleased then to be informed that of all the aforenamed persons of employment, Sir George Somers, that famous seaman, our worthy admiral, that true and constant friend to Virginia, who in his old age left a pleasant seat (in Dorsetshire), a good living, and an easy life to live and die for the good of Virginia, and that godly good preacher, Master Glover, have both of them given their lives in this business, the former in the Barmudaes, the latter in Virginia, crying to their God with the blessed Apostle of the Gentiles (their father whom they followed), "We pass not at all, neither is our life dear unto us, so that we may fulfill our course with joy, and the ministration which we have received of the Lord Jesus, to make way for the Gospel of the Grace of God." (Acts 20) It was the devil that said "Skin for skin, and all that a man hath will he give for his life" (Job 2); and he spake like himself. But these champions of Christ said, "All we have, and even life itself, will we willingly give and consecrate to God, that the Gospel may be preached, and the name of Jesus Christ called upon in Virginia," and so gave up their souls to God and their flesh to nature, honoring and in a sort consecrating those heathenish earths with their happy bodies, more worthy to be esteemed precious relics than thousands that are preserved and adored in the Romish Church. Blessed and glorious shall their portions be at the resurrection of the just, and in the meantime their names shall flourish when the memory of the wicked shall rot.

Of the rest aforenamed, the worthy knights, Sir Thomas Gates and Sir Thomas Dale, lieutenant and marshal, Master Whitaker and Master Bucke, preachers, are now in Virginia and have been some divers years, and everyone almost two years. And of them, Sir Thomas Gates hath been here once and is gone the second time. Master Whitaker went with purpose to stay three years, which, as he resolved here so he there performs, and intends, for ought I perceive, rather to augment than diminish the prefixed number.

This Lord La-war, our honorable general, having spent some time there, for want of health was constrained to come home, but with resolution (as His Lordship spake in an honorable presence at his return, and since hath published) to return again and spend his life in the prosecution of that action. And if the company were as able to furnish and send away His Lordship with a fleet and power sufficient as His Lordship is ready and resolved to engage his person again, and with him many worthy gentlemen and captains, there would soon be not a verbal but a real answer given to that question which is in all men's mouths so common: "Why goes not the Lord La-war again to Virginia?"

And dost thou ask why His Lordship goes not again? I tell thee because thou that askest the question, and others like thee, will not put to your hands to help forward so holy and honorable a work. When the danger is passed and profit comes in, then we shall have partakers enow. But now, for laying of the foundation, the world is content to look on and ask us why we go not forward. We can answer with good consciences we go forward according to our power, we move as we have strength, and we move no faster for want of help. Let the world be like itself, and he that is filthy let him be filthy still: He that rouseth the hog out of the mire or the worldling out of his sensuality doth but trouble himself in vain.

But you, the noble and worthy adventurers, whose hearts God hath touched, whether you be engaged in purse here or person there, go forward and move on, if not so fast as you would, yet as you may. Let this be your comfort, besides the assured hope of gain in due time, that you move not *against* but *for* and *with* God. A little strength doth prevail better with the stream than much against it. So great means should do no good if God were against you, but your weak means shall prevail, seeing you work with God. Go forward in that name and by the strength of the Lord your God, and rest assured that His goodness will either raise you more strength or will make the strength you have already able to prevail. Be not therefore faint-hearted, but remember it is God's cause you have taken in hand. It may therefore be hind'red, but cannot be overthrown. If we then were so base as to betray and forsake it, God whose it is will stir up our children after us and give them that good land to enjoy, which we are not worthy of, and which nothing but our sins and sluggishness can keep from us. Let us not therefore to our own shame leave so blessed a work to them that follow us, lest the ensuing ages say of us, "Why was there such a prize put into the hands of fools who had not hearts to take it?" (Proverbs) Stand to it therefore and be not wanting to yourselves, and God will never be wanting to you nor it, till His blessed providence hath brought it to pass that men shall say, "God hath made His ways known upon earth, and His saving health amongst all nations; and blessed be the Lord God of Virginia, world without end."

And thus, Right Honorable, you may see by that that hath been said in what terms our colony now stand and what they want.

It may hereby appear they have God their friend and protector: They have honorable and worthy governors, godly and painful preachers, a goodly country, and no want of necessaries. Since they had government, they only want the hands and help of men willing and able to do such duties of men as be requisite in a plantation, and the expense that principally and almost only now lies upon us is the charge of sending away a competent number of men, the charge whereof will be about 20 pound a man. If this were done, it would soon appear that our cares and cost were at an end, and that a glorious and comfortable issue is shortly to be looked for; which, howsoever it may be deferred through the backwardness of some, backsliding of others, and coldness of all, yet, that it will come assuredly in the end, the goodness, riches, and excellency of the country doth undoubtedly promise us,[1] as may appear (beside others) in the book lately put out of Captain Smith's—who was there divers years, and whose pains and service there deserves in my judgment high commendations—and by this exhortation and narration of Master Whitaker, who now is there, which by direction of authority is therefore published that the world may see how false and scandalous those imputations be that are laid upon the country and plantation by some base and idle lubbers that come from thence, and some amongst us that are ever opposite to all good public works.

And these true and welcome news from Virginia—as they go out to the world ushered and attended with this my poor preface, so I send them first to Your Lordship, as having a peculiar interest both in them and me; which I do not only because Your Lordship, amongst many other of your rank and quality, is a well-willer, furtherer, and advancer of this noble action, but that hereby I may make good to Your Lordship the truth of something already passed betwixt us in private discourse; and for that Your Lordship knew Master Whitaker in the north and, by your peculiar knowledge of the man and the place where he lived, can be an honorable witness with me, and an evidence beyond all exception to a good part of what I have here said.

And now what remains but that I beseech the God of heaven to bless His own work which we have in hand, and to multiply His heavenly graces upon Your Lordship, that as Your Lordship hath been a Maecenas of learning, a maintainer of true religion, and a furtherer of all honorable actions and good works, so you may continue to the end, and advance forward towards perfection.

And so with humble recommendation of my service, do take my leave, and rest

Your Lordship's devoted in Christ,
W[ILLIAM] CRASHAWE.

[1] "See the book called *The New Life of Virginea.*" (margin note)

GOOD NEWS FROM VIRGINIA

TO THE RIGHT WORSHIPFUL SIR THOMAS SMITH, KNIGHT, TREASURER OF THE ENGLISH COLONY IN VIRGINIA—GRACE AND PEACE BE MULTIPLIED.

RIGHT WORSHIPFUL—The noblest attempts have always had the most doubtful beginnings, most dangerous enemies. For whereso-ever any goodness shall begin to bud forth, the devil will labor by all means to nip it in the head, wherefore I do not marvel though there have been great discouragements and many adversaries of this plantation. For the devil, knowing that where Christ wins he loseth, doth with all his might and policy hinder the publishing and propagation of the Gospel. Such was his practice to discourage the Israelites from the conquest of Canaan, raising up ten of their own princes that weakened the hands of their brethren. By his means also there stood up some of the Disciples that spake against Peter for preaching the Gospel to the Gentiles.

Yea, God himself of purpose suffers the devil to rage thus for a while, that those that are His might be tried. And this hath been the case hitherto of this godly plantation, this the success. But since the affairs of this colony have now taken better footing, and are advanced by the helps of so many honorable adventurers, I was greatly emboldened to write these few lines of exhortation to encourage the noble spirits of so many worthy men to go forward in well-doing.

Wherefore, honored sir, since all the dispatches of our affairs pass thorough your hands, I request you to accept of my poor endeavors, and to publish it to the view of our adventurers, that the prejudicate opinion of some and the disheartened mind of others may be reformed. The God of heaven and earth crown your undaunted spirit with His heavenly reward; and let the beauty of the Lord our God be upon us; and direct thou the works of our hands upon us, even direct thou our handiworks.

From Henrico this 28 of July, 1612.

He that daily prayeth for the prosperity of this plantation,
ALEXANDER WHITAKER.

LIBRARY OF VIRGINIA

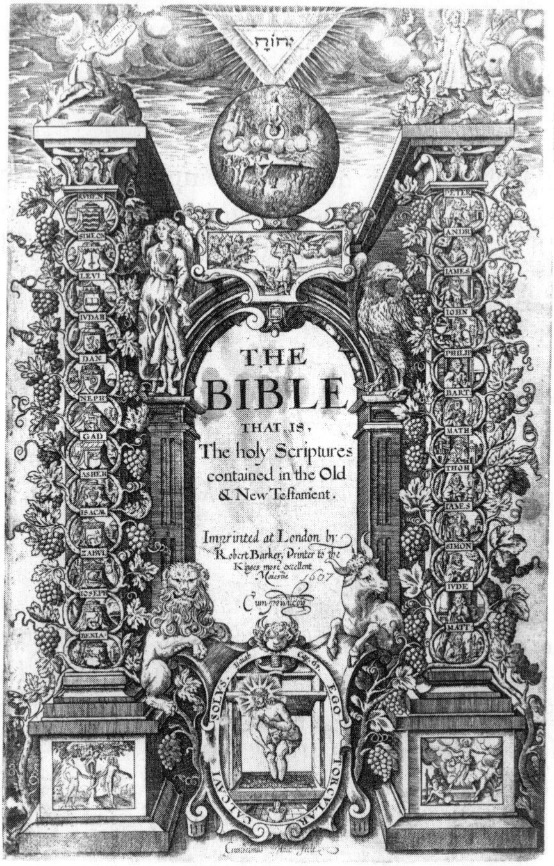

The Geneva Bible
Title Page of Robert Barker's 1607 ediiton

THE LORD IS MY SHEPHERD · THEREFORE I LACK NOTHING · HE SHALL FEED ME IN A GREEN PASTURE AND LEAD ME FORTH BESIDE THE WATERS OF COMFORT · HE SHALL CONVERT MY SOUL AND BRING ME FORTH IN THE PATHS OF RIGHTEOUSNESS FOR HIS NAME'S SAKE · YEA THOUGH I WALK THROUGH THE VALLEY OF THE SHADOW OF DEATH I WILL FEAR NO EVIL · FOR THOU ART WITH ME · THY ROD AND THY STAFF COMFORT ME · THOU SHALT PREPARE A TABLE BEFORE ME AGAINST THEM THAT TROUBLE ME · THOU HAST ANOINTED MY HEAD WITH OIL AND MY CUP SHALL BE FULL · BUT THY LOVING KINDNESS AND MERCY SHALL FOLLOW ME ALL THE DAYS OF MY LIFE AND I WILL DWELL IN THE HOUSE OF THE LORD FOREVER ·

Good News from Virginia

ECCLESIASTES 11:1—Cast thy bread upon the waters: for after many days thou shalt find it.

Aude hospes contemnere opes et quoque dignum
Finge Deo——

"BE BOLD, MY HEARERS, to contemn riches, and frame yourselves to walk worthy of God." For none other be worthy of God but those that lightly esteem of riches. Nakedness is the riches of nature. Virtue is the only thing that makes us rich and honorable in the eyes of wise men. Poverty is a thing which most men fear and covetous men cannot endure to behold. Yet poverty with a contented mind is *great riches!* He truly is the only poor man not that hath little but which continually desireth more. Riches, as they are esteemed, have no limits but still cry *plus ultra!* "still more!" Neither is any man absolutely rich but in comparison of a poorer man, of one, I mean, that hath less than he. For if he make diligent inquiry, he may find divers richer than himself. If riches of gold and the like had been such as the world doth esteem them, it is not likely that Jesus Christ would have taken so poor a state upon Him. When we esteem them at the best, they are but an heavy burthen to some, an idol to others, and profitable to few.

Wherefore Salomon, having before explained the marvelous vanity of riches, and how they are wont to be abused as well of covetous as of prodigal men, in the first six verses of this chapter teacheth us how we may use them well, and God may make the use of them blessed unto us. In the second chapter He hath said, "I have gathered unto me silver and gold, and the chief treasures of kings and provinces. And I was great and increased above all that were before me in Jerusalem. Then I looked and, Behold—all is vanity and vexation of the spirit." In the fifth chapter, "He that loveth silver shall not be satisfied with silver. And he that loveth riches shall be without the fruit of it. And what good cometh to the owners thereof but the beholding thereof with their eyes." And he addeth, "The satiety of the rich will not suffer him to sleep." Again, "There is an evil sickness that I have seen under the sun: riches reserved to the owners thereof for their evil."

Now in the beginning of this chapter, he hath set down a remedy to both these evils, whereby our riches may be made constant unto us. We may take pleasure and profit by them, and our posterity through many descents may enjoy them after us. "Cast thy bread," saith he, "upon the waters." Why? "For after many days thou shalt find it."

The sentence is rhetorical, full of figures, and needs some explaining. *Bread* in Scripture is usually taken for all kind of meat and drink, as may appear, Gen. 18:5, and in divers other places. But here, I take it, it is more generally put for all kind of *alms,* of what nature soever. Not only for meat and drink, money, apparel, or the like, but also for any kind of thing whereby we may relieve the necessity of our neighbor. *Waters* also are here metaphorically put for all those men who stand in need of the alms of our liberality, whether they be such as cannot, but gladly would, requite us; or else such as being able forget to be thankful.

So that the plain meaning of the words is this: Give liberally thine alms to all sorts of men that may stand in need of thy help. Hide not thine eyes at the miserable state of the afflicted. Neither stop thine ears at the cry of the poor, though they be not able to recompense thy well-doing. Reproach not thine enemy when he is punished, but rather overcome his evil deeds with thy goodness. Neither suffer any to return empty-handed from thee whom God shall offer to thy liberality. For though thou canst not presently expect a plentiful reward of thy well-doing, though the persons to whom thou hast cast thine alms be not able to requite thee or forgetful of good turns, yet be assured of it that God beholdeth thy charity and will at His appointed time requite thee. Even in this world, if it be good for thee, thou shalt taste of His bounty, but in the world to come He hath reserved for thee a most glorious crown of blessed immortality. This is the soul and substance of this short sentence.

The words naturally divide themselves into two principal parts. A commandment to be liberal and charitable, and a promise of reward which hereafter we shall find. The commandment also containeth in it five points touching the doctrine of liberality.

1 The duty to be performed: "Cast thy bread"—be liberal to all.
2 The manner of bestowing our alms by casting it away.
3 What is to be given, "bread"—all things needful, yea, and of the best kind.
4 Who may be liberal?—even those that have it: "Thy bread," it must be thine own.
5 To whom we must be liberal: to all, yea, to the "waters."

First, we will briefly speak of these five points of this commandment as they lie in order, and then directly come unto the promise more particularly. The enjoined duty is liberality, which sometimes is termed "alms," sometimes more largely is used for all kind of good works, and very often is signified by the names of "charity" and "brotherly love"; all which being in sense and signification one shall in the naming of them be used all as one.

Liberality is the true practice of Christian humanity and brotherly courtesy, one towards another—a virtue commanded by God and commended by the examples of the best, which makes us accepted of God, and desired of men.

Faith gives comfort to my soul, and ministers peace to my conscience.

Hope teacheth me not to be hasty, but to wait patiently the appointed time of God.

But the practice of love maintains my hope, and assures me that my faith is effectual, and moreover is beneficial unto others, yea, profitable to all. "Now abideth faith, hope, and love, even these three, but the greatest of these is love." (1 Cor. 13) Wherefore hath God made men great, and filled their coffers with His treasures but that they should as faithful stewards of God's store liberally provide for the necessity of His saints? The richest man in the world hath no right by nature to the things he doth possess. For naked he came into the world and he must return naked out of the same again. Why then hath God made thee rich, and commended that to thy liberality which was not thine own but that thou shouldest be bountiful to those whom He hath made poor?

What goodness or excellency did God see in thee more than in the poorest reasonable creature before thou yet wast, that He should make thee rich and him poor? Doth it not befall to thee as to the fool? Yea verily, "The condition of men in this case and the condition of beasts is all one. As one dieth, so dieth the other. All go to one place, and all was of the dust. And all shall return to the dust." (Eccles. 3:19) But that which nature hath not distinguished, the wisdom and bounty of God, hath by a property of calling altered, and lending His treasures to the rich men of the world hath showed to them an example of his liberality to this end that they might be open-handed to others, distributing as faithful stewards of His gifts, according to the necessity of the saints.

Wherefore our Saviour Christ proclaimeth, "Who is a faithful servant and wise, whom his master hath made ruler over his household, t[o give] them meat in season. Blessed is that servant whom his master, when he cometh, shall find so doing." (Matth. 24:45) Saint Paul exhorteth us to do good to all, but specially to the household of faith (Galath. 6), and writeth to Timothy to charge them that be rich in this world that they do good, and be rich in good works, ready to distribute and communicate (1 Tim. 6:17). He showeth Titus also that the end of our redemption is that we might be zealous of good works (Titus 2), and therefore willeth him to affirm that they which have believed in God might be careful to show forth good works, etc. (Titus 3).

But alas, the practice of this age is far otherwise. For those that have wealth either abuse them to the satisfying of their prodigal lusts, in whoring, dicing, or drinking, till all or the most be spent, or else as others use them only to look upon them, or that it might be said they have them. Few or none there be that use them aright to the glory of God and relief of His children. God gave commandment that there should not be a beggar in Israel. But how many idle persons have we in the streets of our cities, in the highways, and corners of our paths, which day and night call upon the passersby and yet remain unprovided for? How many hungry, naked, fatherless, widows, poor men, and oppressed perish for want of that which God hath lent to these rich thieves? For no better than thieves are they, keeping up that which God gave them to disburse to holy and good uses. But what saith Salomon? "He that hideth his eyes from the poor shall have many curses." (Prov. 28:27)

What shall we judge then of those men who being rich in substance and poor in good works? If Paul may be heard, they have not yet believed Christ died for them (Titus 3). If Saint John may judge, they have no love of God in them. "For whosoever," saith he, "hath this world's goods and seeth his brother have need and shutteth up his compassion from him, how dwelleth the love of God in him?" (1 John 3:17) Surely Christ, that shall judge every man according to his works when He shall call them to render an account of their stewardship, will pronounce a heavy sentence against them. "Cast those unprofitable servants into utter darkness. There shall be weeping and gnashing of teeth." (Matth. 25:30)

Go to now, you rich miserable[1] men, weep and howl for the miseries that shall come upon you (James 5:1). Remember the churlishness of Nabal (1 Sam. 25), and forget not the tormented tongue of Dives (Luke 16[:24]). Make haste either to repent betime or make account to hear the dreadful sentence of the Great Judge, "Go, ye cursed, etc., for ye have been uncharitable." (Matth. 25) But you, my brethren, in whose hearts the love of God abideth, show the bowels of your compassion to your fellow servants as need requireth. Remember the afflictions of Joseph, and be assured of this that "He that hath mercy upon the poor, lendeth unto the Lord," etc. (Prov. 19:17)

You will help your friend because he loves you and is the companion of your estate. Nature teacheth us to commiserate the distresses of our brethren because we are of the same flesh and have our parents common. How can we then withhold the hands of our relief from those that stand in need of our help? We are all fellow servants of one lord and master, Jesus Christ. We have all one common father, God the Maker of heaven and earth. We are all members of one mystical body, most unseparably united to our head, Jesus Christ, by the power of the Holy Spirit. How then can we see our fellow servants, our dear brethren, yea, the members of our

---

[1] Miserly.

own body to pass by us hungry and naked, unfed, unclothed? Take heed, I beseech you, that Lazarus starve not at your doors, nor David's messengers return empty (1 Kings 17). If Elijah come to sojourn with you, thrust him not out of doors: Thou knowest not how soon God may alter the times and restore thine estate. The Church of Macedonia is commended because, though they were in want themselves, yet they supplied the extreme want of other churches (2 Cor. 8). Yea, if the saints at Jerusalem want (1 Cor. 16:1), or the churches afar off, lay up the first day of every week somewhat to send to their relief. And so you doing may gather comfort to yourselves that you shall hear that comfortable sentence, *Venite benedicti patris, quoniam fuistis liberales,* "Come you blessed of my father, receive the kingdom prepared for you, for you have been liberal," etc.

I might say much more in the commendation of liberality, but the time requiring less, I come now with haste unto the second point of the commandment.

"Cast thy bread," etc. What? Hath God given us goods to cast them away? Yea, verily, for Salomon saith, "There is a time to seek, and a time to lose; a time to keep, and a time to cast away." (Eccles. 3:6) Which time of losing and casting away the Scripture here noteth. But by this word of casting away is meant no violent rejecting or negligent losing of some things that we hate or do not greatly esteem, but a liberal giving away of such things as we do possess which may appear by these reasons.

First, by the nature of the original word HAY LAMED SHIN,[1] which most usually signifieth "to send out, *mittere & emittere,*" and so it is used by Moses (Gen. 7:7) where he saith that Noah *sent out* the raven, and afterward the dove twice. He useth this word continually, HAY LAMED SHIN YOD KAF, *"et emisit."*[2] And so hath both Pagninus and Mercerus expounded it.

Secondly, it may appear by the agreement of the text with the verses following. For the doctrine handled is touching liberality, allegorically compared to the seed of bread. For so bread may be

---

[1] Hebrew letters spelling left to right.
[2] "And he sent forth." (Latin)

here understood which husbandmen cast not away, but sow as well in moist as in drier grounds. And so Tremelius doth interpret them. Now as husbandmen do not cast away their seed, which they fling into the ground, for hatred or neglect, but under hope of God's blessing, even so liberal men, exercising the works of charity, do not cast away their alms as one that casteth a bone to a dog, or flingeth dead flowers from him, etc., but freely bestow the alms of God without pride, vainglory, or disdain, yea, without hope of any restitution or any other recompense besides the acceptance of God and the reward which God shall give unto him in this life, but especially in the great day of His harvest. And with this doth agree that saying of Salomon, "There is that scattereth and is more increased." (Prov. 17:24) So that the spirit of God teacheth us by this word of casting how we may scatter our good deeds and bestow our alms, as that they may be accepted of God and profitable unto us. As many ask and receive not, because they *ask* amiss (James 4), so the most that cast away find not, because they be illiberal in their liberality, or because they *give* amiss.

Let us then learn from hence to cast away our bread freely. Freely we have received our goods from God, let us freely give. So shall we become followers of God and our liberality draw toward the perfection required of us. The commandment of Christ is that we should be perfect as our Heavenly Father is perfect (Matth. 5:48).

Now then, God's liberality being perfect, let us also be perfect in our good deeds. This is a point very needful for us all to consider. For [that] God requireth liberality from us all, and very few among the divers multitudes of givers give aright, it shall be counted a high point of wisdom in us, first, to inform ourselves thoroughly by what means our charity may become perfect and acceptable in the sight of God, before we reach out our hands to give. Our great Master Christ, the mouth of God to man, handling the doctrine of liberality in his Sermon on the Mount (Matth. 6:1), hath taught us many rules touching the right manner of giving alms, which we may refer to these five points.

1 First, that we give in faith, for without faith it is unpossible to please God (Heb. 11:6); therefore without faith our alms cannot please God. The sum of which faith is this: First, that God will accept of us and our alms for His Son Jesus Christ's sake. For no work of any man can please God before the man himself be approved of Him, and then all our good deeds shall be accepted of Him. Secondly, that we be not hasty in expecting a present recompense of reward, but to wait patiently upon God by faith for the good success of our alms. So husbandmen that cast their seed into the ground stay until the time of harvest, depending upon God for the fruitful increase of their labors (James 5:7). So Paul doth plant and Apollos doth water (1 Cor. 3), but even both these do wait upon God for the blessing of their ministery. This is the cause why heretofore much of our alms bestowed upon the affairs of Virginia have been so cast away that they could never be found again hitherto. For many of us have not been reconciled to God nor approved of Him. Some of our adventurers in London have been most miserable covetous men, sold over to usury, extortion, and oppression. Many of the men sent hither have been murtherers, thieves, adulterers, idle persons, and whatnot besides, all which persons God hateth even from His very soul. How then could their alms or anything else which they do be pleasing unto God? Such men's prayers are abominable in the sight of God, how much more their alms.

2 The second rule in giving is that we give in love, which whosoever lacketh cannot give aright; and saith Saint Paul, "Though I feed the poor with all my goods and have not love, it profiteth me nothing." (1 Cor. 13:3) The sum of which love is that out of mere pity, compassion, and fellow feeling of our neighbor's wants, we cast our bread to him—not for constraint of law and custom of parishioners, neither for any sinister respect of praise or vainglory. Wherefore the same Paul saith, "He that distributeth, let him do it with simplicity." (Rom. 12:8) And our Saviour Christ commandeth that "when thou dost thine alms, let not thy left hand know what thy right hand doth." (Matth. 6:3)

3 Thirdly, we must give our alms bountifully and with a cheerful mind. But as everyone wisheth in his heart, so let him give not grudging or of necessity, for God loveth a cheerful giver (2 Cor. 9:7). He that soweth sparingly shall reap also sparingly, and he that soweth liberally shall reap also liberally. Yet, notwithstanding, this bountifulness hath two proper limits, beyond which it is not to pass.

First, we must be bountiful only according to ability. For if we give all at one time, we may leave ourselves naked, and be disenabled for giving anymore hereafter. Therefore those Papists that give away all and turn begging friars are to be blamed, for God that hath said there shall be poor always with you forbiddeth in the same place that there should be any beggar in Israel (Deut. 15:4); and the rule of John Baptist is that he that hath two coats should not give away both of them, whereby he might be left naked, but he must give one away (Luke 3:11) and reserve the other for himself.

The second limit of our bounty is that we give more or less according to the necessity of the saints, and this Saint Paul teacheth, Romans 12:18.

4 The fourth rule of right giving ariseth from hence, which is that we give our alms with discretion. First, that we communicate such things as the need of our neighbor requireth: The thirsty man must have drink, the hungry and naked meat and apparel, the imprisoned for debt money and the like. Secondly, we must not defer the time of our relief (ωκειαι χαριτες γλυκερωτερας[1]), lest that we give too late when the case of our neighbor is past help: *Bis dat qui cito dat.*[2] The physician comes too late when the patient is dead. "But a word spoken in season is like apples of gold and pictures of silver." (Prov. 25:11) Whilest thou may then, do good—thou knowest not then what may befall afterward. In the morning sow thy seed, and in the afternoon let not thy hand rest, for thou knowest not whether shall prosper this or that. Surely, if there were ever any opportunity given of setting forward this plantation,[3] the season is now most fit. Strike then whilest the iron is hot; do this good work whilest you may, before it be too late. Thirdly, we must choose such a place as may be void of vainglory and hypocrisy. Our left hand may not know what our right hand doth. *Honores palam dandi sunt, eleemosinae clam* (Matth. 6), "Honors may be openly given for the encouragement of others; but alms deeds must be given in secret." Then thy Father that seeth in secret shall reward thee openly.

---

[1] Read γλυκερωτεραι for a printer's error and he means to quote the *Greek Anthology:* "Favors are sweeter for their swiftness."

[2] "Who gives promptly gives doubly." (Latin)

[3] Here at last is the point of the lesson.

5 The last rule of giving is that we give in justice, which is that we cut not large thongs out of another man's leather, that we give not other men's goods, but such as be our own, and those truly gotten. The text saith that the bread must be thine, even thine own, not another man's. The true feasting is to break thine own bread to the hungry, to bring the poor that wander into thine house (Isa. 58:7).

(Thirdly, what is to be given) The next point to be handled is wherein we are to be liberal, what we are to give. Salomon hath shut up all under the name of *bread,* whereby, as I said before, is meant all things wherein we may relieve the necessities of our neighbors. For if a man shall cast his drink, apparel, gold, and the like upon the waters, he shall after many days find them. But Salomon included all these alms under the name of *bread* because he would enforce this doctrine under one allegory of *sowing,* and therefore doth suit his phrase with words of most significancy. Again, bread is the staff of good nourishment, and the most usual kind of alms which we give. This article then of this commandment is that if our neighbors do stand in need of our help in anything wherein we may help them, we are not to withhold our hand from them, but to cast our alms liberally unto them.

And this must needs be the meaning of the Holy Ghost, for Paul teacheth us to distribute according to the necessity of the saints (Rom. 12:13). But the saints need many things very often beside bread, yea, besides food and raiment, wherefore our alms must needs be cast out according to the several necessities of those that want.

The wants of men be divers. Some are of the mind, some of the body, and some be of the outward goods. And thus have the divines divided them.

The distresses of the mind are most grievous and needs the best relief. But of them all, ignorance of spiritual matters is most common, most dangerous. The bread that must relieve this is the mouth of wisdom, which is liberal in instruction, which is as finest silver, which shall be fruitful in understanding, which doth know what is acceptable, which is a tree of life, and which feedeth many (Prov. 10). This was the alms which Paul went to cast away in Macedon, and liberally distributed in Mars his Street in Athens. And this is the alms which may be most profitable unto this barbarous country of Virginia, where the name of God hath been yet scarce heard of.

The wants of the body be many, but not so dangerous. And those be principally hunger, thirst, sickness, and wounds, according to which cases our alms must be bestowed. The sentence of the Great Judge shall be according to the tenor of this: "When I was an-hungry you fed me, when I was athirst, you gave me drink, when I was sick you visited me." (Matth. 25) As for the helping of wounded men, our Saviour Christ hath given us a notable instance and encouragement to be merciful toward them in the case of the wounded Jew, whom, when neither the priest nor the Levite that passed by would relieve, a Samaritan most liberally provided for. (Luke 10:30) Even so let us do. The wants of our neighbor's outward state are most and everywhere common. First, we must freely give to the poor, as clothes to the naked, liberal gleanings to the stranger, fatherless, and widow, justice in judgment to the oppressed, etc.

Secondly, we must freely lend (Mat. 5:42), whereby we may be oftentimes as beneficial to our neighbor as by giving; concerning which our Saviour Christ saith, "From him that would borrow of thee, turn not away thy face." And the commandment of God is, "Thou shalt open thy hands to thy poor brother, and lend him sufficient for his need which he hath." (Deut. 15:8)

Thirdly, we must freely forgive and remit the due debt which our neighbor doth owe unto us, if it so fall out that God bring him into decay and extreme poverty. So the pledge, or pawn, which our neighbor leaveth with us, if it belong to his necessary use, as his raiment or the like, we are to restore it to him again before the sun go down (Exod. 22:26). And this is the exhortation of Nehemiah to the hardhearted rulers of the Jews, that oppressed their brethren with usury and the like (Nehem. 5:11). And thus many ways may we cast away our bread; and for all these kinds of alms, bread is here to be taken.

Wherefore, seeing there be so many ways to exercise our liberality, let us not think it sufficient to be bountiful in one kind of good works and hardhearted in others, but that our liberality may be profitable to us let us give in all, as the present need requireth. Some men will give alms at their gate of the scraps of their table, but will not part with one penny of money to any charitable deed. Others will be ready to spend their voice in the instruction and reproof of their neighbor, or it may be to speak a good word for him, but will part with none of their own goods to help them. And some men will be only liberal in building of churches, hospitals, and the like, which indeed be good works, yet are they neither meritorious nor the most principal, for many times the gift of a piece of bread or a cup of cold water is more needful. Salomon putteth bread the chiefest alms, and Christ at the Day of Judgment will not condemn men for want of buildings but of other more needful alms and less chargeable (Matth. 25). But if the Church of Rome will maintain the merit of their abbeys, nunneries, temples, let them hear a great Schoolman of their own, Thomas Aquinas, who reckoned up the several works of charity belonging to the body [and] hath either forgotten or neglected such buildings. He hath shut them up all in this one verse: *visito, poto, cibo, redimo, tego, colligo, condo* (Aquinas 2.2., quæ. 32, ar. 2), the meaning whereof is that true liberality consisteth in visiting the sick, giving drink to the thirsty, meat to the hungry, in redeeming the captive and imprisoned, in covering the naked, in gathering or calling home poor traveling strangers to his house, and in burial of the dead. But in all these he hath made no mention of those buildings.

Wherefore let us learn not only to spend God's alms but to be such provident stewards or providers for the servants of God as that we may be liberal in all kind to give them meat, drink, and other of God's goods, in necessity according to the several necessities of them.

4 (Who?) The fourth point in order to be considered is who may properly give alms, which may easily be determined if we consider the divers kinds of good works which we have now lately rehearsed. For he that is not able to be liberal in one kind may be fit for another, which may be noted in the alms of Peter and John ent'ring into the temple, when they restored the lame cripple to his health, to whom they said in this manner, "Silver and gold have I none, but such as I have that give I thee." (Acts 3:1) Whence we may conclude that everyone may be a giver of alms. For he that hath not the riches of wealth and cannot give much, let him give a little according to the measure of his ability. Wherefore our Saviour Christ commendeth the liberality of the poor widow which cast into the treasury but two mites,[1] which was all that she had (Mark 12:41).

Those also that have not money and goods to help their neighbor, let them lend the help of their bodily labor, of their callings or the virtues of their soul and body unto them; and this was Peter's alms.

And these whom poverty, age, or subjection unto the hard government of others hath made unfit for these two, let them exercise their liberality in praying for the relief of those that want, which is the proper calling of almsmen and hospital children. Yea, it is the duty of us all.

This is the doctrine, and I beseech God to stir up your minds to the practice of liberality in all things towards all men. And remember the poor estate of the ignorant inhabitants of Virginia. Cast forth your alms, my brethren of England, and extend your liberality on these charitable works which God hath called you to perform. Let not the servants of superstition that think to merit by their good works, as they term them, go beyond us in well-doing. Neither let them be able to open their mouths against us and to condemn the religion of our Protestation for want of charitable deeds.

It may be some men will say, "The work is great, I am not able to relieve it." I answer the work is such, and such order is now taken that those that cannot give much may be liberal in a little. Those that cannot help in monies by reason of their poverty may venture their persons hither, and here not only serve God but help also these poor Indians, and build a sure foundation for themselves. But if you can do neither of these, then send your earnest prayers to God for the prosperity of this work.

5 (To whom?) The first point in order and last article of this commandment remaineth now to be handled, which is concerning the persons to whom we are to be liberal. That is to all men in general, who stand in need of our relief and help. For if corn be cast upon the waters, or very wat'ry grounds, it cannot prosper or bring forth increase. So if good works be bestowed on unthankful or

---

[1] A coin of least value. "Two mites, two drops, yet all her house and land,/Fall from a steady heart, though trembling hand./The other's wanton wealth foams high and brave./The other cast away; she only gave." *The Widow's Mite,* by Richard Crashaw (son of William).

unable persons, we are not to expect a recompense of reward from them. From whence we may gather an argument from the less to the greater, that if we are to be liberal to such as cannot or will not requite us, or to such as will not deserve our kindness, how much more to them that may deserve our good will, or will make conscience, if they can, to be thankful unto us in the best manner. So then if we must be liberal both to good men and bad, to thankful and unthankful, to our enemies and friends, it followeth that we must be charitable to all men.

And this is the rule of St. Paul: "Do good to all, but specially to the household of faith." (Galath. 6:10) Though the children of God be chiefly to be respected, yet are we not to withhold our alms from anyone if they need our help. The rule of Christ is answerable: "Give him that asketh, and from him that would borrow of thee turn not away. Do good to them that hate you, and pray for them which hurt you and persecute you." (Matth. 5:52) And so Paul expoundeth this rule of Christ: "If thine enemy hunger, feed him, if he thirst, give him drink." (Rom. 12:20) If then we must feed and clothe our enemies and persecutors, how much more our friends and helpers. It remaineth then that we must do good to all.

From hence we may take just occasion to blame the uncharitable disposition of hardhearted rich men and wealthy parishes, which suffer multitudes of poor men and women to perish in their quarters for want of their relief. The commandment of God is that there should be no beggars in Israel. But look into the streets of our cities, and pass from them into all the quarters of England, and you shall find neither court nor country, city or village, without the importunate cravings of those that cry GIVE, GIVE!

From hence it is that so many base thieves and petty robbers lurk in every corner until the common trees of execution hang them up. From hence it is that so many poor men's children, wanting the charity of others to see them brought up in learning and some honest vocation, were better if they had never been born than to live in such misorder as most of them do. Repent therefore betimes, you able misers, lest the woe of Saint James fall upon you, lest God hear the cries and curses of the poor, and heap miseries without measure upon such miserable men (James 5:1).

And now let me turn your eyes, my brethren of England, to behold the waters of Virginia, where you may behold a fit subject for the exercise of your liberality, persons enough on whom you may cast away your bread, and yet not without hope after many days to find it. Yea, I will not fear to affirm unto you that those men whom God hath made able any way to be helpful to this plantation, and made known unto them the necessities of our wants, are bound in conscience by virtue of this precept to lay their helping hands to it, either with their purse, persons, or prayers, so far forth as God hath made them fit for it. For it is evident that our wise God hath bestowed no gift upon any man for their private use, but for the good of other men, whom God shall offer to their liberality.

Wherefore, since God hath opened the door of Virginia to our country of England, we are to think that God hath, as it were, by word of mouth called us in to bestow our several charity on them. And that this may the better appear, we have many reasons to encourage us to be liberal-minded and open-handed toward them.

First, if we consider the almost miraculous beginning and continuance of this plantation, we must needs confess that God hath opened this passage unto us, and led us by the hand unto this work. For the mariners that were sent hither first to discover this Bay of Chæsapeac found it only by the mere directions of God's providence. For I heard one of them confess that even then, when they were ent'red within the mouth of the bay, they deemed the place they sought for to have been many degrees further. The finding was not so strange but[1] the continuance and upholding of it hath been most wonderful.

I may fitly compare it to the growth of an infant which hath been afflicted from his birth with some grievous sickness, that many times no hope of life hath remained, and yet it liveth still.

Again, if there were nothing else to encourage us, yet this one thing may stir us up to go on cheerfully with it, that the devil is a capital enemy against it, and continually seeketh which way to hinder the prosperity and good proceedings of it; yea, hath heretofore so far prevailed by his instruments—the covetous hearts of many backsliding adventurers at home, and also by his servants

---

[1] As.

here, some striving for superiority, others by murmurings, mutinies, and plain treasons, and others by fornication,[1] profaneness, idleness, and such monstrous sins—that he had almost thrust us out of this kingdom, and had indeed quitted this land of us, if God had not then, as one awaked out of sleep, stood up and sent us means of great help, when we needed most and expected least relief. The saving of those two honorable knights, Sir Thomas Gates and Sir George Somers, with Captain Newport and the rest of the adventurers in the *Sea Venture,* as also their happy deliverance out of those unhabited and unfrequented, because feared, islands of the Barmudaes, could proceed from none other but the singular providence of God. If this worthy governor, Sir Thomas Gates, had been hind'red but one week longer, it might be feared that the famine, which had by that time devoured the most of our countrymen here, would have consumed the rest. And when he, considering that his weak means was not able to restore or sustain the burthen of such woeful distresses, had shipped the few remaining for England, and had forsaken with Hannibal's sighs the first-builded James-Town, upon the sudden, news met him of the coming in of that honorable Lord La war with a fresh supply. Whereupon he presently returned to the town he had so lately forsaken.

Since when this English colony hath taken better root; and as a spreading herb whose top hath been often cropped off renews her growth, and spreads herself more gloriously than before, so this plantation, which the devil hath so often trodden down, is by the miraculous blessing of God revived, and daily groweth to more happy and more hopeful success.

I have shut up many things in few words, and have alleged this only to prove unto us that the finger of God hath been the only true worker here. That God first showed us the place, God first called us hither, and here God by his special providence hath maintained us; wherefore by Him let us be encouraged to lay our helping hands to this good work, yea, God's work, with all the strength of our ability.

Secondly, let the miserable condition of these naked slaves of the

[1] Could it be Whitaker was the preacher Zuñiga reported was beaten for condemning intermarriage with the Indians? (xv) He had praise for the marriage of Pocahontas and Rolfe.

devil move you to compassion toward them. They acknowledge that there is a great good god, but know him not, having the eyes of their understanding as yet blinded. Wherefore they serve the devil for fear, after a most base manner, sacrificing sometimes (as I have here heard) their own children to him.[1] I have sent one image of their god to the council in England, which is painted upon one side of a toadstool, much like unto a deformed monster.

Their priests, whom they call *quiokosoughs,* are no other but such as our English witches are. They live naked in body as if their shame of their sin deserved no covering. Their names are as naked as their body. They esteem it a virtue to lie, deceive, and steal, as their master the devil teacheth them. Much more might be said of their miserable condition, but I refer the particular narration of these things to some other season.

If this be their life, what think you shall become of them after death but to be partakers with the devil and his angels in hell forevermore? Wherefore my brethren, put on the bowels of compassion, and let the lamentable estate of these miserable people enter in your consideration. One God created us: They have reasonable souls and intellectual faculties as well as we. We all have Adam for our common parent. Yea, by nature the condition of us both is all one: the servants of sin and slaves of the devil. Oh remember, I beseech you, what was the state of England before the Gospel was preached in our country. How much better were we then and concerning our souls' health than these now are? Let the word of the Lord sound out that it may be heard in these parts, and let your faith which is toward God spread itself abroad and show forth the charitable fruits of it in these barren parts of the world. And let him know that he which hath converted a sinner from going astray out of his way shall save a soul from death and hide a multitude of sins.

But if any of us should misdoubt that this barbarous people is uncapable of such heavenly mysteries, let such men know that they are far mistaken in the nature of these men. For besides the promise of God, which is without respect of persons made as well to unwise

[1] See Spelman's *Relation §29–487.* But John Rolfe (882n[3]) told Rev. Purchas that he doubted Whitaker now in 1616, after some years in Virginia, would still claim that.

men after the flesh as to the wise, etc., let us not think that these men are so simple as some have supposed them, for they are of body lusty, strong, and very nimble. They are a very understanding generation, quick of apprehension, sudden in their dispatches, subtle in their dealings, exquisite in their inventions, and industrious in their labor. I suppose the world hath no better mark-men with their bow and arrows than they be. They will kill birds flying, fishes swimming, and beasts running.

They shoot also with marvelous strength: They shot one of our men being unarmed[1] quite through the body and nailed both his arms to his body with one arrow. One of their children also, about the age of 12 or 13 years, killed a bird with his arrow, in my sight.

The service of their god is answerable to their life, being performed with great fear and attention, and many strange dumb shows used in the same, stretching forth their limbs and straining their body, much like to the counterfeit women in England who feign themselves bewitched or possessed of some evil spirit.

They stand in great awe of their quiokosoughs, or priests, which are a generation of vipers, even of Satan's own brood. The manner of their life is much like to the Popish hermits of our age. For they live alone in the woods, in houses sequest'red from the common course of men. Neither may any man be suffered to come into their house or to speak with them but when this priest doth call him. He taketh no care for his victuals, for all such kind of things, both bread and water etc., are brought unto a place near unto his cottage, and there are left, which he fetcheth for his proper need. If they would have rain or have lost anything, they have their recourse to him, who conjureth for them, and many times prevaileth. If they be sick, he is their physician; if they be wounded, he sucketh them; at his command they make war and peace; neither do they anything of moment without him.

I will not be tedious in these strange narrations. When I have more perfectly entered into their secrets, you shall know all.

Finally, there is a civil government amongst them which they strictly observe, and show thereby that the law of nature dwelleth in

[1] Not wearing body armor.

them. For they have a rude kind of commonwealth and rough government, wherein they both honor and obey their kings, parents, and governors; both greater and less, they observe the limits of their own possessions, and encroach not upon their neighbors' dwellings. Murther is a capital crime scarce heard of among them; adultery is most severely punished and so are their other offenses. These unnurtured grounds of reason in them may serve to encourage us to instruct them in the knowledge of the true God, the rewarder of all righteousness, not doubting but that He that was powerful to save us by His word, when we were nothing, will be merciful also to these sons of Adam in His appointed time, in whom there be remaining so many footsteps of God's image.

Wherefore you wealthy men of this world, whose bellies God hath filled with His hidden treasure, trust not in uncertain riches, neither "cast your eyes upon them, for riches taketh her to her wings as an eagle, and flieth into heaven." (Prov. 23:5) But "be rich in good works, ready to distribute or communicate." (1 Tim. 6) How shamefully do the most of you either miserably detain or wickedly misspend God's goods, whereof He made you His stewards. The covetous person seeks to hide his talent from the good of others and himself, honoring it as his god which should be his servant. The prodigal men of our land make haste to fling away God's treasures as a grievous burthen which they desire to be eased of. Some make no scruple at it to spend yearly an hundred pounds, two, three, five hundred and much more about dogs, hawks, and hounds, and such sports, which will not give five hundred *pence* to the relief of God's poor members. Others will not care to lose two or three thousand pound in a night at cards and dice, and yet suffer poor Lazarus to perish in their streets for want of their charitable alms. Yea, divers will hire gardens at great rents, and build stately houses for their whores, which have no compassion on the fatherless and widows. How much better were it for these men to remember the afflictions of Joseph, to extend the bowels of their compassion to the poor, the fatherless afflicted, and the like, than to misspend that which they must give a straight account of at the Day of Judgment. Are not these miserable people here better than hawks, hounds, whores, and the like? O you that spend so much on them, think it no dishonor to your persons, no impoverishing to your state, to bestow somewhat to the raising up of Christ's kingdom, and maintenance of so holy and heavenly an action as this is. God of His goodness, that hath given you ability to perform it, make you willing to help it forward with the best of your power.

"For after many days thou shalt find it." Hitherto have we spoken of the commandment and the several branches of the same. Now follows the reason of this commandment, which the Holy Ghost useth here to stir us up unto liberality, which is taken from the reward which we shall have of our well-doing: "For after many days thou shalt find it"—the sum of which reason is that though God do not presently reward our well-doing, but do defer the requital of it for many days, yet thy good works shall not perish, but God at the appointed time shall abundantly recompense thy liberality.

Out of this reason we may gather two notable conclusions touching the reward of liberality. First, we may conclude from hence that God doth not always give a present reward to the good works. He doth for the most part defer His rewards many days, sometimes many years, yea, sometimes even till death itself, when He will never cease to reward us according to our works with unspeakable joys of blessed immortality. And the wisdom of God doth thus defer His rewards for most singular reasons. For if God should presently reward good works, who then would not be a prodigal giver? Who would be a faithful giver? For when a man is certain of present gain, he will not spare to give abundantly, because he seeth an exceeding profit ready to be put into his hands for so doing. And this would stir up the most covetous wretch in the world to be liberal, gaping out of mere covetousness after an overplus of reward. Wherefore God hath made the time and condition of His rewards doubtful, that we might not be covetous of the benefit, but that He might exercise our faith, and teach us with patience of hope to expect the appointed time of His reward. The principal point of perfect charity is that we give *in faith,* whose true nature is to depend upon God for the good success of our alms. "For faith is the ground of things that are hoped for, and the evidence of things that are not seen." (Heb. 11:1)

Now if we should have the reward of good works in the view of our eyes, and ready, as it were, to be put into our hands, what place would then be left for practice of faith, whose object is unseen, whose hopes be of afterwards? Wherefore St. Paul adviseth Timothy to charge them that be rich in this world to be rich in good works, not for any present reward which they were to have, but only for the benefits to come, laying up, saith he, in store for themselves a good foundation against the time to come, that they may obtain eternal life (1 Tim. 6). The message which God sent to Cornelius by His angel is worthy to be noted of us: "Thy prayers," saith the angel to him, "and thine alms are come up into remembrance before God." (Acts 10:4) Cornelius was a man that had given much alms to the poor, which God did not presently reward, for He did seem rather to have forgotten his liberality. Wherefore now he saith that his alms are come up into remembrance, the meaning whereof must needs be that though God did seem to neglect his liberality, yet He had not forgotten his alms, but now meant to reward them. The Shunammite woman that provided a chamber, table, stool, and candlestick for Elisha (2 Kings 4:10); and Tabitha, which is Dorcas, that was so "full of good works and alms deeds which she did" (Acts 9:36), were both at the first view rather punished for their good works than presently rewarded. For the first lost her only son, the second fell sick and untimely died. But mark the end: God forgat not to requite them even in this world, for the Shunammite had her son restored to her alive by the prayer of Elisha, and Dorcas by the ministery of St. Peter was raised again to life. By this that hath been said, it may easily appear that God doth out of His infinite wisdom defer the time and prolong many days for the most part the reward of our alms and liberality. From whence we may learn that it is the property of true charity to neglect the present reward. For love the mother of liberality is not covetous, but is bountiful; it "believeth all things, it hopeth all things" (1 Cor. 13); and faith, the ground and first pedigree of right giving, doth not make haste, but reposeth itself upon the expectation of hope (Isa. 28:16).

Wherefore in communicating our goods and distributing our alms, let us have no covetous eye aiming at the present profit, but let us depend with faith upon the future blessing which shall come in due season. For if we would thoroughly consider the thing as it is, we shall find that all the reward of our well-doing comes not from any merit or desert of ours, but only from the mere mercy of God.

What man can say that the goods which he possesseth be his own? Or what have we that we have not received? When we have made the most and best of ourselves, we are but the stewards of God's goods, and the almners of his purse. Why then should we look to be paid extraordinarily for the giving of that which is not our own, but which we are commanded by our Master to bestow? We have more need to pray with David, "O Lord, if thou be extreme to mark what is done amiss, who may abide it?" (Psal. 130:3); and to confess that when we have done all that we can, we are but unprofitable servants. It follows then that all the good which we do receive, comes not from our deserts but only from the riches of God's bounty (Luke 17:20), which rewardeth us according to our works done, without any desert of ours whatsoever.

Wherefore the eyes of liberality do not look after the reward of the work, but they search how to do the work, how to give the alms, so as that they may be pleasing to God, and of Him accepted, and by Him, if He see it good, rewarded.

Let then your liberal minds, you honorable and charitable adventurers of Virginia, be stirred up to cast your alms on the waters of Virginia, without hope of present profit. The base affections of the usurer will not look for the overplus of increase until the covenanted time of his loan be expired. The husbandman casting his seed into the earth waiteth upon God until harvest for a fruitful crop. Verily, he that believeth doth not make haste. Be not overhasty with God. God will not yet reward you, that He may make you more famous in the world, that the world may see your zeal, and bear witness to the patience of your faith, not to greedy haste of covetous desires. The work is honorable, and now more than ever sustained by most honorable men. Oh, let us not then be weary of well-doing! Forty years were expired before Israel could plant in Canaan, and yet God had called them by the word of His mouth, had led them Himself by an high hand. Yet may you boldly look for a shorter time of reward. The returns which you have from the East Indies, though they be exceeding rich, yet is the adventure doubtful, the expense chargeable, and the expectation of return of three years' continuance.

Let me advise you to be as liberal in adventure hither, and I dare affirm that by God's assistance your profitable returns shall be of more certainty and much shorter expectation. Remember, I beseech you, how many lives were lost, how many years were spent, what discouragements, what great losses the adventurers of Spain and Portugal suffered and underwent before they could be settled in the West Indies, or receive any profitable return from thence. And now behold what rich loads, what profitable returns are yearly shipped from thence. Shall our nation, hitherto famous for noble attempts and the honorable finishing of what they have undertaken, be now taxed for inconstancy, and blamed by the enemies of our Protestation for uncharitableness? Yea, shall we be a scorn among princes, and a laughingstock among our neighbor nations for basely leaving what we honorably began; yea, for beginning a discovery whose riches other men shall gather so soon as we have forsaken it?

Awake, you true-hearted Englishmen, you servants of Jesus Christ: Remember that the plantation is God's and the reward your country's. Wherefore aim not at your present private gain, but let the Glory of God, whose kingdom you now plant, and good of your country, whose wealth you seek, so far prevail with you that you respect not a present return of gain for this year or two but that you would more liberally supply for a little space this your Christian work, which you so charitably began.

As for those spirits of slander, whom the devil hath stirred up to speak evil of this good land and to weaken the hands of our brethren, lest they should go forward and pull Satan out of his dominions—let them take heed, lest the punishment of Shammua and his nine companions, the faithless searchers of the Land of Canaan, do befall them and that they never live to taste of the commodities of this good land.

But lest I may seem to exhort you to an unprofitable liberality, or to argue God of forgetfulness to those that serve Him faithfully, hear now what a comfortable promise of reward God hath made unto us in these words, which is that after many days we shall *find.*

If God should have commanded us to cast away without finding, some discouragement there might have been to our weak nature. But since God hath assuredly promised us that we shall find in the end, who will not obey the command? Who will not be liberal?

God hath been always found true in His word, most faithful in His promises. If God do promise Abraham that his seed shall inherit the Land of Canaan (Genes. 12), Abraham's posterity shall after many days in the appointed time be planted peaceably in the Land of Canaan. If God promise Salomon wisdom and riches (1 Kings 1), Salomon shall be wiser and richer than any prince of the earth. If God promiseth that He will give His only son, "that whosoever believeth in Him shall not perish, but have life everlasting" (John 3), His Son Jesus Christ shall be born into the world at the appointed time, and undergo the weight of God's wrath for redemption of believers (Rom. 8:32). Shall God then faithfully perform all His promises in so great matters and be unfaithful in lesser matters? Oh, let no such base conceit of the Almighty enter into our minds, as to think that He that spared not His own Son to perform His promises to us will be so unmindful of us in so small a thing!

The promises of God are many and most bountiful. "There is that scattereth," saith Salomon, "and is more increased" (Prov. 10:24)[1]; and in the next verse he addeth, "The liberal person shall have plenty," or, as the Hebrew text is, "The soul of blessing shall be made fat, and he that watereth shall also have rain." Most comfortable is the promise of liberality set down by Isaiah, chapter 58:8. And if thou be liberal, "thy light shall break forth as the morning, and thy health shall grow speedily. Thy righteousness shall go before thee, and the Glory of the Lord shall embrace thee." What can be said more to encourage us? Yet Salomon addeth, "He that hath mercy on the poor lendeth unto the Lord, and the Lord will recompense him what he hath given." (Prov. 19:17)

Wherefore what is with liberality given is not cast away but lent unto the Lord, unto Him that is able to repay us, for both the heaven and the earth are His (Psalm 24), and who is also willing to recompense it, for He hath promised so to do, and confirmed His word and promises by the sacraments, His seals. We do willingly lend to a good creditor, especially if we have his bond, with his hand and seal

[1] 11:24.

to pay us. What, shall we trust man and distrust God? Oh, far be it from us, my brethren! Let no such distrust possess our uncharitable minds. If we desire any more promises, let us observe what counsel Christ gave unto the Pharisees: "Give alms of those things which you have, and behold, all things shall be clean unto you." (Luke 11:41) Which is as much as if He should say Give alms, be liberal, for in so doing your goods shall be sanctified unto you, and you shall attain to an holy and pure use of your goods. The Scripture is plain in this point.

I will now come therefore to give you a view in brief of those commodities and rewards that we shall find here after not many but a few days.

First, our liberality grounded on faith and practiced in love will be a means to help our souls forward in their passage to heaven; for they are the highway and trodden path wherein we must walk to everlasting life. Therefore the more any man abounds in good works, the more comfortable shall be his passage.

Secondly, they are such necessary fruits of faith that faith cannot go without them. For where no good works are, there is no faith; and where true saving faith is, there will be showed good works; yea, we cannot hold true faith from doing good. Read for the proof of this the Epistle of St. James and the First Epistle of St. John, besides the places which we have heretofore alleged.

Thirdly, liberality is a notable means against covetousness. For where true charity dwells, there is no room left for covetousness to harbor in. Two contraries cannot be both at once in one subject; God and the devil will not dwell together, neither can covetousness and liberality be linked together in one breast.

Thus shall the Lord abundantly reward our souls for our liberality, and many ways more besides, if we be truly charitable. But the bounty of God would have us to taste of some temporal blessings besides, and after a few days, if we be cheerful givers, return a plentiful reward home unto us. Wherefore, that I might content the longing minds of every man, I thought it fit in the last place to recite a few commodities which in short time we may find here in Virginia for the charity bestowed in this plantation.

THE WHOLE CONTINENT OF VIRGINIA, situate within the degrees of 34 and 47, is a place beautified by God with all the ornaments of nature, and enriched with his earthly treasures. That part of it which we already possess, beginning at the Bay of Chæsapheac and stretching itself in northerly latitude to the degrees of 39 and 40, is interlined with seven most goodly rivers, the least whereof is equal to our River of Thames. And all these rivers are so nearly joined as that there is not very much distance of dry ground between either of them[1]; and those several mainlands are everywhere watered with many veins, or creeks, of water, which sundry ways do overthwart[2] the land and make it almost navigable from one river to the other; the commodity whereof to those that shall inhabit this land is infinite in respect of the speedy and easy transportance of goods from one river to the other. I cannot better manifest it unto you but in advising you to consider whether the water or land hath been more beneficial to the Low Countries. But here we shall have the commodity both of water and land more ready with less charge and labor than hath been bestowed by them in turning land into water.

The river which we inhabit—commonly called Powhatan's River—ebbeth and floweth 140 miles into the main, at the mouth whereof are the two forts of Henrico[3] and Charles. 42 miles upward is the first and mother Christian town seated, called James-Town, and 70 miles beyond that upward is the new town of Henrico, built and so named in the memory of the noble Prince Henry of lasting and blessed memory.[4] Ten miles beyond this town is a place called the Falls, because the river hath there a great descent, falling down between many mineral rocks which be there. Twelve miles farther beyond this place is there a crystal rock wherewith the Indians do head many of their arrows. Three days' journey from thence is there a rock, or stony hill, found which is in the top covered all over with a perfect and most rich silver ore. Our men that went to discover those parts

[1] "As 14 or 16 miles." (margin note)

[2] Lie across.

[3] More commonly called Fort Henry.

[4] "Crashaw evidently revised this before publication as Whitaker could not have known of the death of Prince Henry when he wrote." (Brown) The Prince of Wales died of typhoid fever, 6 November 1612.

had but two iron pickaxes with them, and those so ill tempered that the points of them turned again and bowed at every stroke, so that we could not search the entrails of the place. Yet some trial was made of that ore, with good success and argument of much hope.

Six days' journey beyond this mine, a great ridge of high hills do run along the mainland, not far from whom the Indians report a great sea doth run—which we commonly call a "south" sea, but in respect of our habitation is a west sea, for there the sun setteth from us.

The higher ground is much like unto the mould of France, clay and sand being proportionably mixed together at the top. But if we dig any depth, as we have done for our bricks, we find it to be red clay, full of glistering spangles. There be many rocky places in all quarters, and more than probable likelihoods of rich mines of all sorts. Though I knew all, yet it were not convenient at this time that I should utter all. Neither have we had means to search for anything as we ought, thorough present want of men and former wants of provision for the belly.

As for iron, steel, antimonium, and terra sigillata, they have rather offered themselves to our eyes and hands than been sought for of us.

The air of the country, especially about Henrico and upward, is very temperate and agreeth well with our bodies. The extremity of summer is not so hot as Spain, nor the cold of winter so sharp as the frosts of England. The spring and harvest are the two longest seasons and most pleasant; the summer and winter are both but short. The winter is for the most part dry and fair, but the summer watered often with many great and sudden showers of rain, whereby the cold of winter is warmed and the heat of summer cooled.

Many have died with us heretofore thorough their own filthiness and want of bodily comforts for sick men; but now very few are sick among us—not above three persons amongst all the inhabitants of Henrico. I would to God our souls were no sicker than our bodies, and that other of God's blessings were as general and common as the bodily health. I have seen it by experience and dare boldly affirm it that sickness doth more rage in England quarterly than here yearly. I doubt that hereafter, when our hospital or guest house is built up, you hear of many more cut off by the sword of justice, unless the better people be sent over, than perished by the diseases of the country.

The natural people of the land are generally such as you heard of before: a people to be feared of those that come upon them without defensive armor, but otherwise faint-hearted—if they see their arrows cannot pierce—and easy to be subdued. Shirts of mail or quilted cotton coats are the best defense against them. There is but one or two of their petty kings that for fear of us have desired our friendship, and those keep good quarter with us, being very pleasant amongst us and, if occasion be, serviceable unto us.

Our eldest friends be Pipsco and Choapoke, who are our overthwart neighbors at James-Town, and have been friendly to us in our great want. The other is the *werewance* of Chescheak, who but lately traded with us peaceably. If we were once the masters of their country, and they stood in fear of us—which might with few hands employed about nothing else be in short time brought to pass—it were an easy matter to make them willingly to forsake the devil to embrace the faith of Jesus Christ and to be baptized. Besides, you cannot easily judge how much they would be available to us in our discoveries of the country, in our buildings and plantings, and quiet provision for ourselves, when we may peaceably pass from place to place without need of arms or guard.

The means for our people to live and subsist here of themselves are many and most certain both for beasts, birds, fish, and herbs. The beasts of the country are for the most part wild, as lions, bears, wolves, and deer, foxes black and red, *rakowns*, beavers, *possowns*, squirrels, wildcats, whose skins are of great price, and muskrats, which yield musk as the muskcats do.

There be two kinds of beasts amongst these most strange. One of them is the female *possown,* which will let forth her young out of her belly and take them up into her belly again at her pleasure without hurt to herself. Neither think this to be a traveler's tale, but the very truth, for nature hath framed her fit for that service. My eyes have been witness unto it, and we have sent of them and their young ones into England.

The other strange-conditioned creature is the flying squirrel, which thorough the help of certain broad flaps of skin growing on each side of her forelegs will fly from tree to tree 20 or 30 paces at one flight and more, if she have the benefit of a small breath of wind.

Besides these, since our coming hither we have brought both kine, goats, and hogs, which prosper well and would multiply exceedingly if they might be provided for.

This country besides is replenished with birds of all sorts, which have been the best sustenance of flesh which our men have had since they came; also eagles, and hawks of all sorts, amongst whom are ausprech (osprey?), fishing hawk, and the cormorant. The woods be everywhere full of wild turkeys, which abound and will run as swift as a greyhound. In winter our fields be full of cranes, herons, pigeons, partridges, and blackbirds.

The rivers and creeks be overspread everywhere with waterfowl of the greatest and least sort, as swans, flocks of geese and brants, duck and mallard, sheldrakes, divers, etc., besides many other kinds of rare and delectable birds whose names and natures I cannot yet recite, but we want the means to take them.

The rivers abound with fish both small and great. The sea fish come into our rivers in March and continue until the end of September; great schools of herrings come in first; shads of a great bigness and rockfish follow them; trouts, bass, flounders, and other dainty fish come in before the other be gone; then come multitudes of great sturgeons, whereof we catch many and should do more but that we want good nets answerable to the breadth and depth of our rivers, besides our channels are so foul in the bottom with great logs and trees that we often break our nets upon them. I cannot reckon nor give proper names to the divers kinds of fresh fish in our rivers. I have caught with mine angle pike, carp, eel, perches of six several kinds, crayfish, and the *torope,* or little turtle, besides many smaller kinds.

Wherefore, since God hath filled the elements of the earth, air, and waters with His creatures good for our food and nourishment, let not the fear of starving hereafter or of any great want dishearten your valiant minds from coming to a place of so great plenty. If the country were ours, and means for the taking of them—which shortly I hope shall be brought to pass—then all these should be ours. We have them now, but we are fain[1] to fight for them. Then should we have them without that trouble. Fear not then to want food, but only provide means to get it here. We have store of wildfowl in England, but what are they better for them that cannot come by them, wanting means to catch them? Even such is and hath been our case heretofore.

But these are not all the commodities which we may find here, for the earth will yield much more fruit to our industrious labors, as hath been proved by the corn and other things which we have planted this last year. I have made proof of it with the help of three more, being a stranger to that business, and having not a body inured to such labor, and set so much corn *horis succisinis unius septimanae,* "in the idle hours of one week," as will suffice me for bread one quarter of a year. And one commodity is besides in this corn: that from the time of setting unto the time of gathering five months will abundantly suffice. For we set corn from the beginning of March until the end of May, and reap or gather in July, August, and September.

Our English seeds thrive very well here, as peas, onions, turnips, cabbages, coleflowers [cauliflowers], carrots, thyme, parsley, hyssop, marjoram, and many other whereof I have tasted and eaten.

What, should I name unto you the divers sorts of trees, sweet woods, and physical[2] plants, the divers kinds of oaks and walnut trees, the pines, pitch trees, soap-ashes trees, sassafras, cedar, ash, maple, cypress, and many more which I daily see, and admire at the beauty and riches which God hath bestowed upon this people that yet know not how to use them.

WHEREFORE you, right wise and noble adventurers of Virginia, whose hearts God hath stirred up to build Him a temple, to make Him an house, to conquer a kingdom for Him here—be not discouraged with those many lamentable assaults that the devil hath made against us. He now rageth most because he knoweth his kingdom is to have a short end. Go forward boldly, and remember that

---

[1] Obliged.

[2] Medicinal.

you fight under the banner of Jesus Christ, that you plant His kingdom who hath already broken the serpent's head. God may defer His temporal reward for a season, but be assured that in the end you shall find riches and honor in this world and blessed immortality in the world to come.

And you my brethren, my fellow laborers, send up your earnest prayers to God for His Church in Virginia, that since His harvest here is great, but the laborers few, He would thrust forth laborers into His harvest. And pray also for me that the ministration of His Gospel may be powerful and effectual by me to the salvation of many and advancement of the Kingdom of Jesus Christ to whom, with the Father and the Holy Spirit, be all honor and glory forevermore. AMEN.

μονωι τωι θεωι δοξα[1]

[1] "Glory to the only God."

44. Don Diego de Molina

Letter [to Don Alonso de Velasco[1]], 28 May 1613

(translated from the Spanish by Maximilian Schele de Vere)

< Simancas Archives 2590–47, **Brown 1890:646**

When he wrote this from Jamestown, poor Don Diego had been a prisoner there two years. His message in confidence was conveyed in a shoe sole by a spy, "a gentleman from Venice," whose identity we cannot guess. He tells us Virginia begs for liberation at the hands of the King of Spain. The colonists live in as much misery as Don Diego himself. Each year half of them die. But do not believe the talk that the rich merchants are going to write off and abandon the colony, the prisoner warns us. Spain will have to deliver the coup de grace or Virginia will linger to become a vast pirate's nest, an "Algiers in America." Hmm.

THE PERSON WHO WILL HAND YOU THIS IS PERFECTLY TRUSTWORTHY AND YOU CAN RELY UPON ALL HE TELLS YOU; AND THUS I SHALL NOT SAY MUCH IN THIS LETTER, BUT ONLY STATE WHAT IS MOST IMPORTANT.

ALTHOUGH my imprisonment, followed by such extraordinary adventures, will have opened His Majesty's eyes and led him to see this new Algiers in America, which is being established here, I do not marvel that he should not have corrected this evil in all this long time, since the delivery would require a voyage—especially as there is wanting all certain knowledge for its carrying out—although I believe that with your own great intelligence and with the going of the caravel to Spain, His Majesty will have been able to decide what is of most importance, and that this would be to cut short the advance of a Hydra in its infancy, since the [English] intention is the destruction of the whole West, by sea as well as on land, and I do not doubt that great results will follow, because the advantages of this place are such as to make it a rendezvous of all the pirates of Europe, where they will be well received.

---

[1] The Spanish ambassador in London.

This nation has great ideas of a league with them, and it will be very powerful even by itself alone, because on the day when there shall be produced here a sufficiency of grain and an abundance of cattle there will not be a man of whatever quality he may be who will not alone or in company with others arm a vessel to come out here and join the others, because, as you know, this kingdom abounds with poor people who abhor peace, and this is necessarily so because in peace they perish; and the rich are so haughty and so selfish that they even covet the wealth of the Indies—their gold and their silver—although this will not be wanting much here, as they have discovered some mines which are considered productive, although they have not yet been able to benefit much by them until they shall be well established here.

There are great expectations of what they will find in the mountains in great abundance, so say the Indians, and offer to show the places which they know.

They [the Indians] say that at the headwaters of the rivers, after they have come forth from the mountains, there is a great quantity of grains of silver and gold. But as they do not attach any value to them, but only to copper, which they esteem very highly, they do not collect them.

Until now these men have not been able to go out to discover them, however eagerly they may desire it—and to pass beyond towards New Mexico, and from thence to the South Sea, where they think of establishing great colonies, and fit[ting] out fleets with which to make themselves masters of those waters (as of this sea by colonizing a few islands of those that lie easterly of the Bahama Channel, and by conquering others like Porto Rico, San Domingo, and Cuba).

Although this may be difficult for them, at least we have already seen evidences of these purposes in the settlement of Bermuda, where it is said they have strong fortifications, because the conformation of the land is such that a few can defend themselves against a large number, especially by preventing a landing and disembarking troops. According to what is understood, the depth is not great enough for ships of a hundred tons. But I believe they make it [out] shallower than it is, because I have described [read a description of] that island from the relation of Captain Diego Ramirez, who was stranded there, and it seems to me that other and larger vessels may enter. I do not remember it well, because it is long ago, but the description is in the house of Don Rodrigo de Aguiar, of the India Board, and the [padron?] in Sevilla, in the house of the licentiate Antonio Moreno, cosmographer of the same.

But above all, this captain will give you a sufficient account of the island, and this is very important on account of the military measures which may hereafter be taken there. Its fertility is great, fish and game abound infinitely, and pork is there as much as they can wish. And thus they are very comfortable in that colony, because they have little need of England, since they are likewise rich in amber and pearls, of which they say they have in very few months sent to this kingdom more than fifty thousand ducats in value, counting the ounce at a moderate value. About four days ago there arrived here [Jamestown] a vessel which brought them men and supplies, and they do not cease praising the good features of this island [Bermuda] and its advantages.

The soil here [in Virginia] is fertile, good for every variety of crops, except for such as require very great heat, because it is cold here. There is much hunting and fishing, but as they have not yet had any profit from the mines—except only [some profits] in timber which is very good—the merchants have not been able to support this colony with such liberality as is required.

And thus they have suffered much want with only a miserable supply of wheat or maize, and dressing wretchedly, so that if today three hundred men should come, the first year consumes a hundred and fifty of them, and there is no year that half of them do not die. Last year there were seven hundred people here, and only three hundred and fifty remain, because the hard work (and the scanty food) on public works kills them, and increases the discontent in which they live, seeing themselves treated like slaves with great cruelty. Hence a good many have gone to the Indians, of whom some have died at their hands. And others have gone out to sea, being sent out to fish. And those who remain do so by force, and are anxious to see a fleet come from Spain to release them from this misery, because from the grievance which they suffer they call upon God and appeal to Your Majesty, in whom they place great hopes.

And thus let a fleet come and give them a passage to that kingdom, not a single person will take up arms. They will rather give up all respect and obedience to their rulers, who think they can keep this up until death. And although there it is understood that the merchants are abandoning this colony, it is not so, because this is a stratagem by which they think they mislead Your Majesty, making it look as if this matter were to finish by itself, and that thus there would be no necessity for going to the expense of fitting out a fleet of any size that might come with eight hundred or a thousand men and settle the matter with great facility—and even with five hundred, because no succor is expected from England to resist, and the fortifications which they have are low and so fragile that a kick would destroy them; and when they are once supported by walls, those on the outside are better than those within because their beams and loopholes are common to both parts,[1] a fortification without skill, and made by people who do not understand it.

Nor are the men soldiers, although the rulers and captains make a great profession of them, because of the great assistance they have rendered in Flanders in favor of Holland, where some of them have companies and castles. The men are badly disciplined and not drilled at all, although their hopes are based upon one of two colonies which they have established twenty leagues from here up the river in a turn of the river on a peninsula [Henrico], which is very rough [strongly situated?], with a small harbor [dock?] for landing, and they are convinced that there they can defend themselves against the whole world. I have not seen it, but I know that the fortifications are like the others, and that one night the Indians broke in and took the whole place without resistance being made, shooting arrows in at all the doors, so that I do not fear any difficulty in taking this place nor Bermuda, especially if my advice is taken in both cases, as coming from a person who has resided here two years, and who has examined all most carefully.

I am looking for the decision of Your Majesty, desirous of being of some service, and I lay no stress upon my captivity nor the suffering

---

[1] At the same convenient height above the ground? If so, that is indeed inept fortification.

which I have endured as a prisoner, by hunger, pain, and illness, because he who suffers from love looks upon his afflictions with indifference.

The Ensign Marco Antonio Perez died fifteen months ago, more from hunger than from sickness, but certainly with the patience of a saint and the spirit of a good soldier.

I have not suffered excessively, although considerably, because since I came here I have been acceptable to the people here, and they have sympathized with me in proportion to their own misery, but with real goodwill. The sailor [Lembri] who came with me is said to be an Englishman and a pilot. He claims to be from Aragon, and really no one would take him to be a foreigner.

This country lies in the midst of thirty-seven degrees and a third, in which lies also the bay which we call Santa Maria. Five rivers fall into it, very wide and very deep. This one measures at the entrance nine fathoms, and inside from five to six.

The others measure five, seven, eight, and twelve. The bay measures eight [leagues] at the mouth, but in some parts it is very wide, up to thirty leagues. There is much valuable timber there and material for shipbuilding, [and] trees fit for such purposes as they may desire [such as] very dark walnut wood, which they esteem very highly, together with other kinds of valuable trees.

The bearer is a gentleman from Venice, very honorable, who having fallen into certain grave errors is now restored to his first religion, and says that God has made me His instrument in this change, for which I am deeply grateful. He desires to go to Spain and to make amends for his sins. If I am restored to freedom, I think I shall assist him as far as I can. I beseech you to do me the favor and to make him some present, since I believe it will be a kindness very acceptable to our Lord.

You see, sire, that I do not believe charity to be extinct yet in Spain, and think it must be excited in you by a man who leaves here poor and sick, who cannot make any use of his good parts, and if I shall have to remain here long, I shall be no less in need of your assistance. By the information of this man, who will tell you what I endure, you might assist me with some ship stores, such as brought here for certain private persons, and especially linen and cloth for clothing ourselves, this man and myself, since we go naked or so ragged that it amounts to the same—not being able to change shirts for a month, because, as the soldiers say, my shirts are odd and do not amount to three.

I trust in God, who will assist me, since He begins already by giving me health after eleven months, during which I had none. I have not space enough to write to His Majesty, and you will be able to do it, informing him of all I state.

May God preserve you, as I desire it.

From Virginia, May 28th (as it is counted in Spain), 1613.

IF YOU HAVE THE KEY TO MY CIPHER, you can write to me in the same cipher. But this letter goes between the soles of a shoe, where it is sewed in. And thus I trust to God that I have not done wrong in writing in this manner.

At first when I came here, I wrote to His Majesty a letter which required some interpretation, and I addressed it with some others to you. I do not know if you have received it. I hoped I would be able to send a description of this country, but the public nature of my lodging does not permit it. But the most important feature is the bay, which extends northwest/southeast. And at the distance of four leagues from the mouth is this river in a southerly direction, with 9 fathoms depth. At the entrance there is a fort, or, to say more correctly a *[flaco de tablas?]* ten hands high, with 25 soldiers and 4 iron guns. Half a league from here there is another one, but smaller, with 15 soldiers without artillery. There is still another smaller one, all of which are inland, half a league off, against the Indians. This has 15 soldiers more. Twenty leagues higher up is this colony [Jamestown] with 150 persons and 6 guns. Still higher up, twenty leagues off, is another strongly situated settlement [Henrico] to which all of them will be taken when the occasion arrives, because there they place their hope. Here there are a hundred persons more, and among them as among the people here there are women, boys, and field laborers, so that there remain not quite two hundred effective men and they are badly disciplined.

DON DIEGO DE MOLINO.

45. Samuel Argall

Letter to Hawes, June 1613

< **Purchas 1625d:1764,** Brown 1890:640

Smith Island lies immediately to the east of Cape Charles. Together with farmland opposite in the Kiptopeake area, it now became "Dale's Gift" plantation. Another Smith Island is 60 miles north of it in the Bay. Both islands were likely named not for Captain John, but for Sir Thomas Smythe, treasurer (chief executive) of the Virginia Company, but John Smith claims as namesake the one off Cape Charles.

We have two other versions of the abduction of Pocahontas—Hamor's §51–802ff and Smith's given on 804 in a footnote. Here it is plain the Patawomeck would go to lengths to keep their alliance intact with Jamestown. The new power was causing the disintegration of Powhatan's authority.

The lack of deep water on the Eastern Shore is why this otherwise rich and securable region was passed over for the bloody James River.

The Pembroke River is the Potomac. Shall we say Argall was the first Washington to admire the site of Mount Vernon?

MASTER HAWES—Within seven weeks after my departure from the coast of England, being the three and twentieth of July, 1612, I fell with the coast of Virginia in the latitude of forty degrees, the twelfth of September, with all my men in good health—the number being sixty-two—and all my victuals very well conditioned, my course being fifty leagues to the northward of the Azores.

The seventeenth, I arrived at Point Comfort, where by the discreet and provident government of Sir Thomas Gates, and great pains and hazard of Sir Thomas Dale, I found both the country and people in far better estate there than the report was by such as came home in Sir Robert Mansfield's ship.

From my arrival until the first of November, I spent my time in helping to repair such ships and boats as I found here decayed for lack of pitch and tar; and in pursuing the Indians with Sir Thomas Dale for their corn, of which we got some quantity—which we were like to have bought very dearly, for by the providence of God Sir

Thomas Dale escaped killing very narrowly.[1]

Then about the beginning of November, by the advice of Sir Thomas Gates, I carried Sir Thomas Dale to Sir Thomas Smith's Island to have his opinion of the inhabiting of it; who, after three days' march in discovering it, approved very well of the place; and so much the better because we found abundance of fish there and very great cod, which we caught in five fathom water, of which we are in hope to get a great quantity this summer for the relief of our men, as also to find safe passage for boats and barges thither by a cut out of the bottom of our bay into the De la Warre Bay; for which fishing and better discovery I have my ship ready with my company in as good health as at my arrival, and as they have continued ever since; for which God be glorified, to whom we give daily thanks for the continuance of His mercy.

After my return from Sir Thomas Smith's Island, I fitted my ship to fetch corn from Patowomeck by trading with the Indians, and so set sail from Point Comfort the first of December.

And being ent'red into Penbrooke River, I met with the King of Pastancie[2] a-hunting, who went presently aboard with me, seeming to be very glad of my coming, and told me that all the Indians there were my very great friends, and that they had good store of corn for me, which they had provided the year before, which we found to be true. Then I carried my ship presently before his town, and there built me a stout shallop to get the corn aboard withal. Which being done, and having concluded a peace with divers other Indian lords, and likewise given and taken hostages,[3] I hasted to James Town, being the first [31st?] of January [1613], and arrived at Point Comfort the first of February.

In this voyage I got 1100 bushels of corn, which I delivered into the several storehouses, according unto the direction of Sir T[homas] Gates, besides the quantity of 300 bushels reserved for mine company.

As soon I had unladen this corn, I set my men to the felling of timber for the building of a frigate, which I left half finished in the

---

1 "This was in the River of Nansamund." (margin note)
2 "Ayapassus, the weroance of Pastancie." (margin note)
3 "Cap. Web, Ensigne Swift, Rob. Sparkes & two boys." (margin note)

hands of the carpenters at Point Comfort, the 19 of March, and returned myself with the ship into Pembrook River, and so discovered to the head of it, which is about 65 leagues into the land, and navigable for any ship. And then marching into the country, I found great store of cattle as big as kine, of which the Indians that were my guides killed a couple which we found to be very good and wholesome meat, and are very easy to be killed in regard they are heavy, slow, and not so wild as other beasts of the wilderness. In this journey I likewise found a mine, of which I have sent a trial into England; and likewise a strange kind of earth, the virtue whereof I know not, but the Indians eat it for physic, alleging that it cureth the sickness and pain of the belly. I likewise found a kind of water issuing out of the earth which hath a tart taste much like unto alum water. It is good and wholesome, for my men did drink much of it and never found it otherwise. I also found an earth like a gum, white and clear, another sort red like terra sigillata, another very white and of so light a substance that being cast into the water it swimmeth.

Whilst I was in this business, I was told by certain Indians my friends that the Great Powhatan's daughter Pokahuntis was with the Great King Patowomeck, whither I presently repaired, resolving to possess myself of her by any stratagem that I could use for the ransoming of so many Englishmen as were prisoners with Powhatan, as also to get such arms and tools as he and other Indians had got by murther and stealing from others of our nation, with some quantity of corn for the colony's relief.

So soon as I came to an anchor before the town, I manned my boat and sent on shore for the King of Pastancy and Ensign Swift, whom I had left as a pledge of our love and truce the voyage before, who presently came and brought my pledge with him; whom after I had received, I brake the matter to this king and told him that if he did not betray Pokohuntis into my hands, we would be no longer brothers nor friends. He alleged that if he should undertake this business, then Powhatan would make wars upon him and his people. But upon my promise that I would join with him against him, he repaired presently to his brother, the great King of Patowomeck, who being made acquainted with the matter called his council together and after some few hours' deliberation concluded rather to deliver her into my hands than lose my friendship.

So presently he betrayed her into my boat, wherein I carried her aboard my ship. This done, an Indian was dispatched to Powhatan to let him know that I had taken his daughter, and if he would send home the Englishmen whom he detained in slavery, with such arms and tools as the Indians had gotten and stol'n, and also a great quantity of corn, that then he should have his daughter restored, otherwise not.

This news much grieved this great king, yet without delay he returned the messenger with this answer, that he desired me to use his daughter well, and bring my ship into his river, and there he would give me my demands; which being performed, I should deliver him his daughter, and we should be friends.

Having received this answer, I presently departed from Patowomeck, being the 13 of April, and repaired with all speed to Sir T[homas] Gates to know of him upon what condition he would conclude this peace, and what he would demand, to whom I also delivered my prisoner, towards whose ransom within few days this king sent home seven of our men, who seemed to be very joyful for that they were freed from the slavery and fear of cruel murther, which they daily before lived in. They brought also three pieces, one broadax, and a long whipsaw, and one canoe of corn.

I being quit of my prisoner went forward with the frigate which I had left at Point Comfort and finished her.

Thus having put my ship in hand to be fitted for an intended fishing voyage, I left that business to be followed by my master with a ging of men, and my lieutenant fortified on shore with another ging to fell timber and clean [cleave] planks to build a fishing boat. My ensign with another ging was employed in the frigate for getting of fish at Cape Charles and transporting it to Henrie's Town[1] for the relief of such men as were there.

And myself with a fourth ging departed out of the river in my shallop, the first of May, for to discover the east side of our bay, which I found to have many small rivers in it, and very good harbors for boats and barges, but not for ships of any great burthen; and also

---

[1] Henrico.

great store of inhabitants who seemed very desirous of our love, and so much the rather because they had received good reports from the Indians of Pembrock River of our courteous usage of them, whom I found trading with me for corn, whereof they had great store.

We also discovered a multitude of islands bearing good meadow ground and, as I think, salt might easily be made there if there were any ponds digged, for that I found salt kerned where the water had overflown in certain places.[1] Here is also great store of fish, both shellfish and other.

So having discovered along the shore some forty leagues northward, I returned again to my ship, the twelfth of May [1613], and hasted forward my business left in hand at my departure, and fitted up my ship, and built my fishing boat, and made ready to take the first opportunity of the wind for my fishing voyage, of which I beseech God of His mercy to bless us.

[entitled:] A letter of Sir Samuell Argoll touching his voyage to Virginia and actions there. Written to Master Nicholas Hawes.

[1] "Kerned salt found. May 12, 1613." (margin note)

46. Thomas Dale

Letter to Sir Thomas Smyth, June 1613
[surviving extract]

< **Library of Congress, Jefferson Papers 8/16;** Stith 1747:132 (in paraphrase); Brown 1890:639; Kingsbury 1906b:399

Dale is a sincere man who believes in the glory of his nation's destiny. He sees the Indian not as England's obstacle but England's mission, looking to the British Commonwealth of our century. He has apparently been adjuring Sir Thomas to supply more men and materiel for the colony.

In the Hundred Years War, England lost France to the French.

From the little we see, this letter would have been written with as much cold passion as the one that follows it, but we have it only because this extract was inserted into the record of the House of Burgesses in May 1623, where first comes Nathaniel Butler's *The Unmasked Face of Our Colony in Virginia,* then the slew of protests and refutations of that, "after which Master Berblock desired that a short passage of Sir Thomas Dale's letter to Sir Thomas Smith might be read, which he had found perusing the books by order of the court; whereupon it was read, being as followeth, vizt.—"

LET[1] ME TELL you all at home this one thing, and I pray remember it: If you give over this country and lose it, you with your wisdoms will leap [at] such a gudgeon[2] as our state hath not done the like since they lost the Kingdom of France. Be not gulled with the clamorous reports of base people; believe Caleb and Joshua! If the glory of God hath not power with them, and the conversion of these poor infidels, yet let the rich Mammon's desire egg them on to inhabit these countries. I protest unto you by the faith of an honest man: The more I range the country the more I admire it. I have seen the best countries in Europe: I protest unto you before the Living God, put them all together, this country will be equivalent unto them if it be inhabitant with good people.

---

[1] "Dated June 1613" (margin note).

[2] False bait.

Following which, the next entry reads: "Which report Master John Smith [not our captain] affirmed to agree with what he had heard from his own mouth delivered to divers worthy persons here in England, protesting from his heart unfeignedly that, in his judgment, out of four of the best kingdoms in Europe there could not be picked out so much good ground as was in Virginia—which speech in effect Master Copland also affirmed Sir Thomas Dale to have spoken to him at Japan in the West [East?] Indies."

47. Thomas Dale

Letter from Henrico, 10 June 1613

< **Magdalene College Library: The Ferrar Papers, 40–1501**

The addressee's name—the Council of Virginia?—is lost, but Nicholas Ferrar, Sr. was especially concerned about the education of Indian children. So Dale's first order of business makes it likely the letter was directed at him in whose papers it is today found.

Marshal Dale (Gates is governor) opens shooting back at something he must have just received to the tune of "we are hearing many an oath and exclamation against you" from settlers (inmates?) at Henrico and the upriver settlements. Dale cannot say he does not *care,* since that would be an affront to the concerns of the Council of Virginia, but says he does not *pass,* pass judgment on how the world, etc. But the word could be *pause.*

From there, Dales does little more than "sigh the lack" and remind us of inadequate and shabby supplies, desperate men forced into pilfering and economic sabotage, all as if to say, "It's not how I treat them, it's how you, the Company, treat us, shortchanging the colony at every turn." Perhaps he had visited his prisoner, Don Diego de Molina, who convinced him that the King of Spain would be all too welcome coming up the James, an abiding nightmare (§38, 44).

Dale, like many a dictator, feels like a hero to stay in the saddle at all, but as his strength is heroic, he says he will never give up, no matter how much it costs him here or at home, for God is just: He will not only tumble the malefactors and slanderers into Hell, He will cause the labor and sacrifice of the patient and good to bear fruit. The marshal expresses himself loud and free enough to suggest he was intimate with his correspondent.[1]

He writes about husbandry matters but does not use husbandry language. Were the swine spayed and the seeds dust, or was Dale just no stock-breeder? I suspect he was not a man of the land, a fundamental lack in doing his job. He was a soldier who had read Plato's *Republic,* and he divided his men into three task companies, one labeled "farmers." But then so did John Rolfe §53, who most certainly *was* a man of the land.

Dale no longer needs two thousand men (§38). Now he needs *three* thousand, which his starving colonists will grow food to feed.

This is another glimpse into the earliest epoch of American life, the collective, propertyless, utopian stage, gone forever everywhere by the end of the decade.[2] It has apparently left a bitter taste. After Henrico, Americans, along with Capt. John Smith, will put their faith in private enterprise and invent the doctrine of rugged individualism, laughing at Dale's one man per sow schemes.

This fascinating letter is published here with the kind and generous permission of the Master and Fellows, Magdalene College, Cambridge, so I have taken the trouble to give it in all three stages—in facsimile facing a literatim (not diplomatic) transcription, followed by a modern text beginning on page 777.

[1] I recall a passage from the sermon on Virginia by Rev. William Symonds: "Sigismund the emperor said well that he merveiled every man avoided all labors and difficulties but only to rule, which is the most difficult of all other labors."

[2] The Plymouth Colony was doomed to revive another attempt a decade later with the same result.

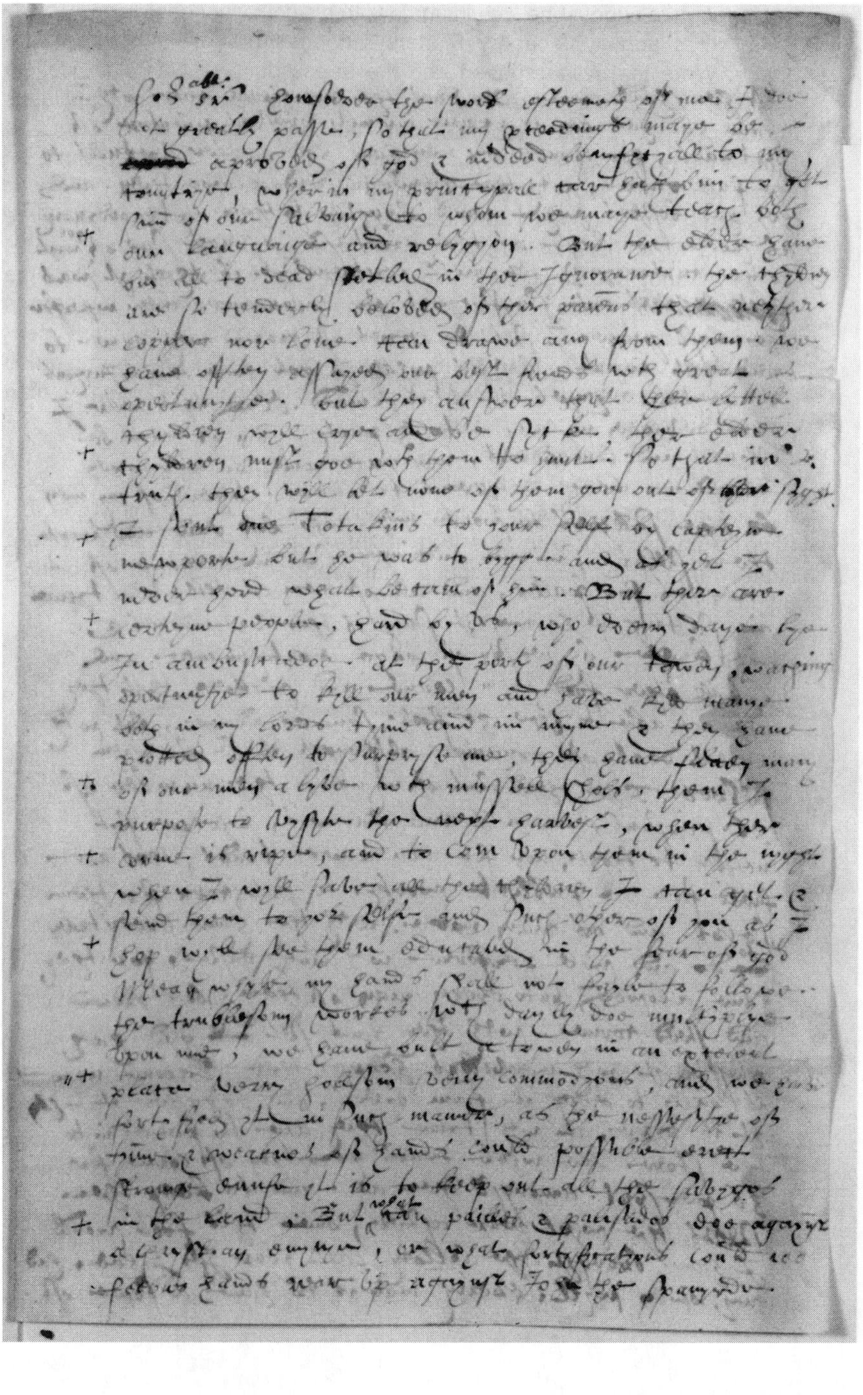

Horable sirs howsoever the world esteemeth of me I doo
not greatly passe, so that my p*ro*ceedings maye be
aproved of god & indeed benyfycyall to my
countrye, wher in my princypall car hath bin to get
sum of our salvaiges to whom we maye teach both
our languaige and relygyon. But the elder have
bin all to dead setled in ther Ignorance. the chyldren
are so tenderly beloved of ther parens that neyther
copper nor love can drawe any from them soe
have offten assayed our best frends with great
opertunytye. but they answer that ther lyttel
chyldren wyll crye and be sycke; ther elder
chyldren must goe with them to hunt. so that in 20.
twnty they wyll let none of them goe out of there syght
I sent one Totakins to your self by Capteyne
newporte but he was to bygg and as yet I
never herd what becam of him. But ther are
certeyne people, hard by us, who every daye lye
In ambuscadoe at the portes of our towen, waching
opertunytye to kill our men and have kild manye
both in my lords tyme and in myne & they have
plotted offten to surpryse me, they have slaen many
of our men a live with mussell shels. them I
purpose to vysyte the next harvest, when ther
corne is ripe, and to com upon them in the nyght
when I wyll save all the chyldren I can get &
send them to yor selfe and such other of you as I
hop wyll see them educated in the fear of god
Mean whyle my hands shall not fayle to followe
the trublesom workes wch dayly doe multyplye
upon me, we have bult a towen in an excelent
place verry hollsom verry commodyous, and we have
fortyfyed yt in such manner, as the nessesytye of
tyme & weaknes of hands could possible erect
strong enufe yt is to keep out all the savyges
in the land; But what can pailles & palisados doe agaynst
a chrystyan enymye, or what fortyfycatyons could 100
feeble hands rear up agaynst John the spanyrde

yt he had come. Besides the particular care wch I
have had ever to retaine our mens present provision of
victualls, for though my men have had all ther victualls to
the full rate, wch heretofore did seldome [illegible]
[illegible] had besides [illegible] to ther extraordinary
as well the least as the greatest (though this is good
to the contrary) yet must I confesse it is that it was
~~[illegible]~~ not sufficient for laborious men. wherefore
for this yeare I sett 80 acres of corne wch come to
[illegible] , besides wch I got from the Indians
[illegible] at Chickahomonie. More this yeare I
have divided my men into 3 parts, some of them be
officers and commanders, who [illegible] of their owne
industrie [illegible] to others. Others of my men
be ther [illegible] in work [illegible], who both [illegible] and work
them selves [illegible] in [illegible] of
quarters for [illegible], and all of them at this present tyme
in setting of corne. It [illegible] is ther [illegible]
[illegible] of [illegible] and
[illegible] ther [illegible] from corne and [illegible] that they
are not able to [illegible] so [illegible], but wth
a great deale of [illegible] although it be for them
selves, the third sort of my men is the number of
36 persons, whom I call Farmers, who are [illegible]
neither to [illegible], nor for mechanick trades, these are
freed from all publick works, to sett corne for them
selves. and as many more, wch they have undertaken
to doe and will performe wth much ease. for they
have allowed unto every man of them. both ground
and seed corne. wch they have sett [illegible]
[illegible] wth [illegible] their labour now
is onely to keep it from weeds, and to gather it when
it is ripe, at wch tyme they are to pay into
the store one whole yeares provision of corne for
36 persons. amongst them all. and to keep them
selves the whole yeare after, [illegible] this [illegible] would
[illegible] brought the Colloney last yeare wch I had. had
my owne will; every man is to have a [illegible] of

If he should come. Bysydes the principall carr wch I have had hath ben to p*ro*cure our men present plentye of vyctuales, for thought my men have had all ther vyctulls to the full rate, wch the generall did alowe them. and they had besydes what could be gyven to them extraordynary as well the least as the greatest (thought sum of you wryt to the contrarye) yet most certeyne yt is that yt was ~~xxxxxxxxx~~ not suffycyent for labouringe men. wherfor the last yeare I set 80 accres of grownd wth corne to help that want, besydes what I got from our inJuryous & capytall enymyes at Nansamond. And this year I have devyded my men in to 3 partes, som of them be offycers and comanders, who guyd and by ther owen Industrye teach dylygens to others. others of my men be ether soldgers or worke men, who both gard and worke them selvs. sum in buldinge sum in cleaving of quarters for palls, and all of them at this seed tyme in setting of cornne. yf such is ther untowardnes & weaknese by reason of longe contynuance and lyttel other food them corne and watter that they are not able to howe 30 foot square adaye, but wth a great deale of gruginge althought yt be for them selves, the thyrd sort of my men to the number of 36 persons, whom I call farmers, who are fyt nether to fyght, nor for meacanyck trads, thes are freed from all publick workes. to set corn for them selves. and as many more. wch they have undertaken ~~do~~ to do and wyll performe wth much ease. for they have alowed unto every man of them. both grownd and seed corne. wch they have set & god hath blessed yt wth mervelous hoapp. ther labour now is onlly to keep yt from byrds, and to gather yt when yt is rype. at wch tyme they are to paye in to the store one whole years provytyon of corne for 36 persons. amongst them all. and to keep them selvs the whol year after, one this foot would I have brought the collony last year If I had. had my only wyll: everry man is to have a sowe of

of the colledge and that he at his owne charge [illegible] yeare
+ two and he is to have to the number of 4 femal servan-
to bring [illegible] so that he is to have all the
+ male servantes [illegible] to kepe for his owne
provision and the female servantes of these 4
servantes and for the colledge to dispose together
[illegible] as they shall come over, so that every man
+ shall [illegible] servantes [illegible] for his provision
and at the [illegible] yeares end he shall have [illegible]
servantes upon his order, and so [illegible] as
[illegible] may be gotten from the Indians or elsewhere
+ [illegible] every man is to have 2 female goates for
himselfe. my worke is to breake up [illegible]
[illegible] follow [illegible] in [illegible]
[illegible]. I have impaled [illegible] since
+ January last a large ~~[illegible]~~ vineyard. many
gardens in the Island and very many about the
towne. and in this case standes our common wealth
of [illegible]. I am now forming all my forces to
[illegible] [illegible] worke of land. [illegible] I meane
+ [illegible]. planting [illegible] one the west side of
our towne one the other side of our river. [illegible]
+ in I have set 60 acres of ground [illegible] comes
the [illegible] is a peninsula. between 7 and 8 myles
in compasse. being quite about [illegible] pleasant
[illegible]. and the [illegible] of it is not [illegible]
+ ~~[illegible]~~ myle from the one side of the river to
the other. the which I meane to Impale and
+ set up 10 blockhouses for 30 men to kepe
before the [illegible] be [illegible]. and let me tell
you the most part of these pales must go [illegible]
+ [illegible]s. or they will never be set up, for that
opinion they have conceived so long. [illegible] ~~[illegible]~~
the worke they [illegible] kept here, they shall ~~[illegible]~~ they
+ [illegible] of [illegible] [illegible] [illegible] England [illegible]
the which they would not be brought to do [illegible]

of the collonyes and to keep her as his owen for v years
and he is to have to the number of 4 femal swyne
to bryng pygges, so that he is to have all the
male pygges every year to kyll for his owen
provytyone and the female swyne of thos 4
sowes are for the collonye to dyspose to other
men as they shall com over, so that every man
shall kyll 12 sweynes every year for his p*ro*vytyons
and at the 5 years end he shall have vi
sowes gyven him for ever, and so soon as
goates can be gotten from the Indyes or encrese
here everry man is to have 2 female goattes for
him selfe. my worke is to knock up palls. the
wch I follow whensoever my leasur wyll
permyte. I have empaled this year syns
Januarye last a larg ~~vyneyard~~ wyneyard. many
gardens in the Island and very many about the
towen. and in this case stands our common wealth
of henryco. I am now torning all my forces to
an other excelent neck of land. wch I named
coxsonndale. flanking us one the west syde of
our towen one the other syde of our ryver. wher
in I have set 60 ackrs of grownd wth corne
the place is a peninsuela. betwen 7 and 8 myls
in compasse. being guirt about wth our pleasant
ryver. and the neck of yt is not aboue one
myle from the one syde of the ryver to
the other. the wch I meane to Impale and
set up 10 blokhouses for 30 men to keep
before the harvest be rype and let me tell
you the most part of thes palls must go thorow
my hands. or they wyll never be set up, for that
opynyon they have concealed so long. that ~~fytt~~ If
they worke they shall be kept here, & they shall then
subsyst of them selvs wth out England
the wch they would not be brought to do If they

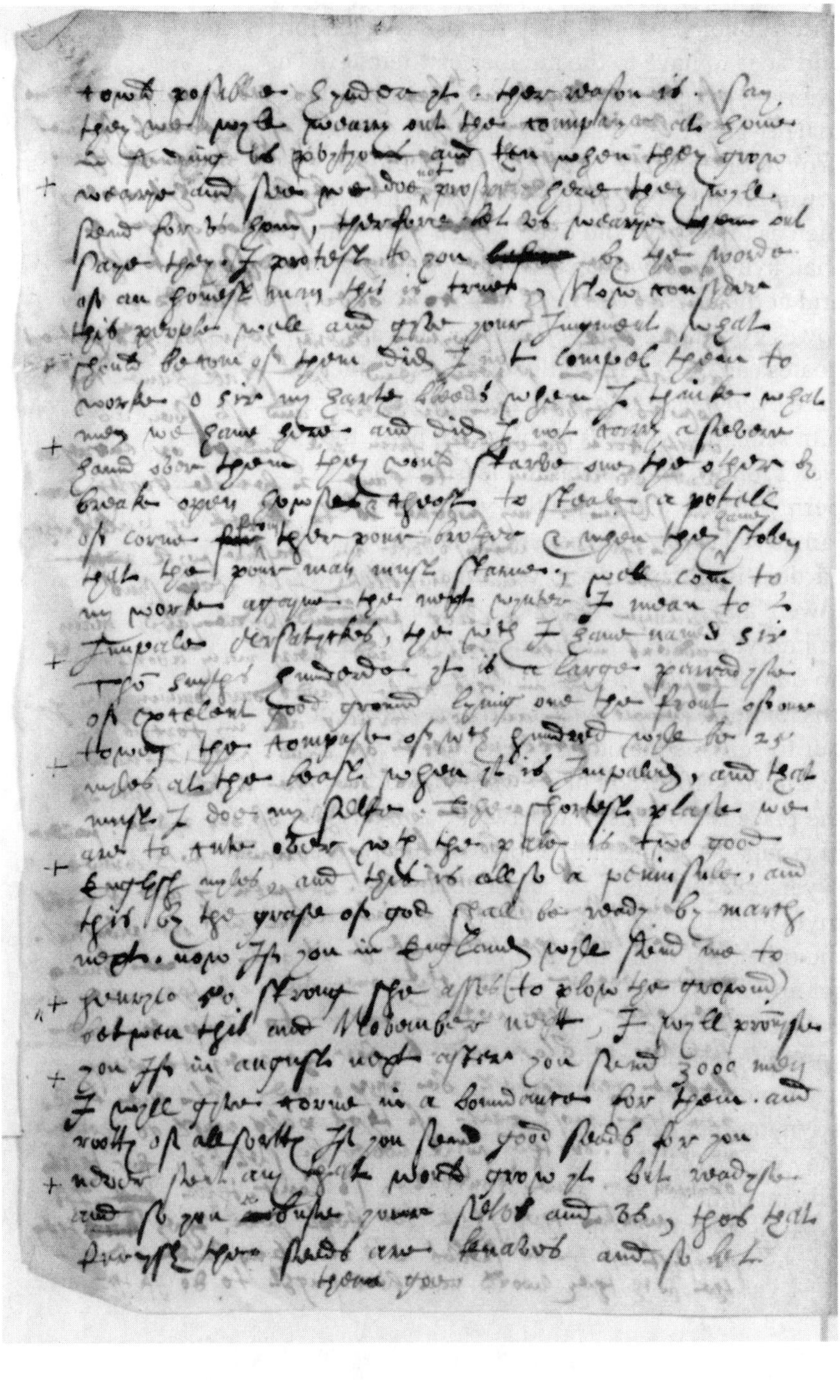

+ tonight possible. hinder it. the reason is, say
they will weary out the company at home
in sending us supplies and then when they grow
+ weary and see we do not prosper here they will
send for us home, therefore lest we weary them out
says they. I protest to you ~~[illegible]~~ by the words
of an honest man this is true. Now consider
this people well and give your judgment what
+ should become of them did I not compel them to
work. O sir my heart bleeds when I think what
men we have here. and did I not cause a severe
+ hand over them they would starve one the other by
break open houses at night to steal a pottle
of corn ~~[illegible]~~ take your orders upon them they stole
that they your man must starve. I will come to
my work again. the next winter I mean to
Impale [illegible], the which I have named Sir
+ Tho. Smiths Hundred. it is a large peninsula
of excellent good ground lying on the front of our
towns. the compass of this hundred will be 25
+ miles all the waste when it is impaled, and that
must I doe my selfe. the shortest place we
are to take over with the pale is two good
+ English miles and this is also a peninsula, and
this by the grace of god shall be ready by march
next. now if you in England will send me to
+ furnish so strong the [illegible] (to plow the ground)
between this and November next, I will promise
+ you if in August next after you send 2000 men
I will give corn in abundance for them. and
roots of all sorts. if you send good seeds for you
+ never shall any fruit well grow it but radishe
and if you [illegible] seeds and [illegible], those that
brought these seeds are knaves and so let
them know

could possiblee hynder yt. ther reason is. say
they. we wyll wearry out the companye at home
in sending us p*ro*vytyons and then when they grow
wearye and see we doe not prosper here they wyll
send for us hom, therfore let us wearye them out
saye they. I protest to you ~~before~~ by the worde
of an honest man this is true, Now consyder
this people well and gyve your Jugment what
should becom of them did I not compel them to
worke o sir my harte bleeds when I thinke what
men we have here and did I not carry a severe
hand over them they would starve one the other by
break~ open howses & cheest to steale a potall
of corne ~~for~~ from ther pour brother & when they have stolen
that the pour man must starve; well com to
my worke agayne the next wynter I mean to
Impale Arsatyckes, the wch I have named sir
Thō Smyths hunderde yt is a large parradyse
of excelent good ground lying one the front of our
towen, the compase of wch hundred wyll be 25
myles at the least when yt is Impaled, and that
must I doe my selfe. The shortest plase we
are to cute over wth the pales is two good
English myles, and this is allso a peninsule; and
this by the grase of god shall be ready by march
next. now If you in England wyll send me to
henryco 50 strong she asses (to plow the grownd)
betwen this and November nextt, I wyll promyse
you If in august next after you send 3000 men
I wyll gyve corne in a boundance for them. and
rootts of all sorttes. If you send good seads for you
never sent any that would grow yt but radyse
and so you abuse your selvs and us, thos that
furnysh thes seeds are knaves and so let
them goe.

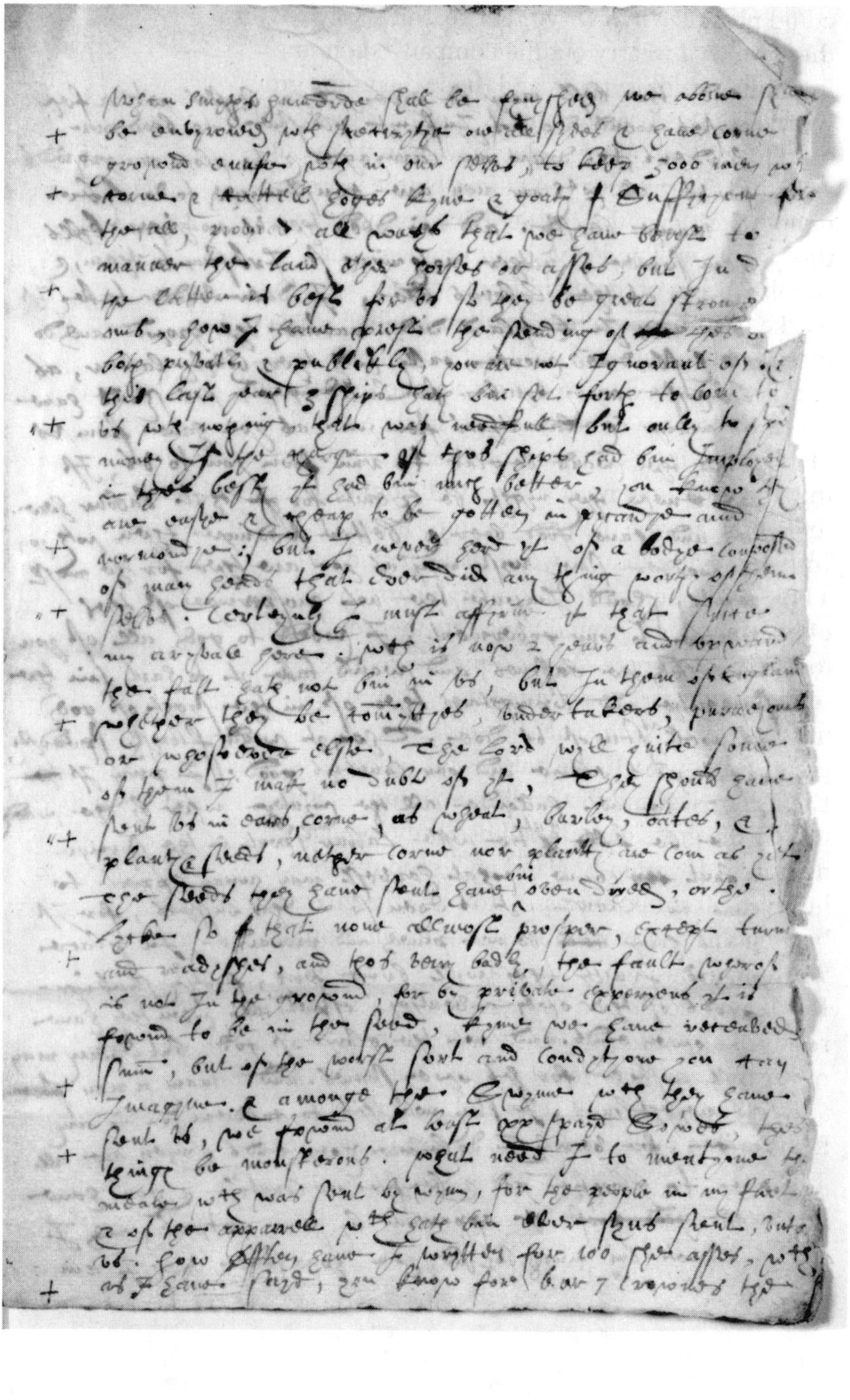

When Smyths hundrde shall be fynyshed we above sha[ll
be envyroned wth scecurytye one all sydes & have corne
grownd enufe wth in our selves, to keep 3000 men wth
corne & cattell hoges kyne & goats & Suffycyent for
them all, provyded all ways that we have beast to
manuer the land ether horses or asses, but In d[eed
the latter is best for us so they be great stronge [
ones, how I have prest the sending of thes o[
both pryvatly and publikly you are not ignorant of &
this last year 3 ships hath bin set forth to com to
us wth nothing, that was needfull but onlly to spe[n]d
money If the charge of thos ships had bin imployed
in thes bestes yt had bin much better, you know th[e]y
are easye & cheap to be gotten in pycardye and
normondye:, but I never herd yt of a bodye conposed
of many heads that ever did any thing worthy of them
selvs. certeynly I must affyrme yt that since
my aryvall here. wch is now 2 years and upward
the falt hath not bin in us, but In them of England
whether they be comyttyes, undertakers, purueyours
or whosoever else, The lord wyll quite some
of them I mak no dubt of yt, They should have
sent us in ears, corne, as wheat, barley, oates, &
plantes & seeds, nather corne nor planttes are com as yet
The seeds they have sent have bin over dryed, or the
lycke so ff that none allmost prosper, except turnip[s
and radyshes, and thes verry badly, the fault wherof
is not In the grownd, for by private experyens yt is
fownd to be in the seed, kyne we have receabed
sum, but of the worst sort and condytyone you can
Imagyne & amonge the Swyne wch they have
sent us, we fownd at least xx spayd Sowes, thes
things be monsterous. what need I to mentyone the
meale wch was sent by wynn, for the people in my fleet
& of the apparrell wch hath bin ever syns sent, unto
us how offten have I wrytten for 100 she asses, wch
as I have sayd, you know for 6 or 7 crownes the

heard the best may be had, these beastes with a few
horses would do us infinite pleasure, to beare our
burdens, to drawe our carriages, & to plowe our grounds
for us, all which our men are constrayned to do, beinge
so many beastes. and in deed there is nothinge better
then seinge, whereas nothinge so irksome to them, &
spent, as these laboures doe, I dare undertake yt
our men in England did manure the grounde and do
all husbandmens worke, only with there bodyly labour, as
we cause carry tymber for buildinge, we should have
as many entertayned from you, as you have from us
& that they would be glad to runn from you to us. yt
is true they might be spent for yt this labour have
we and have good bread & better feedinge then with you
I wonder they which may as you are there for the most
part, should impute the not prosperinge of these
people to our government, I would to God all of you
understood the busines, and would take yt to hart like the
[illegible] and Gentlemen there of, in the sight of God
as well [as] some of us doe, I doubt not would flourish [illegible]
[illegible] to Gods glorye and our countryes good. I pray yt ~~[illegible]~~
ground be not fallowed all the winter which by the words
may be ~~told~~ [that] the whole labour [be] spent in the bringinge
a boute ~~[illegible]~~ come great harvest may away expect to
have in August, yt is even so in this busines, for yt
must have ~~[illegible]~~ bene plowed and prepared. In place
of good fruits they will bringe forth, folly stubborne
weedes of there owne inventions, especially when they have
there owne ends, and not the glorye of God. but every man
shall answer for his owne sinnes. ~~and~~ may a man ~~[illegible]~~
his neighbour, I say not this to condemne you in any
thinge, for surely I do beleave your ends & myne are all
one, to please God & benefit our countrie & you have
made ~~[illegible]~~ yt apparent by your actions, and I
have not bin much behind [illegible] [illegible] some [illegible] I am

head the best may be hade, thes beastes wth a few horses would do us Infynyt pleasuer, to bear owr burdens, to draw our carryages, & to plow our grownds for us, all wch our men are constrayned to do lyke so manye beastes. and in deed ther is nothinge kylls them souner, nather nothynge so Irksom to them, & odyous. as thes labours bee, I daer undertake (If yur men In England did manure the grownd and do all husbandme*ns* workes, onlly wth ther bodyly labour, as lykwyse carry tymber for bulldinges) we should have as manye exclamatyons from you. as you have from us I and they would be glad to run from you to us, If they knew they myght be exemt for ~~s~~ that labour here. yea and have good beer & better feedinge then wth you I wonder. such wyse men as you are ther for the most part, should impute the not prosperinge of thes people to our government, I would to god all of you understod the bussynes, and would take yt to hart, (in the syncerytye and upryghtnes ther of, in the syght of god). as well as som of us doe, Then yt would florysh speedyly both to gods glorye and our countrys good:||I pray If ~~the~~ grownd be not fallowde all the wynter wher by the weeds maye be kylld ~~&~~ that the lesse labour may be spent in the springe about ~~con~~ corne, what harvest may aman expect to have in august, yt is even so in this busynes, for If mens harts be not plued and preparde, In place of good fruictes they wyll bring forth, fylthy stynkinge weeds of ther owen inventyon, espetyally when they have ther owen ends. and not the glorye of god, but everry man shall answer for his owen synnes. and many a man for his neyghtbours, I say not this to condem you in any thinge, for verryly I do beleave your ends & myen are all one, to gloryfye god & benyfyte our countrye & you have mayd ~~good profe~~ yt apparant by your acctyons, and I have not bin much behynd you how some ever I am

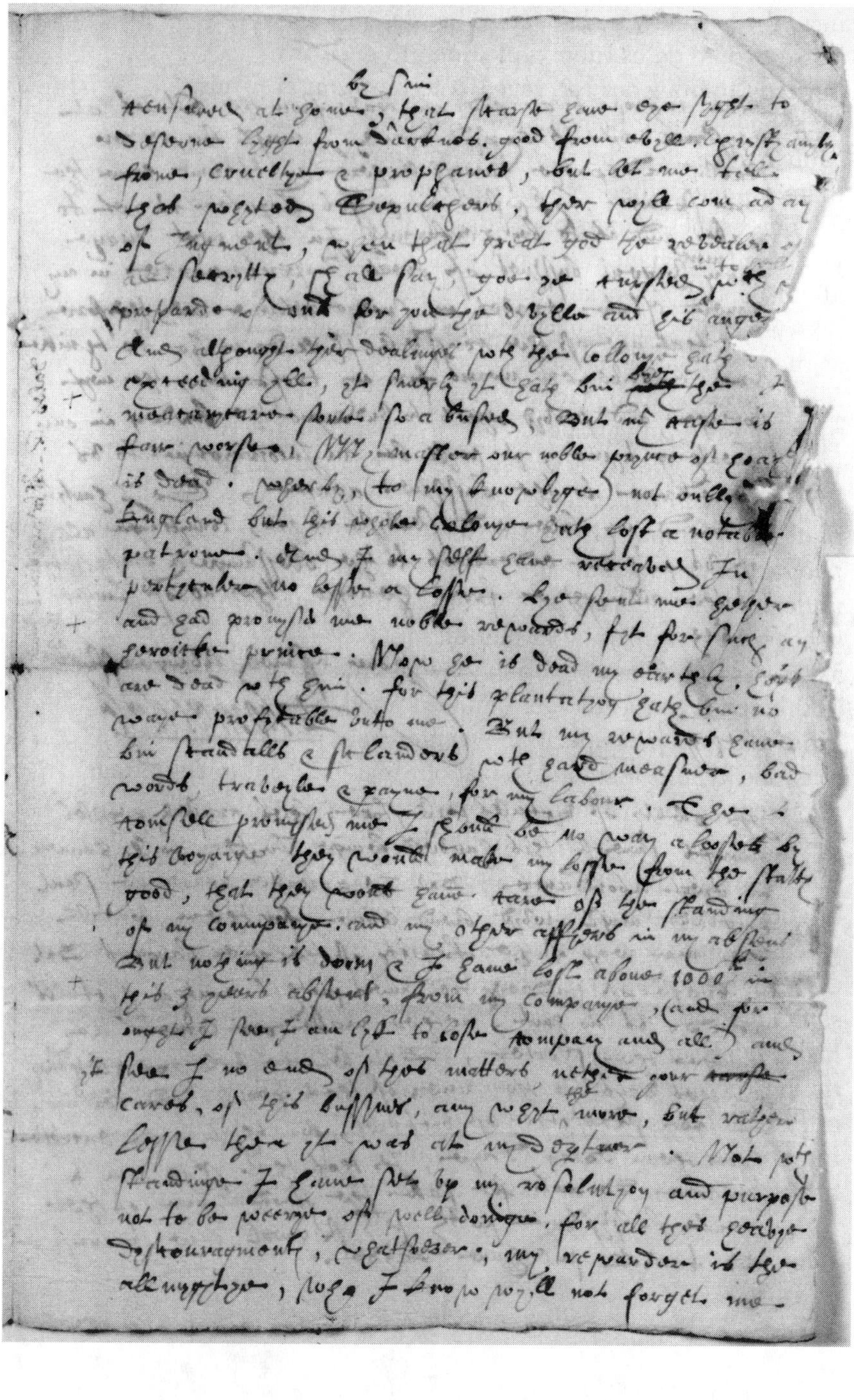

by him
considered at home, that strange have the sight to
discerne light from darknes, good from evill, charity
from cruelty & prophanes, but let me tell
those pretended Reformers, they will come as
of Judgment, when that great god the rewarder of
all secretts, shall say, you ar cursed with
hipocrits for your devill and his angels
And although this dealing with the colonye hath
exceeding ill, yet surely it hath bin
soule for a busines, But my griefe is
far worse. Whereas our noble prince of Wales
is dead, whereby (to my knowledge) not onlye
England but this whole colonye hath lost a notable
patrone. And I my self have received In
perticular no lesse a losse. He sent me hether
and had promised me noble rewards, fit for such a
princelie prince. Now he is dead my ... are
dead with him. for this plantation hath bin no
wayes profitable unto me. But my rewards have
bin scandalls & slanders with hard measure, bad
words, travayles & payne, for my labour. The
counsell promised me I should be no way a loser by
this voyage they would make my losse from the state
good, that they would have care of the standing
of my companye and my other affayres in my absence
But nothing is done & I have lost above 1000li in
this 3 yeares absence, from my companye (and for
ought I see I am like to lose company and all) and
see I no end of these matters unless your ...
care, of this busines, any whit more, but rather
losse then it was at my departure. Notwith
standing I have set by my resolution and purpose
not to be weary of well doinge, for all these greivous
discouragements, whatsoever, my rewarder is the
Almightye, whom I know will not forget me.

censured at home, by sum that scarse have eye syght to
deserne lyght from darknes. good from evyll. chrystyanytye
frome crueltye & prophanes, but let me tell
thos whyted Sepulchers, ther wyll com aday
of Jugment, when that great god the revealer of
all secryttes, shall say, goe ye cursed in to hell wch [is
preparde of ould for you the dyvylle and his ange[ls
And althought ther dealinges with the Collonye hath b[in
exceeding yll, yt suerly yt hath bin ~~wth~~ bye the
meacanycare sorte so a bused, But my case is
farr worse, My master our noble prynce of hoapp
is dead. wher by (to my knowlyge) not onlly
England but this whole colonye hath lost a notable
patrone. And I my self have receaved In
pertyculer no lesse a losse. He sent me hether
and had promysd me noble rewards, fyt for such an
heroicke prince. Now he is dead my earthly hopes
are dead wth him. for this plantatyon hath bin no
waye profytable unto me. But my rewards have
bin scandalls & sclanders wth hard measuer, bad
words, traveyle & payne, for my labour. The
counsell promysed me I should be no way a loose by
this voyaige they would make my losse from the stattes
good, that they would have care of the standing
of my companye. and my other affyers in my absens
But nothing is donn & I have lost aboue 1000^{li} in
this 3 years absens, from my companye, (and for
ought I see I am lyk to lose company and all) and
yf see I no end of thes matters, nether your ~~earse~~
cares, of this bussynes, any whyt the more, but rather
lesse then yt was at my dep*ar*tuer. Not wth
standinge I have set by my resolutyon and purpose
not to be weerye of well doinge. for all thes heavye
dyscouragmentes, whatsoever; my rewarder is the
allmyghtye, who I know wyll not forget me

THOMAS DALE

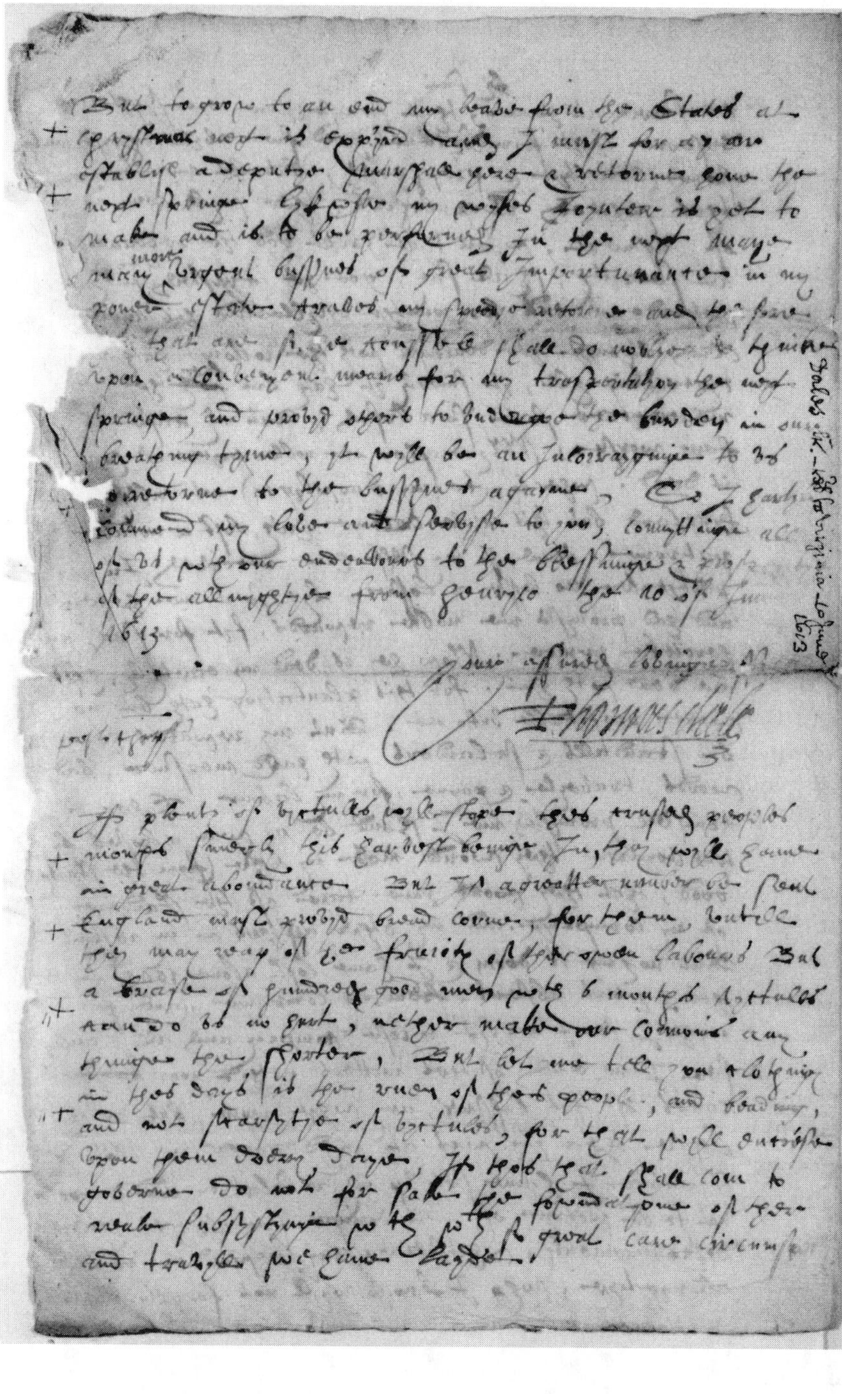
But to growe to an end my leave from the States at
Christmas next is expired, and I must for my [illegible]
stablish a deputie [illegible] returne home the
next springe [illegible]
[illegible]
[illegible]
[illegible]
[illegible]
[illegible]
[illegible]
[illegible]
[illegible]
[illegible]
[illegible] from Henrico the 10 of June
1613

Your assured loving [illegible]
Thomas Dale

[illegible]

But to grow to an end my leave from the States at Chrystmas next is exp'yrd and I must for a year establish a deputye marshall here & retorne home the next springe lykwyse my wyfes Joynter is yet to make and is to be performed In the next maye many more urgent busynes of great Importunance in my pouer estate craves my speedye retorne and therfore [thos] that are of the conssell shall do noblye to thinke upon a convenyent means for my trasportatyon the next* springe, and provyd others to undergoe the burden in our breathing tyme, yt wyll be an incorrayginge to us [t]o retorne to the bussynes agayne, So I hartyly commend my love and servyse to you, comyttinge all of us wth our endeavours to the blessinge & prosper[y]tye of the allmyghtye from henryco the 10 of June 1613

your assured lovinge Fren[d]

[?-]church THOMAS DALE

If plenty of vyctulls wyll stope thes crused peoples mouths suerly this harvest beinge In, they wyll have in great aboundance, But If a greatter nunber be sent England must provyd bread corne, for them, untill they may reap of thes fruictes of ther owen labours But a brase of hundredes good men wth 6 months vyctulls can do us no hurt, nether make our comons any thinge the shorter, But let me tell you clothinges in thes days is the ruen of thes people, and beading, and not scarsytye of vyctules, for that wyll encrese upon them everry daye, If thos that shall com to governe do not for sake the fowndatyone of ther reale subsystynge wch wth so great care circumspecy[on and travyll we have layde

* From here down right margin: "Dales lr–recd fr Virginia–10 June 1613"

VIRGINIA MUSEUM OF FINE ARTS

SIR THOMAS DALE

HONORABLE SIRS—Howsoever the world esteemeth of me I do not greatly pass, so that my proceedings may be approved of God and indeed beneficial to my country—wherein my principal care hath been to get some of our savages to whom we may teach both our language and religion. But the elder have been all too dead settled in their ignorance; the children are so tenderly beloved of their parents that neither copper nor love can draw any from them. So have often assayed our best friends with great opportunity, but they answer that their little children will cry and be sick [and] their elder children must go with them to hunt, so that in twenty they will let none of them go out of their sight. I sent one Totakins to yourself by Captain Newporte, but he was too big. And as yet I never heard what became of him.

But there are certain people hard by us who every day lie in ambuscado at the ports of our town, watching opportunity to kill our men, and have kill'd many both in my lord's time and in mine; and they have plotted often to surprise me. They have slain many of our men alive with mussel shells. Them I purpose to visit the next harvest, when their corn is ripe, and to come upon them in the night, when I will save all the children I can get and send them to yourself and such other of you as I hope will see them educated in the fear of God.

Meanwhile my hands shall not fail to follow the troublesome works which daily do multiply upon me. We have built a town in an excellent place, very wholesome, very commodious, and we have fortified it in such manner as the necessity of time and weakness of hands could possible erect. Strong enough it is to keep out all the savages in the land, but what can pales and palisadoes do against a Christian enemy? Or what fortifications could 100 feeble hands rear up against John the Spaniard, if he should come?

Besides, the principal care which I have had hath been to procure our men present plenty of victuals. For though my men have had all their victuals to the full rate, which the general did allow them, and they had besides what could be given to them extraordinary, as well the least as the greatest (though some of you writ to the contrary), yet most certain it is that it was not sufficient for laboring men. Wherefore the last year I set 80 acres of ground with corn to help that want, besides what I got from our injurious and capital enemies at Nansamond.

And this year I have divided my men into 3 parts: Some of them be officers and commanders, who guide and by their own industry teach diligence to others. Others of my men be either soldiers or workmen, who both guard and work themselves—some in building, some in cleaving of quarters for pales, and all of them at this seed time in setting of corn. If such is their untowardness and weakness by reason of long continuance and little other food than corn and water, that they are not able to hoe 30 foot square a day but with a great deal of grudging, although it be for themselves. The third sort of my men, to the number of 36 persons, whom I call "farmers," who are fit neither to fight nor for mechanic trades, these are freed from all public works to set corn for themselves and as many more, which they have undertaken to do and will perform with much ease. For they have allowed unto every man of them both ground and seed corn, which they have set, and God hath blessed it with marvelous hope. Their labor now is only to keep it from birds, and to gather it when it is ripe, at which time they are to pay into the store one whole year's provision of corn for 36 persons amongst them all, and to keep themselves the whole year after. On this foot would I have brought the colony last year if I had had my only will.

Every man is to have a sow of the colony's and to keep her as his own for v years; and he is to have to the number of 4 female swine to bring pigs, so that he is to have all the male pigs every year to kill for his own provision; and the female swine of those 4 sows are for the colony to dispose to other men as they shall come over; so that every man shall kill 12 swines every year for his provisions, and at the 5 years' end he shall have vi sows given him forever.

And so soon as goats can be gotten from the Indies or increase here, every man is to have 2 female goats for himself.

My work is to knock up pales, the which I follow whensoever my leisure will permit. I have impaled this year since January last a large wineyard, many gardens in the island and very many about the town. And in this case stands our commonwealth of Henryco.

I am now turning all my forces to another excellent neck of land which I named Coxsonndale, flanking us on the west side of our town, on the other side of our river, wherein I have set 60 acres of ground with corn. The place is a peninsula between 7 and 8 miles in compass, being girt about with our pleasant river; and the neck of it is not above one mile from the one side of the river to the other, the which I mean to impale and set up 10 blockhouses for 30 men to keep before the harvest be ripe. And let me tell you the most part of these pales must go thorough my hands or they will never be set up, for that opinion they have concealed so long: that if they work they shall be kept[1] here, and they shall then subsist of themselves without England, the which they would not be brought to do if they could possibly hinder it. Their reason is, say they, "We will weary out the Company at home in sending us provisions, and then, when they grow weary and see we do not prosper here, they will send for us home. Therefore let us weary them out," say they. I protest to you by the word of an honest man this is true! Now consider this people well and give your judgment what should become of them did I not compel them to work. Oh sir, my heart bleeds when I think what men we have here; and did I not carry a severe hand over them they would starve one the other by breaking open houses and chest[s] to steal a pottle of corn from their poor brother, and when they have stolen that the poor man must starve.

Welcome to my work again, the next winter I mean to impale Arsatyckes, the which I have named "Sir Thomas Smyth's Hundred." It is a large paradise of excellent good ground lying on the front of our town, the compass of which hundred will be 25 miles at the least, when it is impaled, and that must I do myself. The shortest place we are to cut over with the pales is two good English miles, and this is also a peninsule—and this by the grace of God shall be ready by March next.

Now if you in England will send me to Henryco 50 strong she-asses to plow the ground between this and November next, I will promise you if in August next after you send 3000 men I will give corn in abundance for them; and roots of all sorts, if you send good seeds, for you never sent any that would grow yet but radice [radishes], and so you abuse yourselves and us. Those that furnish

[1] Make a living.

these seeds are knaves, and so let them go!

When Smyth's Hundred shall be finished, we above shall be environed with security on all sides and have corn ground enough within ourselves to keep 3000 men with corn and cattle, hogs, kine, and goats, and sufficient for them all, provided always that we have beast[s] to manure the land, either horses or asses, but ind[eed] the latter is best for us so they be great strong ones.

How I have press'd the sending of these o[...] both privately and publicly you are not ignorant of—and this last year 3 ships hath been set forth to come to us with nothing that was needful but only to *spend money!* If the charge of those ships had been employed in these beasts, it had been much better. You know they are easy and cheap to be gotten in Picardy and Normandy. But I never heard it of a body composed of many heads that ever did anything worthy of themselves. Certainly I must affirm it that since my arrival here, which is now 2 years and upward, the fault hath not been in us, but in them of England, whether they be committees, undertakers, purveyors, or whosoever else. The Lord will quite some of them, I make no doubt of it. They should have sent us in ears corn, as wheat, barley, oats, and plants and seeds. Neither corn nor plants are come as yet. The seeds they have sent have been overdried or the like, so that none almost prosper except turnip[s] and radishes, and these very badly. The fault whereof is not in the ground, for by private experience it is found to be in the seed.

Kine we have received some, but of the worst sort and condition you can imagine; and among the swine which they have sent us, we found at least xx *spay'd sows!* These things be monstrous! What need I to mention the meal which was sent by Wynn for the people in my fleet, and of the apparel which hath been ever since sent unto us. How often have I written for 100 she-asses, which, as I have said, you know for 6 or 7 crowns the head *the best may be had.* These beasts with a few horses would do us infinite pleasure to bear our burdens, to draw our carriages, and to plow our grounds for us—all which our *men* are constrained to do like so many beasts. And indeed there is nothing kills them sooner, neither nothing so irksome to them and odious as these labors be. I dare undertake if your men in England did manure the ground and do all husbandmen's works only with their bodily labor, as likewise carry timber for buildings, we should have as many exclamations from you as you have from us. Ay, and they would be glad to run from you to *us,* if they knew they might be exempt for that labor here—yea, and have good beer and better feeding than with you! I wonder such wise men as you are there for the most part should impute the not prospering of these people to our government. I would to God all of you understood the business, and would take it to heart in the sincerity and uprightness thereof in the sight of God as well as some of us do. Then it would flourish speedily both to God's glory and our country's good.

I pray if ground be not fallow'd all the winter, whereby the weeds may be kill'd, that the less labor may be spent in the spring about corn, what harvest may a man expect to have in August?[1] It is even so in this business. For if men's hearts be not plowed and prepar'd, in place of good fruits they will bring forth filthy, stinking weeds of their own invention, especially when they have their own ends and not the glory of God. But every man shall answer for his own sins, and many a man for his neighbor's. I say not this to condemn you in anything, for verily I do believe your ends and mine are all one—to glorify God and benefit our country—and you have made it apparent by your actions. And I have not been much behind you, howsomever I am censured at home by some that scarce have eyesight to discern light from darkness, good from evil, Christianity from cruelty and profaneness. But let me tell those whited sepulchers there will come a Day of Judgment when that Great God the Revealer of all secrets shall say, "Go ye cursed into Hell which [is] prepar'd of old for you, the devil, and his ange[ls]." And although their dealings with the colony hath b[een] exceeding ill, yet surely it hath been by the mechanical sort so abused.

But my case is far worse. My master, our noble prince of hope is dead,[2] whereby to my knowledge not only England but this whole colony hath lost a notable patron. And I myself have receaved in particular no less a loss. He sent me hither and had promis'd me noble rewards, fit for such an heroic prince. Now he is dead my

---

[1] This must answer some specific objection as to why land was left fallow.

[2] Henry, Prince of Wales, died the previous November.

earthly hopes are dead with him. For this plantation hath been no way profitable unto me, but my rewards have been scandals and slanders with hard measure, bad words, travail and pain for my labor. The council promised me I should be no way a loss by this voyage, [that] they would make my loss from the States good, that they would have care of the standing of my company,[1] and my other affairs in my absence. But nothing is done and I have lost above £1000 in this 3 years' absence from my company—and for aught I see I am like to lose company and all! And if see I no end of these matters, neither [are] your cares of this business any whit the more, but rather less, than it was at my departure. Notwithstanding, I have set by my resolution and purpose not to be weary of well-doing, for all these heavy discouragements whatsoever. My rewarder is the Almighty, who I know will not forget me.

But to grow to an end, my leave from the States[2] at Christmas next is expir'd, and I must for a year establish a deputy marshal here and return home the next spring. Likewise my wife's jointure is yet to make, and is to be performed in the next May. Many more urgent business' of great importunance in my poor estate craves my speedy return, and therefore [those] that are of the council shall do nobly to think upon a convenient means for my transportation the next spring, and provide others to undergo the burden in our breathing time. It will be an encouraging to us to return to the business again.

So I heartily commend my love and service to you, committing all of us with our endeavors to the blessing and prosperity of the Almighty, from Henryco the 10 of June, 1613.

Your assured loving friend,

[?]church THOMAS DALE

If plenty of victuals will stop these crused [cursed] people's mouths, surely, this harvest being in, they will have in great abundance. But if a greater number be sent, England must provide breadcorn for them until they may reap of these fruits of their own labors. But a brace of hundreds [of] good men with 6 months' victuals can do us no hurt,

---

[1] Dale's military command.

[2] The States of the Netherlands.

neither make our commons anything the shorter. But let me tell you clothings in these days is the ruin of these people, and bedding, and not scarcity of victuals. For that will increase upon them every day, if those that shall come to govern do not forsake the foundation of their real subsisting which with so great care, circumspection, and travail we have laid.

48. Don Diego de Molina

Letter to Velasco, 8 July 1613

(translated from the Spanish by Maximilian Schele de Vere)

< Simancas Archive 2590–141, **Brown 1890:652**

De Molina has complained to the Spanish ambassador in London, Don Diego de Velasco, but the difficulty, he thinks, must lie with the treasurer of the Council of Virginia, who has not conveyed his messages. The tone of this letter, which was sent through non-confidential channels, is a soft contrast to the secret dispatch §44 of six weeks prior. Perhaps it should sound like a plant.

WHEN I WAS CAPTURED in this province, I wrote to you and to His Majesty, and addressed my letters to the care of the President of the Merchants' Board,[1] who have repeatedly assured me that they were handed to you—on which account I am very much astonished that you have never replied to me, even as a comfort in so long a captivity. And thus I determined not to do it again, but to leave in God's hands, as in the hands of a father of mercy and compassion, all my affairs. But having asked Mr. Thomas Gates [Guietz], the governor of this country, to send me on board the ship that is now sailing to that kingdom, he has replied to me and actually ordered

[1] The Treasurer of the Council of Virginia?

me to write to you beseeching you to manage it so that master Clark be restored and I be at once taken to Spain. If it be not for any other reason of yours, I should venture to trust the word of the board, because the men of this nation, who do not like to bind themselves much, pride themselves much to keep their word.[1]

And thus it seems to me that if they offer to send me to Spain as soon as the others (are surrendered) in England, this exchange might be made without any difficulty whatever. I understand very well that you will have left no means untried, but one who is suffering always likes to speak of his own affairs and suggest something that might be of advantage to him. I beseech you to do in this matter all that you can do, since it is a righteous cause. Here they have certainly treated me with great courtesy, and Mr. Thomas Gates has been a father to me, to whom I am greatly indebted. And everybody here in particular have shown me such love that if I had been in need, they would have assisted me with everything that I could have needed. But as all the necessaries of life are provided by the government, and as there are many private persons here, there are given out to them every year provisions and cloth and fine linen for clothes, and I have desired to request that the same be done to me, so that I may not be compelled to weary the governor and to exhaust the goodwill which he shows to myself and to the sailor who came with me, and who they say is an Englishman and a pilot—a thing very new to me who have always taken him for a Spaniard of Aragon, as he himself asserts and, as Marco Antonio Perez, the soldier who died here fifteen months ago told me, has assured him [Perez] that he came from the same country, and on account of their intimacy asked him [Lembri] to embark and to provide him with something from the Havana to Spain. His [Lembri's] captivity and mine are very free and we go about in the same manner as if we were Englishmen. They are certainly courteous and kindly disposed. Captain Adams, who sails in this vessel and, it is understood, will soon return in it, I have asked to speak with you about my business primary and secondary, about food and wearing apparel, because with that, they say, troubles are less. He will carry everything you may give him, for so he has

[1] Gates inspired trust.

promised me. And above all, I beseech you write to me, and if you do not do it, upon my word, this is my last, because although a prisoner, I have my [juntos y collares?]. Pardon me, I pray, my eccentricity, and may our Lord protect you as I desire, since all my affairs are summed up in this letter, and in my previous letters I gave you an account of all that I did until I was captured and the manner in which my misfortune came about.

From Virginia, July 8th, 1613, according to the Gregorian calendar.

DON DIEGO DE MOLINA.

49. Don Diego de Molina

Letter to Gondomar, 30 April 1614

(translated from the Spanish by Maximilian Schele de Vere)

< Simancas Archive 2591–115, **Brown 1890:740**

After nearly three years, de Molina is still languishing a prisoner at Jamestown, and wonders if he is forgotten by those who should long since have seen him and Lembri exchanged for John Clark. He makes mention of Argall's swift and successful raid that wiped out the French settlement of Saint Sauveur on the coast of Maine and ended French ambition south of the Gulf of St. Lawrence. Captives from there all too soon would be joining him and Pocahontas at the fort.

YOUR LETTER, SIR, and the favor which you did me in succoring me, caused me a satisfaction which I cannot express, since it alone was the means to relieve me of a disease which for seventeen months had afflicted me sadly. For all this fell upon me on account of the wrong which the governor did me in not taking me with him to the kingdom where you are,[1] failing thus to comply with the order he had received, which I had so long wished for and solicited from you, and for which I thank you most sincerely, because, [you are] so great a man only to comply with this wish, without my ever having obliged him [you?] by any service of mine, has interested himself [yourself?] so warmly in doing me a favor. I trust, however, I shall still be able one of these days to serve you.

When the governor left here, he told me he had no orders to take me with him, as he should go in the first vessel, a decision which was not made known to me till he was about to embark, so that I might not find means to send a reply to you—because they fancy that every word of mine contains some crafty device, and thus of whatever trifle I may speak they call it tale-bearing and interpret it as deceit concealed under falsehood. I beg our Lord He may well rid me of them!

The chief marshal has told me that I shall go with him. But I rely but little on his good intentions, and therefore I have wished to write this letter and leave it with a friend of mine who will hand it to you, as they mean to carry me to a new colony which they have established this summer fifteen leagues from here up the river, and I shall not be able to write after that.

The sailor who came with me[2] has been taken on board a man-of-war[3] that is here, where they treat him liberally and use much persuasion to make him confess that he is an Englishman. And if this does not succeed, they have assured me they think of making him drunk and then to examine him once more (fine Christian principles!).

Captain Argol, who commands the ship of which I speak, went last year as high as the 44°, where he found a French ship which had come there with some French people to establish a new colony. After some little fighting, he overcame them and captured fifteen persons; the others fled with their governor. After having burnt all their buildings, he returned to this river with his ship and a captured pinnace, with much wheat, clothing, horses, and working tools.

---

[1] Sir Thomas Gates, who left Virginia in April 1614.

[2] Francisco Lembri.

[3] *The Treasurer.* (Brown)

After this he made a second voyage, reaching 45° and a half, and burnt another small fort twenty leagues from the other settlement. All this you will probably have heard already, because the ship and the pinnace, which he took with him on the second expedition, lost their way in a storm and it is understood went to your city with a few prisoners—fathers of the Jesuits. It may be that the governor has taken over others also.

Thus it seems to me these men will have a new cause of complaint with the King of France. As those who commit the offense think they will never be within his reach, these poor people, who suffer from no fault of their own, have nothing to rely upon. Thus they commit here shameless actions as if the forces of Rome and Carthage united were here assembled. I say this with much solicitude, for they have also the intention of going to la Florida and doing the same thing there. But their plans are formed recklessly and without sufficient thought, and thus God will finally pay them according to their works.

All this I write as I get the opportunity to write without having what I write pried into—in like manner to see as they give me a new opportunity without noticing what I may see. I have asked the marshal to leave me here because I have no desire to see his new colonies nor his new fortifications and small forts. For if they keep me a prisoner without charge against me, but merely for having seen what they themselves have shown me, I should not wish their mistakes and ignorances to redound to my injury.

Of myself in special I have nothing to say, thinking only of the favor which I am anxious you should do me.

Since I have left all my affairs in the hands of God, I no longer think of brothers, relatives, property, or honors, because all is fleeting and passes away like the wind. I only wish to do the duty of a good Catholic and to be able to do it among Catholics.

May God enable me to see them through His mercy, and I will serve you as I ought to do—whom may He preserve as I desire.

From Virginia, April 30, 1614.

DIEGO DE MOLINO.

VIRGINIA MUSEUM OF FINE ARTS

DON DIEGO SARMIENTO DE ACUÑA, CONDE DE GONDOMAR

(1567-1625) The Spanish Ambassador from 1613. A friend of Francis Bacon. "He told a merry tale; read Shakespeare's plays, subscribed for a first folio; liked English wines; assured Sir John Digby that he was an Englishman at heart; was very gallant to the ladies; became all things to all men. Perhaps there never was a man who had so much art with so little appearance of it." Granger.

50. Don Diego de Molina

Letter to Gondomar, 14 June 1614
(translated from the Spanish by Maximilian Schele de Vere)

< Simancas Archive 2591–112 & 113, **Brown 1890:743**

Don Diego's courage is there but his patience is giving way. Jamestown is Egypt not only for him but for "these poor people, held captives," with whom he has lived three years in close contact. They cry, "What is the King of Spain doing? Where is his mercy?" That is, when will he send his fleets up the James and free them from the Virginia Company? Virginia's defenses have been dismantled and neglected, her garrisons reduced to a skeleton. But the answer seems to have been "not soon." The whole business came to an end when Dale, accompanied by the Rolfes, returned to England in 1616, taking his prisoners along. He ordered Lembri, English by birth, hanged as a traitor at the yardarm at the first sight of the coast. De Molina was subsequently exchanged for John Clark.

UNTIL NOW I had hoped to go in this ship of Captain Argol, but now they tell me it sailed two days ago and I am not going in it, because the marshal general had many times offered to take me. From this may be seen the want of truthfulness in these men and that they only mean to deceive us! I am amazed at what they have done and how little they have attended to the order of the council, unless it is, as they say, the well-known proverb of the monkey and the cat, etc.[1]

I assume it must be so, that all these are stratagems, for which reason I wish you not to trouble yourself any farther doing me favors. For although I am badly treated and endure much suffering, I reflect that my sins have been great and that I have deserved it all. But as the father of a family, who, while grieving for his own sorrows, suffers those of his children—and considering the intimacy in which I have lived these three years with these poor people, held captives by their masters—I look upon them as my brothers whose sorrows I feel more than my own, because living in their midst and seeing their

[1] "That is, the Spaniards were being made dupes of,—cat's-paws." (Brown)

sufferings, they look me in the face and ask, "What is the King of Spain doing? Where is his mercy? Why does he not show it to so many unfortunate ones by releasing us from our chains or by cutting off all our heads? For would it be more tolerable for us, for every man, to take up arms to defend and maintain our captivity? Certainly not, but to receive with bright faces such a great benefit with all kinds of thanks and everlasting gratitude!"

Now what is there, Sir, that I can answer?—except that in a most Catholic manner the king, our lord, is bound to reply to this petition with a marvelous effect of his Christian mind.[1]

There are here three settlements: this in which I have been three years—although now they have ordered us to a prison in a stockade a mile distant, with orders not to speak to me, because the marshal says I persuade and have persuaded Edward Colaque [Coles] that he should flee with five other persons to Florida as he put him to work; and I believe he did go for the good it did him to escape from here; and he took the complaint of them all, written in his memory. He is a man who knew how to retain them. They have now spread a report that the Indians have killed them so as to terrify the people.

The other settlement is 20 leagues up the river, which they made 3 years ago. They have made still another three leagues higher up this spring, where almost all the people are, who altogether and in all parts amount to two hundred fifty persons—men, women, and children.

Three stockades which they have at the mouth of the river have been dismantled, and thus there are in them only six or seven men.

I take it for granted that the king our master would do a work worthy of his greatness if he were to take these people away from here, and I am convinced that the Lord brought me hither by such extraordinary and unheard of events in order to become the Moses of these unfortunate people—not, as they say, as a spy, because in Spain little or nothing was known of this country when I was made a

---

[1] "The Christian mind of Philip III sustained a wonderful amount of very wonderful special pleading for the removing of the English in Virginia. The determination of the English to hold their grants in America was probably more evident to his Christian mind than was the truth of the special pleas of his servants and agents. He was probably aware of some things not yet known to us." (Brown)

prisoner here. Their own rulers have made it notorious in Spain by my imprisonment and in France by means of the three forts and settlements which Captain Argol has burnt in two years that he has been here with a man-of-war. They have nothing to complain of but their own bad government, because if they wish to settle the country, they ought to do no harm to their neighbors. I, sir, cannot write much longer, because with great labor I have written this with a root from the fields.

I kiss your hands, sir, for the favor you have done me: All came safe and was a great comfort to me.

From Virginia, June 14, 1614.

They have landed the sailor who is here, today, from the vessel on which he has been two months, and they will take him to another stockade, two miles from this.

May God preserve you, as I desire.
DON DIEGO DE MOLINA.

51. Ralph Hamor

A True Discourse of the present estate of Virginia

< **Hamor 1615 [1860,1957]**

A True Discourse was published in 1615 with the letters by Dale, Whitaker, and Rolfe appended. It was popular enough to be reprinted twice in the year, varying only in one passage in Whitaker's letter, which I include in footnotes.

Hamor's tract is the first expression we have of some cocky confidence that Virginia has come through and has enough home support and internal ballast to survive. Those who don't sign on pretty soon, in company with England's worthiest, says Hamor, will regret having missed out on a sure thing. In the long term the Virginia Company was a good investment. In the short term, the road was still rough.

But England is now established in the Chesapeake, France on the St. Lawrence—Canada and the United States are a fact. Other colonies are now in planning and other nations, notably Sweden and the Netherlands, two first-class world powers, are getting interested in our coasts.

Hamor, unlike Delaware and Dale earlier, can give us some "actuals," some accomplishments and successes. Argall's brilliant stroke—the capture of Pocahontas—proved to be the key to solving the whole Indian problem. Peace prevails with a gay little hostage. Now Englishmen can get on with the job of filling the American landscape. Let the immigrants start coming, however wretched at home.[1] Here they will not only find a safety valve but a safety net. And there is this new project called tobacco. Of course the Virginia Company was a disappointment. It was America they were talking about.

---

[1] The Council of Virginia sent a direct appeal to the Lord Mayor of London to offer a chance in the New World to the homeless of the streets: "And if the inmate called before you and enjoined to remove shall allege he hath not place to remove unto, but must lie in the streets, and being off'red to go this journey shall demand what may be their present maintenance, what may be their future hopes—it may please you to let them know that for the present they shall have meat, drink, and clothing, with an house, orchard, and garden, for the meanest family, and a possession of lands to them and their posterity: ONE HUNDRED ACRES for every man's person that hath a trade or a body able to endure day labor, as much for his wife, as much for his child that are of years to do service to the colony, with further particular reward according to their particular merits and industry. (16 March 1609, a great day in the history of the world)

The abjection of the Chickahominy elders, who seem to want to abdicate their *race,* is political expedience throughout. If the English have formed a marriage alliance with Powhatan, what choice do these have? The balance of tribal power, always shaky, is now completely overthrown. Until the marriage of Rolfe and Pocahontas, the Chickahominy paid no tribute and existed as an independent salient against the heart of Powhatan's domain.

Colonies work, says Hamor. If doubts had any basis up to now—Roanoke, Sagadahoc, Jamestown before the arrival of Delaware—all has changed. From now on we must cope with success, growth, permanency.

Dale, however, in the role of the great captain, does not let loose such flagrant optimism. Meanwhile he tells "D. M." that his detractors cannot dive into, fathom, that is, his ends. He is the all-wise dictator with the reins he dare not relax, and the plea for support at home he dare not abandon.

Dale was no man to trifle with. Powhatan had to match wits with John Smith. With Dale he has to match firepower, and utterly he cannot.

Pocahontas is now happy to throw her lot in with the English. In §12 and §17 she was her father's spy and negotiator at John Smith's fort. A few pages back behind us she was an incarcerated captive.[1] Now, always irresistible, she delights in the role of England's peace emissary to her father. She eagerly and quickly becomes a Christian lady and bewitches everybody in sight.

Re Whitaker's letter to Gouge: It is a surprise that Pocahontas' Christian preceptor was not a clergyman, but rather the marshal at Henrico, Sir Thomas Dale, who seems to have taken the role quite seriously (everything Dale did he did *quite seriously).* This accounts for the supine tone of Rolfe's letter ahead, the suitor addressing the girl's guardian.

In the first version of Whitaker's letter he complains about how few clergymen are doing as he did and coming to Virginia. Was the Virginia Company committed to a mission? And why did Dale need defending from slander?

Next is the well-known, oft-printed Pocahontas Letter, in which John Rolfe asks the hand of the Lady America. Rolfe is virtually writing to the father of his bride-to-be in Governor Dale. He took the man's gauge, and this letter doubtless reveals as much about Dale as about Rolfe.

Pious Rolfe the suitor proclaims the cleanliness, all but the sterility, of his passion to be the husband of the gay little Princess Nonparella. He cannot contain his heart—for its holy zeal, that is. God has called him to the altar, etc. Ludicrous in lubricity, humble John Rolfe all the same displays an impressive rate of intellect and a superb command of words in putting all this

[1] Or what was her status? I find it curious that in the small confines of Jamestown she goes unmentioned by another captive, Don Diego de Molina.

together—a well-paced petition in high placatory style. I imagine Dale loved every molecule of it. But, dear reader, keep in mind Pocahontas was the most beautiful woman on earth, and the whole letter falls into place.

As for the marriage of "strange women" by King Solomon, and the prohibition in Joshua 23:12, and a few other passages—Rolfe offers to say he is motivated to an interracial marriage that God approves so as to put the finishing touch on the Christianity of the bride. This is fair, but his prior reservation is a piece of Calvinist austerity. "Strange" women are gentiles! This is either high placatory style or so much early Protestant neo-Hebraism, a hanging onto the Law of the Old Testament that Christ claims He has come to fulfill in the New. The logic-chopping citations from the *Institutes* do not lighten the load of his reason. Alas, these men are Calvinists and Virginia bid fair to be England's first Puritan colony. Compare this with the liberalism of William Strachey's "Præmonition," pp. 583 & 591.

The lovers were married in April 1614 at Jamestown. Pocahontas, alias Matoaka, alias Amonute, baptized Rebecca, died 21 March 1617 at Gravesend (what a name!) on the way returning home from England, §56.

Their son Thomas Rolfe left descendants now numbering in the thousands, such that the first and finest among the planter aristocracy, including some residents of the White House, are the children of Powhatan.

I have printed here Hamor's published text of the letter. Several parties I will not name once passed their time suggesting it was a fake and a fabrication, until the original letter Hamor used was found in the Bodleian collection,[1] and a transcript by Benjamin L. Bowling was published in *The Virginia Magazine* in 1914, in time to commemorate the 300th anniversary of the Rolfes' marriage. So we have two texts. I have preferred the Hamor only for the sake of bringing out the full printed text of §51, and I have placed in quotes in footnotes variances in the Bodleian letter which seemed to me to be of any substance.

[1] Ashmole 830, folios 118–119.

A True Discourse of the Present Estate of Virginia,

and the Success of the Affairs there till the 18 of June, 1614; together with a Relation of the Several English Towns and Forts, the assured Hopes of that Country, and the Peace concluded with the Indians; the Christening of Powhatan's Daughter, and her Marriage with an Englishman.

Written by Raphe Hamor, the Younger, *late Secretary in that Colony.*

ALGET, QUI NON ARDET.[1]

(Printed at London by John Beale for William Welby, dwelling at the sign of the Swan in Paul's churchyard. 1615)

[1] "Cold is he who does not burn." (Latin)

TO THE TRULY HONORABLE AND RIGHT WORTHY KNIGHT, SIR THOMAS SMITH, GOVERNOR OF THE EAST INDIA, MUSCOVIA, NORTHWEST PASSAGES, [AND] SOMER ISLANDS COMPANIES, AND TREASURER FOR THE FIRST COLONY IN VIRGINIA.

HONORABLE SIR—Having in the time of my residence in Virginia (as it is true my employment then invited me hereunto) collected for my own use and benefit some few occurrents and accidents which are obvious in all new employments—a thing which perhaps but few regard there to busy themselves with, and fewer here to peruse—I resolved indeed only to delight myself and some who I am bound to be thankful unto in that kind, with the unworthy view of them the rather because I have seen many publications and impressions of those affairs by those whose books I should be proud to bear after them. But such is the perverseness of mankind, such their incredulity of everything save what their eyes tell them to be true—yea, such their backwardness in the pursuit of honorable enterprises, that though there should be no end of writing but every day should draw forth his line, and every line his real encouragement, as mine may in the state of the colony as it now standeth, it were hard to say whether one of so many thousands as abound in England might be thereby moved to join with others right worthily disposed to become a hearty and devoted furtherer of an action so noble as is this; which thing if I fail in effecting I shall not lose much labor, since when I undertook this task I imagined no such thing, but merely my own delight and content. It shall be reward enough for me to express my endeavors there, though not equal with the best, yet not idly misspent.

I labor not to seduce or betray any into an action or employment wherein once personally engaged they should have any cause to blame me; neither would I force the help of any man's purse more than voluntary, if I could beyond my art use such effectual persuasions. There are enough, in my opinion, and those the worthiest of England, already united (as the way is now laid down to perfect this business) whose endeavors if they proceed without backsliding and therein persist some few years longer shall be requited and paid with such treble interest as it shall not repent him that is now most cold in the pursuit to have refused more competitors to be sharers in the return'd profit.

Your noble self, sir, ever emulous of virtue and honorable enterprises, should shine to the world more noble in the upholding of this employment, though it appeared as in the beginning full of discouragement, which nevertheless I know yourself rests so assured is now more near than ever to perfection. Your innate and habitual virtue needs no spur, your honorable endeavors well witness the same. Would God, as is yours, all men's off'rings, though not so ample, were so free, so heartily sacrificed. Then could they not thus long have wanted their rewards, perhaps for no other end detained but to make others—a thing which God professeth to love and delight in—more cheerful givers.

Accept, worthy sir, this unworthy treatise, the best testimony of my gratuity which as yet my disabilities may render. Truth shall shroud and patronize it from the malevolent detracting multitude, whose blame though it incur, their shame and imputation it scorns and returns unto them.

My zeal to the action, though I may seem to have forsaken it, gives me the heart to publish what I know to the world. To yourself, particularly your own worth and deserts, to me irrequitable, grant but that favorable acceptation which ever accompanies your worth, and I shall ever acknowledge myself wholly yours; in hope whereof I conclude with my service, and rest

At your command to be disposed of,
RALPH HAMOR.

TO THE READER—

IGNORANT OR ENVIOUS if you be, readers, it is not to satisfy the best of you that I now write. A more seasonable time I must take to embark myself in so rough a sea and come off safe. Only his authority who hath power to compel myself and duty hath commanded me to satisfy his affections (covetous of the dignity and truth of this pious plantation) with these particulars. That they are got abroad and become public was no purpose in their first conception (though some respect have made them so now), a naked and unstudied discourse (I acknowledge) without notes, reserved but in memory to help it. Yet thus much I do avow that it hath duty and truth to make good all other the wants and imperfections of it. I will labor in no further excuse.

Concerning the Virginie pious work itself, how it hath thrived under the command both of Sir Thomas Gates, knight, governor, and Sir Thomas Dale, knight and marshal of the colony, these three years and more, let me say, if—setting aside thine own overweening and singularity—thy unhooded eye can now at length look upon it after so many years of her patience and passions,[1] thou wilt easily acknowledge whose finger hath the alone guidance of it; and then, I doubt nothing, be pleased to hear thyself entreated out of those great plenties and havings which God hath lent thee to spare a little little portion to the full settling and finishing up a *sanctum sanctorum,* an holy house, a sanctuary to Him, the God of the spirits, of all flesh, amongst such poor and innocent seduced savages as we treat of, on whom let our hopes be that it hath vouchsafed him now to be sufficiently revenged for their forefathers' ingratitude and treasons, and [that] now in [is] His appointed time to descend in mercy to lighten them that sit in darkness and in the shadow of death, and to direct their feet in the ways of peace.

Sure young though in years and knowledge I may be said to be, yet let me remember to thee perhaps much knowledge, reader: what the wisest man that ever writ or spake (excepting Him that was both God and man) hath said, that such who bring others unto righteousness shall themselves shine as the stars in the firmament. And doubtless I do believe, even amongst the rest of my articles, when these poor heathens shall be brought to entertain the honor of the name and glory of the Gospel of our blessed Saviour; when they shall testify of the true and ever-living God and Jesus Christ to be their salvation, their knowledge so enlarged and sanctified that without Him they confess their eternal death, I do believe I say (and how can it be otherwise?) that they shall break out and cry with rapture of so inexplicable mercy, "Blessed be the King and Prince of England, and blessed be the English nation, and blessed forever be the most high God, possessor of heaven and earth, that sent these English as angels

---

[1] Calm endurance & sufferings.

to bring such glad tidings amongst us!"

These will be doubtless the emp[h]atic effects and exultation of this so Christian work. And may these nothing move? Alas, let Sanballat and Tobiah, Papists and players,[1] Ammonites and Horonites, the scum and dregs of the people—let them mock at this holy business, they that be filthy. Let them be filthy still, and let such swine wallow in the mire! But let not the rod of the wicked fall upon the lot of the righteous! Let not them shrink back and call in their helps from this so glorious enterprise which the Prophet Isaiah calls the declaring of God to the left hand. But let them that know the work rejoice and be glad in the happy success of it, proclaiming that it is the ever-living God that reigneth in England and unto the ends of the world.

Excuse me, courteous reader, if carried beyond my purpose I declaim passionately in this passive[2] and innocently despised work, which I am sure is so full of goodness, and have been almost six years a sufferer[3] and eyewitness of his now well-nigh achieved happiness, the full and unstain'd reportory of every accident whereof, even from his beginning, together with the causes of the backwardness in prosperity thus long, touching at the miraculous delivery of the scattered company cast upon the Bermudas, when those fortunate islands like so many fair Nereids which received our wrack'd company, with the death of that pure and noble-hearted gentleman, Sir George Sumers, dying there, my purpose is shortly at large to publish [so] that at length some one escaped leper amongst so many saved may return back and pay his vows of thanksgiving unto that ever-to-be-praised, merciful Providence that brought us thither; until when I wish thy zealous and fervent thoughts and endeavors to a business so full of piety as is this our Virginie plantation.

RAPHE HAMOR.

---

[1] Stage farce.
[2] Liable to injury.
[3] Partaker.

A True Discourse

of the present estate of Virginia, and the success of the affairs there till the 18 of June, 1614.

THE MANY publications and impressions of Virginia—an employment wherein to this day myself with many other unstay'd heads and thirsty after new designs have been too unprofitably engaged—might justly excuse my silence, did not the filial duty, whereby in all things to the utmost of my power I am bound to obey my father, compel me unwillingly thereunto: A task I know by himself and others, merely because I have been *oculatus testis,*[1] thus imposed upon me; in the undertaking and performance whereof I heartily wish that my poor relation, rich only in truth—as I shall clearly justify myself by eyewitnesses also—may give any credit or encouragement to proceed in a business so full of honor and worth; whereunto, if there were no secondary causes, the already publish'd ends—I mean the glory of God in the conversion of those infidels, and the honor of our king and country, which by right may claim at the least their superfluities from those whom God hath in this world made his dispensers and purse-bearers—might be a sufficient spur to resolved Christians, especially the state and condition of our colony, so standing when I left it.

And I assure myself in this time grown more mature that an honest heart would even relent and mourn to think how poorly (I dare not say unworthily) it is prosecuted. It being true that now after five years intestine war with the revengeful, implacable Indians, a firm peace (not again easily to be broken) hath been lately concluded not only with the neighbor and bordering Indians, as on Pataomecke, Topahanah, and other rivers, but even with that subtle, old, revengeful Powhatan and all the people under his subjection, for all whom Powhatan himself stands firmly engaged; by which means we shall

[1] "An eyewitness." (Latin)

not only be furnished with what commodities their country yieldeth, and [but] have all the helps they may afford us in our endeavors, as they are easily taught, and may by lenity and fair usage—as Sir Thomas Dale, now principal commander there (and most worthy the honor he holds) is well experienced in their dispositions, and accordingly makes use of them—be brought, being naturally, though ingenious, yet idly given, to be no less industrious, nay, to *exceed* our English; especially those which we hitherto and as yet are furnished with, who for the most part no more sensible than beasts would rather starve in idleness (witness their former proceedings) than feast in labor, did not the law compel them thereunto. But also, which will be most for our benefit, our own men may without hazard, I might say with security (by self-experience), follow their several labors, whereby twenty shall now be able to perform more than heretofore hath been forty.

Though I conjecture and assure myself that ye cannot be ignorant by what means this peace hath been thus happily (both for our proceedings and the welfare of the naturals) concluded, yet for the honor of Captain Argol, whose endeavors in the action entituled him most worthy, I judge it no whit impertinent in my discourse to insert them; which with as much brevity as I may, not omitting the circumstances most pertinent and material, I shall endeavor.

The general letters upon my knowledge directed and sent to the honorable Virginia Council, being most of them (though myself most unworthy) by me penned, have intimated how that the ever-worthy gentleman, Captain Argall, in the heat of our home furies and disagreements, by his best experience of the disposition of those people, partly by gentle usage and partly by the composition and mixture of threats, hath ever kept fair and friendly quarter with our neighbors bordering on other rivers of affinity, yea, consanguinity: no less near than brothers to Powhatan. Such is his well-known temper and discretion. Yea, to this pass hath he brought them that they assuredly trust upon what he promiseth, and are as careful in performing their mutual promises as though they contended to make that maxim that there is no faith to be held with infidels a mere and absurd paradox. Nay, as I have heard himself relate, who is *fide dignus*,[1] they have even been pensive and discontented with themselves because they knew not how to do him some acceptable good turn which might not only pleasure him but even be profitable to our whole colony and plantation; yea, ever assuring him that when the times should present occasion they would take hold of her forelock and be the instruments to work him content.

And even thus they proved themselves as honest performers as liberal promisers:

It chanced Powhatan's delight and darling, his daughter Pocahuntas—whose fame hath even been spread in England by the title of "Nonparella of Virginia"—in her princely progress (if I may so term it) took some pleasure, in the absence of Captain Argall, to be among her friends at Pataomecke, as it seemeth by the relation I had, employed thither as shopkeepers to a fair to exchange some of her father's commodities for theirs; where residing some three months or longer, it fortuned upon occasion either of promise or profit Captain Argall to arrive there, whom Pocahuntas, desirous to renew her familiarity with the English, and delighting to see them (as unknown, fearful perhaps to be surprised) would gladly visit as she did. Of whom no sooner had Captain Argall intelligence but he dealt with an old friend and adopted brother of his, Iapazeus, how and by what means he might procure her capture, assuring him that now or never was the time to pleasure him if he intended indeed that love which he had made profession of; that in ransom of her he might redeem some of our Englishmen and arms now in the possession of her father, promising to use her with all fair and gentle entreaty.

Iapazeus, well assured that his brother, as he promised, would use her courteously, promised his best endeavors and secrecy to accomplish his desire; and thus wrought it, making his wife an instrument (which sex have ever been most powerful in beguiling enticements!) to effect his plot which he had thus laid.

He agreed that himself, his wife, and Pocahuntas would accompany his brother to the waterside. Whither come, his wife should feign a great and longing desire to go aboard and see the ship, which

[1] "Trustworthy" (Latin).

being there three or four times before she had never seen; and should be earnest with her husband to permit her. He seemed angry with her making, as he pretended, so unnecessary a request, especially being without the company of women; which denial she taking unkindly, [she] must feign to weep (as who knows not that women can command tears!)—whereupon her husband, seeming to pity those counterfeit tears, gave her leave to go aboard so that it would please Pochahuntas to accompany her. Now was the greatest labor to win her—guilty perhaps of her father's wrongs, though not known as she supposed—to go with her, yet by her earnest persuasions, she assented.[1]

So forthwith aboard they went; the best cheer that could be made was seasonably provided; to supper they went, merry on all hands, especially Iapazeus and his wife, who to express their joy would e'er be treading upon Captain Argal's foot as (who should say 'tis done?) —"She is your own!"

Supper ended, Pochahuntas was lodged in the gunner's room. But Iapazeus and his wife desired to have some conference with their brother, which was only to acquaint him by what stratagem they had betrayed his prisoner, as I have already related; after which discourse to sleep they went; Pochahuntas, nothing mistrusting this policy, who nevertheless, being most possessed with fear and desire of return, was first up, and hastened Iapazeus to be gone.

Captain Argall, having secretly well rewarded him with a small copper kettle and some other less valuable toys so highly by him esteemed that doubtless he would have betrayed his own father for them, permitted both him and his wife to return, but told him that for divers considerations—as for that her father had then eigh[t] of our Englishmen, many swords, pieces, and other tools, which he had at several times by treacherous murdering our men taken from them, which though of no use to him, he would not redeliver—he would reserve Pocahuntas; whereat she began to be exceeding pensive and discontented, yet ignorant of the dealing of Iapazeus, who in outward appearance was no less discontented that he should be the means of

---

[1] I.e., though perhaps an accomplice in her father's wrongs, she was at present unsuspecting, so that by the earnest persuasions of Iapazeus' wife, etc.

her captivity. Much ado there was to persuade her to be patient, which with extraordinary courteous usage, by little and little, was wrought in her.

And so to James town she was brought,[1] [and] a messenger to her father forthwith dispatched to advertise him that his only daughter was in the hands and possession of the English, there to be kept till such time as he would ransom her with our men, swords, pieces, and other tools treacherously taken from us.

The news was unwelcome and troublesome unto him, partly for the love he bare to his daughter and partly for the love he bare to our men his prisoners,[2] of whom, though with us they were unapt for any employment, he made great use—and those swords and pieces of ours which, though of no use to him, it delighted him to view and look upon. He could not without long advice and deliberation with his council resolve upon anything. And it is true we heard nothing of him till three months after, [when] by persuasions of others he returned us seven of our men, with each of them a musket unserviceable, and by them sent us word that whensoever we pleased to deliver his daughter, he would give us in satisfaction of his injuries done to us—and for the rest of our pieces broken and stol'n from him—500 bushels of corn, and be forever friends with us.

The men and pieces in part of payment we received, and returned him answer that his daughter was very well and kindly entreated, and so should be howsoever he dealt with us. But we could not

---

[1] Smith's *General History* tells it: "For though she had seen and been in many ships, yet he caused his wife to feign how desirous she was to see one, and that he offered to beat her for her importunity, till she wept. But at last he told her if Pocahontas would go with her he was content. And thus they betrayed the poor, innocent Pocahontas aboard, where they were all kindly feasted in the cabin. Iapazaws treading oft on the captain's foot to remember he had done his part, the captain, when he saw his time, persuaded Pocahontas to the gun room, feigning to have some conference with Iapazaws, which was only that she should not perceive he was any way guilty of her captivity. So sending for her again, he told her before her friends she must go with him and compound peace betwixt her country and us before she ever should see Powhatan; whereat the old Jew and his wife began to howl and cry as fast as Pocahontas, that upon the captain's fair persuasions by degrees pacifying herself, and Iapazaws and his wife with the kettle and other toys went merrily on shore, and she to James town." (112)

[2] "because he loved both his daughter and our commodities" *ibid.*

VIRGINIA HISTORICAL SOCIETY, RICHMOND, VA

THE ABDUCTION OF POCAHONTAS

Iapazeus and wife (Paupauwiske?), goods in hand, go to work on the girl. In the background are hostilities to which this hostage will be the peace.

believe that the rest of our arms were either lost or stol'n from him, and therefore till he returned them all we would not by any means deliver his daughter; and then it should be at his choice whether he would establish peace or continue enemies with us.

This answer as it seemed pleased him not very well, for we heard no more from him till in March last when with Captain Argall's ship and some other vessels belonging to the colony Sir Thomas Dale with an hundred and fifty men well appointed went up into his own river where his chiefest habitations were, and carried with us his daughter, either to move them to fight for her, if such were their courage and boldness as hath been reported, or to restore the residue of our demands, which were our pieces, swords, tools.

Some of the same men which he returned, as they promised, ran to him again. And because he had put us to the trouble to fetch them five hundred bushels of corn, a great bravado all the way as we went up the river they made, demanding the cause of our coming thither, which we told them was to deliver Pocahuntas, whom purposely we had brought with us, and to receive our arms, men, and corn or else to fight with them, burn their houses, take away their canoas, break down their fishing weirs, and do them what other damages we could.

Some of them, to set a good face on the matter, replied that if we came to fight with them, we were welcome, for they were provided for us, counseling us rather to retire if we loved our safeties than proceed; bragging, as well they might, that we had ever had the worst of them in that river, instancing by Captain Ratliefe (not worthy rememb'ring but to his dishonor) who with most of his company they betrayed and murthered. We told them since they durst remember us of that mischief, unless they made the better and more speedy agreement, we would now revenge that treachery.

And with this discourse by the way as we went, we proceeded, and had no sooner ent'red the narrow of the river, the channel there lying within shot of the shore, but they let their arrows fly amongst us in the ship, themselves unseen to us, and in the forehead hurt one of our men, which might have hazarded his life without the present help of a skillful chirurgeon.

Being thus justly provoked, we presently manned our boats, went ashore, and burned in that very place some forty houses; and of the things we found therein made freeboot and pillage, and as themselves afterward confess'd unto us hurt and killed five or six of their men, with this revenge satisfying ourselves for that their presumption in shooting at us.

And so the next day [we] proceeded higher up the river, the Indians calling unto us and demanding why we went ashore, burnt their houses, killed and hurt their men, and took away their goods. We replied that though we came to them in peaceable manner and would have been glad to have received our demands with love and peace, yet we had hearts and power to take revenge and punish where wrongs should be offered; which having now done, though not so severely as we might, we rested content therewith and are ready to embrace peace with them, if they pleased.

Many excuses they seemed to pretend that they shot not at us, but if any such abuse were offered, it was some straggled Indian, ignorant of our pretense in coming to them, affirming that they themselves would be right glad of our love, and would endeavor to help us to what we came for; which being in the possession of Powhatan their king, they would without delay dispatch messengers to him to know his purpose and pleasure, desiring fair quarter some 24 hours, for so long they pretended it would be before their messengers might return.

This we granted, and what we promised we ever exactly performed. The time now come, we inquired what Powhatan would do, and had for answer that our Englishmen lately with him, fearful to be put to death by us, were run away, and some of Powhatan's men sent abroad in quest of them; but our swords and pieces, so many as he had, should be brought the next day; which merely to delay time they bare us in hand: The next day they came not.

Higher up the river we went, and anchored near unto the chiefest residency Powhatan had, at a town called Matchcot,[1] where were assembled (which we saw) about 400 men well appointed with their bows and arrows to welcome us. Here they dared us to come ashore,

[1] "Matchut" is a town shown on the Smith map near the mouth of the Pamunkey River (modern name) on the W bank, opposite West Point. Also on page 831, where, however, Hamor must cross the river (W to E) to reach it.

a thing which we purposed before; so ashore we went.

Our best landing being up a high steep hill, which might have given the enemy much advantage against us, but it seemed they, as we, were unwilling to begin, and yet would gladly have been at blows.

Being landed, as if they had no show of fear, they stirred not from us, but walked up and down by and amongst us, the best of them inquiring for our *weroance,* or king, with whom they would gladly consult to know the occasion of our coming thither; whereof when they were informed, they made answer that they were there ready to defend themselves, if we pleased to assault them; desiring nevertheless some small time to dispatch two or three men once more to their king to know his resolution, which, if not answerable to our requests, in the morning, if nothing else but blood would then satisfy us, they would fight with us and thereby determine our quarrel—which was but a further delay to procure time to carry away their provisions.

Nevertheless we agreed to this their request, assuring them till the next day by noon we would not molest, hurt, nor detain any of them; and then, before we fought, our drum and trumpets should give them warning; upon which promise of ours, two of Powhatan's sons, being very desirous to see their sister, who was there present ashore with us, came unto us, at the sight of whom and her welfare, whom they suspected to be worse entreated (though they had often heard the contrary), they much rejoiced, and promised that they would undoubtedly persuade their father to redeem her, and to conclude a firm peace forever with us.

And upon this resolution, the two brothers with us retired aboard, we having first dispatched two Englishmen, Master John Rolfe and Master Sparkes, to acquaint their father with the business in hand. The next day being kindly entreated, they returned not at all admitted Powhatan's presence, but spake with his brother Opechankano, his successor—one who hath already the command of all the people—who likewise promised us his best endeavors to further our just requests.

And we, because the time of the year being then April called us to our business at home to prepare ground and set corn for our winter's provision, upon these terms departed, giving them respite till harvest to resolve what was best for them to do, with this proviso that if final agreement were not made betwixt us before that time, we would thither return again and destroy and take away all their corn, burn all the houses upon that river, leave not a fishing weir standing, not a canoa in any creek thereabout, and destroy and kill as many of them as we could.

Long before this time, a gentleman of approved behavior and honest carriage, Master John Rolfe, had been in love with Pocahuntas and she with him; which thing at the instant that we were in parley with them myself made known to Sir Thomas Dale by a letter from him [Rolfe], whereby he entreated his advice and furtherance in his love, if so it seemed fit to him [Dale] for the good of the plantation. And Pocahuntas herself acquainted her brethren therewith. Which resolution Sir Thomas Dale well approving was the only cause he was so mild amongst them, who otherwise would not have departed their river without other conditions.

The bruit of this pretended marriage came soon to Powhatan's knowledge—a thing acceptable to him, as appeared by his sudden consent thereunto, who some ten days after sent an old uncle of hers, named Opachisco, to give her as his deputy in the church, and two of his sons to see the marriage solemnized; which was accordingly done about the fift of April. And ever since we have had friendly commerce and trade not only with Powhatan himself but also with his subjects round about us; so as now I see no reason why the colony should not thrive apace.

Besides this love by this means with Powhatan concluded, it will be worth my pains to run over our friendship with our next neighbors, the Chicohominies, lately confirmed—a lusty and daring people who have long time lived free from Powhatan's subjection, having laws and governors within themselves.

These people, hearing of our concluded peace with Powhatan, as the noise thereof was soon bruited abroad, sent two of their men unto us, and two fat bucks for present to our king, for so Sir Thomas Dale is generally reputed and termed amongst them; and offered themselves and service unto him, alleging that albeit in former times they had been our enemies and we theirs, yet they would now, if we pleased, become not only our trusty friends but even King James his subjects and tributaries, and relinquish their old name of Chicohominies and take upon them, as they call us, the name of *tossantessas.* And because they have no principal commander or weroance, they would entreat Sir Thomas Dale, as King James his deputy, to be their supreme head, king, and governor, and in all just causes and quarrels to defend them, as they would be ready at all times to aid him; only their desire was to enjoy their own laws and liberties; and because himself by reason of his many other employments, beside the charge he hath of his own people, may not be always present amongst them, to be governed as formerly by eight of the elders and principal men amongst them, as his substitutes and councilors. And even this was the sum and effect of their embassy.

Sir Thomas Dale appointed a day to send some men into their river to propose certain conditions unto them, whereunto, if they assented, he would gladly accept of their proffered friendship and be himself their weroance; and with this answer offering them copper for their venison, which they refused to take, dismissed them.

When the appointed day came, Sir Thomas Dale himself and Captain Argall, with 50 men in a barge and frigate, well appointed lest any treachery might be intended, set forward to Chicohominie, an arm of our river some seven miles from James Town, where we found the people according to promise expecting our coming, assembled and met together, who after their best and most friendly manner bade us welcome. And because our business at home would permit us but small time of stay with them, they presently sent for their principal men, some of whom were then absent, which hast'ned unto us.

And the next morning very early, [they] assembled and sat in council about this business, Captain Argall supplying Sir Thomas Dale's place amongst them, who, though there present, for some respects concealed himself and kept aboard his barge. After long discourse of their former proceedings, Captain Argall told them that now since they had entreated peace and promised their love and friendship, he was sent unto them from the great weroance to conclude the same, all former injuries on both sides set apart and forgotten, which he would do upon these conditions:

First, that they should take upon them, as they promised, the name of *tassantasses,* or "Englishmen," and be King James his subjects, and be forever honest, faithful, and trusty unto his deputy in their country.

Secondly, that they should never kill any of our men or cattle. But if either our men or cattle should offend them or run to them, they should bring them home again, and should receive satisfaction for the trespass done them.

Thirdly, they should at all times be ready and willing to furnish us with three or four hundred bowmen to aid us against the Spaniards, whose name is odious amongst them—for Powhatan's father was driven by them from the West Indies into those parts[1]—or against any other Indians which should contrary to the established peace offer us any injury.

Fourthly, they shall not upon any occasion whatsoever break down any of our pales or come into any of our towns or forts by any other ways, issues, or ports than ordinary, but first call, and say the tossantessas are there. And so coming, they shall at all times be let in and kindly entertained.

Fifthly, so many fighting men as they have, which may be at the least five hundred, should yearly bring into our storehouse at the beginning of their harvest two bushels of corn a man, as tribute of their obedience to His Majesty and to his deputy there; for which they should receive so many iron *tomahawkes,* or small hatchets.

Lastly, the eight chief men which govern as substitutes and councilors under Sir Thomas Dale shall at all times see these articles and conditions duly performed, for which they shall receive a red coat, or livery, from our king yearly, and each of them the picture of His Majesty engraven in copper, with a chain of copper to hang it about his neck, whereby they shall be known to be King James his noblemen; so as if these conditions or any of them be broken, the

---

1 A most puzzling statement. The readiest explanation is that Powhatan was the son of Don Luis, but the timing is off. Don Luis was a boy when kidnapped in 1561 and Powhatan was certainly born before he returned in 1570. We may never know the truth.

offenders themselves shall not only be punished but also those *commanders* because they stand engaged for them.

After these articles were thus proposed, the whole assembly assenting thereunto answered with a great shout and noise that they would readily and willingly perform them all. And immediately began the chief of the eight to make an oration to the rest, bending his speech first to the old men, then to the young men, and in conclusion to the women and children, giving them thereby to understand the sum of the proposed conditions and how strictly they were to observe them; in consideration whereof he further declared what we have promised to do for them: not only to defend and keep them from the fury and danger of Powhatan, which thing they most feared, but even from all other enemies domestic or foreign; and that we would yearly by trade furnish them with copper, beads, hatchets, and many other necessaries; yea, which liked them best, that we would permit them to enjoy their own liberties, freedoms, and laws, and to be governed as formerly by eight of their chiefest men.

It shall not be unnecessary to insert the occasion (as we imagine) of this their much desired, unexpected friendship, which was questionless some sudden fear of Powhatan's displeasure, being united with us, now able to revenge their disobedience done unto him. For you must imagine, these people presuming upon their own strength and number (in no one place in those parts which we know so many together) to have a long time neglected Powhatan, and refused—which the place hath been formerly accustomed, and as his right may challenge[1]—the homage and duty of subjects which they ought to have performed; to which obedience, fearing our power might compel them, they chose rather to subject themselves to us than being enemies to both to expose and lay themselves open to Powhatan's tyranny and oppression. For this they did chiefly insist upon that he was an ill weroance, full of cruelty and injustice, covetous of those things they had, and implacable if they denied him whatsoever he demanded; and for these reasons desired to be made one people with us to curb the pride and ambition of Powhatan,

[1] Apparently the Chickahominy once paid Powhatan tribute, and although they have not done so now for a long time, Powhatan, they fear, may still "challenge" them for his right to renew it. Ensuing statements make this clearer.

from whom [we were] to defend them. They told us it would be no breach of peace on our parts, since now they were no longer Chicohomimes, or "naturals," of that place but tossantessars and King James his subjects, whom we are bound to defend.

So soon as there was an end of speaking and the peace firmly concluded and assented unto, Captain Argall, by the gift of eight great pieces of copper and eight great tomahawkes, bound the eight great men, or councilors, to the exact performance and keeping of the same, according to the conditions proclaimed; which they very gladly and thankfully accepted and returned him as testimonies of their loves venison, turkeys, fresh fish, baskets, mats, and suchlike things as they were then furnished with; and so the council broke up. And then every man brought to sell to our men skins, bowls, mats, baskets, tobacco, etc., and became as familiar amongst us as if they had been "Englishmen" indeed.

Thus have I briefly as the matter would permit discoursed our established friendship with the naturals, and the occasions thereof, which I hope will continue so long between us till they shall have the understanding to acknowledge how much they are bound to God for sending us amongst them, than which what work would be more acceptable to God, more honorable to our king and country?

The greatest and many enemies and disturbers of our proceedings, and that which hath hitherto deter'd our people to address themselves into those parts, have been only two: enmity with the naturals and the bruit of famine. One of these two (and that indeed, which was some cause of the other) I have already removed, and shall as easily take away the other, howbeit it were too great folly (I might say impudency in me) to aver that there hath reigned no such infection in the colony, occasioned merely by misgovernment, idleness, and faction, and chiefly by the absence of the ever-worthy commanders, Sir Thomas Gates and Sir George Summers, by the providence of God miraculously wrack'd and saved upon the hopeful Sumer Islands, since myself cannot but witness (of which I had some taste) in what a miserable condition we found the colony at our arrival there from the Bermudas—not living above three score persons therein, and those scarce able to go alone, of well-nigh six hundred not full ten months before. Yet now I dare and will boldly affirm to the greatest adversary of the plantation that shall aver the contrary that there is that plenty of food which every man by his own industry may easily, and doth, procure; that the poorest there and most in want hath not been so much pinched with hunger this 4 years that if he would take any pains, he knew not where to fetch a good meal's meat.

And true it is that every day by the providence and blessing of God and their own industry they have more plenty than other. The reason hereof is at hand. For formerly, when our people were fed out of the common store and labored jointly in the manuring of the ground and planting corn, glad was that man that could slip from his labor. Nay, the most honest of them in a general business would not take so much faithful and true pains in a week as now he will do in a day. Neither cared they for the increase, presuming that howsoever their harvest prospered, the general store must maintain them; by which means we reaped not so much corn from the labors of 30 men as three men have done for themselves; to prevent which mischief hereafter, Sir Thomas Dale hath taken a new course throughout the whole colony, by which means the general store (apparel only excepted) shall not be charged with anything. And this it is he hath allotted to every man in the colony: three English acres of clear corn ground, which every man is to manure and tend, being in the nature of farmers (the Bermuda undertakers only excepted); and they are not called unto any service or labor belonging to the colony more than one month in the year, which shall neither be in seed time or in harvest; for which, doing no other duty to the colony, they are yearly to pay into the store two barrels and a half of corn,[1] there to be reserved to keep new men, which shall be sent over, the first year after their arrival. And even by this means (I daresay) our store will be bountifully furnished to maintain three or four hundred men, whensoever they shall be sent thither to us; so as if that money which hitherto hath been disbursed to provide a twelvemonth's victuals, if there were but now half so much bestowed in clothes and bedding,

---

[1] Smith inserts here in his *General History:* "... from all those farmers, whereof the first was William Spence, an honest, valiant, and an industrious man, and hath continued from 1607 to this present [1624]." (114)

will be such comfort to the men as even thereby the lives of many shall not only be preserved but also themselves kept in strength and heart, able to perform such businesses as shall be imposed upon them. And thus shall also the former charge be well saved and yet more business effected, the action renowned, and more commodity returned to the merchant, as yet faint for want of encouragement.

Concerning the undertaking of the Bermuda City, a business of [the] greatest hope ever begun in our territories there, their patent, which I purposed in this treatise to insert, doth apparently demonstrate upon what terms and conditions they voluntarily have undertaken that employment. How forward that business is, in his due place shall be expressed. Only give me leave with as much brevity as I may, lest any man should divert his mind and be fearful to adventure his person thither for fear of famine and penury, to amplify a little the plenty there.

For if it be true—as most certain it is that those whom I have described under the title of farmers can pay into our store two barrels and a half of corn yearly, and others who labor eleven months in the general business of the colony and but one [for themselves, are able] to provide themselves victuals—why should any man, if he be industrious, mistrust starving, if otherwise, for any part? And I think all that are engaged in the action and understand the business accord with me herein and would not wish his company there. Nay, they shall much wrong themselves and the action if they do not withstand such and deny them passage. For even they, and none else, have been the occasions of the manifold imputations and disgraces which Virginia hath innocently undergone through their defaults. I would therefore by these relations not only encourage honest and industrious but also deter all lazy, impotent, and ill-livers from addressing themselves thither, as being a country too worthy for them and altogether disconsonant to their natures; which must either brook labor or hazard and undergo much displeasure, punishment, and penury, if they escape a thing which few idlers have done: the scurvy disease, with which few or none once infected have recovered.

To proceed therefore in my encouragement to painful people—

such as either through crosses in this world or wrack'd rents, or else [with] great charge of children and family live here, and that not without much care and sweat, into extreme poverty—for those this country hath present remedy: Every such person so well disposed to adventure thither shall soon find the difference between their own and that country.[1] The affairs in the colony being so well ordered, and the hardest tasks already overpass'd, that whosoever now or hereafter shall happily arrive there shall find a handsome house of some four rooms or more, if he have a family, to repose himself in *rent free,* and twelve English acres of ground adjoining thereunto, very strongly impaled; which ground is only allotted unto him for roots, garden herbs, and corn. Neither shall he need to provide himself, as were wont the first planters, of a year's provision of victuals, for that the store there will be able to afford him. And upon these conditions he shall be entertained: He shall have for himself and family a competent twelve months' provision delivered unto him, in which time it must be his care to provide for himself and family ever after, as [do] those already there. To this end he shall be furnished with necessary tools of all sorts. And for his better subsistence he shall have poultry and swine and, if he deserve it, a goat or two, perhaps a cow given him; which once compass'd, how happily he may live, as do many there who I am sure will never return, I submit to their own future well-experienced judgments.

Now, lest any man should yet rest discouraged because as yet no mention is made of any other provision of victuals save only of breadcorn which, grant it may with labor be competently procured, will afford but a bare and miserable living, I think there is no man so ignorant [as] to conceive that such a main continent as is Virginia, boundless for aught we have discovered, and so goodly rivers nowhere else to be paralleled, should be more barren of cattle, fish, and fowl than other lands. Assuredly they are not, for true it is that the land is stored with plenty and variety of wild beasts—lions, bears, deer of all sorts (only differing from ours in their increase, having usual three or four fawns at a time, none that I have seen or heard of

---

[1] This statement, I think, marks the beginning of the United States.

under two; the reason whereof some of our people ascribe to the virtue of some grass or herb which they eat, because our goats oftentimes bring forth three and most of them two. For my part I rather impute their fecundity to the providence of God, who for every mouth provideth meat. And if this increase were not, the naturals would assuredly starve, for of the deer they kill as do we beefs in England: all the year long, neither sparing young nor old—no, not the does ready to fawn, nor the young fawns if but two days old); beavers, otters, foxes, *racounes* (almost as big as a fox; as good meat as a lamb), hares, wildcats, muskrats, squirrels flying and other of three or four sorts, *apossumes* (of the bigness and likeness of a pig of a month old, a beast of as strange as incredible nature. She hath commonly seven young ones, sometimes more and sometimes less, which at her pleasure till they be a month old or more she taketh up into her belly and putteth forth again without hurt to herself or them).

Of each of these beasts, the lion excepted, myself have many times eaten, and can testify that they are not only tasteful but also wholesome and nourishing food.

There are fowl of divers sorts—eagles, wild turkeys much bigger than our English, cranes, herons white and russet, hawks, wild pigeons (in winter beyond number or imagination. Myself have seen three or four hours together flocks in the air so thick that even they have shadowed the sky from us), turkey buzzards, partridge, snipes, owls, swans, geese, brants, duck and mallard, divers, sheldrakes, cormorants, teal, widgeon, curlews, pewits, besides other small birds, as blackbird, hedge sparrows, oxeyes, woodpeckers, and in winter about Christmas many flocks of parakertoths.[1]

For fish, the rivers are plentifully stored with sturgeon, porpoise, bass, rockfish, carp, shad, herring, eel, catfish, perch, flatfish, trout, sheepshead, drummers, garfish, *crevises*, crabs, oysters, and divers other kinds, of all which myself have seen great quantity taken—especially the last summer at Smith's Island at one hale a frigate's lading of sturgeon, bass, and other great fish in Captain Argal's seine. And even at that very place, which is not above fifteen miles from

[1] The Carolina parakeet, now extinct.

Point Comfort, if we had been furnished with salt to have saved it, we might have taken as much fish as would have served us that whole year.

Nor are these provision of bread, flesh, and fish all we have for sustentation of man's life. Behold more change and variety of food which our soil and climate affordeth: carrots, parsnips, turnips, radish, pumpions (of the West Indy kind in great abundance. Of one seed I have seen an hundreth—much better than ours, and lasting all the year), cabbage, parsley, all manner of potherbs and other herbs, marjoram, thyme, winter savory, lettuce, purslane, etc., and besides the natural grain of that country, as wheat, peas, and beans.

It did me much good to view our English wheat, how forward it was, full ear'd, of one grain forty ears or more, a span long, and only wanting ripening in mid June; our English peas then ripe, and beans very forward, and English barley very hopeful, such as mine eyes never beheld better in England. And if that soil bring forth these things—as can those which have been there with me affirm and witness—as plentiful and unchangeable for taste and quantity as England or any other country, why should any man that hath his limbs in a peaceable state as is that so much as *dream* of starving?

To go yet a little further, I myself know no one country yielding without art or industry so many fruits (sure I am England doth not)—wild grapes in abundance all the woods over, their juice sweet and pleasant in taste (some of them we have replanted in a vineyard adjoining to Henrico the quantity of three or four acres, which were this year very plentifully laden. To what perfection they will come, the next return will advertise); cherries little inferior to ours, which if replanted may prove as much better as they are worse; *pissmien* plums [persimmons] in bigness and fashion like a medlar, of a styptic quality; other sorts of plums like to our wheat plums and in goodness answerable; great fields and woods abounding with strawberries much fairer and more sweet than ours; mulberries of great bigness, and about the Bermuda City and hundreds thereunto belonging great store thereof; *maricocks* of the fashion of a lemon, whose blossom may admit comparison with our most delightsome and beautiful flowers, and the fruit exceeding pleasant and tasteful; chestnut trees towards the Falls as many as oaks and as fertile; many goodly groves of *chincomen* trees with a husk like unto a chestnut, raw or boiled luscious and hearty meat; walnuts of three or four sorts whereof there might be yearly made great quantity of oils as useful and good as that of olives; some filberts I have seen; crabs great store, less but not so sour as ours, which grafted with the scions of English apple trees without question would bear very good fruit. And we doubt not but to have scions enough the next year, there being in Sir Thomas Gates his garden at James town many forward apple and pear trees come up of the kernels set the year before.

If all this be not sufficient, lo, further encouragement: The colony is already furnished with two hundred neat cattle, as many goats, infinite hogs in herds all over the woods, besides those to every town belonging in general and every private man; some mares, horses, and colts, poultry great store, besides tame turkeys, peacocks, and pigeons, plentifully increasing and thriving there, in no country better!

Of our young steers, the next winter we doubt not to have three or four plows going, which once compass'd we shall in short time be able to repay England the corn they have lent us.

If I knew yet any further impediments which might seem to give discouragement to adventure thither, I should as easily remove them!

Object that pleaseth the want of clothes?[1] So long as there are wild beasts there and the beasts have skins on their backs, if the necessity were such, why should not we, as do the naturals, clothe ourselves therewith? It is no worse than our forefathers have worn before us, and such as will save us from the cold in winter and heat in summer.

But admit there were no skins or, being there, our people disdain to wear them. If there be any man that hath been so ill an husband here that he cannot furnish himself with a year's provision of apparel, (if I might counsel) he should not be suffered to go thither, for that country is not for him. As for others who can provide apparel for the first year, I hold him a worse husband than the former that shall at any time after be worse clothed than he went over: The valuable commodity of tobacco, of such esteem in Eng-

[1] That = what: "What pleaseth the want of clothes?"

land (if there were nothing else), which every man may plant and with the least part of his labor tend and cure, will return him both clothes and other necessaries, for the goodness whereof answerable to West-Indy, Trinidado, or cracus[1] (admit there hath no such been returned), let no man doubt. Into the discourse whereof, since I am obviously ent'red, I may not forget the gentleman, worthy of much commendations, which first took the pains to make trial thereof: his name Mr. John Rolfe, anno Domini 1612.

Partly for the love he hath a long time borne unto it, and partly to raise commodity to the adventurers, in whose behalf I witness and vouchsafe to hold my testimony, in belief that during the time of his abode there, which draweth near upon six years, no man hath labored to his power by good example there and worthy encouragement into England by his letters than he hath done; witness his marriage with Powhatan's daughter (one of rude education, manners barbarous, and cursed generation) merely for the good and honor of the plantation. And lest any man should conceive that some sinister respects allured him hereunto, I have made bold, contrary to his knowledge, in the end of my treatise to insert the true copy of his letter written to Sir Thomas Dale to acquaint him with his proceedings and purpose therein; the rather to give testimony to the misconstruing and ill-censuring multitude of his integrity in the undertaking, a matter of so great a consequent, who in my hearing have not spared to speak their pleasures. His own letter hits them home, and the better sort who know to censure judiciously cannot but highly commend and approve so worthy an undertaking.

Thus far I have applied myself to encourage personal adventurers. I would gladly now by worthy motives allure the *heavy* undertakers to persist with alacrity and cheerfulness, both for their own reputations, the honor of God, and their king and country. The worthier sort—I mean those nobles and others of that honorable council interessed therein—need no spur. Their own innate virtues drives them apace. The merchant only wants some feeling and present return of those commodities which he is persuaded the country affordeth. To them therefore I will address my speech and, if I may

[1] Principal commercial varieties of tobacco.

persuade them to be constant in their proceedings some small time longer, the benefit will be the greater and the more welcome when it cometh.

It is not for nothing Sir Thomas Dale, so nobly without respect to his living to his lady here in England, pass'd the prefixed time of his resolved return, yet remaineth there. I am sure if he pleased he might return with as much honor as any man from thence; I say not more.

I shall little need, and indeed it were but waste and idle for me, to repeat and mention the commodities which with only labor may be there procured. Many treatises hath them at full, samples have been sent home, and no man disputeth the goodness or the quantity there to be had. Take therefore double courage to yourselves, and let those two years' neglect be restored by a cheerful and new onset; and for your encouragement read yet a little further and view the face of the colony, even superficially portray'd; see what effects these three years have wrought.

In May 1611,[1] Sir Thomas Dale, with a prosperous passage not full eight weeks, arrived there, with him about three hundred people, such as for the present speed and dispatch could then be provided, of worse condition than those formerly there, who (I sorrow to speak it) were not so provident, though once before bitten with hunger and penury, as to put corn into the ground for their winter's bread, but trusted to the store then furnished but with eight months' provision. His first care therefore was to employ all hands about setting of corn at the two forts seated upon Kecoughtan: Henry and Charles; whereby the season then not fully past, though about the end of May, we had there an indifferent crop of good corn.

This business taken order for, and the care and trust of it committed to his under officers, to James Town he hastened, where the most company were, and their daily and usual works bowling in the streets. These he employed about necessary works, as felling of timber, repairing their houses ready to fall upon their heads, and providing pales, posts, and rails to impale his purposed new town, which

[1] May 10th in Smith's *General History,* 110.

by reason of his ignorance in those parts, but newly arrived there, he had not resolved where to seat.

For his better knowledge therefore of those parts, himself with an hundreth men spent some time in discovery. First, Nansamund River, which in despite of the Indians then our enemies he discovered to the head; after that our own river to the Falls, where upon a high land environed with the main river, some sixteen or twenty miles from the head of the Falls, near to an Indian town called Arsahattocke, he resolved to plant his new town, and so did; whereof in his due place I shall make a brief relation.

It was no mean trouble to him to reduce his people so timely to good order, being of so ill a condition as may well witness his severe and strict imprinted book of articles, then needful with all severity and extremity to be executed, now much mitigated.[1] For more deserved death in those days than do now the least punishment, so as if the law should not have restrained by execution, I see not how the utter subversion and ruin of the colony should have been prevented—witness Webbe's and Prise's design the first year, since that Abbot's[2] and others' more dangerous than the former; and even this summer Cole's and Kitchins' plot, with three more bending their course towards the southward to a Spanish plantation reported to be there, who had traveled (it being now a time of peace) some five days' journey to Ocanahoen, there cut off by certain Indians hired by us to bring them home to receive their deserts.

So as Sir Thomas Dale hath not been tyrannous, nor severe at all.

---

[1] *Laws Divine, Moral, and Martial,* etc. Contrast the following passage with the tenor of the *Answer of the General Assembly §58* which Hamor signed in 1623.

[2] Copying these pages into his *General History* (110), Capt. John Smith here pauses to defend his friend: "Here I entreat your patience for an apology, though not a pardon. This Jeffrey Abbots, however this author censures him and the governor executes him, I know he had long served both in Ireland and Netherlands. Here he was a sergeant of my company, and I never saw in Virginia a more sufficient soldier, less turbulent, a better wit, more hardy or industrious, nor any more forward to cut off them that sought to abandon the country or wrong the colony. How ingratefully those deserts might be rewarded, envied, or neglected, or his far inferiors preferred to overtop him, I know not, but such occasions might move a saint, much more a man, to an unadvised passionate impatience. But however, it seems he hath been punished for his offenses that was never rewarded for his deserts."

Indeed the offenses have been capital, and the offenders dangerous, incurable members, for no use so fit as to make examples to others.

But the manner of their death, may some object, hath been cruel, unusual, and barbarous; which indeed they have not been, witness France and other countries for less offenses. What if they have been more severe than usual in England, there was just cause for it. We were rather to have regard to those whom we would have terrified and made fearful to commit the like offenses than to the offenders justly condemned; it being true that amongst those people, who for the most part are sensible only of the body's torment, the fear of a cruel, painful, and unusual death more restrains them than death itself.

Thus much obviously I proceed in his endeavors until Sir Thomas Gates his happy arrival, which was only in preparing timber, pales, posts, and rails for the present impaling [of] this new town to secure himself and men from the malice and treachery of the Indians, in the midst and heart of whom he was resolved to set down. But before he could make himself ready for that business, Sir Thomas Gates (though his passage more long than usual) to second him herein happily arrived about the second of August [1611] with six good ships, men, provisions, and cattle; whom, as yet not fully discovered, we supposed to be a Spanish fleet, thus induced the rather to believe because in company with him were three carvals [caravels] (vessels which never before had been sent thither, and now only for the transportation of the cattle).

It did me much good and gave great courage to the whole company to see the resolution of Sir Thomas Dale, now wholly busied (our land fortifications too weak to withstand a foreign enemy) in lading our provisions aboard the two good ships—the *Star* and *Prosperous,* and our own *Deliverance,* then riding before James town—aboard which ships he had resolved to encounter the supposed enemy, animating his people not only with the hope of victory if they readily obeyed his direction, but also assuring them that if by these means God had ordained to set a period to their lives, they could never be sacrificed in a more acceptable service, himself promising rather to fire the Spanish ships with his own than either basely to yield or to be taken. And in nothing he seemed so much discontent as that we could not possibly lade aboard all our provisions before (the wind being then very fair) they might have been with us.

Whilest therefore the rest were laboring their utmost to lade aboard our provisions, he caused a small shallop to be manned with thirty ready and good shot to discover directly what ships they might be, and with all speed to return him certain word; which within three hours they did, assuring him that it was an *English* fleet, Sir Thomas Gates general thereof; which news how welcome it was unto him, principally because now he doubted not the happy progression of the affairs in hand, let any man equally with him affected to the good and welfare of the action judge and determine.

The worthies being met, after salutation and welcome given and received, Sir Thomas Dale acquainted Sir Thomas Gates both with such businesses as he had affected since his arrival, and also of his resolution to build a new town at the Falls; which design and purpose of his Sir Thomas Gates, then principal governor in Virginia, well approving, [he] furnished him with three hundred and fifty men, such as himself made choice of.

And the beginning of September 1611, he set from James town, and in a day and a half landed at a place where he purposed to seat and build; where he had not been ten days before he had very strongly impaled seven English acres of ground for a town which, in honor of the noble Prince Henrie (of ever happy and blessed memory, whose royal heart was ever strongly affected to that action), he called by the name of "Henrico."

No sooner was he thus fenced and in a manner secured from the Indians, but his next work, without respect to his own health or particular welfare, was building at each corner of the town very strong and high commanders, or watchtowers, a fair and handsome church, and storehouses; which finished, he began to think upon convenient houses and lodgings for himself and men, which, with as much speed as was possible, were more strongly and more handsome than any formerly in Virginia contrived and finished; and even in four months' space he had made Henrico much better and of more worth than all the work ever since the colony began therein done.

I should be too tedious if I should give up the account of every day's labor, which therefore I purposely omit, and will only describe the town in the very state and perfection which I left it. And first for the situation: It stands upon a neck of a very high land, 3 parts thereof environed with the main river, and cut over between the two rivers with a strong pale, which maketh the neck of land an island. There is in this town 3 streets of well framed houses, a handsome church, and the foundation of a more stately one laid—of brick, in length an hundred foot, and fifty foot wide—beside storehouses, watchhouses, and suchlike. There are also, as ornaments belonging to this town, upon the verge of this river, five fair blockhouses, or commanders, wherein live the honester sort of people as in farms in England; and there keep continual sentinel for the town's security; and about two miles from the town into the main, a pale of two miles in length, cut over from river to river, guarded likewise with several commanders, with a great quantity of corn ground impaled, sufficient, if there were no more in the colony secured, to maintain with but easy manuring and husbandry more men than I suppose will be addressed thither (the more is the pity) these 3 years.

For the further enlargement yet of this town on the other side of the river, by impaling likewise—for we make no other fence—is secured to our use, especially for our hogs to feed in, about twelve English miles of ground, by name Coxen-Dale, secured by five forts called Hope in Faith, Charity Fort, Mount Malado (a retreat, or guest house, for sick people—a high seat and wholesome air), El[i]zabeth Fort, and Fort Patience.

And here hath Mr. Whitacres chosen his parsonage, or church land, some hundred acres impaled, and a fair framed parsonage house built thereupon called "Rocke Hall." Of this town and all the forts thereunto belonging hath Captain James Davis the principal command and government.

I proceed to our next and most hopeful habitation, whether we respect commodity or security, which we principally aim at, against foreign designs and invasions. I mean the Bermuda City, begun about Christmas last, which because it is the nearest adjoining to Henrico, though the last undertaken, I hold it pertinent to handle in the next place.

This town, or plantation, is seated by land some 5 miles from Henrico (by water fourteen), being the year before the habitation of the Appamatucks, [but] to revenge the treacherous injury of those people done unto us taken from them, besides all their corn—the former before without the loss of any save only some few of those Indians pretending our hurt; at what time Sir Thomas Dale, being himself upon that service, and duly considering how commodious a habitation and seat it might be for us, took resolution to possess and plant it, and at that very instant gave it the name of the new Bermudas; whereunto he hath laid out and annexed, to be belonging to the freedom[1] and corporation forever, many miles of champion and woodland in several hundreds, as the Upper and Nether Hundreds, Rochdale Hundred, West's Sherly Hundred, and Digges his Hundred.

In the Nether Hundred[2] he first began to plant and inhabit, for that there lieth the most convenient quantity of corn ground. And with a pale cut over from river to river about two miles long, we have secur'd some eight miles circuit of ground, the most part champion and exceeding good corn ground; upon which pale and round about upon the verge of the river in this hundred half a mile distant from each other are very fair houses already builded, besides divers other particular[3] men's houses, not so few as fifty, according to the conditions of the patent granted them; which whoso pleaseth to peruse shall in the end of my discourse find it inserted.[4] In this plantation, next to Sir Thomas Dale is principal in the command Captain Georg Yardley, Sir Thomas Gates his lieutenant, whose endeavors have ever deserved worthy commendations in that employment.

Rochdale Hundred by a cross-pale well-nigh four miles long is also already impaled, with bordering houses all along the pale, in which hundred our hogs and other cattle have twenty miles circuit to graze in securely, the undertaking of the chief city deferred till their harvest

---

[1] Franchise.

[2] Nether Hundred was called Bermuda Hundred.

[3] Privately owned.

[4] None ever was.

be in, which once reaped, all hands shall be employed thereon; which Sir Thomas Dale purposeth; and he may with some labor effect his designs to make an impregnable retreat against any foreign invasion, how powerful soever.

About fifty miles from this seat on the other side of the rivers is James town situate upon a goodly and fertile island which, although formerly scandaled with unhealthful air, we have since approved[1] as healthful as any other place in the country. And this I can say by mine own experience that that corn and garden ground, which with much labor (being when we first seated upon it a thick wood) we have cleared and impaled, is as fertile as any other we have had experience and trial of. The town itself by the care and providence of Sir Thomas Gates, who for the most part had his chiefest residence there, is reduced into a handsome form and hath in it two fair rows of houses, all of framed timber, two stories, and an upper garret, or corn loft, high, besides three large and substantial storehouses joined together in length some hundred and twenty foot, and in breadth forty. And this town hath been lately newly and strongly impaled, and a fair platform for ordnance in the west bulwark raised. There are also without this town in the island some very pleasant and beautiful houses, two blockhouses to observe and watch lest the Indians at any time should swim over the back river and come into the island, and certain other farm houses. The command and government of this town hath Master John Scarpe, lieutenant to Captain Francis West, brother to the Right Honorable the Lord Lawarre.

From James town downwards some forty and odd miles at the mouth of the river near Point Comfort upon Kecoughtan are two pleasant and commodious forts—Henrie and Charles, goodly seats, and much corn ground about them, abounding with the commodities of fish, fowl, deer, and fruits, whereby the men live there with half that maintenance out of the store which in other places is allowed. Certainly this habitation would be no whit inferior to the best we have there, save as yet with the poor means we have we cannot secure it if a foreign enemy, as we have just cause to expect daily, should attempt it. And of these forts Captain Georg Web was

[1] Proved.

lately establish'd the principal commander.

It hath been our greatest care and labor hitherto, and yet but these three years (the former four merely misspent) to compass these businesses, which, being thus settled and brought to such perfection as I have described, now doth the time approach that commodity may be expected, and if means be sent over will assuredly be returned. What honest spirit, having hitherto labored herein, would at the upshot (as I may so term it) be discouraged or desist? I hope none. Rather, more will be animated, if need require, to put to their helping hands and purses.

And even thus I have shadowed I hope, without the guilt of tedious or prolix discourses, as I have been able, the *true condition* (though many circumstances omitted) of Virginia. What may the substance be when the external show is so forward!—so *glorious!?*

I have purposely omitted the relation of the country commodities, which every former treatise hath abundantly: the hope of the better mines, the more base, as iron, alum, and suchlike—perfectly discovered and made trial of. And surely of these things I cannot make so ample relation as others who in the discovery of those affairs have been than myself more often conversant. Only of the hopeful and merchantable commodities of tobacco, silk grass, and silkworms I dare thus much affirm.

And first of tobacco, whose goodness mine own experience and trial induces me to be such that no country under the sun may, or doth, afford more pleasant, sweet, and strong tobacco than I have tasted there, even of mine own planting; which, howsoever being then the first year of our trial thereof, we had not the knowledge to cure and make up; yet are there some now resident there, out of the last year's well observed experience, which both know and, I doubt not, will make and return such tobacco this year that even England shall acknowledge the goodness thereof.

Now I proceed to the silk grass which groweth like unto our flax. I mean not of that kind formerly sent over I have seen, [but] even of the natural and wild plants which Captain Martin, who much delighteth in those businesses, hath made exceeding fine and exceeding strong silk. And himself hath replanted many of the wild plants this year, the silk whereof he purposeth to return for trial.

The silkworms sent thither from England in seeds the last winter came forth many of them the beginning of March, others in April, May, and June, thousands of them grown to great bigness, and a-spinning, and the rest well thriving. Of their increase and commodity well known to be reaped by them, we have almost assurance, since sure I am no country affordeth more store of mulberry trees or a kind with whose leaf they more delight or thrive better.

It may be here happily expected that I should give up the relation of Captain Argall's particular voyages and endeavors, and even as in a plat demonstrate his nor'ward discoveries; from which business I desire to be excused, partly because himself is best able to make his own relations, and partly because my home employments would not permit me leisure to accompany him, though myself desirous, in any of his voyages; whose endeavors, if I should endeavor to make known and publish, could receive no honor at all by my commendations or descriptions. Much might they be impaired through my ignorance or unskillfulness to set them forth. Yet cannot I omit to publish to the world what present relief he hath done to the colony, furnishing us by two trading voyages with three and twenty hundred bushels of corn into our store delivered, beside what he reserved for his men's provision, what he bestowed upon well-deservers, and what his men appropriated.

I pass by the benefit of peace in those parts by reason of his captive Pochahuntas, concluded established, and will only name the commodity by his means done unto us in repairing of our weather-beaten boats, and furnishing us with new, both strong and useful, without whose assistance herein, unless we should have omitted other necessary employments, I see not how we should have had passage one to another.

His nor'ward discoveries towards Sacadehoc, and beyond to Portroyall, Sancta Crux, and thereabout, may not be concealed; in which his adventures, if he had brought home no commodity to the colony—which yet he did very much, both of apparel, victuals, and many other necessaries—the honor which he hath done unto our nation by displanting the French, there beginning to seat and fortify within our limits, and taking off their ship and pinnace, which he brought to James Town, would have been reward enough for his pains, and will ever speak loud his honor and approved valor.

I have heard it credibly reported even from the mouth of Captain Argall that in one small ship and in one voyage the French have cleared eight thousand pounds by trade with the Indians for furs—which benefit will be as easily by us procured.

It is true the savages there inhabiting before Captain Argall's arrival esteemed the French as demigods and had them in great estimation; but seeing them vanquished and overcome by us, forsook them, yea—which is no mean point of policy—desired our friendship, telling Captain Argall that he had undone them forever, for that the French by yearly trade with them for furs furnished them with many necessaries whereof they had great want; which trade by this means might happily be hindered. But Captain Argall hath agreed with them to reserve their furs for him, and promised them once a year to come thither and truck with them. They seemed very well content, assuring him that though the French should at any time arrive there and proffer them trade, they would reserve all their furs for him. And what profit by this means only may be returned to the Virginia adventurers I submit to Captain Argall's own opinion and judgment.

I purposely omitted one thing in the treatise of our concluded peace wherewith I intend to conclude my discourse (which already I have drawn to a longer period than I purposed) whereby we have gathered the better assurance of their honest inward intentions, and this it is:

It pleased Sir Thomas Dale—myself being much desirous before my return for England to visit Powhatan and his court because I would be able to speak somewhat thereof by mine own knowledge—to employ myself and an English boy for my interpreter, one Thomas Salvage, who had lived three years with Powhatan, and speaks the language naturally, one whom Powhatan much affecteth—upon a message unto him, which was to deal with him if by any means I might procure a daughter of his who [might serve] (Pochahuntas being already in our possession is generally reported to be his delight and darling, and surely he esteemeth her as his own soul) for surer pledge of peace.

I departed the fifteenth of May, early in the morning, with the English boy and two Indian guides from the Bermudas, and came to his court or residence—as I judge some threescore miles distant from us, being seated at the head almost of Pamaunkie River at a town called Matchcot—the next night after, about twelve of the clock, the former night lodging in the open woods fearless[1] and without danger. When we were come opposite to his town—the main river between him and us lest at any time we should march by land unto him undiscovered—my Indian guides called for a canoa (a boat made only of one tree, after the fashion of a hollow trough) to transport us, giving them to know that there was two English sent upon business to Powhatan from the English weroance; which once known, a canoa was presently sent and we ferried over, Powhatan himself attending at the landing place to welcome us.

His first salutation was to the boy, whom he very well rememb'red, after this manner: "My child, you are welcome; you have been a stranger to me these four years, at what time I gave you leave to go to Paspahae" (for so was James town called before our seating there) "to see your friends, and till now you never returned. You" (said he) "are my child by the donative of Captain Newport in lieu of one of my subjects, Namontacke, who I purposely sent to King James his land to see him and his country, and to return me the true report thereof. He as yet is not returned, though many ships have arrived here from thence since that time. How ye have dealt with him I know not."

Having thus ended his speech to him, he addressed himself to me, and his first salutation, without any words at all, was about my neck, and with his hand he feeled round about it, so as I might have imagined he would have cut my throat but that I knew he durst not. He asked me where the chain of pearl was; I demanded what chain; "That," said he, "which I sent my brother Sir Thomas Dale for a present at his first arrival; which chain, since the peace concluded, he sent me word [that] if he sent any Englishman upon occasion of

[1] Undisturbed.

business to me, he should wear about his neck; otherwise I had order from him to bind him and send him home again." It is true Sir Thomas Dale had sent him such word (which till then myself never heard of) and for this purpose had given his page order to deliver me the said chain, who forgot it.

I was doubtful at the first how to answer him; yet presently I replied that I was not ignorant of that message from his brother, formerly sent unto him, whereby he only intended that if upon extraordinary and sudden occasion he should be constrained to send an Englishman unto him without an Indian guide, then, in testimony that he sent him, he should wear the chain about his neck. But in case any of his own people should conduct any English unto him, as did me two of his own men—one of them a councilor unto him, who was acquainted with my business—their testimony should be sufficient, and the chain then needless to be worn; which answer pleased him well, and forthwith he brought us to his house, not full a stone's cast from the waterside; whereinto being come, himself sat down on his bedstead side (bed there was none more than a single mat). On each hand of him was placed a comely and personable young woman, not twenty years old the eldest, which they call his "queens" —the house within round about beset with them, the outside guarded with an hundred bowmen with their quivers of arrows at their backs, which at all times and places attend his person.

The first thing he offered us was a pipe of tobacco, which they call *pissimore*, whereof himself first drank and then gave it me. And when I had drank what I pleased I returned his pipe, which with his own hands he vouchsafed to take from me.

Then began he to inquire how his brother Sir Thomas Dale fared; after that of his daughter's welfare, her marriage, his unknown son,[1] and how they liked, lived, and loved together. I resolved him that his brother was very well, and his daughter so well content that she would not change her life to return and live with him, whereat he laughed heartily, and said he was very glad of it.

"Now proceed," said he, "to deliver the cause of your unexpected coming."

---

[1] Thomas Rolfe, the newborn son he had never seen.

I certified him my message was private, to be delivered to himself without the presence of any save one of his councilors: by name Pepaschicher, one of my guides, who was acquainted with my business. He instantly commanded all, both men and women, out of the house, his two queens only excepted, who upon no occasion whatsoever may sequester themselves. "Now," said he, "speak on," and myself by my interpreter thus begun:

"Sir Thomas Dale, your brother, the principal commander of the Englishmen, sends you greeting of love and peace on his part inviolable, and hath in testimony thereof by me sent you a worthy present, *vid[elicet],* two large pieces of copper, five strings of white and blue beads, five wooden combs, ten fishhooks, and a pair of knives," all which I delivered him, one thing after another, that he might have time to view each particular. "He willed me also to certify you that when you pleased to send men he would give you a great grinding stone."

My message and gift hitherto pleased him; I proceeded thus: "The bruit of the exquisite perfection of your youngest daughter, being famous through all your territories, hath come to the hearing of your brother Sir Thomas Dale, who for this purpose hath addressed me hither to entreat you by that brotherly friendship you make profession of to permit her with me to return unto him, partly for the desire which himself hath, and partly for the desire her sister hath to see her, of whom, if fame hath not been prodigal, as like enough it hath not, your brother by your favor would gladly make his nearest companion, wife, and bedfellow—" (many times he would have interrupted my speech, which I entreated him to hear out and then if he pleased to return me answer) "—and the reason hereof is because being now friendly and firmly united together and made one people (as he supposeth and believes), in the band of love he would make a natural union between us principally because himself hath taken resolution to dwell in your country so long as he liveth, and would therefore not only have the firmest assurance he may of perpetual friendship from you but also hereby bind himself thereunto."

When I had thus made an end of speaking (the sooner by his often interruption) I had no need to require his answer, which readily and with no less gravity he returned thus:

"I gladly accept your king's salute of love and peace, which while I live I shall exactly, both myself and my subjects, maintain and conserve. His pledges thereof I receive with no less thanks, albeit they are not so ample—howbeit himself a greater weroance—as formerly Captain Newport, whom I very well love, was accustomed to gratify me with. But to the purpose: My daughter whom my brother desireth I sold within these few days to be wife to a great weroance for two bushels of *roanoake*" (a small kind of beads made of oyster shells, which they use and pass one to another as we do money, a cubit's length valuing sixpence), "and it is true she is already gone with him three days' journey from me."

I replied that I knew his greatness and power to be such that if he pleased herein to gratify his brother, he might—restoring the roanoake without the imputation of injustice—take home his daughter again, the rather because she was not full twelve years old and therefore not marriageable, assuring him, beside the band of peace so much the firmer, he should have treble the price of his daughter in beads, copper, hatchets, and many other things more useful for him.

His answer hereunto was that he loved his daughter as dear as his own life, and though he had many children, he delighted in none so much as in her, whom if he should not often behold, he could not possibly live, which she living with us he knew he could not, having with himself resolved upon no terms whatsoever to put himself into our hands or come amongst us; and therefore entreated me to urge that suit no further, but return his brother this answer:

"I desire no firmer assurance of his friendship than his promise which he hath already made unto me. From me he hath a pledge: one of my daughters, which so long as she lives shall be sufficient. When she dieth, he shall luring[1] have another child of mine. But she yet liveth. I hold it not a brotherly part of your king to desire to bereave me of two of my children at once.

"Further give him to understand that if he had no pledge at all, he should not need to distrust any injury from me or any under my

[1] Hamor inserts this word somewhere after *he* in the sentence, from his table of errata. Meaning?

subjection. There have been too many of his men and my killed, and by my occasion there shall never be more. I, which have power to perform it, have said it: no, not though I should have just occasion offered, for I am now old and would gladly end my days in peace. So as if the English offer me injury, my country is large enough; I will remove myself farther from you. Thus much I hope will satisfy my brother. Now, because yourselves are weary and I sleepy, we will thus end the discourse of this business"; then called to one of his men and willed him to get some bread for us, himself the meanwhile telling us that they not expecting our coming, as usually they do eat up all their other victuals.

Presently the bread was brought in two great wooden bowls: the quantity of a bushel sod bread made up round, of the bigness of a tennis ball, whereof we ate some few and disposed the rest to many of his hungry guard which attended about us. When we had eaten, he caused to be fetched a great glass of sack, some three quarts or better, which Captain Newport had given him five or seven years since, carefully preserved by him, not much above a pint in all this time spent; and gave each of us in a great oyster shell some three spoonfuls; and so giving order to one of his people to appoint us a house to lodge in, took his leave for that night, and we departed.

We had not been half an hour in the house before the fleas began so to torment us that we could not rest there but went forth and under a broad oak upon a mat reposed ourselves that night.

No sooner were we awake and up in the morning but Powhatan himself came to us and asked us how we fared, and immediately led us to his house, where was provided for our breakfast a great bowl of Indian peas and beans boiled together, and as much bread as might have sufficed a dozen hungry men; about an hour after boiled fresh fish, and not long after that roasted oysters, *crevises* and crabs, his men in this time being abroad a-hunting, some venison, others turkeys and suchlike beasts and fowl as their woods afford; who returned before ten of the clock with three does and a buck (very good and fat venison), and two great cock turkeys, all which were dressed that day; and supper ended, scarce a bone to be seen.

Whiles I yet remained there, by great chance came an Englishman thither, almost three years before that time surprised as he was at work near Fort Henrie—one William Parker, grown so like both in complexion and habit to the Indians that I only knew him by his tongue to be an Englishman. He seemed very joyful so happily to meet me there. Of him, when we often inquired, the Indians ever told us that he fell sick and died, which till now we believed. He entreated me to use my best endeavors to procure his return, which thing I was purposed so soon as I knew him, and immediately went with him to Powhatan and told him that we credibly believed that he was dead, but since it was otherwise I must needs have him home, for myself of necessity must acquaint his brother that I had seen him there, who, if he returned not, would make another voyage thither purposely for him.

Powhatan seemed very much discontent, and thus replied: "You have one of my daughters with you, and I am therewith well content. But you can no sooner see or know of any Englishman's being with me but you must have him away or else break peace and friendship. If you must needs have him, he shall go with you. But I will send no guides along with you, so as if any ill befall you by the way, thank yourselves."

I answered that rather than I would go without him I would go alone; the way I knew well enough, and other dangers I feared not, since if I returned not safely, he must expect our revenge upon him and his people; giving him further to know that his brother, our king, might have just occasion to distrust his love to him by his slight respect of me if he returned me home without guides.

He replied not hereunto, but in passion and discontentment went from me, not till supper time speaking anymore unto me; when sending for me, he gave me share of such cates as were for himself provided, and [was of] as good aspect and countenance as before; but not a word concerning my return till himself at midnight, coming to me and the boy where we lay, awaked us and told me that Pepaschechar and another of his men in the morning should accompany us home, earnestly requesting me to remember his brother to send him these particulars: ten pieces of copper, a shaving knife, an iron froe to cleave boards, a grinding stone not so big but four or five men may carry it, which would be big enough for his use; two bone combs such as Captain Newport had given him (the wooden ones his own men can make); an hundred fishhooks or, if he could spare it, rather a fishing seine; and a cat, and a dog—with which things, if his brother would furnish him, he would requite his love with the return of skins, wherewith he was now altogether "unfurnished," as he told me, which yet I knew he was well stored with, but his disposition, mistrustful and jealous, loves to be on the surer hand.

When he had delivered this his message, he asked me if I will [have] rememb'red every particular, which I must repeat to him for his assurance. And yet still doubtful that I might forget any of them, he bade me write them down in such a table-book as he showed me, which was a very fair one. I desired him, it being of no use to him, to give it me, but he told me it did him much good to show it to strangers which came unto him. So in mine own table-book I wrote down each particular. And he departed.

In the morning, himself and we were timely stirring to be gone. To breakfast first we went, with a good boiled turkey; which ended, he gave us a whole turkey besides that we left, and three baskets of bread to carry us home. And when we were ready to depart, he gave each of us an excellent buck's skin very well dressed and white as snow, and sent his son and daughter each of them one, demanding if I well rememb'red his answer to his brother, which I repeated to him. "I hope," said he, "this will give him good satisfaction. If it do not, I will go three days' journey farther from him, and never see Englishman more. If upon any other occasion he send to me again, I will gladly entertain his messengers and to my power accomplish his just requests." And even thus himself conducting us to the waterside, he took leave of us, and we of him. And about ten of the clock the next night after, we were come to the Bermudas.

This discourse I have briefly as I could, and as the matter would permit, the rather related to make known how chary[1] Powhatan is of the conservation of peace—a thing much desired, and I doubt not right welcome news to the undertakers here—as may appear by his answers to my requests, and also by my safe passage thither and homewards without the least show of injury off'red unto us, though

[1] Diligent.

divers times by the way many straggling Indians met us which in former times would gladly have taken so fair occasion to work their mischief and bloody designs upon us.

By all which, as likewise by our forward progression in our affairs, I hope such good success and benefit to be speedily reaped, that myself—though I bless GOD for it, who hath so provided for me that I may live more happily here than many who are fearful to adventure thither—could even willingly make a third voyage thither if by my poor endeavors the business might receive the least furtherance.[1]

God, I hope, will raise up means beyond man's imagination to perfect His own glory and honor in the conversion of those people, of whom undoubtedly, as in all other parts in the world, He hath predestinated some to eternal salvation; and blessed shall those be that are the instruments thereof!

I hope this poor narration will move every honest heart to put his helping hand thereunto. For my part, as I have been five years a personal workman in that building, so shall I ever as my means may permit me be ready to offer my mite towards the furnishing of others, and again, if need require, personally labor therein.

To the Reader—

THERE BE TWO PROPERTIES especially remarkable which should move all men earnestly and constantly with all their means and endeavor to desire the achieving of anything and bringing of the same unto perfection: first, the worth and excellency, secondly, the durableness and continuance thereof. For as that thing which is not durable by reason of fragility and fugacity is not usually esteemed of men, though it be excellent, so that likewise which is not precious is worthily little regarded, though it be never so durable. Now the

---

[1] In fact Hamor returned to Virginia in May 1617.

Virginian plantation hath both these notable properties, if at the least we will and impeach them not ourselves.

For what is more excellent, more precious, and more glorious than to convert a heathen nation from worshiping the devil to the saving knowledge and true worship of God in Christ Jesus? What more praiseworthy and charitable than to bring a savage people from barbarism unto civility? What more honorable unto our country than to reduce a far-disjoined foreign nation under the due obedience of our dread sovereign, the King's Majesty? What more convenient than to have good seats abroad for our ever-flowing multitudes of people at home? What more profitable than to purchase great wealth, which most nowadays gape after overgreedily? All which benefits are assuredly to be had and obtained by well and plentifully upholding of the plantation in Virginia.

And for the durableness of all these great and singular blessings there can by God's assistance be no doubt at all made, if men's hearts unto whom God hath lent ability were but enlarged cheerfully to adventure and send good companies of honest industrious men thither with a mind to enlarge Christ's kingdom. For then will God assuredly maintain His own cause.

But alas, as there was never yet any action so good, so honorable, so glorious, so pious, and so profitable but hath had checks and discouragements both by open enemies abroad and intestine adversaries at home within it own bowels, even so, may I truly say, hath this most glorious, most honorable, most pious, and most profitable enterprise had. For as of old, when Zerubbabel, Ezra, and Nehemiah returned from Babel by allowance of the King of Persia to Jerusalem, and began to repair the walls thereof, and to restore God's service, there wanted not a Sanballat and others to say, "What do these weak Jews? Will they fortify themselves? Will they sacrifice? Will they finish it in a day? No, for although they build, yet if a fox go up, he shall even break down that stony wall."[1] Even so deal many Sanballats and Tobiahs, foreign and domestical enemies of this most religious work.

Yea, there be many who will not seem enemies thereunto, but yet

---

[1] cf. Nehemiah 4:2, 3.

will neither further the business themselves, no, not according to their own engagements, which in conscience and credit they ought, nor quietly suffer others that otherwise would, but discourage them therein all they may, some saying as Judah once did, "The strength of the bearers is weakened, and there is much earth, so as we are not able to build the wall."[1] [And] some saying with the unfaithful spies sent forth to search the land of Canaan, "The land we went through to search it out is a land that eateth up the inhabitants thereof, for all the people we saw in it are strong, and men of great stature."[2]

Yea, and some others say there is much already expended and yet no profit ariseth; neither is there victuals to be had for the preserving of life and soul together. But, O my dear countrymen, be not so far bewitched herewith as to be still discouraged thereat, for those that bring a vild slander upon this action may die by a plague before the Lord, as those men did. But rather rememb'ring your ancient worth, renown, valor, and bounty, hearken unto Caleb and Joshua, who stilled the people's mourning, saying, "Let us go up at once and possess it, for undoubtedly we shall overcome it."[3] Yet not so much now by force of arms as the Israelites did than by warrant from God; nor by utterly destroying of them, as some have cruelly done since, as by gentleness, love, amity, and religion.

As for profit, it shall come abundantly if we can with the husbandman but freely cast our corn into the ground, and with patience wait for a blessing. And of victuals, there is now no complaint at all, and that which was hap'ned by the mere lazy negligence of our own people.

Now to the end that you may the better perceive these things to be true, and be thereby the more animated cheerfully to go forward in the upholding of this holy work, I will no longer detain you from the perusal of some Calebs' and Joshuas' faithful reports writ there in June last this present year 1614, and sent hither by the last ship that came thence—for further encouragement to put hereunto speedily and plentifully your helping hands with all alacrity. As for them that are able and yet will not further but endanger the utter ruining of this

---

[1] v. 10.
[2] cf. Numbers 13:32.
[3] cf. Numbers 13:30.

so glorious a cause—by their miserableness,[1] being without love and charity, to the great dishonor of God and our country's perpetual shame should it now sink and fall to the ground!—I leave them to Him that made them, to dispose of them according to His infinite wisdom; and so come to the letters themselves, the first and chiefest whereof is from Sir Thomas Dale, marshal and governor of Virginia, unto a minister of London.

TO THE R[EVEREND] AND MY MOST ESTEEMED FRIEND, MR. D. M. AT HIS HOUSE AT F. CH. IN LONDON.

RIGHT REVEREND SIR—By Sir Thomas Gates I wrote unto you of such occasions as then presented themselves, and now again by this worthy gentleman, Captain Argall, I salute you. For such is the reverend regard I have of you as I cannot omit any occasion to express the sincere affection I bear you. You have ever given me encouragements to persevere in this religious warfare until your last letters—not for that you are now less well affected thereunto, but because you see the action to be in danger by many of their non-performances who undertook the business.

I have undertaken, and have as faithfully and with all my might endeavored, the prosecution with all alacrity, as God that knoweth the heart can bear me record, what recompense or what rewards, by whom or when I know not where to expect, but from Him in whose vineyard I labor, whose church with greedy appetite I desire to erect. My glorious master[2] is gone that would have enameled with his favors the labors I undertake for God's cause and his immortal honor. He was the great captain of our Israel, the hope to have builded up this heavenly New Jerusalem. He interred (I think) the whole frame of this business [when he] fell into his grave. For most men's forward (at least seeming so) desires are quenched, and Virginia stands in desperate hazard. You there do your duties; I will no

[1] Miserliness.
[2] Prince Henry (margin note)

LIBRARY OF VIRGINIA

HENRY STUART, PRINCE OF WALES
(1594-1612)

way omit mine.

The time I promised to labor is expired. It is not a yoke of oxen hath drawn me from this feast; it is not the marriage of a wife makes me haste home, though that salad give an appetite to cause me return. But I have more care of the stock than to set it upon a die, and rather put myself to the courtesy of noble and worthy censures than ruin this work; and have a jury—nay, a million!—of foul-mouthed detractors scan upon my endeavors, the ends whereof they cannot dive into. You shall briefly understand what hath betide since my last, and how we now stand and are likely to grow to perfection if we be not altogether neglected; my stay grounded upon such reason as had I now returned, it would have hazarded the ruin of all.

Sir Thomas Gates having embarked himself for England, I put myself into Captain Argall's ship; with a hundred and fifty men in my frigate and other boats, went into Pamaunkie River where Powhatan hath his residence, and can in two or three days draw a thousand men together. With me I carried his daughter,[1] who had been long prisoner with us. It was a day or two before we heard of them. At length they demanded why we came; I gave for answer that I came to bring him his daughter, conditionally he would—as had been agreed upon for her ransom—render all the arms, tools, swords, and men (that had run away), and give me a ship full of corn for the wrong he had done unto us. If they would do this, we would be friends; if not, burn all.

They demanded time to send to their king. I assented—I taking, they receiving, two pledges to carry my message to Powhatan. All night my two men lay not far from the waterside. About noon the next day, they told them the great king was three days' journey off, that Opochankano was hard by, to whom they would have had them deliver their message, saying that what he agreed upon and did the great king would confirm. This Opocankano is brother to Powhatan, and is his and their chief captain, and one that can as soon (if not sooner) as Powhatan command the men. But my men refused to do my message unto any save Powhatan. So they were brought back,

[1] Pocahontas.

and I sent theirs to them. They told me that they would fetch Simons to me, who had thrice play'd the runagate, whose lies and villainy much hind'red our trade for corn. But they delayed us so as we went ashore they shot at us. We were not behindhand with them: killed some, hurt others, marched into the land, burnt their houses, took their corn, and quartered all night ashore.

The next day we went further up the river. They dogged us and called to know whither we went. We answered to burn all if they would not do as we demanded and had been agreed upon. They would, they said, bring all the next day. So we forbare all hostility, went ashore, their men in good numbers coming amongst us. But we were very cautious and stood to our arms.

The king's daughter went ashore, but would not talk to any of them, scarce to them of the best sort, and to them only that if her father had loved her, he would not value her less than old swords, pieces, or axes; wherefore she would still dwell with the Englishmen, who loved her.

At last came one from Powhatan, who told us that Simons was run away to Nonsowhaticond[1]—which was a truth, as afterwards appeared; but that the other Englishman was dead, that proved a lie, for, since, Mr. Hamor, whom I employed to Powhatan, brought him to me—our pieces, swords, and tools within fifteen days should be sent to James town with some corn, and that his daughter should be my child and ever dwell with me, desiring to be ever friends; and named such of his people and neighbor kings as he desired to be included and have the benefit of the peace, promising if any of our men came to him without leave from me, he would send them back; and that if any of his men stole from us or killed our cattle, he would send them to us to be punished as we thought fit.

With these conditions we returned, and within the time limited part of our arms were sent and 20 men with corn, and promised more, which he hath also sent.

Opachankano desired I would call him friend and that he might call me so, saying he was a great captain and did always fight; that I was also a great captain, and therefore he loved me, and that my

[1] Nandtaughtacund on the upper Rappahannock River?

friends should be his friends. So the bargain was made, and every eight or ten days I have messages and presents from him, with many appearances that he much desireth to continue friendship.

Now may you judge, sir, if the God of battles have not a helping hand in this, that having our swords drawn, killing their men, burning their houses, and taking their corn, yet they tend'red us peace, and strive with all alacrity to keep us in good opinion of them, by which many benefits arise unto us. First, part of our arms, disgracefully lost long ago, kept by the savages as monuments and trophies of our shames, redelivered—some repair to our honor; our cattle to increase without danger of destroying; our men at liberty to hunt freely for venison, to fish, to do anything else, or go any whither without danger; to follow the husbanding of their corn securely, whereof we have above five hundred acres set and, God be praised, in more forwardness than any of the Indians' that I have seen or heard of this year; roots and herbs we have in abundance. All doubt of want is by God's blessing quite vanished, and much plenty expected. And which is not the least material, we may by this peace come to discover the country better, both by our own travels and by the relation of the savages, as we grow in familiarity with them.

Powhatan's daughter I caused to be carefully instructed in Christian religion, who after she had made some good progress therein renounced publicly her country idolatry, openly confessed her Christian faith, was as she desired baptized, and is since married to an English gentleman of good understanding, as by his letter unto me containing the reasons for his marriage of her you may perceive, another knot to bind this peace the stronger. Her father and friends gave approbation to it, and her uncle gave her to him in the church. She lives civilly and lovingly with him, and I trust will increase in goodness as the knowledge of God increaseth in her. She will go into England with me, and were it but the gaining of this one soul, I will think my time, toil, and present stay well spent.

Since this accident, the governors and people of Checkahomanies, who are five hundred bowmen and better, a stout and warlike nation, have made means to have us come unto them and conclude a peace where all the governors would meet me. They having thus three or four times importuned me, I resolved to go. So, taking Captain Argall with fifty men in my frigate and barge, I went thither. Captain Argall with forty men landed; I kept aboard for some reasons.

Upon the meeting, they told Captain Argall they had longed to be friends, that they had no king but eight great men who govern'd them. He told them that we came to be friends, asked them if they would have King James to be their king, and whether they would be his men. They after some conference between themselves seemed willing of both, demanding if we would fight against their enemies. He told them that if any did them injury, they should send me word, and I would agree them[1]; or if their adversaries would not, then I would let them have as many men as they would to help them. They liked well of that, and told him that all their men should help us. All this being agreed upon, Captain Argall gave every councilor a *tamahawk* and a piece of copper, which was kindly taken. They requested further that if their boats should happen to meet with our boats, and that they said they were the "Chikahominy Englishmen" and King James his men, we would let them pass. We agreed unto it, so that they pronounced themselves "Englishmen" and "King James his men," promising within fifteen days to come unto James town to see me and conclude these conditions; every bowman being to give me as a tribute to King James two measures of corn every harvest, the two measures containing two bushels and a half; and I to give every bowman a small tamahawke, and to every councilor a suit of red cloth, which did much please them. This people never acknowledged any king before, no, nor ever would acknowledge Powhatan for their king—a stout people they be, and a delicate seat they have.

Now, sir, you see our conditions, you and all worthy men may judge whether it would not be a grief to see these fair hopes frost-bitten and these fresh budding plants to wither, which had I returned had assuredly followed. For here is no one that the people

---

[1] Make peace between them.

would have to govern them but myself. For I had now come away had I not found a general desire in the best sort to return for England —letter upon letter, request upon request from their friends to return —so as I knew not upon whom to confer the care of this business in my absence. Whom I thought fit was generally distasted.[1] So as seeing the eminent ensuing danger should I have left this multitude not yet fully refined, I am resolved to stay till harvest be got in, and then settle things according to my poor understanding, and return—if in the interim there come no authorized governor from England.

Consider, I pray you, since things be brought to this pass as you see, and that I should have come away: If then (through their factions, humors, mutinies, or indiscretion of the chiefs I had left behind) this should fall to ruin, I then should receive the imputation, I incur the blame, for quitting the plantation, although I might do it both with my honor (my promised stay of time being expired) and having warrant from my sovereign the King's Majesty. But the precedent reasons moved me, and that this action of such price, such excellency, and assured profit (to mine own knowledge), should not die to the scorn of our nation, and to give cause of laughter to the Papists that desire our ruin.

I can assure you no country of the world affords more assured hopes of infinite riches, which both by mine own people's discovery and the relation of such savages whose fidelity we have often found assureth me.

Oh, why should so many princes and noblemen engage themselves, and thereby intermeddling herein have caused a number of souls transport themselves and be transported hither? Why should they (I say) relinquish this so glorious an action? For if their ends be to build God a church, they ought to persevere. If otherwise, yet their honor engageth them to be constant, howsoever they stand affected. Here is enough to content them: Let their ends be either for God or Mammon.

These things have animated me to stay for a little season, to leave those I am tied in conscience to return unto, to leave the assured benefits of my other fortunes, the sweet society of my friends and

[1] Averse.

acquaintance with all mundal delights, and reside here with much turmoil, which I will constantly do rather than see God's glory diminished, my king and country dishonored, and these poor people I have the charge of ruined.

And so I beseech you to answer for me, if you hear me taxed for my staying, as some may justly do; and that these are my chief motives, God I take to witness.

`Remember me and the cause I have in hand in your daily meditations, and reckon me in the number of those that do sincerely love you and yours, and will ever rest in all offices of a friend to do you service.

From James town in Virginia, the 18 of June, 1614.

THOMAS DALE.

TO MY VERY DEAR AND LOVING COUSIN M[ASTER] G[OUGE], MINISTER OF THE B[LACK] F[RIARS] IN LONDON.

SIR—The colony here is much better. Sir Thomas Dale, our religious and valiant governor, hath now brought that to pass which never before could be effected. For by war upon our enemies and kind usage of our friends, he hath brought them to seek for peace of us, which is made, and they dare not break.

But that which is best, one Pocahuntas, or Matoa[ka], the daughter of Powhatan, is married to an honest and discreet English gentleman, Master Rolfe; and that after she had openly renounced her country idolatry, confessed the faith of Jesus Christ, and was baptized—which thing Sir Thomas Dale had labored a long time to ground in her.

Yet notwithstanding are the virtuous deeds of this worthy knight much debased by the letters which some wicked men have written from hence, and especially by one C. L. If you hear any condemn this noble knight, or do fear to come hither, for those slanderous letters, you may upon my word boldly reprove them. You know that no malefactors can abide the face of the judge, but themselves, scorning to be reproved, do prosecute with all hatred all those that labor their amendment. I marvel much that any men of honest life should fear the sword of the magistrate which is unsheathed only in their defense.

But I much more muse* that so few of our English ministers that were so hot against[1] the supplies and subscription come hither where neither spoken of. Do they not either willfully hide their talents or keep themselves at home for fear of losing a few pleasures? Be there not any amongst them of Moses his mind and of the Apostles' that forsook all to follow Christ? But I refer them to the Judge of all hearts, and to the King that shall reward everyone according to the gain of his talent.[2]

But you, my cousin, hold fast that which you have, and I, though my promise of 3 years' service to my country be expired, will* abide in my vocation here until I be lawfully called from hence.

And so betaking us all unto the mercies of God in Christ Jesus, I rest forever (Virginia, June 18, 1614)

Your most dear and loving cousin,
ALEX[ANDER] WHITAKERS.

---

[1] In favor of.

[2] Whitaker himself had given up a comfortable existence.

* Hamor's *Discourse* had a second printing in the same year which varied from the first only in substituting this passage between the asterisks after "But I much more muse" and "will" in the next paragraph:

> Sir Thomas Dale, with whom I am, is a man of great knowledge in divinity and of a good conscience in all his doings, both which be rare in a martial man. Every Sabbath day we preach in the forenoon and catechize in the afternoon. Every Saturday night I exercise in Sir Thomas Dale's house. Our church affairs be consulted on by the minister and four of the most religious men. Once every month we have a communion, and once a year a solemn fast. For me, though my promise of three years' service to my country be expired, yet I will, etc....

The copy of the gentleman's letters to Sir Thomas Dale, that after married Powhatan's daughter, containing the reasons moving him thereunto.

HONORABLE SIR, AND MOST WORTHY GOVERNOR—When your leisure shall best serve you to peruse these lines, I trust in God the beginning will not strike you into a greater admiration than the end will give you good content. It is a matter of no small moment concerning my own particular which here I impart unto you, and which toucheth me so nearly as the tenderness of my salvation, howbeit, I freely subject myself to your grave and mature judgment, deliberation, approbation, and determination, assuring myself of your zealous admonitions and godly comforts—either persuading me to desist or encouraging me to persist therein with a religious fear and godly care, for which, from the very instant that this began to root itself within the secret bosom of my breast, my daily and earnest prayers have been, still are, and ever shall be proved forthwith as sincere a godly zeal[1] as I possibly may, to be directed, aided, and governed in all my thoughts, words, and deeds to the glory of God; and for my eternal consolation to persevere wherein I never had more need nor till now could ever imagine to have been moved with the like occasion.

But my case standing as it doth, what better worldly refuge can I here seek than to shelter myself under the safety of your favorable protection? And did not my case[2] proceed from an unspotted conscience, I should not dare to offer to your view and approved judgment these passions of my troubled soul, so full of fear and trembling is hypocrisy and dissimulation. But knowing my own innocency and godly fervor in the whole prosecution hereof, I doubt not of your benign acceptance and clement construction.

As for malicious depravers and turbulent spirits to whom nothing is tasteful but what pleaseth their unsavory palate, I pause not for them, being well assured in my persuasion by the often trial and proving of myself in my holiest meditations and prayers that I am

---

[1] "Shall be poured forth with a sincere and godly zeal"

[2] Printed "ease," but written "cause" in the Bodleian MS.

called hereunto by the spirit of God; and it shall be sufficient for me to be protected by yourself in all virtuous and pious endeavors. And for my more happy proceeding herein, my daily oblations shall ever be addressed to bring to pass so good effects that yourself and all the world may truly say this is the work of God and it is marvelous in our eyes.

But to avoid tedious preambles and to come nearer the matter, first suffer me with your patience to sweep and make clean the way wherein I walk from all suspicions and doubts which may be covered therein,[1] and faithfully to reveal unto you what should move me hereunto.

Let therefore this my well-advised protestation, which here I make between God and my own conscience, be a sufficient witness at the dreadful Day of Judgment (when the secret of all men's hearts shall be opened) to condemn me herein if my chiefest intent and purpose be not to strive with all my power of body and mind in the undertaking of so mighty[2] a matter, no way led—so far forth as man's weakness may permit—with the unbridled desire of carnal affection, but for the good of this plantation, for the honor of our country, for the glory of God, for my own salvation, and for the converting to the true knowledge of God and Jesus Christ an unbelieving creature, namely Pokahuntas,[3] to whom my hearty[4] and best thoughts are and have a long time been so entangled and enthralled in so intricate a labyrinth, that I was even a-wearied to unwind myself thereout. But Almighty God, who never faileth His that truly invocate His holy name, hath opened the gate and led me by the hand, that I might plainly see and discern the safe paths wherein to tread.

To you therefore, most noble sir, the patron and father of us in this country, do I utter the effects of this my settled and long continued affection—which hath made a mighty war in my meditations! And here I do truly relate to what issue this dangerous combat is come unto, wherein I have not only examined but throughly tried and

---

[1] "which may lie covered herein,"

[2] "weighty"

[3] "Pohahuntas"

[4] "heart"

LIBRARY OF VIRGINIA

POCAHONTAS

pared my thoughts even to the quick before I could find any fit wholesome and apt applications to cure so dangerous an ulcer. I never failed to offer my daily and faithful prayers to God for His sacred and holy assistance. I forgot not to set before mine eyes the frailty of mankind, his proneness to evil,[1] his indulgency of wicked thoughts, with many other imperfections wherein man is daily ensnared and oftentimes overthrown, and them compared to my present estate.

Nor was I ignorant[2] of the heavy displeasure which Almighty God conceived against the sons of Levi and Israel for marrying strange wives, nor of the inconveniences which may thereby arise with other the like good motions, which made me look about warily and with good circumspection into the grounds and principal agitations which thus should provoke me to be in love with one whose education hath been rude, her manners barbarous, her generation accursed, and so discrepant in all nurtriture from myself that oftentimes with fear and trembling I have ended my private controversy with this: "Surely these are *wicked* instigations, hatched by him who seeketh and delighteth in man's destruction!"—and so with fervent prayers to be ever preserved from such diabolical assaults as I took those to be, I have taken some rest.

Thus, when I had thought I had obtained my peace and quietness, behold, another but more gracious tentation[3] hath made breaches into my holiest and strongest meditations, with which I have been put to a new trial in a straiter[4] manner than the former. For besides the many passions and sufferings which I have daily, *hourly*—yea, and in my sleep endured, even awaking me to astonishment, taxing me with remissness and carelessness, refusing and neglecting to perform the duty of a good Christian, pulling me by the ear and crying, "Why dost not thou endeavor to make her a Christian?" And these have happened to my greater wonder even when she hath been furthest separated from me, which in common reason, were it not an undoubted work of God, might breed forgetfulness of a far

1 "proneness to ill,"
2 "Woe am I ignorant"
3 "temptation"
4 "stricter"

more worthy creature.

Besides, I say the holy spirit of God hath often demanded of me why I was created if not for transitory pleasures and worldly vanities, but to labor in the Lord's vineyard, there to sow and plant, to nourish and increase the fruits thereof, daily adding with the good husband in the Gospel somewhat to the talent, that in the end the fruits may be reaped to the comfort of the laborer in this life and his salvation in the world to come. And if this be, as undoubtedly this is, the service Jesus Christ requireth of his best servant, woe unto him that hath these instruments of piety put[1] into his hands and willfully despiseth to work with them; likewise adding hereunto her great appearance of love to me, her desire to be taught and instructed in the knowledge of God, her capableness of understanding, her aptness and willingness to receive any good impression, and also the spiritual (besides her own) incitements stirring me up hereunto.

What should I do? Shall I be of so untoward a disposition as to refuse to lead the blind into the right way? Shall I be so unnatural as not to give bread to the hungry? or uncharitable[2] as not to cover the naked? Shall I despise to actuate these pious duties of a Christian? Shall the base fear of displeasing the world overpower and withhold me from revealing unto man these spiritual works of the Lord, which in my mediations and prayers I have daily made known unto Him?—God forbid! I assuredly trust He hath thus dealt with me for my eternal felicity and for His glory, and I hope so to be guided by His heavenly grace, that in the end by my faithful pains and Christian-like labor I shall attain to that blessed promise pronounced by that holy prophet Daniel unto the righteous that bring many unto the knowledge of God, namely, that they shall shine like the stars for ever and ever. A sweeter comfort cannot be to a true Christian, nor a greater encouragement for him to labor all the days of his life in the performance thereof, nor a greater gain of consolation to be desired at the hour of death and in the day of judgment.

Again,[3] by my reading and conference with honest and religious

[1] "offered and put"

[2] "so uncharitable"

[3] "Again, for the lawfulness of marriage, I hope I do not far err from the meaning of the holy Apostle that the unbelieving husband is sanctified by the believing wife, and

persons have I received no small encouragement, besides *serena mea conscientia*, "the clearness of my conscience," clean from the filth of impurity, *quae est instar muri ahenei*, "which is unto me as a brazen wall." If I should set down at large the perturbations and godly motions which have striven within me,[1] I should but make a tedious and unnecessary volume. But I doubt not these shall be sufficient both to certify you of my true intents in discharging of my duty to God and to yourself, to whose gracious providence I humbly submit myself, for His glory, your honor, our country's good, the benefit of this plantation, and for the converting of one unregenerate to regeneration—which I beseech God to grant for His dear son Christ Jesus His sake.

Now if the vulgar sort, who square all men's actions by the base rule of their own filthiness, shall tax or taunt me in this my godly labor, let them know it is not any[2] hungry appetite to gorge myself with incontinency. Sure, if I would and were so sensually inclined, I might satisfy such desire (though not without a seared conscience) yet with Christians more pleasing to the eye and less fearful in the offense unlawfully committed. Nor am I in so desperate an estate that I regard not what becometh of me, nor am I out of hope but one day to see my country, nor so void of friends, nor mean in birth but there to obtain a match to my great content, nor have I ignorantly passed over my hopes there, or regardlessly seek to lose the love of my friends by taking this course. I know them all and have not rashly overslipped any.

But shall it please God thus to dispose of me, which I earnestly desire to fulfill my ends before set down, I will heartily accept of it as a godly tax appointed me, and I will never cease—God assisting

---

the unbelieving wife by the believing husband, etc.; upon which place Mr. Calvin in his *Institutions*, lib. 4, cap. 16, sect. 6, sayeth, 'Even as the children of the Jews were called a holy seed because being made heirs of the same covenant which the Lord made with Abraham they were different from the children of the ungodly, for the same reason even yet also the children of Christians are accounted holy, yea, although they be the issue but of one parent faithful, and, as the prophet witnesseth, they differ from the unclean seed of idolatry.' And thus with my reading and conference …"

[1] "within me in this my godly conflict,"

[2] " 'tis not my"

me—until I have accomplished and brought to perfection so holy a work, in which I will daily pray God to bless me to mine and her eternal happiness.

And thus desiring no longer to live to enjoy the blessings of God than this my resolution doth tend to such godly ends as are by me before declared, not doubting of your favorable acceptance, I take my leave, beseeching Almighty God to rain down upon you such plenitude of His heavenly graces as your heart can wish and desire, and so I rest

At your command most willing to be disposed of,
JOHN ROLFE.

VIRGINIA THEREFORE standing now in such a goodly proportion and fair forwardness of thriving as it was never yet hitherto seen in since it began to be first planted cannot but soon come to perfection, to the exceeding great comfort of all well-affected Christians, and no small profit of the planters and adventurers—if it be well seconded and supplied with a good number of able men.

Wherefore let none be hereafter unwilling all they may to further this most honorable action, and be forward to uphold and support it from falling—by their speech and countenance, and freely adventuring thither, both in their persons and also by their purses, as God hath enabled them.

To conclude, as Azariah said once to King Asa, Judah, and Benjamin so say I unto all: "Be ye strong therefore, and let not your hands be weak, for your work shall have a reward."[1] And as the holy Apostle said to the Corinthians, "Be ye therefore steadfast, unmovable, abundant always in the works of the Lord, forasmuch as ye know your labor is not in vain in the Lord,"[2] let us not therefore be weary of well-doing. For in due season we shall reap if we faint not, as the Apostle told the Galatians. FAREWELL.

FINIS

---

[1] 2 Chronicles 15:7.

[2] 1 Corinthians 15:58.

52. John Smith

The General History of Virginia, New England, and the Summer Isles: The Fourth Book (selections)

< **Smith 1624**

Smith opens his Fourth Book (105–119) with the last pages but two of *The Proceedings,* which I have left in the masonry of §17. Omitting the last two pages, he takes up with selections from works with which we are familiar: *A True Declaration §27,* Strachey's *True Reportory §22,* Delaware's letters and his *Short Relation §34,* and Hamor's *Discourse §51,* (more or less the order in which they appear), all which I skip repeating here. However, his not inconsiderable notes inserted in his Hamor text, including his own telling of the abduction of Pocahontas, I have put in footnotes there.

On page 119 he has an anachronistic apostrophe on the Spanish incident at Point Comfort which I quote in my commentary on §36.

Further down the same page he unburdens some feeling on the subject of colonial preferment, and it is there I pick him up for the next four pages ahead of us. After that he gives fresh material from the writings of Captain Powell and others, followed by notes on the Rolfes' trip to London and Smith's own puzzling and spur of the moment visit with the Lady Rebecca in Middlesex—subsequent to his letter on her behalf to Queen Anne. The Virginia Company provided £4 weekly for her expenses, which was small.

If anything passes between them here to indicate Pocahontas was in love with Captain John Smith, as many suppose (some of them even forgetting the man she married was John Rolfe), it is because Smith had been the son by affiliation of her father, Powhatan. Now in England the roles were reversed: He is *her* father, and she is hurt that he has been avoiding her. This is what she is telling him, but she is a princess and Smith, an Englishman in a hard-varnish social order, knows that it is inviting trouble for a commoner to print such things about himself. It is rumored King James was angry that John Rolfe was a commoner.

Smith back in London next (123) runs across Uttamatomakkin (Tomocomo) and recalls a conversation which I have placed not here but at §55–885. After that the Fourth Book begins dealing with Argall's term as governor and events beyond our decade, and I leave off.

[119] SIR THOMAS DALE, having settled to his thinking all things in good order, made choice of one Master George Yearly to be deputy governor in his absence, and so returned for England, accompanied with Pocahontas, the king's daughter, and Master Rolfe, her husband, and arrived at Plymouth the 12 of June 1616.

The government left to Captain Yearly [Yeardley].

NOW A LITTLE TO COMMENTARY upon all these proceedings, let me leave but this as a caveat by the way: If the alteration of government hath subverted great empires, how dangerous is it then in the infancy of a commonweal! The multiplicity of governors is a great damage to any state, but uncertain daily changes are burdensome because their entertainments are chargeable and many will make hay whilst the sun doth shine, however it shall fare with the generality.

This dear-bought land with so much blood and cost hath only made some few rich and all the rest losers. But it was intended at the first [that] the first undertakers should be first preferred and rewarded, and the first adventurers satisfied—and they of all the rest are the most neglected, and those that never adventured a groat, never see the country, nor ever did any service for it, employed in their places, adorned with their deserts, and enriched with their ruins. And when they are fed fat, then in cometh others so lean as they were, who through their omnipotency doth as much. Thus what one officer doth, another undoth, only aiming at their own ends, thinking all the world derides his dignity [who] cannot fill his coffers, being in authority, with anything. Every man hath his mind free, but he can never be a true member to that estate that to enrich himself beg-**[120]**-gars all the country. [Concerning] which bad course, there are many yet in this noble plantation whose true honor and worth [they] as much scorns it as the others loves it.

For the nobility and gentry, there is scarce any of them expects anything but the prosperity of the action. And there are some merchants and others, I am confidently persuaded, do take more care and pains, nay, and at their continual great charge, than they could be hired to for the love of money. So honestly regarding the general good of this great work, they would hold it worse than sacrilege to wrong it but a shilling, or extort upon the common soldier a penny. But to the purpose, and to follow the history.

MASTER GEORGE YEARLY, now invested deputy governor by Sir Thomas Dale, applied himself for the most part in planting tobacco, as the most present commodity they could devise for a present gain, so that every man betook himself to the best place he could for the purpose. Now though Sir Thomas Dale had caused such an abundance of corn to be planted, that every man had sufficient, yet the supplies [that] were sent us came so unfurnished as quickly eased us of our superfluity.

To relieve their necessities, he sent to the Chickahamanias for the tribute corn Sir Thomas Dale and Captain Argall had conditioned for with them. But such a bad answer they returned him that he drew together one hundred of his best shot, with whom he went to Chickahamania.

The people in some places used him indifferently, but in most places with much scorn and contempt, telling him he was but Sir Thomas Dale's man, and they had payed his master according to condition, but to give any to him they had no such order, neither would they obey him as they had done his master. After he had told them his authority, and that he had the same power to enforce them that Dale had, they dared him to come on shore to fight, presuming more of his not daring than their own valors. Yearly, seeing their insolencies, made no great difficulty to go on shore at Ozinies, and they as little to encounter him. But marching from thence towards Mamanahunt, they put themselves in the same order they see us, led by their captain, Kissanacomen, governor of Ozinies, and so marched close along by us, each as threat'ning other who should first begin. But that night we quartered against Mamanahunt, and they passed the river; the next day we followed them.

There are few places in Virginia had then more plain ground together nor more plenty of corn, which although it was but newly gathered, yet they had hid it in the woods where we could not find it. A good time we spent thus in arguing the cause, the savages without fear standing in troops amongst us, seeming as if their countenances had been sufficient to daunt us.

What other practices they had I know not. But to prevent the worst, our captain caused us all to make ready and upon the word to let fly among them where he appointed. Others also he commanded to seize on them they could for prisoners. All which being done according to our direction, the captain gave the word, and we presently discharged, where twelve lay, some dead, the rest for life sprawling on the ground. Twelve more we took prisoners, two whereof were brothers, two of their eight elders, the one took by sergeant Boothe, the other by Robert, a Polonian. Near one hundred bushels of corn we had for their ransoms, which was promised the soldiers for a reward, but it was not performed.

Now Opechankanough had agreed with our captain for the subjecting of those people—that neither he nor Powhatan could ever bring to their obedience—and that he should make no peace with them without his advice. In our return by Ozinies with our prisoners, we met Opechankanough, who with much ado feigned with what pains he had procured their peace, the which to requite they called him the King of Ozinies, and brought him from all parts many presents of beads, copper, and such trash as they had. Here as at many other times we were beholden to Captain Henry Spilman, our interpreter, a gentleman [who] had lived long time in this country, and sometimes a prisoner among the savages, and done much good service, though but badly rewarded.

From hence we march'd towards James town. We had three **[121]** boats loaded with corn and other luggage. The one of them, being more willing to be at James town with the news than the other, was overset, and eleven men cast away with the boat, corn, and all their provision.

Notwithstanding, this put all the rest of the savages in that fear, especially in regard of the great league we had with Opechankanough, that we followed our labors quietly and in such security that divers savages of other nations daily frequented us with what provisions they could get, and would guide our men on hunting and oft hunt for us themselves.

Captain Yearly had a savage or two so well trained up to their pieces they were as expert as any of the English, and one he kept purposely to kill him fowl. There were divers others had savages in like manner for their men. Thus we lived together as if we had been one people all the time Captain Yearley stayed with us, but such grudges and discontents daily increased among ourselves that upon the arrival of Captain Argall, sent by the Council and Company to be our governor, Captain Yearley returned for England in the year 1617.

FROM THE WRITINGS OF CAPTAIN NATHANIEL POWELL,
WILLIAM CANTRILL, SERGEANT BOOTHE, EDWARD GURGANEY.

DURING THIS TIME, the Lady Rebecca, alias Pocahontas, daughter to Powhatan, by the diligent care of Master John Rolfe, her husband, and his friends, [w]as taught to speak such English as might well be understood, well instructed in Christianity, and was become very formal and civil after our English manner. She had also by him a child which she loved most dearly, and the Treasurer and Company took order both for the maintenance of her and it, besides there were divers persons of great rank and quality had been very kind to her.

And before she arrived at London, Captain Smith, to deserve her former courtesies, made her qualities known to the queen's most excellent majesty and her court, and writ a little book to this effect to the queen, an abstract whereof followeth:

TO THE MOST HIGH AND VIRTUOUS PRINCESS, QUEEN ANNE OF GREAT BRITTANY,

MOST ADMIRED QUEEN—The love I bear my God, my king, and country, hath so oft emboldened me in the worst of extreme dangers that now honesty doth constrain me presume thus far beyond myself to present Your Majesty this short discourse. If ingratitude be a deadly poison to all honest virtues, I must be guilty of that crime if I should omit any means to be thankful.

So it is that some ten years ago being in Virginia and taken prisoner by the power of Powhatan, their chief king, I received from this great savage exceeding great courtesy, especially from his son Nantaquaus, the most manliest, comeliest, boldest spirit I ever saw in a savage; and his sister Pocahontas, the king's most dear and well-beloved daughter, being but a child of twelve or thirteen years of age, whose compassionate pitiful heart of my desperate estate gave me much cause to respect her. I being the first Christian this proud king and his grim attendants ever saw, and thus enthralled in their barbarous power, I cannot say I felt the least occasion of want that was in the power of those my mortal foes to prevent, notwithstanding all their threats.

After some six weeks' fatting amongst those savage courtiers, at the minute of my execution, she hazarded the beating out of her own brains to save mine, and not only that, but so prevailed with her father that I was safely conducted to James town, where I found about eight and thirty miserable poor and sick creatures to keep possession of all those large territories of Virginia: Such was the weakness of this poor commonwealth as had the savages not fed us, we directly had starved.

And this relief, most gracious Queen, was commonly brought us by this [122] Lady Pocahontas. Notwithstanding all these passages when inconstant fortune turned our peace to war, this tender virgin would still not spare to dare to visit us, and by her our jars have been oft appeased, and our wants still supplied. Were it the policy of her father thus to employ her, or the ordinance of God thus to make her His instrument, or her extraordinary affection to our nation, I know not, but of this I am sure: When her father with the utmost of his policy and power sought to surprise me, having but eighteen with me, the dark night could not affright her from coming through the irksome woods, and with watered eyes gave me intelligence with her best advice to escape his fury; which had he known, he had surely slain her.

James town with her wild train she as freely frequented as her father's habitation. And during the time of two or three years she next under God was still the instrument to preserve this colony from death, famine, and utter confusion, which, if in those times had once been dissolved, Virginia might have lyen as it was at our first arrival to this day.

Since then this business having been turned and varied by many accidents from that I left it at, it is most certain after a long and troublesome war, after my departure, betwixt her father and our colony, all which time she was not heard of. About two years after, she herself was taken prisoner, [and] being so detained near two years longer, the colony by that means was relieved, peace concluded, and at last, rejecting her barbarous condition, was married to an English gentleman, with whom at this present she is in England—the first Christian ever of that nation, the first Virginian ever spake English, or had a child in marriage by an Englishman, a matter surely, if my meaning be truly considered and well understood, worthy a prince's understanding.

Thus, most gracious Lady, I have related to Your Majesty what at your best leisure our approved histories will account you at large and done in the time of Your Majesty's life. And however this might be presented you from a more worthy pen, it cannot from a more honest heart, as yet I never begged anything of the state or any, and it is my want of ability and her exceeding desert—your birth, means, and authority, her birth, virtue, want, and simplicity—doth make me thus bold humbly to beseech Your Majesty to take this knowledge of her, though it be from one so unworthy to be the reporter as myself, her husband's estate not being able to make her fit to attend Your Majesty.

The most and least I can do is to tell you this, because none so oft hath tried it as myself, and the rather [because she] being of so great a spirit, however her stature: If she should not be well received, seeing this kingdom may rightly have a kingdom by her means, her present love to us and Christianity might turn to such scorn and fury as to divert all this good to the worst of evil. Where[as] finding so great a Queen should do her some honor more than she can imagine [in reward] for being so kind to your servants and subjects would so ravish her with content as endear her dearest blood to effect that [which] Your Majesty and all the King's honest subjects most earnestly desire.

And so I humbly kiss your gracious hands,
[JOHN SMITH]

BEING ABOUT THIS TIME preparing to set sail for New-England, I could not stay to do her that service I desired, and she well deserved. But hearing she was at Branford [Brentford in Middlesex] with divers of my friends, I went to see her.

After a modest salutation, without any word she turned about, obscured her face, as not seeming well contented. And in that humor, her husband with divers others we all left her two or three hours, repenting myself to have writ she could speak English.

But not long after, she began to talk and rememb'red me well what courtesies she had done, saying, "You did promise Powhatan what was yours should be his, and he the like to you. You called him father, being in his land a stranger, and by the same reason so must I do you"; which, though *I* would have excused, I durst not allow of that title because she was a king's daughter. With a well set countenance she said, "Were you not afraid to come into my father's country, and caused fear in him and all his people (but me)? And fear you here I should call you father? I **[123]** tell you then I will, and you shall call me child, and so I will be forever and ever your countryman. They did tell us always you were dead, and I knew no other till I came to Plymouth. Yet Powhatan did command Uttamatomakkin to seek you, and know the truth, because your countrymen will lie much."

[paragraph on Uttamatomakkin removed to 885]

The small time I stay'd in London divers courtiers and others my acquaintances hath gone with me to see her, that generally concluded they did think God had a great hand in her conversion, and they have seen many English ladies worse favored, proportioned, and behaviored. And as since I have heard it pleased both the King and Queen's Majesty honorably to esteem her, accompanied with that honorable lady the Lady De la Ware and that honorable lord her husband, and divers other persons of good qualities, both publicly at the masques[1] and otherwise, to her great satisfaction and content, which doubtless she would have deserved[2] had she lived to arrive in Virginia.

---

[1] She attended the Twelfth Night masque of 6 January 1617, which was attended also by the king. As far as we know she was never given a formal audience.

[2] Recompensed.

53. John Rolfe

A True Relation of the State of Virginia[1]

< **British Library: Royal 18.A.XI–1v–18r,** Southern Literary Messenger 1839:401, Virginia Historical Register I (1848):101, Historical Manuscripts Commission, 8th Report (1881), II, Appendix 208; Taylor 1951 (APVA 1971)

I am puzzled why this oft-printed tract was not printed in full in its own day. Instead, Rev. Purchas adapted it for his chapter on Virginia in his 1617 edition of the *Pilgrimage,* and it went no further.

Rolfe catalogs the prosperity that has unfolded since the second charter. The Indians now trade land for food from the English. And the father of Virginia tobacco calls for tobacco quotas. Rolfe believes in orderly development under wise absolutism, each man at his appointed task. He wants Virginia to be a place where honest people with modest means can get a start. We begin to recognize our nation. Democracy was born in this commonwealth of farmers, among people concerned about corn, hogs, God, and tobacco.

Up to now, America has been described by Englishmen. Rolfe married an American and is the first Englishman to sound to me like an American. He is telling Englishmen about a place where he has struck root—his country. Hamor's lies sound like promotional excess. Rolfe's lies sound like patriotism.

Rolfe tells us all about the boroughs, but like a true Virginian he refused to live anywhere but on his own plantations, one of them across the river from Jamestown. The European village, that easily throve in the northern and middle colonies, was stillborn in Colonial Virginia. Towns emptied out faster than the authorities could plan and fill them. An early American lifestyle is the rural commuter, nowhere so soon as on the James River.

There are three manuscripts. They tally well enough, but it is unfortunate perhaps that Rolfe presented such glowing prospects for the viability of a tobacco colony to a king that hated the "esteemed weed," and who years before had published his own passionate denunciation of it. The APVA edition is a transcription of the Pembroke-Taylor MS.

---

[1] The Pembroke-Taylor MS enlarges the title: " … [when] left by Sir Thomas Dale, knight, in May last, 1616." Rolfe also left with Dale.

TO THE KING'S MOST SACRED MAJESTY.

MAY IT PLEASE YOUR HIGHNESS—There have been of late divulged many impressions judicially and truly penned, partly to take away the ignominy, scandals, and maledictions wherewith this action hath been branded, and partly to satisfy all (especially the best) with the manner of the late proceedings and the prosperity likely to ensue. How happily and plenteously the good blessings of God have fallen upon the people and colony since the last impression (faithfully written by a gentleman of good merit, Mr. Ralph Hamor, sometime an actual member in the plantation, even then departing when the foundation and ground work was new laid of their now thrift and happiness) of[1] the earthy and worldly man is scarcely believed, but of heavenlier minds they are most easily discerned, for they daily attend and mark how those blessings, though sometimes restrained for a time, in the end are poured upon the servants of the Lord. Shall Your Majesty with piety and pity—with piety being zealous for God's glory, and with pity mourning the defects—vouchsafe to read thus much of the estate of this colony as it remained in May last, when Sir Thomas Dale left the same, I shall deem myself most happy in your gracious acceptance, and most readily offer to your approved judgment whether this cause, so much despised and disgraced, do not wrongfully suffer many imputations.

First, to meet with an objection commonly used amongst many men who search truths no farther than by common reports, namely —How is it possible Virginia can now be so good, so fertile a country, so plentifully stored with food and other commodities? Is it not the same still it was when men pined with famine? Can the earth now bring forth such a plentiful increase? Were there not governors, men, and means to have wrought this heretofore? And can it now on the sudden be so fruitful? Surely (say they) these are rather baits to catch and entrap more men into woe and misery than otherwise can be imagined.

These with many as frivolous I have heard instigated and even reproachfully spoken against Virginia. To answer whom—the most

[1] Among.

part of them incredulous worldlings such as believe not unless they feel the goodness of the Lord sensibly to touch them—though it be not much material, yet let them know 'tis true, Virginia is the *same* it was, I mean for the goodness of the seat and fertileness of the land, and will no doubt so continue to the world's end, a country as worthy good report as can be declared by the pen of the best writer, a country spacious and wide, capable of many hundred thousands of inhabitants: for the soil, most fertile to plant in; for air, fresh and temperate, somewhat hotter in summer and not altogether so cold in winter as in England—yet so agreeable it is to our constitutions that now 'tis more rare to hear of a man's death than in England amongst so many people as are there resident—for water, most wholesome and very plentiful; and for fair navigable rivers and good harbors, no country in Christendom in so small a circuit so well stored; for matter fit for buildings and fortifications and for building of shipping with everything thereto appertaining, I may boldly avouch, scarce any or no country known to man of itself more abundantly furnished.

These things (may some say) are of great consequence toward the settling of a plantation, but where are the beasts and cattle to feed and clothe the people? I confess this is a main want. Yet some there are already,[1] as neat cattle, horses, mares, and goats, which are carefully preserved for increase,[2] the number whereof hereafter shall be set down in a particular note by themselves. There are also great store of hogs, both wild and tame, and poultry great plenty, which every man if they will themselves may keep. But the greatest want of all is least thought on, and this is good and sufficient men as well of birth and quality to command soldiers to march, discover, and defend the country from invasions, as also artificers, laborers, and husbandmen with whom, were the colony well provided, then might trial be made what lieth hidden in the womb of the ground. The land might yearly abound with corn and other provisions for man's sustenance; buildings, fortifications, and shipping might be reared,

---

1 "The horses and oxen are employed to the cart and to plough ground for English corn." (margin note)

2 Pembroke-Taylor MS at this point has the statement: "both males and females, the one for the plough, th' other for milk, butter, and cheese"

wrought, and framed; commodities of divers kinds might be reaped yearly and sought after; and many things (God's blessings continuing) might come with ease to establish a firm and perfect commonweal.

But to come again to the matter from which I have a little strayed, and to give a more full answer to the objectors, may you please to take notice that the beginning of this plantation was governed by a president and council aristocratically. The president yearly chosen out of the council which consisted of twelve persons, this government lasted above two years, in which time such envy, dissensions, and jars were daily sown amongst them that they choked the seeds and blasted the fruits of all men's labors. If one were well disposed and gave good advisement to proceed in the business, others out of the malice of their hearts would contradict, interdict, withstand, and dash all. Some rung out and sent home too loud praises of the riches and fertileness of the country before they assayed to plant, to reap, or search the same. Others said nothing, nor did anything thereunto. All would be *Keisars* [Caesars], none inferior to other. Some drew forward; more backward. The vulgar sort looked for supply out of England, neglected husbandry. Some wrote home there was no want of food, yet sought for none. Others that would have sought could not be suffered—in which confusion, much confusion yearly befell them, and in this government happened all the misery.

Afterward a more absolute government was granted monarchically, wherein it still continueth. And although for some few years it stood at a stay, especially in the manuring and tilling of ground, yet men spent not their time idly nor improfitably. For they were daily employed in palisadoing and building of towns, impaling grounds, and other needful businesses, which is now both beneficial to keep the cattle from ranging and preserveth the corn safe from their spoil.

Being thus fitted and prepared to sow corn and to plant other seeds and fruits in all the places of our habitations, one thing, notwithstanding, much troubled our governor, namely, enmity with the Indians. For howsoever we could well defend ourselves—towns and seats—from any assault of the natives, yet our cattle and corn lay too open to their courtesies and too subject to their mercies. Whereupon a peace was concluded which still continueth so firm that our people yearly plant and reap quietly, and travel in the woods a-fowling and a-hunting as freely and securely from fear of danger or treachery as in England. The great blessings of God have followed this peace, and it next under Him hath bred our plenty: every man sitting under his fig tree in safety, gathering and reaping the fruits of their labors with much joy and comfort.

But a question may be demanded what those fruits are. For such as the country affordeth naturally (for variety and goodness comparable to the best in Christendom, growing wild as they do) I pass them over, other discourses having largely manifested them to the view of the world. But for the people's present labors, they have Indian wheat, called *maize* in the West Indies, peas and beans, English wheat, peas, barley, turnips, cabbages, pumpions (West Indian and others), carrots, parsnips, and suchlike, besides herbs and flowers, all of our English seeds, both for pleasure and for the kitchen so good, so fruitful, so pleasant and profitable as the best made ground in England can yield. And that Your Majesty may know what two men's labors with spade and sholve [shovel] only can manure in one year: Fifty pounds in money was offered for their crop, which they refused to take! For hemp and flax none better in England or Holland. Silkworms, some of their labors,[1] and tastes of other good and vendible commodities were now brought home. Likewise tobacco (though an esteemed weed)[2] very commodious, which there thriveth so well that no doubt but after a little more trial and experience in the curing thereof it will compare with the best in the West Indies.

For fish, fowl, deer, and other beasts, reports and writings have rather been too sparing than prodigal. About two years since, Sir Thomas Dale, whose worth and name in concluding this peace and managing of the affairs of this colony will outlast the standing of this plantation, found out two seasons in the year to catch fish, namely, the spring and the fall. He himself took no small pains in the trial, and at one hale with a seine caught five thousand [fish], three

[1] I.e., some people were now laboring at silk culture.
[2] I.e., though once esteemed no better than a weed.

hundred of them as big as cod, the least of the residue a kind of salmon trout two foot long. Yet durst he not adventure on the main school for breaking his net. Likewise two men with axes and suchlike weapons have taken and kill'd near the shore and brought home forty as great as cod in two or three hours' space, so that now there is not so great plenty of victuals in any one of the forenamed kind yearly with small pains to be gotten in any part of England amongst so few people as are there resident.

And whereas heretofore we were constrained yearly to go to the Indians and entreat them to sell us corn, which made them esteem very basely of us, now the case is altered. They seek to us, come to our towns, sell their skins from their shoulders (which is their best garments) to buy corn. Yea, some of their petty kings have this last year borrowed 4 or 500 bushels of wheat, for payment whereof this harvest they have mortgaged their whole countries, some of them not much less in quantity than a shire in England! By this means, plenty and prosperity dwelleth amongst them, and the fear and danger of famine is clean taken away, wherewith the action hath a long time suffered injurious defamations.

Now that Hour Highness may with the more ease understand in what condition the colony standeth, I have briefly set down the manner of all men's several employments, the number of them, and the several places of their abode, which places or seats are all our own ground not so much by conquest, which the Indians hold a just and lawful title, but purchased of them freely, and they very willingly selling it.

The places which are now possessed and inhabited are six: 1. Henrico and the limits, 2. Bermuda Nether Hundred, 3. West and Sherley Hundred (members [of these last two] belonging to the Bermuda town, a place so called there by reason of the strength of the situation, were it indifferently fortified), 4. James Town, 5. Kequoughtan, 6. Dale's Gift.

The general and main body of the planters are divided into l. Officers, 2. Laborers, 3. Farmers.

The officers have the charge and care as well over the farmers as laborers generally, that they watch and ward for their preservations, and that both the one and the other's business may be daily followed to the performance of those employments which from the one are required and the other by covenant are bound unto. These officers are bound to maintain themselves and families with food and raiment by their own and their servants' industry.

The laborers are of two sorts: some employed only in the general works, who are fed and clothed out of the store; others, especially artificers, as smiths, carpenters, shoemakers, tailors, tanners, etc., do work in their professions for the colony, and maintain themselves with food and apparel, having time limited them to till and manure their ground.

The farmers live at most ease, yet by their good endeavors bring yearly much plenty to the plantation. They are bound by covenant both for themselves and servants to maintain Your Majesty's right and title in that kingdom against all foreign and domestic enemies, to watch the ward in the towns where they are resident, to do 31 days' service for the colony when they shall be called thereunto, yet not at all times, but when their own business can best spare them; to maintain themselves and families with food and raiment; and every farmer to pay yearly into the magazine for himself and every manservant two barrels and a half apiece of their best Indian wheat, which amounteth to twelve bushels and a half of English measure.

Thus briefly have I set down every man's particular employment and manner of living. Albeit lest the people, who generally are bent to covet after gain, especially having tasted of the sweets of their labors, should spend too much of their time and labor in planting tobacco (known to them to be very vendible in England) and so neglect their tillage of corn and fall into want thereof, it is provided for by the providence and care of Sir Thomas Dale that no farmer or other who must maintain themselves shall plant any tobacco unless he shall yearly manure, set, and maintain for himself and every manservant two acres of ground with corn; which doing they may plant as much tobacco as they will, else all their tobacco shall be forfeit to the colony; by which means the magazine shall yearly be sure to receive their rent of corn to maintain those who are fed thereout, being but a few, and many others if need be. They themselves will be well stored to keep their families with overplus, and reap tobacco enough to buy clothes and such necessaries as are needful for themselves and household. For an easy laborer will keep and tend two acres of corn and cure good store of tobacco—being yet the principal commodity the colony for the present yieldeth; for which, as for other commodities, the Council and Company for Virginia have already sent a ship thither furnished with all manner of clothing, household stuff, and such necessaries to establish a magazine there, which the people shall buy at easy rates for their commodities, they selling them at such prices that the adventurers may be no losers. This magazine shall be yearly supplied to furnish them, if they will endeavor by their labors to maintain it, which will be much beneficial to the planters and adventurers by interchanging their commodities, and will add much encouragement to them and others to persevere and follow the action, with a constant resolution to uphold the same.

The people which inhabit the said 6 several places are disposed as followeth:

At Henrico and in the precincts (which is seated on the north side the river, 90 odd miles from the mouth thereof, and within 15 or 16 miles of the Falls, or head of the river, being our furthest habitation within the land) are 38 men and boys, whereof 22 are farmers, the rest officers and others, all whom maintain themselves with food and apparel. Of this town one Captain Smaley hath the command (in the absence of Captain James Davis). Mr. William Wickham, minister there, who in his life and doctrine give good examples and godly instructions to the people.

At Bermuda Nether Hundred, seated on the south side the river, crossing it and going by land 5 miles lower than Henrico (by water ten) are 119; which seat containeth a good circuit of ground, the river winding round, so that a pale running 'cross a neck of land from one part of the river to the other maketh it a peninsule. The houses and dwellings of the people are set round about by the river and all along the pale so far distant one from the other that upon any "all-arm" they can second and succor one the other. These people are enjoined by a charter (being incorporated to the Bermuda town, which is made a corporation) to effect and perform such duties and services whereunto they are bound for a certain time and then to have their freedom. This corporation admit no farmers unless they procure

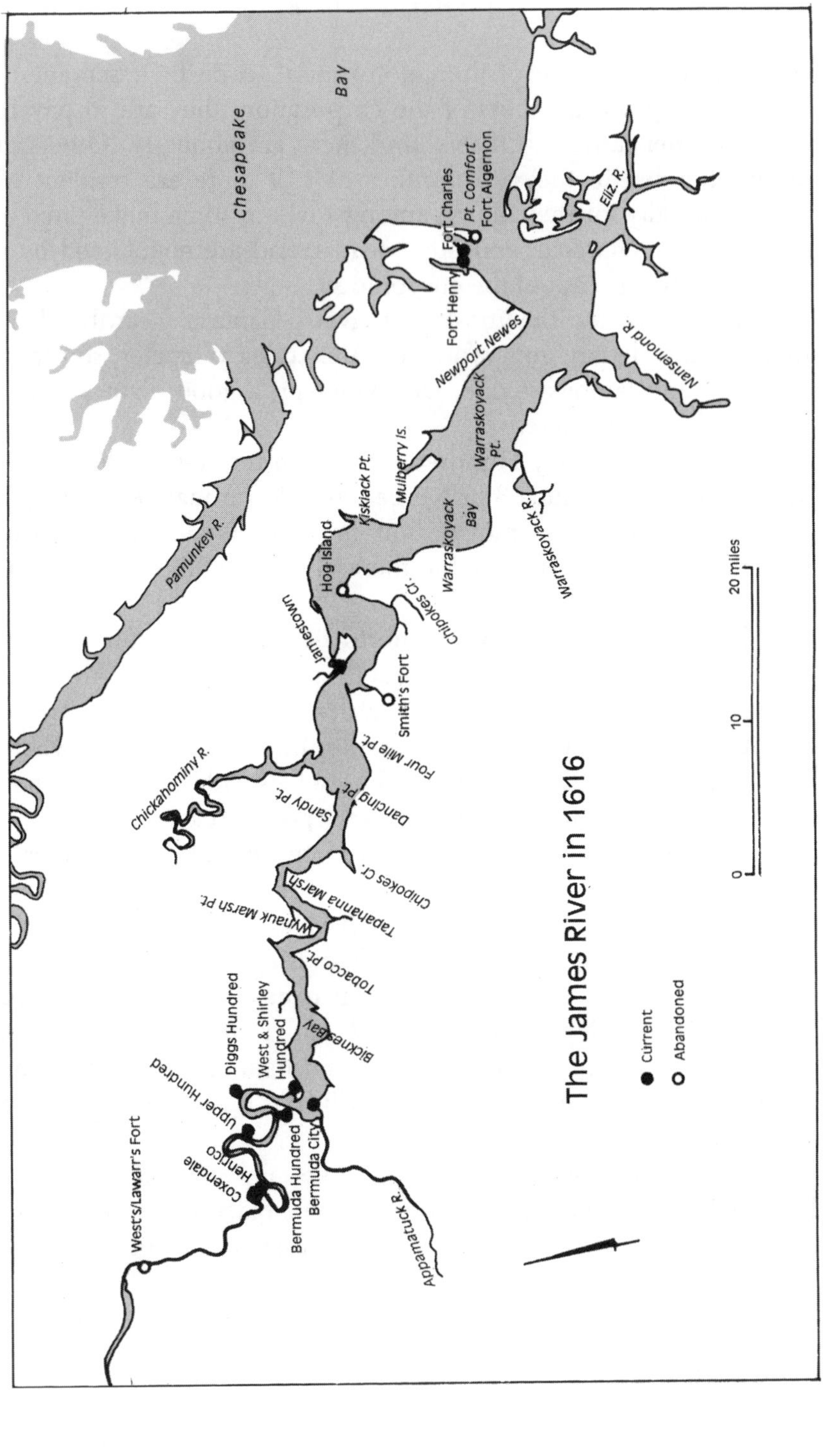

The James River in 1616
Current
Abandoned
0
10
20 miles
Chesapeake
Bay
Pamunkey R.
Chickahominy R.
Hog Island
Kiskiack Pt.
Mulberry Is.
Jamestown
Fort Henry
Fort Charles
Pt. Comfort
Fort Algernon
Newport Newes
Eliz. R.
Nansemond R.
Warraskoyack Pt.
Warraskoyack Bay
Warraskoyack R.
Chipokes Cr.
Smith's Fort
Four Mile Pt.
Dancing Pt.
Sandy Pt.
Chipokes Cr.
Tapahanna Marsh
Wynauk Marsh Pt.
Tobacco Pt.
Bicknes Bay
Diggs Hundred
West & Shirley Hundred
Upper Hundred
Henrico
Coxendale
Bermuda Hundred
Bermuda City
Appamatuck R.
West's/Lawarr's Fort

of the governor some of the colony men[1] to be their servants, for whom, being no members of the corporation, they are to pay rent corn as other farmers. Of this kind there are about 17. Others also comprehended in the said number of 119 there are resident who labor generally for the colony, amongst whom some make pitch and tar, potashes, charcoal, and other works, and are maintained by the magazine, but are not of the corporation.

At this place for the most part liveth Captain Yeardly, deputy marshal and deputy governor. Mr. Alexander Whitaker, son to that reverend and famous divine, Dr. Whitaker, a good divine, hath the ministerial charge there.

At West and Sherley Hundred, seated on the north side the river, lower than the Bermuda 3 or 4 miles, are 25 commanded by Captain Maddeson, who are employed only in planting and curing tobacco, with the profit thereof to clothe themselves and all those who labor about the general business.

At James Town, seated on the north side the river, from West and Sherley Hundred lower down about 37 miles, are 50 under the command of Lieutenant Sharpe (in the absence of Captain Francis West, esquire, brother to the right honorable the Lord Lawarre), whereof 31 are farmers. All these maintain themselves with food and raiment. Mr. Richard Buck, minister there, a very good preacher.

At Kequoughtan, being not far from the mouth of the river, 37 miles below James Town on the same side, are 20, whereof 11 are farmers. All these also maintain themselves as the former. Captain George Webb, commander; Mr. William Mays minister there.

At Dale's Gift, being upon the sea near unto Cape Charles, about 30 miles from Kequoughtan, are 17 under the command of one Lieutenant Cradock. All these are fed and maintained by the colony. Their labor is to make salt, and catch fish at the two seasons before mentioned.

So the number of officers and laborers are 205, the farmers 81, besides [65][2] women and children in every place some, which in all amounteth to 351 persons—a small number to advance so great a

---

[1] Pembroke-Taylor MS has: "four of the colony's men"

[2] *Ibid.,* which is correct for the tally.

work!

These several places are not thus weakly man'd, as capable of no greater number, for they will maintain many 100's more. But because no one can be forsaken without loss and detriment to all, if then so few people thus united, ordered, and governed do live so happily, everyone partaking of the others' labors can keep in possession so much ground as will feed a far greater number in the same or better condition. And seeing too too many poor farmers in England work all the year, rising early and going to bed late, live penuriously, and much ado to pay their landlord's rent, besides a daily carking[1] and caring to feed themselves and families, what happiness might they enjoy in Virginia—were men sensible of these things[2]—where they may have ground for nothing more than they can manure, reap more fruits and profits with half the labor, void of many cares and vexations, and for their rent a matter of small or no moment, I leave to your singular judgment and consideration, nothing doubting but He who by His infinite goodness with so small means hath settled these poor and weak beginnings so happily will animate, stir up, and encourage many others cheerfully to undertake this work, and will assuredly add a daily strength, to uphold and maintain what He hath already begun.

Seeing then this [once] languishing action is now brought to this forwardness and strength (no person but is provided for either by their own or others' labors to subsist themselves for food and to be able to raise commodities for clothing and other necessaries), envy itself, poisoned with the venom of asps, cannot wound it.

Now to draw to a conclusion of this my poor oblation, I would crave Your Highness' patience a little longer, and that you would turn your heart to a more heavenly meditation, wherein much joy and comfort is to be reaped and found of all such as shall truly, sincerely, and unfeignedly seek to advance the honor of God and to propagate His Gospel. There is no small hope by piety, clemency, courtesy, and civil demeanor, by which means some are won to us already, to convert and bring to the knowledge and true worship of

---

[1] Toil and moil.

[2] Aware of these advantages.

Jesus Christ 1000's of poor, wretched, and misbelieving people,[1] on whose faces a good Christian cannot look without sorrow, pity, and commiseration, seeing they bear the image of our heavenly Creator, and we and they come from one and the same mold; especially we knowing that they merely through ignorance of God and Christ do run headlong, yea, with joy, into destruction and perpetual damnation; for which knowledge we are the more bound and indebted to Almighty God (for what were we before the Gospel of Christ shined amongst us?) and cannot better express our duties and thankfulness for so great mercies than by using such means to them as it pleased Him to lend unto others to bring our forefathers and us into the ways of truth.

It is much to be mourned and lamented how lightly the works of God are nowadays generally regarded and less sought after, but the works of the world, as though they were eternal, hung'red for and thirsted after with insatiable greediness. But should we well consider, examine, and search into ourselves what we were and now are, there can be no heart, if not[2] hard'ned as the nether millstone, but would even break itself to pieces and distribute to many poor souls some part thereof to purge them from their lees of sin, and to settle them in the right paths of holiness and righteousness to serve the King of Heaven; by which means, and God's holy assistance, no doubt they will soon be brought to abandon their old superstitions and idolatries, wherein they have been nursed and trained from their infancies—and our greatest adversaries shall not taunt us with this reproach: "Whom of you have you won to Christianity?"[3] What a crown of glory shall be set upon their heads who shall faithfully labor herein I leave to the enjoying of them who shall endeavor unfeignedly to merit the same.

Finally, as Caleb and Joshua, in the very heat of grudgings, murmurings, and assemblies of the Children of Israel, stood stoutly for the Lord's cause, commending the goodness of the land they discovered to the faces of their opposers, and the easiness to obtain it even to the peril of their lives, so many right honorable and worthy

---

[1] The Indians.

[2] Unless.

[3] Pembroke-Taylor begins with "Which of them," which makes better sense.

personages both here and in Virginia, when generally the most part withdrew themselves, that the action was almost sunk down in forgetfulness) have mightily upheld this Christian cause, for God—even our own God—did help them. For neither evil reports nor slanderers, nor murmurings, nor backslidings of others, nor any disaster did once dismay or hinder them from upholding thereof with their good reports, encouragements, and means yearly sent to the planters to nourish life and being in this zealous work. I beseech God to raise up many more such, so zealous for God's glory to forward the same.

We have tasted of some fruits thereof. There are no great nor strong castles, nor men like the sons of Anak[1] to hinder our quiet possession of that land. God's hand hath been mighty in the preservation thereof hitherto. What need we then to fear but to go up at once as a peculiar people marked and chosen by the finger of God to possess it? For undoubtedly He is with us. And as for murmurers, slanderers, and backsliders, a due portion shall be given them for their reward, so the blessings of Caleb and Joshua shall fall upon all those that constantly persevere to the end.

Thus craving your gracious pardon for my rude boldness, beseeching God to send you the fullness of His blessings in this world and in the world to come, I rest

Your Highness' most faithful and loyal subject,
JOHN ROLF

The number of neat cattle, horses, and goats which were alive in Virginia at Sir Thomas Dale his departure thence:

Cows, heifers, cow calves, 83; steers, 41; bulls, 20: in all, 144.

Memorandum—20 of the cows were great with calf at his departure.

Horses, 3; mares, 3: in all, 6.

Goats and kids, male and female in all, 216.

Hogs, wild and tame, not to be numb'red.

Poultry great plenty.

---

[1] Giants. Biblical for "native resistance."

54. Thomas Dale

Letter to Winwood, 3 June 1616

< **Public Records Office: Colonial Office 1/1–113,** Brown 1890:783

Governor Dale arrives on English soil. Aboard with him are the Rolfes, Uttamatomakkin, and Diego de Molina (Lembri was hanged from the yard arm at first sight of the coast of England).

Sir Ralph Winwood (1565–1617) had been the ambassador to the Netherlands, 1608–13, and likely his favors were run up in that connection. He was currently secretary of state. He opposed the king's policy of peace with Spain and longed for a resumption of hostilities.

RIGHT HONORABLE—Having been much bound unto you for many favors as yet not deserved by me, because the occasion hath not been presented whereby I might testify my thankfulness unto Your Honor, I should account myself happy to embrace some subject to demonstrate my faithful love and service unto you.

May it please Your Honor to understand that I am by the mighty power of the Almighty God safely returned from the hardest task that ever I undertook, and by the blessing of God have with poor means left the colony in great prosperity and peace, contrary to many men's expectation.

This ship hath brought home exceeding good tobacco, *sasafrix,* pitch, potashes, sturgeon and caviary, and other suchlike commodities as yet that country yields. I shall with the greatest speed the wind will suffer me present myself unto you and give you full satisfaction of those parts.

How beneficial this admirable country will be for our state I know you are not ignorant of, both for the emptying of our full body and the maintenance of our shipping (all things necessary thereunto, being there to be had), and that country being inhabited by His Majesty's subjects will put such a bit into our ancient enemy's mouth as will curb his haughtiness of monarchy.[1]

I shall give Your Honor great encouragements that this Vergynia affords (at my arrival) to spur us forward to inhabit there, if His Majesty [wishes] to possess one of the goodliest and richest kingdoms of the world and indeed so fit for no state as ours—if it shall please you honorable fathers of our estate to think seriously on it and His Majesty thoroughly to undertake it, the which I becheth [beseech?] the Lord to grant of His infinite mercy, and so I humbly commend my duty and service unto Your Honor.

From Plymouth, this 3 of June, 1616.

Your Honor's to command,
THOMAS DALE

[endorsed:] To the Right Honorable Sir Ralfe Wynwood, knight, Principal Secretary to His Majesty. Plymouth, 3° Junii, 1616, from Sir Thomas Dale.

[1] Spain.

55. Uttamatomakkin (Tomocomo)

An Interview in London

< Purchas 1617:954, 1626:844

Rev. Purchas devoted more than one occasion to examining the opinions of Pocahontas' brother-in-law, who with his delegation accompanied the Rolfes during a stay in London from June 1616 to March 1617. The clergyman barely lets the priest use his own voice, but Uttamatomakkin seems to have warmed to these interviews, and surely held his own "in arguing about religion." Perhaps he asked Purchas why his religion of charity, love, and forgiveness was not the religion of the English. But we learn the Powhatan Indians had a sacred language, that the number twelve held magical significance; and we get a hint of class exploitation. And learn that the Indians of Roanoke set the fashion among English courtiers of wearing lovelocks!

John Rolfe was evidently present and a few of his comments find their way into the text. Along with the excerpts from Percy, White, Spelman, and Wingfield, this makes up the bulk of Purchas' chapter six, eighth book, of the *Pilgrimage*.

I follow it here with a page from the *Pilgrimes* which reworks the same material. After that a morsel from Smith's *General History*, 4th Book.

OF THEIR OPINIONS and ceremonies in religion, who fitter to be heard than a Virginian?—an experienced man and counselor to Opochancanough, their king and governor in Powhatan's absence. Such is Tomocomo, at this present in England, sent hither to observe and bring news of our king and country to his nation. Some others[1] which have been here in former times being more silly,[2] which having seen little else than this city, have reported much of the houses and men, but thought we had small store of corn or trees, the Virginians imagining that our men came into their country for supply of these defects. This man, therefore, being landed in the west parts, found cause of admiration at our plenty in these kinds, and, as

[1] "I was thus told by Sir Thomas Dale." (margin note)

[2] Unsophisticated.

some have reported, began to tell both men and trees till his arithmetic failed. For their numb'ring beyond an hundred is imperfect and somewhat confused. Of him (Sir Thomas Dale's man being our interpreter) I learned that their Okeeus doth often appear to them in his house or temple. The manner of which apparition is thus:

First, four of their priests, or sacred persons, of which he said he was one, go into the house, and by certain words of a strange language—which he repeated very roundly in my hearing, but the interpreter understood not a word, nor do the common people—call or conjure this Okeeus, who appeareth to them out of the air; thence coming into the house, and walking up and down with strange words and gestures, [Okeeus] causeth eight more of the principal persons to be called in; all which twelve standing round about him, he prescribes to them what he would have done.

Of him they depend in all their proceedings, if it be but in a hunting journey,[1] who by winds or other awful tokens of his presence holds them in a superstitious both fear and confidence. His apparition is in form of a personable Virginian, with a long black lock on the left side hanging down near to the foot. This is the cause why the Virginians wear these sinister locks, which some think (I have heard Sir Thomas Dale and Master Rolph of that opinion) was first by our men in the first plantation, little above thirty years since, borrowed from these savages—a fair unlovely generation of the lovelock, Christians imitating savages, and they the devil!—this Virginian so admiring this rite, that in arguing about religion he objected to our god this defect that he had not taught us so to wear our hair. After that he hath stayed with his twelve so long as he thinks fit, he departeth up into the air whence he came.

Tomocomo averred that this was he which made heaven and earth; had taught them to plant so many kinds of corn; was the author of their good; had prophesied to them before of our men's coming; knew all our country; whom he made acquainted with his

---

1 "Sometimes when they are preparing to hunt he will by some known sign manifest himself and direct them to game, they all with great alacrity acknowledging that sign, and following." (margin note)

coming hither,[1] and told him that within so many months he would return. But the devil, or Okeeus, answered that it would be so[2] many more. Neither at his return must he go into that house till Okeeus shall call him.

He is very zealous in his superstition and will hear no persuasions to the truth, bidding us teach the boys and girls which were brought over from thence, he being too old now to learn.

Being asked what became of the souls of dead men, he pointed up to heaven; but of wicked men that they hung between heaven and earth.

This Tomocomo hath Matachanna, one of Powhatan's daughters, to wife.

The vulgar are held in great awe by their ignorance; and when any of them have got a good deer, some of the greater will pretend Okeeus his name, and cause it to be brought to his house, and then share it at their pleasure.

They hold it a disgrace to fear death, and therefore when they must die do it resolutely—as happened to one which had robbed the English, and by Powhatan (upon complaint made to him) was fetched sixscore miles from the place where he lurked, and by this Tomocomo, in the presence of the English, executed, his brains being knocked out, showing no sign of fear or dismayedness.

They use to make "black boys" once in fourteen or fifteen years generally for all the country (this hap'ned the last year, 1615), when all of a certain age that have not been made black boys before are initiated in this ceremony. They use to make some at other times by themselves, as before is showed of Rapahannok out of Captain Smith and Master White, which then mistook it for a sacrifice.[3] Some four months after that rite they live apart and are fed by some appointed to carry them their food.[4] They speak to no man nor come in

---

[1] I.e., Okeeus had acquainted Uttamatomakkin with England before his arrival.

[2] "This proved true, contrary to Tomocomo's mind, being desirous to return in the first ship, which is gone already." (margin note)

[3] Apparently John Rolfe put him straight on this, who also challenged one of Whitaker's assertions that the *quiyoughcosoughs* lived as hermits. But Spelman actually lived among the Patawomeck and Spelman §29–487 reports child sacrifice.

[4] "Master Rolph." (margin note)

company, seem distracted (some think by some devilish apparition scared, certain, to oblige them to that devilish religion, as by a hellish sacrament of the devil's institution) and will offer to shoot at such as come nigh them; and when they come into company, yet are for a certain time of silent and strange behavior, and will do anything never so desperate that they shall be bidden. If they tell them they shall be old men if they go not into the fire, they will do it. There is none of their men but are made black boys at one time or other. Let us observe these things with pity and compassion, and endeavor to bring these silly souls out of the snare of the devil by our prayers, our purses, and all our best endeavors.

This may be added, that their young people have in manner no knowledge, and the vulgar little, of their religion. They use also to beguile them with the Okee or image of him in their houses, into whose mouth they will put a tobacco pipe kindled, and one behind that image draws the smoke, which the sillier, vulgar, and children think to be done by their god or idol.

< Purchas 1625:1774

UTTAMATAMAKIN (commonly called Tomocomo), one of Powhatan's counselors, came over at the same time [as Governor Dale and John and Rebecca Rolfe, arriving in Plymouth in early June 1616]. With this savage I have often conversed at my good friend's, Master Doctor Goldstone, where he was a frequent guest, and where I have both seen him sing and dance his diabolical measures and heard him discourse of his country and religion, Sir Thomas Dale's man being the interpreter, as I have elsewhere showed.

Master Rolfe lent me a discourse which he had written of the estate of Virginia [§51] at that time, out of which I collected those things which I have in my *Pilgrimage* delivered [chapter five]. And his wife did not only accustom herself to civility but still carried herself as the daughter of a king, and was accordingly respected not only by the Company, which allowed provision for herself and her son, but of divers particular persons of honor in their hopeful zeal by her to advance Christianity. I was present when my honorable and reverend patron, the lord bishop of London, Doctor King, entertained her with festival state and pomp, beyond what I have seen in his great hospitality afforded to other ladies.

At her return towards Virginia she came at Gravesend to her end and grave, having given great demonstration of her Christian sincerity, as the first fruits of Virginian conversion, leaving here a godly memory, and the hopes of her resurrection, her soul aspiring to see and enjoy presently in heaven what here she had joyed to hear and believe of her beloved Saviour.

Not such was Tomocomo, but a blasphemer of what he knew not, and preferring his god to ours because he taught them—by his own so appearing—to wear their devil-lock at the left ear. He acquainted me with the manner of that his appearance and believed that this Okee, or devil, had taught them their husbandry, etc.

Powhatan was at this time of their coming gone southwards for fear (as some thought) lest Opachancanough, his brother, should join with the English against him. His age was not so great as some have reported, they reckoning every spring and autumn for distinct years.

Tomocomo was as wise in computation of his sailing, reckoning each night—when he expected they should have anchored by the shore!—as another day. He is said also to have set up with notches on a stick the numbers of men, being sent to see and signify the truth of the multitudes reported to his master. But his arithmetic soon failed, and wonder did no less amaze him at the sight of so much corn and trees in his coming from Plymouth to London, the Virginians imagining that defect thereof here had brought us thither.

< Smith 1624:123

In the Fourth Book of his *General History,* Smith tells us he encountered Uttamatomakkin in London and the man asked an embarrassing question of a kind many an Indian would ask in the years to come: How come east and west can't deal as equals? Can we believe Smith would have reported this if he were not in sympathy? Powhatan's councilor would have seen, if not met, King James at the Twelfth Night masque he attended in company with the Rolfes on 6 January 1617, and Smith apparently reminds him of this below. But neither he nor Pocahontas—Powhatan's royal emissaries—were ever given a royal audience in that capacity.

THIS SAVAGE, one of Powhatan's council, being amongst them held an understanding fellow, the king purposely sent him, as they say, to number the people here and inform him well what we were and our state.

Arriving at Plymouth, according to his directions he got a long stick whereon by notches he did think to have kept the number of all the men he could see, but he was quickly weary of that task.

Coming to London, where by chance I met him, [and] having renewed our acquaintance (where many were desirous to hear and see his behavior), he told me Powhatan did bid him to find me out to show him our god, the king, queen, and prince I so much had told them of. Concerning God I told him the best I could; the king I heard he had seen, and the rest he should see when he would. He denied ever to have seen the king till by circumstances he was satisfied he had. Then he replied very sadly, "You gave Powhatan a white dog, which Powhatan fed as himself. But your king gave me nothing, and I am better than your white dog."

LIBRARY OF VIRGINIA

SIR EDWIN SANDYS

56. John Rolfe

Letter to Sandys, 8 June 1617

< **Magdalene College: The Ferrar Papers 76–960a,** Virginia Magazine X, 1902:134, Kingsbury III, 70–71.

They have taken the northern route across the Atlantic, a route often thwarted by head winds, but the same route the *Mayflower* is to take the Pilgrims in the autumn a few years later—who will come in on the other end of Cape Cod and try unsuccessfully to round it to the south.

The widower on arrival finds shabby prosperity. Ragged men are single men, a sign that women are few or absent.

Rolfe is determined to go ahead, despite the death of his wife, and will bury his grief in the mission work among Indian children. This is an unusual amount of zeal in a lay person. Nicholas Ferrar, Sr., in whose papers this letter is found, had a special interest in this, and held out an endowment of a hundred pounds to establish a school to educate one hundred Indian children. Such was not to be, and the money was sent to Bermuda by his son, Nicholas junior, after his father's death.

Rolfe asks for a "command," but all his land ambition is for his son.

The brand snatched out of the fire is a reference, not altogether apt, to the Greek myth of Althaea and Meleager. Rolfe would have read it in Ovid's *Metamorphoses,* which George Sandys, Sir Edwin's brother, was soon busy translating at Jamestown during the 1620s for a new English edition. He was not quite to replace Golding's, but brought the heroic couplet in fashion.

HONOR'D SIR—The many courtesies and favors I have received at your hands shall during my life bind me to you in my best service, and so often as occasion shall offer itself I will not forget to express the same. At this present I have briefly noted to you in what estate we found the colony, and of our speedy passage hither—

Upon the 10th of April we departed from Plymouth and the next day lost sight of the Lizard, having the *Treaserer* in our company, which kept with us about 3 weeks; at what time we lost her in foggy weather which continued after 20 days, in which time we had hardly a day to make a certain observation. The same day month (according to the day of the week) that we lost the Land's End, we fell with the dangerous shoals of Cape Codd, running in one glass from 20 to 5 and 4 fathom water, not able to see, by reason of the thick fog, half a cable's length from the ship. Here we anchored all night, and the next day with no small peril got clear of them. From hence we shaped our course along our coast of Virginia, keeping our leads all the way—which was our best guide, having so good a pilot as our governor,[1] the fog still continuing—and arrived at Point Comfort the 15 of May, all our company being in good health (only one man died, who was sickly before he came from England).

Thus it pleased God to bless us with a speedy and prosperous passage. Yea, had we not been troubled to free ourselves from those shoals, and with misty weather, we had assuredly by God's help arrived in Virginia in a month's space.

Two or 3 days after, arrived Captain Martyne w[ith the] pinnace, all his men in good health to increase our joys.

We found the colony, God be thanked, in good estate, never enjoying a firmer peace nor more plenty; however, in buildings, fortifications, and of boats much ruined and great want. Our present governor at James town is repairing and making straight what he findeth decayed and crooked, to whose good endeavors and noble disposition our colony hath been, is, and will be much indebted.

All men cheerfully labor about their grounds, their hearts and hands not ceasing from work, though many have scarce rags to cover their naked bodies. English wheat, barley, Indian corn, tobacco—great plenty in the ground; hemp and flax seed distributed to most men by the governor, and is put into the ground; nothing neglected which anyways may be available to advance the colony, and to give encouragement to yourself and the rest of the honorable Company.

The cattle thrive and increase exceeding well, the plows yarely[2] work, and oxen are plentiful; the Indians very loving, and willing to part with their children.

My wife's death is much lamented; my child much desired when it is of better strength to endure so hard a passage, whose life greatly

[1] Deputy Governor Sir Samuel Argall, a fine seaman.
[2] "Quickly." Or read possibly "yearly." The word is written "yerely."

extinguisheth the sorrow of her loss, saying all must die, but 'tis enough that her child liveth.

I know not how I may be censured for leaving my child behind me, nor what hazard I may incur of your noble love and other of my best friends. At my departure from Gravesend, noth[ing] withstanding I was much importuned, I had no such intent. But in our short passage to Plymouth in smooth water I found such fear and hazard of his health, being not fully recovered of his sickness, and lack of attendance—for they who looked to him had need of nurses themselves—and indeed in all our passage [he] prospered no better, that by the advice of Captain Argall, and divers who also foresaw the danger and knew the inconvenience hereof persuaded me to what I did. At Plymouth I found Sir Lewes Stakely[1] is nobly minded towards me [and] that he most earnestly entreated to have the keeping of him until my brother took further order. I thought good to certify you hereof and desire yourself and all the Company for these causes to hold me excused, if in their judgments I may be censured to have erred herein.

A firm continuance of your favor and love towards me I daily pray for. And although great is my loss, and much my sorrow to be deprived of so great a comfort and hopes I had to effect my zealous endeavors and desires as well in others as in her whose soul, I doubt not, resteth in eternal happiness, yet such temperance have I learned in prosperity and patience in adversity, that I will as joyfully receive evil as good at the hand of God; and assuredly trust that He who hath preserved my child even as a brand snatched out of the fire hath further blessings in store for me, and will give me strength and courage to undertake any religious and charitable employment yourself and the honorable Company shall command me, and which in duty I am bound to do.

Now my last request at this time is to yourself, whom I have found a father to me, my wife, and child (and [I] will ever acknowledge it with the best gratefulness my heart and pen can offer), that you would be pleased, as you have begun and been one of the principal

[1] Sir Lewis Stukeley, vice-admiral of Devon.

instruments herein, to continue your noble favor and furtherance even for my child' sake, being the living ashes of his deceased mother, and that you will still be the means that your own free liberality, and all others by your pronouncement, in obtaining so liberal a stipend may not die with my wife, but continue for her child's advancement, which will the better enhable myself and him hereafter to undertake and execute what may be commanded and required from us. Thus referring myself to your approved wisdom, craving pardon for my boldness, desiring no longer to live than when I shall cease from studying and endeavoring to bend my best strength to persevere in this action for the advancement of the honor of God, King, and Country, with my humble remembrance to yourself and your noble and virtuous lady, whose requests I will not forget to satisfy wherein I may when time shall serve.

I take my leave and rest

At your command ever ready,
JO. ROLF

James Town, this 8 of June, 1617.

S[ub] scriptum. May you please, Sire, as occasion shall be offered, to remember me for some place of command and some estate of land to be confirmed to me and my child, wherein I have formerly found your love and readiness, for which I shall rest much bound unto you.

[endorsed:] Mr. John Rolph from Virginia to Sir Edwin Sandys. To my honored and much respected friend, Sir Edwyn Sandys, knight, deliver these. Their journey to Virginia – Good state of the colony – Store of cattle and plows – The Indians loving, and will part with their children – Their comfort of his son – He left at Plymouth with Sir Lewes Stakeley – Desireth the stipend may be continued to him – Praying a place of command for his[

57. The Ancient Planters of Virginia

A Brief Declaration

< State Paper Office, Colonial, 3/21,I; **Colonial Records of Va. 1874:69;** McIlwaine 1915:28

Sir Thomas Smythe's administration had come under increasing criticism until in 1619 the man, in a posture of beleaguerment, offered to turn over his responsibilities and resign. The Smythe faction was still powerful, not least because of its strong attachment to the court party, but had become a minority in the Virginia Company. To Sir Thomas' great disappointment he found his resignation accepted and the Council voted to replace him as treasurer with Sir Edwin Sandys, a leader of the liberals. Sandys was unacceptable to King James and was succeeded a year later by the Earl of Southampton, who remained treasurer until the dissolution of the Company.

After the terrible and devastating massacre of 22 March 1622, the Smythe faction seized the opportunity to lay blame on the Sandys/Southampton administrations. Their first salvo was Capt. Nathaniel Butler's *The Unmasked Face of Our Colony in Virginia,* a report of appalling, of sickening, conditions on the James River, and the leaden apathy in the winter following the massacre. Then came a defense of Smythe in a document by Alderman Johnson early in 1623 entitled *Declaration of the Prosperous State of the Colony,* claiming that for the twelve years of the Smythe administration, 1607–19, excusing initial missteps typical of starting up such undertakings, the colony had prospered and grown and reached accord with the Indians, reminding them that throughout the period careful and accurate accounts were kept. It was endorsed by the signatures of ex-Lieutenant Governor Samuel Argall, Johnson himself, and Samuel Wroth, strong Smythe men, the last a spokesman for the faction. Both papers were spread on the minutes, the latter with replies from the Sandys people.

Captain John Bargrave next spoke up for Sandys and brought itemized accusations against the Smythe years which were answered in Smythe's defense by Sir Nathaniel Rich (April 1623).

Two anti-Smythe salvoes were now fired by the colonists in Virginia, where Smythe was hated. Both are given here. §58 was presented in the spring of 1623, §57 a year later, but they are most important to us as eyewitness accounts of our period, if also the years following. *The Answer* §58 is interesting for the signature of Ralph Hamor, who in his 1615 *Discourse* §51 was all praise for Governor Dale, but now accuses him of having instituted a reign of terror in the early days at Henrico. Thus always the outcome of censorship.

These in turn drew a response from Alderman Johnson in May entitled *An answer to a declaration of the present state of Virginia, which was presented to His Majesty in Easter week last by part of the Company when in truth a 4th part of the whole Company were neither summoned nor present at the publishing of it, and very few had their hands in it.* So the Smythe faction was 25% of the Company.

The third salvo of the Sandys/Southampton supporters, *Discourse of the Old Company,* appeared in April 1625, after the dissolution of the Company and deals with conditions in the 1620s:

> About six years ago, when by reason of the apparent misprospering of the plantation, and the foulness of the accounts here, the then treasurer, being governor of four or five other companies, which excused his neglect of attending this business, the government of the Company was translated from Sir Thomas Smith and Aldran Johnson into Sir Edwin Sandis, and after into the Earl of Southampton's hands, and their deputies. It is notoriously known how they, with Captain Argoll and other of their friends, partly peradventure through fear—their accounts, depredations, piracies, and misgovernment being now question'd before the council and in the Company's courts—perpetually disturbed and disgraced by several ways, both to His Majesty and to the world, all the present proceedings of the Company to the great disheartening of the Company here and no small advantage of the colony.[1]

Notwithstanding, the massacre was a terrible fact; the king supported Sir Thomas Smythe and the court party, and the king did not trust the ambition of Sir Edwin Sandys, the Earl of Southampton, and the liberals. In the end that was all that mattered.

In Sainsbury's calendar of state papers, pp. 65–66, is the following in regard to §57: "1624, July. Petition of Governor Sir Francis Wyatt, the Council, and Assembly of Virginia to the King. Hav[ing] understood that His Majesty, notwithstanding the unjust disparagement of the plantation, has taken it under his especial care, we entreat that credit may not be given to the late declarations presented to His Majesty concerning the happy, but indeed miserable, estate of the colony during the first twelve years, nor to the malicious imputations which have been laid upon the late government, inclose the true state of both, and earnestly request that the present government may be continued, [and we] pray that the King's tender compassion will not allow them to fall into the hands of Sir Thomas Smythe or his confidents." Signed by Sir Francis Wyatt, Captain Francis West, Sir George Yeardley, and eighty-six others. Despite the later date, I feel §57 and §58 are simultaneous expressions, and I give §57 first as the fuller of the two.

---

[1] Kingsbury 1906d: 531–32.

A Brief Declaration

of the

plantation of Virginia during the first twelve years, when Sir Thomas Smith *was governor of the Company, and down to this present time.*

By the Ancient Planters now remaining alive in Virginia.

WHEREAS IN THE BEGINNING of Sir Thomas Smith's twelve years government it was published in print throughout the Kingdom of England that a plantation should be settled in Virginia for the glory of God in the propagation of the Gospel of Christ (the conversion of the savages), to the honor of His Majesty by the enlarging of his territories and future enriching of his kingdom—for which respects many noble and well-minded persons were induced to adventure great sums of money to the advancement of so pious and noble a work, who have from the very first been frustrate of their expectation, as we conceive, by the misgovernment of Sir Thomas Smith, aiming at nothing more than a particular[1] gain to be raised out of the labors of such as both voluntarily adventured themselves and were otherwise sent over at the common charge. This will clearly appear in the examination of the first expedition and several supplies in the time of his government. The first plantation in Virginia consisted of one hundred persons, so slenderly provided for that before they had remained half a year in this new colony they fell into extreme want, not having anything left to sustain them save a little ill-conditioned barley which, ground to meal, and pottage made thereof, one small ladleful was allowed each person for a meal, without bread or aught else whatsoever; so that had not God by His great providence moved the Indians, then our utter enemies, to bring us relief, we had all utterly by famine perished. How unable so small a company of people, so poorly sent over, were to make way for such as should follow may easily be judged.

[1] Private.

The first supply, being two ships, the *John & Francis* and *Phenix,* with one hundred and twenty persons, worse every way provided for than the former, arrived here about eight or nine months after [January 1608] and found the colony consisting of no more than forty persons—of those, ten only able men, the rest at point of death—all utterly destitute of houses, not one as yet built, so that they lodged in cabins and holes within the ground. Victuals they had none save some small relief from the Indians, as some yet living were feeling witnesses. Neither were we for our future and better maintenance permitted to manure or till any ground—a thing in a new plantation *principally* to be regarded—but were by the direction of Sir Thomas Smith and his officers here wholly employed in cutting down of masts, cedar, black walnut, clapboard, etc., and in digging gold ore, as some thought, which being sent for England proved dirt. These works to make return of present profit hindered others of more necessary consequence of plantation.

After this first supply, there were some few poor houses built, and entrance made in clearing of ground to the quantity of four acres for the whole colony, hunger and sickness not permitting any great matters to be done that year.

The second supply was a ship called the *Mary Margett,* which arrived here nine months after, about the time of Michaelmas [29 September 1608], in her sixty persons, most gentlemen, few or no tradesmen, except some Polanders to make pitch, tar, potashes, etc. to be returned for present gain. So meanly likewise were these furnished forth for victuals that in less than two months after their arrival want compelled us to employ our time abroad in trading with the Indians for corn, whereby, though for a time we partly relieved our necessities, yet in May following we were forced—leaving a small guard of gentlemen and some others about the president at James Town—to disperse the whole colony, some amongst the savages, but most to the oyster banks, where they lived upon oysters for the space of nine weeks, with the allowance only of a pint of Indian corn to each man for a week, and that allowance of corn continued to them but two weeks of the nine, which kind of feeding caused all our skins to peel off from head to foot as if we had been flayed.

By this time arrived Captain Samuell Argall in a small bark, with him neither supply of men nor victuals from the Company. But we, understanding that he had some small provisions of bread and wine more than would serve his own company, required him and the master of the bark to remain ashore whilst we might bring his sails ashore, the better to assure us of his ship and such provisions as could be spared, whereunto he seemed willingly to condescend. Those provisions at a small allowance of biscuit, cake, and a small measure of wine or beer to each person for a day somewhat relieved us for the space of a month, at the end of which time arrived the third supply, called Sir Thomas Gates his fleet [August 1609], which consisted of seven ships and near five hundred persons, with whom a small proportion of victual for such a number was landed—houses few or none to entertain them, so that being quartered in the open field they fell upon that small quantity of corn, not being above seven acres, which we with great penury and sufferance had formerly planted, and in three days at the most wholly devoured it.

These numbers thus meanly provided, not being able to subsist and live together, were soon after divided into three parties and dispersed abroad for their better relief: the first, under command of Captain Francis West, to seat at the head of the river; a second, under command of Captain John Smith, then president, at James Town; and the other with Captain John Martin in the river at Nansamun—which divisions gave occasions to the Indians treacherously to cut off divers of our men and boats, and forced the rest at the end of six weeks, having spent those small provisions they had with them, to retire to James Town—and that in the depth of winter when by reason of the cold it was not possible for us to endure to wade in the water as formerly to gather oysters to satisfy our hungry stomachs, but constrained to dig in the ground for unwholesome roots, whereof we were not able to get so many as would suffice us, in respect of the frost at that season and our poverty and weakness; so that famine compelled us wholly to devour those hogs, dogs, and horses that were then in the colony, together with rats, mice, snakes, or what vermin or carrion soever we could light on, as also toadstools, jew's ears,[1] or what else we found growing upon the ground that would fill either mouth or belly; and were driven through unsufferable hunger unnaturally to eat those things which nature most abhorred: the flesh and excrements of man, as well of our own nation as of an Indian digged by some out of his grave after he had lain buried three days, and wholly devoured him. Others, envying the better state of body of any whom hunger had not yet so much wasted as their own, lay wait and threatened to kill and eat them. One among the rest slew his wife as she slept in his bosom, cut her in pieces, powdered [salted] her, and fed upon her till he had clean devoured all parts saving her head, and was for so barbarous a fact and cruelty justly executed.

Some adventuring to seek relief in the woods died as they sought it, and were eaten by others who found them dead. Many put themselves into the Indians' hands, though our enemies, and were by them slain.[2]

In this extremity of famine continued the colony till the twentieth of May [1610] when unexpected yet happily arrived Sir Thomas Gates and Sir George Somers in two small barks—which they built in the Sommer Islands after the wreck of the *Sea Adventure,* wherein they [had] set forth from England—with them one hundred persons barely provided of victual for themselves.

They found the colony consisting then of but sixty persons, most famished and at point of death, of whom many soon after died. The lamentable outcries of theirs so moved the hearts of those worthies, not being in any sort able long to relieve their wants, they soon resolved to embark themselves and this poor remainder of the colony in those two pinnaces and two other small barks then in the river to set sail for Newfoundland, where they might relieve their wants and procure one safer passage for England.

Every man glad of this resolution labored his utmost to further it, so that in three weeks we had fitted those barks and pinnaces the best we could and quitted James Town, leaving the poor buildings in it to the spoil of the Indians, hoping never to return to repossess

[1] An edible tree fungus.

[2] No mention here of the party of Captain Davies at Point Comfort who fared well enough during the "starving time."

them. When we had not sailed down the river above twelve miles but we espied a boat, which afterwards we understood came from the Right Honorable Lord La Ware, who was then arrived at Point Comfort with three good ships, wherein he brought two hundred and fifty persons, with some store of provisions for them; but by reason he found the colony in so great want was forced to put both his own people and the rest of the colony to a very mean allowance, which was seven pound of English meal for a man a week, and five pounds for every woman, without the addition of any victual whatsoever, except in the stead of meal we took valuably[1] either peas or oatmeal.

Upon the arrival of that boat, Sir Thomas Gates, understanding from the Lord La Ware that His Lordship was arrived with commission from the Company to be governor and captain general of Virginia, and had brought men and provisions for the subsisting and advancing of the plantation, he the very next day [8 June 1610] to the great grief of all his company (only except Captain John Martin), as wind and weather gave leave, returned his whole company with charge to take possession again of those poor ruinated habitations at James Town which he had formerly abandoned. Himself in a boat proceeded downward to meet His Lordship, who making all speed up arrived shortly after at James Town.

The time of the year being then most unseasonable by intemperate heat, at the end of June his people suddenly falling generally into most pestilent diseases of calentures and fevers, not less than one hundred and fifty of them died within few months after, and that chiefly for want of means to comfort them in their weak estates. The residue also disabled by reason of sickness could perform nothing that year to the advancement of the colony. Yet with the help of those people which had arrived with Sir Thomas Gates, together with some of the ancient planters, who by use were grown practic in a hard way of living, two small forts were erected near the river's mouth at Kicoughtun, encompassed with small young trees, having for housing, in the one, two formerly built by the Indians and covered with bark by them, in the other a tent with some few

[1] The equivalent measure of.

thatch'd cabins which our people built at our coming thither. We found divers other Indian houses built by the natives which by reason we could make no use of we burnt, killing to the number of twelve or fourteen Indians, and possessing such corn as we found growing of their planting. We remained there until harvest, when we reaped, besides what we spent, about the quantity of one hundred and fifty bushels of corn, which by order from the Lord La Ware was transported to James Town.

His Lordship, intending to send up certain forces to march towards the mountains for the discovery of gold or silver mines at the end of October [1610], sent his patents to Captain Yardley and Captain Holcroft, commanders of those two forts at Kicoughtan, wherein His Lordship gave order that they should be forthwith abandoned and the people with all speed to be brought to James City, there to prepare for his intended march.

At that time there arrived a small ship called the *Dainty,* with twelve men and one woman, some little provision of victual, two or three horses, and some other slight necessaries for the colony.

Soon after, we set forward for our intended march, having for our leaders Captain Edwarde Brewster and Captain George Yeardley, being in number one hundred persons, furnished with all such necessary provisions as the colony at that time out of its poverty was able to provide. This design was hindered by reason of the unfortunate loss of all our chief men skillful in finding out mines, who were treacherously slain by the savages inviting them ashore to eat victuals (which they wanted) even when the meat was in their mouths. They caring only to fill their bellies foresaw not to prevent this danger which befell them.

This injury we revenged for the present as we could by killing some Indians and burning many houses. But by reason of this disaster we proceeded not farther on our journey than the head of the river, where we spent about three months doing little but enduring much.

His Lordship was there in person for the most part of that time. But his disease of body growing much upon him, he resolved to retire to James Town, giving order that the fort which we had built there should be quitted and the troop drawn down, which accordingly was done. His Lordship then in regard of his sickness was advised to put to sea in his ship, the *Delaware,* to seek remedy in some other parts for the health of his body. At his going he left Captain George Percie deputy governor, the people remaining under his command, provided for three months at a short allowance of victuals [April 1611].

The calamities of these times would not any way permit works of great importance to be performed, sith that we did was as much as we could do to live and defend ourselves.

The plantations held at His Lordship's departure were only James Town and Point Comfort, where was a small fort fenced with palisadoes, in it one slight house, a store, and some few thatch'd cabins, which shortly after by casualty was burnt with fire. Some few great ordnance were slenderly mounted at James Town and Point Comfort.

A fortnight after His Lordship's departure arrived a small ship called the *Hercules,* with some thirty people and some provisions for them. The twelve of May [1611] following arrived Sir Thomas Dale with three ships and three hundred persons, his provisions for them of such quality for the most part as hogs refused to eat, some whereof were sent back to England to testify the same. And that the rest was not better was justified upon oath before the Honorable the Lord Chief Justice of the Common Pleas, at Guildhall in London, by Sir Thomas Gates and two other gentlemen.

Sir Thomas Dale, taking into consideration the precedent times not to have succeeded according to the greedy desire of Sir Thomas Smith, presently employed the general colony about the lading of those three ships with such freight as the country then yielded. But a little before the ships were ready to depart, Sir Thomas Gates arrived with three ships and three carvels [caravels], with him three hundred persons meanly provided with victuals for such a number. In this fleet to our remembrance arrived sixty cows and some swine. It was his care to dispatch those ships and carvels freighted as aforesaid to the neglect of works of greater importance. Sir Thomas Dale immediately upon his arrival, to add to that extremity of misery under which the colony from her infancy groaned, made and published most cruel and tyrannous laws, exceeding the strictest rules of martial discipline, which laws were sent over by Sir Thomas Dale to Sir Thomas Smith by the hand of Mr. William Starchey [Strachey], then secretary to the state, and were returned *in print with approbation* for our future government, as in divers books yet extant more fully appeareth.[1]

At Michaelmas then next following [29 September 1611], Sir Thomas Dale removed himself with three hundred persons for the building of Henrico Town, where being landed he oppressed his whole company with such extraordinary labors by day and watching by night as may seem incredible to the ears of any who had not the experimental trial thereof. Want of houses at first landing in the cold of winter and pinching hunger continually biting made those imposed labors most insufferable, and the best fruits and effects thereof to be no better than the slaughter of His Majesty's free subjects by starving, hanging, burning, breaking upon the wheel, and shooting to death. Some, more than half famished, running to the Indians to get relief, being again returned, were burnt to death. Some for stealing to satisfy their hunger were hanged, and one chained to a tree till he starved to death. Others attempting to run away in a barge and a shallop (all the boats that were then in the colony) and therein to adventure their lives for their native country, being discovered and prevented, were shot to death, hanged, and broken upon the wheel; besides continual whippings, extraordinary punishments, working as slaves in irons for term of years—and that for petty offenses!—were daily executed. Many famished in holes and other poor cabins in the ground, not respected because sickness had disabled them for labor, nor was there sufficient for them that were more able to work, our best allowance being but nine ounces of corrupt and putrefied meal and half a pint of oatmeal or peas of like ill condition for each person a day. Those provisions were sent over by one Winne, a draper, and Caswell, a baker, by the appointment (as we conceive) of Sir Thomas Smith.

Under this tyrannous government the colony continued in extreme slavery and misery for the space of five years, in which time many whose necessities enforced the breach of those laws by the strictness

---

[1] *Laws Divine, Moral and Martial,* etc.

and severity thereof suffered death and other punishments. Divers gentlemen both there and at Henrico town and throughout the whole colony, being great adventurers and no friends or alliance to Sir Thomas Smith, were feeling members of those general calamities as far forth as the meanest fellow sent over.

The buildings and fortifications of that town or thereabouts were no way extraordinary, neither could want accompanied with blood and cruelty effect better.

Fortification against a foreign enemy there was none, only two or three pieces of ordnance mounted; and against a domestic no other but a pale enclosing the town to the quantity of four acres, within which those buildings that were erected could not in any man's judgment—neither did—stand above five years, and that not without continual reparations. True it is that there was a brick church intended to be built, but not so much as the foundation thereof ever finished, but we contenting ourselves with a church of wood answerable to those houses. Many other works of like nature were by him done at Henrico and the precincts thereof, but so slightly as, before his departure hence, he himself saw the ruin and desolation of most of them.

Sir Thomas Gates likewise in his time erected some buildings in and about James Town, which by continual cost in repairing of them do yet for the most part in some sort remain.

A framed bridge[1] was also then erected, which utterly decayed before the end of Sir Thomas Smith's government, that being the only bridge any way so to be called that was ever in the country.

At this time in all these labors, the misery throughout the whole colony in the scarcity of food was equal, which penurious and hard kind of living enforced and emboldened some to petition to Sir Thomas Gates, then governor, to grant them that favor that they might employ themselves in husbandry, that thereby they and all others by planting of corn might be better fed than those supplies of victual which were sent from England would afford to do—which request of theirs was denied unless they would pay the yearly rent of three barrels of corn and one month's work to the colony, although

[1] A freight wharf at Jamestown.

many of them had been employed in the general works and services of the colony from the beginning of the plantation, which hard condition of tenantship was then accepted rather than they would continue in those general services and employments no way better than slavery.

Most part of the time that Sir Thomas Gates and Sir Thomas Dale governed we were at war with the natives, so that by them divers times were many of our people slain, whose blood Sir Thomas Dale neglected not to revenge by divers and sundry executions in killing many [Indians], cutting down and taking away their corn, burning their houses, spoiling their weirs, etc.

In this time also the two forts—Fort Henry and Fort Charles—at Kicoughton were again erected with such buildings as were formerly expressed, not fortified at all against a foreign enemy, and against the Indian that common order of a pale, or palisado.

The supplies sent out of England while Sir Thomas Gates and Sir Thomas Dale governed were these: a small bark called the *John & Francis,* which brought few men and less victual; the next a small ship called the *Sarah,* with the like number of men and victual; the next ship called the *Tresorer,* wherein came Captain Samuell Argoll, bringing with him to the number of fifty good men, which ship and men were wholly employed in trade and other services for relieving of the colony; the next ship, called the *Elizabeth,* with about thirteen persons, for them little provision; the next, the same *Elizabeth* came again, with some small store of provisions only. In her Sir Thomas Gates went for England, leaving the government with Sir Thomas Dale [April 1614].

A little before the departure of Sir Thomas Gates, many of the ancient planters, by the instigation of Sir Thomas Dale, upon the promise of an absolute freedom after three years more to be expired, having most of them already served the colony six or seven years in that general slavery, were yet contented to work in the building of Charles City and Hundred, with very little allowance of clothing and victual, and that only for the first year, being promised one month in the year, and one day in the week from May Day till harvest to get our maintenance out of the earth without any further help—which promise of Sir Thomas Dale was not performed, for out of that small time which was allowed for our maintenance we were abridged of near half, so that out of our daily tasks we were forced to redeem time wherein to labor for our sustenance, thereby miserably to purchase our freedom. Yet so fell it out that our state by God's mercy was afterwards more happy than others who continued longer in the aforementioned slavery; in which time we built such houses as before, and in them lived with continual repairs, and building new where the old failed, until the massacre.

For matter of fortification in all this time were only four pieces of ordnance mounted for our defense against the natives.

Soon after we were seated at Charles Hundred, Sir Thomas Dale resolved of a journey to Pamonkey River, there to make with the savages either a firm league of friendship or a present war. They perceiving his intent inclined rather for peace (more for fear than love), which was then concluded betwixt them. That done we returned to our habitations where great want and scarcity oppressed us, that continuing and increasing, our first harvest not yet being ripe, caused in many an intended mutiny, which being by God's mercy discovered, the prime actors were duly examined and convicted, whereof six being adjudged and condemned were executed.

After this arrived for supply a small ship called the *John & Francis,* with about twenty persons and little or no provisions for them. The next ship, called the *Tresorer,* arrived here with the number of twenty persons and as little provisions as the former, in which ship, after many other designs were effected by Sir Thomas Dale, as making spoil of the Keschiacks and Wariscoyacks, impaling some necks of land for defense against the savages, and in fishing for our relief, etc., he departed from Virginia [June 1616], and left the government to Captain George Yardley, under whom the colony lived in peace and best plenty that ever it had till that time, yet most part of the people for that year of his government continued in the general services, following their labors as Sir Thomas Dale left them by order.

At Michaelmas following arrived a small ship called the *Susan,* her lading being the first magazine,[1] consisting of some necessary

---

[1] The *Susan* was the first "magazine ship," a ship sent over to deliver supplies and no new colonists.

provisions of clothing as our wants required, which goods were sold by Sir Thomas Smith's factor, as we suppose, for a sufficient profit, exchanging with us their commodities for our tobacco.

At Christmas then following, just occasion being given by the Indians of Chiquohomini in many and several kinds of abuses, and in deriding of our demands whereunto they had formerly agreed, and conditioned with Sir Thomas Dale to pay us yearly tribute, viz., a bushel of corn for every bowman, for which by agreement we were to give to each man one piece of copper and one iron *tomahawke,* and to the eight chief men each a suit of red cloth, which cloths and trucking stuff we esteemed of more worth than their corn. These and the like gross abuses moved our governor, Captain George Yeardley, to levy a company of men to the number of eighty-four to be revenged upon those contemptuous Indians, which he according to his desire fully executed, and returned home with the spoil of them, concluding before his departure from them a more firm league in appearance than formerly was, for that it continued unviolated almost the space of two years—our people freely traveling from town to town, both men, women, and children, without any arms, and were by the savages lodged in their houses, every way kindly entreated and no way molested.[1]

In March following [1617], our three years time being expired, as it was our due we of Charles Hundred demanded our long-desired freedom from that common and general servitude, unto which request Captain George Yeardley freely and willingly assented, to our great joy and comfort. Yet remained the most part of the colony in the former servitude, part of whom were farmers, the rest employed in such works as Sir Thomas Dale gave order for before his departure.

We that were freed, with our humble thanks to God, fell cheerfully to our particular labors, whereby to our great comfort through His blessing we reaped a plentiful harvest.

In May following arrived Captain Samuel Argoll with commission to be governor. He brought with him to the number of a hundred persons partly at the charge of the Company and partly at the charge

---

[1] See also §52–860, 861.

of private adventures. With them was brought a very little provision for that number. At his arrival here he found the colony in all parts well stored with corn, and at Charles Hundred a granary well furnished by rents lately raised and received from the farmers, which corn he took possession of. But how it was employed himself can best give an account.

Whilest he governed, the colony was slenderly provided of munition, whereby a strict proclamation was made for restraint of wasting or shooting away of powder, under pain of great punishment; which forbidding to shoot at all in our pieces caused the loss of much of our corn then growing upon the ground. The Indians, perceiving our forbearance to shoot as formerly, concluded thereupon that our pieces were, as they said, sick and not to be used. Upon this, not long after, they were bold to presume to assault some of our people, whom they slew, therein breaking that league which before was so fairly kept.

During his time of government most of the people of the colony remained as formerly in the common service, their freedom not being to be obtained without extraordinary payment.

The next ship that arrived here was the *George,* set forth as we suppose at the charge of private adventurers, but came so meanly provided with victual that had not we, the old planters, relieved them, most of them had been starved. The next ships, called the *Neptune* and *Treasurer,* arrived in August following, set out at the charge of the Right Honorable the Lord Laware, his noble associates, and some other private adventurers. The people which arrived were so poorly victualed that had they not been distributed amongst the old planters, they must for want have perished. With them was brought a most pestilent disease called the bloody flux, which infected almost all the whole colony. That disease notwithstanding all our former afflictions was never known before amongst us.[1]

The next supply were two ships called the *William & Thomas* and the *Guift,* which arrived in January [1618], the *Guift* being set forth at the charge of the Society of Martin's Hundred, the other by the magazine and some private adventurers.

---

[1] "The sixth of August [1607], there died John Asbie of the bloody flix." Percy §1–99. And many more that terrible first summer at Jamestown.

The next, a small ship called the *Elinor,* set forth at whose charge we know not, arrived here in April after, and in her Captain Samuell Argoll, leaving his government, ship'd himself for England. Whatsoever else befell in the time of his government we omit to relate, much being upon our oaths already sufficiently examined and our answers sent for England.

By all which hath heretofore been said concerning this colony, from the infancy thereof and until the expiration of Sir Thomas Smith's government, may easily be perceived and plainly understood what just cause he or any else have to boast of the flourishing estate of those times, wherein so great miseries and calamities were endured, and so few works of moment or importance performed, himself being justly to be charged as a prime author thereof by his neglect of providing and allowing better means to proceed in so great a work; and in hindering very many of our friends from sending much relief and means, who being earnestly solicited from hence by our letters, wherein we lamentably complained unto them, have often besought Sir Thomas Smith that they might have leave to supply us *at their own charge,* both with provision of victual and all other necessaries, wherein he utterly denied them so to do!—protesting to them that we were in no want at all, but that we exceeded in abundance and plenty of all things; so that thereby our friends were moved both to desist from sending and to doubt the truth of our letters, most part of which were by him usually intercepted and kept back; farther giving order by his directions to the governor here that all men's letters should be searched at the going away of ships, and if in any of them were found that the true estate of the colony was declared, they were presented to the governor and the inditers of them severely punished; by which means no man durst make any true relation to his friends of his own or the colony's true estate.

Neither was it permitted to any to have pass to go home, but by force were kept here and employed as we have said, save some few, one of whom received his pass from the king, and that closely made up in a garter, lest it should have been seized upon and he kept here notwithstanding. Those whom their friends procured their pass in open court from the Company were by private direction nevertheless made stay of, others procuring private letters having been let go.

We must also note here that Sir Thomas Dale, at his arrival finding himself deluded by the aforesaid protestations, pulled Captain Newport by the beard and threat'ning to hang him, for that he affirmed Sir Thomas Smith's relation to be true, demanding of him whether it were meant that the people here in Virginia should feed upon trees.

So may we here conclude, as some have concluded for him, to what great growth of perfection with the expense of that seventy thousand pounds the plantation was advanced in the time of his 12 years' government. But whether, as it is said, he be to be praised for the managing of these affairs with much unanimity, moderation, integrity and judgment, we leave it to censure.

At the end of this twelve years arrived Sir George Yeardley to be governor, and found the colony in this estate and thus furnished, vizt., for fortification against a foreign enemy there was none at all, two demi-culverin[1] only were mounted upon rotten carriages and placed within James City, fitter to shoot down our houses than to offend an enemy; at Charles Hundred, which were mounted by Sir Thomas Dale, two demi-culverin and one saker[2]; fortifications against a domestic enemy very mean. For forts, towns, and plantations he found these: James City, Henrico, Charles City and Hundred, Shirley Hundred, Arrahattock, Martin Brandon, and Kicoughton—all which were but poorly housed and as ill fortified. For in James City were only those houses that Sir Thomas Gates built in the time of his government, with one wherein the governor always dwelt, an addition being made thereto in the time of Captain Samuel Argoll, and a church built wholly at the charge of the inhabitants of that city—of timber, being fifty foot in length and twenty foot in breadth. At Paspahayes also were some few slight houses built; at Henrico two or three old houses, a poor ruinated church, with some few poor buildings in the island; Coxen Dale and the Maine and at Arrahatocke one house; at Charles City six houses much decayed and, that we may not be too tedious, as these so were

[1] "A kind of cannon ... of about 4½ inches bore." OED
[2] "Smaller than a demi-culverin." OED

the rest of the places furnish'd.

For people then alive about the number of four hundred, very many of them in want of corn, utterly destitute of cattle, swine, poultry, and other provisions to nourish them.

For barks, pinnaces, shallops, barges, and boats he found only one old frigate, which belonged to the Sommer Islands, one old shallop built in Sir Thomas Dale's time, one boat built in Sir Samuel Argoll's time, with two small boats belonging to private men; for munition a very small quantity, the most part thereof being very bad and of little use; for ministers to instruct the people he found only three authorized, two others who never received their orders.

For staple commodities at his arrival he found none afoot save only tobacco. The natives he found upon doubtful terms. Neither did we ever perceive that at any time they voluntarily yielded themselves subjects or servants to our gracious sovereign, neither that ever they took any pride in that title nor paid they at any time any yearly contribution of corn for the sustentation of the colony, nor could we at any time keep them in such good respect or correspondency that they and we did become mutually helpful or profitable each to other; but to the contrary whatsoever at any time was done upon them proceeded from fear without love, for such help as we have had from them have been procured by sword or trade.

And here can we no way approve of that which hath lately been said in the behalf of Sir Thomas Smith by some of his new friends, that a flourishing plantation in Virginia, erected in the time of his 12 years' government, hath since been destroyed through the ignorance of succeeding governors here, for that by what we have already said all the world may judge in what a flourishing estate it was, and to what growth of perfection it was advanced at the arrival of Sir George Yeardley to be governor here, it being then, in our judgments that were members of the colony, in a poor estate.

The whole 12 years expired.

April 1619—arrived Sir George Yeardeley, bringing certain commissions and instructions from the Company for the better establishing of a commonwealth here, wherein order was taken for the removing of all those grievances which formerly were suff'red, and manifested the same by publishing a proclamation that all those that were resident here before the departure of Sir Thomas Dale should be freed and acquitted from such public services and labors which formerly they suffered; and that those cruel laws by which we had so long been governed were now abrogated, and that we were now to be governed by those free laws which His Majesty's subjects live under in England; and farther that free liberty was given to all men to make choice of their dividents of land and, as their abilities and means would permit, to possess and plant upon them.

And that they might have a hand in the governing of themselves, it was granted that a general assembly should be held yearly once, whereat were to be present the governor and council with two burgesses from each plantation freely to be elected by the inhabitants thereof; this assembly to have power to make and ordain whatsoever laws and orders should by them be thought good and profitable for our subsistence[1]—the effect of which proceeding gave such encouragement to every person here that all of them followed their particular labors with singular alacrity and industry, so that through the blessing of God upon our willing labors within the space of three years our country flourished with many new erected plantations from the head of the river to Kicoughtan, beautiful and pleasant to the spectators and comfortable for the relief and succor of all such as by occasion did travel by land or by water, every man giving free entertainment both to friends or others.

The plenty of these times likewise was such that all men generally were sufficiently furnished with corn, and many also had plenty of cattle, swine, poultry, and other good provisions to nourish them.

Monthly courts were held in every precinct to do justice in redressing of all small and petty matters, others of more consequence being referred to the governor, council, and general assembly. Now also were begun and set afoot the erecting of ironworks, planting of vines and mulberry trees for the nourishing of silkworms, a trial made for silk grass, tillage for English grain, gardening, and the like, which gave great hopes of present and future plenty in their several

[1] A first for the New World and nearly so for the whole. Ever since George Yeardley's administration Americans have taken democracy for granted.

particulars, wherein no doubt but much more had been effected had not great sickness and mortality prevented.

Those years falling out to be generally contagious through this continent, the people also sent over arrived here at the most unseasonable time of the year, being at the heat of summer; and divers of the ships brought with them most pestilent infections, whereof many of their people had died at sea, so that these times also of plenty and liberty were mixed with the calamities of sickness and mortality.

In October 1621 arrived Sir Francis Wyatt, knight, with commission to be governor and captain general of Virginia. He ratified and confirmed all the aforementioned liberties, freedoms, and privileges, to our great happiness and content. The country also flourished and increased in her former proceedings, as ironworks, planting of vines and mulberry for silk, etc. A ship also was sent to the Summer Islands for such commodities as that place afforded, as potatoes, fig trees, orange and lemon trees, and suchlike, many of which prosper and grow very likely to increase.

But amidst this happiness was the hand of God set against us, in great part no doubt for the punishment of our ingratitude in not being thankful but forgetful that by His mercy we were delivered from such bondage and calamity as before time we had suffered. Justly likewise were we punished for our greedy desires of present gain and profit, wherein many showed themselves insatiable and covetous—we being too secure in trusting of a treacherous enemy, the savages. They, whilest we entertained them friendly in our houses, took their opportunities and suddenly fell upon us, killing and murdering very many of our people, burning and devasting their houses and plantations. This happening upon the two and twentieth of March following (1622) struck so at the life of our welfare by blood and spoil that it almost generally defaced the beauty of the whole colony, putting us out of the way of bringing to perfection those excellent works wherein we had made so fair a beginning.

This deadly stroke being given to the great amazement and ruin of our state caused our governor and council with all speed for the safety of the rest, lest the Indians should take courage to pursue what they had begun, to recollect the straggling and woeful inhabitants, so dismembered, into stronger bodies and more secure places.

This enforced reducement of the colony into fewer bodies, together with the trouble of war then in hand, caused the year following a slender harvest to be reaped, whereby we were constrained to rely upon hopes for our relief by shipping out of England, and by trading with the more remote savages, most part of which supplies from England unfortunately miscarried by the way.

The savages likewise from whom we hoped to have helps by trade proved our most treacherous enemies, cunningly circumventing and cruelly murdering such as were employed abroad to get relief from them; by all which misaccidents we fell that year into great want and scarcity; which since by the blessing of God through our supplies we have had from the Company together with a plentiful harvest hath been abundantly restored.

Our governor, council, and others have used their uttermost and Christian endeavors in prosecuting revenge against the bloody savages, and have endeavored to restore the colony to her former prosperity, wherein they have used great diligence and industry, employing many forces abroad for the rooting them out of several places, that thereby we may come to live in better security, doubting not but in time we shall clean drive them from these parts, and thereby have the free liberty and range for our cattle, the increase of whom may bring us to plenty, and may also more freely go on again with setting up those staple commodities which we hoped by this time to have brought to good perfection.

For the supplies of shipping, men, cattle, and provisions that have arrived here since Sir Thomas Smith left his government we cannot now well reckon up, they being many, but must refer you to the printed books and to the lists and invoices returned by Sir George Yeardley.

For the state of the colony at this present we leave to the report of such commissioners as are now sent over by the Right Honorable the Lords of His Majesty's Privy Council.

This being read in the general assembly received full approbation.

[endorsed:] Virginia—a relation of its planting.

58. The Virginia General Assembly

The Answer of the General Assembly in Virginia to a "Declaration of the state of the colony in the 12 years of Sir Thomas Smith's government"—exhibited by Alderman Johnsone and others, 20 February 1624

< **Library of Congress, Jefferson Papers 8/20–8,** Neill 1869:407, McIlwaine 1915:21

This is the third salvo at the administration of Sir Thomas Smythe. It is heated and it is deadly, more to the point than the formal, discursive Brief Declaration §57. Alderman Johnson's "Declaration," that claimed that the years 1607–19 all in all were good years, with far better results than what followed under the Sandys/Southampton term that ended in the debacle of the 1622 massacre, brought this stout protest from Virginia.

The New World's first elected legislature makes the correct assertion that the 1609 charter gave no sanction to the harsh "laws divine, moral, and martial," that had suspended English common law in the colony.

HOLDING IT a sin against God and our own suffering to suffer the world to be abused with untrue reports, and to give unto vice the reward of virtue, WE, in the name of the whole Colony of Virginia, in our General Assembly, many of us having been eyewitnesses and patients of those times, have framed out of our duty to this country and love unto truth this dismasking of those praises which are contained in the foresaid declarations.

In those 12 years of Sir Thomas Smith his government we aver that the colony for the most part remained in great want and misery, under most severe and cruel laws sent over in print,[1] and contrary to the express letter of the king in his most gracious charter, and as mercilessly executed, oftentimes without trial or judgment.

---

[1] *Laws Divine, Moral and Martial,* etc., 27.

The allowance in those times for a man was only eight ounces of meal and half a pint of peas for a day, the one and the other moldy, rotten, full of cobwebs and maggots, loathsome to man and not fit for beasts; which forced many to flee for relief to the savage enemy, who being taken again were put to sundry deaths as by h[anging,] shooting, breaking upon the wheel; and others were forced by famine to filch for their bellies, of whom [one] for stealing 2 or 3 pints of oatmeal had a bodkin thrust through his tongue and was tied with a ch[ain] to a tree until he starved. If a man through his sickness had not been able to work, he had no allow[ance] at all. And so consequently perished many, through these extremities being weary of life, [who] digged holes in the earth and there hid themselves till they famished.

We cannot for this our scarcity blame our commanders here, in respect that our sustenance was to come from England. For had they at that time given us better allowance, we had perished in general, so lamentable was our scarcity, that we were constrained to eat dogs, cats, rats, snakes, toadstools, horsehides, and whatnot. One man out of the misery he endured, killing his wife, powdered her up to eat her, for which he was burned. Many besides fed on the corpse' of dead men. And one who had gotten an unsatiable out of custom to that food could not be restrained until such time as he was executed for it. And indeed so miserable was our estate that the happiest day that ever some of us then hoped to see was when the Indians had killed a mare, they wishing whilst she was a-boiling that Sir Thomas Smith were upon her back in the kettle.

And whereas it is affirmed that there were very few of His Majesty's subjects left[1] in those days, and those of the meanest rank, we answer that for one that now dies there then perished *five,* many being of ancient houses and born to estates of £1000 by the year, some more, some less, who likewise perished by famine. Those who survived who had both adventured their estates and persons were constrained to serve the colony (as if they had been slaves!) 7 or 8 years for their freedoms, who underwent as hard and servile labor as the basest fellow that was brought out of Newgate.

---

[1] I.e., brought over and left in Virginia.

And for discovery[1] we say that noth[ing] was discovered in those 12 years, and in these 4 or 5 last years much more than formerly.

For our houses and churches built in those times, they were so mean and poor by reason of those calamities that they could not stand above one or two years, the people never going to work but out of the bitterness of their spirits breathing execrable curses upon Sir Thomas Smith. Neither could a blessing from God be hoped for in those buildings which were founded upon the blood of so many Christians.

The towns were only James City, Henryco, Charles Hundred, West and Sherley Hundred, and Kiccoughtan—all which in those times were ruined also, unless some 10 or 12 houses in the corporation of James City. At this present there are 4 for every one that were there, and forty times exceeding in goodness. Fortifications there were none at all against the foreign enemy, and those that were against the domestic very few and contemptible. Bridges there was only one,[2] and which also decay'd in that time. If through the foresaid calamities many had not perished, we doubt not but there might have been many more than 1000 people in the land when Sir Thomas Smith left the government.

But we conceive that when Sir George Yardley arrived governor, he found not above 400, most of those in want of corn, nearly destitute of cattle, swine, poultry, and other necessary provisions to nourish them.

Ministers to instruct the people there were some whose sufficiency and ability we will not tax, yet divers of them had no orders.

We know not at any time that we exceeded in arms, powder, and munitions, yet that in quality almost altogether useless.

We acknowledge in those times there was a trial made of divers staple commodities. The colony as then not having means to proceed therein, we hope in time there may be some better progressions be made and, had it not been for the massacre, many by this had been brought to perfection.

As for boats in the time of that government, there was only one left

[1] Exploration.
[2] A wharf at Jamestown.

that was serviceable in the colony, for which one, besides 4 or 5 ships and pinnaces, there are now not so few as 40. The barks and barges that then were built were in number few, [and] so unwillingly and weakly by the people effected that in the same time they also perished.

We never perceived that the natives of the country did voluntarily yield themselves subjects to our gracious sovereign—neither that they took pride in that title, nor provide at any time any contribution of corn for sustentation of the colony, nor could [we] at any time keep them in such good respect of correspondency as we became mutually helpful each to other, but contrarily what at any time was done proceeded from fear and not love, and their corn procured by trade or the sword.

To what growth of perfection the colony hath attained at the end of those 22 years[1] we conceive may easily be judged by what we have formerly said. And rather than to be reduced to live under the like government, we desire His Majesty that commissioners may be sent over with authority to hang us.

Alderman Johnson, one of the authors of this declaration, hath reason to commend him to whose offenses and infamies he is so inseparably chained.

By the general report of the country which we never heard contradicted, we affirm this to be true whereof all or the most part were eyewitnesses or resident in the country when every particular within written were effected.

FRANCIS WYATT
GEORGE SANDIS
JOHN POTT
JOHN POWNTIS
ROGER SMITH
RAPHE HAMER[2]

WILLIAM TUCKER
WILLIAM PEERCE

---

[1] Clearly an error for 12.

[2] These six names are the governor and council. The rest are the members of the House of Burgesses.

RAWLEY CROSHAW
SAMUELL MATHEWS
JABEZ WHITTAKER
JOHN WILLCOX
NICHOLAS MARTEN
EDWARD BLANY
ISACK MADISONE
CLEMENT DILKE
LUKE BOYSE
JOHN UTIE
JOHN CHEW
RICHARD STAPLES
GABRIELL HOLLAND
JOHN SOUTHERNE
SAMUELL SHARPE
HENRY WATKINS
NATHANAEL CAUSY
RICHARD BIGGS
RICHARD KINGSWELL
JOHN POLLINGTON
ROBERT ADDAMS
THOMAS MARLOTT

Indians & Firearms

< McIlwaine 1979:28

Minutes of a court held on 1 November 1624—

"Robert Poole, gentleman, sworn and examined, sayeth that when he first lived with Apochankeno, being in the time of Sir Thomas Dale his government, Apochankeno showed this examinate certain trees wherein certain bullets had been shot by Indians which Captain John Smith did teach to shoot in a small petronel [large pistol or carbine].

"And after, in Sir Thomas Dale's government, one Cooss *[Coss]*[1], an Indian, was taught to shoot in a piece by Jo. Powell, servant to Captain Web *[commanding at Kickatan],* and by Captain Webb his appointment.

"And further he sayeth that in the time of Sir Thomas Dale's government one Chacrow, an Indian living with Lieutenant Skarfe, Captain William Powell, and Captain William Peerce, and living with them, he did ordinarily shoot in a piece.

"And further he sayeth that Sir Thomas Dale gave unto Kissacomas [?] a piece called a snaphance [flintlock], wherewithal he did often shoot and killed both fowl and deer, and *[would ordinarily come to James town to Sir Thomas Dale for powder and shot]* and was furnished with powder and shot by Sir Thomas Dale, this examinate having oftentimes carried it to him."

Other instances are then given from the time of Yeardley and Argall—after 1617.

---

[1] Bracketed italics are taken from reiterations on the same page.

Works Cited

American Antiquarian Society

1860 *Achaeologia Americana,* Transactions, volume 4.

1870 Proceedings for October.

Andrews, Charles McLean

1934 *The Colonial Period of American History.* 4 Volumes. New Haven.

Andrews, Kenneth R.

1984 *Trade, Plunder and Settlement. Maritime enterprise and the genesis of the British Empire, 1480–1630.* Cambridge.

Arber, Edward, ed.

1884 *Capt. John Smith of Willoughby by Alford, Lincolnshire,* etc. *Works. 1608-1631.* Birmingham: The English Scholar's Library.

Barbour, Philip L.

1962 "Captain George Kendall: Mutineer or Intelligencer?" The Virginia Magazine of History & Biography, Volume 70, pages 297–313.

1969 *The Jamestown Voyages under the First Charter, 1606–1609.* 2 volumes. 2nd series, no. CXXXVI. Cambridge: The Hakluyt Society.

1986 *The Complete Works of Captain John Smith (1580–1631).* 3 volumes. Chapel Hill.

Bemiss, Samuel M., ed.

1957 *The Three Charters of the Virginia Company of London, with Seven Related Documents, 1606–1621.* Williamsburg: The 350th Anniversary Celebration Corporation.

WORKS CITED

Brown, Alexander

1890 [1964, 1994] *The Genesis of the United States.* 2 volumes. Boston.

1898 *The First Republic in America.* Boston.

Colonial Records, no editor.

1874 *Colonial Records of Virginia.* Senate Document–extra. Richmond.

Culliford, S. G.

1965 *William Strachey 1572–1621.* Charlottesville.

Force, Peter, ed.

1836–1846 [1963] *Tracts and Other Papers, relating principally to the Origin, Settlement, and Progress of the Colonies in North America, from the Discovery of the Country to the Year 1776.* 4 volumes. Washington.

Gayley, Charles Mills

1917 *Shakespeare and the Founders of Liberty in America.* New York.

Gerard, William R.

1907 *Virginia's Indian Contributions to English.* American Anthropologist, n.s., 9, pp. 87–112.

Hamor, Ralph

1615 [1957] *A True Discourse of the Present Estate of Virginia,* etc. London (facsimile edition 1957, A. L. Rowse, ed., Virginia State Library).

Harriott, Thomas

1590 [1972] *A Briefe and True Report of the New Found Land of Virginia,* etc. Frankfurt am Main. (facsimile edition 1972, Paul Hulton, ed., Dover Books).

Hunnewell, James F., ed.

1872 *Relation of Virginia by Henry Spelman, 1609.* London.

Johnson, Robert

1609 *Nova Britannia.* London. Reprinted in Force 1836a:6/1.

1612 *The New Life of Virginea.* London. Reprinted in Force 1836a:7/1.

Jones, Howard Mumford, with Sue Bonner Walcutt

1968 *The Literature of Virginia in the Seventeenth Century.* 2nd edition. Charlottesville.

Kingsbury, Susan Myra, ed.

1906–1935 *The Records of the Virginia Company of London.* 4 volumes. Washington.

McIlwaine, H. R., ed.

1915 *Journals of the House of Burgesses of Virginia, 1619–1658/59.* Richmond.

1979 *Minutes of the Council and General Court of Colonial Virginia.* 2nd Edition. Virginia State Library.

Morison, Samuel Eliot

1971 *The European Discovery of America. The Northern Voyages, A. D. 500–1600.* New York.

Neill, Edward D.

1869 *History of the Virginia Company of London.* Albany.

1878 *Early Settlement of Virginia and Virginiola,* etc. Minneapolis.

1885 *Virginia Vetusta, during the Reign of James the First.* Albany.

Purchas, Samuel

1613 [1614, 1617, 1626] *Purchas his Pilgrimage, or Relations of the World and the Religions,* etc. London.

1625 [1905–07] *Hakluytus Posthumus or Purchas His Pilgrimes, containing a History of the World in Sea Voyages and Lande Travells by Englishmen and others (1625).* [20 volumes. Edinburgh]

Quinn, David Beers, ed.

1967 *George Percy. Observations gathered out of a discourse on the Plantation of the Southern Colony in Virginia by the English, 1606.* Charlottesville.

1979 *New American World. A documentary history of North America to 1612.* 5 volumes. New York.

Rich, R[ichard]

1610 [1976] *Newes from Virginia. The Lost Flock Triumphant,* etc. London (reprinted 1976: Early Accounts of Life in Colonial Virginia, 1609–1613. Scholars' Facsimiles & Reprints)

Siebert, Frank T., Jr.

1975 *Resurrecting Virginia Algonquian from the Dead: The Reconstituted and Historical Phonology of Powhatan.* James M. Crawford, ed. Studies in Southeastern Indian Languages. Athens: University of Georgia Press, pp. 285–453.

Smith, Captain John (modern editions in Barbour 1986)
1608 *A True Relation,* etc.
1612 *A Map of Virginia, with a Description of the Country … Whereunto is Annexed the Proceedings of those Colonies,* etc.
1616 *A Description of New England &c.*
1624 *The General History of Virginia, New England, and the Summer Isles.* See the frontispiece for his title page.
[1627] 1653, 1692 *A Seaman's Grammar.*
1630 *The True Travels, Adventures, and Observations of Captaine John Smith.*
1631 *Advertisements for the Unexperienced Planters of New England, or Any Where.*

Stith, William
1747 [1865, 1969] *The History of the First Discovery and Settlement of Virginia.* Williamsburg.

Strachey, William
1612 *For the Colony in Virginia Britannia: Lavves Diuine, Morall and Martiall, &c.* Printed at London for Walter Burre.

Taylor, Henry C.
1951 [1971] *A True Relation of the State of Virginia,* etc. *by John Rolfe.* J. C. Wylie, et al. eds. New Haven. (Reprinted by the APVA in the Jamestown Documents series in 1971—this is the Pembroke-Taylor MS)

Tyler, Lyon G.
1922 *"A Trewe Relacyon" –Virginia from 1609 to 1612.* Tyler's Quarterly Magazine, volume 3, pp. 259–82.

Whitaker, Rev. Alexander
1613 [1937] *Good Newes from Virginia.* London (reprinted 1937: Early Accounts of Life in Colonial Virginia, 1609–1613. Scholars' Facsimiles & Reprints)

White, Rev. John
1630 [1968] *The Planter's Plea, or the Grounds of the Plantation Examined, and Usual Objections Answered.* London. Printed by William Iones.

Whittingham, C., ed.
1858 *The Relation of the Right Honourable the Lord De-La-Warre,* etc. London reprint of the 1611 William Welbie edition.

Wright, Irene A.
1920 *Spanish Policy toward Virginia, 1606–1612.* The American Historical Review. Volume 25, number 3, April 1920.

Wright, Louis B.
1946 *Newes from the New-World.* San Marino: The Huntington Library.

Wright, Louis B. and Virginia Freund, eds.
1953 *The Historie of Travell into Virginia Britania (1612) by William Strachey, gent.* London: The Hakluyt Society, 2nd Series, No. CIII. Also an earlier edition by R. H. Major, ed. (1849)

Index

SMALL CAPS are Jamestown Narratives texts.
Italic *numbers* refer to commentary material.

INDEX

INDEX

INDEX

Text and layout were done in 11pt Baskerville and **9pt Helvetica** by the editor. Pages were scanned by BookMasters, Inc., from camera-ready hardcopy. Printed on 50# acid-free archival paper.